Copyright Law

Ben Depoorter

1st Ed., 2019

This casebook provides an overview of U.S. federal copyright law as it pertains to works of art, motion pictures, music, literature, and software. The book begins with a discussion of the purposes of copyright law and an overview of the basic rules of copyright law. It then investigates various subject matter areas of copyright protection, focusing on the types of uses of content that authors control under prevailing law. Current controversies in copyright litigation, legislation, and scholarship are also covered.

TABLE OF CONTENTS

1. Foundations of Copyright Law

1.a. Current Issues

1.b. Philosophical Perspectives

Peter Menell, Intellectual Property: General Theories
Encyclopedia of Law & Economics, Bouckaert & De Geest, eds. (2000)

Even copyright law, which implicates a broader array of personal interests of the creator than patent law, may benefit from the application of the utilitarian framework to the extent that society seeks the production and diffusion of literary and artistic works. ... The utilitarian framework has been particularly central to the development of copyright law in the United States. The Congressional Committee reporting on the 1909 Copyright Act stated: 'The enactment of copyright legislation by Congress under the terms of the Constitution is not based upon any natural right that the author has in his writings, ... but upon the ground that the welfare of the public will be served ... by securing to authors for limited periods the exclusive rights to their writings'. (H.R. Rep. No. 2222, 60th Cong., 2nd Sess. 7, 1909. See also Mazer v. Stein, 347 U.S. 201, 219, 1954; MMLJ, 1997, pp. 326-328). ...

The philosophy of intellectual property developed in response to the use of monopoly power to spur innovation. Adam Smith (1776, pp. 277-278), while generally critical of monopoly power as detrimental to the operation of the 'invisible hand', nonetheless justified the need for limited monopolies to promote innovation and commerce requiring substantial up-front investments and risk. Jeremy Bentham (1839, p. 71) went beyond this justification for intellectual property rights, providing a clear explication of the differential fixed costs borne by innovators and imitators:

[T]hat which one man has invented, all the world can imitate. Without the assistance of the laws, the inventor would almost always be driven out of the market by his rival, who finding himself, without any expense, in possession of a discovery which has cost the inventor much time and expense, would be able to deprive him of all his deserved advantages, by selling at a lower price.

... Building upon the growing understanding of oligopoly and the economics of imperfect competition (see, for example, Robinson, 1933; Plant, 1934a, 1934b) offered a more skeptical view of intellectual property rights, questioning whether such rights were in fact needed to stimulate inventive activity and investment in actual as opposed to idealized markets. Plant argued that much invention is spontaneous and hence forthcoming without the provision of patent protection. He contended further that first- mover advantages, imperfections in markets and other factors provided inventors and publishers sufficient rewards to create and market their works even in the absence of intellectual property rights. Plant concluded that patent protection would lead to an overinvestment in research and development that could result in discoveries that fell within the patent domain, wastefully diverting resources from more appropriate endeavors.

Arrow (1962) provides the seminal modern diagnosis of markets for information. In addition to the appropriability problem described by Pigou, Arrow recognized that the marginal cost of increasing the utilization of information is zero.

[A]ny information obtained, say a new method of production, should, from the welfare point of view, be available free of charge (apart from the costs of transmitting information). This insures optimal utilization of the information but of course provides no incentive for investment in research. In a free enterprise economy, inventive activity is supported by using the invention to create property rights; precisely to the extent that it is successful, there is an underutilization of the information. (pp. 616-617)

Reflecting the Chicago tradition of law and economics, a number of scholars questioned whether the 'public goods' attribute of information is the most appropriate starting point for thinking about intellectual property. Demsetz (1969, 1970), applying insights from the property rights literature (Coase, 1960; Demsetz, 1967), argued that strong property rights for intellectual creations should be provided, with the market available to ensure efficient allocation of resources through Coasean bargaining.

1.c. The Economics of Copyright Law

Wendy Gorden & Robert Bone, Copyright Law

Encyclopedia of Law & Economics, Bouckaert & De Geest, eds. (2000)

Once a work is made public, the author cannot easily exclude others from copying. Copiers have an advantage in the market because they avoid creation costs and thus can sell at a price the author cannot match without suffering a loss. Prospective authors anticipating this outcome will hesitate before investing in creative activity and creative products may be undersupplied.

More specifically, if copiers are numerous enough, competition will force the price of copies down to the copier's marginal cost. So long as copying is less costly than creating, the resulting market price will be less than the price the original author must charge to recoup her fixed costs of creation (including opportunity and risk-bearing costs). Therefore, insofar as prospective authors are motivated by the expectation of economic reward and publication is necessary to reap that reward, free access to works of authorship can lead to suboptimal incentives to create ex ante. (In fact, this argument depends on a number of assumptions ...). Gordon (1992a) analyzes this argument as a prisoner's dilemma in which players simultaneously choose between creating a work of their own and copying the work of another. For a plausible payoff structure, copying strictly dominates creation and the result is the Pareto-dominated equilibrium associated with prisoner's dilemma games - in this case, both players choose to copy and nothing is created.

Copyright solves this non-excludability problem and escapes the prisoner's dilemma by giving authors legally enforceable property rights to exclude others from using their works without consent (or at least without paying). This is not the only possible solution .... However, one important benefit of copyright is its compatibility with a market. By eliminating the free-rider obstacle, copyright supports the creation of licensing markets which enable the informational and allocational advantages of a market mechanism. ...

Monopoly Prices and Deadweight Loss: Inexhaustibility

Copyright confers monopoly power and monopolies can result in deadweight loss whenever perfect price discrimination is not possible. The inexhaustibility feature of information only exacerbates this problem. Normally everyone can enjoy an information product without depleting its quantity or quality. In this sense, information differs from tangible goods; for example, giving a particular chair to person A means denying it to person B. It follows from inexhaustibility that information, once created, could be supplied to everyone at the low marginal cost of duplication. Thus, the relatively high price charged by a copyright monopolist excludes consumers who otherwise would have purchased the information, thereby creating a social loss.

There is, therefore, a conflict between ex ante and ex post points of view. From an ex ante perspective, the non-excludability feature of information means that a legal monopoly may be necessary to induce creation. But from an ex post perspective, the inexhaustibility feature means that any such monopoly will create some social loss.

This point has received detailed treatment in the economic literature on the private supply of excludable public goods. In one of the earliest articles, Davis and Whinston (1967) demonstrate that an efficient allocation cannot be achieved by any nondiscriminatory pricing device, even when property rights make exclusion possible at zero cost. Moreover, since consumers have an incentive to lie about their preferences, even a public supplier of information will have difficulty determining how much to supply (Davis and Whinston, 1967, pp. 367-368). In a later article, Demsetz (1970) shows that an efficient result can be achieved with exclusion when the supplier of the inexhaustible good has perfect information about consumer preferences and can perfectly price-discriminate.

Baumol and Ordover (1977) study the same problem when sellers have imperfect information about consumer preferences and face a budget constraint. They show that, under these conditions, prices will be greater than zero in order to induce creation, thus inefficiently excluding consumers who value the information at more than its marginal cost but less than the price. Moreover, Kormendi (1979) shows that it is not possible to escape this loss by using a particular incentive-compatible mechanism to force truthful revelation of preferences.

Chilling Future Creativity: The Cumulative Nature of Information

Information is cumulative in addition to being nonexcludable and inexhaustible: people build on past information to make new creations, adding their own expression to elements borrowed from previous works. Thus, the monopoly created by exclusivity raises the cost of future innovation by requiring prospective innovators to obtain licenses. This burden is especially high for multimedia works, such as digitalized hypertext on CD-ROM, that borrow small amounts from a large number of previous works.

This cumulative feature of information figures prominently in the Landes and Posner (1989) model. There the copyright monopoly has two opposing effects on creation incentives. On the one hand, it enhances the prospective author's economic return from selling copies and thus strengthens the incentive to create. On the other hand, it increases the cost of borrowing from previous works and thus weakens the incentive to create. According to Landes and Posner, copyright entitlements balance these two effects with the ultimate goal of maximizing social benefit net of cost. One way that copyright law attempts to minimize the social cost of exclusivity is by limiting the grant of exclusivity to 'expression' and placing no restraints on the public's use of the most important informational building blocks, namely, general ideas.

1.d. Incentives for Creativity: Evidence

BYE, BYE, MISS AMERICAN PIE?

THE SUPPLY OF NEW RECORDED MUSIC SINCE NAPSTER
Joel Waldfogel

NBER Working Paper No. 16882
Issued in March 2011

In the decade since Napster, file-sharing has undermined the protection that copyright affords recorded music, reducing recorded music sales. What matters for consumers, however, is not sellers' revenue but the surplus they derive from new music. The legal monopoly created by copyright is justified by its encouragement of the creation of new works, but there is little evidence on this relationship. The file-sharing era can be viewed as a large-scale experiment allowing us to check whether events since Napster have stemmed the flow of new works. We assemble a novel dataset on the number of high quality works released annually, since 1960, derived from retrospective critical assessments of music such best-of-the-decade lists. This allows a comparison of the quantity of new albums since Napster to 1) its pre-Napster level, 2) pre-Napster trends, and 3) a possible control, the volume of new songs since the iTunes Music Store's revitalization of the single. We find no evidence that changes since Napster have affected the quantity of new recorded music or artists coming to market. We reconcile stable quantities in the face of decreased demand with reduced costs of bringing works to market and a growing role of independent labels.

http://www.nber.org/papers/w16882

2. The Basics of a Copyright Lawsuit

2.a. Originality

499 U.S. 340 (1991)
FEIST PUBLICATIONS V. RURAL TELEPHONE SERVICE CO.

United States Supreme Court

The sine qua non of copyright is originality. To qualify for copyright protection, a work must be original to the author. See Harper Row, supra, at 471 U. S. 547-549. Original, as the term is used in copyright, means only that the work was independently created by the author (as opposed to copied from other works), and that it possesses at least some minimal degree of creativity. 1 M. Nimmer & D. Nimmer, Copyright §§ 2.01[A], [B] (1990) (hereinafter Nimmer). To be sure, the requisite level of creativity is extremely low; even a slight amount will suffice. The vast majority of works make the grade quite easily, as they possess some creative spark, "no matter how crude, humble or obvious" it might be. Id. § 1.08[C][1]. Originality does not signify novelty; a work may be original even though it closely resembles other works, so long as the similarity is fortuitous, not the result of copying. ... originality is not a stringent standard; it does not require that facts be presented in an innovative or surprising way. It is equally true, however, that the selection and arrangement of facts cannot be so mechanical or routine as to require no creativity whatsoever. The standard of originality is low, but it does exist. See Patterson & Joyce 760, n. 144 ("While this requirement is sometimes characterized as modest, or a low threshold, it is not without effect")...

MESHWERKS, INC. V. TOYOTA MOTOR SALES U.S.A., INC.

United States Court of Appeals for the Tenth Circuit

In 2003, and in conjunction with Saatchi & Saatchi, its advertising agency, Toyota began work on its model-year 2004 advertising campaign. Saatchi and Toyota agreed that the campaign would involve, among other things, digital models of Toyota's vehicles for use on Toyota's website and in various other media. These digital models have substantial advantages over the product photographs for which they substitute. With a few clicks of a computer mouse, the advertiser can change the color of the car, its surroundings, and even edit its physical dimensions to portray changes in vehicle styling; before this innovation, advertisers had to conduct new photo shoots of whole fleets of vehicles each time the manufacturer made even a small design change to a car or truck.

To supply these digital models, Saatchi and Toyota hired Grace & Wild, Inc. ("G & W"). In turn, G & W subcontracted with Meshwerks to assist with two initial aspects of the project—digitization and modeling. Digitizing involves collecting physical data points from the object to be portrayed. In the case of Toyota's vehicles, Meshwerks took copious measurements of Toyota's vehicles by covering each car, truck, and van with a grid of tape and running an articulated arm tethered to a computer over the vehicle to measure all points of intersection in the grid. Based on these measurements, modeling software then generated a digital image resembling a wire-frame model. In other words, the vehicles' data points (measurements) were mapped onto a computerized grid and the modeling software connected the dots to create a "wire frame" of each vehicle.

At this point, however, the on-screen image remained far from perfect and manual "modeling" was necessary. Meshwerks personnel fine-tuned or, as the company prefers it, "sculpted," the lines on screen to resemble each vehicle as closely as possible. Approximately 90 percent of the data points contained in each final model, Meshwerks represents, were the result not of the first-step measurement process, but of the skill and effort its digital sculptors manually expended at the second step. For example, some areas of detail, such as wheels, headlights, door handles, and the Toyota emblem, could not be accurately measured using current technology; those features had to be added at the second "sculpting" stage, and Meshwerks had to recreate those features as realistically as possible by hand, based on photographs. Even for areas that were measured, Meshwerks faced the challenge of converting measurements taken of a three-dimensional car into a two-dimensional computer representation; to achieve this, its modelers had to sculpt, or move, data points to achieve a visually convincing result. The purpose and product of these processes, after nearly 80 to 100 hours of effort per vehicle, were two-dimensional wire-frame depictions of Toyota's vehicles that appeared three-dimensional on screen, but were utterly unadorned-lacking color, shading, and other details. Attached to this opinion as Appendix A are sample screen-prints of one of Meshwerks' digital wire-frame models.

With Meshwerks' wire-frame products in hand, G & W then manipulated the computerized models by, first, adding detail, the result of which appeared on screen as a "tightening" of the wire frames, as though significantly more wires had been added to the frames, or as though they were made of a finer mesh. Next, G & W digitally applied color, texture, lighting, and animation for use in Toyota's advertisements. An example of G & W's work product is attached as Appendix B to this opinion. G & W's digital models were then sent to Saatchi to be employed in a number of advertisements prepared by Saatchi and Toyota in various print, online, and television media.

B

This dispute arose because, according to Meshwerks, it contracted with G & W for only a single use of its models-as part of one Toyota television commercial-and neither Toyota nor any other defendant was allowed to use the digital models created from Meshwerks' wire-frames in other advertisements. Thus, Meshwerks contends defendants improperly-in violation of copyright laws as well as the parties' agreement-reused and redistributed the models created by Meshwerks in a host of other media. In support of the allegations that defendants misappropriated its intellectual property, Meshwerks points to the fact that it sought and received copyright registration on its wire-frame models.

In due course, defendants moved for summary judgment on the theory that Meshwerks' wire-frame models lacked sufficient originality to be protected by copyright. Specifically, defendants argued that any original expression found in Meshwerks' products was attributable to the Toyota designers who conceived of the vehicle designs in the first place; accordingly, defendants' use of the models could not give rise to a claim for copyright infringement.

The district court agreed. It found that the wire-frame models were merely copies of Toyota's products, not sufficiently original to warrant copyright protection, and stressed that Meshwerks' "intent was to replicate, as exactly as possible, the image of certain Toyota vehicles." D. Ct. Op. at 8, 2008 WL 2420869. Because there was no valid copyright, there could be no infringement, and, having granted summary judgment on the federal copyright claim, the district court declined to exercise supplemental jurisdiction over Meshwerks' state-law contract claim. Today, Meshwerks asks us to reverse and hold its digital, wire-frame models sufficiently original to warrant copyright protection.

II

To make a case for copyright infringement, Meshwerks must show (1) it owns a valid copyright, and (2) defendants copied constituent elements of the work that are original to Meshwerks. Autoskill Inc. v. Nat'l Educ. Support Sys., Inc., 994 F.2d 1476, 1487 (10th Cir.1993). Our inquiry in this case focuses on the first of these tests-that is, on the question whether Meshwerks held a valid copyright in its digital wire-frame models. Because Meshwerks obtained registration certificates for its models from the Copyright Office, we presume that it holds a valid copyright. See 17 U.S.C. § 410(c); Palladium Music, Inc. v. EatSleepMusic, Inc., 398 F.3d 1193, 1196 (10th Cir.2005). At the same time, defendants may overcome this presumption by presenting evidence and legal argument sufficient to establish that the works in question were not entitled to copyright protection. Palladium Music, Inc., 398 F.3d at 1196. Because this case comes to us on summary judgment, we review the question whether Meshwerks holds a valid copyright de novo and will affirm the district court's judgment only if, viewing all of the facts in the light most favorable to Meshwerks, we are able to conclude that "there is no genuine issue as to any material fact and that [defendants are] entitled to judgment as a matter of law." Fed.R.Civ.P. 56(c).

Key to our evaluation of this case is the fact that Meshwerks' digital wire-frame computer models depict Toyota's vehicles without any individualizing features: they are untouched by a digital paintbrush; they are not depicted in front of a palm tree, whizzing down the open road, or climbing up a mountainside. Put another way, Meshwerks' models depict nothing more than unadorned Toyota vehicles-the car as car. See Appendix A. And the unequivocal lesson from Feist is that works are not copyrightable to the extent they do not involve any expression apart from the raw facts in the world. As Professor Nimmer has commented in connection with the predecessor technology of photography, "[a]s applied to a photograph of a pre-existing product, that bedrock principle [of originality] means that the photographer manifestly cannot claim to have originated the matter depicted therein. The upshot is that the photographer is entitled to copyright solely based on lighting, angle, perspective, and the other ingredients that traditionally apply to that art-form." Nimmer on Copyright § 3.03[C][3]. It seems to us that exactly the same holds true with the digital medium now before us: the facts in this case unambiguously show that Meshwerks did not make any decisions regarding lighting, shading, the background in front of which a vehicle would be posed, the angle at which to pose it, or the like-in short, its models reflect none of the decisions that can make depictions of things or facts in the world, whether Oscar Wilde or a Toyota Camry, new expressions subject to copyright protection.

...

Confirming this conclusion as well is the peculiar place where Meshwerks stood in the model-creation pecking order. On the one hand, Meshwerks had nothing to do with designing the appearance of Toyota's vehicles, distinguishing them from any other cars, trucks, or vans in the world. That expressive creation took place before Meshwerks happened along, and was the result of work done by Toyota and its designers; indeed, at least six of the eight vehicles at issue are still covered by design patents belonging to Toyota and protecting the appearances of the objects for which they are issued. See 35 U.S.C. § 171; Gorham Mfg. Co. v. White, 14 Wall. 511, 81 U.S. 511, 525, 20 L.Ed. 731 (1871) ("It is the appearance itself, no matter by what agency caused, that constitutes mainly, if not entirely, the contribution to the public which the law deems worthy of recompense."). On the other hand, how the models Meshwerks created were to be deployed in advertising-including the backgrounds, lighting, angles, and colors-were all matters left to those (G & W,

Saatchi, and 3D Recon) who came after Meshwerks left the scene. See infra Section II.C. Meshwerks thus played a narrow, if pivotal, role in the process by simply, if effectively, copying Toyota's vehicles into a digital medium so they could be expressively manipulated by others.

…

It is certainly true that what Meshwerks accomplished was a peculiar kind of copying. It did not seek to recreate Toyota vehicles outright-steel, rubber, and all; instead, it sought to depict Toyota's three-dimensional physical objects in a two-dimensional digital medium. But we hold, as many before us have already suggested, that, standing alone, "[t]he fact that a work in one medium has been copied from a work in another medium does not render it any the less a 'copy.'" Nimmer on Copyright § 8.01[B]; see also Durham Indus., Inc. v. Tomy Corp., 630 F.2d 905, 910 (2d Cir.1980) (holding that "the mere reproduction of the Disney characters in plastic . does not constitute originality as this Court has defined the term"); Entm't Research Group, Inc. v. Genesis Creative Group, Inc., 122 F.3d 1211, 1221-24 (9th Cir.1997) (denying copyright protection to 3-D costumes based on 2-D cartoon characters). After all, the putative creator who merely shifts the medium in which another's creation is expressed has not necessarily added anything beyond the expression contained in the original. See Bridgeman Art Library, Ltd., 36 F.Supp.2d at 199 (noting that "a copy in a new medium is copyrightable only where, as often but not always is the case, the copier makes some identifiable original contribution").

In reaching this conclusion, we do not for a moment seek to downplay the considerable amount of time, effort, and skill that went into making Meshwerks' digital wire-frame models. But, in assessing the originality of a work for which copyright protection is sought, we look only at the final product, not the process, and the fact that intensive, skillful, and even creative labor is invested in the process of creating a product does not guarantee its copyrightability. See Feist, 499 U.S. at 359-60, 111 S.Ct. 1282; Howard B. Abrams, Law of Copyright § 2:8 ("Even if the process is both expensive and intricate, an exact or near-exact duplicate of an original should not qualify for copyright.") (emphasis added); Wojcik, supra, 30 Hastings Comm. & Ent. L.J. at 267 ("This is not to say that [accurately reproducing an underlying image] requires no skill or effort; it simply means that such skill and effort does not suffice to invoke the highly advantageous legal monopoly granted under the Copyright Act."). In the case before us, there is no doubt that transposing the physical appearances of Toyota's vehicles from three dimensions to two, such that computer-screen images accurately reflect Toyota's products, was labor intensive and required a great amount of skill. But because the end-results were unadorned images of Toyota's vehicles, the appearances of which do not owe their origins to Meshwerks, we are unable to reward that skill, effort, and labor with copyright protection.

Meshwerks' intent in making its wire-frame models provides additional support for our conclusion. "In theory, the originality requirement tests the putative author's state of mind: Did he have an earlier work in mind when he created his own?" Paul Goldstein, Goldstein on Copyright § 2.2.1.1. If an artist affirmatively sets out to be unoriginal-to make a copy of someone else's creation, rather than to create an original work-it is far more likely that the resultant product will, in fact, be unoriginal.

2.B. Infringement

2.B.1. Copying in Fact

212 F.3d 477 (9th Cir. 2000)

THREE BOYS MUSIC CORPORATION

v.

MICHAEL BOLTON

United States Court of Appeals for The Ninth Circuit

D.W. Nelson, Circuit Judge:

In 1994, a jury found that Michael Bolton's 1991 pop hit, "Love Is a Wonderful Thing," infringed on the copyright of a 1964 Isley Brothers' song of the same name. The district court denied Bolton's motion for a new trial and affirmed the jury's award of $5.4 million.

Bolton, his co-author, Andrew Goldmark, and their record companies ("Sony Music") appeal, arguing that the district court erred in finding that: (1) sufficient evidence supported the jury's finding that the appellants had access to the Isley Brothers' song, (2) sufficient evidence supported the jury's finding that the songs were substantially similar; ... (4) sufficient evidence supported the jury's attribution of profits to the infringing elements of the song; ...

We affirm.

I. BACKGROUND

The Isley Brothers, one of this country's most well-known rhythm and blues groups, have been inducted into the Rock and Roll Hall of Fame. They helped define the soul sound of the 1960s with songs such as "Shout," "Twist and Shout," and "This Old Heart of Mine," and they mastered the funky beats of the 1970s with songs such as "Who's That Lady, " "Fight the Power," and "It's Your Thing." In 1964, the Isley Brothers wrote and recorded "Love is a Wonderful Thing " for United Artists. The Isley Brothers received a copyright for "Love is a Wonderful Thing" from the Register of Copyrights on February 6, 1964. The following year, they switched to the famous Motown label and had three top-100 hits including "This Old Heart of Mine."

Hoping to benefit from the Isley Brothers' Motown success, United Artists released "Love is a Wonderful Thing" in 1966. The song was not released on an album, only on a 45record as a single. Several industry publications predicted that "Love is a Wonderful Thing" would be a hit -"Cash Box" on August 27, 1966, "Gavin Report" on August 26, 1966, and "Billboard" on September 10, 1966. On September 17, 1966, Billboard listed "Love is a Wonderful Thing" at number 110 in a chart titled "Bubbling Under the Hot 100. " The song was never listed on any other Top 100 charts. In 1991, the Isley Brothers' "Love is a Wonderful Thing" was releasedon compact disc. See Isley Brothers, The Isley Brothers -The Complete UA Sessions, (EMI 1991).

Michael Bolton is a singer/songwriter who gained popularity in the late 1980s and early 1990s by reviving the soul sound of the 1960s. Bolton has orchestrated this soul-music revival in part by covering old songs such as Percy Sledge's "When a Man Love a Woman" and Otis Redding's"(Sittin' on the) Dock of the Bay." Bolton also has written his own hit songs. In early 1990, Bolton and Goldmark wrote a song called "Love Is a Wonderful Thing." Bolton released it as a single in April 1991, and as part of Bolton's album,"Time, Love and Tenderness." Bolton's "Love Is a Wonderful Thing" finished 1991 at number 49 on Billboard's year-end pop chart.

On February 24, 1992, Three Boys Music Corporation filed a copyright infringement action for damages against the appellants under 17 U.S.C. SS 101 et seq. (1988). The parties agreed to a trifurcated trial. On April 25, 1994, in the first phase, the jury determined that the appellants had infringed the Isley Brothers' copyright. At the end of second phase five days later, the jury decided that Bolton's "Love Is a Wonderful Thing" accounted for 28 percent of the profits from "Time, Love and Tenderness." The jury also found that 66 percent of the profits from commercial uses of the song could be attributed to the inclusion of infringing elements. On May 9, 1994, the district court entered judgment in favor of the Isley Brothers based on the first two phases. ...

In the final judgment entered against the appellants, the district court ordered Sony Music to pay $4,218,838; Bolton to pay $932,924; Goldmark to pay $220,785; and their music publishing companies to pay $75,900. They timely appealed.

II. DISCUSSION

Proof of copyright infringement is often highly circumstantial, particularly in cases involving music. A copyright plaintiff must prove (1) ownership of the copyright; and (2) infringement -that the defendant copied protected elements of the plaintiff's work. See Smith v. Jackson , 84 F.3d 1213, 1218 (9th Cir. 1996) (citation omitted). Absent direct evidence of copying, proof of infringement involves fact-based showings that the defendant had "access" to the plaintiff's work and that the two works are "substantially similar." Id.

Given the difficulty of proving access and substantial similarity, appellate courts have been reluctant to reverse jury verdicts in music cases. See, e.g., id. at 1221 (affirming a jury's verdict for the defendants in a copyright infringement case involving Michael Jackson and other musicians); Gaste v. Kaiserman, 863 F.2d 1061, 1071 (2d Cir. 1988) (affirming a jury's damages award against a defendant in a music copyright infringement case). Judge Newman's opinion in Gaste nicely articulated the proper role for an appeals court in reviewing a jury verdict:

The guiding principle in deciding whether to overturn a jury verdict for insufficiency of the evidence is whether the evidence is such that, without weighing the credibility of the witnesses or otherwise considering the weight of the evidence, there can be but one conclusion as to the verdict that reasonable men could have reached.

Id. 1066 (internal quotations omitted). In Arnstein v. Porter, the seminal caseabout musical copyright infringement, Judge Jerome Frank wrote:

Each of these two issues -copying and improper appropriation -is an issue of fact. If there is a trial, the conclusions on those issues of the trier of the facts - of the judge if he sat without a jury, or of the jury if there was a jury trial -bind this court on appeal, provided the evidence supports those findings, regardless of whether we would ourselves have reached the same conclusions. Arnstein v. Porter, 154 F.2d 464, 469 (2d Cir. 1946).

As a general matter, the standard for reviewing jury verdicts is whether they are supported by "substantial evidence" -that is, such relevant evidence as reasonable minds might accept as adequate to support a conclusion. See Poppell v. City of San Diego, 149 F.3d 951, 962 (9th Cir. 1998). The credibility of witnesses is an issue for the jury and is generally not subject to appellate review. See Gilbrook v. City of Westminster, 177 F.3d 839, 856 (9th Cir.), cert. denied, 120 S. Ct. 614 (1999).

We affirm the jury's verdict in this case in light of the standard of review and copyright law's "guiding principles." Although we will address each of the appellant's arguments in turn, we focus on access because it is the most difficult issue in this case. Our decision is predicated on judicial deference -finding that the law has been properly applied in this case, viewing the facts most favorably to the appellees, and not substituting our judgment for that of the jury.

A. Access

[1] Proof of access requires "an opportunity to view or to copy plaintiff's work." Sid and Marty Krofft Television Prods., Inc. v. McDonald's Corp., 562 F.2d 1157, 1172 (9th Cir. 1977). This is often described as providing a "reasonable opportunity" or "reasonable possibility" of viewing the plaintiff's work. 4 Melville B. Nimmer & David Nimmer, Nimmer on Copyright, S 13.02[A], at 13-19 (1999); Jason v. Fonda, 526 F. Supp. 774, 775 (C.D. Cal. 1981), aff'd , 698 F.2d 966 (9th Cir. 1983). We have defined reasonable access as "more than a `bare possibility.' " Jason, 698 F.2d at 967. Nimmer has elaborated on our definition: "Of course, reasonable opportunity as here used, does not encompass any bare possibility in the sense that anything is possible. Access may not be inferred through mere speculation or conjecture. There must be a reasonable possibility of viewing the plaintiff's work -not a bare possibility." 4 Nimmer,S 13.02[A], at 1319. "At times, distinguishing a `bare'

possibility from a `reasonable' possibility will present a close question. " Id. at 1320.

Circumstantial evidence of reasonable access is proven in one of two ways: (1) a particular chain of events is established between the plaintiff's work and the defendant's access to that work (such as through dealings with a publisher or record company), or (2) the plaintiff's work has been widely disseminated. See 4 Nimmer, S 13.02[A], at 13-20-13-21; 2 Paul Goldstein, Copyright: Principles, Law, and Practice S 8.3.1.1., at 90-91 (1989). Goldstein remarks that in music cases the "typically more successful route to proving access requires the plaintiff to show that its work was widely disseminated through sales of sheet music, records, and radio performances." 2 Goldstein, S 8.3.1.1, at 91. Nimmer, however, cautioned that "[c]oncrete cases will pose difficult judgments as to where along the access spectrum a given exploitation falls." 4 Nimmer, S 13.02[A], at 13-22.

Proof of widespread dissemination is sometimes accompanied by a theory that copyright infringement of a popular song was subconscious. Subconscious copying has been accepted since Learned Hand embraced it in a 1924 music infringement case: "Everything registers somewhere in our memories, and no one can tell what may evoke it . . . . Once it appears that another has in fact used the copyright as the source of this production, he has invaded the author's rights. It is no excuse that in so doing his memory has played him a trick." Fred Fisher, Inc. v. Dillingham, 298 F. 145, 147-48 (S.D.N.Y. 1924). In Fred Fisher, Judge Hand found that the similarities between the songs "amount[ed] to identity" and that the infringement had occurred "probably unconsciously, what he had certainly often heard only a short time before." Id. at 147.

In modern cases, however, the theory of subconscious copying has been applied to songs that are more remote in time. ABKCO Music, Inc v. Harrisongs Music, Ltd. , 722 F.2d 988 (2d Cir. 1983) is the most prominent example. In ABKCO, the Second Circuit affirmed a jury's verdict that former Beatle George Harrison, in writing the song "My Sweet Lord," subconsciously copied The Chiffons' "He's So Fine," which was released six years earlier. See id. at 997, 999. Harrison admitted hearing "He's So Fine" in 1963, when it was number one on the Billboard charts in the United States for five weeks and one of the top 30 hits in England for seven weeks. See id. at 998. The court found:"the evidence, standing alone, `by no means compels the conclusion that there was access . . . it does not compel the conclusion that there was not.' " Id. (quoting Heim v. Universal Pictures Co., 154 F.2d 480, 487 (2d Cir. 1946)). In ABKCO, however, the court found that "the similarity was so striking and where access was found, the remoteness of that access provides no basis for reversal." Id. Furthermore, "the mere lapse of a considerable period of time between the moment of access and the creation of defendant's work does not preclude a finding of copying." 4 Nimmer, S 13.02[A], at 13-20 (citing ABKCO, 722 F.2d at 997-98).

The Isley Brothers' access argument was based on a theory of widespread dissemination and subconscious copying. They presented evidence supporting four principal ways that Bolton and Goldmark could have had access to the Isley Brothers' "Love is a Wonderful Thing":

(1) Bolton grew up listening to groups such as the Isley Brothers and singing their songs. In 1966, Bolton and Goldmark were 13 and 15, respectively, growing up in Connecticut. Bolton testified that he had been listening to rhythm and blues music by black singers since he was 10 or 11,"appreciated a lot of Black singers," and as a youth was the lead singer in a band that performed "covers" of popular songs by black singers. Bolton also testified that his brother had a "pretty good record collection."

(2) Three disk jockeys testified that the Isley Brothers' song was widely disseminated on radio and television stations where Bolton and Goldmark grew up. First, Jerry Blavitt testified that the Isley Brothers' "Love is a Wonderful Thing" was played five or six times during a 13-week period on the television show, "The Discophonic Scene," which he said aired in Philadelphia, New York, and Hartford-New Haven. Blavitt also testified that he played the song two to three times a week as a disk jockey in Philadelphia and that the station is still playing the song today. Second, Earl Rodney Jones testified that he played the song a minimum of four times a day during an eight to 14 to 24 week period on WVON radio in Chicago, and that the station is still playing the song today. Finally, Jerry Bledsoe testified that he played the song on WUFO radio in Buffalo, and WWRL radio in New York was playing the song in New York in 1967 when he went there. Bledsoe also testified that he played the song twice on a television show, "Soul," which aired in New York and probably in New Haven, Connecticut, where Bolton lived.

(3) Bolton confessed to being a huge fan of the Isley Brothers and a collector of their music. Ronald Isley testified that when Bolton saw Isley at the Lou Rawls United Negro College Fund Benefit concert in 1988, Bolton said,"I know this guy.I go back with him. I have all his stuff. " Angela Winbush, Isley's wife, testified about that meeting that Bolton said, "This man needs no introduction. I know everything he's done."

(4) Bolton wondered if he and Goldmark were copying a song by another famous soul singer. Bolton produced a work tape attempting to show that he and Goldmark independently created their version of "Love Is a Wonderful Thing." On that tape of their recording session, Bolton asked Goldmark if the song they were composing was Marvin Gaye's "Some Kind of Wonderful."[1] The district court, in affirming the jury's verdict, wrote about Bolton's Marvin Gaye remark:

This statement suggests that Bolton was contemplating the possibility that the work he and Goldmark were creating, or at least a portion of it, belonged to someone else, but that Bolton wasn't sure who it belonged to. A reasonable jury can infer that Bolton mistakenly attributed the work to Marvin Gaye, when in reality Bolton was subconsciously drawing on Plaintiff's song.

The appellants contend that the Isley Brothers' theory of access amounts to a "twenty-five-years-after-the-fact subconscious copying claim." Indeed, this is a more attenuated case of reasonable access and subconscious copying than ABKCO. In this case, the appellants never admitted hearing the Isley Brothers' "Love is a Wonderful Thing." That song never topped the Billboard charts or even made the top 100 for a single week. The song was not released on an album or compact disc until 1991, a year after Bolton and Goldmark wrote their song. Nor did the Isley

Brothers ever claim that Bolton's and Goldmark's song is so "strikingly similar" to the Isley Brothers' that proof of access is presumed and need not be proven.

Despite the weaknesses of the Isley Brothers' theory of reasonable access, the appellants had a full opportunity to present their case to the jury. Three rhythm and blues experts (including legendary Motown songwriter Lamont Dozier of Holland-Dozier-Holland fame) testified that they never heard of the Isley Brothers' "Love is a Wonderful Thing." Furthermore, Bolton produced copies of "TV Guide" from 1966 suggesting that the television shows playing the song never aired in Connecticut. Bolton also pointed out that 129 songs called "Love is a Wonderful Thing" are registered with the Copyright Office, 85 of them before 1964.

The Isley Brothers' reasonable access arguments are not without merit. Teenagers are generally avid music listeners. It is entirely plausible that two Connecticut teenagers obsessed with rhythm and blues music could remember an Isley Brothers' song that was played on the radio and television for a few weeks, and subconsciously copy it twenty years later. Furthermore, Ronald Isley testified that when they met, Bolton said, "I have all his stuff." Finally, as the district court pointed out, Bolton's remark about Marvin Gaye and "Some Kind of Wonderful" indicates that Bolton believed he may have been copying someone else's song.

Finally, with regard to access, we are mindful of Judge Frank's words of caution in Arnstein v. Porter : "The judge characterized plaintiff's story as `fantastic'; and in the light of the references in his opinion to defendant's deposition, the judge obviously accepted the defendant's denial of access and copying . . . . [Y]et plaintiff's credibility, even as to those improbabilities, should be left to the jury." Arnstein, 154 F.2d at 469. In this case, Judge Baird heeded Judge Frank's admonition:

[T]his Court is not in a position to find that the only conclusion that a reasonable jury could have reached is that Defendants did not have access to Plaintiff's song. One must remember that the issue this Court must address is not whether Plaintiff has proven access by a preponderance of evidence, but whether reasonable minds could find that Defendants had a reasonable opportunity to have heard Plaintiff's song before they created their own song.

Although we might not reach the same conclusion as the jury regarding access, we find that the jury's conclusion about access is supported by substantial evidence. We are not establishing a new standard for access in copyright cases; we are merely saying that we will not disturb the jury's factual and credibility determinations on this issue.

B. Substantial Similarity

Under our case law, substantial similarity is inextricably linked to the issue of access. In what is known as the "inverse ratio rule," we "require a lower standard of proof of substantial similarity when a high degree of access is shown." Smith, 84 F.3d at 1218 (citing Shaw v. Lindheim, 919 F.2d 1353, 1361-62 (9th Cir. 1990);

Krofft, 562 F.2d at 1172). Furthermore, in the absence of any proof of access, a copyright plaintiff can still make out a case of infringement by showing that the songs were "strikingly similar." See Smith, 84 F.3d at 1220; Baxter v. MCA, Inc., 812 F.2d 421, 423, 424 n.2 (9th Cir. 1987).

Proof of the substantial similarity is satisfied by a twopart test of extrinsic similarity and intrinsic similarity. See Krofft, 562 F.2d at 1164. Initially, the extrinsic test requires that the plaintiff identify concrete elements based on objective criteria. See Smith, 84 F.3d at 1218; Shaw, 919 F.2d at 1356. The extrinsic test often requires analytical dissection of a work and expert testimony. See Apple Computer, Inc v. Microsoft Corp., 35 F.3d 1435, 1442 (9th Cir. 1994). Once the extrinsic test is satisfied, the factfinder applies the intrinsic test. The intrinsic test is subjective and asks "whether the ordinary, reasonable person would find the total concept and feel of the works to be substantially similar." Pasillas v. McDonald's Corp., 927 F.2d 440, 442 (9th Cir. 1991) (internal quotations omitted).

We will not second-guess the jury's application of the intrinsic test. See Krofft 562 F.3d at 1166 ("Since the intrinsic test for expression is uniquely suited for determination by the trier of fact, this court must be reluctant to reverse it.") (citations omitted). Furthermore, we will not reverse factual determinations regarding the extrinsic test absent a clearly erroneous application of the law. See id. It is well settled that a jury may find a combination of unprotectible elements to be protectible under the extrinsic test because " `the over-all impact and effect indicate substantial appropriation.' " Id. at 1169 (quoting Malkin v. Dubinsky, 146 F. Supp. 111, 114 (S.D.N.Y. 1956)).

1. Evidence of Substantial Similarity

Bolton and Goldmark argue that there was insufficient evidence of substantial similarity because the Isley Brothers' expert musicologist, Dr. Gerald Eskelin, failed to show that there was copying of a combination of unprotectible elements. On the contrary, Eskelin testified that the two songs shared a combination of five unprotectible elements: (1) the title hook phrase (including the lyric, rhythm, and pitch); (2) the shifted cadence; (3) the instrumental figures; (4) the verse/chorus relationship; and (5) the fade ending. Although the appellants presented testimony from their own expert musicologist, Anthony Ricigliano, he conceded that there were similarities between the two songs and that he had not found the combination of unprotectible elements in the Isley Brothers' song "anywhere in the prior art." The jury heard testimony from both of these experts and "found infringement based on a unique compilation of those elements." We refuse to interfere with the jury's credibility determination, nor do we find that the jury's finding of substantial similarity was clearly erroneous.

2. Independent Creation

Bolton and Goldmark also contend that their witnesses rebutted the Isley Brothers' prima facie case of copyright infringement with evidence of independent creation. By establishing reasonable access and substantial similarity, a copyright plaintiff creates a presumption of copying. The burden shifts to the defendant to rebut that presumption through proof of independent creation. See Granite Music Corp. v. United Artists Corp., 532 F.2d 718, 721 (9th Cir. 1976).

The appellants' case of independent creation hinges on three factors: the work tape demonstrating how Bolton and Goldmark created their song, Bolton and Goldmark's history of songwriting, and testimony that their arranger, Walter Afanasieff, contributed two of five unprotectible elements that they allegedly copied. The jury, however, heard the testimony of Bolton, Goldmark, Afanasieff, and Ricigliano about independent creation. The work tape revealed evidence that Bolton may have subconsciously copied a song that he believed to be written by Marvin Gaye. Bolton and Goldmark's history of songwriting presents no direct evidence about this case. And Afanasieff's contributions to Bolton and Goldmark's song were described by the appellants' own expert as "very common." Once again, we refuse to disturb the jury's determination about independent creation. The substantial evidence of copying based on access and substantial similarity was such that a reasonable juror could reject this defense.

3. Inverse-Ratio Rule

Although this may be a weak case of access and a circumstantial case of substantial similarity, neither issue warrants reversal of the jury's verdict. An amicus brief on behalf of the recording and motion picture industries warns against watering down the requirements for musical copyright infringement. This case presents no such danger. The Ninth Circuit's inverse-ratio rule requires a lesser showing of substantial similarity if there is a strong showing of access. See Smith, 84 F.3d at 1218. In this case, there was a weak showing of access. We have never held, however, that the inverse ratio rule says a weak showing of access requires a stronger showing of substantial similarity. Nor are we redefining the test of substantial similarity here; we merely find that there was substantial evidence from which the jury could find access and substantial similarity in this case.

D. Attribution of Profits

Sony Music claims that the district court improperly applied an assumption that all profits from Bolton and Goldmark's song go to the Isley Brothers, and that no evidence supported the jury's apportionment of profits. A successful copyright plaintiff is allowed to recover only those profits that are "attributable to infringement." 17 U.S.C.S 504(b) (1994). "In establishing the infringer's profits, the copyright owner is required to present proof only of the infringer's gross revenue, and the infringer is required to prove his or her deductible expenses and the elements of profit attributable to factors other than the copyrighted work." Id. See also Cream Records, Inc. v. Jos. Schlitz Brewing Co., 754 F.2d 826, 828 (9th Cir. 1985) (holding that when all profits do not clearly derive from the infringing material, the copyright owner is not entitled to recover all of the profits); Gaste , 863 F.2d at 1070 (finding that where there is "imprecision in the computation of expenses, a court should err on the side of guaranteeing the plaintiff a full recovery"). Thus, the statutory burden of proof lies with Sony Music to prove what percentage of their profits were not attributable to copying the Isley Brothers'"Love is a Wonderful Thing." Sony Music presented evidence that Bolton's "Love Is a Wonderful Thing" produced only 5-10% of the profits from his album, "Time, Love and Tenderness," and that the song's infringing elements resulted in only 10-15% of the profits from the song. The Isley Brothers, however, attacked the credibility of one of Sony Music's experts. Furthermore, they presented evidence that Bolton's infringing song was the album's lead single, that it was released 19 days before the album, and that Bolton engaged in telephone promotion of the song. The jury found that 28% of the album's profits derived from the song, and that 66% of the song's profits resulted from infringing elements.

We affirm the jury's apportionment of the profits for several reasons. First, the jury instructions adequately conveyed the burden of proof. Second, the burden of proof was on Sony Music, and the jury chose not to believe Sony Music's experts. Finally, a jury verdict apportioning less than 100% of the profits but more than the percentage estimates of Sony Music's experts does not represent clear error.

...

AFFIRMED.

741 F.2d 896 (1984)

SELLE v. GIBB

US Court of Appeals for the Seventh Circuit

CUDAHY, Circuit Judge.

[1] The plaintiff, Ronald H. Selle, brought a suit against three brothers, Maurice, Robin and Barry Gibb, known collectively as the popular signing group, the Bee Gees, alleging that the Bee Gees, in their hit tune, "How Deep Is Your Love," had infringed the copyright of his song, "Let It End." The jury returned a verdict in plaintiff's favor on the issue of liability in a bifurcated trial. The district court, Judge George N. Leighton, granted the defendants' motion for judgment notwithstanding the verdict and, in the alternative, for a new trial. Selle v. Gibb, 567 F.Supp. 1173 (N.D.Ill. 1983). We affirm the grant of the motion for judgment notwithstanding the verdict.

I

[2] Selle composed his song, "Let It End," in one day in the fall of 1975 and obtained a copyright for it on November 17, 1975. He played his song with his small band two or three times in the Chicago area and sent a tape and lead sheet of the music to eleven music recording and publishing companies. Eight of the companies returned the materials to Selle; three did not respond. This was the extent of the public dissemination of Selle's song. Selle first became aware of the Bee Gees' song, "How Deep Is Your Love," in May 1978 and thought that he recognized the music as his own, although the lyrics were different. He also saw the movie, "Saturday

Night Fever," the sound track of which features the song "How Deep Is Your Love," and again recognized the music. He subsequently sued the three Gibb brothers; Paramount Pictures Corporation, which made and distributed the movie; and Phonodisc, Inc., now known as Polygram Distribution, Inc., which made and distributed the cassette tape of "How Deep Is Your Love."

[3] The Bee Gees are internationally known performers and creators of popular music. They have composed more than 160 songs; their sheet music, records and tapes have been distributed worldwide, some of the albums selling more than 30 million copies. The Bee Gees, however, do not themselves read or write music. In composing a song, their practice was to tape a tune, which members of their staff would later transcribe and reduce to a form suitable for copyrighting, sale and performance by both the Bee Gees and others.

[4] In addition to their own testimony at trial, the Bee Gees presented testimony by their manager, Dick Ashby, and two musicians, Albhy Galuten and Blue Weaver, who were on the Bee Gees' staff at the time "How Deep Is Your Love" was composed. These witnesses described in detail how, in January 1977, the Bee Gees and several members of their staff went to a recording studio in the Chateau d'Herouville about 25 miles northwest of Paris. There the group composed at least six new songs and mixed a live album. Barry Gibb's testimony included a detailed explanation of a work tape which was introduced into evidence and played in court. This tape preserves the actual process of creation during which the brothers, and particularly Barry, created the tune of the accused song while Weaver, a keyboard player, played the tune which was hummed or sung by the brothers. Although the tape does not seem to preserve the very beginning of the process of creation, it does depict the process by which ideas, notes, lyrics and bits of the tune were gradually put together.

[5] Following completion of this work tape, a demo tape was made. The work tape, demo tape and a vocal-piano version taken from the demo tape are all in the key of E flat. Lead sheet music, dated March 6, 1977, is in the key of E. On March 7, 1977, a lead sheet of "How Deep Is Your Love" was filed for issuance of a United States copyright, and in November 1977, a piano-vocal arrangement was filed in the Copyright Office.

[6] The only expert witness to testify at trial was Arrand Parsons, a professor of music at Northwestern University who has had extensive professional experience primarily in classical music. He has been a program annotator for the Chicago Symphony Orchestra and the New Orleans Symphony Orchestra and has authored works about musical theory. Prior to this case, however, he had never made a comparative analysis of two popular songs. Dr. Parsons testified on the basis of several charts comparing the musical notes of each song and a comparative recording prepared under his direction.

[7] According to Dr. Parsons' testimony, the first eight bars of each song (Theme A) have twenty-four of thirty-four notes in plaintiff's composition and twenty-four of forty notes in defendants' composition which are identical in pitch and symmetrical position. Of thirty-five rhythmic impulses in plaintiff's composition and forty in defendants', thirty are identical. In the last four bars of both songs

(Theme B), fourteen notes in each are identical in pitch, and eleven of the fourteen rhythmic impulses are identical. Both Theme A and Theme B appear in the same position in each song but with different intervening material.

[8] Dr. Parsons testified that, in his opinion, "the two songs had such striking similarities that they could not have been written independent of one another." Tr. 202. He also testified that he did not know of two songs by different composers "that contain as many striking similarities" as do the two songs at issue here. However, on several occasions, he declined to say that the similarities could only have resulted from copying.

[9] Following presentation of the case, the jury returned a verdict for the plaintiff on the issue of liability, the only question presented to the jury. Judge Leighton, however, granted the defendants' motion for judgment notwithstanding the verdict and, in the alternative, for a new trial. He relied primarily on the plaintiff's inability to demonstrate that the defendants had access to the plaintiff's song, without which a claim of copyright infringement could not prevail regardless how similar the two compositions are. Further, the plaintiff failed to contradict or refute the testimony of the defendants and their witnesses describing the independent creation process of "How Deep Is Your Love." Finally, Judge Leighton concluded that "the inferences on which plaintiff relies is not a logical, permissible deduction from proof of `striking similarity' or substantial similarity; it is `at war with the undisputed facts,' and it is inconsistent with the proof of nonaccess to plaintiff's song by the Bee Gees at the time in question." 567 F.Supp. at 1183 (citations omitted).

II

[10] Both we and the district court must be reluctant to remove an issue from the purview of the jury on either a directed verdict or a judgment notwithstanding the verdict. Nonetheless, we have a duty to determine whether there is sufficient evidence to support the position of the nonmoving party, in this case, the plaintiff. The standards applicable to a motion for judgment notwithstanding the verdict and to a directed verdict are, of course, the same. All the evidence, taken as a whole, must be viewed in the light most favorable to the nonmoving party. This evidence must provide a sufficient basis from which the jury could have reasonably reached a verdict without speculation or drawing unreasonable inferences which conflict with the undisputed facts. Brady v. Southern Railway, 320 U.S. 476, 480, 64 S.Ct. 232, 234, 88 L.Ed. 239 (1943); United States v. An Article of Device, 731 F.2d 1253, 1257 (7th Cir. 1984); Chillicothe Sand & Gravel Co. v. Martin Marietta Corp., 615 F.2d 427, 430 (7th Cir. 1980); Hohmann v. Packard Instrument Co., 471 F.2d 815, 819 (7th Cir. 1973).

[11] It is, of course, not relevant that, in this case, the trial court denied defendants' motion for a directed verdict and submitted the issue to the jury. It is generally more efficient to proceed in this fashion, so that, in the event the reviewing court reverses, the entire case will not have to be retried. Mattivi v. South African Marine Corp., 618 F.2d 163, 166 (2d Cir. 1980). Since we affirm the district court's grant of

a judgment notwithstanding the verdict, it is not necessary to consider either the grant of the motion, in the alternative, for a new trial or the defendants' cross-appeal on the district court's denial of summary judgment. We note, however, that the cross-appeal with respect to the summary judgment motion is inappropriate and redundant since the issues it raised were incorporated in the motion for judgment notwithstanding the verdict. The cross-appeal may be little more than a device to win an opportunity to file the last brief or to argue the evidence of witnesses not presented at trial who furnished summary judgment affidavits - and is a procedure not to be encouraged.

III

[12] Selle's primary contention on this appeal is that the district court misunderstood the theory of proof of copyright infringement on which he based his claim. Under this theory, copyright infringement can be demonstrated when, even in the absence of any direct evidence of access, the two pieces in question are so strikingly similar that access can be inferred from such similarity alone. Selle argues that the testimony of his expert witness, Dr. Parsons, was sufficient evidence of such striking similarity that it was permissible for the jury, even in the absence of any other evidence concerning access, to infer that the Bee Gees had access to plaintiff's song and indeed copied it.

[13] In establishing a claim of copyright infringement of a musical composition, the plaintiff must prove (1) ownership of the copyright in the complaining work; (2) originality of the work; (3) copying of the work by the defendant, and (4) a substantial degree of similarity between the two works. See Sherman, Musical Copyright Infringement: The Requirement of Substantial Similarity. Copyright Law Symposium, Number 92, American Society of Composers, Authors and Publishers 81-82. Columbia University Press (1977) [hereinafter "Sherman, Musical Copyright Infringement"]. The only element which is at issue in this appeal is proof of copying; the first two elements are essentially conceded, while the fourth (substantial similarity) is, at least in these circumstances, closely related to the third element under plaintiff's theory of the case.

[14] Proof of copying is crucial to any claim of copyright infringement because no matter how similar the two works may be (even to the point of identity), if the defendant did not copy the accused work, there is no infringement. Arnstein v. Edward B. Marks Music Corp., 82 F.2d 275 (2d Cir.), motion to set aside decree denied, 86 F.2d 715 (2d Cir. 1936). However, because direct evidence of copying is rarely available, the plaintiff can rely upon circumstantial evidence to prove this essential element, and the most important component of this sort of circumstantial evidence is proof of access. See generally 3 Nimmer, Copyright § 13.02 at 13-9 (1983) [hereinafter "Nimmer, Copyright"]. The plaintiff may be able to introduce direct evidence of access when, for example, the work was sent directly to the defendant (whether a musician or a publishing company) or a close associate of the defendant. On the other hand, the plaintiff may be able to establish a reasonable possibility of access when, for example, the complaining work has been widely disseminated to the public. See, e.g., Abkco Music, Inc. v. Harrisongs Music,

Ltd., 722 F.2d 988, 998 (2d Cir. 1983) (finding of access based on wide dissemination); Sherman, Musical Copyright Infringement, at 82.

[15] If, however, the plaintiff does not have direct evidence of access, then an inference of access may still be established circumstantially by proof of similarity which is so striking that the possibilities of independent creation, coincidence and prior common source are, as a practical matter, precluded. If the plaintiff presents evidence of striking similarity sufficient to raise an inference of access, then copying is presumably proved simultaneously, although the fourth element (substantial similarity) still requires proof that the defendant copied a substantial amount of the complaining work. The theory which Selle attempts to apply to this case is based on proof of copying by circumstantial proof of access established by striking similarity between the two works.

[16] One difficulty with plaintiff's theory is that no matter how great the similarity between the two works, it is not their similarity per se which establishes access; rather, their similarity tends to prove access in light of the nature of the works, the particular musical genre involved and other circumstantial evidence of access. In other words, striking similarity is just one piece of circumstantial evidence tending to show access and must not be considered in isolation; it must be considered together with other types of circumstantial evidence relating to access.

[17] As a threshold matter, therefore, it would appear that there must be at least some other evidence which would establish a reasonable possibility that the complaining work was available to the alleged infringer. As noted, two works may be identical in every detail, but, if the alleged infringer created the accused work independently or both works were copied from a common source in the public domain, then there is no infringement. Therefore, if the plaintiff admits to having kept his or her creation under lock and key, it would seem logically impossible to infer access through striking similarity. Thus, although it has frequently been written that striking similarity alone can establish access, the decided cases suggest that this circumstance would be most unusual. The plaintiff must always present sufficient evidence to support a reasonable possibility of access because the jury cannot draw an inference of access based upon speculation and conjecture alone.

[18] For example, in Twentieth Century-Fox Film Corp. v. Dieckhaus, 153 F.2d 893 (8th Cir.), cert. denied, 329 U.S. 716, 67 S.Ct. 46, 91 L.Ed. 621 (1946), the court reversed a finding of infringement based solely on the similarities between plaintiff's book and defendant's film. The court stated that the plaintiff herself presented no evidence that the defendant had had access to her book, and the only people to whom the plaintiff had given a copy of her book testified that they had not given it to the defendant. While the court also concluded that the similarities between the book and the film were not that significant, the result turned on the fact that "[t]he oral and documentary evidence in the record . . . establishes the fact that the defendant had no access to plaintiff's book unless the law of plagiarism permits the court to draw an inference contrary to such proof from its finding of similarities on comparison of the book with the picture." Id. at 897. Thus, although proof of striking similarity may permit an inference of access, the plaintiff must

still meet some minimum threshold of proof which demonstrates that the inference of access is reasonable.

...

[20] The possibility of access in the present case is not as remote as that in Dieckhaus because neither side elicited testimony from the individuals (primarily employees of the publishing companies) to whom the plaintiff had distributed copies of his song. Such evidence might have conclusively disproved access. On the other hand, Selle's song certainly did not achieve the extent of public dissemination existing in Cholvin, Jewel Music Publishing Co., or Harrisongs Music, and there was also no evidence that any of the defendants or their associates were in Chicago on the two or three occasions when the plaintiff played his song publicly. It is not necessary for us, given the facts of this case, to determine the number of copies which must be publicly distributed to raise a reasonable inference of access. Nevertheless, in this case, the availability of Selle's song, as shown by the evidence, was virtually de minimis.

[21] In granting the defendants' motion for judgment notwithstanding the verdict, Judge Leighton relied primarily on the plaintiff's failure to adduce any evidence of access and stated that an inference of access may not be based on mere conjecture, speculation or a bare possibility of access. 567 F.Supp. at 1181. Thus, in Testa v. Janssen, 492 F.Supp. 198, 202-03 (W.D.Pa. 1980), the court stated that "[t]o support a finding of access, plaintiffs' evidence must extend beyond mere speculation or conjecture. And, while circumstantial evidence is sufficient to establish access, a defendant's opportunity to view the copyrighted work must exist by a reasonable possibility - not a bare possibility" (citation omitted). See also Ferguson v. National Broadcasting Co., 584 F.2d 111, 113 (5th Cir. 1978); Scott v. Paramount Pictures Corp., 449 F.Supp. 518, 520 (D.D.C. 1978), aff'd mem., 607 F.2d 494 (D.C.Cir. 1979), cert. denied, 449 U.S. 849, 101 S.Ct. 137, 66 L.Ed.2d 60 (1980).

[22] Judge Leighton thus based his decision on what he characterized as the plaintiff's inability to raise more than speculation that the Bee Gees had access to his song. The extensive testimony of the defendants and their witnesses describing the creation process went essentially uncontradicted, and there was no attempt even to impeach their credibility. Judge Leighton further relied on the principle that the testimony of credible witnesses concerning a matter within their knowledge cannot be rejected without some impeachment, contradiction or inconsistency with other evidence on the particular point at issue. Dieckhaus, supra, 153 F.2d at 899-900. See also Chesapeake and Ohio Railroad Co. v. Martin, 283 U.S. 209, 216, 51 S.Ct. 453, 456, 75 L.Ed. 983 (1931). Judge Leighton's conclusions that there was no more than a bare possibility that the defendants could have had access to Selle's song and that this was an insufficient basis from which the jury could have reasonably inferred the existence of access seem correct. The plaintiff has failed to meet even the minimum threshold of proof of the possibility of access and, as Judge Leighton has stated, an inference of access would thus seem to be "at war with the undisputed facts." 567 F.Supp. at 1183.

IV

[23] The grant of the motion for judgment notwithstanding the verdict might, if we were so minded, be affirmed on the basis of the preceding analysis of the plaintiff's inability to establish a reasonable inference of access. This decision is also supported by a more traditional analysis of proof of access based only on the proof of "striking similarity" between the two compositions. The plaintiff relies almost exclusively on the testimony of his expert witness, Dr. Parsons, that the two pieces were, in fact, "strikingly similar." Yet formulating a meaningful definition of "striking similarity" is no simple task, and the term is often used in a conclusory or circular fashion.

[24] Sherman defines "striking similarity" as a term of art signifying "that degree of similarity as will permit an inference of copying even in the absence of proof of access. . . ." Sherman, Musical Copyright Infringement, at 84 n. 15. Nimmer states that, absent proof of access, "the similarities must be so striking as to preclude the possibility that the defendant independently arrived at the same result." Nimmer, Copyright, at 13-14.

[25] "Striking similarity" is not merely a function of the number of identical notes that appear in both compositions. Cf. Wilkie v. Santly Brothers, Inc., 13 F.Supp. 136 (S.D.N.Y. 1935), aff'd, 91 F.2d 978 (2d Cir.), cert. denied, 302 U.S. 735, 58 S.Ct. 120, 82 L.Ed. 568 (1937), aff'd on reargument, 94 F.2d 1023 (2d Cir. 1938) (comparison of note structure demonstrates striking similarity), and Jewel Music Publishing Co. v. Leo Feist, Inc., 62 F.Supp. 596 (S.D.N.Y. 1945) (in light of plaintiff's inability to establish access, degree of similarity despite identity or near identity of several bars was not striking). An important factor in analyzing the degree of similarity of two compositions is the uniqueness of the sections which are asserted to be similar.

[26] If the complaining work contains an unexpected departure from the normal metric structure or if the complaining work includes what appears to be an error and the accused work repeats the unexpected element or the error, then it is more likely that there is some connection between the pieces. See, e.g., Nordstrom v. Radio Corporation of America, 251 F.Supp. 41, 42 (D.Colo. 1965). If the similar sections are particularly intricate, then again it would seem more likely that the compositions are related. Finally, some dissimilarities may be particularly suspicious. See, e.g., Meier Co. v. Albany Novelty Manufacturing Co., 236 F.2d 144, 146 (2d Cir. 1956) (inversion and substitution of certain words in a catalogue in a "crude effort to give the appearance of dissimilarity" are themselves evidence of copying); Blume v. Spear, 30 F. 629, 631 (S.D.N.Y. 1887) (variations in infringing song were placed so as to indicate deliberate copying); Sherman, Musical Copyright Infringement, at 84-88. While some of these concepts are borrowed from literary copyright analysis, they would seem equally applicable to an analysis of music.

[27] The judicially formulated definition of "striking similarity" states that "plaintiffs must demonstrate that `such similarities are of a kind that can only be explained by copying, rather than by coincidence, independent creation, or prior common source.'" Testa v. Janssen, 492 F.Supp. 198, 203 (W.D.Pa. 1980) (quoting

Stratchborneo v. Arc Music Corp., 357 F.Supp. 1393, 1403 (S.D.N.Y. 1973)). See also Scott v. WKJG, Inc., 376 F.2d 467, 469 (7th Cir. 1967) (the similarities must be "so striking and of such nature as to preclude the possibility of coincidence, accident or independent creation."); Arnstein v. Porter, 154 F.2d 464, 468 (2d Cir. 1946) (same); Scott v. Paramount Pictures Corp., 449 F.Supp. 518, 520 (D.D.C. 1978) (same). Sherman adds:

To prove that certain similarities are "striking," plaintiff must show that they are the sort of similarities that cannot satisfactorily be accounted for by a theory of coincidence, independent creation, prior common source, or any theory other than that of copying. Striking similarity is an extremely technical issue - one with which, understandably, experts are best equipped to deal.

[28] Sherman, Musical Copyright Infringement, at 96.

[29] Finally, the similarities should appear in a sufficiently unique or complex context as to make it unlikely that both pieces were copied from a prior common source, Sheldon v. Metro-Goldwyn Pictures Corp., 81 F.2d 49, 54 (2d Cir.), cert. denied, 298 U.S. 669, 56 S.Ct. 835, 80 L.Ed. 1392 (1936), or that the defendant was able to compose the accused work as a matter of independent creation, Nichols v. Universal Pictures Corp., 45 F.2d 119, 122 (2d Cir. 1930), cert. denied, 282 U.S. 902, 51 S.Ct. 216, 75 L.Ed. 795 (1931). See also Darrell v. Joe Morris Music Co., 113 F.2d 80 (2d Cir. 1940) ("simple, trite themes . . . are likely to recur spontaneously . . . and [only few] . . . suit the infantile demands of the popular ear"); Arnstein v. Edward B. Marks Music Corp., 82 F.2d 275, 277 (2d Cir. 1936). Cf. Abkco Music, Inc. v. Harrisongs Music, Ltd., 722 F.2d 988, 998 (2d Cir. 1983) (finding of a "highly unique pattern" makes copying more likely). With these principles in mind, we turn now to an analysis of the evidence of "striking similarity" presented by the plaintiff.

[30] As noted, the plaintiff relies almost entirely on the testimony of his expert witness, Dr. Arrand Parsons. The defendants did not introduce any expert testimony, apparently because they did not think Parsons' testimony needed to be refuted. Defendants are perhaps to some degree correct in asserting that Parsons, although eminently qualified in the field of classical music theory, was not equally qualified to analyze popular music tunes. More significantly, however, although Parsons used the magic formula, "striking similarity," he only ruled out the possibility of independent creation; he did not state that the similarities could only be the result of copying. In order for proof of "striking similarity" to establish a reasonable inference of access, especially in a case such as this one in which the direct proof of access is so minimal, the plaintiff must show that the similarity is of a type which will preclude any explanation other than that of copying.

[31] In addition, to bolster the expert's conclusion that independent creation was not possible, there should be some testimony or other evidence of the relative complexity or uniqueness of the two compositions. Dr. Parsons' testimony did not refer to this aspect of the compositions and, in a field such as that of popular music in which all songs are relatively short and tend to build on or repeat a basic theme, such testimony would seem to be particularly necessary. We agree with the Sixth Circuit which explained that "we do not think the affidavit of [the expert witness],

stating in conclusory terms that `it is extremely unlikely that one set [of architectural plans] could have been prepared without access to the other set,' can fill the gap which is created by the absence of any direct evidence of access." Scholz Homes, Inc. v. Maddox, 379 F.2d 84, 86 (6th Cir. 1967).

[32] To illustrate this deficiency more concretely, we refer to a cassette tape, Plaintiff's Exhibit 27, and the accompanying chart, Plaintiff's Exhibit 26. These exhibits were prepared by the defendants but introduced into evidence by the plaintiff. The tape has recorded on it segments of both themes from both the Selle and the Gibb songs interspersed with segments of other compositions as diverse as "Footsteps," "From Me To You" (a Lennon-McCartney piece), Beethoven's 5th Symphony, "Funny Talk," "Play Down," and "I'd Like To Leave If I May" (the last two being earlier compositions by Barry Gibb). There are at least superficial similarities among these segments, when played on the same musical instrument, and the plaintiff failed to elicit any testimony from his expert witness about this exhibit which compared the Selle and the Gibb songs to other pieces of contemporary, popular music. These circumstances indicate that the plaintiff failed to sustain his burden of proof on the issue of "striking similarity" in its legal sense - that is, similarity which reasonably precludes the possibility of any explanation other than that of copying.

[33] The plaintiff's expert witness does not seem to have addressed any issues relating to the possibility of prior common source in both widely disseminated popular songs and the defendants' own compositions. At oral argument, plaintiff's attorney stated that the burden of proving common source should be on the defendant; however, the burden of proving "striking similarity," which, by definition, includes taking steps to minimize the possibility of common source, is on the plaintiff. In essence, the plaintiff failed to prove to the requisite degree that the similarities identified by the expert witness - although perhaps "striking" in a non-legal sense - were of a type which would eliminate any explanation of coincidence, independent creation or common source, including, in this case, the possibility of common source in earlier compositions created by the Bee Gees themselves or by others. In sum, the evidence of striking similarity is not sufficiently compelling to make the case when the proof of access must otherwise depend largely upon speculation and conjecture.

[34] Therefore, because the plaintiff failed both to establish a basis from which the jury could reasonably infer that the Bee Gees had access to his song and to meet his burden of proving "striking similarity" between the two compositions, the grant by the district court of the defendants' motion for judgment notwithstanding the verdict is affirmed. Because of our doubts concerning the defendants' cross-appeal on the denial of the summary judgment, we order that, under Fed.R.App.P. 38, each party shall bear its own costs.

132 F.3d 1167 (7th Cir. 1997)

TY V. GMA ACCESSORIES

US Court of Appeals for the Seventh Circuit

RICHARD POSNER, Chief Judge.

Ty, the manufacturer of the popular "Beanie Babies" line of stuffed animals, has obtained a preliminary injunction under the Copyright Act against the sale by GMA (and also a retailer, but we can disregard that aspect of the injunction) of "Preston the Pig" and "Louie the Cow." These are bean-bag animals manufactured by GMA that Ty contends are copies of its copyrighted pig ("Squealer") and cow ("Daisy"). Ty began selling the "Beanie Babies" line, including Squealer, in 1993, and it was the popularity of the line that induced GMA to bring out its own line of bean-bag stuffed animals three years later. GMA does not contest the part of the injunction that enjoins the sale of Louie, but asks us on a variety of grounds to vacate the other part, the part that enjoins it from selling Preston.

We have appended to our opinion five pictures found in the appellate record. The first shows Squealer (the darker pig, actually pink) and Preston (white). The second is a picture of two real pigs. The third and fourth are different views of the design for Preston that Janet Salmon submitted to GMA several months before Preston went into production. The fifth is a picture of the two bean-bag cows; they are nearly identical. A glance at the first picture shows a striking similarity between the two bean-bag pigs as well. The photograph was supplied by GMA and actually understates the similarity (the animals themselves are part of the record). The "real" Preston is the same length as Squealer and has a virtually identical snout. The difference in the lengths of the two animals in the picture is a trick of the camera. The difference in snouts results from the fact that the pictured Preston was a manufacturing botch. And GMA put a ribbon around the neck of the Preston in the picture, but the Preston that it sells doesn't have a ribbon.

The two pigs are so nearly identical that if the second is a copy of the first, the second clearly infringes Ty's copyright. But identity is not infringement. The Copyright Act forbids only copying; if independent creation results in an identical work, the creator of that work is free to sell it. Selle v. Gibb, 741 F.2d 896, 901 (7th Cir. 1984); Grubb v. KMS Patriots, L.P., 88 F.3d 1, 3 (1st Cir. 1996). The practical basis for this rule is that unlike the case of patents and trademarks, the creator of an expressive work--an author or sculptor or composer--cannot canvass the entire universe of copyrighted works to discover whether his poem or song or, as in this case, "soft sculpture" is identical to some work in which copyright subsists, especially since unpublished, unregistered works are copyrightable. 17 U.S.C. § 104(a); Harper & Row, Publishers, Inc. v. Nation Enterprises, 471 U.S. 539, 548, 105 S. Ct. 2218, 2224, 85 L. Ed. 2d 588 (1985). But identity can be powerful evidence of copying. Gaste v. Kaiserman, 863 F.2d 1061, 1068 (2d Cir. 1988); Ferguson v. National Broadcasting Co., 584 F.2d 111 (5th Cir. 1978). The more a work is both like an already copyrighted work and--for this is equally important--

unlike anything that is in the public domain, the less likely it is to be an independent creation. As is generally true in the law, circumstantial evidence--evidence merely probabilistic rather than certain--can confer sufficient confidence on an inference, here of copying, to warrant a legal finding.

The issue of copying can be broken down into two subissues. The first is whether the alleged copier had access to the work that he is claimed to have copied; the second is whether, if so, he used his access to copy. CMM Cable Rep, Inc. v. Ocean Coast Properties, Inc., 97 F.3d 1504, 1513 (1st Cir. 1996); Fisher-Price, Inc. v. Well-Made Toy Mfg. Corp., 25 F.3d 119, 123 (2d Cir. 1994). It might seem that access could not be an issue where, as in this case, the allegedly copied work is a mass-produced consumer product purchasable for $5. But we shall see that GMA has attempted to make an issue of access.

Obviously, access does not entail copying. An eyewitness might have seen the defendant buy the copyrighted work; this would be proof of access, but not of copying. But copying entails access. If, therefore, two works are so similar as to make it highly probable that the later one is a copy of the earlier one, the issue of access need not be addressed separately, since if the later work was a copy its creator must have had access to the original. Selle v. Gibb, supra, 741 F.2d at 901; Gaste v. Kaiserman, supra, 863 F.2d at 1068; Ferguson v. National Broadcasting Co., supra. Of course the inference of access, and hence of copying, could be rebutted by proof that the creator of the later work could not have seen the earlier one or (an alternative mode of access) a copy of the earlier one. But unlike the court in Towler v. Sayles, 76 F.3d 579, 584-85 (4th Cir. 1996), and the authors of 4 Nimmer on Copyright § 13.02 [B], pp. 13-24 to 13-25 (1997), we do not read our decision in Selle to hold or imply, in conflict with the Gaste decision, that no matter how closely the works resemble each other, the plaintiff must produce some (other) evidence of access. He must produce evidence of access, all right--but, as we have just said, and as is explicit in Selle itself, see 741 F.2d at 901, a similarity that is so close as to be highly unlikely to have been an accident of independent creation is evidence of access.

What troubled us in Selle but is not a factor here is that two works may be strikingly similar--may in fact be identical--not because one is copied from the other but because both are copies of the same thing in the public domain. In such a case--imagine two people photographing Niagara Falls from the same place at the same time of the day and year and in identical weather--there is no inference of access to anything but the public domain, and, equally, no inference of copying from a copyrighted work. Id. at 904; Gracen v. Bradford Exchange, 698 F.2d 300, 304 (7th Cir. 1983); Warren Publishing, Inc. v. Microdos Data Corp., 115 F.3d 1509, 1516 n. 19 (11th Cir. 1997); Key Publications, Inc. v. Chinatown Today Publishing Enterprises, Inc., 945 F.2d 509, 514 (2d Cir. 1991). A similarity may be striking without being suspicious.

But here it is both. GMA's pig is strikingly similar to Ty's pig but not to anything in the public domain--a real pig, for example, which is why we have included in our appendix a photograph of real pigs. The parties' bean-bag pigs bear little resemblance to real pigs even if we overlook the striking anatomical anomaly of

Preston--he has three toes, whereas real pigs have cloven hooves. We can imagine an argument that the technology of manufacturing bean-bag animals somehow prevents the manufacturer from imitating a real pig. But anyone even slightly familiar with stuffed animals knows that there are many lifelike stuffed pigs on the market, and whether they are stuffed with beans or other materials does not significantly affect their verisimilitude--though here we must emphasize that any factual assertions in this opinion should be treated as tentative, since the case is before us on an appeal from the abbreviated record of a preliminary-injunction proceeding and a full trial may cast the facts in a different light.

Real pigs are not the only pigs in the public domain. But GMA has not pointed to any fictional pig in the public domain that Preston resembles. Preston resembles only Squealer, and resembles him so closely as to warrant an inference that GMA copied Squealer. In rebuttal all that GMA presented was the affidavit of the designer, Salmon, who swears, we must assume truthfully, that she never looked at a Squealer before submitting her design. But it is not her design drawing that is alleged to infringe the copyright on Squealer; it is the manufactured Preston, the soft sculpture itself, which, as a comparison of the first with the third and fourth pictures in the appendix reveals, is much more like Squealer than Salmon's drawing is. And remember that the manufactured Preston in the photograph is a sport, with its stubby snout and its ribbon. Interestingly, these are features of Salmon's drawing but not of the production-model Preston, suggesting design intervention between Salmon's submission and actual production.

It is true that only a few months elapsed between Salmon's submission of the drawing to GMA and the production of Preston. But the record is silent on how long it would have taken to modify her design to make it more like Squealer. For all we know, it might have been done in hours--by someone who had bought a Squealer. The Beanie Babies are immensely popular. They are also, it is true, sometimes hard to find (though not this Christmas, in Chicago at any rate). Ty's practice, apparently, is to create a shortage (that is, to price its bean-bag animals below the market-clearing price) in order to excite the market. But it is unbelievable that a substantial company like GMA which is in the same line of business as Ty could not have located and purchased a Squealer if it wanted to copy it. A glance at the last picture in the appendix shows an identity between Louie the Cow and Ty's Daisy that is so complete (and also not explainable by reference to resemblance to a real cow or other public domain figure) as to compel an inference of copying. If GMA thus must have had access to Daisy, it is probable, quite apart from any inference from the evidence of similarity, that it had access to Squealer as well.

This discussion shows how the tension between Gaste and Selle can be resolved and the true relation between similarity and access expressed. Access (and copying) may be inferred when two works are so similar to each other and not to anything in the public domain that it is likely that the creator of the second work copied the first, but the inference can be rebutted by disproving access or otherwise showing independent creation--and in this connection GMA complains that the district judge refused to conduct an evidentiary hearing at which it might have presented evidence of independent creation. If genuine issues of material fact are created by the response to a motion for a preliminary injunction, an evidentiary hearing is indeed required. Medeco Security Locks, Inc. v. Swiderek, 680 F.2d 37, 38 (7th Cir. 1981) (per curiam); Elliott v. Kiesewetter, 98 F.3d 47, 53 (3d Cir. 1996); Schulz v. Williams, 38 F.3d 657 (2d Cir. 1994) (per curiam). But as in any case in which a party seeks an evidentiary hearing, he must be able to persuade the court that the issue is indeed genuine and material and so a hearing would be productive--he must show in other words that he has and intends to introduce evidence that if believed will so weaken the moving party's case as to affect the judge's decision on whether to issue an injunction. Here is where GMA falters. The only evidence that it seeks to present is the designer's oral testimony in support of the claim of independent creation. Her testimony would presumably have duplicated her affidavit, which was already in evidence; at least, GMA has not indicated what her testimony would add to her affidavit. Affidavits are ordinarily inadmissible at trials but they are fully admissible in summary proceedings, including preliminary-injunction proceedings. Levi Strauss & Co. v. Sunrise Int'l Trading Inc., 51 F.3d 982, 985 (11th Cir. 1995); Asseo v. Pan American Grain Co., 805 F.2d 23, 26 (1st Cir. 1986). So the evidence that GMA wants to put before the district judge was before him when he ruled.

Even if fully credited, the affidavit does not establish the independent creation of Preston but merely the independent creation of a drawing that resembles Squealer much less than the production model of Preston does. This is not to deny that the affidavit is some evidence of independent creation of Preston, so it was relevant evidence.

...

We find no error of law, no clear error of fact, and no abuse of discretion in the grant of the preliminary injunction to Ty. The judgment of the district court is therefore affirmed.

No. C 13-4679 PJH (2014)

BRIGGS v. BLOMKAMP

United States Northern District of California

In January 2006, plaintiff began attempting to market his screenplay. During approximately the next two years, he sent dozens of query letters and emails to literary agents and film companies. He also posted short synopses on screenwriter websites, and entered screenwriting and scriptwriting competitions.

In January 2007, plaintiff again revised his screenplay, and renamed it "Butterfly Driver." He claims that in February 2007, he posted the entire "Butterfly Driver" screenplay on triggerstreet.com, a filmmaker-screenwriter website designed to link filmmakers and screenwriters with industry professionals, by allowing members to post screenplays, short films, and short stories to get feedback from peers and professionals. Plaintiff asserts that at that time, the triggerstreet.com website had approximately 50,000 active members.

On May 27, 2013, plaintiff went to a movie theater, where he watched a trailer for a film called "Elysium," featuring a plot, characters, and settings that appeared to plaintiff to have been misappropriated from "Butterfly Driver."

...

1. Access

Defendants contend that plaintiff has no evidence of access. Direct access is shown if there is proof that the defendant actually viewed, read, or heard the work at issue. Lucky Break Wishbone Corp. v. Sears, Roebuck & Co., 528 F.Supp. 2d 1106, 1122 (W.D. Wash. 14 2007), aff'd, 373 Fed. Appx. 752 (9th Cir. 2010). Here, plaintiff has provided no direct evidence that defendants ever saw the "Butterfly Driver" screenplay. Access may also be demonstrated by circumstantial evidence, which requires a showing that the defendants had a "reasonable opportunity" or a "reasonable possibility" of viewing plaintiff's work prior to the creation of the infringing work. See Three Boys Music, 212 F.3d at 482 (access may be shown by a chain of events connecting plaintiff's work and the defendant's opportunity to view/hear/copy the work, such as dealings through a third party that had access to the plaintiff's work and with whom both the plaintiff and the defendant were dealing; or by the plaintiff's work being widely disseminated). Reasonable access requires more than a "bare possibility," and "may not be inferred through mere speculation or conjecture." Id. (citations and quotations omitted); see also Art Attacks Ink, LLC v. MGA Entm't Inc., 581 F.3d 1138, 1143-44 (9th Cir. 2009). Both in his own motion and in his opposition to defendants' motion, plaintiff relies on the allegations in the FAC. There, he asserts that he posted the "Butterfly Driver" script on a website operated by triggerstreet.com in February 2007, and that triggerstreet.com was "the only place" he ever posted a complete script of "Butterfly Driver." FAC ¶¶ 18-22. At the time, triggerstreet.com allowed members to post screenplays and short films to get feedback from peers and professionals – and gave them "a small hope of being noticed by a Hollywood insider." FAC ¶ 231.

Based on this, plaintiff asserts that triggerstreet.com "is where the [d]efendants had access to [p]laintiff's script." FAC ¶ 23. He claims that he posted four versions of "Butterfly Driver" on triggerstreet.com between February and August 2007, and that after he posted one of the versions in late July 2007, "[a] young director (whose name escapes the [p]laintiff) . . . praised the script through the [website's] message board." FAC ¶ 26.

Plaintiff alleges that this director "MAY have been [d]efendant, Neill Blomkamp[,]" although he also asserts that "Blomkamp, or any associate, may have accessed the work, without a word." FAC ¶ 26 (emphasis in original). He does not believe that the founders of triggerstreet.com "were complicit in the access of his work or the infringement[,] but . . . is certain that one or more of the [d]efendants, or an acquaintance, accessed the [p]laintiff's work on triggerstreet.com." FAC ¶ 226.

In plaintiff's view, Blomkamp, who is credited with writing "Elysium," is "most likely the infringer" because (a) triggerstreet.com is a website for short filmmakers and screenwriters; (b) in 2007 Blomkamp was exclusively a short filmmaker, who was based in Los Angeles (home of Trigger Street); (c) Blomkamp was "perhaps the most social media savvy short filmmaker in the world – and living in the screenwriting hub of the world;" and (d) plaintiff was a screenwriter. See FAC ¶¶ 227, 232, 233.

Defendants contend, however, that plaintiff alleges no facts in the FAC to support his claim that Blomkamp found the "Butterfly Driver" screenplay on triggerstreet.com. They argue further that plaintiff has no evidence that any defendant, including Blomkamp, had a reasonable opportunity or any reasonable possibility of viewing "Butterfly Driver," and that plaintiff is simply speculating when he alleges in the FAC (and argues in these motions) that Blomkamp accessed his screenplay on triggerstreet.com.

Defendants also assert that such a contention is rebutted by Blomkamp's uncontroverted declaration filed in support of defendants' motion. In his declaration, Blomkamp states that before this lawsuit was filed, he had never heard of the website triggerstreet.com; that he has never visited the website; and that he did not obtain a copy of plaintiff's screenplay on that site or anywhere else, and was not given a copy by anyone. Declaration of Neill Blomkamp ("Blomkamp Decl.") ¶¶ 7-8.

Blomkamp briefly explains the genesis of "Elysium" as follows. He states that he was raised in Johannesburg, South Africa, where he lived for 18 years before moving to Vancouver. As a teenager he began pursuing 3D animation and design, which he continued studying in film school. Blomkamp Decl. ¶ 2. He made several short films between 2004 and 2007, with storylines involving extraterrestrials and robotic workers. His first feature film was "District 9," which tells the story of extraterrestrials who are marooned in South Africa when their spacecraft becomes disabled, and are confined to camp outside of Johannesburg, and which explores themes of racism and segregation, and has a main character who transforms into an alien after coming in contact with an extraterrestrial substance. Blomkamp Decl. ¶¶ 3-4. He asserts that he created "Elysium" as he creates all his works, proceeding from visual concepts (in this case, utopian space stations and a robotic police force) and incorporating themes of racial and class segregation (building on his earlier works). Blomkamp Decl. ¶¶ 5-6.

... the allegations in the FAC are entirely speculative as they relate to Blomkamp's access to the screenplay. Plaintiff has failed to provide any evidence supporting his assertion that defendants had access to his screenplay. In his own motion, plaintiff argues that access can be established under the "chain of events" theory. He reiterates that he posted his screenplay on triggerstreet.com; that triggerstreet.com was based in Los Angeles; that the majority of triggerstreet.com members were "short filmmakers and screenwriters;" and that Blomkomp was a short film-maker who was "media-savvy" and who was based in Los Angeles (the "screenwriting hub of the world"). Even assuming for the sake of argument that these factual assertions are judicially noticeable and/or supported by evidence, together they do no more than suggest a bare possibility of access, which is insufficient to sustain a copyright infringement claim. Plaintiff has not provided evidence of a chain of events sufficient to establish a reasonable possibility of access. See Jason v. Fonda, 698 F.2d 966, 967 (9th Cir. 1982); see also Art Attacks, 581 F.3d at 1144.

He also asserts that his screenplay was so widely disseminated that it is reasonably possible that Blomkamp had access to his work. He claims that he emailed the screenplay to his family and friends, and that he posted drafts of the screenplay on triggerstreet.com. However, even were this claim supported by evidence, it does not show wide dissemination sufficient to support an inference that defendants had access to his work, or to raise a triable issue as to access. He also contends that over a 23-month period he sent queries to agents seeking representation, posted short synopses of the storyline on screenwriter websites, and entered screenwriting competitions. Again, these communications and Internet postings do not constitute evidence of wide dissemination of the screenplay.

2.B.2. Improper Appropriation

45 F.2d 119 (1930)

NICHOLS
v.
UNIVERSAL PICTURES CORPORATION

Circuit Court of Appeals, Second Circuit

LEARNED HAND, Circuit Judge

The plaintiff is the author of a play, "Abie's Irish Rose," which it may be assumed was properly copyrighted under section five, subdivision (d), of the Copyright Act, 17 USCA § 5(d). The defendant produced publicly a motion picture play, "The Cohens and The Kellys," which the plaintiff alleges was taken from it. As we think the defendant's play too unlike the plaintiff's to be an infringement, we may assume, arguendo, that in some details the defendant used the plaintiff's play, as will subsequently appear, though we do not so decide. It therefore becomes necessary to give an outline of the two plays.

"Abie's Irish Rose" presents a Jewish family living in prosperous circumstances in New York. The father, a widower, is in business as a merchant, in which his son and only child helps him. The boy has philandered with young women, who to his father's great disgust have always been Gentiles, for he is obsessed with a passion that his daughter-in-law shall be an orthodox Jewess. When the play opens the son, who has been courting a young Irish Catholic girl, has already married her secretly before a Protestant minister, and is concerned to soften the blow for his father, by securing a favorable impression of his bride, while concealing her faith and race. To accomplish this he introduces her to his father at his home as a Jewess, and lets it appear that he is interested in her, though he conceals the marriage. The girl somewhat reluctantly falls in with the plan; the father takes the bait, becomes infatuated with the girl, concludes that they must marry, and assumes that of course they will, if he so decides. He calls in a rabbi, and prepares for the wedding according to the Jewish rite.

Meanwhile the girl's father, also a widower, who lives in California, and is as intense in his own religious antagonism as the Jew, has been called to New York, supposing that his daughter is to marry an Irishman and a Catholic. Accompanied by a priest, he arrives at the house at the moment when the marriage is being celebrated, but too late to prevent it, and the two fathers, each infuriated by the proposed union of his child to a heretic, fall into unseemly and grotesque antics. The priest and the rabbi become friendly, exchange trite sentiments about religion, and agree that the match is good. Apparently out of abundant caution, the priest celebrates the marriage for a third time, while the girl's father is inveigled away. The second act closes with each father, still outraged, seeking to find some way by which the union, thus trebly insured, may be dissolved.

The last act takes place about a year later, the young couple having meanwhile been abjured by each father, and left to their own resources. They have had twins, a boy and a girl, but their fathers know no more than that a child has been born. At Christmas each, led by his craving to see his grandchild, goes separately to the young folks' home, where they encounter each other, each laden with gifts, one for a boy, the other for a girl. After some slapstick comedy, depending upon the insistence of each that he is right about the sex of the grandchild, they become reconciled when they learn the truth, and that each child is to bear the given name of a grandparent. The curtain falls as the fathers are exchanging amenities, and the Jew giving evidence of an abatement in the strictness of his orthodoxy.

"The Cohens and The Kellys" presents two families, Jewish and Irish, living side by side in the poorer quarters of New York in a state of perpetual enmity. The wives in both cases are still living, and share in the mutual animosity, as do two small sons, and even the respective dogs. The Jews have a daughter, the Irish a son; the Jewish father is in the clothing business; the Irishman is a policeman. The children are in love with each other, and secretly marry, apparently after the play opens. The Jew, being in great financial straits, learns from a lawyer that he has fallen heir to a large fortune from a great-aunt, and moves into a great house, fitted luxuriously. Here he and his family live in vulgar ostentation, and here the Irish boy seeks out his Jewish bride, and is chased away by the angry father. The Jew then abuses the Irishman over the telephone, and both become hysterically excited. The extremity of his feelings makes the Jew sick, so that he must go to Florida for a rest, just before which the daughter discloses her marriage to her mother.

On his return the Jew finds that his daughter has borne a child; at first he suspects the lawyer, but eventually learns the truth and is overcome with anger at such a low alliance. Meanwhile, the Irish family who have been forbidden to see the grandchild, go to the Jew's house, and after a violent scene between the two fathers in which the Jew disowns his daughter, who decides to go back with her husband, the Irishman takes her back with her baby to his own poor lodgings. [45 F.2d 121] The lawyer, who had hoped to marry the Jew's daughter, seeing his plan foiled, tells the Jew that his fortune really belongs to the Irishman, who was also

39

related to the dead woman, but offers to conceal his knowledge, if the Jew will share the loot. This the Jew repudiates, and, leaving the astonished lawyer, walks through the rain to his enemy's house to surrender the property. He arrives in great dejection, tells the truth, and abjectly turns to leave. A reconciliation ensues, the Irishman agreeing to share with him equally. The Jew shows some interest in his grandchild, though this is at most a minor motive in the reconciliation, and the curtain falls while the two are in their cups, the Jew insisting that in the firm name for the business, which they are to carry on jointly, his name shall stand first.

It is of course essential to any protection of literary property, whether at common-law or under the statute, that the right cannot be limited literally to the text, else a plagiarist would escape by immaterial variations. That has never been the law, but, as soon as literal appropriation ceases to be the test, the whole matter is necessarily at large, so that, as was recently well said by a distinguished judge, the decisions cannot help much in a new case. Fendler v. Morosco, 253 N. Y. 281, 292, 171 N. E. 56. When plays are concerned, the plagiarist may excise a separate scene Daly v. Webster, 56 F. 483 (C. C. A. 2); Chappell v. Fields, 210 F. 864 (C. C. A. 2); Chatterton v. Cave, L. R. 3 App. Cas. 483; or he may appropriate part of the dialogue (Warne v. Seebohm, L. R. 39 Ch. D. 73). Then the question is whether the part so taken is "substantial," and therefore not a "fair use" of the copyrighted work; it is the same question as arises in the case of any other copyrighted work. Marks v. Feist, 290 F. 959 (C. C. A. 2); Emerson v. Davies, Fed. Cas. No. 4436, 3 Story, 768, 795-797. But when the plagiarist does not take out a block in situ, but an abstract of the whole, decision is more troublesome. Upon any work, and especially upon a play, a great number of patterns of increasing generality will fit equally well, as more and more of the incident is left out. The last may perhaps be no more than the most general statement of what the play is about, and at times might consist only of its title; but there is a point in this series of abstractions where they are no longer protected, since otherwise the playwright could prevent the use of his "ideas," to which, apart from their expression, his property is never extended. Holmes v. Hurst, 174 U. S. 82, 86, 19 S. Ct. 606, 43 L. Ed. 904; Guthrie v. Curlett, 36 F.(2d) 694 (C. C. A. 2). Nobody has ever been able to fix that boundary, and nobody ever can. In some cases the question has been treated as though it were analogous to lifting a portion out of the copyrighted work (Rees v. Melville, MacGillivray's Copyright Cases 1911-1916, 168); but the analogy is not a good one, because, though the skeleton is a part of the body, it pervades and supports the whole. In such cases we are rather concerned with the line between expression and what is expressed. As respects plays, the controversy chiefly centers upon the characters and sequence of incident, these being the substance.

...

In the two plays at bar we think both as to incident and character, the defendant took no more - assuming that it took anything at all - than the law allowed. The stories are quite different. One is of a religious zealot [45 F.2d 122] who insists upon his child's marrying no one outside his faith; opposed by another who is in this respect just like him, and is his foil. Their difference in race is merely an obbligato to the main theme, religion. They sink their differences through grandparental pride and affection. In the other, zealotry is wholly absent; religion does not even appear. It is true that the parents are hostile to each other in part because they differ in race; but the marriage of their son to a Jew does not apparently offend the Irish family at all, and it exacerbates the existing animosity of the Jew, principally because he has become rich, when he learns it. They are reconciled through the honesty of the Jew and the generosity of the Irishman; the grandchild has nothing whatever to do with it. The only matter common to the two is a quarrel between a Jewish and an Irish father, the marriage of their children, the birth of grandchildren and a reconciliation.

If the defendant took so much from the plaintiff, it may well have been because her amazing success seemed to prove that this was a subject of enduring popularity. Even so, granting that the plaintiff's play was wholly original, and assuming that novelty is not essential to a copyright, there is no monopoly in such a background. Though the plaintiff discovered the vein, she could not keep it to herself; so defined, the theme was too generalized an abstraction from what she wrote. It was only a part of her "ideas."

Nor does she fare better as to her characters. It is indeed scarcely credible that she should not have been aware of those stock figures, the low comedy Jew and Irishman. The defendant has not taken from her more than their prototypes have contained for many decades. If so, obviously so to generalize her copyright, would allow her to cover what was not original with her. But we need not hold this as matter of fact, much as we might be justified. Even though we take it that she devised her figures out of her brain de novo, still the defendant was within its rights.

There are but four characters common to both plays, the lovers and the fathers. The lovers are so faintly indicated as to be no more than stage properties. They are loving and fertile; that is really all that can be said of them, and anyone else is quite within his rights if he puts loving and fertile lovers in a play of his own, wherever he gets the cue. The plaintiff's Jew is quite unlike the defendant's. His obsession is his religion, on which depends such racial animosity as he has. He is affectionate, warm and patriarchal. None of these fit the defendant's Jew, who shows affection for his daughter only once, and who has none but the most superficial interest in his grandchild. He is tricky, ostentatious and vulgar, only by misfortune redeemed into honesty. Both are grotesque, extravagant and quarrelsome; both are fond of display; but these common qualities make up only a small part of their simple pictures, no more than any one might lift if he chose. The Irish fathers are even more unlike; the plaintiff's a mere symbol for religious fanaticism and patriarchal pride, scarcely a character at all. Neither quality appears in the defendant's, for while he goes to get his grandchild, it is rather out of a truculent determination not to be forbidden, than from pride in his progeny. For the rest he is only a grotesque hobbledehoy, used for low comedy of the most conventional sort, which any one might borrow, if he chanced not to know the exemplar.

... We assume that the plaintiff's play is altogether original, even to an extent that in fact it is hard to believe. We assume further that, so far as it has been anticipated by earlier plays of which she knew nothing, that fact is immaterial. Still, as we have

41

already said, her copyright did not cover everything that might be drawn from her play; its content went to some extent into the public domain. We have to decide how much, and while we are as aware as anyone that the line, whereever it is drawn, will seem arbitrary, that is no excuse for not drawing it; it is a question such as courts must answer in nearly all cases. Whatever may be the difficulties a priori, we have no question on which side of the line this case falls. A comedy based upon conflicts between Irish and Jews, into which the marriage of their children enters, is no more susceptible of copyright than the outline of Romeo and Juliet.

The plaintiff has prepared an elaborate analysis of the two plays, showing a "quadrangle" of the common characters, in which each is represented by the emotions which he discovers. She presents the resulting parallelism as proof of infringement, but the adjectives employed are so general as to be quite useless. Take for example the attribute of "love" ascribed to both Jews. The plaintiff has depicted her father as deeply attached [45 F.2d 123] to his son, who is his hope and joy; not so, the defendant, whose father's conduct is throughout not actuated by any affection for his daughter, and who is merely once overcome for the moment by her distress when he has violently dismissed her lover. "Anger" covers emotions aroused by quite different occasions in each case; so do "anxiety," "despondency" and "disgust." It is unnecessary to go through the catalogue for emotions are too much colored by their causes to be a test when used so broadly. ...

Decree affirmed.

462 F.3d 1072 (2006)

FUNKY FILMS v. Time Warner

United States Court of Appeals, Ninth Circuit

BETTY B. FLETCHER, Circuit Judge.

Gwen O'Donnell and Funky Films, Inc. (collectively, "appellants"), creators of the screenplay "The Funk Parlor," appeal the district court's summary judgment to Time Warner Entertainment Company and Home Box Office (collectively, "HBO"), creators of the award-winning television mini-series "Six Feet Under," for copyright infringement. Appellants assert that the district court erred in concluding that "The Funk Parlor" and "Six Feet Under" are not substantially similar. They also appeal the district court's denial of a request for additional discovery. For the reasons set forth below, we affirm the judgment of the district court.

I

Between October 1997 and July 1999, Gwen O'Donnell drafted "The Funk Parlor," a screenplay tracing the lives of a small, family-run funeral parlor in Connecticut. Sometime in 1998, O'Donnell was injured in an automobile accident and sought treatment from Stacey Smith, a chiropractor. During these appointments, the two discussed O'Donnell's screen-play; eventually, Smith took an interest in the script and asked O'Donnell if she would like him to give a copy to his friend and client Chris Albrecht, the President of Original Programing at HBO. O'Donnell agreed and gave Smith a copy of "The Funk Parlor." Three months later, Carolyn Strauss, Albrecht's top lieutenant, solicited Alan Ball to develop "Six Feet Under" for HBO.[1]

Appellants allege that "The Funk Parlor" and "Six Feet Under" are substantially similar and that HBO unlawfully infringed upon appellants' copyrighted work. "As a determination of substantial similarity requires a detailed examination of the works themselves," Williams v. Crichton, 84 F.3d 581, 583 (2d Cir.1996) (internal citation and quotation marks omitted), we begin with a discussion of the works at issue.

A

"The Funk Parlor" takes place in a small, family-run funeral home in Connecticut. John Funk Sr., the patriarch, has committed suicide, and the deteriorating funeral parlor has been handed down to his two sons, John Jr. and Tom. John, the older brother who had moved away to start his own business promoting nightclubs in Los Angeles, reluctantly decides to remain in Connecticut after his father's death to help out with the struggling venture. Applying his business acumen, John revives it, all the while staving off an attempted takeover by a larger competitor. Meanwhile, he attracts the attention of Sophie, a neighbor and longtime acquaintance, and the two become romantically involved. Sophie repeatedly talks of entering a convent to become a nun, although in actuality she is a psychopathic murderer whose killing sprees breathe new life (as it were) into the Funk business. John and Sophie intend to marry, but John eventually figures out that he is Sophie's next target and that he must kill her (which he does) to spare his own life.

Tom, who had been running the funeral home during John's absence and who expresses an interest in Sophie as well, is murdered midway through the play. After Tom's death, John continues operating the business to bring it out of debt. After Sophie's death, John sells the business, moves to New York, and returns to the nightclub business.

Like "The Funk Parlor," "Six Feet Under" takes place in a funeral home and begins with the death of the patriarch, Nathaniel Fisher, and return of the "prodigal son," Nate, who receives an equal share of the business along with his younger brother, David. Nate decides to stay and help David maintain the business, which, like the Funk business, struggles against a larger competitor. The story traces the interpersonal relationships and romantic lives of each of the Fisher sons. It also revolves around the lives of the mother, Ruth, and sister, Claire, as well as other characters who come into contact with members of the Fisher family. The father, though deceased, reemerges throughout the drama. He continues to interact with each remaining character of the Fisher family, often helping them piece together problems that seemed irresolvable during his lifetime.

At the beginning of the drama, Nate begins a relationship with Brenda Chenowith, a massage therapist he meets on an airplane. David, who is gay, struggles with his sexuality and begins a relationship with Keith, a police officer he meets at church.

B

The district court conducted an independent analysis of the "The Funk Parlor" and the first three episodes of "Six Feet Under," comparing the two works for their setting, plot, characters, theme, mood, pace, dialogue, and sequence of events. The court determined that the works' few similarities operate at a general, abstract level and that no jury could reasonably find substantial similarities between the two works. Accordingly, the court granted HBO's motion for summary judgment. Appellants filed a timely notice of appeal.

II

We review the district court's grant of summary judgment de novo, see Government of Guam v. United States, 179 F.3d 630, 632 (9th Cir.1999), viewing the evidence in the light most favorable to the non-moving party to determine the presence of any issues of material fact. See Kouf v. Walt Disney Pictures & Television, 16 F.3d 1042, 1044 (9th Cir.1994). Summary judgment is appropriate only when "there is no genuine issue as to any material fact," see Fed.R.Civ.P. 56(c), and only if "the evidence . is so one-sided that one party must prevail as a matter of law." Anderson v. Liberty Lobby, Inc., 477 U.S. 242, 251-52, 106 S.Ct. 2505, 91 L.Ed.2d 202 (1986).

A

A plaintiff bringing a claim for copyright infringement must demonstrate "(1) ownership of a valid copyright, and (2) copying of constituent elements of the work that are original." Feist Pubs., Inc. v. Rural Tel. Serv. Co., 499 U.S. 340, 361, 111 S.Ct. 1282, 113 L.Ed.2d 358 (1991). Appellants' ownership in the copyright is undisputed; they need only demonstrate a triable issue of fact whether HBO "cop[ied] anything that was 'original' to" their work. Id. Absent evidence of direct copying, "proof of infringement involves fact-based showings that the defendant had 'access' to the plaintiff's work and that the two works are 'substantially similar.'" See, e.g., Three Boys Music Corp. v. Bolton, 212 F.3d 477, 481 (9th Cir.2000). Because the district court assumed, without deciding, appellees' access to "The Funk Parlor," we must decide whether the two works are substantially similar.

"When the issue is whether two works are substantially similar, summary judgment is appropriate if no reasonable juror could find substantial similarity of ideas and expression." Kouf, 16 F.3d at 1045 (internal citations and punctuation omitted). Although "summary judgment is not highly favored on the substantial similarity issue in copyright cases," Berkic v. Crichton, 761 F.2d 1289, 1292 (9th Cir.1985), substantial similarity "may often be decided as a matter of law." Sid & Marty Krofft Television Prods., Inc. v. McDonald's Corp., 562 F.2d 1157, 1164 (9th Cir.1977). Indeed, "[w]e have frequently affirmed summary judgment in favor of copyright defendants on the issue of substantial similarity." Shaw v. Lindheim, 919 F.2d 1353, 1355 (9th Cir.1990). See Berkic, 761 F.2d at 1292 ("we have frequently affirmed summary judgments in favor of copyright defendants on the

44

substantial similarity issue") (citing cases); see also Kouf, 16 F.3d at 1045-1046 (finding no substantial similarity as a matter of law).

B

The substantial-similarity test contains an extrinsic and intrinsic component. At summary judgment, courts apply only the extrinsic test; the intrinsic test, which examines an ordinary person's subjective impressions of the similarities between two works, is exclusively the province of the jury. See Shaw, 919 F.2d at 1360-61. A "plaintiff who cannot satisfy the extrinsic test necessarily loses on summary judgment, because a jury may not find substantial similarity without evidence on both the extrinsic and intrinsic tests." Kouf, 16 F.3d at 1045.

Extrinsic analysis is objective in nature. "[I]t depends not on the responses of the trier of fact, but on specific criteria which can be listed and analyzed." Krofft, 562 F.2d at 1164. The extrinsic test focuses on "articulable similarities between the plot, themes, dialogue, mood, setting, pace, characters, and sequence of events" in the two works. Kouf, 16 F.3d at 1045 (citations omitted). In applying the extrinsic test, this court "compares, not the basic plot ideas for stories, but the actual concrete elements that make up the total sequence of events and the relationships between the major characters." Berkic, 761 F.2d at 1293.

"[P]rotectable expression includes the specific details of an author's rendering of ideas." Metcalf v. Bochco, 294 F.3d 1069, 1074 (9th Cir.2002). However, scenes à faire, which flow naturally from generic plot-lines, are not protectable. See id. We "must take care to inquire only whether 'the protectable elements, standing alone, are substantially similar.'" Cavalier v. Random House, 297 F.3d 815, 822 (9th Cir.2002) (quoting Williams, 84 F.3d at 588 (emphasis in original)). In so doing, we "filter out and disregard the non-protectable elements in making [our] substantial similarity determination." Id.

C

Appellants allege a number of similarities between "The Funk Parlor" and "Six Feet Under." According to appellants, both works concern "a narrative about a small funeral home, and the lives of the family members who operate it"; plot-lines involving "the death of the father . [who] has for decades run the business"; a father whose death is "unexpected and not attributable to natural causes" (suicide in "The Funk Parlor" and a car accident in "Six Feet Under"); and the presence of "two sons" who receive equal shares of the business, with the "older son . liv[ing] in a distant city, working outside the funeral industry." In both works, the older son initially "has no interest in becoming involved with the funeral business"; moreover, "[t]he family business is financially fragile, and in both works the funeral home is pointedly shown to be in debt and operating out of a substandard facility with obsolete equipment and a hearse that stalls." Both works also contain an attempt by a "rival funeral home," spearheaded by "the female principal of the rival business" to "take[ ] advantage of their vulnerable financial condition," "bluntly mak[ing] a lowball offer" and "approaching one of the brothers at the father's funeral with a proposal to buy the family business." In both works, the older brother initially "expresses his desire to sell" but "changes his mind and commits himself to help his brother keep the business afloat." Finally, appellants point out the older brother's creativity, which stands in "pointed contrast to the leaden conservatism of the younger brother"; that the funeral home in both works is used as a "site for musical entertainment"; that the "younger brother . change[s] his church affiliation in order to increase their client base" in both works; and that "the rival's takeover attempt does not succeed."

D

At first blush, these apparent similarities in plot appear significant; however, an actual reading of the two works reveals greater, more significant differences and few real similarities at the levels of plot, characters, themes, mood, pace, dialogue, or sequence of events.

1. Plot

Both "Six Feet Under" and "The Funk Parlor" commence with the death of the father and return of the "prodigal son." Aside from that rather uneventful similarity, the plots of the two stories develop quite differently. The father's suicide in "The Funk Parlor" sets the stage for a series of additional murders, including several of the central characters in the play. The story revolves around the life of the older brother, John, who rehabilitates the fledgling business, falls in love with Sophie, proposes to her and then, upon discovering that she is a serial murderer, kills her in an effort to spare his own life.

"Six Feet Under," unlike "The Funk Parlor," is not a murder mystery, nor does it revolve around any plot-line in particular. Rather, "Six Feet Under" explores the intimate lives of each member of the Fisher family by examining each character's complex psyche and his or her interpersonal interactions and emotional attachments. "Six Feet Under" develops separate plot-lines around each member of the Fisher family, including the mother and daughter, for whom there are no comparable characters in "The Funk Parlor." "Six Feet Under" is not so much a story about death as it is about the way the characters struggle with life in the wake of the cataclysmic death of the father.

2. Characters

Although appellants attempt to link up the various characters of the two works, there are very few real similarities between any of them. John Funk, Sr., is a minor character who vanishes at the start of "The Funk Parlor" and does not reappear except during one quick flashback scene; his relationships with the other characters are not consciously explored. Nathaniel Fisher, Sr., by contrast, appears throughout the drama and continues to interact with each character separately. In that regard, "Six Feet Under" traces each character's unique set of relationships with the deceased father, exploring issues that were apparently not resolvable during life.

The "prodigal son" characters of the two works, while similar at the abstract level, are markedly different in the two scripts. Nate Fisher's search for meaning originally led him away from the family business; prior to his return home, he

46

remained somewhat adrift in Seattle. Although he reluctantly agrees to remain in Los Angeles to help his brother David run the business, he shows little interest or skill. John Funk, Jr., by contrast, is a talented and creative businessperson whose efforts quickly restore the moribund business. Unlike Nate, John graduated from mortuary school and took on an active role in the business before decamping for Los Angeles to become a club promoter.

The characters of David Fisher and Tom Funk, both younger brothers, are remarkably different. Tom's role in "The Funk Parlor" is less developed (in part because he is killed roughly midway through the story), though he is clearly less skilled than his brother at maintaining the family business. Although Tom is rumored to be gay, his homosexuality remains a matter of speculation and is never pursued through any relationship or meaningful dialogue. David, by contrast, is deeply enmeshed in a struggle with sexual identity, which he hides from his family and explores privately. His coming-out process and his relationship with Keith occupy a central plot-line of the story. The complexity of David's character has no equivalent in "The Funk Parlor."

Appellants equate Sophie Zemlaskas with Brenda Chenowith, both of whom are romantically involved with the older brother in each story. However, the two have little in common. Sophie, a devout and obsessive Catholic who plans to enter the convent, is a psychopathic killer. Unlike Sophie, Brenda is not homicidal. Brenda, a massage therapist, is psychologically astute and expresses no interest in religion. While Sophie expresses deep conflict over her sexuality, Brenda engages in an apparently conflict-free sexual life with Nate (and others).

Appellants also try to draw connections between Jamie, a twelve- or thirteen-year-old cousin who works at the funeral home, and Claire Fisher, the younger sister in "Six Feet Under." But Jamie is a very minor character; Claire, by contrast, is a central character who develops relationships of her own. Her struggle to define herself within the family, while rejecting any place within the family business, is a recurring theme in "Six Feet Under."

Completely missing from "The Funk Parlor" is any character similar to Ruth Fisher, the mother and one of the central characters of "Six Feet Under." Ruth is presented as a strong-willed woman who struggles to overcome her lingering maternal instincts over her now-grown children. Her own romantic attachments and relationships form an important part of the plot-line as well.

Additional characters within "Six Feet Under" that have no counterpart in "The Funk Parlor" are Fredrico Diaz, an employee of the Fisher business who eventually becomes a partner, and Keith Charles, David's boyfriend who struggles to remain in the relationship despite David's conflicts in coming to terms with his sexuality.

3. Themes

Although both works explore themes of death, relationships, and sex, they do so in very different ways. "The Funk Parlor," a murder mystery, is driven by a series of murders, which catalyze the salvation of the business. The use of death in "Six Feet

Under" is quite different: there, death provides the focal point for exploring relationships and existential meaning. As noted by the district court, the general theme of "Six Feet Under" "is that sex and death provide focal points for relationships," while the predominant theme of "The Funk Parlor" is that "sex and religion don't mix."

In addition to the numerous murders that take place, "The Funk Parlor" traces a number of religious themes (tension between members of the Protestant and Catholic communities, religious conversion, and a general fear of God). Much of the story takes place at the Polish deli owned by Sophie's family, and several of the deaths take place at "Overlook Point." Characters continually brush up against law-enforcement officials investigating the series of murders. Meanwhile, the religious themes serve as a conscious moral structure against the backdrop of the mass killings that take place. The characters must come to grips with religious expectations, agonizing that they will "burn in Hell" and that "God is punishing us." John Funk considers religious conversion and seeks confession as a source of absolution. Sophie, meanwhile, is obsessed with religion and, for much of the story, appears ready to enter the convent to become a nun.

"Six Feet Under," by contrast, is a neo-realistic, postmodern account of family and romantic relationships, without any overarching religious themes or overtones. Themes of love, romance, death, and sexuality are explored entirely through the characters' complex interactions. The story focuses on the characters' longing for connection, their insecurities, and their complaints. Unlike "The Funk Parlor," none of the main characters are murderers or murder victims.

4. Setting, Mood, and Pace

Although both works take place in a contemporary, family-run funeral home, the similarities in setting end there. "Six Feet Under" takes place in a well-maintained funeral home in Los Angeles. Although the business struggles against a competitor and is, at times, somewhat sluggish, "The Funk Parlor," located in Connecticut, is in shambles. The moods of the two works are drastically different as well. "The Funk Parlor" is a farcical mystery, while "Six Feet Under" is serious, dramatic, and introspective. "The Funk Parlor" moves at a rapid clip, while "Six Feet Under" evolves slowly and often in repetitive fashion. Beyond the basic premise of a family-run funeral home, there are no similarities in the setting, mood or pace of the two works.

5. Dialogue

The encounters explored in "The Funk Parlor" are at times pedestrian, and the dialogue, at times, rather trite. The characters play beer-drinking games like "I never" and express concern about "burning in hell" and that "God is punishing us." "Six Feet Under," by contrast, is full of complex and subtle dialogue, including ironic turns of phrases that heighten the already-fraught interactions among the characters.

48

6. Sequence of Events

The sequence of events in the two works are different as well. "The Funk Parlor" opens with a younger John Funk attempting to seduce Jennifer Angeli at "Overlook Point." Their automobile crashes; John is blamed for the death; he leaves home; and returns only later at the death of his father. "Six Feet Under" begins with a montage of different scenes depicting each character's reaction to the death of Nathaniel Sr., who is killed in an automobile accident on the way to pick up Nate Jr. at the airport. Minutes before finding out, Nate engages in a sexual encounter with Brenda in an airport broom closet; Claire smokes crystal methamphetamine with a group of friends; and Ruth broods over dinner and Nate's favorite breakfast cereal.   Shortly after these scenes, the Fisher children are reunited with their mother at the hospital to identify their father's body, thus beginning the exploration of their complex relationships. While "The Funk Parlor" unfolds in a straight, linear trajectory, "Six Feet Under" employs repetition, dreams, and flashbacks to intensify certain scenes and conflate the real with the unreal.

E

At a very high level of generality, both works share certain plot similarities: the family-run funeral home, the father's death, and the return of the "prodigal son," who assists his brother in maintaining the family business. But "[g]eneral plot ideas are not protected by copyright law; they remain forever the common property of artistic mankind."   See Berkic, 761 F.2d at 1293.   See also Cavalier, 297 F.3d at 824 ("basic plot ideas, such as this one, are not protected by copyright law");   Shaw, 919 F.2d at 1356 ("Copyright law protects an author's expression; facts and ideas within a work are not protected.").   Beyond that, "[t]he stories do not share any detailed sequence of events." Cavalier, 297 F.3d at 824. See Berkic, 761 F.2d at 1293 ("Both deal with criminal organizations that murder healthy young people, then remove and sell their vital organs to wealthy people in need of organ transplants. To some extent, both works take their general story from the adventures of a young professional who courageously investigates, and finally exposes, the criminal organization. But this degree of similarity between the basic plots of two works cannot sustain a plaintiff's claim that the works are 'substantially similar.' "). The similarities recounted throughout appellants' brief rely heavily on scenes à faire-not concrete renderings specific to "The Funk Parlor"-and are, at best, coincidental. Consequently, the two works are not substantially similar.

..

III

For the reasons stated above, the district court's summary judgment in appellees' favor is AFFIRMED.

2.C. Defenses

641 F.Supp.2d 250 (2009)

J.D. SALINGER v. COLTING

United States District Court, S.D. New York

DEBORAH A. BATTS, District Judge.

Plaintiff J.D. Salinger brings suit against Defendants Fredrik Colting, writing under the name John David California, Windupbird Publishing Ltd., Nicotext A.B., and ABP, Inc., doing business as SCB Distributors Inc., alleging claims for Copyright Infringement and common law Unfair Competition. Plaintiff alleges that Defendants' novel, 60 Years Later: Coming [254] Through the Rye (hereinafter "60 Years"), is a derivative work of his novel, The Catcher in the Rye (hereinafter "Catcher"), and that the character of Mr. C from 60 Years, is an infringement on his character, Holden Caulfield, from Catcher.

Plaintiff now moves for a preliminary injunction preventing Defendants from publishing, advertising, or otherwise distributing 60 Years in the United States of America during the pendency of this suit. For the following reasons, a preliminary injunction is GRANTED.

INTRODUCTION

As set forth on the record of June 17, 2009, and for the reasons stated therein, the Court found that Plaintiff possesses a valid Copyright in the novel The Catcher in the Rye, that the character of Holden Caulfield ("Holden" or "Caulfield") is sufficiently delineated so that a claim for infringement will lie. 2 Nimmer on Copyright § 2.12 (2009) ("[I]n those cases recognizing such protection, the character appropriated was distinctively delineated in the plaintiff's work."). Additionally, for the reasons stated on the record of June 17, 2009, the Court found that the Plaintiff had access to Catcher and that there are similarities that are probative of copying between the works. Castle Rock Entertainment, Inc. v. Carol Pub. Group, Inc., 150 F.3d 132, 137 (2d Cir.1998). Finally, the Court found that Plaintiff has shown that there is substantial similarity between Catcher and 60 Years, as well as between the character Holden Caulfield from Catcher, and the character Mr. C from 60 Years, such that it was an unauthorized infringement of Plaintiff's copyright. Suntrust Bank v. Houghton Mifflin Company, 268 F.3d 1257, 1266 (11th Cir.2001) (finding that "substantial similarity" exists where "an average lay observer would recognize the alleged copy as having been appropriated from the copyrighted work"); Castle Rock, 150 F.3d at 139 ("Under the `ordinary observer' test ... two works are substantially similar where the ordinary observer, unless he set out to detect the disparities, would be disposed to overlook them, and regard the aesthetic appeal of the two works as the same.") (internal quotations omitted).

DISCUSSION

The Preliminary Injunction Standard

Under Rule 65, "[t]o obtain a preliminary injunction a party must demonstrate: (1) that it will be irreparably harmed if an injunction is not granted, and (2) either (a) a likelihood of success on the merits or (b) sufficiently serious questions going to the merits to make them a fair ground for litigation, and a balance of the hardships tipping decidedly in its favor." Bronx Household of Faith v. Board of Educ. of City of New York, 331 F.3d 342, 349 (2d Cir.2003) (citing Forest City Daly Housing, Inc. v. Town of North Hempstead, 175 F.3d 144, 149 (2d Cir.1999)).

[The Court addresses Defendants' claim that their novel 60 Years and its protagonist Mr. C constitute fair use of Plaintiff's copyrighted work under 17 U.S.C. §§ 107(1)-(4). The Court finds some limited transformative character in 60 Years, but holds that the alleged parodic content is not reasonably perceivable, and that the limited non-parodic transformative content is unlikely to overcome the obvious commercial nature of the work, the likely injury to the potential market for derivative works of Catcher, and especially the substantial and pervasive extent to which 60 Years borrows from Catcher and the character of Holden Caulfield.]

Irreparable Harm

When a Plaintiff establishes a prima facie case of copyright infringement, irreparable harm may be presumed. ABKCO Music, Inc. v. Stellar Records, Inc., 96 F.3d 60, 66 (2d Cir.1996); Warner Bros. Entertainment, Inc., 575 F.Supp.2d at 552; E Gluck Corp. v. Rothenhaus, 585 F.Supp.2d 505, 519 (S.D.N.Y.2008). Because [269]. Plaintiff has established a prima facie case of copyright infringement, irreparable harm from that infringement is presumed.

CONCLUSION

Given the Court's finding that Plaintiff is likely to succeed on the merits of its Copyright claim, as well as the presumption of irreparable harm, the Court preliminarily enjoins Defendants from manufacturing, publishing, distributing, shipping, advertising, promoting, selling, or otherwise disseminating any copy of 60 Years or any portion thereof, in or to the United States.

SO ORDERED.

921 F. Supp. 1065 (1995)

BANFF v. EXPRESS.

United States District Court, S.D. New York

SCHEINDLIN, District Judge:

After a six day trial in this copyright and trademark action, the jury returned a verdict for plaintiff Banff Ltd. ("Banff"), a knitwear manufacturer. The jury found that Defendant Express, Inc. ("Express"), a retail clothing chain, had infringed Plaintiff's copyright by selling a knockoff of Plaintiff's Aran fisherman's sweater. The jury awarded Plaintiff $200,685 in actual damages and $1,017,240 in profits it determined Defendant earned from the infringement. ...

Express now moves, pursuant to Fed. R.Civ.P. 50(b), for judgment as a matter of law on a number of Banff's claims. ... Express contends that it is entitled to judgment on Banff's claim for actual damages under the Copyright Act.

A. Factual Background

In late 1990, Jeffrey Gray, an employee of Banff's Vanessa Division, designed the sweater that is the subject of this lawsuit. Trial Transcript ("Tr.") at 79-80. The sweater Mr. Gray designed conformed to the Aran style of knitting, and featured a combination of cabled patterns, traditional stitching and hand crocheted roses. See Banff Ltd. v. Limited, Inc., 869 F. Supp. 1103, 1105 (S.D.N.Y.1994); Tr. at 205.[2] Banff produced both wool and cotton versions of this sweater, and sold it to a number of retailers, including Neiman Marcus, Bergdorf Goodman and Bloomingdale's. Tr. at 82, 84-85.

In December 1992, a Banff employee named Lois Adelman noticed a similar sweater in the window of one of Express' Manhattan stores. Tr. at 90. She notified Herbert Vanefsky, the President of Banff's Vanessa division. Mr. Vanefsky purchased one of Express' sweaters, and brought it back to his showroom to compare it with Banff's sweater. Tr. at 92. Although the Express sweater was made of a combination of ramie and cotton, a less expensive material than Banff used, Mr. Vanefsky was convinced that its design was identical to that of the Banff sweater. Tr. at 92, 95, 105. Mr. Vanefsky called his attorneys, and promptly filed for a copyright of Banff's sweater. Tr. at 92. Soon thereafter, in April 1993, Banff brought this action.

At trial, Banff offered evidence as to the originality of Mr. Gray's design. Kathleen Sibrizzi, a designer with seventeen years experience, testified that it was one of the most unique sweaters she had ever seen. Tr. at 316, 317. Ms. Sibrizzi also testified that the sweater sold by Express was virtually identical to that designed by Mr. Gray. Tr. at 324.

In addition, Banff offered evidence suggesting that Express' employees were aware of Banff's sweater. The evidence established that Banff's sweater was advertised in both Bergdorf Goodman's and Bloomingdale's catalogues, and that the employee in charge of purchasing sweaters for Express read these catalogues. Tr. at 83, 87, 236. The evidence also established that Banff's sweater was featured in Glamour magazine, another publication which Express' sweater purchaser read. Tr. at 235.

The evidence presented at trial clearly supported the jury's determination that Express infringed Banff's copyright. Notably, Express does not challenge this determination. Express challenges only the damages the jury awarded under the Copyright Act, and the jury's finding that its actions violated § 43(a) of the Lanham Act.

...

C. Actual Damages

Express contends that there was no "legally sufficient evidentiary basis" for the jury's award of actual damages, and that it is entitled to judgment as a matter of law on Banff's claim for such damages. The Court rejects this argument, but finds that the jury's verdict was both "seriously erroneous" and contrary to the "weight of evidence." Accordingly, Express' alternative motion for a new trial on Banff's claim for actual damages is granted.

Section 504(b) of the Copyright Act enables a prevailing plaintiff "to recover the actual damages suffered by him or her as a result of the infringement." 17 U.S.C. § 504(b). In general, a copyright owner's actual damages are equal to the profits she would have accrued but for defendant's infringement. See 3 Nimmer, Nimmer on Copyright § 14.02[A] at 14-10 (1995).

The plain language of § 504(b) contemplates that actual damages are only available where there is a causal connection between the infringement and the copyright owner's losses. In order to sustain an award for actual damages, Banff was required to prove that it would have made the sweater sales in question but for the infringing activity. See Stevens Linen Assocs., Inc. v. Mastercraft Corp., 656 F.2d 11, 15 (2d Cir.1981) (the inquiry on the issue of damages focuses on "what sales probably would have been made without the infringement").

At trial, Banff asserted that it was ready, willing and able to provide Express with sweaters of the copyrighted design. However, it offered little probative evidence suggesting that Express would actually have bought sweaters from Banff. In fact, the evidence at trial indicated that this would have been highly unlikely.

Notably, Express had never done any business with the division of Banff that designed the fisherman's sweaters. Tr. at 99. Moreover, the evidence demonstrated that the two parties sold different products at significantly different prices. Banff's sweaters were sold in high end stores like Saks Fifth Avenue and Bergdorf Goodman, whereas Express was a retailer of moderately priced merchandise. Tr. at 82, 245, 421. Banff sold the cotton version of its sweater to Bloomingdale's at a wholesale price of $63.75 per sweater. Tr. at 108. By contrast, the retail price of Express' sweater never exceeded $60, and averaged only $48.51. Tr. at 490. Thus,

Banff's wholesale price was higher than the highest price at which Express sold its sweater to the public.

Additionally, Banff offered little evidence that it could have supplied the quantity of sweaters Express needed. Express purchased between 39,262 and 40,137 of the knockoff sweaters. By contrast, Banff sold only about 400 of its cotton sweaters. Tr. at 143. Banff claimed it could have supplied the necessary quantity through a factory in Turkey. However, the evidence suggested that this would not have been acceptable to Express. Because of production delays in Turkey, Express did not purchase Turkish sweaters. Tr. at 426.

There are other reasons to question Banff's ability to supply Express with the sweaters it needed. At trial, Banff offered no evidence that it had ever made any sweaters out of the ramie cotton material used in the sweaters Express sold. Moreover, the evidence indicated that, during the time Express purchased its sweaters, Banff was experiencing financial difficulties. Express ordered the infringing sweaters from Mast Industries from November 1991 until August 1992. See Pl.Ex. 19. Yet the evidence demonstrated that by the late 1980s, Banff was experiencing financial difficulties. Tr. at 116-17. Jeffrey Gray testified that by April 1992, when Banff laid him off, he knew the company was experiencing financial problems. Tr. at 211, 212. Indeed, Banff began to wind its business down in late 1992, and went out of business in January 1993. Tr. at 122, 141.

The evidence at trial provided a very weak basis for the jury's finding of actual damages. Although the Court cannot say that the jury's finding had no "legally sufficient" basis, it was both "seriously erroneous" and against the "weight of evidence." Here, the jury's verdict was indisputably egregious. From 1991 until it went out of business in 1993, Banff sold only about 400 of its cotton sweaters. It never made a sweater comparable to the infringing sweater and never demonstrated that it had the capacity to do so. The verdict of actual damages is nothing but an undeserved windfall as there was no realistic possibility that Banff would ever have made the sales and profits awarded by the jury but for the Defendant's infringing conduct. Accordingly, Express' motion for a new trial on Banff's claim for actual damages is granted.

...

[court denies the Express' motion for judgment as a matter of law on Banff's claim for actual damages under the Copyright Act but grants the motion for a new trial for judgment as a matter of law on Banff's trade dress claim].

SO ORDERED.

409 F.Supp.2d 484 (2006)

CAFFEY v. COOK

United States District Court, S.D. New York

HOLWELL, District Judge.

Plaintiffs Marion J. Caffey and Willette Klausner (collectively "plaintiffs") brought this copyright action pursuant to 17 U.S.C. § 101 et seq. against Victor Trent Cook, Rodrick Dixon and Thomas Young (collectively "defendants"), asserting that defendants infringed on plaintiffs' copyright in a compilation of pre-existing musical compositions and bridge dialogue embodied in a musical show styled as "The Three Mo' Tenors" (the "Show"). Following the denial of plaintiffs' motion for summary judgment on this claim, the Court conducted a bench trial on various dates between June 14, 2005 and July 15, 2005. This Memorandum Opinion and Order sets forth the findings of fact and conclusions of law in accordance with Rule 52 of the Federal Rules of Civil Procedure.

FINDINGS OF FACT

I. The Parties

Plaintiff Marion J. Caffey has been a writer, choreographer, producer and director of live musical theater and concerts since 1981. He has directed and/or choreographed numerous musical stage shows, including Bowfire, Storyville, Forever Plaid, Jelly Roll: The Music and the Man, Little Shop of Horrors, Tintypes, The All Night Strut, Ain't Misbehavin', Purlie Victorious, Ruthless, Lady Day at Emerson's Bar & Grill, and Spunk. He has also conceived and written the musical shows Street Corner Symphony which opened on Broadway, Cookin' at the Cookery (The Music and Times of Alberta Hunter), Blackbirds of Broadway, and Three Mo' Divas. (Declaration of Marion J. Caffey ("Caffey Decl.") 1, 2.)

...

Defendant Victor Trent Cook is a classically trained counter-tenor by profession. Following high school, Cook was crowned the "$100,000 Male Vocal Champion!" by the popular television series Star Search. Cook has since appeared in numerous off-Broadway and Broadway productions and has received a Tony Award nomination for his role in the Broadway production Smokey Joe's Café. (Declaration of Victor Trent Cook ("Cook Decl.")

Defendant Rodrick Dixon is a classically trained lyric tenor with a Master of Art degree. (Declaration of Rodrick Dixon ("Dixon Decl.") Dixon has performed as a vocalist with symphonies throughout the world and has appeared in a wide variety of genres including opera, Broadway and musical theater. (Id.)

Defendant Thomas Young is also a classically trained lyric tenor and has appeared as a principal soloist in major concert halls and opera houses in approximately twenty countries. (Declaration of Thomas Young ("Young Decl."). Young is a tenured professor at Sarah Lawrence College and has worked in musical theater, including productions of Porgy and Bess, The Wiz and Evita. He has extensive recording and jazz credits including a 1992 album, High Standards, which featured two songs, Twisted and Send in the Clowns that were among the songs subsequently incorporated into the show. (Id.)

II. Creation of the Show

In 1997, Caffey developed the idea for a musical stage show which he ultimately named Three Mo' Tenors. He was inspired by the performances of "The Three Tenors" — Luciano Pavarotti, Placido Domingo and Jose Carreras — and sought to create a similar concert involving three African-American tenors performing diverse musical genres, including classical, Broadway, jazz, blues, soul and gospel. (Caffey Decl. ¶ 4.) Caffey believed that African-American tenors "were more likely to be able to adapt to the many various musical genres and could sing Broadway, blues, etc. without sounding like opera singers, making the concept and the show unique." (Id.) All of the parties agree that Caffey "conceived" the idea for the Show. (Young Decl.)

Caffey had known Young for over ten years, admired his work, and invited him to participate in the project in early 1998. (Id. 12; Young Tr. 316-18.) Caffey was also familiar with Cook's work and had produced a concert for him in which Cook sang multiple musical genres. (Caffey Decl.) When Caffey approached Cook, Caffey stated that "[h]e told me he got an idea from the actual three tenors. And he knew of three specially trained African-American tenors who he thought would be tailor-made for this idea, he had, which was a take-off for the Three Tenors." (Victor Trent Cook Trial Testimony ("Cook Tr.") 143; Thomas Young Trial Testimony ("Young Tr.") 316.) Caffey also stated that he wanted the show to include a "multitude" of genres. (Cook Tr. 144.) Upon Cook's recommendation, Caffey invited Dixon to participate in a "showcase performance" in 1998 which had been arranged by Caffey to solicit investors in the Show. (Cook Tr. 150; Caffey Decl. 18.)

The showcase performance took place on November 19, 1998. Cook, Dixon and Young participated in the performance along with a fourth tenor, Jeff Haerston. (Id.) Caffey asked each of the performers to suggest songs from their own repertoire. (Caffey Decl. ¶ 18.) He [selected and] sequenced fourteen songs. (Pls.' Ex. 35). Cook testified that he, Young and Dixon "came to the table with our own repertoire." (Cook Tr. 195.) Young performed two of the songs in his standard repertoire — Nessun Dorma!, and Send in the Clowns. (Young Tr. 320.) Dixon performed Ah Mes Amis and Make Them Hear You, the latter of which came from the repertoire he performed in the Broadway musical Ragtime and had been specifically arranged for him by Ragtime's author. (Dixon Tr. 383.) Cook sang O'Lessate di Piagermi, (Pls.' Ex. 35; Dixon Tr. 490.) All three tenors sang La Donna e Mobile, a universal piece standard in each tenor's repertoire. (Dixon Tr. 387.) These songs from the defendants' repertoire were ultimately included in the thirty-two songs that were performed in the Show and listed in Caffey's subsequent copyright application. (Pls.' Ex. 1.) Caffey, however, insists that the showcase was not intended to be a precursor or version of the Show. (Caffey Decl. 19).

56

Following the showcase, Caffey, Cook, Dixon and Young engaged in a series of workshops to develop the Show. (Cook Tr. 151, 158.) Cook testified that the workshop was intended, in part, to demonstrate to Caffey which songs they wanted to include in the Show. (Id. at 158.) Over the course of three years, defendants and Caffey collaborated together in selecting the solo pieces, group numbers and some of the spoken dialogue to segue the songs. (Dixon Decl. ¶ 5; Dixon Tr. 486; Young Decl. ¶¶ 5-6; Defs.' Proposed Findings of Fact and Conclusions of Law ¶ 6.) The primary factors in determining the selection and ordering of the songs were (1) musicality; (2) familiarity and commercial popularity with the general public; and (3) the physical demands of performance. (Caffey Decl. ¶¶ 9, 11; Young Tr. 322.) Caffey felt that it was important to maintain "an `arc,' i.e., a pattern that resonates with and moves the audience in the most effective manner." (Caffey Decl. ¶ 11.) Dixon stated that "as far as crafting this concert from beginning to end, the arc, it had to [as] with, can you physically sing the repertoire, what do you feel comfortable singing, and number three, can you maintain the standard over four concerts in one week." (Dixon Tr. 486.)

The Show evolved into a collection of solos, group numbers and medleys linked together with a minimal amount of bridge dialogue. A script for the show prepared by Caffey identified thirty-two songs to be performed ...

...

It is undoubtedly true that defendants actively participated in the selection and sequencing of the songs that comprised the Show. The Show was a collaborative undertaking that included primarily Caffey and the three tenors, but included musical arrangers and directors, set, costume and lighting designers. (Caffey Decl. ¶ 19; Caffey Tr. 288-89.) It is also true that approximately seven of the songs were taken directly from the established repertoires of the defendants. However, a number of other songs from defendants' repertoires were suggested but ultimately rejected by Caffey. (Caffey Decl. ¶ 20.) Thus, it was Caffey who had the decision making authority on what went in the Show and what did not. As Cook conceded, "Caffey arranged the show" (Cook Tr. 486) and had the "final decision" as to what songs were to be in the Show and in what sequence (Id. at 155-156, 206-207).

The bridge dialogue for the show was minimal, amounting to about a page and one-half of text, and was also a collaborative effort. Caffey, however, actually penned the text and had the final say as to what spoken words would be incorporated into the Show. (Cook Tr. 208; Caffey Decl. ¶ 22.)

At the time of their involvement in the workshops, defendants never asked Caffey to be included as joint authors. This was based on their belief that there was nothing copyrightable in the performance of other people's songs. (Cook Tr. 198) ("So I didn't think there was going to be a copyright. I wasn't asked or told."); (Young Tr. 347; Dixon Tr. 442.)

...

A. The In-Concert Performances

After defendants completed their performances on the dates set forth by the July and September Settlement Agreements, they performed seven "In Concert" shows as Cook, Dixon & Young, which shows were in substance the Show they had performed as the Three Mo' Tenors. (Cook Tr. 160.) Specifically, defendants performed in Naples, Florida (December 2, 2003); Chicago, Illinois (December 5, 2003); Phoenix, Arizona (March 31, 2004); Philadelphia, Pennsylvania (May 9, 2004); Naperville, Illinois (September 25, 2004); Memphis, Tennessee (October 2, 2004); and New Orleans, Louisiana (October 4, 2004). (Pls.' Exs. 4, 5.) Defendants did not request, and Caffey did not give his permission to defendants to perform the compilation of songs or dialogue that had been used in the Show. (Caffey Decl. ¶ 47.)

For the first six dates, defendants performed the same show with the exception of substituting one aria (Di Quella Pira for Ah! Mes Amis, Pour Mon Ame) and altering the underlying musical arrangements for certain of the songs for these concerts. (Dixon Tr. 460-68; Pls.' Exs. 3, 4, 20; Caffey Decl. ¶ 52.) However, with respect to the New Orleans concert, defendants performed only a 45-50-minute set, the Show normally being two hours and fifteen minutes, and changed the order of the songs that were sung. (Dixon Tr. 468; Cook Decl. ¶ 14.)

The parties agree that defendants grossed the following amounts for these performances:

Naples, Florida	$ 40,000
Chicago, Illinois	$115,000
Phoenix, Arizona	$ 45,000
Philadelphia, Pennsylvania	$ 40,000
Naperville, Illinois	$ 50,000
Memphis, Tennessee	$ 40,000
New Orleans, Louisiana	$ 50,000

(Pls.' Ex. 5; Defs.' Proposed Findings of Fact and Conclusions of Law ¶ 41; Pls.' Proposed Findings of Fact and Conclusions of Law ¶ 66.) For each performance, defendants paid a 10% booking fee to the William Morris Agency from the gross revenues received from these concerts. (Declaration of Karl Graham ("Graham Decl.") ¶ 5; Cook Tr. 507.) Defendants further paid out 20% of their gross income to their personal manager, CD Enterprises, and 5% of their gross income to Padell Nadell, their business manager. (Graham Decl. ¶ 6.) In addition, defendants paid general overhead costs from December of 2003 through December of 2004 as follows: $1,000.00 for legal fees; $6,408.88 for insurance; $6,000.00 for public relations; $23,391.91 for rehearsals; $3,475.00 for travel; and $10,363.31 for reimbursements to CD Enterprises. (Graham Decl., Ex. A.) During this period there were seven "In Concert" and ten abbreviated "private" performances. Graham attested that "it would be fair to allocate one-seventeenth of the total overhead expenses to each date." (Graham Decl. ¶ 11.) Defendants also paid state, local and federal taxes ranging 30-35% of their net income. (Graham Decl. ¶ 12; Cook Tr. 513.)

With respect to the Naples, Florida performance, defendants paid $14,000.00 in commissions, $3,563.64 in disbursements regarding per diem expenses and other costs, $3,850.28 in salaries to the musicians and $140.62 as royalty payments to Caffey. (Graham Decl., Ex. A; Cook Tr. 510-11; Pls.' Exs. 14, 36.)

With respect to the Chicago, Illinois performance, defendants paid $40,250.00 in commissions, $1,977.33 in disbursements, $11,279.17 in check disbursements including salaries to musicians and $140.62 in royalties to Caffey. (Graham Decl., Ex. A; Cook Tr. 510-11; Pls.' Exs. 14 and 37.)

With respect to the Phoenix, Arizona performance, defendants paid $15,750.00 in commissions, $2,502.18 in disbursements, $4,329.29 in hotel expenses and $4,831.60 in check disbursements. (Graham Decl., Ex. A.)

With respect to the Philadelphia, Pennsylvania performance, defendants paid $13,825.00 in commissions, $4,034.45 in disbursements, $5,489.28 in check disbursements. (Graham Decl., Ex. A.)

With respect to the Naperville, Florida, Memphis, Tennessee and New Orleans, Louisiana performances, defendants paid a total of $42,500.00 in commissions, $7,601.41 in disbursements and $25,318.66 in check disbursements. (Graham Decl., Ex. A.)

...

CONCLUSIONS OF LAW

[Court finds infringement]

V. Damages

A copyright owner who succeeds on the merits of his infringement claim is entitled to recover (1) compensatory damages or (2) statutory damages. 17 U.S.C. §§ 504(b) and (c). Plaintiffs have elected to recover compensatory damages. (Pls.' Proposed Findings of Fact and Conclusions of Law ¶¶ 21-32.) Section 504 of the Act sets forth two categories of compensatory damages: infringer's profits that are attributable to the infringement, and the copyright owner's "actual damages." On Davis v. Gap, Inc., 246 F.3d 152, 159 (2d Cir.2001). The distinction between these types of damages is important since:

The award of the infringer's profits examines the facts only from the infringer's point of view. If the infringer has earned a profit, this award makes him disgorge the profit to insure that he not benefit from his wrongdoing. The award of the owner's actual damages looks at the facts from the point of view of [the] copyright owner; it undertakes to compensate the owner for any harm he suffered by reason of the infringer's illegal act. Id.; see also Hamil America v. GFI, 193 F.3d 92, 103 (2d Cir.1999) ("These two methods of recovery available under § 504(b) serve two distinct purposes: [d]amages are awarded to compensate the copyright owner for losses from the infringement, and profits are awarded to prevent the infringer from unfairly benefiting from a wrongful act.") (quoting H.R.Rep. No. 94-1476, at 161, 1976 U.S.Code Cong. & Admin.News, p. 5557). Plaintiffs do not bother to seek recovery of their actual losses, presumably because Caffey's author fee was only $93.75 per performance.

A. Defendants' Profits

Section 504 provides that to establish the infringer's profits, the copyright owner must "present proof only of the infringer's gross revenue." 17 U.S.C. § 504(b) (2000). The infringer must then prove his "deductible expenses and the elements of profit attributable to factors other than the copyrighted work." Id. As the Second Circuit has stated, the "infringer's profits are calculated as the gross sales of infringing goods minus the costs that the infringer proves are attributable to the production and sale of those goods." Hamil, 193 F.3d at 104.

1. Plaintiffs' Burden in Showing Gross Revenues

In discharging their burden, plaintiffs must show "gross revenue reasonably related to the infringement, not unrelated revenues." On Davis, 246 F.3d at 160. For instance, the Second Circuit posited: Thus, if a publisher published an anthology of poetry which contained a poem covered by the plaintiff's copyright, we do not think the plaintiff's statutory burden would be discharged by submitting the publisher's gross revenue resulting from its publication of hundreds of titles, including trade books, textbooks, cookbooks, etc. In our view, the owner's burden would require evidence of the revenues realized from the sale of the anthology containing the infringing poem. The publisher would then bear the burden of proving its costs attributable to the anthology and the extent to which its profits from the sale of the anthology were attributable to factors other than the infringing poem, including particularly the other poems contained in the volume.

Since plaintiffs have proven that defendants infringed his copyright by incorporating the compilation embodied in the Show in six in-concert performances, plaintiffs must show the gross revenues flowing from those performances. The parties have introduced evidence regarding the gross revenues for each of those performances:

Naples, Florida	$ 40,000
Chicago, Illinois	$115,000
Phoenix, Arizona	$ 45,000
Philadelphia, Pennsylvania	$ 40,000
Naperville, Illinois	$ 50,000
Memphis, Tennessee	$ 40,000

(Pls.' Ex. 5; Defs.' Proposed Findings of Fact and Conclusions of Law ¶ 41; Pls.' Proposed Findings of Fact and Conclusions of Law ¶ 66.) Accordingly, plaintiffs have met their burden in showing the total gross revenues associated with the performances of $330,000.

2. Defendants' Burden in Offsetting Gross Revenues

To discharge their burden in showing costs, defendants must demonstrate "with some specificity" "that the expense was incurred in the production of the infringing work." Nimmer § 14.03[A] at 14-42; On Davis, 246 F.3d at 160. Moreover, "any uncertainty as to profits that is caused by the defendant's failure to keep adequate records of costs will be resolved in favor of the plaintiff." Yurman Design v. Chaindom Enterprises, Inc., No. 99 Civ. 9307(JFK), 2003 WL 22047843, at *4 (S.D.N.Y. Aug. 29, 2003) (internal citations omitted). In this instance, defendants have adduced evidence of commissions, disbursements, check disbursements for musician salaries, royalty payments and general overhead costs for these six performances. (See Graham Decl., Ex. A.)

(a) Commissions, Disbursements and Salaries for each Performance

Plaintiffs have not contested the specificity of defendants' direct costs. With respect to commissions for each performance, defendants' accountant, Karl Graham, and Cook, who was in charge of expenses, both testified that they paid (1) a 10 booking fee to the William Morris Agency from the gross revenues received; (2) 20% of their gross income to CD Enterprises; and (3) 5% of their gross income to their business manager, Padell Nadell. (Graham Decl. ¶¶ 5, 6; Cook Tr. 507.) Defendants also submitted sufficiently detailed statements for disbursements regarding per diem expenses and other costs, as well as salaries to musicians playing in the performances. (Graham Decl., Ex A.)

For the six infringing shows, defendants have established that their direct costs including commissions, salaries and disbursements totaled $174,995.95. (Id.)

(b) Overhead Expenses

With respect to overhead expenses, the Court must first determine "what overhead expense categories (such as rent, business, entertainment, personnel and public relations) are actually implicated by the production of the infringing product." Hamil Am. Inc., 193 F.3d at 106. Once the overhead categories are identified, the infringer must then propose a "fair and acceptable formula" for allotting a share of overhead expenses to the infringed work. Id. at 106 (citation omitted). Where the infringement is willful, the Court's analysis must be applied with "particular vigor." See id. (citing cases).

To establish willfulness under the Act, "the plaintiff must show (1) that the defendant was actually aware of the infringing activity, or (2) that the defendant's actions were the result of reckless disregard for, or willful blindness to, the copyright holder's rights." Island Software and Computer Serv., Inc. v. Microsoft Corp., 413 F.3d 257, 263 (2d Cir.2005) (internal citations omitted). Indeed, the plaintiff is not required to prove defendants' "actual knowledge that it was infringing" on his copyright. Knitwaves, Inc. v. Lollytogs Ltd. (Inc.), 71 F.3d 996, 1010-11 (2d Cir. 1995). Rather, "[k]nowledge of infringement may be constructive rather than actual; that is, it need not be proven directly but may be inferred from the defendant's conduct." Id.

The Court has found that defendants were not aware of Caffey's claimed copyright at the time of the Show's rehearsals. See discussion supra. However, on May 13, 2003, Caffey's attorney, Erach F. Screwvala, wrote a letter to defendants' agent, CD Enterprises, Inc., claiming Caffey's right in "the continued performance of THREE MO' TENORS," including any copyrights or trademarks associated with THREE MO' TENORS. (Pls.' Ex. 32.) Robert Cinque, attorney for Cook, Dixon and Young, responded by letter dated May 28, 2003, stating "To the extent that you possess copyright registrations or a trademark application with any supporting documents, kindly furnish them to me. You have my assurances that whatever you provide will be promptly reviewed and a further response given to you." (Pls.' Ex. 33.) Screwvala refused to provide further information, stating only that "[w]e are confident of our client's rights . . . Proceed at your peril." (Pls.' Ex 34.)

The question, then, is whether the foregoing exchange of letters establishes willfulness on the part of the defendants. The Court thinks not. At best, the letters reveal that defendants, through their counsel, were aware that Caffey was claiming undefined copyright and trademark interests in the Show. They, or more accurately their counsel, did not demonstrate willful blindness; to the contrary, the letter demonstrates that defendants would have received and considered evidence to support Caffey's claims. In light of what has transpired, it may well have been the better course to ignore Screwala's hostile response and examine the matter further, but this does not mean that defendants conduct was willful or reckless. Moreover, having listened to defendants' testimony, the Court concludes that they in fact believed they had as much right as Caffey to perform the selected songs.8 As Caffey himself noted, they had "their truth" (Caffey Tr. 289), though in the end their belief was misplaced. Since plaintiffs have failed to establish willful infringement, defendants are entitled to deduct their reasonable overhead expenses in calculating their net profit.

...

(c) Income Taxes

With respect to defendants' payment of income taxes, no willful infringer may deduct such costs. See In Design v. K-Mart Apparel Corp., 13 F.3d 559, 566-67 (2d Cir.1994). As the Court therein noted: "[W]hen a claim is made for infringing profits, [t]his means profits actually made. A book profit of a dollar is not a profit actually made when from the dollar the government takes twenty cents as the price for the right to make any profit at all." However, where the infringement was willful, income tax paid from profits is not deductible. Id. at 566. Since the Court has found that defendants did not engage in willful infringement, deduction of income taxes is appropriate. Defendants' accountant provided affidavit testimony that their rates of taxation (federal, state and local) ranged between 30 and 35 of their net income. The Court accepts the low-end of the range as a deductible expense in the amount of $43,616.22.

3. Total Profits

The Court calculates net profit after deduction of direct and overhead expenses and taxes of $101,771.18.

B. Defendants' Burden in Showing Profits Attributable to Other Factors

Section 504(b) permits defendants to prove "the elements of profit attributable to factors other than the copyrighted work." 17 U.S.C. § 504(b). Defendants herein contend that apportionment of the profits is appropriate since Caffey's copyrighted compilation was a minor factor in the success of the Show. In situations "where an infringer's profits are not entirely due to the infringement, and the evidence suggests some division which may rationally be used as a springboard it is the duty of the [trier-of-fact] to make some apportionment." Orgel v. Clark Boardman Co., 301 F.2d 119, 121 (2d Cir.1962); Frank Music Corp. v. Metro-Goldwyn-Mayer, Inc., 886 F.2d 1545, 1549 (9th Cir. 1989) ("[C]ourts cannot be expected to determine with mathematical exactness an apportionment of profits.") (internal citations omitted).

Apportionment is "not an area susceptible to precise measurement," ABKCO Music v. Harrisongs Music, Ltd., 508 F.Supp. 798, 801 (S.D.N.Y.1981), particularly where the analysis does not rest on quantifiable factors such as minutes, pages or lines incorporating the infringed work,9 but rather on the incorporation of the infringed work into a new presentation. The Second Circuit has considered several factors in apportioning those "elements of profit attributable to factors other than the copyrighted work." Rogers v. Koons, 960 F.2d 301, 313 (2d Cir.1992). Relevant factors include (1) defendants' "own notoriety and ability to command high prices for [their] work," id.; see also ABKCO Music, 508 F.Supp. at 801;10 (2) the "expert and creative operations involved in the production and direction of the Show," Sheldon v. Metro-Goldwyn Pictures Corp., 309 U.S. 390, 406, 60 S.Ct. 681, 84 L.Ed. 825 (1940), see also Abend v. MCA, Inc., 863 F.2d 1465, 1480 (9th Cir.1988), aff'd sub. Nom. Stewart v. Abend, 495 U.S. 207, 110 S.Ct. 1750, 109 L.Ed.2d 184 (1990); (3) the outstanding performances, talent and drawing power of defendants, Sheldon, 309 U.S. at 406, 60 S.Ct. 681; and (4) the creativity of defendants in staging the Show, Frank Music Corp. v. Metro-Goldwyn-Mayer Inc., 886 F.2d 1545, 1549 (9th Cir.1989); Twentieth Century-Fox Film Corp. v. Stonesifer, 140 F.2d 579, 583-84 (9th Cir.1944) ("It is now settled that where a portion of the profits of an infringing work is attributable to the appropriated work, to avoid an unjust course by giving the originator all profits where the infringer's labor and artistry have also to an extent contributed to the ultimate result").

The Second Circuit has further stated that the extent to which plaintiff "worked over old material" already in the "public demesne" may also "count towards reducing the percentage of the profits recoverable." Sheldon v. Metro-Goldwyn Pictures Corp., 106 F.2d 45, 51 (2d Cir.1939), aff'd 309 U.S. 390, 60 S.Ct. 681, 84 L.Ed. 825 (1940). In Sheldon, defendants produced a movie that infringed on a play written and copyrighted by plaintiffs. However, the Second Circuit noted that:

[T]he plaintiffs worked over old material; the general skeleton was already in the public demesne. A wanton girl kills her lover to free herself for a better match; she is brought to trial for the murder and escapes. Nobody can say how far this basic plot is to be credited with whatever the play contributed to the drawing power of the picture. That consideration must therefore count towards reducing the percentage of profits recoverable. Id. at 51. In light of those considerations, as well as defendants' employment of actors, scenery, directors and producers in adding to the creativity of the film, the Second Circuit awarded plaintiffs 20% of defendants' profits arising from the infringing motion picture. Id. at 52; Stonesifer, 140 F.2d at 583-84 (awarding 20 of defendants' profits from motion picture that infringed upon plaintiff's copyrighted play).

The Court discerns several "profit-making features, apart from the use of any infringing material," that contributed to the profits of defendants' six in-concert performances. Sheldon, 309 U.S. at 406, 60 S.Ct. 681.

First, as is evident from the recorded PBS performance, defendants possess tremendous talent. While praising the Show as "sensational," newspaper clippings submitted by plaintiffs indicate that all three defendants were "standout" performers. Id. Young was reviewed as "a magical singer in every idiom"; "Cook tore the house down"; and Dixon gave "the most stirring performance." Id. In addition, each of defendants entered the Show as performers with impressive resumes including educational pedigrees at the top musical performance schools, Broadway appearances and performances with elite conductors such as Zubin Mehta and Simon Rattle. Id. As such, defendants' talent, accolade-laden performances and growing notoriety played a significant role in generating profits for their six performances as Cook, Dixon Young. See Sheldon, 309 U.S. at 406, 60 S.Ct. 681.

Second, plaintiffs admitted that Caffey's concept was intended to piggyback off the idea of "The Three Tenors," popularized by the famous tenors Pavarotti, Domingo and Carreras. (Caffey Decl. ¶ 4.) Certainly, the bankable name and concept of the "Three Mo' Tenors" was, to some extent, already in the "public demesne," as evidenced by the fact that each newspaper article describing the "Three Mo' Tenors" also mentioned "The Three Tenors." (See Pls.' Ex. 11 at 1909) ("Who can ignore the success of the Three Tenors concept?") Indeed, the very point of the Show was to offer an African-American alternative to the Three Tenors. (See Pls.' Ex. 11 ("Three Mo' Tenors go much farther afield than Domingo or Pavarotti ever did")); Sheldon, 106 F.2d at 51. This concept undoubtedly created value in the Show and contributed to the Show's profitability. Caffey, however, does not claim a copyright in the idea of three African-American tenors singing multiple genres; nor does it appear that the idea itself is copyrightable. 17 U.S.C. § 102(B); Harper & Row Publishers, Inc. v. Nation Enterprises, 471 U.S. 539, 556, 105 S.Ct. 2218, 85 L.Ed.2d 588 (1985); Nimmer § 1.10[B][2]. Moreover, the concept was not entirely novel. Cook frequently sang multiple genres in concert and had even done a show with Caffey in 1991 when he sang classical, jazz, show tunes, pop and gospel. (Dixon Tr. 192; Dixon Decl., Ex. 2.)

Third, a very substantial factor contributing to the Show's profitability was the songs themselves. The show is essentially the performance of other artists' copyrighted works written and made famous by the likes of Verdi, Puccini, Ellington and Calloway. Without the prior works, there is no Show.

Finally, and against this backdrop, the Court must evaluate the nature of plaintiffs' copyright and its contribution to the profits generated by defendants' infringing performances. The copyright covers three elements: selection, sequencing and bridge dialogue. The defendants contend that the brief lines of dialogue between songs add little value to the Show. Caffey does not seriously dispute this claim, noting only one piece of dialogue that he claims generated significant audience reaction. (Pls.' Proposed Findings of Fact and Conclusions of Law, ¶ 23.) Having reviewed the passages as well as the parties' testimony, and without putting too fine a point on it, the Court finds that the bridge dialogue contributed minimal value to the success of the Show or to the profits generated by the infringing performances.

Defendants also testified that the selection and ordering of the songs had no independent value. (Defs.' Proposed Findings of Fact and Conclusions of Law ¶ 22.) Defendants overstate their case, however, and the Court accepts Caffey's testimony that the selection and ordering of the songs creates an "arc" to the Show. But it is also true that a different ordering of the songs might also result in a successful performance. This is best evidenced by the televised broadcast of a performance on PBS which drastically rearranged the order of the songs with no apparent diminution in effect; indeed it is this telecast that is credited with popularizing the Show. (Pls.' Ex. 11 at 1909; Pls.' Ex. 17). Moreover, the ordering of some of the songs was dictated in part by physical constraints, not creativity. As all parties agreed, the classical numbers put such strain on the performers' voices that they had to be performed first. Indeed the first four classical numbers in the Show were performed in the same order in the 1998 showcase that Caffey admits was "never intended . . . to be either a precursor or a version of what would eventually become the [Show]." (Caffey Decl. ¶ 19.) Caffey goes on to explain that the purpose of the showcase "[was] to introduce my concept for the Show . . ." (Id.) But the concept for the Show — three African-American tenors performing a variation of the immensely popular Three Tenors — is not the subject of plaintiffs' copyright, which is limited to the selection and ordering of preexisting copyrighted materials with bridge dialogue. The selection and ordering of the particular songs was not valueless as defendants claim, but the Court concludes that it was of comparable value to the concept for the Show, the defendants' performances and the artistry of the songs themselves.

The apportionment of profits derived from these qualitative factors is an inexact science. And while it would be "certainly unjust" to award plaintiffs all the profits from the infringing shows, it is also true that the Court "must make an award which by no possibility shall be too small." Sheldon, 106 F.2d at 51. Accordingly, the share of net profits attributable to the copyrighted element of the Show is fixed at one-third (33.3%) or $33,889.80.

...

VII. Punitive Damages

Finally, plaintiffs seek punitive damages arguing that defendants acted with "malice" and with "personal animosity" towards plaintiffs. (Pls.' Proposed Findings of Fact and Conclusions of Law ¶ 32.) It is unclear whether punitive damages may be awarded under the Act where the plaintiff has elected to receive actual damages. See Blanch v. Koons, 329 F.Supp.2d 568, 569 (S.D.N.Y.2004) (remarking that "[c]onventional authority holds that punitive damages are unavailable in copyright infringement actions, regardless of whether plaintiff is seeking statutory damages or the alternative of actual damages plus profits.") Some cases in the Southern District of New York suggest that punitive damages may be awarded where (1) the plaintiff has elected to receive actual damages; and (2) defendants engaged in willful infringement. TVT Records v. Island DEF Jam Music Group, 262 F.Supp.2d 185, 187 (S.D.N.Y. 2003) (concluding that plaintiff's "claims for punitive damages for copyright infringement found to be willful are not precluded as a matter of law and can be presented to the jury."). Even under this theory, however, the Court has already concluded that defendants did not act willfully in infringing on plaintiffs' copyright. Accordingly, the Court denies plaintiffs' request for punitive damages.

...

CONCLUSION

Subject to ruling upon any renewed motion for injunctive relief, the Court directs entry of judgment in favor of plaintiffs and against defendants jointly and severally in the amount of $33,889.80.11

603 F.3d 135 (2010)

BRYANT v. MEDIA RIGHT PRODUCTIONS

United States Court of Appeals, Second Circuit

KIMBA M. WOOD, District Judge:

Appellants produced two copyrighted albums of music, each of which was composed of ten songs. Appellee Media Right Productions, Inc. ("Media Right") gave the albums to Appellee Orchard Enterprises, Inc. ("Orchard"), who copied and sold them without authorization. The Court awarded Appellants one statutory damage award for each album infringed by each Appellee, a total of four awards, rather than one statutory damage award for each of the songs on the albums (which would have totaled forty awards), as Appellants had sought. The Court also found that Appellants had not proven that the infringement was willful, that Orchard had proven that its infringement was innocent, and that profits from infringing sales were low; the Court thus awarded a total of only $2400 in damages. We conclude that the District Court (1) correctly awarded statutory damages for each album infringed; (2) did not commit clear error in finding that Appellants had failed to prove willfulness and that Orchard had proven its innocence; and (3) correctly calculated damages. We also conclude that the District Court did not abuse its discretion by denying attorneys fees. Accordingly, we affirm.

I. Background

Appellants Anne Bryant and Ellen Bernfeld are songwriters who own a record label, Appellant Gloryvision Ltd (collectively with Bryant and Bernfeld, "Appellants"). In the late 1990s, Appellants created and produced two albums, Songs for Dogs and Songs for Cats (the "Albums"). They registered the Albums with the United States Copyright Office. They also separately registered at least some of the twenty songs on the Albums.

On February 24, 2000, Appellants entered into an agreement with Media Right ("Media Right Agreement"), which authorized Media Right to market the Albums in exchange for twenty percent of the proceeds from any sales. The Agreement did not grant Media Right permission to make copies of the Albums. If Media Right needed more copies of the Albums, Appellants would provide them.

The Media Right Agreement resulted from conversations between Appellant Ellen Bernfeld ("Bernfeld") and Appellee Douglas Maxwell ("Maxwell"), President of Media Right, during which Maxwell told Bernfeld that Media Right would be distributing music through Orchard, a music wholesaler.

Media Right entered into an agreement with Orchard on February 1, 2000 ("Orchard Agreement"). The Orchard Agreement authorized Orchard to distribute on Media Right's behalf eleven albums listed in the Agreement, two of which were the Albums (apparently in anticipation of the Media Right Agreement). The Orchard Agreement provided, in relevant part, that:

[Media Right] grant[s] [Orchard] non-exclusive rights to sell, distribute and otherwise exploit [Media Right's albums] by any and all means and media (whether now known or existing in the future), including throughout E-stores including those via the Internet, as well as all digital storage, download and transmission rights, whether now known or existing in the future.

In the Orchard Agreement, Media Right warranted that Orchard's use of the Albums would not infringe any copyrights. Maxwell gave Orchard physical copies of the Albums, which bore copyright notices stating that the copyrights for the Albums were held by Appellants.

When Media Right entered into the Orchard Agreement in 2000, Orchard sold only physical copies of recordings. In about April 2004, however, Orchard began making digital copies of the Albums to sell through internet-based music retailers such as iTunes. Internet customers were able to purchase and download digital copies of the Albums and individual songs on the Albums. Orchard did not inform Media Right or Appellants that it was selling digital copies of the Albums and individual songs on the Albums.

From April 1, 2002 to April 8, 2008, Orchard generated $12.14 in revenues from sales of physical copies of the Albums, and $578.91 from downloads of digital copies of the Albums and of individual songs. Media Right's share of these revenues was $413.82, of which $331.06 should have been forwarded to Appellants pursuant to the Media Right Agreement. Because the $413.82 was aggregated with other monies Orchard paid to Media Right, Media Right overlooked that it owed a portion of the payments to Appellants. Media Right, therefore, did not pay Appellants the $331.06 to which they were entitled.

In 2006, Appellants discovered that digital copies of the Albums were available online. On April 16, 2007, Appellants filed a complaint against Appellees in the Southern District of New York, alleging direct and contributory copyright infringement, and seeking statutory damages.

In 2008, Appellants and Appellees both moved for summary judgment in the case. They agreed to permit the District Court to treat the motions as a case stated. The Court conducted two evidentiary hearings before issuing its order. The Court held, in relevant part, that Appellees had committed direct copyright infringement by making and selling digital copies of the Albums and the individual songs on the Albums.

The Court awarded Appellants statutory damages in the total amount of $2400, pursuant to Section 504 of the Copyright Act of 1976 (the "Act"). 17 U.S.C. § 504(c). The Act provides that a court can award statutory damages of not less than $750 or more than $30,000, "as the court considers just," for all infringements with respect to one work, and that all parts of a "compilation" constitute one work. 17 U.S.C. § 504(c)(1). If the infringer proves that his infringement was innocent, the court may reduce damages to an amount not less than $200. 17 U.S.C. § 504(c)(2). If the copyright holder proves that infringement was willful, the court may increase the award to no more than $150,000. Id.

The District Court made the following three rulings regarding damages, all of which Appellants contest on appeal.

First, the Court held that the Albums were compilations, and thus that each Appellee was liable for only one award of statutory damages per Album, rather than one award per song, as Appellants had sought. Bryant v. Europadisk Ltd., 07 Civ. 3050(WGY), 2009 WL 1059777, *6-8 (S.D.N.Y. Apr. 15, 2009).

Second, the Court found that Orchard had proven that its infringement was innocent, and thus ordered Orchard to pay only minimal statutory damages of $200 per Album, for a total of $400. Id. at *8-9.

Third, the Court found that Maxwell and Media Right had failed to prove that their infringement was innocent, but that Appellants had failed to prove that Maxwell and Media Right's infringement was willful. Id. The Court found that because neither side had met its burden of proof, and because Appellees' revenues from the Albums were very low, Media Right and Maxwell were jointly and severally liable for an award of only $1000 per Album, for a total of $2000. Id.

The Court did not award Appellants attorneys fees. Dist. Ct. Order, May 12, 2009. Accordingly, the total award to Appellants was $2400. This appeal followed.

II. Discussion

Appellants argue that we should vacate the District Court's statutory damage award, contending that: (1) the Court erred in refusing to grant a separate statutory damage award for each song on the Albums; (2) the Court erred in its findings on intent; and (3) the Court erred in determining the amount of damages. Appellants also argue that the Court abused its discretion by refusing to award them attorneys' fees. We address each of these arguments in turn.

A. The District Court's Decision to Award Statutory Damages on a Per-Album Basis

Appellants contend that the District Court erred in holding that the Albums were compilations, and thus limiting statutory damages to one award for each Album. Appellants argue that each song on the Albums qualifies as a separate work because, according to Appellants, each song is separately copyrighted, and because Orchard sold the songs individually.

The question of whether a work constitutes a "compilation" for the purposes of statutory damages pursuant to Section 504(c)(1) of the Copyright Act is a mixed question of law and fact. See Gamma Audio & Video, Inc. v. Ean-Chea, 11 F.3d 1106, 1116 (1st Cir.1993). We thus review de novo the District Court's decision that the Albums are "compilations." See APL Co. PTF Ltd. v. Blue Water Shipping U.S. Inc., 592 F.3d 108, 110 (2d Cir.2010). We conclude that the District Court's ruling was correct.

The Copyright Act allows only one award of statutory damages for any "work" infringed. 17 U.S.C. § 504(c)(1). It states that "all the parts of a compilation constitute one work." Id. § 504(c)(1). It defines a "compilation" as "a work formed by the collection and assembling of preexisting materials or of data that are selected, coordinated, or arranged in such a way that the resulting work as a whole constitutes an original work of authorship ." Id. § 101. The term compilation includes collected works, which are defined as works "in which a number of contributions, constituting separate and independent works in themselves, are assembled into a collective work." Id. The Conference Report that accompanied the Act and explains many of its provisions, states that a "compilation" "results from a process of selecting, bringing together, organizing, and arranging previously existing material of all kinds, regardless of whether . the individual items in the material have been or ever could have been subject to copyright." H.R.Rep. No. 1476, 94th Cong., 2d Sess. 162, reprinted in 1976 U.S.C.C.A.N. 5659 (emphasis added).

An album falls within the Act's expansive definition of compilation. An album is a collection of preexisting materials-songs-that are selected and arranged by the author in a way that results in an original work of authorship-the album. Based on a plain reading of the statute, therefore, infringement of an album should result in only one statutory damage award. The fact that each song may have received a separate copyright is irrelevant to this analysis. See H.R.Rep. No. 1476, 94th Cong., 2d Sess. 162, reprinted in 1976 U.S.C.C.A.N. 5659.

We have addressed in two previous decisions the issue of what constitutes a compilation subject to Section 504(c)(1)'s one-award restriction. See Twin Peaks Prods., Inc. v. Publ'ns. Int'l Ltd., 996 F.2d 1366, 1381 (2d Cir.1993); WB Music Corp. v. RTV Comm. Group, Inc., 445 F.3d 538, 541 (2d Cir.2006). In both decisions, we focused on whether the plaintiff-the copyright holder-issued its works separately, or together as a unit.

In Twin Peaks, the plaintiff issued each episode of a television series sequentially, each at a different time. The defendant printed eight teleplays from the series in one book. 996 F.2d at 1381. We held that the plaintiff could receive a separate award of statutory damages for each of the eight teleplays because the plaintiff had issued the works separately, as independent television episodes. Id. In WB Music Corp., the plaintiff had separately issued each of thirteen songs. 445 F.3d at 541. It was the defendant who issued the songs in album form. Id. We held that the plaintiff could receive a separate statutory damage award for each song, because there was "no evidence that any of the separately copyrighted works were included in a compilation authorized by the [plaintiff]." Id. (emphasis added).

Here, it is the copyright holders who issued their works as "compilations"; they chose to issue Albums. In this situation, the plain language of the Copyright Act limits the copyright holders' statutory damage award to one for each Album.

Appellants argue that the District Court should have allowed a statutory damage award for each song, because each song has "independent economic value": internet customers could listen to and purchase copies of each song, each of which Appellants claim was independently copyrighted. Plaintiffs point to a decision from the First Circuit, Gamma Audio, in which the Court held that a work that is part of a multi-part product can constitute a separate work for the purposes of statutory damages if it has "independent economic value and is viable." 11 F.3d at 1116-17. Applying what that court described as a "functional" test, the court held that each episode of a television show, although released on videotape as part of a complete series, could be the subject of a separate statutory damage award because each episode could be rented and viewed separately. Id. at 1117-18. At least three other circuits have adopted the "independent economic value" test, although to date none has applied the test to an album of music. See MCA Television Ltd. v. Feltner, 89 F.3d 766, 769 (11th Cir.1996) (holding that each episode of a television show can be the subject of a separate statutory damage award because each episode has independent economic value); Columbia Pictures Television v. Krypton Broad. of Birmingham, Inc., 106 F.3d 284, 295 (9th Cir.1997) (same) (reversed on other grounds, 523 U.S. 340, 118 S.Ct. 1279, 140 L.Ed.2d 438 (1998)); Walt Disney Co. v. Powell, 897 F.2d 565, 569 (D.C.Cir.1990) (holding that plaintiff could not receive a separate statutory damage award for each, separate picture of Mickey Mouse and Minnie Mouse in different poses, because each picture did not have independent economic value). Appellants argue that it is particularly appropriate to apply the "independent economic value" test to music albums, because music is increasingly available in digital form, which has made it easier for infringers to break apart albums and sell the album's songs individually, as Appellees did here.

This Court has never adopted the independent economic value test, and we decline to do so in this case. The Act specifically states that all parts of a compilation must be treated as one work for the purpose of calculating statutory damages. This language provides no exception for a part of a compilation that has independent economic value, and the Court will not create such an exception. See UMG Recordings, Inc., 109 F.Supp.2d at 225 (stating that to award statutory damages on a per-song basis would "make a total mockery of Congress' express mandate that all parts of a compilation must be treated as a single 'work' for purposes of computing statutory damages"). We cannot disregard the statutory language simply because digital music has made it easier for infringers to make parts of an album available separately. This interpretation of the statute is consistent with the

Congressional intent expressed in the Conference Report that accompanied the 1976 Copyright Act, which states that the one-award restriction applies even if the parts of the compilation are "regarded as independent works for other purposes." H.R.Rep. No. 1476, 94th Cong., 2d Sess. 162, reprinted in 1976 U.S.C.C.A.N. 5659, 5778.

Accordingly, we affirm the District Court's decision to treat each Album as a compilation, subject to only one award of statutory damages.

B. The District Court's Decision on Intent and the Amount of Damages

Appellants contend that the District Court erred in finding that Orchard proved that its conduct was innocent, and that Appellants failed to prove that Appellees' conduct amounted to willful infringement.

Pursuant to Section 504(c)(2) of the Copyright Act, an infringer's intent can affect the amount of statutory damages awarded: only a minimal award may be warranted where the infringment is innocent; a higher award may be warranted where the infringer acted willfully.

We review the district court's findings on intent for clear error. See Fitzgerald Pbl'g Co. v. Baylor Pbl'g Co., 807 F.2d 1110, 1115 (2d Cir.1986). The burden of proving innocence is on the alleged infringer. The burden of proving willfulness is on the copyright holder. See 17 U.S.C. § 504(c).

1. Innocence

The District Court found that Orchard acted innocently because Orchard, in making digital copies, reasonably relied on two provisions of the Orchard Agreement: (1) a provision permitting Orchard to distribute the Albums "by any and all means and media including digital storage, download and transmission," Orchard Agreement, Appellants App., A-174; and (2) a provision warranting that Orchard's use of the Albums in accordance with the Agreement would not infringe any copyrights, Orchard Agreement, Appellants App., A-174.

We hold that it was not clear error for the District Court to find that it was reasonable for Orchard to believe that it had received the right to copy the Albums.

2. Willfulness

A copyright holder seeking to prove that a copier's infringement was willful must show that the infringer "had knowledge that its conduct represented infringement or recklessly disregarded the possibility." Twin Peaks, 996 F.2d at 1382.

The District Court found that Appellees did not prove that Maxwell and Media Right acted willfully in infringing Appellees' copyright. The District Court found that it was not unreasonable for Maxwell not to have anticipated that Orchard would distribute digital copies of the Albums, notwithstanding that the Orchard Agreement granted Orchard the right to do so, because Orchard did not distribute digital music in 2000, when the Orchard Agreement was signed. The District Court also found credible Maxwell's testimony at the evidentiary hearing that he had never before marketed recordings that were not his own, and that, in allowing Orchard broad distribution rights, he focused only on his belief that Appellants wanted him to do everything possible to market their Albums. This testimony shows that Maxwell did not have experience marketing music owned by a third party; that he did not fully understand the rights he had obtained under the Media Right Agreement; and that his focus was on maximizing sales of the Albums.

We hold that it was not clear error for the District Court to find that Maxwell and Media Right's infringement was not willful.

C. The District Court's Calculation of Statutory Damages

Appellants also argue that the statutory damages awarded by the District Court were too low. District courts "enjoy wide discretion in setting the amount of statutory damages." Fitzgerald Pbl'g Co., 807 F.2d at 1116. We review for clear error the District Court's factual findings supporting its determination of the appropriate level of statutory damages, and we review an award of those damages for abuse of discretion. Lyons Parntership, L.P. v. Morris Costumes, Inc., 243 F.3d 789, 799 (4th Cir.2001); see also Knitwaves, Inc. v. Lollytogs Ltd. (Inc.), 71 F.3d 996, 1012 (2d Cir.1995).

When determining the amount of statutory damages to award for copyright infringement, courts consider: (1) the infringer's state of mind; (2) the expenses saved, and profits earned, by the infringer; (3) the revenue lost by the copyright holder; (4) the deterrent effect on the infringer and third parties; (5) the infriger's cooperation in providing evidence concerning the value of the infringing material; and (6) the conduct and attitude of the parties. See N.A.S. Impor. Corp. v. Chenson Enter., Inc., 968 F.2d 250, 252-53 (2d Cir.1993).

The District Court awarded a total of $2400 in statutory damages, based on its finding that Appellees' profits from infringing sales of the Albums and songs were meager, and that the award did not need to be higher to achieve deterrence, because deterrence was effectuated here by Appellees having to pay their own attorneys fees. We hold that the District Court did not abuse its discretion in calculating statutory damages.

...

III. Conclusion

For the reasons stated above, the order of the District Court is AFFIRMED.

761 F.3d 789 (2014)

KLINGER v. CONAN DOYLE ESTATE

United States Court of Appeals, Seventh Circuit

This opinion is a sequel to Klinger v. Conan Doyle Estate, Ltd., 2014 WL 2726187 (7th Cir. June 16, 2014), where we held that Leslie Klinger was entitled to a declaratory judgment that he would not be infringing copyrights on fictional works published by Arthur Conan Doyle before 1923 by anthologizing stories written long after Doyle's death in 1930 that feature Sherlock Holmes and other characters depicted in Doyle's pre–1923 fiction. Even though the modern (post-Doyle) Sherlock Holmes stories copy copyrightable material in the pre–1923 fiction, the copyrights on that fiction, which cover copyrightable elements in it that include original depictions of characters (like Holmes and Dr. Watson), have expired. We rejected the Doyle estate's argument that because stories published by Doyle between 1923 and his death—and still under copyright—depicted those characters in a more "rounded form" than found in the pre–1923 fiction, the "flat" characters of the earlier stories were protected by the copyrights still in force on the "rounded" characters of the later stories.

Once the copyright on a work expires, the work becomes a part of the public domain and can be copied and sold without a license from the holder of the expired copyright. So when Klinger published his first anthology of modern Sherlock Holmes stories he didn't think he needed a license. But the Doyle estate told Random House, which had agreed to publish Klinger's book, that it would have to pay the estate $5,000 for a copyright license. Random House yielded to the demand, obtained the license, and published the book.

Klinger arranged for a sequel to the anthology to be published by Pegasus Books and distributed by W.W. Norton & Company to booksellers. When the Doyle estate learned of this project, it told Pegasus, as it had told Random House, that Pegasus would have to obtain a $5,000 license from the estate in order to be legally authorized to publish the new book. The estate didn't explicitly threaten to sue Pegasus for copyright infringement if the publisher didn't obtain a license, but did explicitly threaten to prevent distribution of the book. It did not mince words. It told Pegasus: "If you proceed to bring out [the sequel] unlicensed, do not expect to see it offered for sale by Amazon, Barnes & Noble, and similar retailers. We work with those compan[ies] routinely to weed out unlicensed uses of Sherlock Holmes from their offerings, and will not hesitate to do so with your book as well." There was also a latent threat to sue Pegasus for copyright infringement if it published Klinger's book without a license, and to sue Internet service providers who distributed it. See Digital Millennium Copyright Act, 17 U.S.C. § 512(i)(1)(A). Pegasus yielded to the threat, as Random House had done, and refused to publish the anthology until Klinger obtained a license from the Doyle estate.

Instead of obtaining a license Klinger sued the estate, seeking declaratory relief against being adjudged an infringer of any valid copyrights of the estate—and won, both in the district court and, on the estate's appeal, in this court. We could find no basis in statute or case law for extending a copyright beyond its expiration. When a story falls into the public domain, story elements—including characters covered by the expired copyright—become fair game for follow-on authors. There is no ground known to American law for extending copyright protection beyond the limits fixed by Congress. The estate's appeal bordered on the quixotic.

Now Klinger asks us to order the Doyle estate to reimburse the attorneys' fees he incurred in the appeal, amounting to $30,679.93. (He has filed a separate petition for fees and related costs incurred in his litigation in the district court, totaling

$39,123.44. That petition is not before us.) The estate opposes Klinger's request on the same hopeless grounds that it had urged in its appeal, but does not question the amount of fees as distinct from Klinger's entitlement to an award of any amount of fees in this case.

The Copyright Act authorizes the "award [of] a reasonable attorney's fee to the prevailing party as part of the costs." 17 U .S.C. § 505. We said in Assessment Technologies of Wisconsin, LLC v. WIREdata, Inc., 361 F.3d 434, 436–37 (7th Cir.2004) (and reaffirmed in DeliverMed Holdings, LLC v. Schaltenbrand, 734 F.3d 616, 625–26 (7th Cir.2013)) that the two most important considerations in deciding whether to award fees "are the strength of the prevailing party's case and the amount of damages or other relief the party obtained. If the case was a toss-up and the prevailing party obtained generous damages, or injunctive relief of substantial monetary value, there is no urgent need to add an award of attorneys' fees. But if at the other extreme the claim or defense was frivolous and the prevailing party obtained no relief at all, the case for awarding attorneys' fees is compelling" (citations omitted). We said that as a consequence of the successful defense of an infringement suit the defendant is entitled to a "very strong" presumption in favor of receiving attorneys' fees, in order to ensure that an infringement defendant does not abandon a meritorious defense in situations in which "the cost of vindication exceeds the private benefit to the party." 361 F.3d at 437. "For without the prospect of such an award, [an infringement defendant] might be forced into a nuisance settlement or deterred altogether from exercising [its] rights." Id.

We're not alone in expressing these concerns. See Michael J. Meurer, "Controlling Opportunistic and Anti–Competitive Intellectual Property Litigation," 44 Boston College L.Rev. 509, 521 (2003). See also Ben Depoorter & Robert Kirk Walker, "Copyright False Positives," 89 Notre Dame L.Rev. 319, 343–45 (2013), where we read that many persons or firms accused of copyright infringement find that "it is more cost-effective to simply capitulate" than to fight, even when the alleged claim is of dubious merit. Copyright holders, the authors explain, have larger potential upsides and smaller downside risks to filing suit, since if they win they obtain damages but if they lose they don't have to pay damages (although a loss, especially if recorded in a published opinion as in this case, may make it more difficult for them to play their extortionate game in future cases). So copiers or alleged copiers may be "induced into licensing [that is, paying a fee for a license to reproduce] the underlying work, even if this license is unnecessary or conveys non-existent rights." Id. at 345. Depoorter and Walker (id. at 345 n. 172) give the example of the Summy–Brichard Company, a subsidiary of Warner Music Group, which "receives approximately $2 million per year in royalty payments for licenses to the song 'Happy Birthday to You,' despite the fact that the song is most likely in the public domain," as argued in Robert Brauneis, "Copyright and the World's Most Popular Song," 56 J. Copyright Society U.S.A. 335, 338–40 (2009).

This case illustrates the concerns expressed both in the articles we've just cited...

The Doyle estate's business strategy is plain: charge a modest license fee for which there is no legal basis, in the hope that the "rational" writer or publisher asked for the fee will pay it rather than incur a greater cost, in legal expenses, in challenging the legality of the demand. The strategy had worked with Random House; Pegasus was ready to knuckle under; only Klinger (so far as we know) resisted. In effect he was a private attorney general, combating a disreputable business practice—a form of extortion—and he is seeking by the present motion not to obtain a reward but merely to avoid a loss. He has performed a public service—and with substantial risk to himself, for had he lost he would have been out of pocket for the $69,803.37 in fees and costs incurred at the trial and appellate levels ($30,679.93 + $39,123.44). The willingness of someone in Klinger's position to sue rather than pay Doyle's estate a modest license fee is important because it injects risk into the estate's business model. As a result of losing the suit, the estate has lost its claim to own copyrights in characters in the Sherlock Holmes stories published by Arthur Conan Doyle before 1923. For exposing the estate's unlawful business strategy, Klinger deserves a reward but asks only to break even.

...

It's time the estate, in its own self-interest, changed its business model.

Klinger's motion is granted and the Doyle estate ordered to pay him $30,679.93 for the legal fees that he incurred in his successful defense of the district court's judgment in his favor.

POSNER, Circuit Judge.

3. Limiting Concepts

3.A. Idea-Expression

101 U.S. 99 (1879)

BAKER V. SELDEN

U.S. Supreme Court

MR. JUSTICE BRADLEY delivered the opinion of the Court.

Charles Selden, the testator of the complainant in this case, in the year 1859 took the requisite steps for obtaining the copyright of a book, entitled "Selden's Condensed Ledger, or Bookkeeping Simplified," the object of which was to exhibit and explain a peculiar system of bookkeeping. In 1860 and 1861, he took the copyright of several other books, containing additions to and improvements upon the said system. The bill of complaint was filed against the defendant, Baker, for an alleged infringement of these copyrights. The latter, in his answer, denied that Selden was the author or designer of the books, and denied the infringement charged, and contends on the argument that the matter alleged to be infringed is not a lawful subject of copyright.

The parties went into proofs, and the various books of the complainant, as well as those sold and used by the defendant, were exhibited before the examiner, and witnesses were examined to both sides. A decree was rendered for the complainant, and the defendant appealed.

The book or series of books of which the complainant claims the copyright consists of an introductory essay explaining the system of bookkeeping referred to, to which are annexed certain forms or banks, consisting of ruled lines, and headings, illustrating the system and showing how it is to be used and carried out in practice. This system effects the same results as bookkeeping by double entry, but, by a peculiar arrangement of columns and headings, presents the entire operation, of a day, a week, or a month on a single page or on two pages facing each other, in an account book. The defendant uses a similar plan so far as results are concerned, but makes a different arrangement of the columns, and uses different headings. If the complainant's testator had the exclusive right to the use of the system explained in his book, it would be difficult to contend that the defendant does not infringe it, notwithstanding the difference in his form of arrangement; but if it be assumed that the system is open to public use, it seems to be equally difficult to contend that the books made and sold by the defendant are a violation of the copyright of the complainant's book considered merely as a book explanatory of the system. Where the truths of a science or the methods of an art are the common property of the whole world, any author has the right to express the one, or explain and use the other, in his own way. As an author, Selden explained the system in a particular way. It may be conceded that Baker makes and uses account books arranged on substantially the same system, but the proof fails to show that he has violated the copyright of Selden's book, regarding the latter merely as an explanatory work, or that he has infringed Selden's right in any way, unless the latter became entitled to an exclusive right in the system.

The evidence of the complainant is principally directed to the object of showing that Baker uses the same system as that which is explained and illustrated in Selden's books. It becomes important, therefore, to determine whether, in obtaining the copyright of his books, he secured the exclusive right to the use of the system or method of bookkeeping which the said books are intended to illustrate and explain. It is contended that he has secured such exclusive right because no one can use the system without using substantially the same ruled lines and headings which he was appended to his books in illustration of it. In other words, it is contended that the ruled lines and headings, given to illustrate the system, are a part of the book, and as such are secured by the copyright, and that no one can make or use similar ruled lines and headings, or ruled lines and headings made and arranged on substantially the same system, without violating the copyright. And this is really the question to be decided in this case. Stated in another form, the question is whether the exclusive property in a system of bookkeeping can be claimed under the law or copyright by means of a book in which that system is explained? The complainant's bill, and the case made under it, are based on the hypothesis that it can be.

...

There is no doubt that a work on the subject of bookkeeping, though only explanatory of well known systems, may be the subject of a copyright, but then it is claimed only as a book. Such a book may be explanatory either of old systems or of an entirely new system, and, considered as a book, as the work of an author, conveying information on the subject of bookkeeping, and containing detailed explanations of the art, it may be a very valuable acquisition to the practical knowledge of the community. But there is a clear distinction between the book as such and the art which it is intended to illustrate. The mere statement of the proposition is so evident that it requires hardly any argument to support it. The same distinction may be predicated of every other art as well as that of bookkeeping. A treatise on the composition and use of medicines, be they old or new; on the construction and use of ploughs, or watches, or churns; or on the mixture and application of colors for painting or dyeing; or on the mode of drawing lines to produce the effect of perspective -- would be the subject of copyright; but no one would contend that the copyright of the treatise would give the exclusive right to the art or manufacture described therein. The copyright of the book, if not pirated from other works, would be valid without regard to the novelty, or want of novelty, of its subject matter. The novelty of the art or thing described or explained has nothing to do with the validity of the copyright. To give to the author of the book an exclusive property in the art described therein when no examination of its novelty has ever been officially made would be a surprise and a fraud upon the public. That is the province of letters patent, not of copyright. The claim to an invention or discovery of an art or manufacture must be subjected to the examination of the Patent Office before an exclusive right therein can be obtained, and it can only be secured by a patent from the government.

The difference between the two things, letters patent and copyright, may be illustrated by reference to the subjects just enumerated. Take the case of medicines. Certain mixtures are found to be of great value in the healing art. If the discoverer writes and publishes a book on the subject (as regular physicians generally do), he gains no exclusive right to the manufacture and sale of the medicine; he gives that to the public. If he desires to acquire such exclusive right, he must obtain a patent for the mixture as a new art, manufacture, or composition of matter. He may copyright his book if he pleases, but that only secures to him the exclusive right of printing and publishing his book. So of all other inventions or discoveries.

The copyright of a book on perspective, no matter how many drawings and illustrations it may contain, gives no exclusive right to the modes of drawing described, though they may never have been known or used before. By publishing the book without getting a patent for the art, the latter is given to the public. The fact that the art described in the book by illustrations of lines and figures which are reproduced in practice in the application of the art makes no difference. Those illustrations are the mere language employed by the author to convey his ideas more clearly. Had he used words of description instead of diagrams (which merely stand in the place of words), there could not be the slightest doubt that others, applying the art to practical use, might lawfully draw the lines and diagrams which were in the author's mind, and which he thus described by words in his book.

The copyright of a work on mathematical science cannot give to the author an exclusive right to the methods of operation which he propounds, or to the diagrams which he employs to explain them, so as to prevent an engineer from using them whenever occasion requires. The very object of publishing a book on science or the useful arts is to communicate to the world the useful knowledge which it contains. But this object would be frustrated if the knowledge could not be used without incurring the guilt of piracy of the book. And where the art it teaches cannot be used without employing the methods and diagrams used to illustrate the book, or such as are similar to them, such methods and diagrams are to be considered as necessary incidents to the art, and given therewith to the public -- not given for the purpose of publication in other works explanatory of the art, but for the purpose of practical application.

Of course these observations are not intended to apply to ornamental designs or pictorial illustrations addressed to the taste. Of these it may be said that their form is their essence, and their object, the production of pleasure in their contemplation. This is their final end. They are as much the product of genius and the result of composition as are the lines of the poet or the historian's period. On the other hand, the teachings of science and the rules and methods of useful art have their final end in application and use, and this application and use are what the public derive from the publication of a book which teaches them. But as embodied and taught in a literary composition or book, their essence consists only in their statement. This alone is what is secured by the copyright. The use by another of the same methods of statement, whether in words or illustrations, in a book published for teaching the art would undoubtedly be an infringement of the copyright.

Recurring to the case before us, we observe that Charles Selden, by his books, explained and described a peculiar system of bookkeeping, and illustrated his method by means of ruled lines and blank columns, with proper headings on a page or on successive pages. Now whilst no one has a right to print or publish his book, or any material part thereof, as a book intended to convey instruction in the art, any person may practice and use the art itself which he has described and illustrated therein. The use of the art is a totally different thing from a publication of the book explaining it. The copyright of a book on bookkeeping cannot secure the exclusive right to make, sell, and use account books prepared upon the plan set forth in such book. Whether the art might or might not have been patented is a question which is not before us. It was not patented, and is open and free to the use of the public. And of course, in using the art, t bhe ruled lines and headings of accounts must necessarily be used as incident to it.

The plausibility of the claim put forward by the complainant in this case arises from a confusion of ideas produced by the peculiar nature of the art described in the books which have been made the subject of copyright. In describing the art, the illustrations and diagrams employed happen to correspond more closely than usual with the actual work performed by the operator who uses the art. Those illustrations and diagrams consist of ruled lines and headings of accounts, and it is similar ruled lines and headings of accounts which, in the application of the art, the bookkeeper makes with his pen, or the stationer with his press, whilst in most other cases the diagrams and illustrations can only be represented in concrete forms of wood, metal, stone, or some other physical embodiment. But the principle is the same in all. The description of the art in a book, though entitled to the benefit of copyright, lays no foundation for an exclusive claim to the art itself. The object of the one is explanation; the object of the other is use. The former may be secured by copyright. The latter can only be secured, if it can be secured at all, by letters patent.

...

The conclusion to which we have come is that blank account books are not the subject of copyright, and that the mere copyright of Selden's book did not confer upon him the exclusive right to make and use account books, ruled and arranged as designated by him and described and illustrated in said book.

The decree of the circuit court must be reversed and the cause remanded with instructions to dismiss the complainant's bill, and it is

So ordered.

618 F.2d 972 (1980)

HOEHLING v. UNIVERSAL CITY STUDIOS

United States Court of Appeals, Second Circuit

IRVING R. KAUFMAN, Chief Judge:

A grant of copyright in a published work secures for its author a limited monopoly over the expression it contains. The copyright provides a financial incentive to those who would add to the corpus of existing knowledge by creating original works. Nevertheless, the protection afforded the copyright holder has never extended to history, be it documented fact or explanatory hypothesis. The rationale for this doctrine is that the cause of knowledge is best served when history is the common property of all, and each generation remains free to draw upon the discoveries and insights of the past. Accordingly, the scope of copyright in historical accounts is narrow indeed, embracing no more than the author's original expression of particular facts and theories already in the public domain. As the case before us illustrates, absent wholesale usurpation of another's expression, claims of copyright infringement where works of history are at issue are rarely successful.

I.

This litigation arises from three separate accounts of the triumphant introduction, last voyage, and tragic destruction of the Hindenburg, the colossal dirigible constructed in Germany during Hitler's reign. The zeppelin, the last and most sophisticated in a fleet of luxury airships, which punctually floated its wealthy passengers from the Third Reich to the United States, exploded into flames and disintegrated in 35 seconds as it hovered above the Lakehurst, New Jersey Naval Air Station at 7:25 p. m. on May 6, 1937. Thirty-six passengers and [618 F.2d 975] crew were killed but, fortunately, 52 persons survived. Official investigations conducted by both American and German authorities could ascertain no definitive cause of the disaster, but both suggested the plausibility of static electricity or St. Elmo's Fire, which could have ignited the highly explosive hydrogen that filled the airship. Throughout, the investigators refused to rule out the possibility of sabotage.

The destruction of the Hindenburg marked the concluding chapter in the chronicle of airship passenger service, for after the tragedy at Lakehurst, the Nazi regime permanently grounded the Graf Zeppelin I and discontinued its plan to construct an even larger dirigible, the Graf Zeppelin II.

The final pages of the airship's story marked the beginning of a series of journalistic, historical, and literary accounts devoted to the Hindenburg and its fate. Indeed, weeks of testimony by a plethora of witnesses before the official investigative panels provided fertile source material for would-be authors. Moreover, both the American and German Commissions issued official reports, detailing all that was then known of the tragedy. A number of newspaper and magazine articles had been written about the Hindenburg in 1936, its first year of trans-Atlantic service, and they, of course, multiplied many fold after the crash. In addition, two passengers Margaret Mather and Gertrud Adelt published separate and detailed accounts of the voyage, C. E. Rosendahl, commander of the Lakehurst Naval Air Station and a pioneer in airship travel himself, wrote a book titled What About the Airship?, in which he endorsed the theory that the Hindenburg was the victim of sabotage. In 1957, Nelson Gidding, who would return to the subject of the Hindenburg some 20 years later, wrote an unpublished "treatment" for a motion picture based on the deliberate destruction of the airship. In that year as well, John Toland published Ships in the Sky which, in its seventeenth chapter, chronicled the last flight of the Hindenburg. In 1962, Dale Titler released Wings of Mystery, in which he too devoted a chapter to the Hindenburg.

Appellant A. A. Hoehling published Who Destroyed the Hindenburg?, a full-length book based on his exhaustive research in 1962. Mr. Hoehling studied the investigative reports, consulted previously published articles and books, and conducted interviews with survivors of the crash as well as others who possessed information about the Hindenburg. His book is presented as a factual account, written in an objective, reportorial style.

The first half recounts the final crossing of the Hindenburg, from Sunday, May 2, when it left Frankfurt, to Thursday, May 6, when it exploded at Lakehurst. Hoehling describes the airship, its role as an instrument of propaganda in Nazi Germany, its passengers and crew, the danger of hydrogen, and the ominous threats received by German officials, warning that the Hindenburg would be destroyed. The second portion, headed The Quest, sets forth the progress of the official investigations, followed by an account of Hoehling's own research. In the final chapter, spanning eleven pages, Hoehling suggests that all proffered explanations of the explosion, save deliberate destruction, are unconvincing. He concludes that the most likely saboteur is one Eric Spehl, a "rigger" on the Hindenburg crew who was killed at Lakehurst.

According to Hoehling, Spehl had motive, expertise, and opportunity to plant an explosive device, constructed of dry-cell batteries and a flashbulb, in "Gas Cell 4," the location of the initial explosion. An amateur photographer with access to flashbulbs, Spehl could have destroyed the Hindenburg to please his ladyfriend, a suspected communist dedicated to exploding the myth of Nazi invincibility.

Ten years later appellee Michael MacDonald Mooney published his book, The Hindenburg. [618 F.2d 976] Mooney's endeavor might be characterized as more literary than historical in its attempt to weave a number of symbolic themes through the actual events surrounding the tragedy. His dominant theme contrasts the natural beauty of the month of May, when the disaster occurred, with the cold, deliberate progress of "technology." The May theme is expressed not simply by the season, but also by the character of Spehl, portrayed as a sensitive artisan with needle and thread. The Hindenburg, in contrast, is the symbol of technology, as are its German creators and the Reich itself. The destruction is depicted as the ultimate triumph of nature over technology, as Spehl plants the bomb that ignites the hydrogen. Developing this theme from the outset, Mooney begins with an extended review of man's efforts to defy nature through flight, focusing on the evolution of the zeppelin. This story culminates in the construction of the Hindenburg, and the Nazis' claims of its indestructibility. Mooney then traces the fateful voyage, advising the reader almost immediately of Spehl's scheme. The book concludes with the airship's explosion.

Mooney acknowledges, in this case, that he consulted Hoehling's book, and that he relied on it for some details. He asserts that he first discovered the "Spehl-as-saboteur" theory when he read Titler's Wings of Mystery. Indeed, Titler concludes that Spehl was the saboteur, for essentially the reasons stated by Hoehling. Mooney also claims to have studied the complete National Archives and New York Times files concerning the Hindenburg, as well as all previously published material. Moreover, he traveled to Germany, visited Spehl's birthplace, and conducted a number of interviews with survivors.

After Mooney prepared an outline of his anticipated book, his publisher succeeded in negotiations to sell the motion picture rights to appellee Universal City Studios. Universal then commissioned a screen story by writers Levinson and Link, best known for their television series, Columbo, in which a somewhat disheveled, but wise detective unravels artfully conceived murder mysteries. In their screen story, Levinson and Link created a Columbo-like character who endeavored to identify the saboteur on board the Hindenburg. Director Robert Wise, however, was not satisfied with this version, and called upon Nelson Gidding to write a final screenplay. Gidding, it will be recalled, had engaged in preliminary work on a film about the Hindenburg almost twenty years earlier.

The Gidding screenplay follows what is known in the motion picture industry as a "Grand Hotel" formula, developing a number of fictional characters and subplots involving them. This formula has become standard fare in so-called "disaster" movies, which have enjoyed a certain popularity in recent years. In the film, which was released in late 1975, a rigger named "Boerth," who has an anti-Nazi ladyfriend, plans to destroy the airship in an effort to embarrass the Reich. Nazi officials, vaguely aware of sabotage threats, station a Luftwaffe intelligence officer on the zeppelin, loosely resembling a Colonel Erdmann who was aboard the Hindenburg. This character is portrayed as a likable fellow who soon discovers that Boerth is the saboteur. Boerth, however, convinces him that the Hindenburg should be destroyed and the two join forces, planning the explosion for several hours after the landing at Lakehurst, when no people would be on board. In Gidding's version, the airship is delayed by a storm, frantic efforts to defuse the bomb fail, and the Hindenburg is destroyed. The film's subplots involve other possible suspects, including a fictional countess who has had her estate expropriated by the Reich, two fictional confidence men wanted [618 F.2d 977] by New York City police, and an advertising executive rushing to close a business deal in America.

Upon learning of Universal's plans to release the film, Hoehling instituted this action against Universal for copyright infringement and common law unfair competition in the district court for the District of Columbia in October 1975. Judge Smith declined to issue an order restraining release of the film in December, and it was distributed throughout the nation.

In January 1976, Hoehling sought to amend his complaint to include Mooney as a defendant. The district court, however, decided that it lacked personal jurisdiction over Mooney. In June 1976, Hoehling again attempted to amend his complaint, this time to add Mooney's publishers as defendants. Judge Smith denied this motion as well, but granted Hoehling's request to transfer the litigation to the Southern District of New York, 28 U.S.C. § 1404(a), where Mooney himself was successfully included as a party. Judge Metzner, with the assistance of Magistrate Sinclair, supervised extensive discovery through most of 1978. After the completion of discovery, both Mooney and Universal moved for summary judgment, Fed.R.Civ.P. 56, which was granted on August 1, 1979.

II.

It is undisputed that Hoehling has a valid copyright in his book. To prove infringement, however, he must demonstrate that defendants "copied" his work and that they "improperly appropriated" his "expression." See Arnstein v. Porter, 154 F.2d 464, 468 (2d Cir. 1946). Ordinarily, wrongful appropriation is shown by proving a "substantial similarity" of copyrightable expression. See Nichols v. Universal Pictures Corp., 45 F.2d 119, 121 (2d Cir. 1930), cert. denied, 282 U.S. 902, 51 S.Ct. 216, 75 L.Ed. 795 (1931). Because substantial similarity is customarily an extremely close question of fact, see Arnstein, supra, 154 F.2d at 468, summary judgment has traditionally been frowned upon in copyright litigation, id. at 474. Nevertheless, while Arnstein 's influence in other areas of the law has been diminished, see SEC v. Research Automation Corp., 585 F.2d 31 (2d Cir. 1978); 6 Moore's Federal Practice P 56.17(14) (2d ed. 1976), a series of copyright cases in the Southern District of New York have granted defendants summary judgment when all alleged similarity related to non -copyrightable elements of the plaintiff's work, see, e. g., Alexander v. Haley, 460 F.Supp. 40 (S.D.N.Y.1978); Musto v. Meyer, 434 F.Supp. 32 (S.D.N.Y.1977); Gardner v. Nizer, 391 F.Supp. 940 (S.D.N.Y.1975); Fuld v. National Broadcasting Co., 390 F.Supp. 877

(S.D.N.Y.1975). These cases signal an important development in the law of copyright, permitting courts to put "a swift end to meritless litigation" and to avoid lengthy and costly trials. Quinn v. Syracuse Model Neighborhood Corp., 613 F.2d 438, 445 (2d Cir. 1980); accord, Donnelly v. Guion, 467 F.2d 290, 293 (2d Cir. 1972); American Manufacturers Mutual Insurance Co. v. American Broadcasting-Paramount Theatres, Inc., 388 F.2d 272, 278 (2d Cir. 1967). Drawing on these cases, Judge Metzner assumed both copying and substantial similarity, but concluded that all similarities pertained to various categories of non-copyrightable material. Accordingly, he granted appellees' motion for summary judgment. We affirm the judgment of the district court.

A

Hoehling's principal claim is that both Mooney and Universal copied the essential plot of his book i. e., Eric Spehl, influenced by his girlfriend, sabotaged the Hindenburg by placing a crude bomb in Gas Cell 4. In their briefs, and at oral argument, appellees have labored to convince us that their plots are not substantially similar to Hoehling's. While Hoehling's Spehl destroys the airship to please his communist girlfriend, Mooney's character is motivated by an aversion to the technological age. Universal's [618 F.2d 978] Boerth, on the other hand, is a fervent anti-fascist who enlists the support of a Luftwaffe colonel who, in turn, unsuccessfully attempts to defuse the bomb at the eleventh hour.

Although this argument has potential merit when presented to a fact finder adjudicating the issue of substantial similarity, it is largely irrelevant to a motion for summary judgment where the issue of substantial similarity has been eliminated by the judge's affirmative assumption. Under Rule 56(c), summary judgment is appropriate only when "there is no genuine issue as to any material fact." Accord, Heyman v. Commerce & Industry Insurance Co., 524 F.2d 1317 (2d Cir. 1975). Perhaps recognizing this, appellees further argue that Hoehling's plot is an "idea," and ideas are not copyrightable as a matter of law. See Sheldon v. Metro-Goldwyn Pictures Corp., 81 F.2d 49, 54 (2d Cir.), cert. denied, 298 U.S. 669, 56 S.Ct. 835, 80 L.Ed. 1392 (1936).

Hoehling, however, correctly rejoins that while ideas themselves are not subject to copyright, his "expression" of his idea is copyrightable. Id. at 54. He relies on Learned Hand's opinion in Sheldon, supra, at 50, holding that Letty Lynton infringed Dishonored Lady by copying its story of a woman who poisons her lover, and Augustus Hand's analysis in Detective Comics, Inc. v. Bruns Publications, Inc., 111 F.2d 432 (2d Cir. 1940), concluding that the exploits of "Wonderman" infringed the copyright held by the creators of "Superman," the original indestructible man. Moreover, Hoehling asserts that, in both these cases, the line between "ideas" and "expression" is drawn, in the first instance, by the fact finder.

Sheldon and Detective Comics, however, dealt with works of fiction, where the distinction between an idea and its expression is especially elusive. But, where, as here, the idea at issue is an interpretation of an historical event, our cases hold that such interpretations are not copyrightable as a matter of law. In Rosemont Enterprises, Inc. v. Random House, Inc., 366 F.2d 303 (2d Cir. 1966), cert. denied, 385 U.S. 1009, 87 S.Ct. 714, 17 L.Ed.2d 546 (1967), we held that the defendant's biography of Howard Hughes did not infringe an earlier biography of the reclusive alleged billionaire. Although the plots of the two works were necessarily similar, there could be no infringement because of the "public benefit in encouraging the development of historical and biographical works and their public distribution." Id. at 307; accord, Oxford Book Co. v. College Entrance Book Co., 98 F.2d 688 (2d Cir. 1938). To avoid a chilling effect on authors who contemplate tackling an historical issue or event, broad latitude must be granted to subsequent authors who make use of historical subject matter, including theories or plots. Learned Hand counseled in Myers v. Mail & Express Co., 36 C.O.Bull. 478, 479 (S.D.N.Y.1919), "(t)here cannot be any such thing as copyright in the order of presentation of the facts, nor, indeed, in their selection."

In the instant case, the hypothesis that Eric Spehl destroyed the Hindenburg is based entirely on the interpretation of historical facts, including Spehl's life, his girlfriend's anti-Nazi connections, the explosion's origin in Gas Cell 4, Spehl's duty station, discovery of a dry-cell battery [618 F.2d 979] among the wreckage, and rumors about Spehl's involvement dating from a 1938 Gestapo investigation. Such an historical interpretation, whether or not it originated with Mr. Hoehling, is not protected by his copyright and can be freely used by subsequent authors.

B

The same reasoning governs Hoehling's claim that a number of specific facts, ascertained through his personal research, were copied by appellees. The cases in this circuit, however, make clear that factual information is in the public domain. See, e. g., Rosemont Enterprises, Inc., supra, 366 F.2d at 309; Oxford Book Co., supra, 98 F.2d at 691. Each appellee had the right to "avail himself of the facts contained" in Hoehling's book and to "use such information, whether correct or incorrect, in his own literary work." Greenbie v. Noble, 151 F.Supp. 45, 67 (S.D.N.Y.1957). Accordingly, there is little consolation in relying on cases in other circuits holding that the fruits of original research are copyrightable. See, e. g., Toksvig v. Bruce Publications Corp., 181 F.2d 664, 667 (7th Cir. 1950); Miller v. Universal City Studios, Inc., 460 F.Supp. 984 (S.D.Fla.1978). Indeed, this circuit has clearly repudiated Toksvig and its progeny. In Rosemont Enterprises, Inc., supra, 366 F.2d at 310, we refused to "subscribe to the view that an author is absolutely precluded from saving time and effort by referring to and relying upon prior published material. . . . It is just such wasted effort that the proscription against the copyright of ideas and facts . . . . are designed to prevent." Accord, 1 Nimmer on Copyright § 2.11 (1979).

C

The remainder of Hoehling's claimed similarities relate to random duplications of phrases and sequences of events. For example, all three works contain a scene in a German beer hall, in which the airship's crew engages in revelry prior to the voyage. Other claimed similarities concern common German greetings of the period, such as "Heil Hitler," or songs, such as the German National anthem. These elements, however, are merely scenes a faire, that is, "incidents, characters or settings which are as a practical matter indispensable, or at least standard, in the treatment of a given topic." Alexander, supra, 460 F.Supp. at 45; accord, Bevan v.

Columbia Broadcasting System, Inc., 329 F.Supp. 601, 607 (S.D.N.Y.1971). Because it is virtually impossible to write about a particular historical era or fictional theme without employing certain "stock" or standard literary devices, we have held that scenes a faire are not copyrightable as a matter of law. See Reyher v. Children's Television Workshop, 533 F.2d 87, 91 (2d Cir.), cert. denied, 429 U.S. 980, 97 S.Ct. 492, 50 L.Ed.2d 588 (1976).

D

All of Hoehling's allegations of copying, therefore, encompass material that is non-copyrightable as a matter of law, rendering summary judgment entirely appropriate. We are aware, however, that in distinguishing between themes, facts, and scenes a faire on the one hand, and copyrightable expression on the other, courts may lose sight of the forest for the trees. By factoring out similarities based on non-copyrightable elements, a court runs the risk of overlooking wholesale usurpation of a prior author's expression. A verbatim reproduction of another work, of course, even in the realm of nonfiction, is actionable as copyright infringement. See Wainwright Securities, Inc. v. Wall Street Transcript Corp., 558 F.2d 91 (2d Cir. 1977), cert. denied, 434 U.S. 1014, 98 S.Ct. 730 (1978). Thus, in granting or reviewing a grant of summary judgment for defendants, courts should assure themselves that the works before them are not virtually identical. In this case, it is clear that all three authors relate the story of the Hindenburg differently.

In works devoted to historical subjects, it is our view that a second author may make significant use of prior work, so long as he does not bodily appropriate the expression of another. Rosemont Enterprises, Inc., supra, 366 F.2d at 310. This principle is justified by the fundamental policy undergirding the copyright laws the encouragement of contributions to recorded knowledge. The "financial reward guaranteed to the copyright holder is but an incident of this general objective, rather than an end in itself." Berlin v. E. C. Publications, Inc., 329 F.2d 541, 543-44 (2d Cir.), cert. denied, 379 U.S. 822, 85 S.Ct. 46, 13 L.Ed.2d 33 (1964). Knowledge is expanded as well by granting new authors of historical works a relatively free hand to build upon the work of their predecessors.[7]

III

Finally, we affirm Judge Metzner's rejection of Hoehling's claims based on the common law of "unfair competition." Where, as here, historical facts, themes, and research have been deliberately exempted from the scope of copyright protection to vindicate the overriding goal of encouraging contributions to recorded knowledge, the states are pre-empted from removing such material from the public domain. See, e. g., Sears, Roebuck & Co. v. Stiffel Co., 376 U.S. 225, 83 S.Ct. 1868, 10 L.Ed.2d 1050 (1964); Compco Corp. v. Day-Brite Lighting, Inc., 376 U.S. 234, 84 S.Ct. 779, 11 L.Ed.2d 669 (1964). "To forbid copying" in this case, "would interfere with the federal policy . . . of allowing free access to copy whatever the federal patent and copyright laws leave in the public domain." Id. at 237, 84 S.Ct. at 782.

The judgment of the district court is affirmed.

694 F. Supp. 2d 1071 (2010)

BISSOON v. SONY COMPUTER ENTERTAINMENT AMERICA

United States District Court, N.D. California

MARILYN HALL PATEL, District Judge.

In this action, Jonathan Bissoon-Dath ("Bissoon-Dath") and Jennifer B. Dath ("Dath") (collectively "plaintiffs") allege that Sony Computer Entertainment America, Inc. ("Sony") and its former employee David Jaffe (collectively "defendants") misappropriated plaintiffs' original copyrighted works to develop the popular God of War video game. Defendants now move for summary judgment. Having considered the parties' arguments and extensive submissions, the court enters the following memorandum and order.

BACKGROUND

I. Parties

Plaintiffs Bissoon-Dath and Dath are individuals living in Davis, California. At some or all times relevant to this action, Dath acted as an agent for Bissoon-Dath. Defendant Sony is a corporation headquartered in Foster City, California, which distributes PlayStation 2 and PlayStation Portable ("PSP") video game consoles and related games. Defendant Jaffe was at all times relevant to this action an employee of Sony. He was the lead designer of the God of War video game, which Sony commercially launched in March 2005. Docket No. 35 (Jaffe Dec.) ¶¶ 3-4; Docket No. 33 (Becker Dec.) ¶ 5.

II. Plaintiffs' Works

Plaintiffs allege defendants infringed their copyrights to one or more of five specific works. These include two treatments, "Theseus: A Screenplay Treatment" ("Theseus") and "The Adventures of Owen" ("Owen"), and two screenplays, "Olympiad Version A" ("Olympiad A") and "Olympiad" ("Olympiad"). Bissoon-Dath Dec. ¶ 10. "Owen" included an original illustrated map of the "Island at the Edge of the Living World" ("the map"), which was created by Dath with input from Bissoon-Dath in February or March 2002. Id. ¶ 21; Docket No. 85 (Dath Dec.) ¶ 21. The five works, including the map, are collectively referred to herein as "plaintiffs' works." Plaintiffs began distributing the works in January or February 2002. Bissoon-Dath Dec. ¶¶ 20-22 & 24.

With certain variations, each of plaintiffs' works tells a similar story. The works open with a Spartan attack on Athens led by the Spartan co-king and/or general Gaylon and the Spartan colonel Balzak. Docket No. 44 (Oliver Moving Dec.), *1076 Exh. D ("Owen") at 6; id., Exh. E ("Theseus") at 5; id., Exh. F ("Olympiad") at 4; id., Exh. G ("Olympiad A") at 5. It is later revealed that the Spartan kings are loyal to the god Ares. See Olympiad at 50 (The Spartan solders "must only obey one cause. . . the honor and glory of following their kings in the service of Ares."); id. at 86 (The Spartan kings "get the soldiers to do whatever they want by brainwashing them into believing that the war god, Ares, is the one true god."); see also Olympiad A at 52; Owen at 7; Theseus at 23. As the temporarily beaten Spartan army retreats from Athens, the gods gather and discuss the situation, with Zeus and Athena expressing distaste for the state of war in Greece. Olympiad at 12-13; Olympiad A at 13; Owen at 7; Theseus at 9. In order to restore peace, Zeus decides to order all Greece to declare a truce and participate in an Olympiad. Olympiad at 13; Olympiad A at 14; Owen at 7; Theseus at 9. When Ares and Apollo (and Hermes, in three of the works) object to the plan, the gods agree that Zeus will instead choose a mortal whose quest will be to convince Athens and Sparta to declare a truce. Olympiad at 14-15, 19; Olympiad A at 14-17; Owen at 7; Theseus at 9.

The champion is informed of the quest by a magical nymph before being sent to Athens and then sent forth by the Athenian Council to perform a series of tasks culminating in the truce and the Olympic Games. Olympiad at 19, 35; Olympiad A at 20-21, 37; Owen at 8, 9; Theseus at 10, 13. During his quest, the champion must capture the Nemean Lion, rescue a hostage from the Amazons, rescue a hostage held by Hades in the underworld (in "Owen" and "Theseus" only) and convince Sparta to participate in the truce. Olympiad at 36, 44, 50; Olympiad A at 38, 46, 52; Owen at 10, 12; Theseus at 13, 16, 19. A truce is eventually declared and the Olympic Games are held in Sparta. Olympiad at 57; Olympiad A at 59; Owen at 13; Theseus at 21. While the games are in progress, Sparta secretly attacks Athens. Olympiad at 81; Olympiad A at 83; Owen at 16; Theseus at 19-20. In the end, the protagonist is crowned the Olympic champion, the Spartan co-kings (or General and Dictator, in "Owen" and "Theseus") are removed from power, and the sneak attack on Athens is thwarted. Olympiad at 102, 104; Olympiad A at 104, 106; Owen at 19; Theseus at 41-43. In "Owen," Zeus orders the Spartans to adopt democracy and lift the siege of Athens. Owen at 19. In "Theseus," the Spartan royal guard champion, tired of the sacrifice of justice and freedom in service to Ares, first seizes the Spartan Dictator and then convinces the Spartan army to withdraw from Athens. Theseus at 42-43. In "Olympiad" and "Olympiad A," the stadium crowd overwhelms the Spartans and "an army of the united people of Greece" liberates Athens. Olympiad at 104; Olympiad A at 106. Peace and democracy then reign over Greece. See Olympiad at 104 ("Sparta, never again, threatened [sic] the rest of Greece, which enjoyed the longest period of peace and prosperity in its history, as city after city adopted the Athenian political system called . . . democracy.") (ellipsis in original); see also Olympiad A at 106; Owen at 20; Theseus at 43.

III. Defendants' God of War Video Game

God of War is a multi-hour video game. JSUF at 3. Sony released God of War in March 2005. Id. The game is rated "M" for a "MATURE 17+ " audience. Id. at 5.

In the game, also set in ancient Greece, the warrior Kratos fights myriad human and mythical opponents and ultimately replaces Ares as the god of war. Oliver Moving Dec., Exh. W (Merged Script) at 45. In a series of flashbacks, the player learns that Kratos was once a captain in the Spartan military but rose to command an entire army. Id. at 15. With his army almost annihilated and a barbarian king about to kill him, Kratos offered his life to Ares in exchange for the destruction of his enemies. Id. at 22-23. Thereafter, Kratos led armies in conquest, serving Ares as "a beast, his humanity robbed," until Ares tricked Kratos into killing and burning his own wife and child. Id. at 29, 31. Kratos then rejected Ares and began serving other gods, hoping they would relieve his nightmares of his family's murder. Id. at 4. The action of God of War game-play begins with Kratos awakening from a nightmare and imploring a statue of Athena to relieve his nightmares. Id. Speaking through the statue, Athena offers divine forgiveness to Kratos if he kills Ares. Id. The game manual includes a gathering-of-the-gods scene that explains Athena's request: Zeus, Athena and Ares are gathered to discuss Kratos, and Athena complains that Ares is preparing forces to attack Athens. Jaffe Dec., Exh. E (Game Manual) at 3. This scene does not appear in the game itself.

Having accepted Athena's offer, Kratos travels to Athens and finds that Ares is attacking the city with an army of mythical beasts including Minotaurs and Zombies. Id. at 6-7. The Oracle in Athens tells Kratos he must find Pandora's Box, the only weapon capable of killing Ares. Id. at 16. At the edge of the Desert of Lost Souls, a statue of Athena informs Kratos that he must cross the desert, following and then killing four Sirens to do so, and find a Titan crawling around the desert with the Temple of Pandora chained to his back. Id. at 17-18. Liberally extinguishing his adversaries with his "Blades of Chaos," Kratos quests to find Pandora's Box. He locates it and is dragging it out of the temple when Ares, still attacking Athens but aware of Kratos' achievement, launches a column that impales Kratos. Id. at 32-33. Kratos dies and begins to fall to the underworld, but he scrambles onto the stairway leading into Hades and crawls back to life through a grave near Athens. Id. at 35-36. There he recovers Pandora's Box from Ares, opens the lid and becomes a giant, and defeats Ares in battle. Id. at 38, 42. Later, Kratos attempts suicide by jumping off a cliff into the sea because the gods, despite forgiving him for murdering his family, did not relieve his nightmares. Id. at 43-44. He is then lifted from the sea and directed up a flight of stairs to assume the now-vacant throne of the god of war, from whence he oversees various modern wars, including World War II and the Vietnam war. Id. at 44-45. Bonus scenes reveal that Kratos is actually the son of Zeus and a mortal woman who moved to Sparta when driven out of her village, that Kratos had a weaker brother who died when turned out by the Spartans, and that the ruins of Pandora's Temple were discovered in modern times. Id. at 48-49, 50.

IV. Procedural History

Plaintiffs initiated this action in February 2008. The parties stipulated to a number of continuances to pursue alternative dispute resolution. The parties did not reach a settlement, and defendants thereafter filed the instant motion for summary judgment.

LEGAL STANDARD

Summary judgment may be granted only when, drawing all inferences and resolving all doubts in favor of the non-moving party, there are no genuine issues *1078 of material fact and the moving party is entitled to judgment as a matter of law. Fed.R.Civ.P. 56(c); see generally Anderson v. Liberty Lobby, Inc., 477 U.S. 242, 247-255, 106 S. Ct. 2505, 91 L. Ed. 2d 202 (1986). A fact is "material" if it may affect the outcome of the proceedings, and an issue of material fact is "genuine" if the evidence is such that a reasonable jury could return a verdict for the non-moving party. Id. at 248, 106 S. Ct. 2505. The court may not make credibility determinations. Id. at 255, 106 S. Ct. 2505. The moving party bears the burden of identifying those portions of the pleadings, discovery and affidavits that demonstrate the absence of a genuine issue of material fact. Celotex Corp. v. Catrett, 477 U.S. 317, 323, 106 S. Ct. 2548, 91 L. Ed. 2d 265 (1986). Once the moving party meets its initial burden, the non-moving party must go beyond the pleadings and, by its own affidavits or discovery, set forth specific facts showing that there is a genuine issue for trial. Fed R. Civ. P. 56(e); see Anderson, 477 U.S. at 250, 106 S. Ct. 2505.

"Although summary judgment is not highly favored on questions of substantial similarity in copyright cases, summary judgment is appropriate if the court can conclude, after viewing the evidence and drawing inferences in a manner most favorable to the non-moving party, that no reasonable juror could find substantial similarity of ideas and expression." Shaw v. Lindheim, 919 F.2d 1353, 1355 (9th Cir.1990) (quoting Narell v. Freeman, 872 F.2d 907, 909-10 (9th Cir.1989)). "Where reasonable minds could differ on the issue of substantial similarity, however, summary judgment is improper." Id. (citations omitted). The Ninth Circuit "ha[s] frequently affirmed summary judgment in favor of copyright defendants on the issue of substantial similarity." Funky Films, Inc. v. Time Warner Entm't Co., L.P., 462 F.3d 1072, 1077 (9th Cir.2006) (citations omitted).

DISCUSSION

Plaintiffs have advanced claims for copyright infringement, contributory copyright infringement and unfair business practices in violation of section 17200 of the California Business and Professions Code. The allegations of copyright infringement form the basis for the latter two claims. Under the Copyright Act, as amended in 1976, "copyright protection subsists . . . in original works of authorship fixed in any tangible medium of expression . . . from which they can be perceived, reproduced, or otherwise communicated. . . ." 17 U.S.C. § 102(a). To prevail on a claim of copyright infringement, a plaintiff must show that (1) he or she owns a valid copyright in the work in question and (2) that the defendant copied protected elements of that work. Cavalier v. Random House, 297 F.3d 815, 822 (9th Cir.2002). Defendants do not dispute that plaintiffs' works are original works of authorship for purposes of the Copyright Act or that plaintiffs own a valid copyright in those works.

A plaintiff may establish copying either (1) by presenting direct evidence of copying or (2) by showing that the defendant had access to the work and that the works at issue are substantially similar. Id. Plaintiffs have not presented direct evidence of copying and so seek to establish copying with a showing of access and substantial similarity. Access may be established by showing that the defendant had a reasonable possibility to view the plaintiff's work. Three Boys Music Corp. v. Bolton, 212 F.3d 477, 482 (9th Cir.2000). Such a possibility can arise either where there has been wide dissemination of a plaintiff's work or where there is a particular chain of events linking the work to the defendant. Id. The evidence must rise beyond mere speculation or a bare possibility, but it may be proved circumstantially *1079 such as by showing a chain of events linking the plaintiff's work and the defendant's alleged access. Id. The Ninth Circuit applies an "inverse ratio rule," requiring a "lower standard of proof of substantial similarity when a high degree of access is shown." Rice v. Fox Broad. Co., 330 F.3d 1170, 1178 (9th Cir.2003). Absent evidence of access, a "striking similarity" between the works may give rise to a permissible inference of copying. Baxter v. MCA, Inc., 812 F.2d 421, 423 (9th Cir.1987) (citations omitted).

Substantial similarity is analyzed using a two-part test with "extrinsic" and "intrinsic" components. Apple Computer, Inc. v. Microsoft Corp., 35 F.3d 1435, 1442 (9th Cir.1994). "[T]he extrinsic test . . . objectively considers whether there are substantial similarities in both ideas and expression." Id. The extrinsic test requires a comparison of specific, concrete elements, focusing on "articulable similarities between the plot, themes, dialogue, mood, settings, pace, characters, and sequence of events." Funky Films, 462 F.3d at 1077 (quoting Kouf v. Walt Disney Pictures & Television, 16 F.3d 1042, 1045 (9th Cir.1994)). Analytic dissection of a work and expert testimony are appropriate to the extrinsic test. Smith v. Jackson, 84 F.3d 1213, 1218 (9th Cir.1996). The intrinsic prong "test[s] for similarity of expression from the standpoint of the ordinary reasonable observer, with no expert assistance." Funky Films, 462 F.3d at 1077. On summary judgment, only the extrinsic test is relevant: if the plaintiff satisfies the extrinsic test, the intrinsic test's subjective inquiry must be left to the jury and summary judgment must be denied. Smith v. Jackson, 84 F.3d at 1218; Kouf, 16 F.3d at 1045.

"Because only those elements of a work that are protectable and used without the author's permission can be compared when it comes to the ultimate question of illicit copying, [the court] use[s] analytic dissection to determine the scope of copyright protection before works are considered `as a whole.'" Apple Computer, 35 F.3d at 1443. Copyright law protects a writer's expression of ideas, but not the ideas themselves. Kouf, 16 F.3d at 1045. "General plot ideas are not protected by copyright law; they remain forever the common property of artistic mankind." Berkic v. Crichton, 761 F.2d 1289, 1293 (9th Cir.1985). Nor does copyright law protect "scenes a faire," scenes that flow naturally from unprotectable basic plot premises. Id.; See v. Durang, 711 F.2d 141, 143 (9th Cir.1983). "[P]rotectable expression includes the specific details of an author's rendering of ideas, or `the actual concrete elements that make up the total sequence of events and the relationships between the major characters.'" Metcalf v. Bochco, 294 F.3d 1069, 1074 (9th Cir.2002) (quoting Berkic, 761 F.2d at 1293). "However, the presence of so many generic similarities and the common patterns in which they arise [can help to] satisfy the extrinsic test. The particular sequence in which an author strings a significant number of unprotectable elements can itself be a protectable element." Id.

The parties have briefed both the issues of access and substantial similarity. The court concludes below that no reasonable juror could find substantial similarity of ideas and expression, even if access to all of plaintiffs' works were proven. Accordingly, the court does not reach the question of access.

...

II. Copyright Infringement: Substantial Similarity

Plaintiffs contend that God of War is substantially similar to their works. On a motion for summary judgment in a copyright infringement action, the "extrinsic test" is applied. This test examines "articulable similarities between the plot, themes, dialogue, mood, settings, pace, characters, and sequence of events."[6]Funky Films, 462 F.3d at 1077; Smith v. Jackson, 84 F.3d at 1218. Non-protectable elements are filtered out and disregarded.[7]Funky Films, 462 F.3d at 1077 (citing Cavalier, 297 F.3d at 822).

A. Plot

Plaintiffs' works and God of War both involve a mortal human questing at the behest of a Greek god. In plaintiffs' works, Zeus initiates a quest to restore peace after a human Spartan army attacks Athens, by convincing Athens and Sparta to participate in Olympic Games. See, e.g., Olympiad at 4-19. In God of War, the goddess Athena assigns a quest to kill the god Ares while Ares is attacking Athens with mythical beasts. Merged Script at 4-7. A scene in which the gods gather together for discussion is provided as a background for the assignment in both stories.[8] Early in "Olympiad," eleven gods are gathered around a pool of water on whose surface the Spartan army is seen after its attack on Athens, and Zeus expresses his displeasure at the state of war in the mortal world. Olympiad at 12-13. Zeus ultimately decides to order all of Greece to participate in the Olympic Games as a means to achieve peace, choosing the mortal Owen to convince Athens and Sparta to declare a truce for the games. Id. at 13, 19. In "Owen," this decision is made after the gods "argue back and forth" about Zeus's intervention in mortal affairs. Owen at 7. In "Theseus," Ares "threatens to start a war among the gods" unless *1082 Zeus agrees to the mortal champion scheme. Theseus at 9. In "Olympiad," Ares and Apollo morph into giant cobras and physically fight Athena and Zeus until Zeus agrees to choose a mortal champion. Olympiad at 14-15. In "Olympiad A," Ares, Apollo, and Hermes threaten to remove Zeus by force but Hestia intervenes and averts this outcome by suggesting the selection of a mortal champion. Olympiad A at 15-17. The God of War gathering-of-the-gods scene, which occurs only in the game manual and not the game itself, is quite different. Only Zeus, Athena and Ares are present to discuss the "mortal" Kratos, who appears alone in a pool of water[9] resembling a well; the gods discuss Kratos's strength and Ares's impending attack on Athens, but they make no mention of choosing mortals for any purpose. Game Manual at 3. There is no physical battle among any of the gods in the God of War scene nor any threat of overthrowing Zeus; the only argument is a brief "quibble" between Ares and Athena which pertains to Ares's impending attack on Athens, not the selection of any mortal champion. See id. Athena appears to Kratos only later and asks him to kill Ares in return for forgiveness. Merged Script at 4-5.

In both works, the protagonists must accomplish various tasks to achieve their goals: the participation of Athens and Sparta in the Olympic Games in plaintiffs' works, and the death of Ares in God of War. In "Olympiad," the Athenian Council, as a condition of the city's participation in the Games, requires that the protagonist capture the Nemean lion, retrieve a hostage from the Amazons, and convince Sparta to agree to a truce. Olympiad at 35, 44, 50. In God of War, the protagonist is not given specific tasks to perform; rather, he is told that Pandora's Box, hidden in the desert, is the only weapon capable of killing Ares. Merged Script at 16. While seeking this weapon, Kratos must cross the Desert of Lost Souls and navigate through Pandora's Temple. Merged Script at 16-18. All of plaintiffs' works end with the protagonist winning the Olympics, Athens saved from destruction by the Spartans, and all of Greece experiencing lasting peace and prosperity. Owen at 20; Theseus at 43; Olympiad A at 106; Olympiad at 104. In contrast, God of War ends with Athens destroyed and Kratos killing Ares, becoming the new god of war, and overseeing a series of modern wars. Merged Script at 45-46.

There is some similarity between the two stories. As have stories since time immemorial, both involve a questing hero acting in accord with a divine power or powers. See generally Joseph Campbell, The Hero With A Thousand Faces (2d ed. 1968). Yet the motivations, tasks and accomplishments of the respective questing heroes are quite different. Both stories involve antagonism between Athena, the goddess of wisdom, and Ares, the god of war, and between Athens and Sparta. The latter antagonism is surely not protectable, as the historical Athens and Sparta famously fought the Peloponnesian War. More generally, as plaintiffs note, popular culture iterations of classical Greek mythology such as Thor and Wonder Woman, as well as ancient stories such as Hesiod's Theogony, contain plot lines involving various combinations of wars and rivalries among the Greek gods. See Docket No. 47-1 (Martin Report) at 26-27. Once the unprotectable elements are filtered, the two stories' plots are similar only at a level of abstraction that is barely meaningful, if at all.

B. Themes

Plaintiffs contend that their works and God of War share the themes of "heroic savior, the dark side of religious fanaticism, of a seemingly impossible quest, the avoidance of conflict and the triumph over evil." Pl.'s Opp. at 21. In reality, the themes of plaintiffs' works are peace, democracy and the establishment of the same. All of the works begin with Zeus desiring peace in the mortal world, proceed with the protagonist striving to create conditions for peace while the Spartans scheme with Ares to perpetuate war, and end with peace and democracy spreading over Greece. Owen at 20 ("Coexisting peacefully as sister democracies, Sparta and Athens both flourished economically and socially as never before."); Theseus at 43 ("Coexisting peacefully as sister democracies Sparta and Athens both flourished as never before."); Olympiad at 104 ("Greece . . . enjoyed . . . peace and prosperity. . . as city after city adopted the Athenian political system called . . . democracy."); Olympiad A at 106 (same).

The primary themes in God of War are violence, the search for divine forgiveness and the continuation of war. Violence pervades the game, the ultimate goal of which is to kill Ares. See Merged Script at 2 ("An arrow slams into the Fisherman's head, shattering his skull."); id. at 3 ("Slaughtered like animals, the victims lay before him."); id. at 4 ("A rapid succession of violent images."); id. at 6 ("The axe lops off the second Redshirt's head."); id. at 18 ("Kratos . . . must destroy all four

Sirens."); id. at 22 ("A Spartan is decapitated."); id. at 24 ("Kratos pulls the lever, igniting the burners and setting the Redshirt on fire, who screams as his cage is lowered to the ground."); id. at 42 ("Kratos thrusts the sword upwards, ripping through Ares."). While violence is not absent from plaintiffs' works, it lacks the thematic centrality and intensity seen in God of War. For instance, plaintiffs' protagonist refuses to kill such an "amazing animal" as the rampaging Nemean Lion and instead transforms the beast into his "tamed pet." Olympiad at 44. Indeed, outside of the generic battle scenes in which the Spartan army attacks Athens, very few deaths occur in plaintiffs' works; instead, most fights end with the antagonists merely unconscious. See, e.g., Olympiad at 27-28 (Spartan soldiers knocked unconscious), 47 (Amazon knocked unconscious).

Kratos's motivation for accepting the quest to kill Ares is divine forgiveness for murdering his family. Merged Script at 4-5. To the extent that the motivations of plaintiffs' protagonist are revealed, they appear to be the desire to abide by Zeus's wishes and to prove himself capable. See Olympiad at 22; Olympiad A at 24; Theseus at 6; Owen at 9. Plaintiffs attempt to equate Kratos's desire to end the nightmares of his family's murder at his own hands with the self-doubt of plaintiffs' protagonist, engendered either by his failure at age eight to protect his family from bandits, see Theseus at 23-24, or by his parents' ridicule, see Owen at 16. This attempt is unpersuasive: the self-doubt of plaintiffs' protagonist has no discernable similarity to Kratos's suicidal anguish, wrenching guilt and murderous violence. This is in keeping with the fact that plaintiffs' works culminate in an era of peace and prosperity, while God of War ends with a new god of war overseeing wars throughout the ages. Merged Script at 45. Moreover, democracy plays absolutely no thematic role in God of War. Thematically, the two stories are quite different.

C. Dialogue

1. A Cruel, Brutish Spartan Commander

Plaintiffs attempt to illustrate similarities in dialogue by comparing Kratos, a former Spartan commander, with a Spartan commander found in plaintiffs' works, alleging that both demonstrate their cruelty by killing a "terrified" Spartan innocent who is "dragged" to his death, despite "protests" against the "barbarism" of the act. See Bissoon-Dath Dec., Exh. 4 (comparison charts) at 4-5. Yet only one word quoted by plaintiff (or rather a form of it)—"barbarian"—appears on the cited pages of the Merged Script. Compare id. with Merged Script at 24-25. Additionally, plaintiffs are not comparing dialogue but rather scene descriptions. Plaintiffs also note that the respective Spartan commanders both act "in the name of" or "in the service of" Ares at some point. Such phrases are ordinarily used to express loyalty to a divinity and are not, standing alone, protectable by copyright. Plaintiffs also compare the statement in "Olympiad A" that the Spartan commander's "thirst for war knew no bounds" with the statement that Kratos's "desire for conquest knew no bounds." This is misleading in that the quote from "Olympiad A" is referring to the "Spartans" generally, not a Spartan commander. See Olympiad A at 52. The phrase "knew no bounds" is also ordinary and clichéd.

2. Gathering of the Gods

Plaintiffs also endeavor to point out similarities in the stories' respective gathering-of-the-gods scenes. Indeed, plaintiffs' counsel represented at oral argument that these scenes "read verbatim." They do not. For example, plaintiffs assert that the dialogue in both scenes begins with Zeus expressing concern about the impending destruction of Athens. See Pl.'s Opp. at 20. In fact, Zeus expresses no concern about Athens in any of the works at issue. In God of War, Zeus says he has gathered the gods to discuss a "mortal whose actions I sense could have grave implications to all of us here on Mount Olympus." Game Manual at 3. As discussed below in the analysis of the characters, Zeus expresses absolutely no concern for Athens in this scene. In "Olympiad" and "Olympiad A," Zeus is concerned about the "sorry state" of Greece, the "whole of Greece" and "peace in the mortal world," not Athens specifically. See Olympiad at 13; Olympiad A at 13-14.[10]

Plaintiffs also assert that statements made by Zeus to Athena and Ares are similar in the two stories. In "Olympiad" and "Olympiad A," Zeus says, "Stop it . . . right now . . . the two of you. There has been more than enough argument between mortals . . . and among us Gods." Olympiad at 13, Olympiad A at 14. In the God of War game manual, Zeus says, "Enough, both of you. Your childish quibbles are your own, but I do not want this war encroaching on the steps of Mount Olympus." Game Manual at 3. While the first sentences of these statements are somewhat similar, the language is ordinary, clichéd and has likely been spoken by every mother of multiple children. The second sentences are not substantially similar. The first speaks to the unfortunate prevalence of contentious natures among both mortals and gods. The latter speaks to the potential spread of a particular war against Athens.

Plaintiffs also point to dialogue in "Olympiad A" in which the goddess Hestia asks, "You would risk war on Olympus . . . from which many among us will surely meet a terrible end?" Olympiad A at 16. Plaintiffs assert that God of War includes a similar statement by Athena, namely "Civil war on Olympus would mean an end to us all." In fact, this statement is nowhere to be found in God of War. The statement appears in the story boards for *1085 "Dark Odyssey," an early prototype for God of War, but it was not included in the final work. Docket No. 93 (Jacobs Opp. Dec.), Exh. 16 ("Dark Odyssey" story boards) at 10. The fact that a strikingly similar excerpt of dialogue was used in an earlier version of an allegedly infringing work, but not the work itself, could be probative of a defendant's assertion that he did not have access to the plaintiff's work. In this case, the words of the dialogue are dissimilar, and the notion of a war on earth leading to a war among the gods has been clichéd for a while—perhaps five thousand years or more.

Finally, plaintiffs compare Athena's remark in "Olympiad" and "Olympiad A" that "Owen is perfect to undertake this noble quest" to Zeus's remark in the God of War game manual that "Athena has chosen well, no doubt. Perhaps Athens will survive after all." Compare Olympiad at 20 and Olympiad A at 22 with Game Manual at 12. This dialogue is simply not similar.

3. The Quest

During his quest, plaintiffs' protagonist tells the leader of the Athenian Council that he must "make [the Council] listen. All of Greece depends on it." Olympiad at

33; Olympiad A at 35. In God of War, the Oracle tells Kratos, "You must find me . . . Athens depends on it. . . ." Merged Script at 11. Any moviegoer can attest that the snippet of dialogue stating that something "depends on it" is clichéd. Moreover, the context of these statements is quite different. The first is spoken by plaintiffs' protagonist as he seeks to convince the Athenian Council that he truly is on a mission from Zeus, after the Council has laughed at his story. Olympiad at 33. The statement refers to all of Greece. The God of War statement refers only to Athens and is spoken by the Oracle to the protagonist as the Oracle is being carried away by Harpies. Merged Script at 11.

Later in the quest, plaintiffs' protagonist is warned: "through there many have entered . . . but none has returned." Olympiad at 40; Olympiad A at 42. "There" refers to the entrance to the Nemean Lion's cave. In God of War, Kratos is warned: "Many have gone in search of Pandora's Box. None have returned." Merged Script at 17. These statements refer to very different things (entering a cave versus searching for Pandora's Box), and the phrase "none has/have returned" is clichéd and unprotectable.

Plaintiffs' comparison of language regarding a javelin in plaintiffs' works and a column in God of War does not refer to dialogue and is thus irrelevant to the analysis of similarities in dialogue.

D. Mood

The mood of plaintiffs' works is generally light-hearted, with elements of romance and comedy. While plaintiffs accurately point to some dark scenes, plaintiffs' characterization of both works as "extremely dark, violent, gloomy and filled with dread" is hyperbolic at best. See Pl.'s Opp. at 21. Plaintiffs describe some "lighter, even comic" scenes as being "sprinkled" throughout their works, but such terms more accurately describe the works as a whole with some darker scenes sprinkled in for contrast. See, e.g., Olympiad at 15-16 (protagonist and side-kick chat about girls while drinking "brew, racing to finish."); id. at 30-31 (Owen runs into a merchant's stall while staring at a beautiful girl; "Mercante notices the attraction between Aria and Owen. It amuses and pleases him. . . . [Meanwhile,] corpulent Medea comes up behind Camden and pinches his butt."); Owen at 19 ("The entertaining pole vault competition proceeds with drama, comedy, and mishap.").

In contrast, the mood of God of War is dark and extremely violent. There are virtually no light-hearted or comic moments in the game. Indeed, the game begins with Kratos attempting suicide, repeatedly references Kratos's memories of and guilt over his past violent deeds, and ends with images of World War II and Vietnam. Merged Script at 1, 4, 45.

At oral argument, plaintiffs' counsel represented that the Olympic Games are depicted as extremely violent events in plaintiffs' works. Plaintiffs' counsel noted, for example, that the chariot race includes an intentional collision and that the javelin throw is aimed at a captive Spartan. See, e.g., Olympiad at 80, 90. Such elements are not surprising in an action-adventure script and serve to temporarily heighten the tension of the story. However, they fall short of establishing a pervasive mood of dark violence throughout plaintiffs' works. Furthermore, the protagonist, though injured in the chariot collision, is healthy enough to participate in the next day's event, id. at 88-89, and the protagonist and another competitor intentionally avoid hitting the captive Spartan with their javelins, id. at 92-95—not a decision one would expect from Kratos.

E. Settings

Both stories are set in ancient and mythical Greece, including scenes in Athens and on Mount Olympus. God of War and two of plaintiffs' works, "Owen" and "Theseus," also include scenes set in the Underworld. Significant portions of plaintiffs' works—e.g., approximately half of "Olympiad"—are set in Sparta, which appears in God of War only in two short bonus scenes. Compare Olympiad at 50-104 with Merged Script at 47-50. Plaintiffs' works also include scenes in and near the protagonist's village, a Nemean Village and the island of the Amazons; these settings are absent from God of War. God of War includes scenes set on bluffs overlooking the Aegean Sea, on a boat on the Aegean Sea and in the Desert of Lost Souls where Pandora's Temple is located; these settings are absent from plaintiffs' works.

While the shared settings of Greece, Athens, Mount Olympus, Sparta, and the Underworld do establish some similarity between the works at issue, these settings are generic and clichéd for stories involving ancient Greece and Greek gods. While the action in God of War is spread over several locations, the bulk of the action appears to occur inside Pandora's Temple in the Desert of Lost Souls, and in Athens.

Contrary to plaintiffs' assertion, the respective depictions of Mount Olympus are also dissimilar. In plaintiffs' works, a meeting hall of the gods is located on Mount Olympus. See Olympiad at 12. In "Olympiad," eleven golden statues of the gods face a pool of water in the meeting hall. Id. The "flesh and blood" gods "morph" out of these statues. Id. at 12-13. In "Olympiad A," the pool is "enormous" and no statues are mentioned.[11] Olympiad A at 13. In God of War, Mount Olympus is merely glimpsed at the top of the stairs Kratos must climb to take his place as the new god of war. Merged Script at 45. In the God of War game manual, three humanlike gods stand in the open air beside a round, well-like structure. Game Manual at 3. A jagged mountain range is visible over their shoulders and low columns stand close behind them. Id. Two notable differences distinguish these two depictions of Mount Olympus: plaintiffs' setting is indoors while God of *1087 War's is outdoors; and plaintiffs' pool is large enough to be faced by eleven large ("twice the size of a man") statues while God of War's well-like structure is quite small.

Plaintiffs also note that their works contain a "Meadow of Lost Souls" while God of War contains a "Desert of Lost Souls." The meadow appears only in "Owen" and on the accompanying map. In "Owen," the protagonist and his party "proceed inland down a road, passing through meadows that contain lost souls wandering aimlessly." Owen at 12. God of War features a Desert of Lost Souls, through which the titan Chronos crawls with Pandora's Temple chained to his back. Merged Script at 18. The concept of characters encountering lost souls is hardly original to either plaintiffs or defendants, and a meadow is not a desert. It is notable that the meadow is referenced in only one sentence of "Owen," whereas a significant portion of the action in God of War takes place in the desert.[12]

Plaintiffs also note that their works contain a "Bottomless Valley" and assert that God of War allegedly contains a similar "Bottomless Chasm." Like the Meadow of Lost Souls, the Bottomless Valley appears only in "Owen" and the accompanying map, and it is referenced in only one sentence. In "Owen," "satyrs take their captives, up the Steps to the Underworld, past the Bottomless Valley and Fiery Lake." Owen at 12. Plaintiffs assert that the "Bottomless Chasm" in God of War appears just before Pandora's Temple. The screen image provided by plaintiffs, however, simply shows a rope bridge spanning a wide gap. See Bissoon-Dath Dec., Exh. 6 at 2. Although the bottom is not visible, there is no indication that the void is bottomless.[13]

F. Pace

Plaintiffs' works are relatively fast-paced action-adventure epics in which high-tension scenes are interspersed with scenes of levity. For instance, scenes featuring the initial Spartan attack on Athens and the argument among the gods are followed by a scene in which the protagonist and his sidekick drink and joke about girls. Olympiad at 4-16. God of War is a video game, and its pace is driven at least in part by the individual player. The game is generally very past-paced with few if any lulls in the action other than those caused by a novice player. Such a fast pace is hardly surprising in a violent video game and is not readily indicative of *1088 any copying of plaintiffs' works. In addition, the storyline is pieced together through repeated and disordered flashbacks rather than presented in a linear fashion as in plaintiffs' works.

...

H. Sequence of Events

There are also significant differences in the respective sequences of events in plaintiffs' works and God of War. Plaintiffs' works are all told in a linear, narrative fashion with scenes occurring one after another in logical sequence. The story in God of War, in contrast, jumps around repeatedly and is told largely through flashbacks. For instance, God of War opens with what will ultimately be the second-to-last scene; in this scene, Kratos jumps off a cliff. Before Kratos reaches the rocks below (and presumably his death), the story jumps three weeks into the past to depict Kratos battling a Hydra at Poseidon's behest. Merged Script at 1-2.

Plaintiffs' works begin with the Spartans attacking Athens, then retreating for the winter when repulsed by the city's forces. Olympiad at 4-12. The retreating army is visible in a pool of water on Mount Olympus. Id. at 12. The Spartan army returns the next year and attacks Athens while the Olympic Games are in progress in Sparta, but Athens is not conquered. Id. at 81, 104. According to the God of War game manual, Ares (not the Spartans) is preparing his forces to attack Athens (not retreating) when the gods meet to discuss Kratos. Game Manual at 3. Once the storyline *1091 begins in God of War, Ares is actively attacking Athens; he continues to do so for most of the game and has completed his conquest of the city when Kratos arrives to defeat him. Merged Script at 4, 32, 37.

Plaintiffs assert that in both stories "Athens is saved from destruction by a Spartan commander who was once loyal exclusively to Ares but renounces Ares in a climatic [sic] one-on-one battle." Pl.'s Opp. at 23. This assertion is misleading in several ways. Firstly, Athens is not saved by anyone in God of War; the city is conquered and "lies in ruins" before Kratos fights Ares. Merged Script at 37. Secondly, Kratos is not a Spartan commander when he fights Ares. Id. at 4, 15. Thirdly, Kratos does not renounce Ares in one-on-one battle; although he rejected Ares in the past, the rejection occurred ten years before God of War's action and involved no personal combat with the god. Id. at 1, 31. Fourthly, in "Theseus," the only one of plaintiffs' works in which a Spartan leader betrays Ares to rescue Athens, no character is referred to as a Spartan "commander." While the work features a Spartan General and a Spartan Dictator, it is the previously silent Royal Guard Captain who decides that justice and freedom have too long been sacrificed in Ares's name, orders the guard to seize the Dictator, and later defeats the Spartan Colonel in one-on-one combat at Athens. Theseus at 6, 23-24, 42-43. Fifthly, the Royal Guard Captain speaks of the Dictator's affinity for Ares, but reveals no exclusive loyalty of his own to the god. Id. at 42. Sixthly, the adjective "clima[c]tic" is belied by the fact that the one-on-one battle with the Colonel is referenced only in the epilogue. Id. at 43.

Plaintiffs' other contentions regarding the stories' respective sequences of events are no more availing. To the extent that plaintiffs accurately portray similarities, those similarities refer to clichéd and unprotected elements.

I. Summary

An examination of articulable similarities between the plot, themes, dialogue, mood, settings, pace, characters and sequence of events of God of War and plaintiffs' works reveals far less similarity than would be required to overcome summary judgment, even if plaintiffs had proven access. Plaintiffs have pointed to no persuasive similarity in dialogue or narration that would suggest actual copying. As in Berkic v. Crichton, 761 F.2d at 1293, there is some degree of similarity between the plots at an extremely generalized level. Yet, as that court admonished, "No one can own the basic idea for a story. General plot ideas are not protected by copyright law; they remain forever the common property of artistic mankind." Id. This is particularly true when virtually all of the elements comprising plaintiffs' works are stock elements that have been used in literary and artistic works for years, if not millennia. As noted, the particular sequence in which an author strings a significant number of unprotectable elements can itself be a protectable element. Metcalf, 294 F.3d at 1074. Here, the sequences of elements, and the relationships between them, are entirely dissimilar. No reasonable trier of fact could conclude that God of War is substantially similar to any of plaintiffs' works.

...

CONCLUSION

For the foregoing reasons, defendants' motion for summary judgment is GRANTED. Judgment shall be entered accordingly.

IT IS SO ORDERED.

635 F.3d 290 (2011)

KELLEY v. CHICAGO PARK DIST.

United States Court of Appeals, Seventh Circuit

SYKES, Circuit Judge.

Chapman Kelley is a nationally recognized artist known for his representational paintings of landscapes and flowers—in particular, romantic floral and woodland interpretations set within ellipses. In 1984 he received permission from the Chicago Park District to install an ambitious wildflower display at the north end of Grant Park, a prominent public space in the heart of downtown Chicago. "Wildflower Works" was thereafter planted: two enormous elliptical flower beds, each nearly as big as a football field, featuring a variety of native wildflowers and edged with borders of gravel and steel.

Promoted as "living art," Wildflower Works received critical and popular acclaim, and for a while Kelley and a group of volunteers tended the vast garden, pruning and replanting as needed. But by 2004 Wildflower Works had deteriorated, and the City's goals for Grant Park had changed. So the Park District dramatically modified the garden, substantially reducing its size, reconfiguring the oval flower beds into rectangles, and changing some of the planting material.

Kelley sued the Park District for violating his "right of integrity" under the Visual Artists Rights Act of 1990 ("VARA"), 17 U.S.C. § 106A, and also for breach of contract. The contract claim is insubstantial; the main event here is the VARA claim, which is novel and tests the boundaries of copyright law. Congress enacted this statute to comply with the nation's obligations under the Berne Convention for the Protection of Literary and Artistic Works. VARA amended the Copyright Act, importing a limited version of the civil-law concept of the "moral rights of the artist" into our intellectual-property law. In brief, for certain types of visual art— paintings, drawings, prints, sculptures, and exhibition photographs—VARA confers upon the artist certain rights of attribution and integrity. The latter include the right of the artist to prevent, during his lifetime, any distortion or modification of his work that would be "prejudicial to his . . . honor or reputation," and to recover for any such intentional distortion or modification undertaken without his consent. See 17 U.S.C. § 106A(a)(3)(A).

The district court held a bench trial and entered a split judgment. The court rejected Kelley's moral-rights claim for two reasons. First, the judge held that although Wildflower Works could be classified as both a painting and a sculpture and therefore a work of visual art under VARA, it lacked sufficient originality to be eligible for copyright, a foundational requirement in the statute. Second, following the First Circuit's decision in Phillips v. Pembroke Real Estate, Inc., 459 F.3d 128 (1st Cir.2006), the court concluded that site-specific art like Wildflower Works is categorically excluded from protection under VARA. The court then held for Kelley on the contract claim, but found his evidence of damages uncertain and entered a nominal award of $1. Both sides appealed.

We affirm in part and reverse in part. There is reason to doubt several of the district court's conclusions: that Wildflower Works is a painting or sculpture; that it flunks the test for originality; and that all site-specific art is excluded from VARA. But the court was right to reject this claim; for reasons relating to copyright's requirements of expressive authorship and fixation, a living garden like Wildflower Works is not copyrightable. The district court's treatment of the contract claim is another matter; the Park District is entitled to judgment on that claim as well.

I. Background

Kelley is a painter noted for his use of bold, elliptical outlines to surround scenes of landscapes and flowers. In the late-1970s and 1980s, he moved from the canvas to the soil and created a series of large outdoor wildflower displays that resembled his paintings. He planted the first in 1976 alongside a runway at the Dallas-Fort Worth International Airport and the second in 1982 outside the Dallas Museum of Natural History. The wildflower exhibit at the museum was temporary; the one at the airport just "gradually petered out."

In 1983 Kelley accepted an invitation from Chicago-based oil executive John Swearingen and his wife, Bonnie—collectors of Kelley's paintings—to come to Chicago to explore the possibility of creating a large outdoor wildflower display in the area. He scouted sites by land and by air and eventually settled on Grant Park, the city's showcase public space running along Lake Michigan in the center of downtown Chicago. This location suited Kelley's artistic, environmental, and educational mission; it also provided the best opportunity to reach a large audience. Kelley met with the Park District superintendent to present his proposal, and on June 19, 1984, the Park District Board of Commissioners granted him a permit to install a "permanent Wild Flower Floral Display" on a grassy area on top of the underground Monroe Street parking garage in Daley Bicentennial Plaza in Grant Park. Under the terms of the permit, Kelley was to install and maintain the exhibit at his own expense. The Park District reserved the right to terminate the installation by giving Kelley "a 90 day notice to remove the planting."

Kelley named the project "Chicago Wildflower Works I." The Park District issued a press release announcing that "a new form of `living' art" was coming to Grant Park—"giant ovals of multicolored wildflowers" created by Kelley, a painter and "pioneer in the use of natural materials" who "attracted national prominence for his efforts to incorporate the landscape in artistic creation." The announcement explained that "[o]nce the ovals mature, the results will be two breathtaking natural canvases of Kelley-designed color patterns."

In the late summer of 1984, Kelley began installing the two large-scale elliptical flower beds at the Grant Park site; they spanned 1.5 acres of parkland and were set within gravel and steel borders. A gravel walkway bisected one of the ovals, and each flower bed also accommodated several large, preexisting air vents that were flush with the planting surface, providing ventilation to the parking garage below. For planting material Kelley selected between 48 and 60 species of self-sustaining wildflowers native to the region. The species were selected for various aesthetic, environmental, and cultural reasons, but also to increase the likelihood that the garden could withstand Chicago's harsh winters and survive with minimal maintenance. Kelley designed the initial placement of the wildflowers so they would blossom sequentially, changing colors throughout the growing season and increasing in brightness towards the center of each ellipse. He purchased the initial planting material—between 200,000 and 300,000 wildflower plugs—at a cost of between $80,000 and $152,000. In September of 1984, a battery of volunteers planted the seedlings under Kelley's direction.

When the wildflowers bloomed the following year, Wildflower Works was greeted with widespread acclaim. Chicago's mayor, the Illinois Senate, and the Illinois Chapter of the American Society of Landscape Artists issued commendations. People flocked to see the lovely display—marketed by the Park District as "living landscape art"—and admiring articles appeared in national newspapers. Wildflower Works was a hit. Here's a picture:

For the next several years, Kelley's permit was renewed and he and his volunteers tended the impressive garden. They pruned and weeded and regularly planted new seeds, both to experiment with the garden's composition and to fill in where initial specimen had not flourished. Of course, the forces of nature—the varying bloom periods of the plants; their spread habits, compatibility, and life cycles; and the weather—produced constant change. Some wildflowers naturally did better than others. Some spread aggressively and encroached on neighboring plants. Some withered and died. Unwanted plants sprung up from seeds brought in by birds and the wind. Insects, rabbits, and weeds settled in, eventually taking a toll. Four years after Wildflower Works was planted, the Park District decided to discontinue the exhibit. On June 3, 1988, the District gave Kelley a 90-day notice of termination.

Kelley responded by suing the Park District in federal court, claiming the termination of his permit violated the First Amendment. The parties quickly settled; in exchange for dismissal of the suit, the Park District agreed to extend Kelley's permit for another year. On September 14, 1988, the Park District issued a "Temporary Permit" to Kelley and Chicago Wildflower Works, Inc., a nonprofit organization formed by his volunteers. This permit authorized them "to operate and maintain a two ellipse Wildflowers Garden Display . . . at Daley Bicentennial Plaza in Grant Park" until September 1, 1989. The permit stipulated that Kelley "will have responsibility and control over matters relating to the aesthetic design and content of Wildflower Works I," and Wildflower Works, Inc. "shall maintain the Wildflower Works I at no cost to the Chicago Park District including, without limitation, weeding and application of fertilizer." Although it did not contain a notice-of-termination provision, the permit did state that "[t]he planting material is the property of Mr. Chapman Kelley" and that Kelley "may remove the planting material" if the permit was not extended. Finally, the permit provided that "[t]his agreement does not create any proprietary interest for Chicago Wildflower Works, Inc., or Mr. Chapman Kelley in continuing to operate and maintain the Wildflower Garden Display after September 1, 1989."

The Park District formally extended this permit each succeeding year through 1994. After that point Kelley and his volunteers continued to cultivate Wildflower Works without a permit, and the Park District took no action, adverse or otherwise, regarding the garden's future. In March 2004 Kelley and Jonathan Dedmon, president of Wildflower Works, Inc., attended a luncheon to discuss the 20th anniversary of Wildflower Works. At the luncheon Dedmon asked Park District Commissioner Margaret Burroughs if Wildflower Works needed a new permit. Commissioner Burroughs responded, "You're still there, aren't you? That's all you need to do."

Three months later, on June 10, 2004, Park District officials met with Kelley and Dedmon to discuss problems relating to inadequate maintenance of the garden and forthcoming changes to Grant Park necessitated by the construction of the adjacent Millennium Park. The officials proposed reconfiguring Wildflower Works—decreasing its size from approximately 66,000 square feet to just under 30,000 square feet and remaking its elliptical flower beds into rectangles. The District's director of development invited Kelley's views on this proposal but made it clear that the District planned to go forward with the reconfiguration with or without Kelley's approval. Kelley objected to the proposed changes, but did not request an opportunity to remove his planting material before the reconfiguration took place. A week later the Park District proceeded with its plan and reduced Wildflower Works to less than half its original size. The elliptical borders became rectilinear, weeds were removed, surviving wildflowers were replanted in the smaller-scale garden, and some new planting material was added. Dedmon sent a letter of protest to the Park District.

Kelley then sued the Park District for violating his moral rights under VARA. He claimed that Wildflower Works was both a painting and a sculpture and therefore a "work of visual art" under VARA, and that the Park District's reconfiguration of it was an intentional "distortion, mutilation, or other modification" of his work and was "prejudicial to his . . . honor or reputation." See 17 U.S.C. § 106A(a)(3)(A). He also alleged breach of contract; he claimed that Commissioner Burroughs's remark created an implied contract that the Park District had breached when it altered Wildflower Works without providing reasonable notice.1 On the VARA claim Kelley sought compensation for the moral-rights violation, statutory damages, and attorney's fees; on the contract claim he sought the fair-market value of the planting material removed in the reconfiguration. He later quantified his damages, estimating the value of the plants at $1.5 million and requesting a staggering $25 million for the VARA violation.

The case proceeded to a bench trial, and the district court entered judgment for the Park District on the VARA claim and for Kelley on the contract claim. See Kelley v. Chi. Park Dist., No. 04 C 07715, 2008 WL 4449886 (N.D.Ill. Sept. 29, 2008). The judge first concluded that Wildflower Works could be classified as both a painting and a sculpture and therefore qualified as a work of visual art under VARA. Id. at *4-5. But he also held that Wildflower Works was insufficiently original for copyright, a prerequisite to moral-rights protection under VARA. Id. at *6. ...

II. Discussion

This case comes to us from a judgment entered after a bench trial; we review the district court's factual findings for clear error and its conclusions of law de novo. Spurgin-Dienst v. United States, 359 F.3d 451, 453 (7th Cir.2004). In this circuit, questions of copyright eligibility are issues of law subject to independent review. Schrock v. Learning Curve Int'l, Inc., 586 F.3d 513, 517 (7th Cir.2009).

...

[The court discusses the claim under VARA]

4. Is Wildflower Works copyrightable?

To merit copyright protection, Wildflower Works must be an "original work[ ] of authorship fixed in a[ ] tangible medium of expression . . . from which [it] can be perceived, reproduced, or otherwise communicated." 17 U.S.C. § 102(a). The district court held that although Wildflower Works was both a painting and a sculpture, it was ineligible for copyright because it lacked originality. There is a contradiction here. As we have explained, VARA supplements general copyright protection and applies only to artists who create the specific subcategories of art enumerated in the statute. VARA-eligible paintings and sculptures comprise a discrete subset of otherwise copyrightable pictorial and sculptural works; the statute designates these works of fine art as worthy of special protection. If a work is so lacking in originality that it cannot satisfy the basic requirements for copyright, then it can hardly qualify as a painting or sculpture eligible for extra protection under VARA. See Cronin, Dead on the Vine, 12 VAND. J. ENT. & TECH. L. at 239 ("[I]f a work does not evince sufficient original expression to be copyrightable, the work should belong in a category other than `visual art' as this term is contemplated under VARA.").

That point aside, the district court's conclusion misunderstands the originality requirement. Originality is "the touchstone of copyright protection today," an implicit constitutional and explicit statutory requirement. Feist Publ'ns, Inc. v.

Rural Tel. Serv. Co., 499 U.S. 340, 347, 346, 111 S.Ct. 1282, 113 L.Ed.2d 358 (1991) ("Originality is a constitutional requirement."); id. at 355 (The Copyright Act of 1976 made the originality requirement explicit.); see also Schrock, 586 F.3d at 518-19 ("As a constitutional and statutory matter, `[t]he sine qua non of copyright is originality.'" (quoting Feist, 499 U.S. at 345, 111 S.Ct. 1282)). Despite its centrality in our copyright regime, the threshold for originality is minimal. See Feist, 499 U.S. at 345, 111 S.Ct. 1282; Am. Dental Ass'n v. Delta Dental Plans Ass'n, 126 F.3d 977, 979 (7th Cir.1997) ("The necessary degree of `originality' is low. . . ."). The standard requires "only that the work was independently created by the author (as opposed to copied from other works), and that it possesses at least some minimal degree of creativity." Feist, 499 U.S. at 345, 111 S.Ct. 1282 (citation omitted). The "requisite level of creativity is extremely low; even a slight amount will suffice. The vast majority of works make the grade quite easily, as they possess some creative spark." Id. (citation omitted).

The district court took the position that Wildflower Works was not original because Kelley was not "the first person to ever conceive of and express an arrangement of growing wildflowers in ellipse-shaped enclosed area[s]." Kelley, 2008 WL 4449886, at *6. This mistakenly equates originality with novelty; the law is clear that a work can be original even if it is not novel. Feist, 499 U.S. at 345, 111 S.Ct. 1282 ("Originality does not signify novelty; a work may be original even though it closely resembles other works so long as the similarity is fortuitous, not the result of copying."). No one argues that Wildflower Works was copied; it plainly possesses more than a little creative spark.

... "Authorship + Fixation"

The real impediment to copyright here is not that Wildflower Works fails the test for originality (understood as "not copied" and "possessing some creativity") but that a living garden lacks the kind of authorship and stable fixation normally required to support copyright. Unlike originality, authorship and fixation are explicit constitutional requirements; the Copyright Clause empowers Congress to secure for "authors" exclusive rights in their "writings." U.S. CONST. art 1, § 8, cl. 8; see also 2 PATRY § 3:20 (2010) ("[T]he Constitution uses the terms `writings' and `authors;' `originality' is not used."); id. § 3:22 (2010); 1 NIMMER § 2.03[A]-[B] (2004). The originality requirement is implicit in these express limitations on the congressional copyright power. See Feist, 499 U.S. at 346, 111 S.Ct. 1282 (The constitutional reference to "authors" and "writings" "presuppose[s] a degree of originality."). The Supreme Court has "repeatedly construed all three terms in relation to one another [or] perhaps has collapsed them into a single concept"; therefore, "[w]ritings are what authors create, but for one to be an author, the writing has to be original." 2 PATRY § 3:20.

"Without fixation," moreover, "there cannot be a `writing.'" Id. § 3:22. The Nimmer treatise elaborates:

Fixation in tangible form is not merely a statutory condition to copyright. It is also a constitutional necessity. That is, unless a work is reduced to tangible form it cannot be regarded as a writing within the meaning of the constitutional clause authorizing federal copyright legislation. Thus, certain works of conceptual art stand outside of copyright protection.

1 NIMMER § 2.03[B]. A work is "fixed" in a tangible medium of expression "when its embodiment in a copy or phonorecord . . . is sufficiently permanent or stable to permit it to be perceived, reproduced, or otherwise communicated for a period of more than transitory duration." 17 U.S.C. § 101. As William Patry explains:

Fixation serves two basic roles: (1) easing problems of proof of creation and infringement, and (2) providing the dividing line between state common law protection and protection under the federal Copyright Act, since works that are not fixed are ineligible for federal protection but may be protected under state law. The distinction between the intangible intellectual property (the work of authorship) and its fixation in a tangible medium of expression (the copy) is an old and fundamental and important one. The distinction may be understood by examples of multiple fixations of the same work: A musical composition may be embodied in sheet music, on an audio-tape, on a compact disc, on a computer hard drive or server, or as part of a motion picture soundtrack. In each of the fixations, the intangible property remains a musical composition. 2 PATRY § 3:22 (internal quotation marks omitted).

Finally, "authorship is an entirely human endeavor." Id. § 3:19 (2010). Authors of copyrightable works must be human; works owing their form to the forces of nature cannot be copyrighted. Id. § 3:19 n. 1; see also U.S. COPYRIGHT OFFICE, COMPENDIUM II: COPYRIGHT OFFICE PRACTICES § 503.03(a) ("[A] work must be the product of human authorship" and not the forces of nature.) (1984); id. § 202.02(b).

Recognizing copyright in Wildflower Works presses too hard on these basic principles. We fully accept that the artistic community might classify Kelley's garden as a work of postmodern conceptual art. We acknowledge as well that copyright's prerequisites of authorship and fixation are broadly defined. But the law must have some limits; not all conceptual art may be copyrighted. In the ordinary copyright case, authorship and fixation are not contested; most works presented for copyright are unambiguously authored and unambiguously fixed. But this is not an ordinary case. A living garden like Wildflower Works is neither "authored" nor "fixed" in the senses required for copyright. See Toney v. L'Oreal USA, Inc., 406 F.3d 905, 910 (7th Cir.2005) ("A person's likeness—her persona— is not authored and it is not fixed."); see also Cronin, Dead on the Vine, 12 VAND. J. ENT. & TECH. L. at 227-39.

Simply put, gardens are planted and cultivated, not authored. A garden's constituent elements are alive and inherently changeable, not fixed. Most of what we see and experience in a garden—the colors, shapes, textures, and scents of the plants—originates in nature, not in the mind of the gardener. At any given moment in time, a garden owes most of its form and appearance to natural forces, though the gardener who plants and tends it obviously assists. All this is true of Wildflower Works, even though it was designed and planted by an artist.

Of course, a human "author"—whether an artist, a professional landscape designer, or an amateur backyard gardener—determines the initial arrangement of the plants in a garden. This is not the kind of authorship required for copyright. To the extent that seeds or seedlings can be considered a "medium of expression," they originate in nature, and natural forces—not the intellect of the gardener—determine their form, growth, and appearance. Moreover, a garden is simply too changeable to satisfy the primary purpose of fixation; its appearance is too inherently variable to supply a baseline for determining questions of copyright creation and infringement. If a garden can qualify as a "work of authorship" sufficiently "embodied in a copy," at what point has fixation occurred? When the garden is newly planted? When its first blossoms appear? When it is in full bloom? How—and at what point in time—is a court to determine whether infringing copying has occurred?

In contrast, when a landscape designer conceives of a plan for a garden and puts it in writing—records it in text, diagrams, or drawings on paper or on a digital-storage device—we can say that his intangible intellectual property has been embodied in a fixed and tangible "copy." This writing is a sufficiently permanent and stable copy of the designer's intellectual expression and is vulnerable to infringing copying, giving rise to the designer's right to claim copyright. The same cannot be said of a garden, which is not a fixed copy of the gardener's intellectual property. Although the planting material is tangible and can be perceived for more than a transitory duration, it is not stable or permanent enough to be called "fixed." Seeds and plants in a garden are naturally in a state of perpetual change; they germinate, grow, bloom, become dormant, and eventually die. This life cycle moves gradually, over days, weeks, and season to season, but the real barrier to copyright here is not temporal but essential. The essence of a garden is its vitality, not its fixedness. It may endure from season to season, but its nature is one of dynamic change.

We are not suggesting that copyright attaches only to works that are static or fully permanent (no medium of expression lasts forever), or that artists who incorporate natural or living elements in their work can never claim copyright. Kelley compares Wildflower Works to the Crown Fountain, a sculpture by Spanish artist Jaume Plensa that sits nearby in Chicago's Millennium Park. The surfaces of Plensa's fountain are embedded with LED screens that replay recorded video images of the faces of 1,000 Chicagoans. See http://www.explorechicago.org/city/en/ things_see_do/attractions/dca_tourism/ Crown_Fountain.html (last visited Feb. 10, 2011). But the Copyright Act specifically contemplates works that incorporate or consist of sounds or images that are broadcast or transmitted electronically, such as telecasts of sporting events or other live performances, video games, and the like. See 17 U.S.C. § 101 (defining "fixed" as including a "work consisting of sounds, images, or both, that are being transmitted. . . if a fixation of the work is being made simultaneously with its transmission"); see also Balt. Orioles, Inc. v. Major League Baseball Players Ass'n, 805 F.2d 663, 675 (7th Cir.1986); Midway Mfg. Co. v. Artic Int'l, Inc., 704 F.2d 1009, 1013-14 (7th Cir.1983). Wildflower Works does not fit in this category; the Crown Fountain is not analogous.

Though not addressing the requirement of fixation directly, the district court compared Wildflower Works to "[t]he mobiles of Alexander Calder" and "Jeff Koons' `Puppy,' a 43-foot flowering topiary." Kelley, 2008 WL 4449886, at *4. These analogies are also inapt. Although the aesthetic effect of a Calder mobile is attributable in part to its subtle movement in response to air currents, see http://en.wikipedia.org/ wiki/Alexander_Calder (last visited Feb. 10, 2011), the mobile itself is obviously fixed and stable. In "Puppy" the artist assembled a huge metal frame in the shape of a puppy and covered it with thousands of blooming flowers sustained by an irrigation system within the frame. See http://en.wikipedia.org/wiki/Jeff_Koons (last visited Feb. 10, 2011). This may be sufficient fixation for copyright (we venture no opinion on the question), but Wildflower Works is quite different. It is quintessentially a garden; "Puppy" is not.

In short, Wildflower Works presents serious problems of authorship and fixation that these and other examples of conceptual or kinetic art do not. Because Kelley's garden is neither "authored" nor "fixed" in the senses required for basic copyright, it cannot qualify for moral rights protection under VARA.

...

3.C. Usefulness

347 U.S. 201 (1954)

MAZER v. STEIN

United States Supreme Court

Respondents are engaged in the manufacture and sale of electric lamps. One of the respondents created original works of sculpture, from the models of which china statuettes were made. The statuettes were used as bases for fully equipped electric lamps, which respondents sold. Respondents submitted the statuettes, without any lamp components added, for registration under the copyright law as "works of art" or reproductions thereof. Held: The statuettes were copyrightable. Pp. 202-219.

...

MR. JUSTICE REED

This case involves the validity of copyrights obtained by respondents for statuettes of male and female dancing figures made of semivitreous china. The controversy centers around the fact that although copyrighted as "works of art," the statuettes were intended for use and used as bases for table lamps, with electric wiring, sockets and lamp shades attached.

Respondents are partners in the manufacture and sale of electric lamps. One of the respondents created original works of sculpture in the form of human figures by traditional clay-model technique. From this model, a production mold for casting copies was made. The resulting statuettes, without any lamp components added, were submitted by the respondents to the Copyright Office for registration as "works of art" or reproductions thereof under 5 (g) or 5 (h) of the copyright law, 1 and certificates [347 U.S. 201, 203] of registration issued. Sales (publication in accordance with the statute) as fully equipped lamps preceded the applications for copyright registration of the statuettes. 17 U.S.C. (Supp. V, 1952) 10, 11, 13, 209; Rules and Regulations, 37 CFR, 1949, 202.8 and 202.9. Thereafter, the statuettes were sold in quantity throughout the country both as lamp bases and as statuettes. The sales in lamp form accounted for all but an insignificant portion of respondents' sales.

Petitioners are partners and, like respondents, make and sell lamps. Without authorization, they copied the statuettes, embodied them in lamps and sold them.

The instant case is one in a series of reported suits brought by respondents against various alleged infringers of the copyrights, all presenting the same or a similar question. Because of conflicting decisions, we granted certiorari. 346 U.S. 811 . In the present case respondents sued petitioners for infringement in Maryland. Stein v. Mazer, 111 F. Supp. 359. ...

Petitioners, charged by the present complaint with infringement of respondents' copyrights of reproductions of their works of art, seek here a reversal of the Court of Appeals decree upholding the copyrights. Petitioners in their petition for certiorari present a single question:

"Can statuettes be protected in the United States by copyright when the copyright applicant intended primarily to use the statuettes in the form of lamp bases to be made and sold in quantity and carried the intentions into effect?

"Stripped down to its essentials, the question presented is: Can a lamp manufacturer copyright his lamp bases?"

The first paragraph accurately summarizes the issue. The last gives it a quirk that unjustifiably, we think, broadens the controversy. The case requires an answer, not as to a manufacturer's right to register a lamp base but as to an artist's right to copyright a work of art intended to be reproduced for lamp bases. As petitioners say in their brief, their contention "questions the validity of the copyright based upon the actions of the respondents." Petitioners question the validity of a copyright of a work of art for "mass" production. "Reproduction of a work of art" does not mean to them unlimited reproduction. Their position is that a copyright does not cover industrial reproduction of the protected article. Thus their reply brief states:

"When an artist becomes a manufacturer or a designer for a manufacturer he is subject to the limitations of design patents and deserves no more consideration than any other manufacturer or designer."

It is not the right to copyright an article that could have utility under 5 (g) and (h), note 1, supra, that petitioners oppose. Their brief accepts the copyrightability of the great carved golden saltcellar of Cellini but adds:

"If, however, Cellini designed and manufactured this item in quantity so that the general public could have salt cellars, then an entirely different conclusion would be reached. In such case, the salt cellar becomes an article of manufacture having utility in addition to its ornamental value and would therefore have to be protected by design patent."

It is publication as a lamp and registration as a statue to gain a monopoly in manufacture that they assert is such a misuse of copyright as to make the registration invalid.

No unfair competition question is presented. The constitutional power of Congress to confer copyright protection on works of art or their reproductions is not questioned. Petitioners assume, as Congress has in its [347 U.S. 201, 207] enactments and as do we, that the constitutional clause empowering legislation "To promote the Progress of Science and useful Arts, by securing for limited Times to Authors and Inventors the exclusive Right to their [347 U.S. 201, 208] respective Writings and Discoveries," Art. I, 8, cl. 8, includes within the term "Authors" the creator of a picture or a statue. The Court's consideration will be limited to the question presented by the petition for the writ of certiorari. In recent years the question as to utilitarian use of copyrighted articles has been much discussed.

In answering that issue, a review of the development of copyright coverage will make clear the purpose of the Congress in its copyright legislation. In 1790 the First Congress conferred a copyright on "authors of any map, chart, book or books already printed." Later, designing, engraving and etching were included; in 1831 musical compositions; dramatic compositions in 1856; and photographs and negatives thereof in 1865.

The Act of 1870 defined copyrightable subject matter as:

". . . any book, map, chart, dramatic or musical composition, engraving, cut, print, or photograph or negative thereof, or of a painting, drawing, chromo, statue, statuary, and of models or designs intended to be perfected as works of the fine arts." (Emphasis supplied.)

The italicized part added three-dimensional work of art to what had been protected previously. In 1909 Congress again enlarged the scope of the copyright statute. The new Act provided in 4:

"That the works for which copyright may be secured under this Act shall include all the writings of an author."

Some writers interpret this section as being coextensive with the constitutional grant, but the House Report, while inconclusive, indicates that it was "declaratory of existing law" only. Section 5 relating to classes of writings in 1909 read as shown in the margin with subsequent additions not material to this decision. Significant for our purposes was the deletion of the fine-arts clause of the 1870 Act. Verbal distinctions between purely aesthetic articles and useful works of art ended insofar as the statutory copyright language is concerned.

The practice of the Copyright Office, under the 1870 and 1874 Acts and before the 1909 Act, was to allow registration "as works of the fine arts" of articles of the same character as those of respondents now under challenge. Seven examples appear in the Government's brief amicus curiae. In 1910, interpreting the 1909 Act, the pertinent Copyright Regulations read as shown in the margin. Because, as explained by the Government, this regulation "made no reference to articles which might fairly be considered works of art although they might also serve a useful purpose," it was reworded in 1917 as shown below. The amicus brief gives sixty examples selected at five-year intervals, 1912-1952, said to be typical of registrations of works of art possessing utilitarian aspects. The current pertinent regulation, published in 37 CFR, 1949, 202.8, reads thus:

"Works of art (Class G) - (a) In General. This class includes works of artistic craftsmanship, in so far as their form but not their mechanical or utilitarian aspects are concerned, such as artistic jewelry, enamels, glassware, and tapestries, as well as all works belonging to the fine arts, such as paintings, drawings and sculpture. . . ."

So we have a contemporaneous and long-continued construction of the statutes by the agency charged to administer them that would allow the registration of such a statuette as is in question here.

This Court once essayed to fix the limits of the fine arts. That effort need not be appraised in relation to this copyright issue. It is clear Congress intended the scope of the copyright statute to include more than the traditional fine arts. ...

The successive acts, the legislative history of the 1909 Act and the practice of the Copyright Office unite to show] that "works of art' and "reproductions of works of art" are terms that were intended by Congress to include the authority to copyright these statuettes. Individual perception of the beautiful is too varied a power to permit a narrow or rigid concept of art. As a standard we can hardly do better than the words of the present Regulation, 202.8, supra, naming the things that appertain to the arts. They must be original, that is, the author's tangible expression of his ideas. Compare Burrow-Giles Lithographic Co. v. Sarony, 111 U.S. 53, 59 -60. Such expression, whether meticulously delineating the model or mental image or conveying the meaning by modernistic form or color, is copyrightable. What cases there are confirm this coverage of the statute.

... petitioners assert that congressional enactment of the design patent laws should be interpreted as denying protection to artistic articles embodied or reproduced in manufactured articles. They say:

"Fundamentally and historically, the Copyright Office is the repository of what each claimant considers to be a cultural treasure, whereas the Patent Office is the repository of what each applicant considers to be evidence of the advance in industrial and technological fields."

... As petitioner sees the effect of the design patent law:

"If an industrial designer can not satisfy the novelty requirements of the design patent laws, then his design as used on articles of manufacture can be copied by anyone."

Petitioner has furnished the Court a booklet of numerous design patents for statuettes, bases for table lamps and similar articles for manufacture, quite indistinguishable in type from the copyrighted statuettes here in issue. 35 Petitioner urges that overlapping of patent and copyright legislation so as to give an author or inventor a choice between patents and copyrights should not be permitted. We assume petitioner takes the position that protection for a statuette for industrial use can only be obtained by patent, if any protection can be given. 36 [347 U.S. 201, 217]

As we have held the statuettes here involved copyrightable, we need not decide the question of their patentability. Though other courts have passed upon the issue as to whether allowance by the election of the author or patentee of one bars a grant of the other, we do not. We do hold that the patentability of the statuettes, fitted as lamps or unfitted, does not bar copyright as works of art. Neither the Copyright Statute nor any other says that because a thing is patentable it may not be copyrighted. We should not so hold.

Unlike a patent, a copyright gives no exclusive right to the art disclosed; protection is given only to the expression of the idea - not the idea itself. Thus, in Baker v. Selden, 101 U.S. 99 , the Court held that a copyrighted book on a peculiar system of bookkeeping was not infringed by a similar book using a similar plan which achieved similar results where the alleged infringer made a different arrangement of the columns and used different headings. The distinction is illustrated in Fred Fisher, Inc. v. Dillingham, 298 F. 145, 151, when the court speaks of two men, each a perfectionist, independently making maps of the same territory. Though the maps are identical, each may obtain the exclusive right to make copies of his own particular map, and yet neither will infringe the other's copyright. Likewise a copyrighted directory is not infringed by a similar directory which is the product of independent work. The copyright protects originality rather than novelty or invention - conferring only "the sole right of multiplying copies." Absent copying there can be no infringement of copyright. Thus, respondents may not exclude others from using statuettes of human figures in table lamps; they may only prevent use of copies of their statuettes as such or as incorporated in some other article. Regulation 202.8, supra, makes clear that artistic articles are protected in "form but not their mechanical or utilitarian aspects." See Stein v. Rosenthal, 103 F. Supp. 227, 231. The dichotomy of protection for the aesthetic is not beauty and utility but art for the copyright and the invention of original and ornamental design for design patents. We find nothing in the copyright statute to support the argument that the intended use or use in industry of an article eligible for copyright bars or invalidates its registration. We do not read such a limitation into the copyright law.

Nor do we think the subsequent registration of a work of art published as an element in a manufactured article, is a misuse of the copyright. This is not different from the registration of a statuette and its later embodiment in an industrial article.

...

The economic philosophy behind the clause empowering Congress to grant patents and copyrights is the conviction that encouragement of individual effort by personal gain is the best way to advance public welfare through the talents of authors and inventors in "Science and useful Arts." Sacrificial days devoted to such creative activities deserve rewards commensurate with the services rendered.

Affirmed.

834 F.2d 1142 (1987)

BRANDIR INTERNATIONAL
v.
CASCADE PACIFIC LUMBER

United States Court of Appeals, Second Circuit

OAKES, Circuit Judge:

In passing the Copyright Act of 1976 Congress attempted to distinguish between [1143] protectable "works of applied art" and "industrial designs not subject to copyright protection." See H.R.Rep. No. 1476, 94th Cong., 2d Sess. 54, reprinted in 1976 U.S.Code Cong. & Admin.News 5659, 5667 (hereinafter H.R.Rep. No. 1476). The courts, however, have had difficulty framing tests by which the fine line establishing what is and what is not copyrightable can be drawn. Once again we are called upon to draw such a line, this time in a case involving the "RIBBON Rack," a bicycle rack made of bent tubing that is said to have originated from a wire sculpture. (A photograph of the rack is contained in the appendix to this opinion.) We are also called upon to determine whether there is any trademark protection available to the manufacturer of the bicycle rack, appellant Brandir International, Inc. The Register of Copyright, named as a third-party defendant under the statute, 17 U.S.C. § 411, but electing not to appear, denied copyrightability. In the subsequent suit brought in the United States District Court for the Southern District of New York, Charles S. Haight, Jr., Judge, the district court granted summary judgment on both the copyright and trademark claims to defendant Cascade Pacific Lumber Co., d/b/a Columbia Cascade Co., manufacturer of a similar bicycle rack. We affirm as to the copyright claim, but reverse and remand as to the trademark claim.

Against the history of copyright protection well set out in the majority opinion in Carol Barnhart Inc. v. Economy Cover Corp., 773 F.2d 411, 415-18 (2d Cir.1985), and in Denicola, Applied Art and Industrial Design: A Suggested Approach to Copyright in Useful Articles, 67 Minn.L.Rev. 707, 709-17 (1983), Congress adopted the Copyright Act of 1976. The "works of art" classification of the Copyright Act of 1909 was omitted and replaced by reference to "pictorial, graphic, and sculptural works," 17 U.S.C. § 102(a)(5). According to the House Report, the new category was intended to supply "as clear a line as possible between copyrightable works of applied art and uncopyrighted works of industrial design." H.R.Rep. No. 1476, at 55, U.S.Code Cong. & Admin.News 1976, p. 5668. The statutory definition of "pictorial, graphic, and sculptural works" states that "the design of a useful article, as defined in this section, shall be considered a pictorial, graphic, or sculptural work only if, and only to the extent that, such design incorporates pictorial, graphic, or sculptural features that can be identified separately from, and are capable of existing independently of, the utilitarian aspects of the article." 17 U.S.C. § 101.[2] The legislative history added gloss on the criteria of separate identity and independent existence in saying:

On the other hand, although the shape of an industrial product may be aesthetically satisfying and valuable, the Committee's intention is not to offer it copyright protection under the bill. Unless the shape of an automobile, airplane, ladies' dress, food processor, television set, or any other industrial product contains some element that, physically or conceptually, can be identified as separable from the utilitarian aspects of that article, the design would not be copyrighted under the bill. H.R.Rep. No. 1476, at 55, U.S.Code Cong. & Admin.News 1976, p. 5668.

As courts and commentators have come to realize, however, the line Congress attempted to draw between copyrightable art and noncopyrightable design "was neither clear nor new." Denicola, supra, 67 Minn.L.Rev. at 720. One aspect of the distinction that has drawn considerable attention is the reference in the House Report to "physically or conceptually" (emphasis added) separable elements. The District of Columbia Circuit in Esquire, Inc. v. Ringer, 591 F.2d 796, 803-04 (D.C.Cir.1978) (holding outdoor lighting fixtures ineligible for copyright), cert. denied, 440 U.S. 908, 99 S.Ct. 1217, 59 L.Ed.2d 456 (1979), called this an "isolated reference" and gave it no significance. Professor Nimmer, however, [1144] seemed to favor the observations of Judge Harold Leventhal in his concurrence in Esquire, who stated that "the overall legislative policy ... sustains the Copyright Office in its effort to distinguish between the instances where the aesthetic element is conceptually severable and the instances where the aesthetic element is inextricably interwoven with the utilitarian aspect of the article." 591 F.2d at 807; see 1 Nimmer on Copyright § 2.08[B] at 2-93 to 2-96.2 (1986). But see Gerber, Book Review, 26 U.C.L.A.L.Rev. 925, 938-43 (1979) (criticizing Professor Nimmer's view on conceptual separability). Looking to the section 101 definition of works of artistic craftsmanship requiring that artistic features be "capable of existing independently of the utilitarian aspects," Professor Nimmer queries whether that requires physical as distinguished from conceptual separability, but answers his query by saying "[t]here is reason to conclude that it does not." See 1 Nimmer on Copyright § 2.08[B] at 2-96.1. In any event, in Kieselstein-Cord v. Accessories by Pearl, Inc., 632 F.2d 989, 993 (2d Cir.1980), this court accepted the idea that copyrightability can adhere in the "conceptual" separation of an artistic element. Indeed, the court went on to find such conceptual separation in reference to ornate belt buckles that could be and were worn separately as jewelry. Kieselstein-Cord was followed in Norris Industries, Inc. v. International Telephone & Telegraph Corp., 696 F.2d 918, 923-24 (11th Cir.), cert. denied, 464 U.S. 818, 104 S.Ct. 78, 78 L.Ed.2d 89 (1983), although there the court upheld the Register's refusal to register automobile wire wheel covers, finding no "conceptually separable" work of art. See also Transworld Mfg. Corp. v. Al Nyman & Sons, Inc., 95 F.R.D. 95 (D.Del.1982) (finding conceptual separability sufficient to support copyright in denying summary judgment on copyrightability of eyeglass display cases).

In Carol Barnhart Inc. v. Economy Cover Corp., 773 F.2d 411 (2d Cir.1985), a divided panel of this circuit affirmed a district court grant of summary judgment of noncopyrightability of four life-sized, anatomically correct human torso forms. Carol Barnhart distinguished Kieselstein-Cord, but it surely did not overrule it. The distinction made was that the ornamented surfaces of the Kieselstein-Cord belt buckles "were not in any respect required by their utilitarian functions," but the features claimed to be aesthetic or artistic in the Carol Barnhart forms were "inextricably intertwined with the utilitarian feature, the display of clothes." 773 F.2d at 419. But cf. Animal Fair, Inc. v. Amfesco Indus., Inc., 620 F.Supp. 175, 186-88 (D.Minn.1985) (holding bear-paw design conceptually separable from the utilitarian features of a slipper), aff'd mem., 794 F.2d 678 (8th Cir.1986). As Judge Newman's dissent made clear, the Carol Barnhart majority did not dispute "that `conceptual separability' is distinct from `physical separability' and, when present, entitles the creator of a useful article to a copyright on its design." 773 F.2d at 420.

"Conceptual separability" is thus alive and well, at least in this circuit. The problem, however, is determining exactly what it is and how it is to be applied. Judge Newman's illuminating discussion in dissent in Carol Barnhart, see 773 F.2d at 419-24, proposed a test that aesthetic features are conceptually separable if "the article ... stimulate[s] in the mind of the beholder a concept that is separate from the concept evoked by its utilitarian function." Id. at 422. This approach has received favorable endorsement by at least one commentator, W. Patry, Latman's The Copyright Law 43-45 (6th ed. 1986), who calls Judge Newman's test the "temporal displacement" test. It is to be distinguished from other possible ways in which conceptual separability can be tested, including whether the primary use is as a utilitarian article as opposed to an artistic work, whether the aesthetic aspects of the work can be said to be "primary," and whether the article is marketable as art, none of which is very satisfactory. But Judge Newman's test was rejected outright by the majority as "a standard so ethereal as to amount to a `nontest' that would be extremely difficult, if not impossible, to administer or apply." 773 F.2d at 419 n. 5.

Perhaps the differences between the majority and the dissent in Carol Barnhart might have been resolved had they had before them the Denicola article on Applied Art and Industrial Design: A Suggested Approach to Copyright in Useful Articles, supra. There, Professor Denicola points out that although the Copyright Act of 1976 was an effort "to draw as clear a line as possible,'" in truth "there is no line, but merely a spectrum of forms and shapes responsive in varying degrees to utilitarian concerns." 67 Minn.L.Rev. at 741. Denicola argues that "the statutory directive requires a distinction between works of industrial design and works whose origins lie outside the design process, despite the utilitarian environment in which they appear." He views the statutory limitation of copyrightability as "an attempt to identify elements whose form and appearance reflect the unconstrained perspective of the artist," such features not being the product of industrial design. Id. at 742. "Copyrightability, therefore, should turn on the relationship between the proffered work and the process of industrial design." Id. at 741. He suggests that "the dominant characteristic of industrial design is the influence of nonaesthetic, utilitarian concerns" and hence concludes that copyrightability "ultimately should depend on the extent to which the work reflects artistic expression uninhibited by functional considerations." Id. To state the Denicola test in the language of conceptual separability, if design elements reflect a merger of aesthetic and functional considerations, the artistic aspects of a work cannot be said to be conceptually separable from the utilitarian elements. Conversely, where design elements can be identified as reflecting the designer's artistic judgment exercised independently of functional influences, conceptual separability exists.

We believe that Professor Denicola's approach provides the best test for conceptual separability and, accordingly, adopt it here for several reasons. First, the approach is consistent with the holdings of our previous cases. In Kieselstein-Cord, for example, the artistic aspects of the belt buckles reflected purely aesthetic choices, independent of the buckles' function, while in Carol Barnhart the distinctive features of the torsos — the accurate anatomical design and the sculpted shirts and collars — showed clearly the influence of functional concerns. Though the torsos bore artistic features, it was evident that the designer incorporated those features to further the usefulness of the torsos as mannequins. Second, the test's emphasis on the influence of utilitarian concerns in the design process may help, as Denicola notes, to "alleviate the de facto discrimination against nonrepresentational art that has regrettably accompanied much of the current analysis." Id. at 745.[4] Finally, and perhaps most importantly, we think Denicola's test will not be too difficult to administer in practice. The work itself will continue to give "mute testimony" of its origins. In addition, the parties will be required to present evidence relating to the design process and the nature of the work, with the trier of fact making the determination whether the aesthetic design elements are significantly influenced by functional considerations.

Turning now to the facts of this case, we note first that Brandir contends, and its chief owner David Levine testified, that the original design of the RIBBON Rack stemmed from wire sculptures that Levine had created, each formed from one continuous undulating piece of wire. These sculptures were, he said, created and displayed in his home as a means of personal expression, but apparently were never sold or displayed elsewhere. He also created a wire sculpture in the shape of a bicycle and states that he did not give any thought to the utilitarian application of any of his sculptures until he accidentally juxtaposed the bicycle sculpture with one of the self-standing wire sculptures. It was not until November 1978 that Levine seriously began pursuing the utilitarian application of his sculptures, when a friend, G. Duff Bailey, a bicycle buff and author of numerous articles about urban cycling, was at Levine's home and informed him that the sculptures would make excellent bicycle racks, permitting bicycles to be parked under the overloops as well as on top of the underloops. Following this meeting, Levine met several times with Bailey and others, completing the designs for the RIBBON Rack by the use of a vacuum cleaner hose, and submitting his drawings to a fabricator complete with dimensions. The Brandir RIBBON Rack began being nationally advertised and promoted for sale in September 1979.

In November 1982 Levine discovered that another company, Cascade Pacific Lumber Co., was selling a similar product. Thereafter, beginning in December 1982, a copyright notice was placed on all RIBBON Racks before shipment and on

December 10, 1982, five copyright applications for registration were submitted to the Copyright Office. The Copyright Office refused registration by letter, stating that the RIBBON Rack did not contain any element that was "capable of independent existence as a copyrightable pictorial, graphic or sculptural work apart from the shape of the useful article." An appeal to the Copyright Office was denied by letter dated March 23, 1983, refusing registration on the above ground and alternatively on the ground that the design lacked originality, consisting of "nothing more than a familiar public domain symbol." In February 1984, after the denial of the second appeal of the examiner's decision, Brandir sent letters to customers enclosing copyright notices to be placed on racks sold prior to December 1982.

Between September 1979 and August 1982 Brandir spent some $38,500 for advertising and promoting the RIBBON Rack, including some 85,000 pieces of promotional literature to architects and landscape architects. Additionally, since October 1982 Brandir has spent some $66,000, including full-, half-, and quarter-page advertisements in architectural magazines such as Landscape Architecture, Progressive Architecture, and Architectural Record, indeed winning an advertising award from Progressive Architecture in January 1983. The RIBBON Rack has been featured in Popular Science, Art and Architecture, and Design 384 magazines, and it won an Industrial Designers Society of America design award in the spring of 1980. In the spring of 1984 the RIBBON Rack was selected from 200 designs to be included among 77 of the designs exhibited at the Katonah Gallery in an exhibition entitled "The Product of Design: An Exploration of the Industrial Design Process," an exhibition that was written up in the New York Times.

Sales of the RIBBON Rack from September 1979 through January 1985 were in excess of $1,367,000. Prior to the time Cascade Pacific began offering for sale its bicycle rack in August 1982, Brandir's sales were $436,000. The price of the RIBBON Rack ranges from $395 up to $2,025 for a stainless steel model and generally depends on the size of the rack, one of the most popular being the RB-7, selling for $485.

Applying Professor Denicola's test to the RIBBON Rack, we find that the rack is not copyrightable. It seems clear that [1147] the form of the rack is influenced in significant measure by utilitarian concerns and thus any aesthetic elements cannot be said to be conceptually separable from the utilitarian elements. This is true even though the sculptures which inspired the RIBBON Rack may well have been — the issue of originality aside — copyrightable.

Brandir argues correctly that a copyrighted work of art does not lose its protected status merely because it subsequently is put to a functional use. The Supreme Court so held in Mazer v. Stein, 347 U.S. 201, 74 S.Ct. 460, 98 L.Ed. 630 (1954), and Congress specifically intended to accept and codify Mazer in section 101 of the Copyright Act of 1976. See H.R.Rep. No. 1476 at 54-55. The district court thus erred in ruling that, whatever the RIBBON Rack's origins, Brandir's commercialization of the rack disposed of the issue of its copyrightability.

Had Brandir merely adopted one of the existing sculptures as a bicycle rack, neither the application to a utilitarian end nor commercialization of that use would have caused the object to forfeit its copyrighted status. Comparison of the RIBBON Rack with the earlier sculptures, however, reveals that while the rack may have been derived in part from one or more "works of art," it is in its final form essentially a product of industrial design. In creating the RIBBON Rack, the designer has clearly adapted the original aesthetic elements to accommodate and further a utilitarian purpose. These altered design features of the RIBBON Rack, including the spacesaving, open design achieved by widening the upper loops to permit parking under as well as over the rack's curves, the straightened vertical elements that allow in- and above-ground installation of the rack, the ability to fit all types of bicycles and mopeds, and the heavy-gauged tubular construction of rustproof galvanized steel, are all features that combine to make for a safe, secure, and maintenance-free system of parking bicycles and mopeds. Its undulating shape is said in Progressive Architecture, January 1982, to permit double the storage of conventional bicycle racks. Moreover, the rack is manufactured from 2 3/8-inch standard steam pipe that is bent into form, the six-inch radius of the bends evidently resulting from bending the pipe according to a standard formula that yields bends having a radius equal to three times the nominal internal diameter of the pipe.

Brandir argues that its RIBBON Rack can and should be characterized as a sculptural work of art within the minimalist art movement. Minimalist sculpture's most outstanding feature is said to be its clarity and simplicity, in that it often takes the form of geometric shapes, lines, and forms that are pure and free of ornamentation and void of association. As Brandir's expert put it, "The meaning is to be found in, within, around and outside the work of art, allowing the artistic sensation to be experienced as well as intellectualized." People who use Foley Square in New York City see in the form of minimalist art the "Tilted Arc," which is on the plaza at 26 Federal Plaza. Numerous museums have had exhibitions of such art, and the school of minimalist art has many admirers.

It is unnecessary to determine whether to the art world the RIBBON Rack properly would be considered an example of minimalist sculpture. The result under the copyright statute is not changed. Using the test we have adopted, it is not enough that, to paraphrase Judge Newman, the rack may stimulate in the mind of the reasonable observer a concept separate from the bicycle rack concept. While the RIBBON Rack may be worthy of admiration for its aesthetic qualities alone, it remains nonetheless the product of industrial design. Form and function are inextricably intertwined in the rack, its ultimate design being as much the result of utilitarian pressures as aesthetic choices. Indeed, the visually pleasing proportions and symmetricality of the rack represent design changes made in response to functional concerns. Judging from the awards the rack has received, it would seem in fact that Brandir has achieved with the RIBBON Rack the highest goal of modern industrial design, that is, the harmonious fusion of function and aesthetics. Thus there remains no artistic element of the RIBBON [1148] Rack that can be identified as separate and "capable of existing independently, of, the utilitarian aspects of the article." Accordingly, we must affirm on the copyright claim.

...

Here, the district court limited its inquiry to determining whether portions of the RIBBON Rack performed the function of a bicycle rack. But the fact that a design feature performs a function does not make it essential to the performance of that function; it is instead the absence of alternative constructions performing the same function that renders the feature functional. Thus, the true test of functionality is not whether the feature in question performs a function, but whether the feature "is dictated by the functions to be performed," Warner Bros. Inc. v. Gay Toys, Inc., 724 F.2d 327, 331 (2d Cir.1983) (quoted in LeSportsac, Inc. v. K mart Corp., 754 F.2d at 76), as evidenced by available alternative constructions. See Metro Kane Imports, Ltd. v. Rowoco, Inc., 618 F.Supp. 273, 275-76 (S.D.N.Y.1985), aff'd mem., 800 F.2d 1128 (2d Cir.1986) (finding high-tech design of orange juice squeezer not dictated by function to be performed as there was no evidence that design permitted juicer to be manufactured at lower price or with altered performance). There are numerous alternative bicycle rack constructions. The nature, price, and utility of these constructions are material issues of fact not suitable for determination by summary judgment.[6] For example, while it is true that the materials used by Brandir are standard-size pipes, we have no way of knowing whether the particular size and weight of the pipes used is the best, the most economical, or the only available size and weight pipe in the marketplace. We would rather think the opposite might be the case. So, too, with the dimension of the bends being dictated by a standard formula corresponding to the pipe size; it could be that there are many standard radii and that the particular radius of Brandir's RIBBON Rack actually required new tooling. This issue of functionality on remand should be viewed in terms of bicycle racks generally and not one-piece undulating bicycle racks specifically. See id. at 330-32; see also In re DC Comics, Inc., 689 F.2d 1042, 1045 (C.C.P.A.1982) (dolls generally and not Superman dolls are the class by [1149] which functionality is determined). We reverse and remand as to the trademark and unfair competition claims.

137 S. Ct. 1002 (2017)

STAR ATHLETICA v. VARSITY BRANDS

United States Supreme Court

Justice Thomas:

Congress has provided copyright protection for original works of art, but not for industrial designs. The line between art and industrial design, however, is often difficult to draw. This is particularly true when an industrial design incorporates artistic elements. Congress has afforded limited protection for these artistic elements by providing that "pictorial, graphic, or sculptural features" of the "design of a useful article" are eligible for copyright protection as artistic works if those features "can be identified separately from, and are capable of existing independently of, the utilitarian aspects of the article." 17 U. S. C. §101.

We granted certiorari to resolve widespread disagreement over the proper test for implementing §101's separate-identification and independent-existence requirements. 578 U. S. ____ (2016). We hold that a feature incor-porated into the design of a useful article is eligible for copyright protection only if the feature (1) can be perceived as a two- or three-dimensional work of art separate from the useful article and (2) would qualify as a protectable pictorial, graphic, or sculptural work—either on its own or fixed in some other tangible medium of expression—if it were imagined separately from the useful article into which it is incorporated. Because that test is satisfied in this case, we affirm.

I

Respondents Varsity Brands, Inc., Varsity Spirit Corporation, and Varsity Spirit Fashions & Supplies, Inc., design, make, and sell cheerleading uniforms. Respondents have obtained or acquired more than 200 U. S. copyright registrations for two-dimensional designs appearing on the surface of their uniforms and other garments. These designs are primarily "combinations, positionings, and arrangements of elements" that include "chevrons . . . , lines, curves, stripes, angles, diagonals, inverted [chevrons], coloring, and shapes." App. 237. At issue in this case are Designs 299A, 299B, 074, 078, and 0815. See Appendix, infra.

Petitioner Star Athletica, L. L. C., also markets and sells cheerleading uniforms. Respondents sued petitioner for infringing their copyrights in the five designs. The District Court entered summary judgment for petitioner on respondents' copyright claims on the ground that the designs did not qualify as protectable pictorial, graphic, or sculptural works. It reasoned that the designs served the useful, or "utilitarian," function of identifying the garments as "cheerleading uniforms" and therefore could not be "physically or conceptually" separated under §101 "from the utilitarian function" of the uniform. 2014 WL 819422, *8–*9 (WD Tenn., Mar. 1, 2014).

The Court of Appeals for the Sixth Circuit reversed. 799 F. 3d 468, 471 (2015). In its view, the "graphic designs" were "separately identifiable" because the designs "and a blank cheerleading uniform can appear 'side by side'—one as a graphic design, and one as a cheerleading uniform." Id., at 491 (quoting Compendium of U. S. Copyright Office Practices §924.2(B) (3d ed. 2014) (Compendium)). And it determined that the designs were " 'capable of existing independently' " because they could be incorporated onto the surface of different types of garments, or hung on the wall and framed as art. 799 F. 3d, at 491, 492.

Judge McKeague dissented. He would have held that, because "identifying the wearer as a cheerleader" is a utilitarian function of a cheerleading uniform and the surface designs were "integral to" achieving that function, the designs were inseparable from the uniforms. Id., at 495–496.

II

The first element of a copyright-infringement claim is "ownership of a valid copyright." Feist Publications, Inc. v. Rural Telephone Service Co., 499 U. S. 340, 361 (1991). A valid copyright extends only to copyrightable subject matter. See 4

M. Nimmer & D. Nimmer, Copyright §13.01[A] (2010) (Nimmer). The Copyright Act of 1976 defines copyrightable subject matter as "original works of authorship fixed in any tangible medium of expression." 17 U. S. C. §102(a).

"Works of authorship" include "pictorial, graphic, and sculptural works," §102(a)(5), which the statute defines to include "two-dimensional and three-dimensional works of fine, graphic, and applied art, photographs, prints and art reproductions, maps, globes, charts, diagrams, models, and technical drawings, including architectural plans," §101. And a work of authorship is " 'fixed' in a tangible medium of expression when it[is] embodi[ed] in a" "material objec[t] . . . from which the work can be perceived, reproduced, or otherwise communicated." Ibid. (definitions of "fixed" and "copies").

The Copyright Act also establishes a special rule for copyrighting a pictorial, graphic, or sculptural work incorporated into a "useful article," which is defined as "an article having an intrinsic utilitarian function that is not merely to portray the appearance of the article or to convey information." Ibid. The statute does not protect useful articles as such. Rather, "the design of a useful article" is "considered a pictorial, graphical, or sculptural work only if, and only to the extent that, such design incorporates pictorial, graphic, or sculptural features that can be identified separately from, and are capable of existing independently of, the utilitarian aspects of the article." Ibid.

Courts, the Copyright Office, and commentators have described the analysis undertaken to determine whether a feature can be separately identified from, and exist independently of, a useful article as "separability." In this case, our task is to determine whether the arrangements of lines, chevrons, and colorful shapes appearing on the surface of respondents' cheerleading uniforms are eligible for copyright protection as separable features of the design of those cheerleading uniforms.

A

As an initial matter, we must address whether separability analysis is necessary in this case.

Respondents argue that "[s]eparability is only implicated when a [pictorial, graphic, or sculptural] work is the 'design of a useful article.' " Brief for Respondents 25. They contend that the surface decorations in this case are "two-dimensional graphic designs that appear on useful articles," but are not themselves designs of useful articles. Id., at 52. Consequently, the surface decorations are protected two-dimensional works of graphic art without regard to any separability analysis under §101. Ibid.; see 2 W. Patry, Copyright §3:151, p. 3–485 (2016) (Patry) ("Courts looking at two-dimensional design claims should not apply the separability analysis regardless of the three-dimensional form that design is embodied in"). Under this theory, two-dimensional artistic features on the surface of useful articles are "inherently separable." Brief for Respondents 26.

This argument is inconsistent with the text of §101. The statute requires separability analysis for any "pictorial, graphic, or sculptural features" incorporated into the "design of a useful article." "Design" refers here to "the combination" of "details" or "features" that "go to make up" the useful article. 3 Oxford English Dictionary 244 (def. 7, first listing) (1933) (OED). Furthermore, the words "pictorial" and "graphic" include, in this context, two-dimensional features such as pictures, paintings, or drawings. See 4 id., at 359 (defining "[g]raphic" to mean "[o]f or pertaining to drawing or painting"); 7 id., at 830 (defining "[p]ictorial" to mean "of or pertaining to painting or drawing"). And the statute expressly defines "[p]ictorial, graphical, and sculptural works" to include "two-dimensional . . . works of . . . art." §101. The statute thus provides that the "design of a useful article" can include two-dimensional "pictorial" and "graphic" features, and separability analysis applies to those features just as it does to three-dimensional "sculptural" features.

The United States makes a related but distinct argument against applying separability analysis in this case, which respondents do not and have not advanced. As part of their copyright registrations for the designs in this case, respondents deposited with the Copyright Office drawings and photographs depicting the designs incorporated onto cheerleading uniforms. App. 213–219; Appendix, infra. The Government argues that, assuming the other statutory requirements were met, respondents obtained a copyright in the deposited drawings and photographs and have simply reproduced those copyrighted works on the surface of a useful article, as they would have the exclusive right to do under the Copyright Act. See Brief for United States as Amicus Curiae 14–15, 17–22. Accordingly, the Government urges, separability analysis is unnecessary on the record in this case. We generally do not entertain arguments that were not raised below and that are not advanced in this Court by any party, Burwell v. Hobby Lobby Stores, Inc., 573 U. S. ___, ___ (2014), because "[i]t is not the Court's usual practice to adjudicate either legal or predicate factual questions in the first instance," CRST Van Expedited, Inc. v. EEOC, 578 U. S. ___, ___ (2016) (slip op., at 16). We decline to depart from our usual practice here.

B

We must now decide when a feature incorporated into a useful article "can be identified separately from" and is "capable of existing independently of" "the utilitarian aspects" of the article. This is not a free-ranging search for the best copyright policy, but rather "depends solely on statutory interpretation." Mazer v. Stein, 347 U. S. 201, 214 (1954). "The controlling principle in this case is the basic and unexceptional rule that courts must give effect to the clear meaning of statutes as written." Estate of Cowart v. Nicklos Drilling Co., 505 U. S. 469, 476 (1992). We thus begin and end our inquiry with the text, giving each word its "ordinary, contemporary, common meaning." Walters v. Metropolitan Ed. Enterprises, Inc., 519 U. S. 202, 207 (1997) (internal quotation marks omitted). We do not, however, limit this inquiry to the text of §101 in isolation. "[I]nterpretation of a phrase of uncertain reach is not confined to a single sentence when the text of the whole statute gives instruction as to its meaning." Maracich v. Spears, 570 U. S. ___, ___ (2013) (slip op., at 15). We thus "look to the provisions of the whole law" to determine §101's meaning. United States v. Heirs of Boisdoré, 8 How. 113, 122 (1849).

The statute provides that a "pictorial, graphic, or sculptural featur[e]" incorporated into the "design of a useful article" is eligible for copyright protection if it (1) "can be identified separately from," and (2) is "capable of existing independently of, the utilitarian aspects of the article." §101. The first requirement—separate identification—is not onerous. The decisionmaker need only be able to look at the useful article and spot some two- or three-dimensional element that appears to have pictorial, graphic, or sculptural qualities. See 2 Patry §3:146, at 3–474 to3–475.

The independent-existence requirement is ordinarily more difficult to satisfy. The decisionmaker must determine that the separately identified feature has the capacity to exist apart from the utilitarian aspects of the article. See 2 OED 88 (def. 5) (defining "[c]apable" of as "[h]aving the needful capacity, power, or fitness for"). In other words, the feature must be able to exist as its own pictorial, graphic, or sculptural work as defined in §101 once it is imagined apart from the useful article. If the feature is not capable of existing as a pictorial, graphic, or sculptural work once separated from the useful article, then it was not a pictorial, graphic, or sculptural feature of that article, but rather one of its utilitarian aspects.

Of course, to qualify as a pictorial, graphic, or sculptural work on its own, the feature cannot itself be a useful article or "[a]n article that is normally a part of a useful article" (which is itself considered a useful article). §101. Nor could someone claim a copyright in a useful article merely by creating a replica of that article in some other medium—for example, a cardboard model of a car. Al-though the replica could itself be copyrightable, it would not give rise to any rights in the useful article that inspired it.

The statute as a whole confirms our interpretation. The Copyright Act provides "the owner of [a] copyright" with the "exclusive righ[t] ... to reproduce the copyrighted work in copies." §106(1). The statute clarifies that this right "includes the right to reproduce the [copyrighted] work in or on any kind of article, whether useful or otherwise." §113(a). Section 101 is, in essence, the mirror image of §113(a). Whereas §113(a) protects a work of authorship first fixed in some tangible medium other than a useful article and subsequently applied to a useful article, §101 protects art first fixed in the medium of a useful article. The two provisions make clear that copyright protection extends to pictorial, graphic, and sculptural works regardless of whether they were created as freestanding art or as features of useful articles. The ultimate separability question, then, is whether the feature for which copyright protection is claimed would have been eligible for copyright protection as a pictorial, graphic, or sculptural work had it originally been fixed in some tangible medium other than a useful article before being applied to a useful article.

This interpretation is also consistent with the history of the Copyright Act. In Mazer, a case decided under the 1909 Copyright Act, the respondents copyrighted a statuette depicting a dancer. The statuette was intended for use as a lamp base, "with electric wiring, sockets and lamp shades attached." 347 U. S., at 202. Copies of the statuette were sold both as lamp bases and separately as statuettes. Id., at 203. The petitioners copied the statuette and sold lamps with the statuette as the base. They defended against the respondents' infringement suit by arguing that the respondents did not have a copyright in a statuette intended for use as a lamp base. Id., at 204–205.

Two of Mazer's holdings are relevant here. First, the Court held that the respondents owned a copyright in the statuette even though it was intended for use as a lamp base. See id., at 214. In doing so, the Court approved the Copyright Office's regulation extending copyright protection to works of art that might also serve a useful purpose. See ibid. (approving 37 CFR §202.8(a) (1949) (protect-ing "works of artistic craftsmanship, in so far as theirform but not their mechanical or utilitarian aspects are concerned")).

Second, the Court held that it was irrelevant to the copyright inquiry whether the statuette was initially created as a freestanding sculpture or as a lamp base. 347 U. S., at 218–219 ("Nor do we think the subsequent registration of a work of art published as an element in a manufactured article, is a misuse of copyright. This is not different from the registration of a statuette and its later embodiment in an industrial article"). Mazer thus interpreted the 1909 Act consistently with the rule discussed above: If a design would have been copyrightable as a standalone pictorial, graphic, or sculptural work, it is copyrightable if created first as part of a useful article.

Shortly thereafter, the Copyright Office enacted a regulation implementing the holdings of Mazer. See 1 Nimmer §2A.08[B][1][b] (2016). As amended, the regulation introduced the modern separability test to copyright law:

"If the sole intrinsic function of an article is its utility, the fact that the article is unique and attractively shaped will not qualify it as a work of art. However, if the shape of a utilitarian article incorporates features, such as artistic sculpture, carving, or pictorial representation, which can be identified separately and are capable of existing independently as a work of art, such features will be eligible for registration." 37 CFR §202.10(c) (1960) (punctuation altered).

Congress essentially lifted the language governing protection for the design of a useful article directly from the post-Mazer regulations and placed it into §101 of the 1976 Act. Consistent with Mazer, the approach we outline today interprets §§101 and 113 in a way that would afford copyright protection to the statuette in Mazer regardless of whether it was first created as a standalone sculptural work or as the base of the lamp. See 347 U. S., at 218–219.

C

In sum, a feature of the design of a useful article is eligible for copyright if, when identified and imagined apart from the useful article, it would qualify as a pictorial, graphic, or sculptural work either on its own or when fixed in some other tangible medium.

Applying this test to the surface decorations on the cheerleading uniforms is straightforward. First, one can identify the decorations as features having pictorial, graphic, or sculptural qualities. Second, if the arrangement of colors, shapes, stripes, and chevrons on the surface of the cheerleading uniforms were separated from the uniform and applied in another medium—for example, on a painter's canvas—they would qualify as "two-dimensional . . . works of . . . art," §101. And imaginatively removing the surface decorations from the uniforms and applying them in another medium would not replicate the uniform itself. Indeed, respondents have applied the designs in this case to other media of expression— different types of clothing—without replicating the uniform. See App. 273–279. The decorations are therefore separable from the uniforms and eligible for copyright protection. 1

The dissent argues that the designs are not separable because imaginatively removing them from the uniforms and placing them in some other medium of expression—a canvas, for example—would create "pictures of cheerleader uniforms." Post, at 10 (opinion of Breyer, J.). Petitioner similarly argues that the decorations cannot be copyrighted because, even when extracted from the useful article,they retain the outline of a cheerleading uniform. Brief for Petitioner 48–49.

This is not a bar to copyright. Just as two-dimensional fine art corresponds to the shape of the canvas on which it is painted, two-dimensional applied art correlates to the contours of the article on which it is applied. A fresco painted on a wall, ceiling panel, or dome would not lose copyright protection, for example, simply because it was designed to track the dimensions of the surface on which it was painted. Or consider, for example, a design etched or painted on the surface of a guitar. If that entire design is imaginatively removed from the guitar's surface and placed on an album cover, it would still resemble the shape of a guitar. But the image on the cover does not "replicate" the guitar as a useful article. Rather, the design is a two-dimensional work of art that corresponds to the shape of the useful article to which it was applied. The statute protects that work of art whether it is first drawn on the album cover and then applied to the guitar's surface, or vice versa. Failing to protect that art would create an anomaly: It would extend protection to two-dimensional designs that cover a part of a useful article but would not protect the same design if it covered the entire article. The statute does not support that distinction, nor can it be reconciled with the dissent's recognition that "artwork printed on a t-shirt" could be protected. Post, at 4 (internal quotation marks omitted).

To be clear, the only feature of the cheerleading uniform eligible for a copyright in this case is the two-dimensional work of art fixed in the tangible medium of the uniform fabric. Even if respondents ultimately succeed in establishing a valid copyright in the surface decorations at issue here, respondents have no right to prohibit any person from manufacturing a cheerleading uniform of identical shape, cut, and dimensions to the ones on which the decorations in this case appear. They may prohibit only the reproduction of the surface designs in any tangible medium of expression—a uniform or otherwise. 2

D

Petitioner and the Government raise several objections to the approach we announce today. None is meritorious.

Petitioner first argues that our reading of the statute is missing an important step. It contends that a feature may exist independently only if it can stand alone as a copyrightable work and if the useful article from which it was extracted would remain equally useful. In other words, copyright extends only to "solely artistic" features of useful articles. Brief for Petitioner 33. According to petitioner, if a feature of a useful article "advance[s] the utility of the article," id., at 38, then it is categorically beyond the scope of copyright, id., at 33. The designs here are not protected, it argues, because they are necessary to two of the uniforms' "inherent, essential, or natural functions"—identifying the wearer as a cheerleader and enhancing the wearer's physical appearance. Id., at 38, 48; Reply Brief 2, 16. Because the uniforms would not be equally useful without the designs, petitioner contends that the designs are inseparable from the "utilitarian aspects" of the uniform. Brief for Petitioner 50.

The Government raises a similar argument, although it reaches a different result. It suggests that the appropriate test is whether the useful article with the artistic feature removed would "remai[n] similarly useful." Brief for United States as Amicus Curiae 29 (emphasis added). In the view of the United States, however, a plain white cheerleading uniform is "similarly useful" to uniforms with respondents' designs. Id., at 27–28.

The debate over the relative utility of a plain white cheerleading uniform is unnecessary. The focus of the separability inquiry is on the extracted feature and not on any aspects of the useful article that remain after the imaginary extraction. The statute does not require the decisionmaker to imagine a fully functioning useful article without the artistic feature. Instead, it requires that the separated feature qualify as a nonuseful pictorial, graphic, or sculptural work on its own.

Of course, because the removed feature may not be a useful article—as it would then not qualify as a pictorial, graphic, or sculptural work—there necessarily would be some aspects of the original useful article "left behind" if the feature were conceptually removed. But the statute does not require the imagined remainder to be a fully functioning useful article at all, much less an equally useful one. Indeed, such a requirement would deprive the Mazer statuette of protection had it been created first as a lamp base rather than as a statuette. Without the base, the "lamp" would be just a shade, bulb, and wires. The statute does not require that we imagine a nonartistic replacement for the removed feature to determine whether that feature is capable of an independent existence.

Petitioner's argument follows from its flawed view that the statute protects only "solely artistic" features that have no effect whatsoever on a useful article's utilitarian function. This view is inconsistent with the statutory text. The statute expressly protects two- and three-dimensional "applied art." §101. "Applied art" is art "employed in the decoration, design, or execution of useful objects," Webster's Third New International Dictionary 105 (1976) (emphasis added), or "those arts or crafts that have a primarily utilitarian function, or . . . the designs and decorations used in these arts," Random House Dictionary 73 (1966) (emphasis added); see also 1 OED 576 (2d ed. 1989) (defining "applied" as "[p]ut to practical use"). An artistic feature that would be eligible for copyright protection on its own cannot lose that protection simply because it was first created as a feature of the design of a useful article, even if it makes that article more useful.

Indeed, this has been the rule since Mazer. In holding that the statuette was protected, the Court emphasized that the 1909 Act abandoned any "distinctions between purely aesthetic articles and useful works of art." 347 U. S., at 211. Congress did not enact such a distinction in the 1976 Act. Were we to accept petitioner's argument that the only protectable features are those that play absolutely no role in an article's function, we would effectively abrogate the rule of Mazer and read "applied art" out of the statute.

Because we reject the view that a useful article must remain after the artistic feature has been imaginatively separated from the article, we necessarily abandon the distinction between "physical" and "conceptual" separability, which some courts and commentators have adopted based on the Copyright Act's legislative history. See H. R. Rep. No. 94–1476, p. 55 (1976). According to this view, a feature is physically separable from the underlying useful article if it can "be physically separated from the article by ordinary means while leaving the utilitarian aspects of the article completely intact." Compendium §924.2(A); see also Chosun Int'l, Inc. v. Chrisha Creations, Ltd., 413 F. 3d 324, 329 (CA2 2005). Conceptual separability applies if the feature physically could not be removed from the useful article by ordinary means. See Compendium §924.2(B); but see 1 P. Goldstein, Copyright §2.5.3, p. 2:77 (3d ed. 2016) (explaining that the lower courts have been unable to agree on a single conceptual separability test); 2 Patry §§3:140–3:144.40 (surveying the various approaches in the lower courts).

The statutory text indicates that separability is a conceptual undertaking. Because separability does not require the underlying useful article to remain, the physical-conceptual distinction is unnecessary.

Petitioner next argues that we should incorporate two "objective" components, Reply Brief 9, into our test to provide guidance to the lower courts: (1) "whether the design elements can be identified as reflecting the designer's artistic judgment exercised independently of functional influence," Brief for Petitioner 34 (emphasis deleted and internal quotation marks omitted), and (2) whether "there is [a] substantial likelihood that the pictorial, graphic, or sculptural feature would still be marketable to some significant segment of the community without its utilitarian function," id., at 35 (emphasis deleted and internal quotation marks omitted).

We reject this argument because neither consideration is grounded in the text of the statute. The first would require the decisionmaker to consider evidence of the creator's design methods, purposes, and reasons. Id., at 48. The statute's text makes clear, however, that our inquiry is limited to how the article and feature are perceived, not how or why they were designed. See Brandir Int'l, Inc. v. Cascade Pacific Lumber Co., 834 F. 2d 1142, 1152 (CA2 1987) (Winter, J., concurring in part and dissenting in part) (The statute "expressly states that the legal test is how the final article is perceived, not how it was developed through various stages").

The same is true of marketability. Nothing in the statute suggests that copyrightability depends on market surveys. Moreover, asking whether some segment of the market would be interested in a given work threatens to prize popular art over other forms, or to substitute judicial aesthetic preferences for the policy choices embodied in the Copyright Act. See Bleistein v. Donaldson

Lithographing Co., 188 U. S. 239, 251 (1903) ("It would be a dangerous undertaking for persons trained only to the law to constitute themselves final judges of the worth of pictorial illustrations, outside of the narrowest and most obvious limits").

Finally, petitioner argues that allowing the surface decorations to qualify as a "work of authorship" is inconsistent with Congress' intent to entirely exclude industrial design from copyright. Petitioner notes that Congress refused to pass a provision that would have provided limited copyright protection for industrial designs, including clothing, when it enacted the 1976 Act, see id., at 9–11 (citing S. 22, Tit. II, 94th Cong., 2d Sess., 122 Cong. Rec. 3856–3859 (1976)), and that it has enacted laws protecting designs for specific useful articles—semiconductor chips and boat hulls, see 17 U. S. C. §§901–914, 1301–1332—while declining to enact other industrial design statutes, Brief for Petitioner 29, 43. From this history of failed legislation petitioner reasons that Congress intends to channel intellectual property claims for industrial design into design patents. It therefore urges us to approach this question with a presumption against copyrightability. Id., at 27.

We do not share petitioner's concern. As an initial matter, "[c]ongressional inaction lacks persuasive significance" in most circumstances. Pension Benefit Guaranty Corporation v. LTV Corp., 496 U. S. 633, 650 (1990) (internal quotation marks omitted). Moreover, we have long held that design patent and copyright are not mutually exclusive. See Mazer, 347 U. S., at 217. Congress has provided for limited copyright protection for certain features of industrial design, and approaching the statute with presumptive hostility toward protection for industrial design would undermine Congress' choice. In any event, as explained above, our test does not render the shape, cut, and physical dimensions of the cheerleading uniforms eligible for copyright protection.

III

We hold that an artistic feature of the design of a useful article is eligible for copyright protection if the feature (1) can be perceived as a two- or three-dimensional work of art separate from the useful article and (2) would qualify as a protectable pictorial, graphic, or sculptural work either on its own or in some other medium if imagined separately from the useful article. Because the designs on the surface of respondents' cheerleading uniforms in this case satisfy these requirements, the judgment of the Court of Appeals is affirmed.

It is so ordered.

3.D. First Sale Doctrine

86 F.3d 1447 (1996)

ProCD v. ZEIDENBERG

United States Court of Appeals, Seventh Circuit

EASTERBROOK, Circuit Judge.

Must buyers of computer software obey the terms of shrinkwrap licenses? The district court held not, for two reasons: first, they are not contracts because the licenses are inside the box rather than printed on the outside; second, federal law forbids enforcement even if the licenses are contracts. 908 F.Supp. 640 (W.D.Wis.1996). The parties and numerous amici curiae have briefed many other issues, but these are the only two that matter — and we disagree with the district judge's conclusion on each. Shrinkwrap licenses are enforceable unless their terms are objectionable on grounds applicable to contracts in general (for example, if they violate a rule of positive law, or if they are unconscionable). Because no one argues that the terms of the license at issue here are troublesome, we remand with instructions to enter judgment for the plaintiff.

I

ProCD, the plaintiff, has compiled information from more than 3,000 telephone directories into a computer database. We may assume that this database cannot be copyrighted, although it is more complex, contains more information (nine-digit zip codes and census industrial codes), is organized differently, and therefore is more original than the single alphabetical directory at issue in Feist Publications, Inc. v. Rural Telephone Service Co., 499 U.S. 340, 111 S.Ct. 1282, 113 L.Ed.2d 358 (1991). See Paul J. Heald, The Vices of Originality, 1991 Sup.Ct. Rev. 143, 160-68. ProCD sells a version of the database, called SelectPhone (trademark), on CD-ROM discs. (CD-ROM means "compact disc — read only memory." The "shrinkwrap license" gets its name from the fact that retail software packages are covered in plastic or cellophane "shrinkwrap," and some vendors, though not ProCD, have written licenses that become effective as soon as the customer tears the wrapping from the package. Vendors prefer "end user license," but we use the more common term.) A proprietary method of compressing the data serves as effective encryption too. Customers decrypt and use the data with the aid of an application program that ProCD has written. This program, which is copyrighted, searches the database in response to users' criteria (such as "find all people named Tatum in Tennessee, plus all firms with `Door Systems' in the corporate name"). The resulting lists (or, as ProCD prefers, "listings") can be read and manipulated by other software, such as word processing programs.

The database in SelectPhone (trademark) cost more than $10 million to compile and is expensive to keep current. It is much more valuable to some users than to others. The combination of names, addresses, and SIC codes enables manufacturers to compile lists of potential customers. Manufacturers and retailers pay high prices to specialized information intermediaries for such mailing lists; ProCD offers a potentially cheaper alternative. People with nothing to sell could use the database as a substitute for calling long distance information, or as a way to look up old friends who have moved to unknown towns, or just as an electronic substitute for the local phone book. ProCD decided to engage in price discrimination, selling its database to the general public for personal use at a low price (approximately $150 for the set of five discs) while selling information to the trade for a higher price. It has adopted some intermediate strategies too: access to the SelectPhone (trademark) database is available via the America Online service for the price America Online charges to its clients (approximately $3 per hour), but this service has been tailored to be useful only to the general public.

If ProCD had to recover all of its costs and make a profit by charging a single price — that is, if it could not charge more to commercial users than to the general public —it would have to raise the price substantially over $150. The ensuing reduction in sales would harm consumers who value the information at, say, $200. They get consumer surplus of $50 under the current arrangement but would cease to buy if the price rose substantially. If because of high elasticity of demand in the consumer segment of the market the only way to make a profit turned out to be a price attractive to commercial users alone, then all consumers would lose out — and so would the commercial clients, who would have to pay more for the listings because ProCD could not obtain any contribution toward costs from the consumer market.

To make price discrimination work, however, the seller must be able to control arbitrage. An air carrier sells tickets for less to vacationers than to business travelers, using advance purchase and Saturday-night-stay requirements to distinguish the categories. A producer of movies segments the market by time, releasing first to theaters, then to pay-per-view services, next to the videotape and laserdisc market, and finally to cable and commercial tv. Vendors of computer software have a harder task. Anyone can walk into a retail store and buy a box. Customers do not wear tags saying "commercial user" or "consumer user." Anyway, even a commercial-user-detector at the door would not work, because a consumer could buy the software and resell to a commercial user. That arbitrage would break down the price discrimination and drive up the minimum price at which ProCD would sell to anyone.

Instead of tinkering with the product and letting users sort themselves — for example, furnishing current data at a high price that would be attractive only to commercial customers, and two-year-old data at a low price — ProCD turned to the institution of contract. Every box containing its consumer product declares that the software comes with restrictions stated in an enclosed license. This license, which is encoded on the CD-ROM disks as well as printed in the manual, and which appears on a user's screen every time the software runs, limits use of the application program and listings to non-commercial purposes.

Matthew Zeidenberg bought a consumer package of SelectPhone (trademark) in 1994 from a retail outlet in Madison, Wisconsin, but decided to ignore the license.

He formed Silken Mountain Web Services, Inc., to resell the information in the SelectPhone (trademark) database. The corporation makes the database available on the Internet to anyone willing to pay its price — which, needless to say, is less than ProCD charges its commercial customers. Zeidenberg has purchased two additional SelectPhone (trademark) packages, each with an updated version of the database, and made the latest information available over the World Wide Web, for a price, through his corporation. ProCD filed this suit seeking an injunction against further dissemination that exceeds the rights specified in the licenses (identical in each of the three packages Zeidenberg purchased). The district court held the licenses ineffectual because their terms do not appear on the outside of the packages. The court added that the second and third licenses stand no different from the first, even though they are identical, because they might have been different, and a purchaser does not agree to — and cannot be bound by — terms that were secret at the time of purchase. 908 F.Supp. at 654.

II

Following the district court, we treat the licenses as ordinary contracts accompanying the sale of products, and therefore as governed by the common law of contracts and the Uniform Commercial Code.... Notice on the outside, terms on the inside, and a right to return the software for a refund if the terms are unacceptable (a right that the license expressly extends), may be a means of doing business valuable to buyers and sellers alike. See E. Allan Farnsworth, 1 Farnsworth on Contracts § 4.26 (1990); ....

Transactions in which the exchange of money precedes the communication of detailed terms are common. Consider the purchase of insurance. The buyer goes to an agent, who explains the essentials (amount of coverage, number of years) and remits the premium to the home office, which sends back a policy. On the district judge's understanding, the terms of the policy are irrelevant because the insured paid before receiving them. Yet the device of payment, often with a "binder" (so that the insurance takes effect immediately even though the home office reserves the right to withdraw coverage later), in advance of the policy, serves buyers' interests by accelerating effectiveness and reducing transactions costs. Or consider the purchase of an airline ticket. The traveler calls the carrier or an agent, is quoted a price, reserves a seat, pays, and gets a ticket, in that order. The ticket contains elaborate terms, which the traveler can reject by canceling the reservation. To use the ticket is to accept the terms, even terms that in retrospect are disadvantageous. See Carnival Cruise Lines, Inc. v. Shute, 499 U.S. 585, 111 S.Ct. 1522, 113 L.Ed.2d 622 (1991); see also Vimar Seguros y Reaseguros, S.A. v. M/V Sky Reefer, ___ U.S. ___, 115 S.Ct. 2322, 132 L.Ed.2d 462 (1995) (bills of lading). Just so with a ticket to a concert. The back of the ticket states that the patron promises not to record the concert; to attend is to agree. A theater that detects a violation will confiscate the tape and escort the violator to the exit. One could arrange things so that every concertgoer signs this promise before forking over the money, but that cumbersome way of doing things not only would lengthen queues and raise prices but also would scotch the sale of tickets by phone or electronic data service.

...

What then does the current version of the UCC have to say? We think that the place to start is § 2-204(1): "A contract for sale of goods may be made in any manner sufficient to show agreement, including conduct by both parties which recognizes the existence of such a contract." A vendor, as master of the offer, may invite acceptance by conduct, and may propose limitations on the kind of conduct that constitutes acceptance. A buyer may accept by performing the acts the vendor proposes to treat as acceptance. And that is what happened. ProCD proposed a contract that a buyer would accept by using the software after having an opportunity to read the license at leisure. This Zeidenberg did. He had no choice, because the software splashed the license on the screen and would not let him proceed without indicating acceptance. So although the district judge was right to say that a contract can be, and often is, formed simply by paying the price and walking out of the store, the UCC permits contracts to be formed in other ways. ProCD proposed such a different way, and without protest Zeidenberg agreed. Ours is not a case in which a consumer opens a package to find an insert saying "you owe us an extra $10,000" and the seller files suit to collect. Any buyer finding such a demand can prevent formation of the contract by returning the package, as can any consumer who concludes that the terms of the license make the software worth less than the purchase price. Nothing in the UCC requires a seller to maximize the buyer's net gains.... Competition among vendors, not judicial revision of a package's contents, is how consumers are protected in a market economy. Digital Equipment Corp. v. Uniq Digital Technologies, Inc., 73 F.3d 756 (7th Cir.1996). ProCD has rivals, which may elect to compete by offering superior software, monthly updates, improved terms of use, lower price, or a better compromise among these elements. As we stressed above, adjusting terms in buyers' favor might help Matthew Zeidenberg today (he already has the software) but would lead to a response, such as a higher price, that might make consumers as a whole worse off.

III

The district court held that, even if Wisconsin treats shrinkwrap licenses as contracts, § 301(a) of the Copyright Act, 17 U.S.C. § 301(a), prevents their enforcement. 908 F.Supp. at 656-59. The relevant part of § 301(a) preempts any "legal or equitable rights [under state law] that are equivalent to any of the exclusive rights within the general scope of copyright as specified by section 106 in works of authorship that are fixed in a tangible medium of expression and come within the subject matter of copyright as specified by sections 102 and 103". ProCD's software and data are "fixed in a tangible medium of expression", and the district judge held that they are "within the subject matter of copyright". The latter conclusion is plainly right for the copyrighted application program, and the judge thought that the data likewise are "within the subject matter of copyright" even if, after Feist, they are not sufficiently original to be copyrighted. 908 F.Supp. at 656-57. Baltimore Orioles, Inc. v. Major League Baseball Players Ass'n, 805 F.2d 663, 676 (7th Cir.1986), supports that conclusion, with which commentators agree. E.g., Paul Goldstein, III Copyright § 15.2.3 (2d ed.1996); Melville B. Nimmer & David Nimmer, Nimmer on Copyright § 101[B] (1995); William F. Patry, II Copyright Law and Practice 1108-09 (1994). One function of § 301(a) is to prevent states from giving special protection to works of authorship that Congress has decided should be in the public domain, which it can accomplish only if "subject matter of copyright" includes all works of a type covered by sections 102 and 103, even if federal law does not afford protection to them. Cf. Bonito Boats, Inc. v. Thunder Craft Boats, Inc., 489 U.S. 141, 109 S.Ct. 971, 103 L.Ed.2d 118 (1989) (same principle under patent laws).

But are rights created by contract "equivalent to any of the exclusive rights within the general scope of copyright"? Three courts of appeals have answered "no." National Car Rental System, Inc. v. Computer Associates International, Inc., 991 F.2d 426, 433 (8th Cir.1993); Taquino v. Teledyne Monarch Rubber, 893 F.2d 1488, 1501 (5th Cir.1990); Acorn Structures, Inc. v. Swantz, 846 F.2d 923, 926 (4th Cir.1988). The district court disagreed with these decisions, 908 F.Supp. at 658, but we think them sound. Rights "equivalent to any of the exclusive rights within the general scope of copyright" are rights established by law — rights that restrict the options of persons who are strangers to the author. Copyright law forbids duplication, public performance, and so on, unless the person wishing to copy or perform the work gets permission; silence means a ban on copying. A copyright is a right against the world. Contracts, by contrast, generally affect only their parties; strangers may do as they please, so contracts do not create "exclusive rights." Someone who found a copy of SelectPhone (trademark) on the street would not be affected by the shrinkwrap license — though the federal copyright laws of their own force would limit the finder's ability to copy or transmit the application program.

...

A law student uses the LEXIS database, containing public-domain documents, under a contract limiting the results to educational endeavors; may the student resell his access to this database to a law firm from which LEXIS seeks to collect a much higher hourly rate? Suppose ProCD hires a firm to scour the nation for telephone directories, promising to pay $100 for each that ProCD does not already have. The firm locates 100 new directories, which it sends to ProCD with an invoice for $10,000. ProCD incorporates the directories into its database; does it have to pay the bill? Surely yes; Aronson v. Quick Point Pencil Co., 440 U.S. 257, 99 S.Ct. 1096, 59 L.Ed.2d 296 (1979), holds that promises to pay for intellectual property may be enforced even though federal law (in Aronson, the patent law) offers no protection against third-party uses of that property. See also Kennedy v. Wright, 851 F.2d 963 (7th Cir. 1988). But these illustrations are what our case is about. ProCD offers software and data for two prices: one for personal use, a higher price for commercial use. Zeidenberg wants to use the data without paying the seller's price; if the law student and Quick Point Pencil Co. could not do that, neither can Zeidenberg.

Although Congress possesses power to preempt even the enforcement of contracts about intellectual property — or railroads, on which see Norfolk & Western Ry. v. Train Dispatchers, 499 U.S. 117, 111 S.Ct. 1156, 113 L.Ed.2d 95 (1991) — courts usually read preemption clauses to leave private contracts unaffected. American Airlines, Inc. v. Wolens, ____ U.S. ___, 115 S.Ct. 817, 130 L.Ed.2d 715 (1995), provides a nice illustration. A federal statute preempts any state "law, rule, regulation, standard, or other provision ... relating to rates, routes, or services of any air carrier." 49 U.S.C.App. § 1305(a)(1). Does such a law preempt the law of contracts — so that, for example, an air carrier need not honor a quoted price (or a contract to reduce the price by the value of frequent flyer miles)? The Court allowed that it is possible to read the statute that [1455] broadly but thought such an interpretation would make little sense. Terms and conditions offered by contract reflect private ordering, essential to the efficient functioning of markets. ____ U.S. at ____-____, 115 S.Ct. at 824-25. Although some principles that carry the name of contract law are designed to defeat rather than implement consensual transactions, id. at ____ n. 8, 115 S.Ct. at 826 n. 8, the rules that respect private choice are not preempted by a clause such as § 1305(a)(1). Section 301(a) plays a role similar to § 1301(a)(1): it prevents states from substituting their own regulatory systems for those of the national government. Just as § 301(a) does not itself interfere with private transactions in intellectual property, so it does not prevent states from respecting those transactions. Like the Supreme Court in Wolens, we think it prudent to refrain from adopting a rule that anything with the label "contract" is necessarily outside the preemption clause: the variations and possibilities are too numerous to foresee. National Car Rental likewise recognizes the possibility that some applications of the law of contract could interfere with the attainment of national objectives and therefore come within the domain of § 301(a). But general enforcement of shrinkwrap licenses of the kind before us does not create such interference.

Aronson emphasized that enforcement of the contract between Aronson and Quick Point Pencil Company would not withdraw any information from the public domain. That is equally true of the contract between ProCD and Zeidenberg. Everyone remains free to copy and disseminate all 3,000 telephone books that have been incorporated into ProCD's database. Anyone can add SIC codes and zip codes. ProCD's rivals have done so. Enforcement of the shrinkwrap license may even make information more readily available, by reducing the price ProCD charges to consumer buyers. To the extent licenses facilitate distribution of object code while concealing the source code (the point of a clause forbidding disassembly), they serve the same procompetitive functions as does the law of trade secrets. Rockwell Graphic Systems, Inc. v. DEV Industries, Inc., 925 F.2d 174, 180 (7th Cir.1991). Licenses may have other benefits for consumers: many licenses permit users to make extra copies, to use the software on multiple computers, even to incorporate the software into the user's products. But whether a particular license is generous or restrictive, a simple two-party contract is not "equivalent to any of the exclusive rights within the general scope of copyright" and therefore may be enforced.

REVERSED AND REMANDED.

Guy Rub, Copyright Survives: Rethinking the Copyright- Contract Conflict

103 Virginia Law Review 1141 (2017)

Twenty-one years ago, copyright died. More accurately, it was killed. In 1996, in ProCD v. Zeidenberg, Judge Easterbrook, writing for the Seventh Circuit, held that a contract that restricted the use of factual information was not preempted by the Copyright Act and therefore enforceable. The reaction among copyright scholars was swift and passionate. In dozens of articles and books, spreading over two decades, scholars cautioned that if the ProCD approach is broadly adopted, the results would be dire. Through contracts, the rights of copyright owners would run amok, expand, and in doing so they would invade, shrink, and possibly destroy the public domain. Contracts, we were repeatedly warned throughout the years, would kill copyright law.

This Article challenges this scholarly consensus by studying the court opinions that have dealt with the copyright-contract conflict over the past four decades. This examination reveals surprising facts: notwithstanding the scholars' warnings, ProCD's approach won the day and was embraced by most federal circuit courts. The doomsday scenarios scholars warned against, however, did not materialize.

...

Surprisingly, a close examination of the case law suggests that the doomsday scenarios many scholars predicted did not come to fruition. Indeed, there is a clear discrepancy between the parade of horribles that commentators warned about and the actual reality, as reflected in the case law.

The vast majority of the contracts litigated since ProCD embody commercially reasonable transactions that do not seem to pose any real threat to the goals or policies of federal copyright law. For example, a common form of such contracts includes a promise by the defendant to pay the plaintiff if the defendant decides to use a creative idea pitched by the plaintiff, such as an idea for a movie script or an advertising campaign. Although such a contract regulates the use of ideas, it does not stand in the way of copyright policy and therefore there is little reason to find it preempted. Other typical arrangements that have been litigated, such as obligations to pay for certain usages, promises of confidentiality, or promises to refrain from copyright infringement, are also commercially reasonable and should not be preempted.

The study of the case law also indicates that the contracts subject to preemption litigation were entered into by sophisticated parties or, at least, in situations where the parties have likely read, or should have read, the contract prior to its acceptance. In other words, the contracts that have been litigated are typically not the type of standard-form agreements that commonly raise serious policy concerns: click-wraps, browser-wraps, shrink-wraps, and other form documents which are routinely accepted without being read and usually without much thought. The type of contracts that commentators warned about—for example, a mass of long and complicated standard-form agreements that would force all users, without reading or noticing, to promise not to criticize the underlying work, parody it, or use the idea expressed therein—are nowhere to be found among the litigated contracts.

4. Authorship in Copyright Law

52 U.S.P.Q.2d 1609 (S.D.N.Y. 1999)

LINDSAY V. R.M.S. TITANIC

United States District Court Southern District of New York

HAROLD BAER, JR., District Judge:

The plaintiff, Alexander Lindsay, commenced this lawsuit in 1997, seeking damages based upon his share of the revenues generated by the salvage operations conducted at the wreck site of the famous sunken vessel, the R.M.S. Titanic. Defendants R.M.S. Titanic, Inc. ("RMST") and Suarez Corporation Inc. ("SCI") answered and asserted counterclaims against the plaintiff for copyright infringement. The plaintiffs' amended complaint joined defendant Discovery Communications, Inc. ("DCI") and added claims of copyright infringement against RMST, SCI and DCI. Pursuant to Rule 12(b)(6) of the Federal Rules of Civil Procedure, the defendants now move [2] to dismiss the plaintiffs copyright claims alleged in the amended complaint. The plaintiff crossmoves for summary judgment as to both his salvage and copyright claims. For the reasons discussed below, the defendants' motions are DENIED in part and GRANTED in part, and the Court reserves decision on the plaintiff's motion.

I. BACKGROUND

The plaintiff, a citizen of the United Kingdom and resident of the State of New York, is an independent documentary film maker engaged in the business of creating, producing, directing, and filming documentaries: Defendant R.M.S. Titanic, Inc. ("RMST") is a publicly traded U.S. corporation, organized under the laws of the State of Florida, which conducts business within and has its office and principal place of business in New York City. Defendant George Tulloch ("Tulloch") is a shareholder, president and member of the board of directors of RMST. Defendant Titanic Ventures Limited Partnership ("TVLP") is a limited partnership organized under the laws of Connecticut and currently doing business in the State of New York. Defendant Oceanic Research and Exploration Limited ("OREL") is a Delaware corporation and general partner of TVLP. Defendant Tullqch is also the president and sole shareholder of OREL (defendants RMST, Tulloc, TVLP and OREL collectively as "RMST"). Defendant Suarez Corporation, Inc. ("SCI") is an Ohio corporation doing business in the State of New York. Defendant Discovery Communications, Inc. ("DCI") is a Maryland corporation doing business as "The Discovery Channel", and is engaged in the business of making, financing and distributing documentary films.

In 1993, RMST was awarded exclusive status as salvor-in-possession of the Titanic wreck site and is therefore authorized to carry on salvage operations at the vessel's wreck site. As a condition of obtaining these rights, RMST allegedly agreed to maintain all the artifacts it recovered during the salvage operations for historical verification, scientific education, and public awareness.

In 1994, the plaintiff, under contract with a British television company, filmed and directed the British documentary film, "Explorers of the Titanic," a chronicle of RMST's third salvage expedition of the Titanic. To film this documentary, Lindsay sailed with RMST and the salvage expedition crew to the wreck site and remained at sea for approximately one month. The plaintiff alleges that during and after filming this documentary in 1994, he conceived a new film project for the Titanic wreck using high illumination lighting equipment.

The plaintiff later discussed his idea with defendant George Tulloch and, according to the plaintiff, the two agreed to work together on the venture. In March 1995, the plaintiff traveled to New York and developed a comprehensive business plan for the new film project entitled, "Titanic: A Memorial Tribute." Tulloch allegedly informed the plaintiff that he would agree to the plan — which purported to include provisions for compensating Lindsay for his work on the project — but that Tulloch would have to obtain approval from the RMST Board of Directors. The plaintiff agreed to join RMST to raise money not only for the film project, but for other aspects of the 1996 salvage operation as well.

Lindsay moved into an office at RMST in and around April 1995. Around this time, tulloch repeatedly told Lindsay that he would obtain approval from RMSTs Board of Directors for a contract for the plaintiff based upon the terms of Lindsay's film plan. \ The contract was to include terms of Lindsay's compensation, including sharing in the profits derived from any film, video and still photographs obtained from the 1996 salvage operation. This contract was never executed.

As part of his pre-production efforts, the plaintiff created various storyboards for the film, a series of drawings which incorporated images of the Titanic by identifying specific camera angles and shooting sequences "that reflect[ed] Plaintiff's [sic] creative inspiration and force behind his concept for shooting the Subject Work." The plaintiff also alleges that he, along with members of his film team, designed the huge underwater light towers that were later used to make the film. Lindsay also "personally constructed the light towers" and thereafter "for approximately 3-4 weeks directed, produced, and acted as the cinematographer of the Subject Work; underwater video taping of the Titanic wreck site, and otherwise participated in the 1996 salvage operation." He also directed the filming of the wreck site from on board the salvage vessel "Ocean Voyager" after leading daily planning sessions with the crew of the Nautile, the submarine used to transport the film equipment and photographers to the underwater wreck site. The purpose of these sessions was to provide the photographers with "detailed instructions for positioning and utilizing the light towers." Id.)

The plaintiff now alleges that he was never fully compensated for his services and that, inter alia, the defendants are now "unlawfully profiting from the exploitation of the" film project at issue.

The plaintiff originally brought this action under the Court's admiralty jurisdiction to enforce his salvage claims against defendants RMS Titanic, Inc., Titanic Ventures Limited Partners, Oceanic Research and Exploration Limited (collectively as "RMST"), and Suarez Corporation.

These defendants moved to dismiss the plaintiffs salvage claims. By order dated September 2, 1998, I denied the motion to dismiss, having found that the plaintiff had met his burden of pleading all the necessary elements for bringing a salvage claim. See Lindsay v. Titanic, No. 97 Civ. 9248, 1998 WL 557591 (S.D.N.Y. Sept. 2, 1998).

RMST and SCI then answered the complaint and included counterclaims for copyright infringement arising from the plaintiff's use of certain video footage taken from the wreck during the 1996 expedition. By order dated April 9, 1999, I granted the plaintiffs motion to amend his complaint to add copyright infringement claims against RMST and SCI and to join Discovery Communications, Inc. ("DCI") d/b/a The Discovery Channel, for copyright infringement of what appears to be the same footage at issue in the defendants' counterclaims.

The plaintiffs amended complaint now includes 13 causes of action, including those based on copyright infringement, salvage claims, and state law causes of action for fraud, breach of contract, and conversion. The defendants now move pursuant to Rule 12(b)(6) of the Federal Rules of Civil Procedure to dismiss Lindsay's copyright claims, and the plaintiff cross-moves for summary judgment on his copyright and salvage claims. ...

II. DISCUSSION

...

B. Copyright Claims

...

2. Authorship

The defendants first argue that the plaintiff cannot have any protectable right in the illuminated footage since he did not dive to the ship and thus did not himself actually photograph the wreckage. This argument, however, does not hold water.

The Copyright Act of 1976 provides that copyright ownership "vests initially in the author or authors of the work." 17 U.S.C. §201(a). Generally speaking, the author of a work is the person "who actually creates the work, that is, the person who translates an idea into a fixed, tangible expression entitled to copyright protection." Community for Creative Non-Violence v. Reid, 490 U.S. 730, 737 (1989) (citing 17 U.S.C. §102). In the context of film footage and photography, it makes intuitive sense that the "author" of a work is the individual or individuals who took the pictures, i.e. the photographer. However, the concept is broader than as argued by the defendants.

For over 100 years, the Supreme Court has recognized that photographs may receive copyright protection in "so far as they are representatives of original intellectual conceptions of the author" Burrow-Giles Lithographic Co. v. Sarony, 111 U.S . 53, 58 (1884). An individual claiming to be an author for copyright purposes must show "the existence of those facts of originality, of intellectual production, of thought, and conception." Feist Publications. Inc. v. Rural Telephone Service Company Inc., 499 U.S. 340, 346-347 (1991) (citing Burrow-Giles, 111 U.S. at 59-60). [9] Some elements of originality in a photograph includes "posing the subjects, lighting, angle, selection of film and camera, evoking the desired expression, and almost any variant involved." Rogers v. Koons, 960 F.2d 301, 307 (2d Cir.), cert. denied, 506 U.S. 934 (1992). Taken as true, the plaintiffs allegations meet this standard. Lindsay's alleged storyboards and the specific directions he provided to the film crew regarding the use of the lightowers and the angles from which to shoot the wreck all indicate that the final footage would indeed be the product of Lindsay's "original intellectual conceptions."

The fact that Lindsay did not literally perform the filming, i.e. by diving to the wreck and operating the cameras, will not defeat his claims of having "authored" the illuminated footage. The plaintiff alleges that as part of his pre-production efforts, he created so-called "storyboards," a series of drawings which incorporated images of the Titanic by identifying specific camera angles and shooting sequences. During the expedition itself, Lindsay claims to have been "the director, producer and cinematographer" of the underwater footage. As part of this role, Lindsay alleges that he directed daily planning sessions with the film crew to provide them with "detailed instructions for positioning and utilizing the light towers." Moreover, the plaintiff actually "directed the filming" of the Titanic from on board the Ocean Voyager, the salvage vessel that held the crew and equipment. Finally, Lindsay screened the footage at the end of each day to "confirm that he had obtained the images he wanted."

All else being equal, where a plaintiff alleges that he exercised such a high degree of control over a film operation — including the type and amount of lighting used, the specific camera angles to be employed, and other detail-intensive artistic elements of a film — such that the final product duplicates his conceptions and visions of what the film should look like, the plaintiff may be said "author" within the meaning of the Copyright Act.

...

3. Joint-Authorship

In the alternative, the defendants argue that Lindsay is, at best, a joint author of the underwater footage with RMST. This contention is based on the notion that

Christian Petron, the main photographer of the film, was at least a joint-author of the footage with the plaintiff. Since Petron's participation was accomplished under the auspices of a work for hire agreement with RMST, the defendants' argument continues, any rights to authorship Petron may have received via his filming were conferred upon RMST. As a joint author with the plaintiff then, RMST cannot be liable for copyright infringement since each co-author acquires an undivided interest in the entire work and has the right to use the work as he or she pleases. Thomson v. Larson, 147 F .3d 195; 199 (2d Cir. 1998); Weissman v. Freeman, 868 F.2d 1313, 1318 (2d Cir.) ("[A]n action for infringement between joint owners will not lie because an individual cannot infringe his own copyright."), cert. denied, 493 U.S. 883 (1989). Similarly, any copyright claim against DCI would fail since RMST, as a joint author, has the right to license the joint work to third parties. Thomson, 147 F.3d at 199.

A "joint work" under the Copyright Act is one "prepared by two or more authors with the intention that their contributions be merged into inseparable or interdependent parts of a unitary whole." 17 U.S.C. §101. To prove co-authorship status, it must be shown by the individual claiming co-authorship status that each of the putative co-authors (1) fully intended to be co-authors, and (2) made independently copyrightable contributions to the work. Thomson, 147 F.3d at 200 (citing Childress v. Taylor, 945 F.2d 500, 507-508 (2d Cir. 1991)).

Drawing all inferences in favor of Lindsay, I conclude that no such status existed in the case at bar. With regard to the intent prong of the analysis, "[a]n important indicator of authorship is a contributor's decision making authority over what changes are made and what is included in a work." Id. at 202-3 (citing Erickson v. Trinity Theatre. Inc., 13 F.3d 1061, 1071-72 (7th Cir. 1994) (actor's suggestions of text did not support a claim of co-authorship where the sole author determined whether and where such suggestions were included in the work)). In other words, where one contributor retains a so-called "veto" authority over what is included in a work, such control is a strong indicator that he or she does not intend to be co-authors with the other contributor. According to the pleadings, the plaintiff exercised virtually total control over the content of the film as "the director, producer and cinematographer" of the production. Additionally, he briefed the photographers with regards to, inter alia, the specific camera angles they were to employ, and Lindsay screened the film each day to make sure the proper footage was obtained. Based on these allegations, and implicit in the notion that the film crew was simply "following directions," Lindsay retained what appeared to be exclusive authority over what was included in the footage. Assuming as I must at this stage of the litigation that this is true, it can hardly be said that the plaintiff intended Petron — or any other contributor — to be a coauthor. Accordingly, the claims by RMST that it — by virtue of Petron's role as a photographer under a work-for-hire agreement — was a joint-author within the meaning of the Copyright Act must fail.

...

13 F.3d 1061 (1994)

ERICKSON v. TRINITY THEATRE

Court of Appeals of the Seventh Circuit

RIPPLE, Circuit Judge.

[1] The plaintiff Karen Erickson brought this action seeking a preliminary and permanent injunction to prevent the defendant Trinity Theatre d/b/a Trinity Square Ensemble ("Trinity") from performing three plays and using two videotapes to which she owned the copyrights. The magistrate judge recommended enjoining the performance of the plays but not the use of the videotapes. Both parties filed objections. The district court sustained Ms. Erickson's objections to the portions of the recommendation addressing the videotapes but denied Trinity's objections to the portion of the recommendation addressing performance of the plays. Accordingly, the district court enjoined Trinity from using either the plays or the videotapes. Trinity now appeals. We now affirm.

I

[2] BACKGROUND

[3] A. Facts

[4] Ms. Erickson was one of the founders of a theatre company in Evanston, Illinois, that ultimately became known as Trinity Theatre. Between 1981 and January 1991, Ms. Erickson served Trinity in various capacities: as playwright, artistic director, actress, play director, business manager, and member of the board of directors. This suit revolves around Ms. Erickson's role as playwright.

[5] At issue here are the rights to three plays: Much Ado About Shakespeare ("Much Ado"); The Theatre Time Machine ("Time Machine"); and Prairie Voices: Tales from Illinois ("Prairie Voices"). Much Ado is a compilation of scenes and sonnets from William Shakespeare and other writers of his time. Ms. Erickson revised this work from an earlier script entitled Sounds and Sweet Aires. Michael Osborne, a Trinity actor, testified that Ms. Erickson compiled Much Ado in 1988 and that many decisions about what was to be included were made during rehearsals. Osborne identified two portions of the copyrighted script that resulted from his suggestions: a passage to Macbeth and the introduction to the play. The editing of the text, Osborne continued, was accomplished largely by consensus; however, when a consensus could not be had, Ms. Erickson made the final decisions. Osborne further testified that he understood at the time that the play was being created for Trinity and not for Ms. Erickson. Ms. Erickson does not dispute the process described by Osborne, but characterizes it differently. She perceived the process only as actors making suggestions for her script.

[6] Time Machine is a play of five scenes based on a public domain Native American folk tale. Each scene depicts dramatic styles from different historical periods. Ms. Erickson received a copyright registration for Time Machine on September 12, 1988. She described the development of the play as beginning in

1977 when she was in school. At that time, she wrote the Greek-style drama scene. Later, while teaching high school drama, she wrote the second scene based on commedia dell'arte. She also began work on the melodrama and improvisational scenes of the play at that time. Ms. Erickson started producing the play independently of Trinity in 1984 with two other actors, Paddy Lynn and Will Clinger. Ms. Erickson claimed that she worked to develop the scenes alone; however, the evidence shows that the actors were involved in the development of the melodrama and improvisational scenes. The improvisational process, as described by Ms. Lynn, is a form of theatre in which there is no script. Rather, actors work with an idea and a loose structure to create a play. Ms. Lynn described the development of the improvisational scene in Time Machine as a collaborative effort. However, she conceded that Ms. Erickson took all of the notes from rehearsals and compiled them into the script; furthermore, nothing was included in the script without Ms. Erickson's approval. Initially, Ms. Erickson attributed the script to both herself and to Ms. Lynn. Ms. Lynn also received royalties for performances of the play. Ms. Erickson denied that she ever intended to include Ms. Lynn as joint author. She conceded that Ms. Lynn was credited on publicity materials as an author but denied that she approved such credit. The later change in attribution, Ms. Erickson claims, merely corrected the initial error.

[7] In 1990, Ms. Erickson developed Prairie Voices, a play based on tales from Illinois history. She had the idea to develop the play as a Trinity production. Her original intent was to launch a collaborative effort in which each of the actors would contribute a story to the play. However, none of the actors initiated writing a script and the play, as it resulted, was based entirely on tales provided by Ms. Erickson. As with Time Machine, Ms. Erickson worked with the actors in the improvisational format. Although testifying that she alone wrote the play, Ms. Erickson admitted that the actors provided ideas for the dialogue. Another actor, Ruth Ann Weyna, testified that the writing of the play was a creative process involving a number of actors. However, she conceded that Ms. Erickson controlled what eventually was put in the script.

[8] In 1987, Trinity began paying Ms. Erickson royalties for its performances of her plays. On July 5, 1988, Ms. Erickson entered into a two-year licensing agreement with Trinity that designated her as a "playwright" entitling her to royalties for performances of two of her plays, Much Ado and Time Machine. Trinity stipulated that it also paid Erickson royalties for its performances of Prairie Voices, although that play was not expressly covered by the licensing agreement. Trinity continued to pay Ms. Erickson royalties after the expiration of the licensing agreement. Trinity discontinued making royalty payments on November 15, 1990.

[9] Ms. Erickson was also subject to an actors' agreement with Trinity. In July 1988, Ms. Erickson signed the agreement which stated: "The actor expressly agrees that Trinity reserves the rights to any recording, audio, video or both of the Production. . . ." The contract covered the tour which was forecast to run through June 30, 1989.

[10] Ms. Erickson left Trinity Theatre in January 1991. Shortly thereafter, she applied for and was issued copyright registration for Much Ado and Prairie Voices.

Concurrently, she received registration for the video productions of Time Machine, taped in October 1989, and Prairie Voices, taped in November 1990. She had previously obtained a copyright certificate for Time Machine on September 12, 1988. On January 21, 1991, Ms. Erickson's attorneys wrote Trinity a letter demanding that the theatre discontinue performing the plaintiff's plays. Trinity refused to comply with the request.

[11] On April 3, 1991, Ms. Erickson filed a seventeen-count complaint against Trinity Theatre, members of Trinity's management, and individual Trinity actors seeking injunctive and legal relief in which she alleged copyright infringement, unfair competition, and other related tortious activity. In October 1992, Ms. Erickson filed a motion for a preliminary injunction to prevent the defendant from producing or performing five plays for which Ms. Erickson claimed exclusive copyright ownership, from displaying videotapes, photographs, and brochures regarding these plays, and from reproducing any materials from a copyrighted work entitled "Drama/Learning Process." After a partial settlement agreement, the parties stipulated that the district court did not need to resolve the plaintiff's request for injunctive relief as to two of the five plays. As a result, the only plays at issue for purposes of the plaintiff's motion for preliminary injunction were Time Machine, Much Ado, and Prairie Voices, as well as videotapes of Time Machine and Prairie Voices.

...

[30] B. Joint Work

[31] We now turn to the issue of whether any of the material in question is a "joint work." In a joint work, the joint authors hold undivided interests in a work, despite any differences in each author's contribution. 17 U.S.C. § 201. Each author as co-owner has the right to use or to license the use of the work, subject to an accounting to the other co-owners for any profits. Childress v. Taylor, 945 F.2d 500, 505 (2d Cir. 1991); Weinstein v. University of Illinois, 811 F.2d 1091, 1095 (7th Cir. 1987); 1 Nimmer on Copyright, § 6.02, at 6-7 to 6-8. Thus, even a person whose contribution is relatively minor, if accorded joint authorship status, enjoys a significant benefit. See Community for Creative Non-Violence v. Reid, 846 F.2d 1485, 1498 (D.C.Cir. 1988), aff'd on other grounds, 490 U.S. 730, 109 S.Ct. 2166, 104 L.Ed.2d 811 (1989); Nimmer, § 6.08, at 6-24.

[32] In determining whether any of the works at issue in this case may be classified as a "joint work," our starting point must be the language of the statute. Section 101 of the Copyright Act defines a "joint work" as

a work prepared by two or more authors with the intention that their contributions be merged into inseparable or interdependent parts of a unitary whole.

[34] Neither the Act nor its legislative history defines "inseparable" or "interdependent." The legislative history states that examples of inseparable parts are the joint contributions of two authors to a single novel or the contributions of two painters to a single work; an example of interdependent parts are the lyrics and music for a song. Apart from these examples, the reports do little to clarify the

criteria for determining joint authorship. Indeed, they increase the ambiguity. The committee reports state:

[A] work is "joint" if the authors collaborated with each other, or if each of the authors prepared his or her contribution with the knowledge and intention that it would be merged with the contributions of other authors as "inseparable or interdependent parts of a unitary whole." The touchstone here is the intention, at the time the writing is done, that the parts be absorbed or combined into an integrated unit. . . .

[35] House Report at 120; Senate Report at 103, U.S. Code Cong. & Admin.News 1976, pp. 5736 (emphasis added). The statute clearly requires a focus on the intention to collaborate. However, the disjunctive first sentence in the legislative reports, set out directly above, seemingly contradicts that statutory language by focusing on collaboration and not mentioning intent to create a joint work.

[36] This ambiguity presents analytical problems in cases such as this one, in which the parties have collaborated in some sense but dispute whether there was a mutual intent to create a joint work. In resolving this ambiguity, we believe that it is important to note, at the outset, that the statute itself requires that there be an intent to create a joint work. Therefore, reliance on collaboration alone, as Trinity suggests, would be incompatible with the clear statutory mandate. On this point, we find ourselves in agreement with the analysis of Judge Newman writing for the Second Circuit in Childress. He pointed out that a disjunctive standard based solely on the legislative history would not square with the plain meaning of the statute:

This passage appears to state two alternative criteria - one focusing on the act of collaboration and the other on the parties' intent. However, it is hard to imagine activity that would constitute meaningful "collaboration" unaccompanied by the requisite intent on the part of both participants that their contributions be merged into a unitary whole, and the case law has read the statutory language literally so that the intent requirement applies to all works of joint authorship. Childress, 945 F.2d at 505-06. ... Like the Second Circuit in Childress, we believe that the statutory language clearly requires that each author intend that their respective contributions be merged into a unitary whole. Focusing solely upon the fact of contemporaneous input by several parties does not satisfy the statutory requirement that the parties intend to merge their contributions into a unified work. In addition, the "collaboration alone" standard would frustrate the goal of the Act "[t]o promote the Progress of Science and the useful Arts." U.S. CONST. art. I, § 8, cl. 8. Seldom would an author subject his work to pre-registration peer review if this were the applicable test. Those seeking copyrights would not seek further refinement that colleagues may offer if they risked losing their sole authorship. Thus, we cannot accept Trinity's proposed "collaboration alone" test as compatible with the language and purpose of the Act.

[38] Even if two or more persons collaborate with the intent to create a unitary work, the product will be considered a "joint work" only if the collaborators can be considered "authors." Courts have applied two tests to evaluate the contributions of authors claiming joint authorship status: Professor Nimmer's de minimis test and Professor Goldstein's copyrightable subject matter ("copyrightability") test.

The de minimis and copyrightability tests differ in one fundamental respect. The de minimis test requires that only the combined product of joint efforts must be copyrightable. By contrast, Professor Goldstein's copyrightability test requires that each author's contribution be copyrightable. We evaluate each of these tests in turn.

[39] In undertaking this task, we focus on how well the test promotes the primary objective of the Act. This objective is not to reward an author for her labors, but "[t]o promote the Progress of Science and useful Arts." U.S. CONST. art. I, § 8, cl. 8; see also Feist Publications, Inc. v. Rural Tel. Serv. Co., Inc., 499 U.S. 340, 350, 111 S.Ct. 1282, 1290, 113 L.Ed.2d 358 (1991). This objective is accomplished by "assur[ing] authors the right to their original expression," but also by "encourag[ing] others to build freely upon the ideas and information conveyed by a work." Feist Publications, 499 U.S. at 349-50, 111 S.Ct. at 1290 (citing Harper & Row, Publishers, Inc. v. Nation Enters., 471 U.S. 539, 556-57, 105 S.Ct. 2218, 2228-29, 85 L.Ed.2d 588 (1984)). It is in light of this goal that § 102(b) exempts ideas from protection under the Copyright Act.

[40] In addition to promoting the Act's primary objective, we must consider how well the test will further goals of administrative and judicial efficiency. In this inquiry, we must adopt a standard that is sufficiently clear to enable parties to predict whether their contributions to a work will receive copyright protection. A standard satisfying these aims will allow contributors to avoid post-contribution disputes concerning authorship, and to protect themselves by contract if it appears that they would not enjoy protections of the Act itself.

[41] a. Professor Nimmer's de minimis standard

[42] Professor Nimmer, the late scholar on copyright, took the position that all that should be required to achieve joint author status is more than a de minimis contribution by each author. "De minimis" requires that "more than a word or line must be added by one who claims to be a joint author." Nimmer § 6.07, at 6-21. Professor Nimmer distinguishes his de minimis standard from the standard for copyrightability. Id. As an example, Professor Nimmer asserts that if two authors collaborate, with one contributing only uncopyrightable plot ideas and another incorporating those ideas into a completed literary expression, the two authors should be regarded as joint authors of the resulting work. Id.

[43] This position has not found support in the courts. The lack of support in all likelihood stems from one of several weaknesses in Professor Nimmer's approach. First, Professor Nimmer's test is not consistent with one of the Act's premises: ideas and concepts standing alone should not receive protection. Because the creative process necessarily involves the development of existing concepts into new forms, any restriction on the free exchange of ideas stifles creativity to some extent. Restrictions on an author's use of existing ideas in a work, such as the threat that accepting suggestions from another party might jeopardize the author's sole entitlement to a copyright, would hinder creativity. Second, contribution of an idea is an exceedingly ambiguous concept. Professor Nimmer provides little guidance to courts or parties regarding when a contribution rises to the level of joint

144

authorship except to state that the contribution must be "more than a word or a line." Nimmer, § 6.07, at 6-20.

[44] Professor Nimmer's approach is of little pragmatic use in resolving actual cases. Rarely will minor contributors have the presumption to claim authorship status. In such easy cases, the parties' intent as to authorship status likely will be apparent without resort to any formal test evaluating the parties' respective contributions to discern intent. In the more complex situations, such as the case before us, in which the improvisational process undoubtedly yielded valuable insights to the primary author, the test gives no guidance on how we are to assess the respective contributions of the parties to distinguish the author from the critic or advisor. For these reasons, we, as the majority of the other courts, cannot accept Professor Nimmer's test as an adequate judicial tool to ascertain joint authorship.

[45] b. Professor Goldstein's copyrightability test

[46] The copyrightable subject matter test was formulated by Professor Paul Goldstein and has been adopted, in some form, by a majority of courts that have considered the issue. According to Professor Goldstein, "[a] collaborative contribution will not produce a joint work, and a contributor will not obtain a co-ownership interest, unless the contribution represents original expression that could stand on its own as the subject matter of copyright." Paul Goldstein, Copyright: Principles, Law, and Practice § 4.2.1.2, at 379 (1989). Furthermore, the parties must have intended to be joint authors at the time the work was created. Id. Professor Goldstein and the courts adopting his test justify this position by noting that § 101's and § 302(b)'s use of the word "authors" suggests that each collaborator's contribution must be a copyrightable "work of authorship" within the meaning of § 102(a).

[47] We agree that the language of the Act supports the adoption of a copyrightability requirement. Section 101 of the Act defines a "joint work" as a "work prepared by two or more authors" (emphasis added). To qualify as an author, one must supply more than mere direction or ideas. An author is "the party who actually creates the work, that is, the person who translates an idea into a fixed, tangible expression entitled to copyright protection." Community for Creative Non-Violence v. Reid, 490 U.S. 730, 737, 109 S.Ct. 2166, 2171, 104 L.Ed.2d 811 (1989). As to the requirement of fixation, § 101 states:

A work is "fixed" in a tangible medium of expression when its embodiment in a copy or phonorecord, by or under the authority of the author, is sufficiently permanent or stable to permit it to be perceived, reproduced, or otherwise communicated for a period of more than transitory duration. ...

[49] The copyrightable subject matter test does not suffer from the same infirmities as Professor Nimmer's de minimis test. The copyrightability test advances creativity in science and art by allowing for the unhindered exchange of ideas, and protects authorship rights in a consistent and predictable manner. It excludes contributions such as ideas which are not protected under the Copyright

Act. 17 U.S.C. § 102(b) ("In no case does copyright protection for an original work of authorship extend to any idea . . . embodied in such work."); see also Feist Publications v. Rural Tel. Serv. Co., 499 U.S. 340, 344-45, 111 S.Ct. 1282, 1287, 113 L.Ed.2d 358 (1991) (stating that the "most fundamental axiom of copyright law is that `[n]o author may copyright his ideas or the facts he narrates'"); Harper & Row, Publishers, Inc. v. Nation Enters., 471 U.S. 539, 556, 105 S.Ct. 2218, 2228, 85 L.Ed.2d 588 (1985) (discussing idea/expression dichotomy). This test also enables parties to predict whether their contributions to a work will entitle them to copyright protection as a joint author. Compared to the uncertain exercise of divining whether a contribution is more than de minimis, reliance on the copyrightability of an author's proposed contribution yields relatively certain answers. See 17 U.S.C. § 101; Feist Publications, 499 U.S. at 344-50, 111 S.Ct. at 1287-90. The copyrightability standard allows contributors to avoid post-contribution disputes concerning authorship, and to protect themselves by contract if it appears that they would not enjoy the benefits accorded to authors of joint works under the Act.

[50] We agree with the Childress court's observation that the copyrightability test "strikes an appropriate balance in the domains of both copyright and contract law." 945 F.2d at 507. Section 201(b) of the Act allows any person to contract with another to create a work and endow the employer with authorship status under the Act. 17 U.S.C. § 201(b). A contributor of uncopyrightable ideas may also protect her rights to compensation under the Act by contract. Section 201(d) of the Act provides in part that any of the exclusive ownership rights comprised in a copyright may be transferred from the person who satisfied the requirements for obtaining the copyright to one who contracts for such rights. 17 U.S.C. § 201(d). Thus, anyone who contributes to the creation of a work, either as patron, employer, or contributor of ideas, has the opportunity to share in the profits produced by the work through an appropriate contractual arrangement.

[51] C. Application

[52] We now address Trinity's claims of joint authorship under the copyrightability test. As stated above, Trinity must clear two hurdles in order to establish that the plays at issue are joint works. First, it must show the parties intended to be joint authors at the time the work was created. Second, Trinity must show that its contributions to the works were independently copyrightable.

[53] It is clear that, with regard to at least two works, Much Ado and Prairie Voices, Trinity cannot clear the first hurdle. Much Ado is based on a work that Ms. Erickson had largely completed before Trinity actors improvised based on Ms. Erickson's creation. The fact that one actor, Michael Osborne, suggested that Ms. Erickson include a passage from Macbeth and an introduction to the play does not make him a joint author. He conceded that whether his contributions were included and where they went into the compilation were entirely Ms. Erickson's decisions. Furthermore, neither Ms. Erickson nor Trinity considered any of the actors to be co-authors with her in Much Ado, as is evidenced by the licensing agreement. Similarly with Prairie Voices, Ms. Erickson provided the stories on which the play was based, and she decided which of the actors' suggestions were

incorporated into the script. The actors did not consider themselves to be joint authors with Ms. Erickson, and there is no evidence that Ms. Erickson considered the actors as co-authors of the script. Because Trinity cannot establish the requisite intent for Much Ado or Prairie Voices, the actors cannot be considered joint authors for the purposes of copyright protection.

[54] Time Machine, as both the magistrate judge and the district court noted, is more problematic. Paddy Lynn testified that at least two scenes from Time Machine were developed through a collaborative process. Ms. Lynn considered the created dialogue to be hers as well as well as Ms. Erickson's. Furthermore, there is evidence that Ms. Erickson, too, intended at the time to create a joint work because she initially attributed the script to both Ms. Lynn and herself. Consequently, Trinity has produced some evidence that there was the requisite intent for joint authorship with regard to Time Machine. In Childress, the Second Circuit specifically acknowledged that "`billing' or `credit'" may be evidence of intent to create a joint work. Id. at 508. Here there is evidence that Ms. Lynn was credited with authorship of Time Machine.

[55] In order for the plays to be joint works under the Act, Trinity also must show that actors' contributions to Ms. Erickson's work could have been independently copyrighted. Trinity cannot establish this requirement for any of the above works. The actors, on the whole, could not identify specific contributions that they had made to Ms. Erickson's works. Even when Michael Osborne was able to do so, the contributions that he identified were not independently copyrightable. Ideas, refinements, and suggestions, standing alone, are not the subjects of copyrights. Consequently, Trinity cannot establish the two necessary elements of the copyrightability test and its claims must fail.

[56] Trinity cannot establish joint authorship to the plays at issue. As a result, Trinity cannot overcome the presumption in favor of the validity of Ms. Erickson's copyrights. Consequently, Ms. Erickson is very likely to succeed on the merits of her claims for copyright infringement.

[57] Conclusion

[58] For the foregoing reasons, the judgment of the district court is affirmed.

[59] AFFIRMED.

202 F.3d 1227 (2000)

AALMUHAMMED

v.

Spike LEE & WARNER BROTHERS

United States Court of Appeals, Ninth Circuit

KLEINFELD, Circuit Judge:

This is a copyright case involving a claim of coauthorship of the movie Malcolm X. We reject the "joint work" claim but remand for further proceedings on a quantum meruit claim.

I. FACTS

In 1991, Warner Brothers contracted with Spike Lee and his production companies to make the movie Malcolm X, to be based on the book, The Autobiography of Malcolm X. Lee co-wrote the screenplay, directed, and co-produced the movie, which starred Denzel Washington as Malcolm X. Washington asked Jefri Aalmuhammed to assist him in his preparation for the starring role because Aalmuhammed knew a great deal about Malcolm X and Islam. Aalmuhammed, a devout Muslim, was particularly knowledgeable about the life of Malcolm X, having previously written, directed, and produced a documentary film about Malcolm X.

Aalmuhammed joined Washington on the movie set. The movie was filmed in the New York metropolitan area and Egypt. Aalmuhammed presented evidence that his involvement in making the movie was very extensive. He reviewed the shooting script for Spike Lee and Denzel Washington and suggested extensive script revisions. Some of his script revisions were included in the released version of the film; others were filmed but not included in the released version. Most of the revisions Aalmuhammed made were to ensure the religious and historical accuracy and authenticity of scenes depicting Malcolm X's religious conversion and pilgrimage to Mecca.

Aalmuhammed submitted evidence that he directed Denzel Washington and other actors while on the set, created at least two entire scenes with new characters, translated Arabic into English for subtitles, supplied his own voice for voice-overs, selected the proper prayers and religious practices for the characters, and edited parts of the movie during post production. Washington testified in his deposition that Aalmuhammed's contribution to the movie was "great" because he "helped to rewrite, to make more authentic." Once production ended, Aalmuhammed met with numerous Islamic organizations to persuade them that the movie was an accurate depiction of Malcolm X's life.

Aalmuhammed never had a written contract with Warner Brothers, Lee, or Lee's production companies, but he expected Lee to compensate him for his work. He did not intend to work and bear his expenses in New York and Egypt gratuitously. Aalmuhammed ultimately received a check for $25,000 from Lee, which he cashed, and a check for $100,000 from Washington, which he did not cash.

During the summer before Malcolm X's November 1992 release, Aalmuhammed asked for a writing credit as a co-writer of the film, but was turned down. When the film was released, it credited Aalmuhammed only as an "Islamic Technical Consultant," far down the list. In November 1995, Aalmuhammed applied for a copyright with the U.S. Copyright Office, claiming he was a co-creator, co-writer, and co-director of the movie. The Copyright Office issued him a "Certificate of Registration," but advised him in a letter that his "claims conflict with previous registrations" of the film.

On November 17, 1995, Aalmuhammed filed a complaint against Spike Lee, his production companies, and Warner Brothers, (collectively "Lee"), as well as Largo International, N.V., and Largo Entertainment, Inc. (collectively "Largo"), and Victor Company of Japan and JVC Entertainment, Inc. (collectively "Victor"). The suit sought declaratory relief and an accounting under the Copyright Act. In addition, the complaint alleged breach of implied contract, quantum meruit, and unjust enrichment, and federal (Lanham Act) and state unfair competition claims. The district court dismissed some of the claims under Rule 12(b)(6) and the rest on summary judgment.

II. ANALYSIS

A. Copyright claim

Aalmuhammed claimed that the movie Malcolm X was a "joint work" of which he was an author, thus making him a co-owner of the copyright. He sought a declaratory judgment to that effect, and an accounting for profits. He is not claiming copyright merely in what he wrote or contributed, but rather in the whole work, as a co-author of a "joint work." The district court granted defendants summary judgment against Mr. Aalmuhammed's copyright claims. We review de novo.

Defendants argue that Aalmuhammed's claim that he is one of the authors of a joint work is barred by the applicable statute of limitations. A claim of authorship of a joint work must be brought within three years of when it accrues. Because creation rather than infringement is the gravamen of an authorship claim, the claim accrues on account of creation, not subsequent infringement, and is barred three years from "plain and express repudiation" of authorship.

The movie credits plainly and expressly repudiated authorship, by listing Aalmuhammed far below the more prominent names, as an "Islamic technical consultant." That repudiation, though, was less than three years before the lawsuit was filed. The record leaves open a genuine issue of fact as to whether authorship was repudiated before that. Aalmuhammed testified in his deposition that he discussed with an executive producer at Warner Brothers his claim to credit as one of the screenwriters more than three years before he filed suit. Defendants argue that this discussion was an express repudiation that bars the claim. It was not. Aalmuhammed testified that the producer told him "there is nothing I can do for you," but "[h]e said we would discuss it further at some point." A trier of fact could construe that communication as leaving the question of authorship open for further discussion. That leaves a genuine issue of fact as to whether the claim is barred by limitations, so we must determine whether there is a genuine issue of fact as to whether Aalmuhammed was an author of a "joint work."

Aalmuhammed argues that he established a genuine issue of fact as to whether he was an author of a "joint work," Malcolm X. The Copyright Act does not define "author," but it does define "joint work":

A "joint work" is a work prepared by two or more authors with the intention that their contributions be merged into inseparable or interdependent parts of a unitary whole.

"When interpreting a statute, we look first to the language." The statutory language establishes that for a work to be a "joint work" there must be (1) a copyrightable work, (2) two or more "authors," and (3) the authors must intend their contributions be merged into inseparable or interdependent parts of a unitary whole. A "joint work" in this circuit "requires each author to make an independently copyrightable contribution" to the disputed work. Malcolm X is a copyrightable work, and it is undisputed that the movie was intended by everyone involved with it to be a unitary whole. It is also undisputed that Aalmuhammed made substantial and valuable contributions to the movie, including technical help, such as speaking Arabic to the persons in charge of the mosque in Egypt, scholarly and creative help, such as teaching the actors how to pray properly as Muslims, and script changes to add verisimilitude to the religious aspects of the movie. Speaking Arabic to persons in charge of the mosque, however, does not result in a copyrightable contribution to the motion picture. Coaching of actors, to be copyrightable, must be turned into an expression in a form subject to copyright. The same may be said for many of Aalmuhammed's other activities. Aalmuhammed has, however, submitted evidence that he rewrote several specific passages of dialogue that appeared in Malcolm X, and that he wrote scenes relating to Malcolm X's Hajj pilgrimage that were enacted in the movie. If Aalmuhammed's evidence is accepted, as it must be on summary judgment, these items would have been independently copyrightable. Aalmuhammed, therefore, has presented a genuine issue of fact as to whether he made a copyrightable contribution. All persons involved intended that Aalmuhammed's contributions would be merged into interdependent parts of the movie as a unitary whole. Aalmuhammed maintains that he has shown a genuine issue of fact for each element of a "joint work."

But there is another element to a "joint work." A "joint work" includes "two or more authors." Aalmuhammed established that he contributed substantially to the film, but not that he was one of its "authors." We hold that authorship is required under the statutory definition of a joint work, and that authorship is not the same thing as making a valuable and copyrightable contribution. We recognize that a contributor of an expression may be deemed to be the "author" of that expression for purposes of determining whether it is independently copyrightable. The issue we deal with is a different and larger one: is the contributor an author of the joint work within the meaning of 17 U.S.C. § 101.

By statutory definition, a "joint work" requires "two or more authors." The word "author" is taken from the traditional activity of one person sitting at a desk with a pen and writing something for publication. It is relatively easy to apply the word "author" to a novel. It is also easy to apply the word to two people who work together in a fairly traditional pen-and-ink way, like, perhaps, Gilbert and Sullivan. In the song, "I Am the Very Model of a Modern Major General," Gilbert's words and Sullivan's tune are inseparable, and anyone who has heard the song knows that it owes its existence to both men, Sir William Gilbert and Sir Arthur Sullivan, as its creative originator. But as the number of contributors grows and the work itself becomes less the product of one or two individuals who create it without much help, the word is harder to apply.

Who, in the absence of contract, can be considered an author of a movie? The word is traditionally used to mean the originator or the person who causes something to come into being, or even the first cause, as when Chaucer refers to the "Author of Nature." For a movie, that might be the producer who raises the money. Eisenstein thought the author of a movie was the editor. The "auteur" theory suggests that it might be the director, at least if the director is able to impose his artistic judgments on the film. Traditionally, by analogy to books, the author was regarded as the person who writes the screenplay, but often a movie reflects the work of many screenwriters. Grenier suggests that the person with creative control tends to be the person in whose name the money is raised, perhaps a star, perhaps the director, perhaps the producer, with control gravitating to the star as the financial investment in scenes already shot grows. Where the visual aspect of the movie is especially important, the chief cinematographer might be regarded as the author. And for, say, a Disney animated movie like "The Jungle Book," it might perhaps be the animators and the composers of the music.

The Supreme Court dealt with the problem of defining "author" in new media in Burrow-Giles Lithographic Co. v. Sarony. The question there was, who is the author of a photograph: the person who sets it up and snaps the shutter, or the person who makes the lithograph from it. Oscar Wilde, the person whose picture was at issue, doubtless offered some creative advice as well. The Court decided that the photographer was the author, quoting various English authorities: "the person who has superintended the arrangement, who has actually formed the picture by putting the persons in position, and arranging the place where the people are to be—the man who is the effective cause of that"; "`author' involves originating, making, producing, as the inventive or master mind, the thing which is to be protected"; "the man who really represents, creates, or gives effect to the idea, fancy, or imagination." The Court said that an "author," in the sense that the Founding Fathers used the term in the Constitution, was "`he to whom anything owes its origin; originator; maker; one who completes a work of science or literature.'

Answering a different question, what is a copyrightable "work," as opposed to who is the "author," the Supreme Court held in Feist Publications that "some minimal level of creativity" or "originality" suffices. But that measure of a "work" would be too broad and indeterminate to be useful if applied to determine who are "authors" of a movie. So many people might qualify as an "author" if the question were limited to whether they made a substantial creative contribution that that test would not distinguish one from another. Everyone from the producer and director to casting director, costumer, hairstylist, and "best boy" gets listed in the movie credits because all of their creative contributions really do matter. It is striking in Malcolm X how much the person who controlled the hue of the lighting contributed, yet no one would use the word "author" to denote that individual's relationship to the movie. A creative contribution does not suffice to establish authorship of the movie.

Burrow-Giles, in defining "author," requires more than a minimal creative or original contribution to the work. Burrow-Giles is still good law, and was recently reaffirmed in Feist Publications. Burrow-Giles and Feist Publications answer two distinct questions; who is an author, and what is a copyrightable work. Burrow-Giles defines author as the person to whom the work owes its origin and who superintended the whole work, the "master mind." In a movie this definition, in the absence of a contract to the contrary, would generally limit authorship to someone at the top of the screen credits, sometimes the producer, sometimes the director, possibly the star, or the screenwriter—someone who has artistic control. After all, in Burrow-Giles the lithographer made a substantial copyrightable creative contribution, and so did the person who posed, Oscar Wilde, but the Court held that the photographer was the author.

The Second and Seventh Circuits have likewise concluded that contribution of independently copyrightable material to a work intended to be an inseparable whole will not suffice to establish authorship of a joint work. Although the Second and Seventh Circuits do not base their decisions on the word "authors" in the statute, the practical results they reach are consistent with ours. These circuits have held that a person claiming to be an author of a joint work must prove that both parties intended each other to be joint authors. In determining whether the parties have the intent to be joint authors, the Second Circuit looks at who has decision making authority, how the parties bill themselves, and other evidence.

In Thomson v. Larson, an off-Broadway playwright had created a modern version of La Boheme, and had been adamant throughout its creation on being the sole author. He hired a drama professor for "dramaturgical assistance and research," agreeing to credit her as "dramaturg" but not author, but saying nothing about "joint work" or copyright. The playwright tragically died immediately after the final dress rehearsal, just before his play became the tremendous Broadway hit, Rent. The dramaturg then sued his estate for a declaratory judgment that she was an author of Rent as a "joint work," and for an accounting. The Second Circuit noted that the dramaturg had no decision making authority, had neither sought nor was billed as a co-author, and that the defendant entered into contracts as the sole author. On this reasoning, the Second Circuit held that there was no intent to be joint authors by the putative parties and therefore it was not a joint work.

Considering Burrow-Giles, the recent cases on joint works (especially the thoughtful opinion in Thomson v. Larson), and the Gilbert and Sullivan example, several factors suggest themselves as among the criteria for joint authorship, in the absence of contract. First, an author "superintend[s]" the work by exercising control This will likely be a person "who has actually formed the picture by putting the persons in position, and arranging the place where the people are to be—the man who is the effective cause of that," or "the inventive or master mind" who "creates, or gives effect to the idea." Second, putative coauthors make objective manifestations of a shared intent to be coauthors, as by denoting the authorship of The Pirates of Penzance as "Gilbert and Sullivan." We say objective manifestations because, were the mutual intent to be determined by subjective intent, it could become an instrument of fraud, were one coauthor to hide from the other an intention to take sole credit for the work. Third, the audience appeal of the work turns on both contributions and "the share of each in its success cannot be appraised." Control in many cases will be the most important factor. The best objective manifestation of a shared intent, of course, is a contract saying that the parties intend to be or not to be co-authors. In the absence of a contract, the inquiry must of necessity focus on the facts. The factors articulated in this decision and the Second and Seventh Circuit decisions cannot be reduced to a rigid formula, because the creative relationships to which they apply vary too much. Different people do creative work together in different ways, and even among the same people working together the relationship may change over time as the work proceeds.

Aalmuhammed did not at any time have superintendence of the work. Warner Brothers and Spike Lee controlled it. Aalmuhammed was not the person "who has actually formed the picture by putting the persons in position, and arranging the place ...." Spike Lee was, so far as we can tell from the record. Aalmuhammed, like Larson's dramaturg, could make extremely helpful recommendations, but Spike Lee was not bound to accept any of them, and the work would not benefit in the slightest unless Spike Lee chose to accept them. Aalmuhammed lacked control over the work, and absence of control is strong evidence of the absence of co-authorship.

Also, neither Aalmuhammed, nor Spike Lee, nor Warner Brothers, made any objective manifestations of an intent to be coauthors. Warner Brothers required Spike Lee to sign a "work for hire" agreement, so that even Lee would not be a co-author and co-owner with Warner Brothers. It would be illogical to conclude that Warner Brothers, while not wanting to permit Lee to own the copyright, intended to share ownership with individuals like Aalmuhammed who worked under Lee's control, especially ones who at the time had made known no claim to the role of co-author. No one, including Aalmuhammed, made any indication to anyone prior to litigation that Aalmuhammed was intended to be a co-author and co-owner.

Aalmuhammed offered no evidence that he was the "inventive or master mind" of the movie. He was the author of another less widely known documentary about Malcolm X, but was not the master of this one. What Aalmuhammed's evidence showed, and all it showed, was that, subject to Spike Lee's authority to accept them, he made very valuable contributions to the movie. That is not enough for co-authorship of a joint work.

The Constitution establishes the social policy that our construction of the statutory term "authors" carries out. The Founding Fathers gave Congress the power to give authors copyrights in order "[t]o promote the progress of Science and useful arts." Progress would be retarded rather than promoted, if an author could not consult with others and adopt their useful suggestions without sacrificing sole ownership of the work. Too open a definition of author would compel authors to insulate themselves and maintain ignorance of the contributions others might make. Spike Lee could not consult a scholarly Muslim to make a movie about a religious conversion to Islam, and the arts would be the poorer for that.

The broader construction that Aalmuhammed proposes would extend joint authorship to many "overreaching contributors," like the dramaturg in Thomson, and deny sole authors "exclusive authorship status simply because another person render[ed] some form of assistance." Claimjumping by research assistants, editors, and former spouses, lovers and friends would endanger authors who talked with people about what they were doing, if creative copyrightable contribution were all that authorship required.

...

Because the record before the district court established no genuine issue of fact as to Aalmuhammed's co-authorship of Malcolm X as a joint work, the district court correctly granted summary judgment dismissing his claims for declaratory judgment and an accounting resting on co-authorship.

...

C. Unfair competition

Aalmuhammed claimed that defendants passed off his scriptwriting, directing and other work as that of other persons, in violation of the Lanham Act and the California statute prohibiting unfair competition. The dismissal was under Rule 12(b)(6), for failure to state a claim upon which relief can be granted, so we review de novo, on the basis of allegations in the complaint.

We have held that, at least in some circumstances, failure to give appropriate credit for a film is "reverse palming off" actionable under the Lanham Act. And we have held that "actions pursuant to California Business and Professions Code § 17200 are substantially congruent to claims made under the Lanham Act." Defendants argue that not enough of Aalmuhammed's proposed script was used verbatim to amount to a violation. But this argument goes to the evidence, not the complaint, so it cannot sustain the 12(b)(6) dismissal. The complaint alleged that Aalmuhammed "substantially rewrote and expanded the dialogue for various entire scenes" and otherwise alleged extensive and substantial use of his work in the final movie. We need not determine whether Aalmuhammed established a genuine issue of fact regarding unfair competition, because the claim never got as far as summary judgment in the district court. We reverse the dismissal of these two claims.

...

AFFIRMED in part, REVERSED and REMANDED in part. Each party to bear its own costs.

COMMUNITY FOR CREATIVE NON-VIOLENCE v. REID

United States Supreme Court

MARSHALL, J.,

[1] In this case, an artist and the organization that hired him to produce a sculpture contest the ownership of the copyright in that work. To resolve this dispute, we must construe the "work made for hire" provisions of the Copyright Act of 1976 (Act or 1976 Act), 17 U.S.C. §§ 101 and 201(b), and in particular, the provision in § 101, which defines as a "work made for hire" a "work prepared by an employee within the scope of his or her employment" (hereinafter § 101(1)). [p*733]

I

[2] Petitioners are the Community for Creative Non-Violence (CCNV), a nonprofit unincorporated association dedicated to eliminating homelessness in America, and Mitch Snyder, a member and trustee of CCNV. In the fall of 1985, CCNV decided to participate in the annual Christmastime Pageant of Peace in Washington, D.C., by sponsoring a display to dramatize the plight of the homeless. As the District Court recounted:

Snyder and fellow CCNV members conceived the idea for the nature of the display: a sculpture of a modern Nativity scene in which, in lieu of the traditional Holy Family, the two adult figures and the infant would appear as contemporary homeless people huddled on a streetside steam grate. The family was to be black (most of the homeless in Washington being black); the figures were to be life-sized, and the steam grate would be positioned atop a platform "pedestal," or base, within which special effects equipment would be enclosed to emit simulated "steam" through the grid to swirl about the figures. They also settled upon a title for the work -- "Third World America" -- and a legend for the pedestal: "and still there is no room at the inn." 652 F.Supp. 1453, 1454 (DC 1987).

[3] Snyder made inquiries to locate an artist to produce the sculpture. He was referred to respondent James Earl Reid, a Baltimore, Maryland, sculptor. In the course of two telephone calls, Reid agreed to sculpt the three human figures. CCNV agreed to make the steam grate and pedestal for the statue. Reid proposed that the work be cast in bronze, at a total cost of approximately $100,000 and taking six to eight months to complete. Snyder rejected that proposal because CCNV did not have sufficient funds, and because the statue had to be completed by December 12 to be included in the pageant. Reid then suggested, and Snyder agreed, that the [p*734] sculpture would be made of a material known as "Design Cast 62," a synthetic substance that could meet CCNV's monetary and time constraints, could be tinted to resemble bronze, and could withstand the elements. The parties agreed that the project would cost no more than $15,000, not including Reid's services, which he offered to donate. The parties did not sign a written agreement. Neither party mentioned copyright.

155

[4] After Reid received an advance of $3,000, he made several sketches of figures in various poses. At Snyder's request, Reid sent CCNV a sketch of a proposed sculpture showing the family in a creche-like setting: the mother seated, cradling a baby in her lap; the father standing behind her, bending over her shoulder to touch the baby's foot. Reid testified that Snyder asked for the sketch to use in raising funds for the sculpture. Snyder testified that it was also for his approval. Reid sought a black family to serve as a model for the sculpture. Upon Snyder's suggestion, Reid visited a family living at CCNV's Washington shelter, but decided that only their newly born child was a suitable model. While Reid was in Washington, Snyder took him to see homeless people living on the streets. Snyder pointed out that they tended to recline on steam grates, rather than sit or stand, in order to warm their bodies. From that time on, Reid's sketches contained only reclining figures.

[5] Throughout November and the first two weeks of December, 1985, Reid worked exclusively on the statue, assisted at various times by a dozen different people who were paid with funds provided in installments by CCNV. On a number of occasions, CCNV members visited Reid to check on his progress and to coordinate CCNV's construction of the base. CCNV rejected Reid's proposal to use suitcases or shopping bags to hold the family's personal belongings, insisting instead on a shopping cart. Reid and CCNV members did not discuss copyright ownership on any of these visits.

[6] On December 24, 1985, 12 days after the agreed-upon date, Reid delivered the completed statue to Washington. There it was joined to the steam grate and pedestal prepared by CCNV, and placed on display near the site of the pageant. Snyder paid Reid the final installment of the $15,000. The statue remained on display for a month. In late January, 1986, CCNV members returned it to Reid's studio in Baltimore for minor repairs. Several weeks later, Snyder began making plans to take the statue on a tour of several cities to raise money for the homeless. Reid objected, contending that the Design Cast 62 material was not strong enough to withstand the ambitious itinerary. He urged CCNV to cast the statue in bronze at a cost of $35,000, or to create a master mold at a cost of $5,000. Snyder declined to spend more of CCNV's money on the project.

[7] In March, 1986, Snyder asked Reid to return the sculpture. Reid refused. He then filed a certificate of copyright registration for "Third World America" in his name, and announced plans to take the sculpture on a more modest tour than the one CCNV had proposed. Snyder, acting in his capacity as CCNV's trustee, immediately filed a competing certificate of copyright registration.

[8] Snyder and CCNV then commenced this action against Reid and his photographer, Ronald Purtee, seeking return of the sculpture and a determination of copyright ownership. The District Court granted a preliminary injunction, ordering the sculpture's return. After a 2-day bench trial, the District Court declared that "Third World America" was a "work made for hire" under § 101 of the Copyright Act, and that Snyder, as trustee for CCNV, was the exclusive owner of the copyright in the sculpture. 652 F.Supp. at 1457. The court reasoned that Reid had been an "employee" of CCNV within the meaning of § 101(1) because CCNV

156

was the motivating force in the statue's production. Snyder and [p*736] other CCNV members, the court explained, "conceived the idea of a contemporary Nativity scene to contrast with the national celebration of the season," and "directed enough of [Reid's] effort to assure that, in the end, he had produced what they, not he, wanted." Id. at 1456.

[9] The Court of Appeals for the District of Columbia Circuit reversed and remanded, holding that Reid owned the copyright because "Third World America" was not a work for hire. 270 U.S.App.D.C. 26, 35, 846 F.2d 1485, 1494 (1988). Adopting what it termed the "literal interpretation" of the Act as articulated by the Fifth Circuit in Easter Seal Society for Crippled Children and Adults of Louisiana, Inc. v. Playboy Enterprises, 815 F.2d 323, 329 (1987), cert. denied, 485 U.S. 981 (1988), the court read § 101 as creating "a simple dichotomy in fact between employees and independent contractors." 270 U.S.App.D.C. at 33, 846 F.2d at 1492. Because, under agency law, Reid was an independent contractor, the court concluded that the work was not "prepared by an employee" under § 101(1). Id. at 35, 846 F.2d at 1494. Nor was the sculpture a "work made for hire" under the second subsection of § 101 (hereinafter § 101(2)): sculpture is not one of the nine categories of works enumerated in that subsection, and the parties had not agreed in writing that the sculpture would be a work for hire. Ibid. The court suggested that the sculpture nevertheless may have been jointly authored by CCNV and Reid, id. at 36, 846 F.2d at 1495, and remanded for a determination whether the sculpture is indeed a joint work under the Act, id. at 39-40, 846 F.2d at 1498-1499.

[10] We granted certiorari to resolve a conflict among the Courts of Appeals over the proper construction of the "work made for hire" provisions of the Act. 488 U.S. 940 (1988). We now affirm.

II

A

[11] The Copyright Act of 1976 provides that copyright ownership "vests initially in the author or authors of the work." 17 U.S.C. § 201(a). As a general rule, the author is the party who actually creates the work, that is, the person who translates an idea into a fixed, tangible expression entitled to copyright protection. § 102. The Act carves out an important exception, however, for "works made for hire." If the work is for hire, "the employer or other person for whom the work was prepared is considered the author," and owns the copyright, unless there is a written agreement to the contrary. § 201(b). Classifying a work as "made for hire" determines not only the initial ownership of its copyright, but also the copyright's duration, § 302(c), and the owners' renewal rights, § 304(a), termination rights, § 203(a), and right to import certain goods bearing the copyright, § 601(b)(1). See 1 M. Nimmer & D. Nimmer, Nimmer on Copyright § 5.03 [A], pp. 5-10 (1988). The contours of the work for hire doctrine therefore carry profound significance for freelance creators -- including artists, writers, photographers, designers, composers, and computer programmers -- and for the publishing, advertising, music, and other industries which commission their works.

[12] Section 101 of the 1976 Act provides that a work is "for hire" under two sets of circumstances:

(1) a work prepared by an employee within the scope of his or her employment; or

(2) a work specially ordered or commissioned for use as a contribution to a collective work, as a part of a motion picture or other audiovisual work, as a translation, as a supplementary work, as a compilation, as an instructional text, as a test, as answer material for a test, or as an atlas, if the parties expressly agree in a written instrument signed by them that the work shall be considered a work made for hire.

[13] Petitioners do not claim that the statue satisfies the terms of § 101(2). Quite clearly, it does not. Sculpture does not fit within any of the nine categories of "specially ordered or commissioned" works enumerated in that subsection, and no written agreement between the parties establishes "Third World America" as a work for hire.

[14] The dispositive inquiry in this case therefore is whether "Third World America" is "a work prepared by an employee within the scope of his or her employment" under § 101(1). The Act does not define these terms. In the absence of such guidance, four interpretations have emerged. The first holds that a work is prepared by an employee whenever the hiring party retains the right to control the product. See Peregrine v. Lauren Corp., 601 F.Supp. 828, 829 (Colo.1985); Clarkstown v. Reeder, 566 F.Supp. 137, 142 (SDNY 1983). [p*739] Petitioners take this view. Brief for Petitioners 15; Tr. of Oral. Arg. 12. A second, and closely related, view is that a work is prepared by an employee under § 101(1) when the hiring party has actually wielded control with respect to the creation of a particular work. This approach was formulated by the Court of Appeals for the Second Circuit, Aldon Accessories Ltd. v. Spiegel, Inc., 738 F.2d 548, cert. denied, 469 U.S. 982 (1984), and adopted by the Fourth Circuit, Brunswick Beacon, Inc. v. Schock-Hopchas Publishing Co., 810 F.2d 410 (1987), the Seventh Circuit, Evans Newton, Inc. v. Chicago Systems Software, 793 F.2d 889, cert. denied, 479 U.S. 949 (1986), and, at times, by petitioners, Brief for Petitioners 17. A third view is that the term "employee" within § 101(1) carries its common law agency law meaning. This view was endorsed by the Fifth Circuit in Easter Seal Society for Crippled Children and Adults of Louisiana, Inc. v. Playboy Enterprises, 815 F.2d 323 (1987), and by the Court of Appeals below. Finally, respondent and numerous amici curiae contend that the term "employee" only refers to "formal, salaried" employees. See, e.g., Brief for Respondent 23-24; Brief for Register of Copyrights as Amicus Curiae 7. The Court of Appeals for the Ninth Circuit recently adopted this view. See Dumas v. Gommerman, 865 F.2d 1093 (1989).

[15] The starting point for our interpretation of a statute is always its language. Consumer Product Safety Comm'n v. GTE Sylvania, Inc., 447 U.S. 102, 108 (1980). The Act nowhere defines the terms "employee" or "scope of employment." It is, however, well established that

[w]here Congress uses terms that have accumulated settled meaning under . . . the common law, a court must infer, unless the statute otherwise dictates, that Congress means to incorporate the established meaning of these terms.

NLRB v. Amax Coal Co., 453 U.S. 322, 329 (1981); see also Perrin v. United States, 444 U.S. 37, 42 (1979). In the past, when Congress has used the term "employee" without defining it, we have concluded that Congress intended to describe the conventional master-servant relationship as understood by common law agency doctrine. See, e.g., Kelley v. Southern Pacific Co., 419 U.S. 318, 322-323 (1974); Baker v. Texas & Pacific R. Co., 359 U.S. 227, 228 (1959) (per curiam); Robinson v. Baltimore & Ohio R. Co., 237 U.S. 84, 94 (1915). Nothing in the text of the work for hire provisions indicates that Congress used the words "employee" and "employment" to describe anything other than "'the conventional relation of employer and employe.'" Kelley, supra, at 323, quoting Robinson, supra, at 94; compare NLRB v. Hearst Publications, Inc., 322 U.S. 111, 124-132 (1944) (rejecting agency law conception of employee for purposes of the National Labor Relations Act where structure and context of statute indicated broader definition). On the contrary, Congress' intent to incorporate the agency law definition is suggested by § 101(1)'s use of the term, "scope of employment," a widely used term of art in agency law. See Restatement (Second) of Agency § 228 (1958) (hereinafter Restatement).

[16] In past cases of statutory interpretation, when we have concluded that Congress intended terms such as "employee," "employer," and "scope of employment" to be understood in light of agency law, we have relied on the general common law of agency, rather than on the law of any particular State, to give meaning to these terms. See, e.g., Kelley, 419 U.S. at 323-324, and n. 5; id. at 332 (Stewart, J., concurring in judgment); Ward v. Atlantic Coast Line R. Co., 362 U.S. 396, 400 (1960); Baker, supra, at 228. This practice reflects the fact that "federal statutes are generally intended to have uniform nationwide application." Mississippi Band of Choctaw Indians v. Holyfield, ante at 43. Establishment of a federal rule of agency, rather than reliance on state agency law, is particularly appropriate here, given the Act's express objective of creating national, uniform copyright law by broadly preempting state statutory and common law copyright regulation. See 17 U.S.C. § 301(a). We thus agree with the Court of Appeals that the term "employee" should be understood in light of the general common law of agency.

[17] In contrast, neither test proposed by petitioners is consistent with the text of the Act. The exclusive focus of the right to control the product test on the relationship between the hiring party and the product clashes with the language of § 101(1), which focuses on the relationship between the hired and hiring parties. The right to control the product test also would distort the meaning of the ensuing subsection, § 101(2). Section 101 plainly creates two distinct ways in which a work can be deemed for hire: one for works prepared by employees, the other for those specially ordered or commissioned works which fall within one of the nine enumerated categories and are the subject of a written agreement. The right to control the product test ignores this dichotomy by transforming into a work for hire under § 101(1) any "specially ordered or commissioned" work that is subject

159

to the supervision and control of the hiring party. Because a party who hires a "specially ordered or commissioned" work by definition has a right to specify the characteristics of the product desired, at the time the commission is accepted, and frequently until it is completed, the right to control the product test would mean that many works that could satisfy § 101(2) would already have been deemed works for hire under § 101(1). Petitioners' interpretation is particularly hard to square with § 101(2)'s enumeration of the nine specific categories of specially ordered or commissioned works eligible to be works for hire, e.g., "a contribution to a collective work," "a part of a motion picture," and "answer material for a test." The unifying feature of these works is that they are usually prepared at the instance, direction, and risk of a publisher or producer. [By their very nature, therefore, these types of works would be works by an employee under petitioners' right to control the product test. *※ why "actual control test" is bad*

[18] The actual control test, articulated by the Second Circuit in Aldon Accessories, fares only marginally better when measured against the language and structure of § 101. Under this test, independent contractors who are so controlled and supervised in the creation of a particular work are deemed "employees" under § 101(1). Thus, work for hire status under § 101(1) depends on a hiring party's actual control of, rather than right to control, the product. Aldon Accessories, 738 F.2d at 552. Under the actual control test, a work for hire could arise under § 101(2), but not under § 101(1), where a party commissions, but does not actually control, a product which falls into one of the nine enumerated categories. Nonetheless, we agree with the Fifth Circuit Court of Appeals that "[t]here is simply no way to milk the `actual control' test of Aldon Accessories from the language of the statute." Easter Seal Society, 815 F.2d at 334. Section 101 clearly delineates between works prepared by an employee and commissioned works. Sound though other distinctions might be as a matter of copyright policy, there is no statutory support for an additional dichotomy between commissioned works that are actually controlled and supervised by the hiring party and those that are not.

[19] We therefore conclude that the language and structure of § 101 of the Act do not support either the right to control the product or the actual control approaches. The structure of [p*743] § 101 indicates that a work for hire can arise through one of two mutually exclusive means, one for employees and one for independent contractors, and ordinary canons of statutory interpretation indicate that the classification of a particular hired party should be made with reference to agency law.

This reading of the undefined statutory terms finds considerable support in the Act's legislative history. Cf. Diamond v. Chakrabarty, 447 U.S. 303, 315 (1980). The Act, which almost completely revised existing copyright law, was the product of two decades of negotiation by representatives of creators and copyright-using industries, supervised by the Copyright Office and, to a lesser extent, by Congress. See Mills Music, Inc. v. Snyder, 469 U.S. 153, 159 (1985); Litman, Copyright, Compromise, and Legislative History, 72 Cornell L.Rev. 857, 862 (1987). Despite the lengthy history of negotiation and compromise which ultimately produced the Act, two things remained constant. First, interested parties and Congress at all times viewed works by employees and commissioned works by independent contractors as separate entities. Second, in using the term "employee," the parties and Congress meant to refer to a hired party in a conventional employment relationship. These factors militate in favor of the reading we have found appropriate.

[21] In 1955, when Congress decided to overhaul copyright law, the existing work for hire provision was § 62 of the 1909 Copyright Act, 17 U.S.C. § 26 (1976 ed.) (1909 Act). It provided that "the word `author' shall include an employer in [p*744] the case of works made for hire." Because the 1909 Act did not define "employer" or "works made for hire," the task of shaping these terms fell to the courts. They concluded that the work for hire doctrine codified in § 62 referred only to works made by employees in the regular course of their employment. As for commissioned works, the courts generally presumed that the commissioned party had impliedly agreed to convey the copyright, along with the work itself, to the hiring party. See, e.g., Shapiro, Bernstein & Co. v. Jerry Vogel Music Co., 221 F.2d 569, 570, aff'd, 223 F.2d 252 (CA2 1955); Yardley v. Houghton Mifflin Co., 108 F.2d 28, 31 (CA2 1939), cert. denied, 309 U.S. 686 (1940).

[22] In 1961, the Copyright Office's first legislative proposal retained the distinction between works by employees and works by independent contractors. See Report of the Register of Copyrights on the General Revision of the U.S. Copyright Law, 87th Cong., 1st Sess., Copyright Law Revision 86-87 (H. Judiciary Comm. Print 1961). After numerous meetings with representatives of the affected parties, the Copyright Office issued a preliminary draft bill in 1963. Adopting the Register's recommendation, it defined "work [p*745] made for hire" as

a work prepared by an employee within the scope of the duties of his employment, but not including a work made on special order or commission.

Preliminary Draft for Revised U.S. Copyright Law and Discussions and Comments on the Draft, 88th Cong., 2d Sess., Copyright Law Revision, Part 3, p. 15, n. 11 (H. Judiciary Comm. Print 1964) (hereinafter Preliminary Draft).

[23] In response to objections by book publishers that the preliminary draft bill limited the work for hire doctrine to "employees," the 1964 revision bill expanded the scope of the work for hire classification to reach, for the first time, commissioned works. The bill's language, proposed initially by representatives of the publishing industry, retained the definition of work for hire insofar as it referred to "employees," but added a separate clause covering commissioned works, without regard to the subject matter, "if the parties so agree in writing." S. 3008, H.R. 11947, H.R. 12354, 88th Cong., 2d Sess., § 54 (1964), reproduced in 1964 Revision Bill with Discussions and Comments, 89th Cong., 1st Sess., Copyright Law Revision, pt. 5, p. 31 (H.R. Judiciary Comm. Print 1965). Those representing authors objected that the added provision would allow publishers to use their superior bargaining position to force authors to sign work for hire agreements, thereby relinquishing all copyright rights as a condition of getting their books published. See Supplementary Report, at 67.

[24] In 1965, the competing interests reached an historic compromise, which was embodied in a joint memorandum submitted to Congress and the Copyright Office,

incorporated into the 1965 revision bill, and ultimately enacted in the same form and nearly the same terms 11 years later, as § 101 of the 1976 Act. The compromise retained as subsection (1) the language referring to "a work prepared by an employee within the scope of his employment." However, in exchange for concessions from publishers on provisions relating to the termination of transfer rights, the authors consented to a second subsection which classified four categories of commissioned works as works for hire if the parties expressly so agreed in writing: works for use "as a contribution to a collective work, as a part of a motion picture, as a translation, or as supplementary work." S. 1006, H.R. 4347, H.R. 5680, H.R. 6835, 89th Cong., 1st Sess., § 101 (1965). The interested parties selected these categories because they concluded that these commissioned works, although not prepared by employees, and thus not covered by the first subsection, nevertheless should be treated as works for hire because they were ordinarily prepared "at the instance, direction, and risk of a publisher or producer." Supplementary Report, at 67. The Supplementary Report emphasized that only the "four special cases specifically mentioned" could qualify as works made for hire; "[o]ther works made on special order or commission would not come within the definition." Id. at 67-68.

[25] In 1966, the House Committee on the Judiciary endorsed this compromise in the first legislative report on the revision bills. See H.R.Rep. No. 2237, 89th Cong., 2d Sess., 114, 116 (1966). Retaining the distinction between works by employees and commissioned works, the House Committee focused instead on

how to draw a statutory line between those works written on special order or commission that should be considered as works made for hire, and those that should not.

Id. at 115. The House Committee added four other enumerated categories of commissioned works that could be treated as works for hire: compilations, instructional texts, tests, and atlases. Id. at 116. With the single addition of "answer material for a test," the 1976 Act, as enacted, contained the same definition of works made for hire as did the 1966 revision bill, and had the same structure and nearly the same terms as the 1966 bill. Indeed, much of the language of the 1976 House and Senate Reports was borrowed from the Reports accompanying the earlier drafts. See, e.g., H.R.Rep. No. 94-1476, p. 121 (1976); S.Rep. No. 94-473, p. 105 (1975).

[26] Thus, the legislative history of the Act is significant for several reasons. First, the enactment of the 1965 compromise with only minor modifications demonstrates that Congress intended to provide two mutually exclusive ways for works to acquire work for hire status: one for employees and [p*748] the other for independent contractors. Second, the legislative history underscores the clear import of the statutory language: only enumerated categories of commissioned works may be accorded work for hire status. The hiring party's right to control the product simply is not determinative. See Note, The Creative Commissioner: Commissioned Works Under the Copyright Act of 1976, 62 N.Y.U.L.Rev. 373, 388 (1987). Indeed, importing a test based on a hiring party's right to control, or actual control of, a product would unravel the "`carefully worked-out compromise aimed

at balancing legitimate interests on both sides.'" H.R.Rep. No. 2237, supra, at 114, quoting Supplemental Report, at 66.

[27] We do not find convincing petitioners' contrary interpretation of the history of the Act. They contend that Congress, in enacting the Act, meant to incorporate a line of cases decided under the 1909 Act holding that an employment relationship exists sufficient to give the hiring party copyright ownership whenever that party has the right to control or supervise the artist's work. See, e.g., Siegel v. National Periodical Publications, Inc., 508 F.2d 909, 914 (CA2 1974); Picture Music, Inc. v. Bourne, Inc., 457 F.2d 1213, 1216 (CA2), cert. denied, 409 U.S. 997 (1972); Scherr v. Universal Match Corp., 417 F.2d 497, 500 (CA2 1969), cert. denied, 397 U.S. 936 (1970); Brattleboro Publishing Co. v. Winmill Publishing Corp., 369 F.2d 565, 567-568 (CA2 1966). In support of this position, petitioners note:

Nowhere in the 1976 Act or in the Act's legislative history does Congress state that it intended to jettison the control standard or otherwise to reject the pre-Act judicial approach to identifying a work for hire employment relationship.

Brief for Petitioners 20, citing Aldon Accessories, 738 F.2d at 552.

[28] We are unpersuaded. Ordinarily, "Congress' silence is just that -- silence." Alaska Airlines, Inc. v. Brock, 480 U.S. 678, 686 (1987). Petitioners' reliance on legislative silence is particularly misplaced here, because the text and structure of § 101 counsel otherwise. See Bourjaily v. United States, 483 U.S. 171, 178 (1987); Harrison v. PPG Industries, Inc., 446 U.S. 578, 592 (1980). Furthermore, the structure of the work for hire provisions was fully developed in 1965, and the text was agreed upon in essentially final form by 1966. At that time, however, the courts had applied the work for hire doctrine under the 1909 Act exclusively to traditional employees. Indeed, it was not until after the 1965 compromise was forged and adopted by Congress that a federal court for the first time applied the work for hire doctrine to commissioned works. See, e.g., Brattleboro Publishing Co., supra, at 567-568. Congress certainly could not have "jettisoned" a line of cases that had not yet been decided.

[29] Finally, petitioners' construction of the work for hire provisions would impede Congress' paramount goal in revising the 1976 Act of enhancing predictability and certainty of copyright ownership. See H.R.Rep. No. 94-1476, supra, at 129. In a "copyright marketplace," the parties negotiate with an expectation that one of them will own the copyright in the completed work. Dumas, 865 F.2d at 1104-1105, n. 18. With that expectation, the parties at the outset can settle on relevant contractual terms, such as the price for the work and the ownership of reproduction rights.

[30] To the extent that petitioners endorse an actual control test, CCNV's construction of the work for hire provisions prevents such planning. Because that test turns on whether the hiring party has closely monitored the production process, the parties would not know until late in the process, if not until the work is completed, whether a work will ultimately fall within § 101(1). Under petitioners' approach, therefore, parties would have to predict in advance whether the hiring party will sufficiently control a given work to make it the author.

If they guess incorrectly, their reliance on "work for hire" or an assignment may give them a copyright interest that they did not bargain for.

Easter Seal Society, 815 F.2d at 333; accord, Dumas, 865 F.2d at 1103. This understanding of the work for hire provisions clearly thwarts Congress' goal of ensuring predictability through advance planning. Moreover, petitioners' interpretation

leaves the door open for hiring parties, who have failed to get a full assignment of copyright rights from independent contractors falling outside the subdivision (2) guidelines, to unilaterally obtain work-made-for-hire rights years after the work has been completed as long as they directed or supervised the work, a standard that is hard not to meet when one is a hiring party.

Hamilton, Commissioned Works as Works Made for Hire Under the 1976 Copyright Act: Misinterpretation and Injustice, 135 U.Pa.L.Rev. 1281, 1304 (1987).

[31] In sum, we must reject petitioners' argument. Transforming a commissioned work into a work by an employee on the basis of the hiring party's right to control, or actual control of, the work is inconsistent with the language, structure, and legislative history of the work for hire provisions. To [p*751] determine whether a work is for hire under the Act, a court first should ascertain, using principles of general common law of agency, whether the work was prepared by an employee or an independent contractor. After making this determination, the court can apply the appropriate subsection of § 101.

B

[32] We turn, finally, to an application of § 101 to Reid's production of "Third World America." In determining whether a hired party is an employee under the general common law of agency, we consider the hiring party's right to control the manner and means by which the product is accomplished. Among the other factors relevant to this inquiry are the skill required; the source of the instrumentalities and tools; the location of the work; the duration of the relationship between the parties; whether the hiring party has the right to assign additional projects to the hired party; the extent of the hired party's discretion over when and how long to work; the method of payment; the hired party's role in hiring and [p*752] paying assistants; whether the work is part of the regular business of the hiring party; whether the hiring party is in business; the provision of employee benefits; and the tax treatment of the hired party. See Restatement § 220(2) (setting forth a nonexhaustive list of factors relevant to determining whether a hired party is an employee). No one of these factors is determinative. See Ward, 362 U.S. at 400; Hilton Int'l Co. v. NLRB, 690 F.2d 318, 321 (CA2 1982).

[33] Examining the circumstances of this case in light of these factors, we agree with the Court of Appeals that Reid was not an employee of CCNV, but an independent contractor. 270 U.S.App.D.C. at 35, n. 11, 846 F.2d at 1494, n. 11. True, CCNV members directed enough of Reid's work to ensure that he produced a sculpture that met their specifications. 652 F.Supp. at 1456. But the extent of control the hiring party exercises over the details of the product is not dispositive. Indeed, all the other circumstances weigh heavily against finding an employment

relationship. Reid is a sculptor, a skilled occupation. Reid supplied his own tools. He worked in his own studio in Baltimore, making daily supervision of his activities from Washington practicably impossible. Reid was retained for less than two months, a relatively short period of time. During and after this time, CCNV had no right to assign additional projects to Reid. Apart from the deadline for completing the sculpture, Reid had absolute freedom to decide when and how long to work. CCNV paid Reid $15,000, a sum dependent on "completion of a specific job, a method by which independent contractors are often compensated." Holt v. Winpisinger, 258 U.S.App.D.C. 343, 351, 811 F.2d 1532, 1540 (1987). Reid had total discretion in hiring and paying assistants. "Creating sculptures was hardly `regular business' for CCNV." 270 U.S.App.D.C. at 35, n. 11, 846 F.2d at 1494, n. 11. Indeed, CCNV is not a business at all. Finally, CCNV did not pay payroll or Social Security taxes, provide any employee benefits, or contribute to unemployment insurance or workers' compensation funds.

[34] Because Reid was an independent contractor, whether "Third World America" is a work for hire depends on whether it satisfies the terms of § 101(2). This petitioners concede it cannot do. Thus, CCNV is not the author of "Third World America" by virtue of the work for hire provisions of the Act. However, as the Court of Appeals made clear, CCNV nevertheless may be a joint author of the sculpture if, on remand, the District Court determines that CCNV and Reid prepared the work "with the intention that their contributions be merged into inseparable or interdependent parts of a unitary whole." 17 U.S.C. § 101. In that case, CCNV and Reid would be co-owners of the copyright in the work. See § 201(a).

[35] For the aforestated reasons, we affirm the judgment of the Court of Appeals for the District of Columbia Circuit.

[36] It is so ordered.

531 F.3d 962 (2008)

RICHLIN V. METRO-GOLDWYN-MAYER PICTURES

Court of Appeals for the Ninth Circuit

WARDLAW, Circuit Judge:

Inspector Jacques Clouseau, famously unable to crack the simplest of murder cases, would most certainly be confounded by the case we face. While Inspector Clouseau searched for the answer to the question, "Who did it?", we must search for the answer to the question, "Who owns it?" In 1962, Maurice Richlin coauthored a story treatment (the "Treatment") involving the bumbling inspector. Later that year, before publication, Richlin assigned all rights in the Treatment — including copyright and the right to renew that copyright — to a corporation that used it to create the smash-hit film, The Pink Panther (the "Motion Picture"). The Richlin heirs now claim federal statutory renewal rights in the Treatment and derivative works, including the Motion Picture. They assert that Richlin's coauthorship of the Treatment makes him a coauthor of the Motion Picture. Alternatively, they contend that, because the Motion Picture secured statutory protection for the portions of the Treatment incorporated into the Motion Picture, and because the copyright in the Motion Picture was renewed for a second term, they are co-owners of the Motion Picture's renewal copyright and all derivative works thereof. Although the Richlin heirs have developed several theories that could supply the answer to the question, "Who owns it?", unlike Inspector Clouseau, they have not quite stumbled upon a theory that favors them. We therefore affirm the district court's conclusion that the Richlin heirs have no interest in the copyright to the Motion Picture.

I. BACKGROUND

The material facts are largely undisputed. In April 1962, Maurice Richlin and Blake Edwards coauthored a fourteen-page Treatment initially entitled The Pink Rajah, but later renamed The Pink Panther. The Treatment served as the basis for the well-known motion picture, The Pink Panther, and numerous derivative works. It appears that the Treatment set forth many of the plot elements and characters, including Inspector Clouseau himself, developed into the screenplay and incorporated into the Motion Picture.

Richlin and Edwards entered into an employment agreement dated May 14, 1962 (the "Employment Agreement") with the Mirisch Corporation of Delaware ("Mirisch") to write the screenplay for the Motion Picture. They agreed to create the screenplay as a "work made for hire." Under this contract, Richlin and Edwards combined received $150,000 for their work on the Treatment and the screenplay.

Later that month, on May 24, 1962, Richlin and Edwards executed a literary assignment agreement (the "Assignment") whereby they transferred and assigned "forever ... that certain story (which term shall cover all literary material written by [Richlin and Edwards] in connection therewith including any adaptations, treatments, scenarios, dialogue, scripts and/or screenplays) entitled: `Pink Rajah' also entitled or known as `Pink Panther'" in exchange for $1 "and other good and valuable consideration in hand" paid by Mirisch. Mirisch also received "the right to use [Richlin's and Edwards's] name[s] as the author of the literary composition upon which said adaptations, or any of them, are based." The Assignment further provided that if Mirisch copyrighted the Treatment, Mirisch "shall enjoy its rights hereunder for the full duration of such copyright or copyrights, including any and all renewals thereof."

In 1963, The Pink Panther was released and distributed in theaters to great acclaim. It was followed by nine movie sequels, many of which gave screen credit to Richlin and Edwards for creating the characters. The original Motion Picture bears a copyright notice of 1963 in the name of Mirisch and G & E Productions. In 1964, the U.S. Copyright Office issued a certificate of registration for the "motion picture" entitled "The Pink Panther" under the Copyright Act of 1909 ("1909 Act").

The Certificate of Registration identifies the claimant and author as "Mirisch-G & E Productions." The certificate lists the date of publication as March 18, 1964, but notes that the copyright notice on the Motion Picture bears a date of 1963. The Richlin heirs concede that neither the Treatment nor the screenplay was ever separately published or registered for federal copyright protection.

Richlin died on November 13, 1990. The original term of copyright in the Motion Picture — twenty-eight years from the first date of publication — was set to expire in 1991, but it was renewed that year by the successors-in-interest to Mirisch-G & E Productions, MGM-Pathe Communications Co./ Geoffrey Productions Inc. (collectively, "MGM"). A Renewal Certificate issued, which identified MGM as the claimant and "proprietor of copyright in a work made for hire" and the author and original claimant as Mirisch-G & E Productions. None of the Richlin heirs attempted to secure a renewal interest in the Treatment or screenplay, and there is no separate renewal certificate for either.

The Richlin heirs filed suit in the United States District Court for the Central District of California seeking declaratory relief and an accounting. They claim a 50 percent renewal interest in the Treatment and all derivative works. During the course of this litigation, the theories undergirding this claim have evolved. The complaint relies on the theory that publication of the derivative work (the Motion Picture) effectuated publication of the underlying work (the Treatment). Under this theory, when MGM renewed the Motion Picture's statutory copyright in 1991, this renewed the copyright in the Treatment on behalf of the Richlin heirs, which gave the Richlin heirs an interest in the Motion Picture's renewal copyright. These principles carry some theoretical weight in copyright law; however, the Richlin heirs failed to renew their statutory copyright, if any, in the Treatment in 1991. That may explain why, by the time the district court granted summary judgment in favor of MGM, the Richlin heirs had abandoned their argument based on a statutory copyright in the Treatment. Instead, they argued that they have a copyright interest in the Motion Picture as coauthors based on Richlin's coauthorship of the Treatment, which was incorporated into the Motion Picture. The district court analyzed the requirements of a "joint work" prepared by coauthors, who under copyright law would each be deemed an owner of the copyright. The court rejected this theory because, under the factors set forth in Aalmuhammed v. Lee, 202 F.3d 1227, 1234 (9th Cir.2000), Richlin had no control over the Motion Picture, and there was no manifestation of intent — by contract or otherwise — that Richlin and Edwards would be coauthors of the Motion Picture. See id. at 1234 (analyzing coauthorship under three factors: control, objective manifestation of intent to be coauthors, and whether the audience appeal of the work can be attributed to all coauthors). Because the coauthorship theory failed, the district court awarded summary judgment in favor of MGM, declining to reach any other issues. The Richlin heirs timely appeal.

II. JURISDICTION AND STANDARD OF REVIEW

The district court had jurisdiction pursuant to 28 U.S.C. § 1338, which confers subject matter jurisdiction over copyright actions. We have jurisdiction over final judgments of the district courts pursuant to 28 U.S.C. § 1291.

We review a district court's grant of summary judgment de novo. Bagdadi v. Nazar, 84 F.3d 1194, 1197 (9th Cir.1996). In reviewing the grant of summary judgment, we "must determine, viewing the evidence in the light most favorable to the nonmoving party, whether genuine issues of material fact exist and whether the district court correctly applied the relevant substantive law." Id.

III. DISCUSSION

On appeal, the Richlin heirs maintain their contention that because Richlin and Edwards jointly authored the Treatment, and the Treatment became a critical component of the Motion Picture, Richlin was a co-author of the Motion Picture, and was therefore a co-owner on whose heirs' behalf MGM secured a renewal interest in the Motion Picture's copyright in 1991. Alternatively, the Richlin heirs resort to the theory underlying their complaint. They contend that publication of the Treatment with the Motion Picture secured a statutory copyright for the Treatment, which was renewed on their behalf by MGM when it renewed the Motion Picture's copyright. We address each argument in turn.

A. Coauthorship of the Motion Picture

To determine whether Richlin had an interest in the Motion Picture's federal statutory copyright, we must consider the question of coauthorship. The Richlin heirs argue that because Richlin coauthored the Treatment, which was a substantial component of the Motion Picture, he is also a coauthor of the Motion Picture. This coauthorship, according to the Richlin heirs, gives them an interest in the Motion Picture's copyright. Under this facially appealing, but legally unsustainable, argument, an interest in the renewal term of copyright and all subsequent motion pictures and adaptations based on that copyright would revert to the Richlin heirs.[8]See 17 U.S.C. § 201(a) (1976) ("The authors of a joint work are co-owners of copyright in the work.").

We agree with the district court that Richlin and Edwards were not coauthors of the Motion Picture. Richlin and Edwards wrote the Treatment in 1962, and the Motion Picture was copyrighted when published with notice in 1963; therefore, the Richlin heirs' claim of coauthorship is governed by the 1909 Act. The 1909 Act, however, did not expressly mention or define joint works or coauthorship. Nevertheless, as early as 1915, in Maurel v. Smith, Judge Learned Hand applied the universally adopted common law definition of joint authors to the 1909 Act, holding that they "undertake jointly to write a play, agreeing on the general outline and design and sharing the labor of working it out." 220 F. 195, 199 (S.D.N.Y.1915) (quoting Levy v. Rutley, L.R. 6 C.P. 523 (1871)); see also Edward B. Marks Music Corp. v. Jerry Vogel Music Co., 140 F.2d 266, 267 (2d Cir.1944) ("[I]t is enough that they mean their contributions to be complementary in the sense that they are to be embodied in a single work to be performed as such."); LIOR ZEMER, THE IDEA OF AUTHORSHIP IN COPYRIGHT 190 n. 15 (2007) ("In Levy v. Rutley, the earliest recorded case on joint authorship, Byles[,] J[.] found joint authorship to exist although one person had contributed a very small amount of work to the execution."). Then, in Picture Music, Inc. v. Bourne, Inc., a district court suggested a "statutory revision[ ] of the copyright law [that] would define a `joint work' as one `prepared by two or more authors with the intention that their contributions be merged into inseparable or interdependent parts of a unitary whole.'" 314 F.Supp. *968 640, 646 (S.D.N.Y.1970). This was the precise wording that Congress used to define "joint work" when it enacted the 1976 Act. See 17 U.S.C. § 101 (1976). As Professor Nimmer explains, "[t]he 1909 Act did not expressly refer to the doctrine of joint ownership, but its principles, largely unchanged under the current Act, were firmly established by case law, and were applicable to common law as well as statutory copyright." 1 M. NIMMER & D. NIMMER, NIMMER ON COPYRIGHT § 6.01 n. 1 (2007). Because the 1976 Act incorporated the well-established case law interpreting the definition of "joint work" under the 1909 Act, we may assess the Richlin heirs' claim under the more fully developed rubric of the 1976 Act.

Section 101 of the 1976 Act defines "joint work" as "a work prepared by two or more authors with the intention that their contributions be merged into inseparable or interdependent parts of a unitary whole." 17 U.S.C. § 101 (1976). A "joint work" requires each author to make "an independently copyrightable contribution." Ashton-Tate Corp. v. Ross, 916 F.2d 516, 521 (9th Cir.1990). "The authors of a joint work are co-owners of copyright in the work." 17 U.S.C. § 201(a) (1976). Even if a person's contribution is minor, once he is accorded joint authorship status, he enjoys all benefits of joint authorship. See Erickson v. Trinity Theatre, Inc., 13 F.3d 1061, 1068 (7th Cir. 1994); Cmty. for Creative Non-Violence v. Reid, 846 F.2d 1485, 1498 (D.C.Cir.1988), aff'd on other grounds, 490 U.S. 730, 109 S. Ct. 2166, 104 L. Ed. 2d 811 (1989); Bencich v. Hoffman, 84 F. Supp. 2d 1053, 1055 (D.Ariz.2000); 1 NIMMER § 6.08.

In Aalmuhammed v. Lee, 202 F.3d 1227, 1234 (9th Cir.2000), we set forth three criteria for determining whether a work is jointly authored under § 101. First, we determine whether the "putative coauthors ma[de] objective manifestations of a shared intent to be coauthors." Id. A contract evidencing intent to be or not to be coauthors is dispositive. Id. Second, we determine whether the alleged author superintended the work by exercising control. Id. Control will often be the most important factor. Id. Third, we analyze whether "the audience appeal of the work" can be attributed to both authors, and whether "the share of each in its success cannot be appraised." Id. (quotations omitted).

The plain language of § 101 makes clear that Richlin is a coauthor of the Treatment. Viewing the facts in the light most favorable to the Richlin heirs, Richlin and Edwards could have secured statutory copyright for the Treatment before assigning it to Mirisch, as it was a fourteen-page original creative story written jointly by Richlin and Edwards. See 17 U.S.C. § 4 (1909) ("The works for which copyright may be secured under this title shall include all the writings of an author."); 17 U.S.C. § 102 (1976) ("Copyright protection subsists ... in original works of authorship fixed in any tangible medium of expression...."); 1 NIMMER §§ 2.04 and 6.01 (articulating standards for "literary works" and "joint works"). Moreover, the Treatment "was prepared by two or more authors," Richlin and Edwards, who clearly intended that it be "merged into inseparable or interdependent parts of a unitary whole." 17 U.S.C. § 101 (1976). Indeed, this is what Richlin and Edwards accomplished when they presented the completed Treatment to Mirisch.

But the Treatment is not the appropriate reference point. The Richlin heirs' claim for declaratory relief and an accounting rests on their argument that, by virtue of his contribution to the Treatment, Richlin is coauthor of the Motion Picture. Thus, the work that must be examined to determine joint authorship is the Motion Picture, not the Treatment. The plain language of § 101 does not shed light on whether Richlin was a coauthor of the Motion Picture. Applying the Aalmuhammed factors to Richlin's involvement in the Motion Picture, however, confirms that Richlin and Edwards were not coauthors of that work.

We must first determine whether "putative coauthors ma[de] objective manifestations of a shared intent to be coauthors." Aalmuhammed, 202 F.3d at 1234. A contract evidencing intent to be or not to be coauthors is dispositive. Id. In the absence of a contract, we look to other objective evidence of intent. Id. The district court found that the Assignment was contractual evidence of an objective manifestation that the parties did not intend to be coauthors. The district court reasoned that the Assignment conveyed forever "that certain story ... including any adaptations, treatments, scenarios, dialogue and/or screenplays." Professor Nimmer clarifies that "forever," when used in conjunction with conveyance of a copyrighted work (which the Treatment was not), "should be considered a shorthand for `the original and renewal term of copyright, plus any extensions, reversions, resurrections, or other circumstances that prolong the term.'" 3 NIMMER § 10.14[N]. Although the Treatment was not the subject of a federal statutory copyright, we agree with the district court that when Richlin and Edwards conveyed all present and future interests in the Treatment and derivative works to Mirisch, the parties to the contract could not consistently entertain the intent that Richlin and Edwards would be coauthors of the Motion Picture. Rather, Mirisch was given the right to exploit the Treatment in any way he chose. In any event, no language in the Assignment indicates any intent that Richlin and Edwards were to coauthor the Motion Picture.

In light of the Assignment, the Employment Agreement, and the surrounding circumstances, there were no "objective manifestations of a shared intent to be coauthors." Aalmuhammed, 202 F.3d at 1234. The Assignment conveyed to Mirisch all present and future rights in the Treatment and derivative works, including the common law "copyright." Neither the Assignment nor the Employment Agreement said anything about Richlin becoming a coauthor of the Motion Picture. None of The Pink Panther sequels lists Richlin as coauthor; rather, they simply give him screen credit as the creator of the original story and characters. Both the initial- and renewal-term statutory copyright registrations list Mirisch and its successors-in-interest as authors of the Motion Picture, not Richlin. Furthermore, the Employment Agreement specified that Richlin and Edwards were Mirisch's "employees," rendering the screenplay a "work made for hire," which is also inconsistent with the view that Richlin coauthored the Motion Picture. See 17 U.S.C. § 26 (1909); Warren v. Fox Family Worldwide, Inc., 328 F.3d 1136, 1140 (9th Cir.2003) ("[I]f the work is made for hire, `the employer or other person for whom the work was prepared is considered the author ..., and, unless

170

the parties have expressly agreed otherwise in a written instrument signed by them, owns all the rights in the copyright.'" (quoting 17 U.S.C. § 201(b) (1976))).

The second factor — whether Richlin supervised the Motion Picture by exercising control — favors MGM as well. Richlin did not exercise any supervisory powers over the Motion Picture, a factor that Aalmuhammed indicates will often be the most important. Aalmuhammed, 202 F.3d at 1234. The Assignment granted to Mirisch "forever … the absolute and unqualified right to use the [Treatment], in whole or in part, in whatever manner said purchaser may desire." Thus, while Richlin may have had control over the Treatment as originally written, he had no control over how the Treatment was incorporated into the Motion Picture. Moreover, although Richlin and Edwards cowrote the screenplay, the screenplay was a work made for hire pursuant to the Employment Agreement, making Mirisch the author/owner of the screenplay. 17 U.S.C. § 26 (1909); Warren, 328 F.3d at 1140. Any control that Richlin may have had over the screenplay does not lend support to his claim that he exercised any control over the creation of the Motion Picture.

We agree with the district court that the third factor, whether "the audience appeal of the work" can be attributed to both authors, and whether "the share of each in its success cannot be appraised," favors the Richlin heirs, in light of the summary judgment standard. Aalmuhammed, 202 F.3d at 1234. As the district court noted, it is nearly impossible to determine how much of the Motion Picture's audience appeal and success can be attributed to the Treatment. Although the characters that Richlin helped to create formed the basis for the Motion Picture's success, perhaps it was Peter Sellers's legendary comedic performance, Henry Mancini's memorable score, or Blake Edwards's award-winning direction— none of which can be attributed to Richlin — that was the main draw. Nevertheless, given that the Motion Picture adopted the characters and original story from the Treatment, and that, absent the Treatment, the Motion Picture likely would not exist, we cannot say the district court erred in finding that this factor favors the Richlin heirs.

Given that the two primary Aalmuhammed factors weigh most heavily in favor of Appellees, we hold that Richlin was not a coauthor of the Motion Picture. Therefore, there is no renewal interest in the Motion Picture that might conceivably have vested in the Richlin heirs under a theory of coauthorship.

…

Indeed, the Copyright Office has rejected the Richlin heirs' theory that previously unpublished components of a motion picture receive independent statutory copyright protection by virtue of incorporation into a motion picture that itself becomes the subject of federal statutory copyright protection. In Husbands, the Copyright Office Board of Appeals ("BOA") expressly ruled that an unpublished underlying work that is incorporated into a statutorily copyrighted motion picture does not receive a statutory copyright independent of the motion picture's copyright. Husbands, Copyright Office Board of Appeals Letter, Control No. 10-600-754-2(C), at 6 (May 14, 2002), available at http://www.ipmall.info/ hosted—resources/CopyrightAppeals. There, John Cassavetes authored a screenplay, but did not secure statutory copyright in the work. Id. at 1. He transferred "the rights" to Faces Music Inc., which incorporated the screenplay into the motion picture, Husbands. The motion picture received federal statutory copyright protection in 1970. Id. at 2. In 1998, when it came time to renew the motion picture's copyright for its second term, Cassavetes's heirs filed two renewal copyright registrations, one for the screenplay and one for the motion picture. Id. at 1. The Copyright Office issued the renewal registration in the motion picture, but denied the application for renewal of copyright in the screenplay. Id. The Cassavetes heirs appealed to the BOA, making the identical arguments as the Richlin heirs.

The BOA upheld the Copyright Office's rejection of the heirs' application for a renewal copyright interest in the screenplay, reasoning:

The Copyright Office considered a motion picture to be a unified work of authorship for purposes of registration under the 1909 law. The Office's Compendium I (1973) described a motion picture as "ordinarily ... embod[ying] a large number of contributions, including those of the author of the story, author of the screenplay, director, editor, cameraman, individual producer, etc. These persons are not regarded as the `author' of the film in the copyright sense. Compendium I further states that most motion pictures were works made for hire, with the production company's [sic] being the employer in most cases. The Office's understanding of motion picture authorship ... as consisting of contributions or parts, each of which is meant to be joined to other contributions or parts, in order to produce an integrated entity underlies this understanding.

....

The failure of the screenplay author ... to have reserved via registration the copyright in the unpublished version of the screenplay ..., thus rendering the screenplay's copyright for purposes of the public registration record separate and apart from the copyright in the motion picture, means that the Office, viewing the motion picture as an integrated entity, cannot now insert into the public record a claim to renewal rights owned by a party different from the owner of record of the rights in the integrated entity, i.e., in the motion picture as a whole.

Even absent the principle of deference to the views of the Copyright Office, we would find the BOA's analysis persuasive. A motion picture is a work to which many contribute; however, those contributions ultimately merge to create a unitary whole. As one district court explained, "it is impossible to cleave the story, screenplay and musical score of a motion picture film from the film itself." Classic Film Museum, Inc. v. Warner Bros., Inc., 453 F. Supp. 852, 855-56 (D.Me.1978). Though publication of a motion picture with notice secures federal statutory copyright protection *976 for all of its component parts, see 17 U.S.C. § 3 (1909), that does not mean that the component parts necessarily each secure an independent federal statutory copyright. The component parts may or may not be copyrightable; they may or may not be the subject of an independent statutory copyright when they are incorporated into the motion picture. As Abend itself demonstrates, the author of a work at common law must secure a federal copyright for that work for the right to renew to vest in either him or his heirs. The statutory copyright of a motion picture precludes the public from copying or otherwise infringing upon the statutory rights in the motion picture, including its component parts. However, when Mirisch secured federal statutory copyright for the Motion Picture, it did not also secure a federal statutory copyright for the Treatment. Assuming the Treatment is a copyrightable work, Richlin and Edwards simply failed to secure federal copyright for it.

...

IV. CONCLUSION

For the foregoing reasons, we affirm the district court's decision.

AFFIRMED.

771 F.3d 647 (9th Cir. 2014)

GARCIA V. GOOGLE

United States Court of Appeals for The Ninth Circuit

McKEOWN, Circuit Judge:

44

In this case, a heartfelt plea for personal protection is juxtaposed with the limits of copyright law and fundamental principles of free speech. The appeal teaches a simple lesson—a weak copyright claim cannot justify censorship in the guise of authorship.

45

By all accounts, Cindy Lee Garcia was bamboozled when a movie producer transformed her five-second acting performance into part of a blasphemous video proclamation against the Prophet Mohammed. The producer—now in jail on unrelated matters—uploaded a trailer of the film, Innocence of Muslims, to YouTube. Millions of viewers soon watched it online, according to Garcia. News outlets credited the film as a source of violence in the Middle East. Garcia received death threats.

46

Asserting that she holds a copyright interest in her fleeting performance, Garcia sought a preliminary injunction requiring Google to remove the film from all of its platforms, including YouTube. The district court denied the injunction, finding that Garcia did not establish likely success on the merits for her copyright claim. Nor did she demonstrate that the injunction would prevent any alleged harm in light of the film's five-month presence on the Internet. A divided panel of our court reversed, labeled her copyright claim as "fairly debatable," but then entered a mandatory injunction requiring Google to remove the film. That injunction was later limited to versions of the film featuring Garcia's performance.

47

As Garcia characterizes it, "the main issue in this case involves the vicious frenzy against Ms. Garcia that the Film caused among certain radical elements of the Muslim community." We are sympathetic to her plight. Nonetheless, the claim against Google is grounded in copyright law, not privacy, emotional distress, or tort law, and Garcia seeks to impose speech restrictions under copyright laws meant to foster rather than repress free expression. Garcia's theory can be likened to "copyright cherry picking," which would enable any contributor from a costume designer down to an extra or best boy to claim copyright in random bits and pieces of a unitary motion picture without satisfying the requirements of the Copyright Act. Putting aside the rhetoric of Hollywood hijinks and the dissent's dramatics, this case must be decided on the law.

48

In light of the Copyright Act's requirements of an "original work of authorship fixed in any tangible medium," 17 U.S.C. § 102(a), the mismatch between Garcia's copyright claim and the relief sought, and the Copyright Office's rejection of Garcia's application for a copyright in her brief performance, we conclude that the district court did not abuse its discretion in denying Garcia's request for the preliminary injunction. As a consequence, the panel's mandatory injunction against Google was unjustified and is dissolved upon publication of this opinion.

49

BACKGROUND AND PROCEDURAL HISTORY

50

In July 2011, Cindy Lee Garcia responded to a casting call for a film titled Desert Warrior, an action-adventure thriller set in ancient Arabia. Garcia was cast in a cameo role, for which she earned $500. She received and reviewed a few pages of script. Acting under a professional director hired to oversee production, Garcia spoke two sentences: "Is George crazy? Our daughter is but a child?" Her role was to deliver those lines and to "seem concerned."

51

Garcia later discovered that writer-director Mark Basseley Youssef (a.k.a. Nakoula Basseley Nakoula or Sam Bacile) had a different film in mind: an anti-Islam polemic renamed Innocence of Muslims. The film, featuring a crude production, depicts the Prophet Mohammed as, among other things, a murderer, pedophile, and homosexual. Film producers dubbed over Garcia's lines and replaced them with a voice asking, "Is your Mohammed a child molester?" Garcia appears on screen for only five seconds.

52

Almost a year after the casting call, in June 2012, Youssef uploaded a 13-minute-and-51-second trailer of Innocence of Muslims to YouTube, the video-sharing website owned by Google, Inc., which boasts a global audience of more than one billion visitors per month. After it was translated into Arabic, the film fomented outrage across the Middle East, and media reports linked it to numerous violent protests. The film also has been a subject of political controversy over its purported connection to the September 11, 2012, attack on the United States Consulate in Benghazi, Libya.

53

Shortly after the Benghazi attack, an Egyptian cleric issued a fatwa against anyone associated with Innocence of Muslims, calling upon the "Muslim Youth in America and Europe" to "kill the director, the producer, and the actors and everyone who helped and promoted this film." Garcia received multiple death threats.

54

Legal wrangling ensued. Garcia asked Google to remove the film, asserting it was hate speech and violated her state law rights to privacy and to control her likeness. Garcia also sent Google five takedown notices under the Digital Millenium Copyright Act, 17 U.S.C. § 512, claiming that YouTube's broadcast of Innocence of Muslims infringed her copyright in her "audio-visual dramatic performance." Google declined to remove the film.

55

On September 19, 2012, Garcia first sued Google, Youssef, and other unnamed production assistants in Los Angeles Superior Court. Her complaint alleged a compendium of torts and assorted wrongdoing under California law. As against Google, Garcia made claims for invasion of privacy, false light, and violating her right to publicity. She brought the same claims against Youssef and added fraud, unfair business practices, slander, and intentional infliction of emotional distress. The state court denied Garcia's motion for a "temporary restraining order and for an order to show cause re preliminary injunction," because she had "not shown a likelihood of success on the merits." On September 25, 2012, Garcia voluntarily dismissed her state court suit.

56

One day later, Garcia turned to federal court. She filed suit in the United States District Court for the Central District of California and again named Google and Youssef as co-defendants. Garcia alleged copyright infringement against both defendants and revived her state law claims against Youssef for fraud, unfair business practices, libel, and intentional infliction of emotional distress.

57

Garcia then moved for a temporary restraining order and for an order to show cause on a preliminary injunction—but only on the copyright claim. She sought to bar Google from hosting Innocence of Muslims on YouTube or any other Google-run website.

58

On November 30, 2012, the district court denied Garcia's motion for a preliminary injunction. As an initial matter, the court concluded that "Garcia ha[d] not demonstrated that the requested relief would prevent any alleged harm," because, by that point, the film trailer had been on the Internet for five months. Nor did Garcia establish a likelihood of success on the merits. In particular, the district court found that the nature of Garcia's copyright interest was unclear, and even if she could establish such a copyright, she granted the film directors an implied license to "distribute her performance as a contribution incorporated into the indivisible whole of the Film."

59

A divided panel of our court reversed. More than a year and a half after the film was first uploaded, the panel majority first issued a secret takedown order, giving Google twenty-four hours to remove all copies of Innocence of Muslims from YouTube and other Google-controlled platforms. The panel embargoed disclosure of the order until it issued its opinion. The panel later amended the order to allow YouTube to post any version of the film that did not include Garcia's performance.

60

In its later-issued opinion, the panel majority reversed the district court and granted Garcia's preliminary injunction.

61

Garcia v. Google, Inc., 743 F.3d 1258, amended by Garcia v. Google, Inc., 766 F.3d 929 (9th Cir. 2014). Despite characterizing Garcia's copyright claim as "fairly debatable," the panel majority nonetheless concluded that Garcia was likely to prevail on her copyright claim as to her individual performance in Innocence of Muslims. 766 F.3d at 935. In contrast to the district court's factual finding of an implied license from Garcia to Youssef, the panel opinion held that the license ran in the opposite direction: "Youssef implicitly granted [Garcia] a license to perform his screenplay," and that Garcia did not grant Youssef an implied license to incorporate her performance into the film. Id. at 935–38. Finally, the panel majority held that, because of the death threats against her, Garcia had established irreparable harm and the equities and public interest favored an injunction. Id. at 938–40. The opinion did not address the First Amendment consequences of the mandatory takedown injunction, beyond stating that the First Amendment does not protect copyright infringement.

62

Judge N.R. Smith dissented. He wrote that Garcia had not met the high burden required for a mandatory preliminary injunction because she was unlikely to succeed on her copyright claim. Id. at 941 (N.R. Smith, J., dissenting). Specifically, Garcia was not likely to prove her performance was a "work," nor would she likely meet the copyright requirements of authorship and fixation, among other shortcomings with her claim. Id. at 946. In sum, "[b]ecause the facts and law do not 'clearly favor' issuing a preliminary injunction to Garcia, the district court did not abuse its discretion in denying Garcia's requested relief." Id. at 940.

63

We granted rehearing en banc. Garcia v. Google, Inc., 771 F.3d 647 (9th Cir. 2014).

ANALYSIS

...

A. COPYRIGHT

78

The central question is whether the law and facts clearly favor Garcia's claim to a copyright in her five-second acting performance as it appears in Innocence of Muslims. The answer is no. This conclusion does not mean that a plaintiff like Garcia is without options or that she couldn't have sought an injunction against different parties or on other legal theories, like the right of publicity and defamation.[5]

79

Under the Copyright Act, "[c]opyright protection subsists . . . in original works of authorship fixed in any tangible medium of expression . . . [including] motion pictures." 17 U.S.C. § 102(a). That fixation must be done "by or under the authority of the author." 17 U.S.C. § 101. Benchmarked against this statutory standard, the law does not clearly favor Garcia's position.

80

The statute purposefully left "works of authorship" undefined to provide for some flexibility. See 1 Nimmer on Copyright § 2.03. Nevertheless, several other provisions provide useful guidance. An audiovisual work is one that consists of "a series of related images which are intrinsically intended to be shown" by machines or other electronic equipment, plus "accompanying sounds." 17 U.S.C. § 101. In turn, a "motion picture" is an "audiovisual work[] consisting of a series of related images which, when shown in succession, impart an impression of motion, together with accompanying sounds, if any." Id. These two definitions embody the work here: Innocence of Muslims is an audiovisual work that is categorized as a motion picture and is derivative of the script. Garcia is the author of none of this and makes no copyright claim to the film or to the script.[6]

81

Instead, Garcia claims that her five-second performance itself merits copyright protection.

82

In the face of this statutory scheme, it comes as no surprise that during this litigation, the Copyright Office found that Garcia's performance was not a copyrightable work when it rejected her copyright application. The Copyright Office explained that its "longstanding practices do not allow a copyright claim by an individual actor or actress in his or her performance contained within a motion picture." Thus, "[f]or copyright registration purposes, a motion picture is a single integrated work. . . . Assuming Ms. Garcia's contribution was limited to her acting performance, we cannot register her performance apart from the motion picture."

83

We credit this expert opinion of the Copyright Office— the office charged with administration and enforcement of the copyright laws and registration.[7] See Inhale, Inc. v. Starbuzz Tobacco, Inc., 755 F.3d 1038, 1041–42 (9th Cir. 2014). The Copyright Office's well-reasoned position "reflects a 'body of experience and informed judgment to which courts and litigants may properly resort for guidance.'" Southco, Inc. v. Kanebridge Corp., 390 F.3d 276, 286 n.5 (3d Cir. 2004) (en banc) (Alito, J.) (quoting Yates v. Hendon, 541 U.S. 1, 3 (2004)).[8]

84

In analyzing whether the law clearly favors Garcia, Aalmuhammed v. Lee, 202 F.3d 1227 (9th Cir. 2000), provides a useful foundation. There, we examined the meaning of "work" as the first step in analyzing joint authorship of the movie Malcolm X. The Copyright Act provides that when a work is "prepared by two or more authors with the intention that their contributions be merged into inseparable or interdependent parts of a unitary whole," the work becomes a "joint work" with two or more authors. 17 U.S.C. § 101 (emphasis added). Garcia unequivocally disclaims joint authorship of the film.

85

In Aalmuhammed, we concluded that defining a "work" based upon "some minimal level of creativity or originality. . . would be too broad and indeterminate to be useful."[9] 202 F.3d at 1233 (internal quotation marks omitted). Our animating concern was that this definition of "work" would fragment copyright protection for the unitary film Malcolm X into many little pieces:

86

So many people might qualify as an "author" if the question were limited to whether they made a substantial creative contribution that that test would not distinguish one from another. Everyone from the producer and director to casting director, costumer, hairstylist, and "best boy" gets listed in the movie credits because all of their creative contributions really do matter. ...

88

Garcia's theory of copyright law would result in the legal morass we warned against in Aalmuhammed—splintering a movie into many different "works," even in the absence of an independent fixation. Simply put, as Google claimed, it "make[s] Swiss cheese of copyrights."

89

Take, for example, films with a large cast—the proverbial "cast of thousands"[10]— such as Ben-Hur or Lord of the Rings.[11]1 The silent epic Ben-Hur advertised a cast of 125,000 people. In the Lord of the Rings trilogy, 20,000 extras tramped around Middle-Earth alongside Frodo Baggins (played by Elijah Wood). Treating every acting performance as an independent work would not only be a logistical and financial nightmare, it would turn cast of thousands into a new mantra: copyright of thousands.

90

The dissent spins speculative hypotheticals about copyright protection for book chapters, movie outtakes, baseball games, and Jimi Hendrix concerts. See Dissent at 35, 38. This hyperbole sounds a false alarm. Substituting moral outrage and colorful language for legal analysis, the dissent mixes and matches copyright concepts such as collective works, derivative works, the requirement of fixation, and sound recordings. The statutory definitions and their application counsel precision, not convolution. See, e.g., 17 U.S.C. §§ 101, 103, 114, 201. The citation to Effects Associates, Inc. v. Cohen, 908 F.2d 555 (9th Cir. 1990) (Kozinski, J.), is particularly puzzling. There, neither party disputed the plaintiff's copyright, and the plaintiff independently fixed the special-effects footage and licensed it to the filmmakers. See id. at 556 n.2

91

The reality is that contracts and the work-made-for-hire doctrine govern much of the big-budget Hollywood performance and production world. See 1 Nimmer on Copyright § 6.07[B][2]. Absent these formalities, courts have looked to implied licenses. See Effects Assocs., 908 F.2d at 559–60. Indeed, the district court found that Garcia granted Youssef just such an implied license to incorporate her performance into the film.[12] But these legal niceties do not necessarily dictate whether something is protected by copyright, and licensing has its limitations. As filmmakers warn, low-budget films rarely use licenses. Even if filmmakers diligently obtain licenses for everyone on set, the contracts are not a panacea. Third-party content distributors, like YouTube and Netflix, won't have easy access to the licenses; litigants may dispute their terms and scope; and actors and other content contributors can terminate licenses after thirty five years. See 17 U.S.C. § 203(a)(3). Untangling the complex, difficult-to-access, and often phantom chain of title to tens, hundreds, or even thousands of standalone copyrights is a task that could tie the distribution chain in knots. And filming group scenes like a public parade, or the 1963 March on Washington, would pose a huge burden if each of the thousands of marchers could claim an independent copyright.

92

Garcia's copyright claim faces yet another statutory barrier: She never fixed her acting performance in a tangible medium, as required by 17 U.S.C. § 101 ("A work is 'fixed' in a tangible medium of expression when its embodiment in a copy or phonorecord, by or under the authority of the author, is sufficiently permanent or stable to permit it to be perceived, reproduced, or otherwise communicated for a period of more than transitory duration.") (emphasis added). According to the Supreme Court, "the author is the party who actually creates the work, that is, the person who translates an idea into a fixed, tangible expression entitled to copyright protection." Cmty. for Creative Non-Violence v. Reid, 490 U.S. 730, 737 (1989). Garcia did nothing of the sort.[13]

93

For better or for worse, Youssef and his crew "fixed" Garcia's performance in the tangible medium, whether in physical film or in digital form. However one might characterize Garcia's performance, she played no role in fixation. On top of this, Garcia claims that she never agreed to the film's ultimate rendition or how she was portrayed in Innocence of Muslims, so she can hardly argue that the film or her cameo in it was fixed "by or under [her] authority." 17 U.S.C. § 101.

94

In sum, the district court committed no error in its copyright analysis. Issuance of the mandatory preliminary injunction requires more than a possible or fairly debatable claim; it requires a showing that the law "clearly favor[s]" Garcia. See Stanley, 13 F.3d at 1320. Because neither the Copyright Act nor the Copyright Office's interpretation supports Garcia's claim, this is a hurdle she cannot clear.

95

B. IRREPARABLE HARM

96

Although we could affirm the district court solely on the copyright issue, see DISH Network, 653 F.3d at 776–77, we address irreparable harm because the grave danger Garcia claims cannot be discounted and permeates the entire lawsuit.

97

At first blush, irreparable harm looks like Garcia's strongest argument. Garcia understandably takes seriously the fatwa and threats against her and her family, and so do we. The difficulty with Garcia's claim is that there is a mismatch between her substantive copyright claim and the dangers she hopes to remedy through an injunction. Garcia seeks a preliminary injunction under copyright law, not privacy, fraud, false light or any other tort-based cause of action. Hence, Garcia's harm must stem from copyright— namely, harm to her legal interests as an author. Salinger v. Colting, 607 F.3d 68, 81 & n.9 (2d Cir. 2010) ("The relevant harm is the harm that . . . occurs to the parties' legal interests . . . .").

98

Looking to the purpose of copyright underscores the disjunction Garcia's case presents. Article 1, Section 8 of the U.S. Constitution provides that copyrights "promote the Progress of Science and useful arts." Hence, the "Framers intended copyright itself to be the engine of free expression. By establishing a marketable right to the use of one's expression, copyright supplies the economic incentive to create and disseminate ideas." Harper & Row Publishers, Inc. v. Nation Enters., 471 U.S. 539, 558 (1985); see also Eldred v. Ashcroft, 537 U.S. 186, 219 (2003) (noting that "copyright's purpose is to promote the creation and publication of free expression") (emphasis in original). In keeping with copyright's function, "the justification of the copyright law is the protection of the commercial interest of the []author. It is not to . . . protect secrecy, but to stimulate creation by protecting its rewards." Salinger, 607 F.3d at 81 n.9 (quoting New Era Publ'ns Int'l, ApS v. Henry Holt & Co., 695 F. Supp. 1493, 1526 (S.D.N.Y. 1988)).

99

As Garcia frames it, "the main issue in this case involves the vicious frenzy against Ms. Garcia that the Film caused among certain radical elements of the Muslim community," which has caused "severe emotional distress, the destruction of her career and reputation" and credible death threats. With respect to irreparable harm, she argues that "[t]he injuries sheseeks to avoid—damage to her reputation, unfair[,] forced promotion of a hateful Film, and death—will be avoided if any injunction issues."

100

This relief is not easily achieved under copyright law. Although we do not take lightly threats to life or the emotional turmoil Garcia has endured, her harms are untethered from—and incompatible with—copyright and copyright's function as the engine of expression.

101

In broad terms, "the protection of privacy is not a function of the copyright law. . . . To the contrary, the copyright law offers a limited monopoly to encourage ultimate public access to the creative work of the author." Bond v. Blum, 317 F.3d 385, 395 (4th Cir. 2003); see also Monge v. Maya Magazines, Inc., 688 F.3d 1164, 1177 (9th Cir. 2012) (quoting Bond and "pointedly" noting copyright cases are analyzed "only under copyright principles, not privacy law").

102

Likewise, authors cannot seek emotional distress damages under the Copyright Act, because such damages are unrelated to the value and marketability of their works. See In re Dawson, 390 F.3d 1139, 1146 n.3 (9th Cir. 2004) (noting that "'actual damages' in the context of the Copyright Act . . . cover only economic damages" (internal citation omitted));

103

Mackie v. Rieser, 296 F.3d 909, 917 (9th Cir. 2002) (rejecting copyright damages where "the infringement did not in any way influence the market value" of a piece of outdoor artwork but instead boiled down to the author's "personal objections to the manipulation of his artwork").

104

By way of example, erstwhile professional wrestler and reality TV star Hulk Hogan wanted to enjoin Gawker.com from posting a sex tape of Hogan with a mistress, claiming copyright infringement. Bollea v. Gawker Media, LLC, 913 F. Supp. 2d 1325, 1327 (M.D. Fla. 2012). The district court found an absence of irreparable harm because Hogan "produced no evidence demonstrating that he will suffer irreparable harm in the copyright sense absent a preliminary injunction. The only evidence in the record reflecting harm to [Hogan] relates to harm suffered by him personally and harm to his professional image due to the 'private' nature of the Video's content. This evidence does not constitute irreparable harm in the context of copyright infringement."

105

Id. at 1329; cf. New Era Publ'ns, 695 F. Supp. at 1499 (denying injunction sought "not in good faith for its intended purpose of protecting the value of publication rights, but rather to suppress a derogatory study of the founder of the Church of Scientology").

106

Privacy laws, not copyright, may offer remedies tailored to Garcia's personal and reputational harms. On that point, we offer no substantive view. Ultimately, Garcia would like to have her connection to the film forgotten and stripped from YouTube. Unfortunately for Garcia, such a "right to be forgotten," although recently affirmed by the Court of Justice for the European Union, is not recognized in the United States. See Case C-131/12, Google Spain SL v. Agencia Española de Protección de Datos (AEPD), ECLI:EU:C:2014:616 (May 13, 2014) (requiring Google to consider individual requests to remove personal information from its search engine); Internet Law—Protection of Personal Data—Court of Justice of the European Union Creates Presumption that Google Must Remove Links to Personal Data Upon Request, 128 Harv. L. Rev. 735 (2014).

107

Nor is Garcia protected by the benefits found in many European countries, where authors have "moral rights" tocontrol the integrity of their works and to guard against distortion, manipulation, or misappropriation. See Kelley v. Chicago Park Dist., 635 F.3d 290, 296 (7th Cir. 2011) (describing differences in moral rights in American copyright law versus other countries). Except for a limited universe of works of visual art, such as paintings and drawings protected under the Visual Artists Rights Act of 1990, United States copyright law generally does not recognize moral rights. 17 U.S.C. § 106A. Motion pictures specifically are excluded from moral rights protection. § 106A; § 101 ("[W]ork of visual art does not include . . . any . . . motion picture or other audiovisual work . . . .").

108

In short, Garcia's harms are too attenuated from the purpose of copyright. We do not foreclose that in a different circumstance with a strong copyright claim, a court could consider collateral consequences as part of its irreparable harm analysis and remedy. 17 U.S.C. § 502 (providing that the court may grant injunctions "as it may deem reasonable to prevent or restrain infringement of a copyright"). But such a case is not before us.

109

Garcia waited months to seek an injunction after Innocence of Muslims was uploaded to YouTube in July 2012; she did not seek emergency relief when the film first surfaced on the Internet. The district court did not abuse its discretion by finding this delay undercut Garcia's claim of irreparable harm. See Oakland Tribune, Inc. v. Chronicle Publ'g Co., 762 F.2d 1374, 1377 (9th Cir. 1985) ("Plaintiff's long delay before seeking a preliminary injunction implies a lack of urgency and irreparable harm."); 4 Nimmer on Copyright § 14.06[A][3][c] (noting unreasonable delay can defeat irreparable injury and the length of time "need not be great"). Garcia notes that she moved swiftly once the film was translated into Arabic and sparked death threats against her. But that proves the point: the gravamen of Garcia's harm is untethered from her commercial interests as a performer, and instead focuses on the personal pain caused by her association with the film.

110

The district court did not abuse its discretion in determining that Garcia failed to muster a clear showing of irreparable harm. See Flexible Lifeline Sys., Inc. v. Precision Lift, Inc., 654 F.3d 989, 999–1000 (9th Cir. 2011) ("Harm must be proved, not presumed." (quoting 4 Nimmer on Copyright § 14.06[A][5])).

111

In the face of a doubtful copyright claim and the absence of irreparable harm to Garcia's interests as an author, we need not consider the final two Winter factors, the balance of equities and public interest.

112

II. THE PANEL'S INJUNCTION

113

In February 2014, the panel majority issued the following injunction: "Google, Inc. shall take down all copies of 'Innocence of Muslims' from YouTube.com and from any other platforms under Google's control, and take all reasonable steps to prevent further uploads of 'Innocence of Muslims' to those platforms." Soon after, the panel amended the order to state that the prohibition did "not preclude the posting or display of any version of 'Innocence of Muslims' that does not include Cindy Lee Garcia's performance."

114

Although the first order was more sweeping, the second cast the court in the uneasy role of film editor. The amendment only mattered if Google assumed authority to change the content of someone else's copyrighted film. To no one's surprise, the end result was the same: the entire film remained removed from YouTube.

115

The takedown order was unwarranted and incorrect as a matter of law, as we have explained above. It also gave short shrift to the First Amendment values at stake. The mandatory injunction censored and suppressed a politically significant film— based upon a dubious and unprecedented theory of copyright. In so doing, the panel deprived the public of the ability to view firsthand, and judge for themselves, a film at the center of an international uproar.

116

Although the intersection between copyright and the First Amendment is much-debated,[14] the Supreme Court teaches that copyright is not "categorically immune from challenges under the First Amendment." Eldred, 537 U.S. at 221 (internal citation omitted). To be sure, this is not a case of garden-variety copyright infringement, such as seeking to restrain the use of copyrighted computer code. The panel's takedown order of a film of substantial interest to the public is a classic prior restraint of speech. Alexander v. United States, 509 U.S. 544, 550 (1993) ("Temporary restraining orders and permanent injunctions—i.e., court orders that actually forbid speech activities—are classic examples of prior restraints."). Prior restraints pose the "most serious and the least tolerable infringement on First Amendment rights," Hunt v. NBC, 872 F.2d 289, 293 (9th Cir. 1989) (citation omitted), and Garcia cannot overcome the historical and heavy presumption against such restraints with a thin copyright claim in a five-second performance.

117

The amended injunction issued February 28, 2014 is dissolved immediately and has no force or effect.

118

CONCLUSION

119

At this stage of the proceedings, we have no reason to question Garcia's claims that she was duped by an unscrupulous filmmaker and has suffered greatly from her disastrous association with the Innocence of Muslims film. Nonetheless, the district court did not abuse its discretion when it denied Garcia's motion for a preliminary injunction under the copyright laws.

120

AFFIRMED.

...

KOZINSKI, Circuit Judge, dissenting:

131

Garcia's dramatic performance met all of the requirements for copyright protection: It was copyrightable subject matter, it was original and it was fixed at the moment it was recorded. So what happened to the copyright? At times, the majority says that Garcia's performance was not copyrightable at all. And at other times, it seems to say that Garcia just didn't do enough to gain a copyright in the scene. Either way, the majority is wrong and makes a total mess of copyright law, right here in the Hollywood Circuit. In its haste to take internet service providers off the hook for infringement, the court today robs performers and other creative talent of rights Congress gave them. I won't be a party to it. ...

133

Youssef handed Garcia a script. Garcia performed it. Youssef recorded Garcia's performance on video and saved the clip. Until today, I understood that the rights in such a performance are determined according to elementary copyright principles: An "original work[] of authorship," 17 U.S.C. § 102(a), requires only copyrightable subject matter and a "minimal degree of creativity." Feist Publ'ns,

Inc. v. Rural Tel. Serv. Co., 499 U.S. 340, 345 (1991). The work is "fixed" when it is "sufficiently permanent or stable to permit it to be perceived, reproduced, or otherwise communicated for a period of more than transitory duration." 17 U.S.C. § 101. And at that moment, the "author or authors of the work" instantly and automatically acquire a copyright interest in it. 17 U.S.C. § 201(a). This isn't exactly String Theory; more like Copyright 101.

134

Garcia's performance met these minimal requirements; the majority doesn't contend otherwise. The majority nevertheless holds that Garcia's performance isn't a "work," apparently because it was created during the production of a later-assembled film, Innocence of Muslims. Maj. Op. 17–20. But if you say something is not a work, it means that it isn't copyrightable by anyone. Under the majority's definition of "work," no one (not even Youssef) can claim a copyright in any part of Garcia's performance, even though it was recorded several months before Innocence of Muslims was assembled. Instead, Innocence of Muslims—the ultimate film—is the only thing that can be a "work." If this is what my colleagues are saying, they are casting doubt on the copyrightability of vast swaths of material created during production of a film or other composite work.

135

The implications are daunting. If Garcia's scene is not a work, then every take of every scene of, say, Lord of the Rings is not a work, and thus not protected by copyright, unless and until the clips become part of the final movie. If some dastardly crew member were to run off with a copy of the Battle of Morannon, the dastard would be free to display it for profit until it was made part of the final movie. And, of course, the take-outs, the alternative scenes, the special effects never used, all of those things would be fair game because none of these things would be "works" under the majority's definition. And what about a draft chapter of a novel? Is there no copyright in the draft chapter unless it gets included in the published book? Or if part of the draft gets included, is there no copyright in the rest of it?

136

This is a remarkable proposition, for which the majority provides remarkably little authority. Aalmuhammed v. Lee, 202 F.3d 1227 (9th Cir. 2000), the only case that the majority cites, says just the opposite. In Aalmuhammed, we considered a claim by a contributor to the movie Malcolm X that he was a joint author of the entire movie. Id. at 1230. Everyone in Aalmuhammed agreed that the relevant "work" was Malcolm X. The only question was whether the contributor was a joint author of that work. We went out of our way to emphasize that joint authorship of a movie is a "different question" from whether a contribution to the movie can be a "work" under section 102(a). Id. at 1233. And we clearly stated that a contribution to a movie can be copyrightable (and thus can be a "work"). Id. at 1232.

137

The majority's newfangled definition of "work" is directly contrary to a quarter-century-old precedent that has never been questioned, Effects Associates, Inc. v.

Cohen, 908 F.2d 555 (9th Cir. 1990). There, we held that a company that created special effects footage during film production retained a copyright interest in the footage even though it became part of the film. Id. at 556–58; see also Oddo v. Ries, 743 F.2d 630, 633–34 (9th Cir. 1984). The majority tries to distinguish Effects Associates by arguing that the footage there was a "standalone work[] that [was] separately fixed and incorporated into a film." Maj Op. 22 n.13. But Garcia's performance was also "separately fixed and incorporated into" Innocence of Muslims. Why then are the seven shots "featuring great gobs of alien yogurt oozing out of a defunct factory" interspersed in The Stuff, 908 F.2d at 559, any more a "standalone work" than Garcia's performance? Youssef wasn't required to use any part of Garcia's performance in the film; he could have sold the video clip to someone else. The clip might not have had much commercial value, but neither did the special effects scenes in Effects Associates. Nothing in the Copyright Act says that special effects scenes are "works" entitled to copyright protection but other scenes are not. And what about scenes that have actors and special effects? Are those scenes entitled to copyright protection (as in Effects Associates), or are they denied copyright protection like Garcia's scene?

138

II

139

A. The majority also seems to hold that Garcia is not entitled to copyright protection because she is not an author of the recorded scene. According to the majority, Garcia can't be an author of her own scene because she "played no role in [her performance's] fixation." Maj. Op. 22–23.

140

But a performer need not operate the recording equipment to be an author of his own performance. See H.R. Rep. No. 94-1476, at 56 (1976); S. Rep. No. 94-473, at 53–54 (1975); see also 1 Nimmer on Copyright § 2.10[A][3] at 2-178.4 to 2-178.5. Without Garcia's performance, all that existed was a script. To convert the script into a video, there needed to be both an actor physically performing it and filmmakers recording the performance. Both kinds of activities can result in copyrightable expression. See 1 Nimmer on Copyright 09[F] at 2-165 to 2-171 (discussing Baltimore Orioles, Inc. v. Major League Baseball Players Ass'n, 805 F.2d 663 (7th Cir. 1986)).[15] Garcia's performance had at least "some minimal degree of creativity" apart from the script and Youssef's direction. See Feist, 499 U.S. at 345. One's "[p]ersonality always contains something unique. It expresses its singularity even in handwriting, and a very modest grade of art has in it something which is one man's alone." Bleistein v. Donaldson Lithographing Co., 188 U.S. 239, 250 (1903). To dispute this is to claim that Gone With the Wind would be the same movie if Rhett Butler were played by Peter Lorre.

141

Actors usually sign away their rights when contracting to do a movie, but Garcia didn't and she wasn't Youssef's employee. I'd therefore find that Garcia acquired a copyright in her performance the moment it was fixed. When dealing with material created during production of a film or other composite work, the absence of a contract always complicates things. See Effects Associates, 908 F.2d at 556 ("Moviemakers do lunch, not contracts."). Without a contract the parties are left with whatever rights the copyright law gives them. It's not our job to take away from performers rights Congress gave them. Did Jimi Hendrix acquire no copyright in the recordings of his concerts because he didn't run the recorder in addition to playing the guitar? Garcia may not be as talented as Hendrix—who is?— but she's no less entitled to the protections of the Copyright Act.

142

B. While the Copyright Office claims that its "longstanding practices" don't recognize Garcia's copyright interest, it doesn't seem that the Register of Copyrights got the memo. The Register was a member of the U.S. delegation that signed the Beijing Treaty on Audiovisual Performances. See U.S. Copyright Office, Annual Report of the Register of Copyrights 8 (2012). The Treaty would recognize Garcia's rights in her performance. It provides that "performers" have the "exclusive right of authorizing . . . the fixation of their unfixed performances," and "reproduction of their performances fixed in audiovisual fixations, in any manner or form." World Intellectual Property Organization, Beijing Treaty on Audiovisual Performances, Art. 6(ii), 7 (2012).

143

The Patent Office, which led the delegation, states that U.S. law is "generally compatible" with the Treaty, as "actors and musicians are considered to be 'authors' of their performances providing them with copyright rights." U.S. Patent & Trademark Office, Background and Summary of the 2012 WIPO Audiovisual Performances Treaty 2 (2012). Although the Copyright Office hasn't issued a statement of compatibility, it's hard to believe that it would sign on if it believed that the Treaty's key provisions are inconsistent with U.S. copyright law. In fact, the Copyright Office praised the Treaty as "an important step forward in protecting the performances of television and film actors throughout the world." U.S. Copyright Office, NewsNet: Beijing Audiovisual Performances Treaty (2 0 1 2) , http://copyright.gov/newsnet/2012/460.html. Except in the Ninth Circuit.

144

The Copyright Office's position is thus inconsistent at best. And, in any event, neither the Copyright Office's reasoning nor the authority it relies on in its letter to Garcia fare any better than the majority's. The Copyright Office would refuse copyright registration to an actor like Garcia because "an actor or an actress in a motion picture is either a joint author in the entire work or, as most often is the case, is not an author at all by virtue of a work made for hire agreement." However, Garcia isn't a joint author of the entire movie and didn't sign any agreements. She doesn't fit into either category. Like the majority, the Copyright Office would wish this problem away by refusing registration unless the copyright claimant personally recorded his performance. But nothing in the legislative history relied on by the Copyright Office (which concerned joint authorship of an entire film) suggests that a non-employee doesn't retain any copyright interest in a video clip of his acting performance because it's recorded by the film's producer. See H.R. Rep. No. 94-1476, at 120

145

III

146

The harm the majority fears would result from recognizing performers' copyright claims in their fixed, original expression is overstated. The vast majority of copyright claims by performers in their contributions are defeated by a contract and the work for hire doctrine. See 1 Nimmer on Copyright § 6.07[B][2] at 6-28 to 6-29; 2 William F. Patry, Patry on Copyright § 5:17 (2010). And most of the performers that fall through the cracks would be found to have given an implied license to the film's producers to use the contribution in the ultimate film. See Effects Associates, 908 F.2d at 558. Very few performers would be left to sue at all, and the ones that remain would have to find suing worth their while. They wouldn't be able to claim the valuable rights of joint authorship of the movie, such as an undivided share in the movie or the right to exploit the movie for themselves. See 1 Nimmer on Copyright § 6.08 at 6-34 to 6-36. Rather, their copyright claims would be limited to the original expression they created. See Aalmuhammed, 202 F.3d at 1232; Effects Associates, 908 F.2d at 559. Which is why filmmaking hasn't ground to a halt even though we held a quarter-century ago that "where a non-employee contributes to a book or movie, . . . the exclusive rights of copyright ownership vest in the creator of the contribution, unless there is a written agreement to the contrary." Effects Associates, 908 F.2d at 557.

147

Regardless, the Supreme Court has reminded us that "speculation about future harms is no basis for [courts] to shrink authorial rights." N.Y. Times Co. v. Tasini, 533 U.S. 483, 505–06 (2001). In Tasini, freelance authors argued that the inclusion in databases of their articles that originally appeared in periodicals infringed their copyrights in the works. Id. at 487. Publishers warned that "'devastating' consequences," including massive damages awards, would result if the Court were to hold for the freelancers. Id. at 504. The Court nonetheless held for the freelancers, turning back the parade of horribles deployed by the publishers. The Court explained that there are "numerous models for distributing copyrighted works and remunerating authors for their distribution." Id. at 504–05. Tasini is a powerful reminder that movie producers, publishers and distributors will always claim that the sky is falling in cases that might recognize an individual contributor's copyright interest in material he created.[16] They will always say, as Google says here, that holding in the contributor's favor will make "Swiss cheese" of copyrights. Maj. Op. 20.

148

But under our copyright law, the creators of original, copyrightable material automatically acquire a copyright interest in the material as soon as it is fixed. There's no exception for material created during production of a film or other composite work. When modern works, such as films or plays, are produced, contributors will often create separate, copyrightable works as part of the process. Our copyright law says that the copyright interests in this material vest initially with its creators, who will then have leverage to obtain compensation by contract. The answer to the "Swiss cheese" bugbear isn't for courts to limit who can acquire copyrights in order to make life simpler for producers and internet service providers. It's for the parties to allocate their rights by contract. See Effects Associates, 908 F.2d at 557. Google makes oodles of dollars by enabling its users to upload almost any video without pre-screening for potential copyright infringement. Google's business model, like that of the database owners in Tasini, assumes the risk that a user's upload infringes someone else's copyright, and that it may have to take corrective action if a copyright holder comes forward.

149

The majority credits the doomsday claims at the expense of property rights that Congress created. Its new standard artificially shrinks authorial rights by holding that a performer must personally record his creative expression in order to retain any copyright interest in it, speculating that a contrary rule might curb filmmaking and burden the internet. But our injunction has been in place for over a year; reports of the internet's demise have been greatly exaggerated. For the reasons stated here and in the majority opinion in Garcia v. Google, Inc., 766 F.3d 929, 933–36 (9th Cir. 2014), I conclude that Garcia's copyright claim is likely to succeed. I'd also find that Garcia has made an ample showing of irreparable harm. It's her life that's at stake. See id. at 938–39.

5. Copyright on Photography

111 U.S. 53 (1884)

BURROW-GILES LITHOGRAPHIC COMPANY V. SARONY

U.S. Supreme Court

MR. JUSTICE MILLER delivered the opinion of the Court.

This is a writ of error to the Circuit Court for the Southern District of New York.

Plaintiff is a lithographer, and defendant a photographer, with large business in those lines in the City of New York. The suit was commenced by an action at law in which Sarony was plaintiff and the lithographic company was defendant, the plaintiff charging the defendant with violating his copyright in regard to a photograph, the title of which is "Oscar Wilde, No. 18." A jury being waived, the court made a finding of facts on which a judgment in favor of the plaintiff was rendered for the sum of $600 for the plates and 85,000 copies sold and exposed to sale, and $10 for copies found in his possession, as penalties under section 4965 of the Revised Statutes. Among the finding of facts made by the court, the following presents the principal question raised by the assignment of errors in the case:

"3. That the plaintiff, about the month of January, 1882, under an agreement with Oscar Wilde, became and was the author, inventor, designer, and proprietor of the photograph in suit, the title of which is 'Oscar Wilde, No. 18,' being the number used to designate this particular photograph and of the negative thereof; that the same is a useful, new, harmonious, characteristic, and graceful picture, and that said plaintiff made the same at his place of business in said City of New York, and within the United States, entirely from his own original mental conception, to which he gave visible form by posing the said Oscar Wilde in front of the camera, selecting and arranging the costume, draperies, and other various accessories in said photograph, arranging the subject so as to present graceful outlines, arranging and disposing the light and shade, suggesting and evoking the desired expression, and from such disposition, arrangement, or representation, made entirely by the plaintiff, he produced the picture in suit, Exhibit A, April 14, 1882, and that the terms 'author,' 'inventor,' and 'designer,' as used in the art of photography and in the complaint, mean the person who so produced the photograph."

Other findings leave no doubt that plaintiff had taken all the steps required by the act of Congress to obtain copyright of this photograph, and section 4952 names photographs, among other things, for which the author, inventor, or designer may obtain copyright, which is to secure him the sole privilege of reprinting, publishing, copying, and vending the same. That defendant is liable, under that section and section 4965, there can be no question if those sections are valid as they relate to photographs.

...

The third finding of facts says, in regard to the photograph in question, that it is a

"useful, new, harmonious, characteristic, and graceful picture, and that plaintiff made the same . . . entirely from his own original mental conception, to which he gave visible form by posing the said Oscar Wilde in front of the camera, selecting and arranging the costume, draperies, and other various accessories in said photograph, arranging the subject so as to present graceful outlines, arranging and disposing the light and shade, suggesting and evoking the desired expression, and from such disposition, arrangement, or representation, made entirely by plaintiff, he produced the picture in suit."

These findings, we think, show this photograph to be an original work of art, the product of plaintiff's intellectual invention, of which plaintiff is the author, and of a class of inventions for which the Constitution intended that Congress should secure to him the exclusive right to use, publish, and sell it...

The question here presented is one of first impression under our Constitution, but an instructive case of the same class is that of Nottage v. Jackson, 11 Q.B.D. 627, decided in that court on appeal, August, 1883.

The first section of the Act of 25 & 26, Vict. c. 68, authorizes the author of a photograph, upon making registry of it under the Copyright Act of 1882, to have a monopoly of its reproduction and multiplication during the life of the author.

The plaintiffs in that case described themselves as the authors of the photograph which was pirated in the registration of it. It appeared that they had arranged with the captain of the Australian cricketers to take a photograph of the whole team in a group, and they sent one of the artists in their employ from London to some country town to do it. The question in the case was whether the plaintiffs, who owned the establishment in London where the photographs were made from the negative and were sold, and who had the negative taken by one of their men, were the authors or the man who, for their benefit, took the negative. It was held that the latter was the author, and the action failed because plaintiffs had described themselves as authors.

Brett, M.R., said in regard to who was the author:

"The nearest I can come to is that it is the person who effectively is as near as he can be the cause of the picture which is produced -- that is, the person who has superintended the arrangement, who has actually formed the picture by putting the persons in position, and arranging the place where the people are to be -- the man who is the effective cause of that."

Lord Justice Cotton said:

"In my opinion, 'author' involves originating, making, producing, as the inventive or mastermind, the thing which is to be protected, whether it be a drawing, or a painting, or a photograph,"

and Lord Justice Bowen says that photography is to be treated for the purposes of the act as an art, and the author is the man who really represents, creates, or gives effect to the idea, fancy, or imagination.

The appeal of plaintiffs from the original judgment against them was accordingly dismissed.

These views of the nature of authorship and of originality, intellectual creation, and right to protection confirm what we have already said.

The judgment of the circuit court is accordingly affirmed

<hr>

377 F.Supp.2d 444 (S.D.N.Y. 2006)

MANNION V. COORS BREWING CO.

Southern District of New York

LEWIS A. KAPLAN, District Judge.

The parties dispute whether a photograph used in billboard advertisements for Coors Light beer infringes the plaintiff's copyright in a photograph of a basketball star. The defendants almost certainly imitated the plaintiff's photograph. The major question is whether and to what extent what was copied is protected. The case requires the Court to consider the nature of copyright protection in photographs. The matter is before the Court on cross motions for summary judgment.

Facts

Jonathan Mannion is a freelance photographer who specializes in portraits of celebrity athletes and musicians in the rap and rhythm-and-blues worlds. In 1999 he was hired by SLAM, a basketball magazine, to photograph basketball star Kevin Garnett in connection with an article that the maga- zine planned to publish about him. The article, entitled "Above the Clouds," appeared as the cover story of the December 1999 issue of the magazine. It was accompanied by a number of Mannion's photographs of Garnett, including the one at issue here (the "Garnett Photograph"), which was printed on a two-page spread introducing the article.

The Garnett Photograph, which is reproduced below, is a three-quarter-length portrait of Garnett against a backdrop of clouds with some blue sky shining through. The view is up and across the right side of Garnett's torso, so that he appears to be towering above earth. He wears a white T-shirt, white athletic pants, a black close-fitting cap, and a large amount of platinum, gold, and diamond jewelry ("bling bling" in the vernacular), including several necklaces, a Rolex watch and bracelet on his left wrist, bracelets on his right wrist, rings on one finger of each hand, and earrings. His head is cocked, his eyes are closed, and his heavily-veined hands, nearly all of which are visible, rest over his lower abdomen, with the thumbs hooked on the waistband of the trousers. The light is from the viewer's left, so that Garnett's right shoulder is the brightest area of the photograph and his hands cast slight shadows on his trousers. As reproduced in the magazine, the photograph cuts off much of Garnett's left arm.

In early 2001, defendant Carol H. Williams Advertising ("CHWA") began developing ideas for outdoor billboards that would advertise Coors Light beer to young black men in urban areas. One of CHWA's "comp boards"- a "comp board" is an image created by an advertising company to convey a proposed design - used a manipulated version of the Garnett Photograph and superimposed on it the words "Iced Out" ("ice" being slang for diamonds) and a picture of a can of Coors Light beer (the "Iced Out Comp Board"). CHWA obtained authorization from Mannion's representa- tive to use the Garnett Photograph for this purpose.

The Iced Out Comp Board, reproduced below, used a black-and-white, mirror image of the Gar- nett Photograph, but with the head cropped out on top and part of the fingers cropped out below. CHWA forwarded its comp boards to, and solicited bids for the photograph for the Coors advertising from, various photographers including Mannion, who submitted a bid but did not receive the assignment.

Coors and CHWA selected for a Coors billboard a photograph (the "Coors Billboard"), repro- duced below, that resembles the Iced Out Comp Board. The Coors Billboard depicts, in black-and- white, the torso of a muscular black man, albeit a model other than Garnett, shot against a cloudy

backdrop. The pose is similar to that in the Garnett Photograph, and the view also is up and across the left side of the torso. The model in the billboard photograph also wears a white T-shirt and white athletic pants. The model's jewelry is prominently depicted; it includes a necklace of platinum or gold and diamonds, a watch and two bracelets on the right wrist, and more bracelets on the left wrist. The light comes from the viewer's right, so that the left shoulder is the brightest part of the photograph, and the right arm and hand cast slight shadows on the trousers.

Mannion subsequently noticed the Coors Billboard at two locations in the Los Angeles area. He applied for registration of his copyright of the Garnett Photograph in 2003 and brought this action for infringement in February of 2004. The registration was completed in May 2004. The parties each move for summary judgment.

Discussion

...

B. The Elements of Copyright Infringement

"To prove infringement, a plaintiff with a valid copyright must demonstrate that: (1) the defendant has actually copied the plaintiff's work; and (2) the copying is illegal because a substantial similarity exists between the defendant's work and the protectible elements of plaintiff's." "Actual copying" - which is used as a term of art to mean that "the defendant, in creating its work, used the plaintiff's material as a model, template, or even inspiration" - may be shown by direct evidence, which rarely is available, or by proof of access and probative similarities (as distinguished from "substantial similarity") between the two works.

Mannion concededly owns a valid copyright in the Garnett photograph. Access is undisputed. There is ample evidence from which a trier of fact could find that CHWA actually copied the Garnett Photograph for the Coors Billboard. Thus, the major questions presented by these motions are whether a trier of fact could or must find substantial similarity between protected elements of the Coors Billboard and the Garnett Photograph. ...

...

C. Determining the Protectible Elements of the Garnett Photograph

The first question must be: in what respects is the Garnett Photograph protectible?

1. Protectible Elements of Photographs

It is well-established that "the sine qua non of copyright is originality" and, accordingly, that "copyright protection may extend only to those components of a work that are original to the author." 'Original' in the copyright context "means only that the work was independently created by the author (as opposed to copied from other works), and that it possesses at least some minimal degree of creativity."

It sometimes is said that "copyright in the photograph conveys no rights over the subject matter conveyed in the photograph." But this is not always true. It of course is correct that the photographer of a building or tree or other pre-existing object has no right to prevent others from photographing the same thing. That is because originality depends upon independent creation, and the photographer did not create that object. By contrast, if a photographer arranges or otherwise creates the subject that his camera captures, he may have the right to prevent others from producing works that depict that subject.

Almost any photograph "may claim the necessary originality to support a copyright." Indeed, ever since the Supreme Court considered an 1882 portrait by the celebrity photographer Napoleon Sarony of the 27-year-old Oscar Wilde, courts have articulated lists of potential components of a photograph's originality. These lists, however, are somewhat unsatisfactory.

First, they do not deal with the issue, alluded to above, that the nature and extent of a photograph's protection differs depending on what makes that photograph original.

Second, courts have not always distinguished between decisions that a photographer makes in creating a photograph and the originality of the final product. Several cases, for example, have included in lists of the potential components of photographic originality "selection of film and camera," "lens and filter selection," and "the kind of camera, the kind of film, [and] the kind of lens." Having considered the matter fully, however, I think this is not sufficiently precise. Decisions about film, camera, and lens, for example, often bear on whether an image is original. But the fact that a photographer made such choices does not alone make the image original. "Sweat of the brow" is not the touchstone of copyright. Protection derives from the features of the work itself, not the effort that goes into it.

This point is illustrated by Bridgeman Art Library, Ltd. v. Corel Corp., in which this Court held that there was no copyright in photographic transparencies that sought to reproduce precisely paintings in the public domain. To be sure, a great deal of effort and expertise may have been poured into the production of the plaintiff's images, including decisions about camera, lens, and film. But the works were "slavish copies." They did not exhibit the originality necessary for copyright.

The Court therefore will examine more closely the nature of originality in a photograph. In so doing, it draws on the helpful discussion in a leading treatise on United Kingdom copyright law, which is similar to our own with respect to the requirement of originality.

a. Rendition

First, "there may be originality which does not depend on creation of the scene or object to be photographed . . . and which resides [instead] in such specialties as angle of shot, light and shade, exposure, effects achieved by means of filters, developing techniques etc." I will refer to this type of originality as originality in the rendition because, to the extent a photograph is original in this way, copyright protects not what is depicted, but rather how it is depicted.

It was originality in the rendition that was at issue in SHL Imaging, Inc. v. Artisan House, Inc. That case concerned photographs of the defendants' mirrored picture frames that the defendants commissioned from the plaintiff. The photographs were to be used by the defendants' sales force for in-person pitches. When the defendants reproduced the photographs in their catalogues and brochures, the court found infringement: "Plaintiff cannot prevent others from photographing the same frames, or using the same lighting techniques and blue sky reflection in the mirrors. What makes plaintiff's photographs original is the totality of the precise lighting selection, angle of the camera, lens and filter selection." Again, what made the photographs original was not the lens and filter selection themselves. It was the effect produced by the lens and filters selected, among other things. In any case, those effects were the basis of the originality of the works at issue in SHL Imaging.

By contrast, in Bridgeman Art Library, the goal was to reproduce exactly other works. The photographs were entirely unoriginal in the rendition, an extremely unusual circumstance. Unless a photograph replicates another work with total or near-total fidelity, it will be at least somewhat original in the rendition.

b. Timing

A photograph may be original in a second respect. "[A] person may create a worthwhile photograph by being at the right place at the right time." I will refer to this type of originality as originality in timing.

One case that concerned originality in timing, among other things, was Pagano v. Chas. Beseler Co., which addressed the copyrightability of a photograph of a scene in front of the New York Public Library at Fifth Avenue and Forty-Second Street:

"The question is not, as defendant suggests, whether the photograph of a public building may properly be copyrighted. Any one may take a photograph of a public building and of the surrounding scene. It undoubtedly requires originality to determine just when to take the photograph, so as to bring out the proper setting for both animate and inanimate objects . . . . The photographer caught the men and women in not merely lifelike, but artistic, positions, and this is especially true of the traffic policeman. . . . There are other features, which need not be discussed in detail, such as the motor cars waiting for the signal to proceed."

ous also that the plaintiff's case is not affected by the fact, if it be one, that the pictures represent actual groups-visible things. They seem from the testimony to have been composed from hints or description, not from sight . . . . But even if they had been drawn from the life, that fact would not deprive them of protection. The opposite proposition would mean that a portrait by Velasquez or Whistler was common property because others might try their hand on the same face. Others are free to copy the original. They are not free to copy the copy."); Franklin Mint Corp. v. Nat'l Wildlife Art Exchange, Inc., 575 F.2d 62, 65 (3d Cir. 1978) (same); F. W. Woolworth Co. v. Contemporary Arts, Inc., 193 F.2d 162, 164 (1st Cir. 1951) ("It is the well established rule that a copyright on a work of art does not protect a subject, but only the treatment of a subject."); BENJAMIN KAPLAN, AN UNHURRIED VIEW OF COPYRIGHT 56 (1967) (observing that, with respect to "works of 'fine art,'" "the manner of execution is usually of more interest than the subject pictured.").

A modern work strikingly original in timing might be Catch of the Day, by noted wildlife photographer Thomas Mangelsen, which depicts a salmon that appears to be jumping into the gaping mouth of a brown bear at Brooks Falls in Katmai National Park, Alaska.An older example is Alfred Eisenstaedt's photograph of a sailor kissing a young woman on VJ Day in Times Square, the memorability of which is attributable in significant part to the timing of its creation.

Copyright based on originality in timing is limited by the principle that copyright in a photograph ordinarily confers no rights over the subject matter. Thus, the copyright in Catch of the Day does not protect against subsequent photographs of bears feasting on salmon in the same location. Furthermore, if another photographer were sufficiently skilled and fortunate to capture a salmon at the precise moment that it appeared to enter a hungry bear's mouth - and others have tried, with varying degrees of success- that photographer, even if inspired by Mangelsen, would not neces- sarily have infringed his work because Mangelsen's copyright does not extend to the natural world he captured.

In practice, originality in timing gives rise to the same type of protection as originality in the rendition. In each case, the image that exhibits the originality, but not the underlying subject, qualifies for copyright protection.

c. Creation of the Subject

The principle that copyright confers no right over the subject matter has an important limitation. A photograph may be original to the extent that the photographer created "the scene or subject to be photographed." This type of originality, which I will refer to as originality in the creation of the sub-ject, played an essential role in Rogers v. Koons and Gross v. Seligman.

196

In Rogers, the court held that the copyright in the plaintiff's photograph Puppies, which depicted a contrived scene of the photographer's acquaintance, Jim Scanlon, and his wife on a park bench with eight puppies on their laps, protected against the defendants' attempt to replicate precisely, albeit in a three dimensional sculpture, the content of the photograph. Although the Circuit noted that Puppies was original because the artist "made creative judgments concerning technical matters with his camera and the use of natural light" - in other words, because it was original in the rendition - its originality in the creation of the subject was more salient. The same is true of the works at issue in Gross v. Seligman, in which the Circuit held that the copyright in a photograph named Grace of Youth was infringed when the same artist created a photograph named Cherry Ripe using "the same model in the identical pose, with the single exception that the young woman now wears a smile and holds a cherry stem between her teeth."

To conclude, the nature and extent of protection conferred by the copyright in a photograph will vary depending on the nature of its originality. Insofar as a photograph is original in the rendition or timing, copyright protects the image but does not prevent others from photographing the same object or scene. Thus, the copyright at issue in SHL Imaging does not protect against subsequent photographs of the picture frames because the originality of the plaintiffs' photographs was almost purely in the rendition of those frames, not in their creation or the timing of the scene captured. In Pagano, the timing of the capture of the scene in front of the New York Public Library and its rendition were original, but the copyright in the Pagano photograph does not protect against future attempts to capture a scene in front of the same building, just as a copyright in Catch of the Day would not protect against other photographers capturing images of salmon-eating bears.

By contrast, to the extent that a photograph is original in the creation of the subject, copyright extends also to that subject. Thus, an artist who arranges and then photographs a scene often will have the right to prevent others from duplicating that scene in a photograph or other medium.

2. Originality of the Garnett Photograph

There can be no serious dispute that the Garnett Photograph is an original work. The photograph does not result from slavishly copying another work and therefore is original in the rendition. Mannion's relatively unusual angle and distinctive lighting strengthen that aspect of the photograph's originality. His composition - posing man against sky - evidences originality in the creation of the subject. Furthermore, Mannion instructed Garnett to wear simple and plain clothing and as much jewelry as possible, and "to look 'chilled out.'" His orchestration of the scene contributes additional originality in the creation of the subject.

Of course, there are limits to the photograph's originality and therefore to the protection conferred by the copyright in the Garnett Photograph. For example, Kevin Garnett's face, torso, and hands are not original with Mannion, and Mannion therefore may not prevent others from creating photographic portraits of Garnett. Equally obviously, the existence of a cloudy sky is not original, and Mannion therefore may not prevent others from using a cloudy sky as a backdrop.

The defendants, however, take this line of reasoning too far. They argue that it was Garnett, not Mannion, who selected the specific clothing, jewelry, and pose. In consequence, they maintain, the Garnett Photograph is not original to the extent of Garnett's clothing, jewelry, and pose. They appear to be referring to originality in the creation of the subject.

There are two problems with the defendants' argument. The first is that Mannion indisputably orchestrated the scene, even if he did not plan every detail before he met Garnett, and then made the decision to capture it. The second difficulty is that the originality of the photograph extends beyond the individual clothing, jewelry, and pose viewed in isolation. It is the entire image - depicting man, sky, clothing, and jewelry in a particular arrangement - that is at issue here, not its individual components. The Second Circuit has rejected the proposition that:

"in comparing designs for copyright infringement, we are required to dissect them into their separate components, and compare only those elements which are in them- selves copyrightable. . . . If we took this argument to its logical conclusion, we might have to decide that 'there can be no originality in a painting because all colors of paint have been used somewhere in the past."

3. The Idea / Expression Difficulty

Notwithstanding the originality of the Garnett Photograph, the defendants argue that the Coors Billboard does not infringe because the two, insofar as they are similar, share only "the generalized idea and concept of a young African American man wearing a white T-shirt and a large amount of jewelry."

It is true that an axiom of copyright law is that copyright does not protect "ideas," only their expression. Furthermore, when "a given idea is inseparably tied to a particular expression" so that "there is a 'merger' of idea and expression," courts may deny protection to the expression in order to avoid conferring a monopoly on the idea to which it inseparably is tied. But the defendants' reliance on these principles is misplaced.

The "idea" (if one wants to call it that) postulated by the defendants does not even come close to accounting for all the similarities between the two works, which extend at least to angle, pose, background, composition, and lighting. It is possible to imagine any number of depictions of a black man wearing a white T-shirt and "bling bling" that look nothing like either of the photographs at issue here.

This alone is sufficient to dispose of the defendants' contention that Mannion's claims must be rejected because he seeks to protect an idea rather than its expression. But the argument reveals an analytical difficulty in the case law about which more ought to be said. One of the main cases upon which the defendants rely is Kaplan v. Stock Market Photo Agency, Inc.,in which two remarkably similar photographs of a businessman's shoes and lower legs, taken from the top of a tall building looking down on a street below (the plaintiff's and defendants' photographs are reproduced below), were held to be not substantially similar as a matter of law because all of the similarities flowed only from an unprotected idea rather than from the expression of that idea.

But what is the "idea" of Kaplan's photograph? Is it (1) a businessman contemplating suicide by jumping from a building, (2) a businessman contemplating suicide by jumping from a building, seen from the vantage point of the businessman, with his shoes set against the street far below, or perhaps something more general, such as (3) a sense of desperation produced by urban professional life?

If the "idea" is (1) or, for that matter, (3), then the similarities between the two photographs flow from something much more than that idea, for it have would been possible to convey (1) (and (3)) in any number of ways that bear no obvious similarities to Kaplan's photograph. (Examples are a businessman atop a building seen from below, or the entire figure of the businessman, rather than just his shoes or pants, seen from above.) If, on the other hand, the "idea" is (2), then the two works could be said to owe much of their similarity to a shared idea.

...

The idea/expression distinction arose in the context of literary copyright. For the most part, the Supreme Court has not applied it outside that context. The classic Hand formulations reviewed above also were articulated in the context of literary works. And it makes sense to speak of the idea conveyed by a literary work and to distinguish it from its expression. To take a clear example, two different authors each can describe, with very different words, the theory of special relativity. The words will be protected as expression. The theory is a set of unprotected ideas.

In the visual arts, the distinction breaks down. For one thing, it is impossible in most cases to speak of the particular "idea" captured, embodied, or conveyed by a work of art because every observer will have a different interpretation. Furthermore, it is not clear that there is any real distinction between the idea in a work of art and its expression. An artist's idea, among other things, is to depict a particular subject in a particular way. As a demonstration, a number of cases from this Circuit have observed that a photographer's "conception" of his subject is copyrightable. By "conception," the courts must mean originality in the rendition, timing, and creation of the subject - for that is what copyright protects in photography. But the word "conception" is a cousin of "concept," and both are akin to "idea." In other words, those elements of a photograph, or indeed, any work of visual art protected by copyright, could just as easily be labeled "idea" as "expression."

This Court is not the first to question the usefulness of the idea/expression terminology in the context of non-verbal media. Judge Hand pointed out in Peter Pan Fabrics that whereas "in the case of verbal 'works', it is well settled that . . . there can be no copyright in the 'ideas' disclosed but only in their 'expression[,]'" "in the case of designs, which are addressed to the aesthetic sensibilities of the observer, the test is, if possible, even more intangible." Moreover, Judge Newman has written:

"I do not deny that all of these subject matters [computer programs, wooden dolls, advertisements in a telephone directory] required courts to determine whether the first work was copyrightable and whether the second infringed protectable elements. What I question is whether courts should be making those determinations with the same modes of analysis and even the same vocabulary that was appropriate for writings. . . . It is not just a matter of vocabulary. Words convey concepts, and if we use identical phrases from one context to resolve issues in another, we risk failing to notice that the relevant concepts are and ought to be somewhat different."

He then referred to dicta from his own decision in Warner Bros. v. American Broadcasting Compa- nies, explaining: "I was saying . . . [that] one cannot divide a visual work into neat layers of abstraction in precisely the same manner one could with a text." The Third Circuit has made a similar point:

"Troublesome, too, is the fact that the same general principles are applied in claims involving plays, novels, sculpture, maps, directories of information, musical compositions, as well as artistic paintings. Isolating the idea from the expression and determining the extent of copying required for unlawful appropriation necessarily depend to some degree on whether the subject matter is words or symbols written on paper, or paint brushed onto canvas."

For all of these reasons, I think little is gained by attempting to distinguish an unprotectible "idea" from its protectible "expression" in a photograph or other work of visual art. It remains, then, to consider just what courts have been referring to when they have spoken of the "idea" in a photograph.

A good example is Rogers v. Koons, in which the court observed that "it is not . . . the idea of a couple with eight small puppies seated on a bench that is protected, but rather Rogers' expression of this idea - as caught in the placement, in the particular light, and in the expressions of the subjects . . . ." But "a couple with eight small puppies seated on a bench" is not necessarily the idea of Puppies, which just as easily could be "people with dogs on their laps," "the bliss of owning puppies," or even a sheepishly ironic thought such as "Ha ha! This might look cute now, but boy are these puppies going to be a lot of work!"

Rather, "a couple with eight small puppies seated on a bench" is nothing more or less than what "a young African American man wearing a white T-shirt and a large amount of jewelry" is: a description of the subject at a level of generality sufficient to avoid implicating copyright protection for an original photograph. Other copyright cases that have referred to the "idea" of a photograph also used "idea" to mean a general description of the subject or subject matter. The Kaplan decision even used these terms interchangeably: "The subject matter of both photographs is a business- person contemplating a leap from a tall building onto the city street below. As the photograph's central idea, rather than Kaplan's expression of the idea, this subject matter is unprotectable in and of itself." Thus another photographer may pose a couple with eight puppies on a bench, depict a businessman contemplating a leap from an office building onto a street, or take a picture of a black man in white athletic wear and showy jewelry. In each case, however, there would be infringement (assuming actual copying and ownership of a valid copyright) if the subject and rendition were sufficiently like those in the copyrighted work.

This discussion of course prompts the question: at what point do the similarities between two photographs become sufficiently general that there will be no infringement even though actual copying has occurred? But this question is precisely the same, although phrased in the opposite way, as one that must be addressed in all infringement cases, namely whether two works are substantially similar with respect to their protected elements. It is nonsensical to speak of one photograph being substantially similar to another in the rendition and creation of the subject but somehow not infringing because of a shared idea. Conversely, if the two photographs are not substantially similar in the rendition and creation of the subject, the distinction between idea and expression will be irrelevant because there can be no infringement. The idea/expression distinction in photography, and probably the other visual arts, thus achieves nothing beyond what other, clearer copyright principles already accomplish.

I recognize that those principles sometimes may pose a problem like that Judge Hand identified with distinguishing idea from expression in the literary context. As Judge Hand observed, however, such line-drawing difficulties appear in all areas of the law. The important thing is that the categories at issue be useful and relevant, even if their precise boundaries are sometimes difficult to delineate. In the context of photography, the idea/expression distinction is not useful or relevant.

D. Comparison of the Coors Billboard and the Garnett Photograph

The next step is to determine whether a trier of fact could or must find the Coors Billboard substantially similar to the Garnett Photograph with respect to their protected elements.

Substantial similarity ultimately is a question of fact. "The standard test for substantial similarity between two items is whether an ' ordinary observer, unless he set out to detect the disparities, would be disposed to overlook them, and regard [the] aesthetic appeal as the same.'" The Second Circuit sometimes has applied a "more discerning observer" test when a work contains both protectible and unprotectible elements. The test "requires the court to eliminate the unprotectible elements from its consideration and to ask whether the protectible elements, standing alone, are substantially similar." The Circuit, however, is ambivalent about this test. In several cases dealing with fabric and garment designs, the Circuit has cautioned that:

"ideas, and artistic dexterity and skill in their representation in the chosen medium. It is not the law that copyright protects the second kind of ingredient only. If that were so a debased copy which failed to capture the artist's dexterity and skill would not infringe, which plainly is not the case. Unless an artist is content merely to represent a pre-existent object (e.g. a building) or scene, it is part of his task as artist to exercise his imagination and in so doing he may create a pattern of ideas for incorporation in his finished work. This idea-pattern may be as much part of his work, and deserving of copyright protection, as the brushstrokes, pencil-lines, etc. The true proposition is that there is no copyright in a general idea, but that an original combination of ideas may [be protected]." 1 LADDIE ß 4.43, at 212 (footnote omitted).

...

Dissecting the works into separate components and comparing only the copyrightable elements, however, appears to be exactly what the "more discerning observer" test calls for.

The Circuit indirectly spoke to this tension in the recent case of Tufenkian Import/Export Ventures, Inc. v. Einstein Moomjy, Inc. There the trial court purported to use the more discerning observer test but nonetheless compared the "total-concept-and-feel" of carpet designs. The Circuit observed that the more discerning observer test is "intended to emphasize that substantial similarity must exist between the defendant's allegedly infringing design and the protectible elements in the plaintiff's design." In making its own comparison, the Circuit did not mention the "more discerning observer" test at all, but it did note that:

"the total-concept-and-feel locution functions as a reminder that, while the infringement analysis must begin by dissecting the copyrighted work into its component parts in order to clarify precisely what is not original, infringement analysis is not simply a matter of ascertaining similarity between components viewed in isolation. . . . The court, confronted with an allegedly infringing work, must analyze the two works closely to figure out in what respects, if any, they are similar, and then determine whether these similarities are due to protected aesthetic expressions original to the allegedly infringed work, or whether the similarity is to something in the original that is free for the taking."

In light of these precedents, the Court concludes that it is immaterial whether the ordinary or more discerning observer test is used here because the inquiries would be identical. The cases agree that the relevant comparison is between the protectible elements in the Garnett Photograph and the Coors Billboard, but that those elements are not to be viewed in isolation.

The Garnett Photograph is protectible to the extent of its originality in the rendition and creation of the subject. Key elements of the Garnett Photograph that are in the public domain - such as Kevin Garnett's likeness - are not replicated in the Coors Billboard. Other elements arguably in the public domain - such as the existence of a cloudy sky, Garnett's pose, his white T-shirt, and his specific jewelry - may not be copyrightable in and of themselves, but their existence and arrangement in this photograph indisputably contribute to its originality. Thus the fact that the Garnett Photograph includes certain elements that would not be copyrightable in isolation does not affect the nature of the comparison. The question is whether the aesthetic appeal of the two images is the same.

The two photographs share a similar composition and angle. The lighting is similar, and both use a cloudy sky as backdrop. The subjects are wearing similar clothing and similar jewelry arranged in a similar way. The defendants, in other words, appear to have recreated much of the subject that Mannion had created and then, through imitation of angle and lighting, rendered it in a similar way. The similarities here thus relate to the Garnett Photograph's originality in the rendition and the creation of the subject and therefore to its protected elements.

There of course are differences between the two works. The similarity analysis may take into account some, but not all, of these. It long has been the law that "no plagiarist can excuse the wrong by showing how much of his work he did not pirate." Thus the addition of the words "Iced Out" and a can of Coors Light beer may not enter into the similarity analysis.

Other differences, however, are in the nature of changes rather than additions. One image is black and white and dark, the other is in color and bright. One is the mirror image of the other. One depicts only an unidentified man's torso, the other the top three-fourths of Kevin Garnett's body. The jewelry is not identical. One T-shirt appears to fit more tightly than the other. These changes may enter the analysis because "if the points of dissimilarity not only exceed the points of similarity, but indicate that the remaining points of similarity are, within the context of plaintiff's work, of minimal importance . . . then no infringement results."

The parties have catalogued at length and in depth the similarities and differences between these works. In the last analysis, a reasonable jury could find substantial similarity either present or absent. As in Kisch v. Ammirati & Puris Inc., which presents facts as close to this case as can be imagined, the images are such that infringement cannot be ruled out - or in - as a matter of law.

... The plaintiff's cross motion for summary judgment is denied.

1-The Garnett Photograph

2- The Iced Out Comp Board

3- The Coors Billboard and detail

883 F.3d 1111 (2018)

RENTMEESTER v. NIKE

United States Court of Appeals, Ninth Circuit

WATFORD, Circuit Judge:

This is a copyright infringement action brought by the renowned photographer Jacobus Rentmeester against Nike, Inc. The case involves a famous photograph Rentmeester took in 1984 of Michael Jordan, who at the time was a student at the University of North Carolina. The photo originally appeared in Life magazine as part of a photo essay featuring American athletes who would soon be competing in the 1984 Summer Olympic Games. We are asked to decide whether Nike infringed Rentmeester's copyright when it commissioned its own photograph of Jordan and then used that photo to create one of its most iconic trademarks.

I

The allegations in Rentmeester's complaint, which we accept as true at this stage of the proceedings, establish the following. Rentmeester's photograph of Jordan, reproduced in the Appendix, is highly original. It depicts Jordan leaping toward a basketball hoop with a basketball raised above his head in his left hand, as though he is attempting to dunk the ball. The setting for the photo is not a basketball court, as one would expect in a shot of this sort. Instead, Rentmeester chose to take the photo on an isolated grassy knoll on the University of North Carolina campus. He brought in a basketball hoop and backboard mounted on a tall pole, which he planted in the ground to position the hoop exactly where he wanted. Whether due to the height of the pole or its placement within the image, the basketball hoop appears to tower above Jordan, beyond his reach.

Rentmeester instructed Jordan on the precise pose he wanted Jordan to assume. It was an unusual pose for a basketball player to adopt, one inspired by ballet's grand jeté, in which a dancer leaps with legs extended, one foot forward and the other back. Rentmeester positioned the camera below Jordan and snapped the photo at the peak of his jump so that the viewer looks up at Jordan's soaring figure silhouetted against a cloudless blue sky. Rentmeester used powerful strobe lights and a fast shutter speed to capture a sharp image of Jordan contrasted against the sky, even though the sun is shining directly into the camera lens from the lower right-hand corner of the shot.

Not long after Rentmeester's photograph appeared in Life magazine, Nike contacted him and asked to borrow color transparencies of the photo. Rentmeester provided Nike with two color transparencies for $150 under a limited license authorizing Nike to use the transparencies "for slide presentation only." It is unclear from the complaint what kind of slide presentation Nike may have been preparing, but the company was then beginning its lucrative partnership with Jordan by promoting the Air Jordan brand of athletic shoes.

In late 1984 or early 1985, Nike hired a photographer to produce its own photograph of Jordan, one obviously inspired by Rentmeester's. In the Nike photo, Jordan is again shown leaping toward a basketball hoop with a basketball held in his left hand above his head, as though he is about to dunk the ball. See Appendix. The photo was taken outdoors and from a similar angle as in Rentmeester's photo, so that the viewer looks up at Jordan's figure silhouetted against the sky. In the Nike photo, though, it is the city of Chicago's skyline that appears in the background, a nod to the fact that by then Jordan was playing professionally for the Chicago Bulls. Jordan wears apparel reflecting the colors of his new team, and he is of course wearing a pair of Nike shoes. Nike used this photo on posters and billboards as part of its marketing campaign for the new Air Jordan brand.

When Rentmeester saw the Nike photo, he threatened to sue Nike for breach of the limited license governing use of his color transparencies. To head off litigation, Nike entered into a new agreement with Rentmeester in March 1985, under which the company agreed to pay $15,000 for the right to continue using the Nike photo on posters and billboards in North America for a period of two years. Rentmeester alleges that Nike continued to use the photo well beyond that period.

In 1987, Nike created its iconic "Jumpman" logo, a solid black silhouette that tracks the outline of Jordan's figure as it appears in the Nike photo. See Appendix. Over the past three decades, Nike has used the Jumpman logo in connection with the sale and marketing of billions of dollars of merchandise. It has become one of Nike's most recognizable trademarks.

Rentmeester filed this action in January 2015. He alleges that both the Nike photo and the Jumpman logo infringe the copyright in his 1984 photo of Jordan. His complaint asserts claims for direct, vicarious, and contributory infringement, as well as a claim for violation of the Digital Millennium Copyright Act, 17 U.S.C. § 1202. Rentmeester seeks damages only for acts of infringement occurring within the Copyright Act's three-year limitations period (January 2012 to the present). Doing so avoids the defense of laches that would otherwise arise from his 30–year delay in bringing suit. See Petrella v. Metro–Goldwyn–Mayer, Inc., 134 S. Ct. 1962, 1970 (2014).

The district court granted Nike's motion to dismiss under Federal Rule of Civil Procedure 12(b)(6). The court dismissed Rentmeester's claims with prejudice after concluding that neither the Nike photo nor the Jumpman logo infringe Rentmeester's copyright as a matter of law. We review that legal determination de novo.

II

To state a claim for copyright infringement, Rentmeester must plausibly allege two things: (1) that he owns a valid copyright in his photograph of Jordan, and (2) that Nike copied protected aspects of the photo's expression. See Feist Publications,

Inc. v. Rural Telephone Service Co., 499 U.S. 340, 361 (1991); Shaw v. Lindheim, 919 F.2d 1353, 1356 (9th Cir. 1990).

Although our cases have not always made this point explicit, the second element has two distinct components: "copying" and "unlawful appropriation." Sid & Marty Krofft Television Productions, Inc. v. McDonald's Corp., 562 F.2d 1157, 1164–65 (9th Cir. 1977); Arnstein v. Porter, 154 F.2d 464, 468 (2d Cir. 1946); 4 Melville B. Nimmer & David Nimmer, Nimmer on Copyright § 13.01[B] (2017). Proof of copying by the defendant is necessary because independent creation is a complete defense to copyright infringement. No matter how similar the plaintiff's and the defendant's works are, if the defendant created his independently, without knowledge of or exposure to the plaintiff's work, the defendant is not liable for infringement. See Feist, 499 U.S. at 345–46. Proof of unlawful appropriation—that is, illicit copying—is necessary because copyright law does not forbid all copying. The Copyright Act provides that copyright protection does not "extend to any idea, procedure, process, system, method of operation, concept, principle, or discovery, regardless of the form in which it is described, explained, illustrated, or embodied in [the copyrighted] work." 17 U.S.C. § 102(b). Thus, a defendant incurs no liability if he copies only the "ideas" or "concepts" used in the plaintiff's work. To infringe, the defendant must also copy enough of the plaintiff's expression of those ideas or concepts to render the two works "substantially similar." Mattel, Inc. v. MGA Entertainment, Inc., 616 F.3d 904, 913–14 (9th Cir. 2010).

When the plaintiff lacks direct evidence of copying, he can attempt to prove it circumstantially by showing that the defendant had access to the plaintiff's work and that the two works share similarities probative of copying. See Baxter v. MCA, Inc., 812 F.2d 421, 423 (9th Cir. 1987); 4 Nimmer on Copyright § 13.01[B]. Such proof creates a presumption of copying, which the defendant can then attempt to rebut by proving independent creation. Three Boys Music Corp. v. Bolton, 212 F.3d 477, 486 (9th Cir. 2000).

Unfortunately, we have used the same term—"substantial similarity"—to describe both the degree of similarity relevant to proof of copying and the degree of similarity necessary to establish unlawful appropriation. The term means different things in those two contexts. To prove copying, the similarities between the two works need not be extensive, and they need not involve protected elements of the plaintiff's work. They just need to be similarities one would not expect to arise if the two works had been created independently. Laureyssens v. Idea Group, Inc., 964 F.2d 131, 140 (2d Cir. 1992); 4 Nimmer on Copyright § 13.01[B]. To prove unlawful appropriation, on the other hand, the similarities between the two works must be "substantial" and they must involve protected elements of the plaintiff's work. Laureyssens, 964 F.2d at 140.1

In this case, Rentmeester has plausibly alleged the first element of his infringement claim—that he owns a valid copyright. The complaint asserts that he has been the sole owner of the copyright in his photo since its creation in 1984. And the photo obviously qualifies as an "original work of authorship," given the creative choices Rentmeester made in composing it. See 17 U.S.C. § 102(a)(5); Burrow–Giles Lithographic Co. v. Sarony, 111 U.S. 53, 60 (1884). Rentmeester alleges that he registered his photo with the Copyright Office in 2014, which permits him to bring this suit. 17 U.S.C. § 411(a).

Rentmeester has also plausibly alleged the "copying" component of the second element. He alleges that he provided color transparencies of his photo to Nike's creative director shortly before production of the Nike photo. That allegation establishes that Nike had access to Rentmeester's photo, which in this context means a reasonable opportunity to view it. L.A. Printex Industries, Inc. v. Aeropostale, Inc., 676 F.3d 841, 846 (9th Cir. 2012). Nike's access to Rentmeester's photo, combined with the obvious conceptual similarities between the two photos, is sufficient to create a presumption that the Nike photo was the product of copying rather than independent creation.

The remaining question is whether Rentmeester has plausibly alleged that Nike copied enough of the protected expression from Rentmeester's photo to establish unlawful appropriation. To prove this component of his claim, Rentmeester does not have to show that Nike produced an exact duplicate of his photo. See Rogers v. Koons, 960 F.2d 301, 307 (2d Cir. 1992). But, as mentioned, he does have to show that Nike copied enough of the photo's protected expression to render their works "substantially similar." See Mattel, 616 F.3d at 913–14.

In our circuit, determining whether works are substantially similar involves a two-part analysis consisting of the "extrinsic test" and the "intrinsic test." The extrinsic test assesses the objective similarities of the two works, focusing only on the protectable elements of the plaintiff's expression. Cavalier v. Random House, Inc., 297 F.3d 815, 822 (9th Cir. 2002). Before that comparison can be made, the court must "filter out" the unprotectable elements of the plaintiff's work—primarily ideas and concepts, material in the public domain, and scènes à faire (stock or standard features that are commonly associated with the treatment of a given subject). Id. at 822–23. The protectable elements that remain are then compared to corresponding elements of the defendant's work to assess similarities in the objective details of the works. The intrinsic test requires a more holistic, subjective comparison of the works to determine whether they are substantially similar in "total concept and feel." Id. at 822 (internal quotation marks omitted). To prevail, a plaintiff must prove substantial similarity under both tests. Funky Films, Inc. v. Time Warner Entertainment Co., 462 F.3d 1072, 1077 (9th Cir. 2006).

Only the extrinsic test's application may be decided by the court as a matter of law, McCulloch v. Albert E. Price, Inc., 823 F.2d 316, 319 (9th Cir. 1987), so that is the only test relevant in reviewing the district court's ruling on a motion to dismiss. Before applying the extrinsic test ourselves, a few words are in order about the filtering process that the test demands.

Certain types of works can be dissected into protected and unprotected elements more readily than others. With novels, plays, and motion pictures, for instance, even after filtering out unprotectable elements like ideas and scènes à faire, many protectable elements of expression remain that can be objectively compared. "[P]lot, themes, dialogue, mood, setting, pace, characters, and sequence of events" are elements we have previously identified. Funky Films, 462 F.3d at 1077 (internal quotation marks omitted).

Photographs cannot be dissected into protected and unprotected elements in the same way. To be sure, photos can be broken down into objective elements that reflect the various creative choices the photographer made in composing the image—choices related to subject matter, pose, lighting, camera angle, depth of field, and the like. See Ets–Hokin v. Skyy Spirits, Inc., 225 F.3d 1068, 1074–75 (9th Cir. 2000). But none of those elements is subject to copyright protection when viewed in isolation. For example, a photographer who produces a photo using a highly original lighting technique or a novel camera angle cannot prevent other photographers from using those same techniques to produce new images of their own, provided the new images are not substantially similar to the earlier, copyrighted photo. With respect to a photograph's subject matter, no photographer can claim a monopoly on the right to photograph a particular subject just because he was the first to capture it on film. A subsequent photographer is free to take her own photo of the same subject, again so long as the resulting image is not substantially similar to the earlier photograph.

That remains true even if, as here, a photographer creates wholly original subject matter by having someone pose in an unusual or distinctive way. Without question, one of the highly original elements of Rentmeester's photo is the fanciful (non-natural) pose he asked Jordan to assume. That pose was a product of Rentmeester's own "intellectual invention," Burrow–Giles, 111 U.S. at 60; it would not have been captured on film but for Rentmeester's creativity in conceiving it. The pose Rentmeester conceived is thus quite unlike the pose at issue in Harney v. Sony Pictures Television, Inc., 704 F.3d 173 (1st Cir. 2013), which consisted of nothing more than a daughter riding piggyback on her father's shoulders. The photographer there did not orchestrate the pose and, even if he had, the pose is so commonplace as to be part of the public domain. Id. at 187; see also Leibovitz v. Paramount Pictures Corp., 137 F.3d 109, 116 (2d Cir. 1998) (pose of a nude, pregnant woman in profile is part of the public domain).

Without gainsaying the originality of the pose Rentmeester created, he cannot copyright the pose itself and thereby prevent others from photographing a person in the same pose. He is entitled to protection only for the way the pose is expressed in his photograph, a product of not just the pose but also the camera angle, timing, and shutter speed Rentmeester chose. If a subsequent photographer persuaded Michael Jordan to assume the exact same pose but took her photo, say, from a bird's eye view directly above him, the resulting image would bear little resemblance to Rentmeester's photo and thus could not be deemed infringing.

What is protected by copyright is the photographer's selection and arrangement of the photo's otherwise unprotected elements. If sufficiently original, the combination of subject matter, pose, camera angle, etc., receives protection, not any of the individual elements standing alone. In that respect (although not in others), photographs can be likened to factual compilations. 1 Nimmer on Copyright § 2A.08[E][3][c]; Justin Hughes, The Photographer's Copyright—Photograph as Art, Photograph as Database, 25 Harv. J. L. & Tech. 339, 350–51 (2012). An author of a factual compilation cannot claim copyright protection for the underlying factual material—facts are always free for all to use. Feist, 499 U.S. at 347–48. If sufficiently original, though, an author's selection and arrangement of the material are entitled to protection. Id. at 348–49. The individual elements that comprise a photograph can be viewed in the same way, as the equivalent of unprotectable "facts" that anyone may use to create new works. A second photographer is free to borrow any of the individual elements featured in a copyrighted photograph, "so long as the competing work does not feature the same selection and arrangement" of those elements. Id. at 349. In other words, a photographer's copyright is limited to "the particular selection and arrangement" of the elements as expressed in the copyrighted image. Id. at 350–51.2

This is not to say, as Nike urges us to hold, that all photographs are entitled to only "thin" copyright protection, as is true of factual compilations. A copyrighted work is entitled to thin protection when the range of creative choices that can be made in producing the work is narrow. Mattel, 616 F.3d at 913–14. In Mattel, we noted by way of illustration that "there are only so many ways to paint a red bouncy ball on blank canvas." Id. at 914. We contrasted that with the "gazillions of ways to make an aliens-attack movie," a work that would be entitled to "broad" protection given the much wider range of creative choices available in producing it. Id. at 913–14. When only a narrow range of expression is possible, copyright protection is thin because the copyrighted work will contain few protectable features.

Some photographs are entitled to only thin protection because the range of creative choices available in selecting and arranging the photo's elements is quite limited. That was the case in Ets–Hokin v. Skyy Spirits, Inc., 323 F.3d 763 (9th Cir. 2003), where we held that the plaintiff's commercial product shots of a vodka bottle were entitled to only thin protection. Given the constraints imposed by the subject matter and conventions of commercial product shots, there were relatively few creative choices a photographer could make in producing acceptable images of the bottle. As a result, subtle differences in lighting, camera angle, and background were sufficient to render the defendant's otherwise similar-looking photos of the same bottle non-infringing. Id. at 766.

With other photographs, however, the range of creative choices available to the photographer will be far broader, and very few of those choices will be dictated by subject matter or convention. On the spectrum we set out in Mattel—the relatively small number of ways "to paint a red bouncy ball on blank canvas" on one end, and the "gazillions of ways to make an aliens-attack movie" on the other—many photos will land more on the "aliens-attack movie" end of the range. 616 F.3d at 913–14. As with any other work, the greater the range of creative choices that may be made, the broader the level of protection that will be afforded to the resulting image. See id. at 916; McCulloch, 823 F.2d at 321.

Rentmeester's photo is undoubtedly entitled to broad rather than thin protection. The range of creative choices open to Rentmeester in producing his photo was exceptionally broad; very few of those choices were dictated by convention or subject matter. In fact, Rentmeester's photo is distinctive precisely because he chose not to be bound by the conventions commonly followed in photographing a basketball player attempting to dunk a basketball. Such photos would typically call for a basketball court as the setting, whether indoors or out. Rentmeester chose instead to place Jordan on an open, grassy knoll with a basketball hoop inserted as a prop, whimsically out of place and seeming to tower well above regulation height. Rentmeester also departed from convention by capturing Jordan in a fanciful, highly original pose, one inspired more by ballet's grand jeté than by any pose a basketball player might naturally adopt when dunking a basketball. These creative choices—along with the other choices Rentmeester made with respect to lighting, camera angle, depth of field, and selection of foreground and background elements—resulted in a photo with many non-standard elements. Rentmeester's selection and arrangement of those elements produced an image entitled to the broadest protection a photograph can receive.

With those preliminary observations out of the way, we can now turn to whether Rentmeester has plausibly alleged that his photo and the Nike photo are substantially similar under the extrinsic test. As discussed, that inquiry requires us to assess similarities in the selection and arrangement of the photos' elements, as reflected in the objective details of the two works. We do not have a well-defined standard for assessing when similarity in selection and arrangement becomes "substantial," and in truth no hard-and-fast rule could be devised to guide determinations that will necessarily turn on the unique facts of each case. See Peter Pan Fabrics, Inc. v. Martin Weiner Corp., 274 F.2d 487, 489 (2d Cir. 1960). The best we can do is borrow from the standard Judge Learned Hand employed in a case involving fabric designs: The two photos' selection and arrangement of elements must be similar enough that "the ordinary observer, unless he set out to detect the disparities, would be disposed to overlook them." Id.

We conclude that the works at issue here are as a matter of law not substantially similar. Just as Rentmeester made a series of creative choices in the selection and arrangement of the elements in his photograph, so too Nike's photographer made his own distinct choices in that regard. Those choices produced an image that differs from Rentmeester's photo in more than just minor details.

Let's start with the subject matter of the photographs. The two photos are undeniably similar in the subject matter they depict: Both capture Michael Jordan in a leaping pose inspired by ballet's grand jeté. But Rentmeester's copyright does not confer a monopoly on that general "idea" or "concept"; he cannot prohibit other photographers from taking their own photos of Jordan in a leaping, grand jeté-inspired pose. Because the pose Rentmeester conceived is highly original, though, he is entitled to prevent others from copying the details of that pose as expressed in the photo he took. Had Nike's photographer replicated those details in the Nike photo, a jury might well have been able to find unlawful appropriation even though other elements of the Nike photo, such as background and lighting, differ from the corresponding elements in Rentmeester's photo.

But Nike's photographer did not copy the details of the pose as expressed in Rentmeester's photo; he borrowed only the general idea or concept embodied in the photo. Thus, in each photo Jordan is holding a basketball above his head in his left hand with his legs extended, in a pose at least loosely based on the grand jeté. The position of each of his limbs in the two photos is different, however, and those differences in detail are significant because, among other things, they affect the visual impact of the images. In Rentmeester's photo, Jordan's bent limbs combine with the background and foreground elements to convey mainly a sense of horizontal (forward) propulsion, while in the Nike photo Jordan's completely straight limbs combine with the other elements to convey mainly a sense of vertical propulsion. While the photos embody a similar idea or concept, they express it in different ways. See Folkens v. Wyland Worldwide, LLC, ––– F.3d ––––, 2018 WL 841431, at 4–5 (9th Cir. Feb. 13, 2018).

As to the other highly original element of Rentmeester's photo—the unusual outdoor setting he chose—Nike's photographer did not copy the details of that element either. The two photos again share undeniable similarities at the conceptual level: Both are taken outdoors without the usual trappings of a basketball court, other than the presence of a lone hoop and backboard. But when comparing the details of how that concept is expressed in the two photos, stark differences are readily apparent. Rentmeester set his shot on a grassy knoll with a whimsically out-of-place basketball hoop jutting up from a pole planted in the ground. The grassy knoll in the foreground of Rentmeester's photo is wholly absent from the Nike photo. In fact, in the Nike photo there is no foreground element at all. The positioning of the basketball hoops is also materially different in the two photos. In Rentmeester's photo, the hoop is positioned at a height that appears beyond the ability of anyone to dunk on (even someone as athletic as Jordan), which further contributes to the whimsical rather than realistic nature of the depiction. The hoop in the Nike photo, by contrast, appears to be easily within Jordan's reach.

The other major conceptual similarity shared by the two photos is that both are taken from a similar angle so that the viewer looks up at Jordan's soaring figure silhouetted against a clear sky. This is a far less original element of Rentmeester's photo, as photographers have long used similar camera angles to capture subjects silhouetted against the sky. But even here, the two photos differ as to expressive details in material respects. In Rentmeester's photo, the background is a cloudless blue sky; in the Nike photo, it is the Chicago skyline silhouetted against the orange and purple hues of late dusk or early dawn. In Rentmeester's photo, the sun looms large in the lower right-hand corner of the image; in the Nike photo the sun does not appear at all. And in Rentmeester's photo, parts of Jordan's figure are cast in shadow, while in the Nike photo every inch of Jordan's figure is brightly lit.

Finally, the arrangement of the elements within the photographs is materially different in two further respects. In Rentmeester's photo, Jordan is positioned slightly left of center and appears as a relatively small figure within the frame. In the Nike photo, he is perfectly centered and dominates the frame. In Rentmeester's photo, the basketball hoop stands atop a tall pole planted in the ground, and the hoop's position within the frame balances Jordan's left-of-center placement. In the Nike photo, the hoop takes up the entire right border of the frame, highlighting Jordan's dominant, central position. The hoops are also lit and angled differently toward the viewer, further distinguishing their expressive roles in the photographs.

In our view, these differences in selection and arrangement of elements, as reflected in the photos' objective details, preclude as a matter of law a finding of infringement. Nike's photographer made choices regarding selection and arrangement that produced an image unmistakably different from Rentmeester's photo in material details—disparities that no ordinary observer of the two works would be disposed to overlook. What Rentmeester's photo and the Nike photo share are similarities in general ideas or concepts: Michael Jordan attempting to dunk in a pose inspired by ballet's grand jeté; an outdoor setting stripped of most of the traditional trappings of basketball; a camera angle that captures the subject silhouetted against the sky. Rentmeester cannot claim an exclusive right to ideas or concepts at that level of generality, even in combination. Permitting him to claim such a right would withdraw those ideas or concepts from the "stock of materials" available to other artists, 4 Nimmer on Copyright § 13.03[B][2][a], thereby thwarting copyright's "fundamental objective" of "foster[ing] creativity." Warner Bros. Inc. v. American Broadcasting Cos., 720 F.2d 231, 240 (2d Cir. 1983). Copyright promotes the progress of science and the useful arts by "encourag [ing] others to build freely upon the ideas and information conveyed by a work." Feist, 499 U.S. at 349–50. That is all Nike's photographer did here.

If the Nike photo cannot as a matter of law be found substantially similar to Rentmeester's photo, the same conclusion follows ineluctably with respect to the Jumpman logo. The logo is merely a solid black silhouette of Jordan's figure as it appears in the Nike photo, which, as we have said, differs materially from the way Jordan's figure appears in Rentmeester's photo. Isolating that one element from the Nike photo and rendering it in a stylized fashion make the Jumpman logo even less similar to Rentmeester's photo than the Nike photo itself.3

III

Rentmeester makes three additional arguments in support of reversal, none of which we find persuasive.

A

First, Rentmeester contends that dismissal at the pleading stage is rarely appropriate in copyright infringement cases and that he should have been allowed to take discovery before the district court assessed substantial similarity. It is true that dismissal of copyright infringement claims occurs more commonly at the summary judgment stage, but dismissal at the pleading stage is by no means unprecedented. See, e.g., Peters v. West, 692 F.3d 629, 631 (7th Cir. 2012); Peter F. Gaito Architecture, LLC v. Simone Development Corp., 602 F.3d 57, 64–65 (2d Cir. 2010); Christianson v. West Publishing Co., 149 F.2d 202, 203 (9th Cir. 1945). Dismissal is appropriate here because the two photos and the Jumpman logo are properly before us and thus "capable of examination and comparison." Christianson, 149 F.2d at 203. Nothing disclosed during discovery could alter the fact that the allegedly infringing works are as a matter of law not substantially similar to Rentmeester's photo.

This is not a case in which discovery could shed light on any issues that actually matter to the outcome. In some cases, the defendant claims independent creation as a defense and thus denies having had access to the plaintiff's work. In that scenario, disputed factual issues will often require discovery to flesh out. Here,

Nike does not contest that it had access to Rentmeester's photo, so that issue is not in dispute.

In other cases, more may need to be known about the range of creative choices available to the plaintiff photographer in order to determine the breadth of protection available to his work. Here, we have accepted as true all of Rentmeester's allegations concerning the creative choices he made in producing his photograph. But even granting his photo the broad protection it deserves, a comparison of the works at issue makes clear that Nike's photographer made creative choices of his own, which resulted in an image and derivative logo not substantially similar to Rentmeester's photo. Nothing disclosed during discovery could strengthen Rentmeester's arguments on this score.

...

C

Finally, Rentmeester contends that the district court should have granted him leave to amend his complaint, rather than dismissing the action with prejudice. The district court did not abuse its discretion in dismissing Rentmeester's suit with prejudice because amending the complaint would have been futile. Rentmeester's photo and the allegedly infringing works are as a matter of law not substantially similar. None of the new allegations Rentmeester proposed to add would have changed that dispositive fact.

AFFIRMED.

Partial Concurrence and Partial Dissent by Judge Owens:

I agree with most of the majority's analysis, and with its holding that Rentmeester cannot prevail on his Jumpman logo copyright infringement claim. However, I respectfully disagree with the majority's conclusion as to the Nike photo.

After correctly (1) setting out the law of copyright as applied to photographs, and (2) recognizing that Rentmeester's photo is entitled to "broad" copyright protection, the majority then dissects why, in its view, the Rentmeester and Nike photos are, as a matter of law, not substantially similar. This section of the majority reads like a compelling motion for summary judgment or closing argument to a jury, and it may be correct at the end of the day. Yet such questions of substantial similarity are inherently factual, and should not have been made at this stage of the game.

Where no discovery has taken place, we should not say that, as a matter of law, the Nike photo could never be substantially similar to the Rentmeester photo. This is an inherently factual question which is often reserved for the jury, and rarely for a court to decide at the motion to dismiss stage. See, e.g., L.A. Printex Indus., Inc. v. Aeropostale, Inc., 676 F.3d 841, 848 (9th Cir. 2012) ("Summary judgment is 'not highly favored' on questions of substantial similarity in copyright cases." (citation omitted)); Sturdza v. United Arab Emirates, 281 F.3d 1287, 1296 (D.C. Cir. 2002) ("Because substantial similarity is customarily an extremely close question of fact, summary judgment has traditionally been frowned upon in copyright litigation." (citation and alteration omitted)); Leigh v. Warner Bros., Inc., 212 F.3d 1210, 1213

(11th Cir. 2000) ("Copyright infringement is generally a question of fact for the jury to decide . and the court erred in holding as a matter of law that no reasonable jury could find that the Warner Brothers promotional single-frame images were substantially similar to the aspects of [the photographer's] work protected by copyright.").

"Although it may be easy to identify differences between" the two photos, the Nike photo also has "much in common" with the broadly protected Rentmeester photo. Leigh, 212 F.3d at 1216 (reversing summary judgment for defendant with respect to its alleged infringement of a photograph notwithstanding "undeniably[ ] significant differences between the pictures"). For example, in addition to the similarity of both photos capturing Michael Jordan doing a grand-jeté pose while holding a basketball, both photos are taken from a similar angle, have a silhouette aspect of Jordan against a contrasting solid background, and contain an outdoor setting with no indication of basketball apart from an isolated hoop and backboard.

I cannot say that no reasonable jury could find in favor of Rentmeester regarding the Nike photo, so I would hesitate in granting summary judgment. Here, the majority did not permit the case even to go that far. Rather, it substituted its own judgment—with no factual record development by the parties—as to why the photos are not substantially similar.

While I disagree with the majority's ruling as to the Nike photo, I agree with its holding as to the Jumpman logo. The only element of the Rentmeester photo which Nike possibly could have copied to create the Jumpman logo is the outline of Jordan doing a grand-jeté pose while holding a basketball. As the cases that the majority cites make clear, the outline of a pose isolated from a photograph enjoys, at best, "thin" copyright protection. A grand-jeté dunking pose cannot receive the broad protection that Rentmeester claims, even if Rentmeester encouraged Jordan to strike it. The pose is ultimately no different from the Vulcan salute of Spock, the double thumbs up of Arthur Fonzarelli, or John Travolta's iconic Saturday Night Fever dance pose. See, e.g., Harney v. Sony Pictures Television, Inc., 704 F.3d 173, 187 (1st Cir. 2013) (holding that piggyback pose in photograph was unprotected element); Mattel, Inc. v. Azrak–Hamway Int'l, Inc., 724 F.2d 357, 360 (2d Cir. 1983) (per curiam) (holding that figurine's "traditional fighting pose" was unprotected element); Reece v. Island Treasures Art Gallery, Inc., 468 F. Supp. 2d 1197, 1206–07 (D. Haw. 2006) (holding that hula pose in photograph was unprotected element); cf. Bikram's Yoga College of India, L.P. v. Evolation Yoga, LLC, 803 F.3d 1032, 1036–44 (9th Cir. 2015) (holding that yoga sequence fell outside of copyright protection).

All of these poses can exist independently of the photographer taking them. It does not matter that Rentmeester told Jordan to pose that way—standing alone, a photograph of a mannequin or marionette in that same pose would receive the same thin protection. Cf. Folkens v. Wyland Worldwide, LLC, ––– F.3d ––––, 2018 WL 841431, at *3–4 (9th Cir. Feb. 13, 2018) (holding that two dolphins crossing each other was an unprotected element because that pose can be found in nature and it was irrelevant that the dolphins were posed by animal trainers). Indeed, Rentmeester cannot cite any cases to suggest that Jordan's pose, in isolation, enjoys anything more than the thinnest of copyright protection. To hold otherwise would mean that a photographer would own a broad copyright over photos of human movements, including facial expressions. I cannot find any authority in our cases or the relevant copyright statutes that would permit such a radical change in our intellectual property laws. Cf. id. at *4 (reaffirming that "ideas, 'first expressed in nature, are the common heritage of humankind, and no artist may use copyright law to prevent others from depicting them'") (quoting Satava v. Lowry, 323 F.3d 805, 813 (9th Cir. 2003)).

At this stage of the litigation, we assume that (1) Nike traced the Jumpman logo directly from the Nike photo, and (2) that Nike based its photo on the Rentmeester photo. Even assuming all of this to be true, the Jumpman logo is not "virtually identical" to the image of Jordan in the Rentmeester photo. Mattel, Inc. v. MGA Entm't, Inc., 616 F.3d 904, 914 (9th Cir. 2010). For example, there are differences in the angles of Jordan's arms and legs, and the Jumpman logo is a black silhouette. And without being virtually identical, the Jumpman logo—the outline of a pose by Jordan in the Nike photo—cannot infringe upon any thin copyright protection enjoyed by the few elements of the Rentmeester photo allegedly copied. See id. Accordingly, while I agree with the majority regarding the Jumpman logo, I think that whether the Nike photo is substantially similar is not an uncontested breakaway layup, and therefore dismissal of that copyright infringement claim is premature.

6. Copyright on Literary Works

471 U.S. 539, 105 S.Ct. 2218

HARPER & ROW v. NATION

U.S. Supreme Court of the United States

Justice O'CONNOR:

This case requires us to consider to what extent the "fair use" provision of the Copyright Revision Act of 1976, (here [542] inafter the Copyright Act) 17 U.S.C. § 107, sanctions the unauthorized use of quotations from a public figure's unpublished manuscript. In March 1979, an undisclosed source provided The Nation Magazine with the unpublished manuscript of "A Time to Heal: The Autobiography of Gerald R. Ford." Working directly from the purloined manuscript, an editor of The Nation produced a short piece entitled "The Ford Memoirs — Behind the Nixon Pardon." The piece was timed to "scoop" an article scheduled shortly to appear in Time Magazine. Time had agreed to purchase the exclusive right to print prepublication excerpts from the copyright holders, Harper & Row Publishers, Inc. (hereinafter Harper & Row), and Reader's Digest Association, Inc. (hereinafter Reader's Digest). As a result of The Nation article, Time canceled its agreement. Petitioners brought a successful copyright action against The Nation. On appeal, the Second Circuit reversed the lower court's finding of infringement, holding that The Nation's act was sanctioned as a "fair use" of the copyrighted material. We granted certiorari, 467 U.S. 1214, 104 S.Ct. 2655, 81 L.Ed.2d 362 (1984), and we now reverse.

I

In February 1977, shortly after leaving the White House, former President Gerald R. Ford contracted with petitioners Harper & Row and Reader's Digest, to publish his as yet unwritten memoirs. The memoirs were to contain "significant hitherto unpublished material" concerning the Watergate crisis, Mr. Ford's pardon of former President Nixon and "Mr. Ford's reflections on this period of history, and the morality and personalities involved." App. to Pet. for Cert. C-14 — C-15. In addition to the right to publish the Ford memoirs in book form, the agreement gave petitioners the exclusive right to license prepublication excerpts, known in the trade as "first serial rights." Two years later, as the memoirs were nearing completion, petitioners negotiated a prepublication licensing agreement with Time, a weekly news magazine. Time agreed to pay $25,000, $12,500 in advance and an additional $12,500 at publication, in exchange for the right to excerpt 7,500 words from Mr. Ford's account of the Nixon pardon. The issue featuring the excerpts was timed to appear approximately one week before shipment of the full length book version to bookstores. Exclusivity was an important consideration; Harper & Row instituted procedures designed to maintain the confidentiality of

217

the manuscript, and Time retained the right to renegotiate the second payment should the material appear in print prior to its release of the excerpts.

Two to three weeks before the Time article's scheduled release, an unidentified person secretly brought a copy of the Ford manuscript to Victor Navasky, editor of The Nation, a political commentary magazine. Mr. Navasky knew that his possession of the manuscript was not authorized and that the manuscript must be returned quickly to his "source" to avoid discovery. 557 F.Supp. 1067, 1069 (SDNY 1983). He hastily put together what he believed was "a real hot news story" composed of quotes, paraphrases, and facts drawn exclusively from the manuscript. Ibid. Mr. Navasky attempted no independent commentary, research or criticism, in part because of the need for speed if he was to "make news" by "publish[ing] in advance of publication of the Ford book." App. 416-417. The 2,250-word article, reprinted in the Appendix to this opinion, appeared on April 3, 1979. As a result of The Nation's article, Time canceled its piece and refused to pay the remaining $12,500.

Petitioners brought suit in the District Court for the Southern District of New York, alleging conversion, tortious interference with contract, and violations of the Copyright Act. After a 6-day bench trial, the District Judge found that "A Time to Heal" was protected by copyright at the time of The Nation publication and that respondents' use of the copyrighted material constituted an infringement under the Copyright Act, §§ 106(1), (2), and (3), protecting respectively the right to reproduce the work, the right to license preparation of derivative works, and the right of first distribution of [544] the copyrighted work to the public. App. to Pet. for Cert. C-29 C-30. The District Court rejected respondents' argument that The Nation's piece was a "fair use" sanctioned by § 107 of the Act. Though billed as "hot news," the article contained no new facts. The magazine had "published its article for profit," taking "the heart" of "a soon-to-be-published" work. This unauthorized use "caused the Time agreement to be aborted and thus diminished the value of the copyright." 557 F.Supp., at 1072. Although certain elements of the Ford memoirs, such as historical facts and memoranda, were not per se copyrightable, the District Court held that it was "the totality of these facts and memoranda collected together with Ford's reflections that made them of value to The Nation, [and] this . . . totality . . . is protected by the copyright laws." Id., at 1072-1073. The court awarded actual damages of $12,500.

A divided panel of the Court of Appeals for the Second Circuit reversed. The majority recognized that Mr. Ford's verbatim "reflections" were original "expression" protected by copyright. But it held that the District Court had erred in assuming the "coupling [of these reflections] with uncopyrightable fact transformed that information into a copyrighted 'totality.'" 723 F.2d 195, 205 (CA2 1983). The majority noted that copyright attaches to expression, not facts or ideas. It concluded that, to avoid granting a copyright monopoly over the facts underlying history and news, "'expression' [in such works must be confined] to its barest elements — the ordering and choice of the words themselves." Id., at 204. Thus similarities between the original and the challenged work traceable to the copying or paraphrasing of uncopyrightable material, such as historical facts, memoranda and other public documents, and quoted remarks of third parties, must be disregarded in evaluating whether the second author's use was fair or infringing.

"When the uncopyrighted material is stripped away, the article in The Nation contains, at most, approximately 300 words that are copyrighted. These remaining paragraphs and scattered phrases are all verbatim quotations from the memoirs which had not appeared previously in other publications. They include a short segment of Ford's conversations with Henry Kissinger and several other individuals. Ford's impressionistic depictions of Nixon, ill with phlebitis after the resignation and pardon, and of Nixon's character, constitute the major portion of this material. It is these parts of the magazine piece on which [the court] must focus in [its] examination of the question whether there was a 'fair use' of copyrighted matter." Id., at 206.

Examining the four factors enumerated in § 107, see infra, at 547, n. 2, the majority found the purpose of the article was "news reporting," the original work was essentially factual in nature, the 300 words appropriated were insubstantial in relation to the 2,250-word piece, and the impact on the market for the original was minimal as "the evidence [did] not support a finding that it was the very limited use of expression per se which led to Time's decision not to print the excerpt." The Nation's borrowing of verbatim quotations merely "len[t] authenticity to this politically significant material . . . complementing the reporting of the facts." 723 F.2d, at 208. The Court of Appeals was especially influenced by the "politically significant" nature of the subject matter and its conviction that it is not "the purpose of the Copyright Act to impede that harvest of knowledge so necessary to a democratic state" or "chill the activities of the press by forbidding a circumscribed use of copyrighted words." Id., at 197, 209.

...

III

A.

Fair use was traditionally defined as "a privilege in others than the owner of the copyright to use the copyrighted material in a reasonable manner without his consent." H. Ball, Law of Copyright and Literary Property 260 (1944) (hereinafter Ball). The statutory formulation of the defense of fair use in the Copyright Act reflects the intent of Congress to codify the common-law doctrine. 3 Nimmer § 13.05. Section 107 requires a case-by-case determination whether a particular use is fair, and the statute notes four nonexclusive factors to be considered. This approach was "intended to restate the [pre-existing] judicial doctrine of fair use, not to change, narrow, or enlarge it in any way." H.R.Rep. No. 94-1476, p. 66 (1976) (hereinafter House Report), U.S.Code Cong. & Admin.News 1976, pp. 5659, 5680.

"[T]he author's consent to a reasonable use of his copyrighted works ha[d] always been implied by the courts as a necessary incident of the constitutional policy of promoting the progress of science and the useful arts, since a prohibition of such use would inhibit subsequent writers from attempting to improve upon prior works and thus . . . frustrate the very ends sought to be attained." Ball 260. Professor Latman, in a study of the doctrine of fair use commissioned by Congress for the revision effort, see Sony Corp. of America v. Universal City Studios, Inc., 464 U.S., at 462-463, n. 9, 104 S.Ct., at 781, n. 9 (dissenting opinion), summarized prior law as turning on the "importance [550] of the material copied or performed from the point of view of the reasonable copyright owner. In other words, would the reasonable copyright owner have consented to the use?" Latman 15.

As early as 1841, Justice Story gave judicial recognition to the doctrine in a case that concerned the letters of another former President, George Washington.

"[A] reviewer may fairly cite largely from the original work, if his design be really and truly to use the passages for the purposes of fair and reasonable criticism. On the other hand, it is as clear, that if he thus cites the most important parts of the work, with a view, not to criticise, but to supersede the use of the original work, and substitute the review for it, such a use will be deemed in law a piracy." Folsom v. Marsh, 9 F.Cas. 342, 344-345 (No. 4,901) (CC Mass.)

As Justice Story's hypothetical illustrates, the fair use doctrine has always precluded a use that "supersede[s] the use of the original." Ibid. Accord, S.Rep. No. 94-473, p. 65 (1975) (hereinafter Senate Report).

Perhaps because the fair use doctrine was predicated on the author's implied consent to "reasonable and customary" use when he released his work for public consumption, fair use traditionally was not recognized as a defense to charges of copying from an author's as yet unpublished works. Under common-law copyright, "the property of the author . . . in his intellectual creation [was] absolute until he voluntarily part[ed] with the same." American Tobacco Co. v. Werckmeister, 207 U.S. 284, 299, 28 S.Ct. 72, 77, 52 L.Ed. 208 (1907); 2 Nimmer § 8.23, at 8-273. This absolute rule, however, was tempered in practice by the equitable nature of the fair use doctrine. In a given case, factors such as implied consent through de facto publication on performance or dissemination of a work may tip the balance of equities in favor of prepublication use. See Copyright Law Revision — Part 2: Discussion and Comments on Report of the Register of Copyrights on General Revision of the U.S. Copyright Law, 88th Cong., 1st Sess., 27 (H.R.Comm. Print 1963) (discussion suggesting works disseminated to the public in a form not constituting a technical "publication" should nevertheless be subject to fair use); 3 Nimmer § 13.05, at 13-62, n. 2. But it has never been seriously disputed that "the fact that the plaintiff's work is unpublished . . . is a factor tending to negate the defense of fair use." Ibid. Publication of an author's expression before he has authorized its dissemination seriously infringes the author's right to decide when and whether it will be made public, a factor not present in fair use of published works. Respondents contend, however, that Congress, in including first publication among the rights enumerated in § 106, which are expressly subject to fair use under § 107, intended that fair use would apply in pari materia to published and unpublished works. The Copyright Act does not support this proposition.

The Copyright Act represents the culmination of a major legislative reexamination of copyright doctrine. See Mills Music, Inc. v. Snyder, 469 U.S. 153, 159-160, 105 S.Ct. 638, at —, 83 L.Ed.2d 556 (1985); Sony Corp. of America v. Universal City Studios, Inc., 464 U.S., at 462-463, n. 9, 104 S.Ct., at 781, n. 9 (dissenting opinion). Among its other innovations, it eliminated publication "as a dividing line between common law and statutory protection," House Report, at 129 U.S.Code Cong. & Admin.News 1976, p. 5745, extending statutory protection to all works from the time of their creation. It also recognized for the first time a distinct statutory right of first publication, which had previously been an element of the common-law protections afforded unpublished works. The Report of the House Committee on the Judiciary confirms that "Clause (3) of section 106, establishes the exclusive right of publications. . . . Under this provision the copyright owner would have the right to control the first public distribution of an authorized copy . . . of his work." Id., at 62 U.S.Code Cong. & Admin.News 1976, p. 5675.

Though the right of first publication, like the other rights enumerated in § 106, is expressly made subject to the fair use provision of § 107, fair use analysis must always be tailored to the individual case. Id., at 65; 3 Nimmer § 13.05[A]. The nature of the interest at stake is highly relevant to whether a given use is fair. From the beginning, those entrusted with the task of revision recognized the "overbalancing reasons to preserve the common law protection of undisseminated works until the author or his successor chooses to disclose them." Copyright Law Revision, Report of the Register of Copyrights on the General Revision of the U.S. Copyright Law, 87th Cong., 1st Sess., 41 (Comm. Print 1961). The right of first publication implicates a threshold decision by the author whether and in what form to release his work. First publication is inherently different from other § 106 rights in that only one person can be the first publisher; as the contract with Time illustrates, the commercial value of the right lies primarily in exclusivity. Because the potential damage to the author from judicially enforced "sharing" of the first publication right with unauthorized users of his manuscript is substantial, the balance of equities in evaluating such a claim of fair use inevitably shifts.

...

B

Respondents, however, contend that First Amendment values require a different rule under the circumstances of this case. The thrust of the decision below is that "[t]he scope of [fair use] is undoubtedly wider when the information conveyed relates to matters of high public concern." Consumers Union of the United States, Inc. v. General Signal Corp., 724 F.2d 1044, 1050 (CA2 1983) (construing 723 F.2d 195 (CA2 1983) (case below) as allowing advertiser to quote Consumer Reports), cert. denied, 469 U.S. 823, 104 S.Ct. 2655, 81 L.Ed.2d 362 (1984). Respondents advance the substantial public import of the subject matter of the Ford memoirs as grounds for excusing a use that would ordinarily not pass muster as a fair use — the piracy of verbatim quotations for the purpose of "scooping" the authorized first serialization. Respondents explain their copying of Mr. Ford's expression as essential to reporting the news story it claims the book itself represents. In respondents' view, not only the facts contained in Mr. Ford's memoirs, but "the precise manner in which [he] expressed himself [were] as newsworthy as what he had to say." Brief for Respondents 38-39. Respondents argue that the public's interest in learning this news as fast as possible outweighs the right of the author to control its first publication.

The Second Circuit noted, correctly, that copyright's idea/expression dichotomy "strike[s] a definitional balance between the First Amendment and the Copyright Act by permitting free communication of facts while still protecting an author's expression." 723 F.2d, at 203. No author may copyright his ideas or the facts he narrates. 17 U.S.C. § 102(b). See, e.g., New York Times Co. v. United States, 403 U.S. 713, 726, n., 91 S.Ct. 2140, 2147, n., 29 L.Ed.2d 822 (1971) (BRENNAN, J., concurring) (Copyright laws are not restrictions on freedom of speech as copyright protects only form of expression and not the ideas expressed); 1 Nimmer § 1.10[B][2]. As this Court long ago observed: "[T]he news element — the information respecting current events contained in the literary production — is not the creation of the writer, but is a report of matters that ordinarily are publici juris; it is the history of the day." International News Service v. Associated Press, 248 U.S. 215, 234, 39 S.Ct. 68, 71, 63 L.Ed. 211 (1918). But copyright assures those who write and publish factual narratives such as "A Time to Heal" that they may at least enjoy the right to market the original expression contained therein as just compensation for their investment. Cf. Zacchini v. Scripps-Howard Broadcasting Co., 433 U.S. 562, 575, 97 S.Ct. 2849, 2857, 53 L.Ed.2d 965 (1977).

Respondents' theory, however, would expand fair use to effectively destroy any expectation of copyright protection in the work of a public figure. Absent such protection, there would be little incentive to create or profit in financing such memoirs, and the public would be denied an important source of significant historical information. The promise of copyright would be an empty one if it could be avoided merely by dubbing the infringement a fair use "news report" of the book. See Wainwright Securities Inc. v. Wall Street Transcript Corp., 558 F.2d 91 (CA2 1977), cert. denied, 434 U.S. 1014, 98 S.Ct 730, 54 L.Ed.2d 759 (1978).

Nor do respondents assert any actual necessity for circumventing the copyright scheme with respect to the types of works and users at issue here. Where an author and publisher have invested extensive resources in creating an original work and are poised to release it to the public, no legitimate aim is served by pre-empting the right of first publication. The fact that the words the author has chosen to clothe his narrative may of themselves be "newsworthy" is not an independent justification for unauthorized copying of the author's expression prior to publication. To paraphrase another recent Second Circuit decision:

"[Respondent] possessed an unfettered right to use any factual information revealed in [the memoirs] for the purpose of enlightening its audience, but it can claim no need to 'bodily appropriate' [Mr. Ford's] 'expression' of that information by utilizing portions of the actual [manuscript]. The public interest in the free flow of information is assured by the law's refusal to recognize a valid copyright in facts. The fair use doctrine is not a license for corporate theft, empowering a court to ignore a copyright whenever it determines the underlying work contains material of possible public importance." Iowa State University Research Foundation, Inc. v. American Broadcasting Cos., Inc., 621 F.2d 57, 61 (CA2 1980) (citations omitted).

Accord, Roy Export Co. Establishment v. Columbia Broadcasting System, Inc., 503 F.Supp. 1137 (SDNY 1980) ("newsworthiness" of material copied does not justify copying), aff'd, 672 F.2d 1095 (CA2), cert. denied, 459 U.S. 826, 103 S.Ct. 60, 74

L.Ed.2d 63 (1982); Quinto v. Legal Times of Washington, Inc., 506 F.Supp. 554 (DC 1981) (same).

In our haste to disseminate news, it should not be forgotten that the Framers intended copyright itself to be the engine of free expression. By establishing a marketable right to the use of one's expression, copyright supplies the economic incentive to create and disseminate ideas. This Court stated in Mazer v. Stein, 347 U.S. 201, 219, 74 S.Ct. 460, 471, 98 L.Ed. 630 (1954):

"The economic philosophy behind the clause empowering Congress to grant patents and copyrights is the conviction that encouragement of individual effort by personal gain is the best way to advance public welfare through the talents of authors and inventors in 'Science and useful Arts.'"

And again in Twentieth Century Music Corp. v. Aiken:

"The immediate effect of our copyright law is to secure a fair return for an 'author's' creative labor. But the ultimate aim is, by this incentive, to stimulate [the creation of useful works] for the general public good." 422 U.S., at 156, 95 S.Ct., at 2043.

[559] It is fundamentally at odds with the scheme of copyright to accord lesser rights in those works that are of greatest importance to the public. Such a notion ignores the major premise of copyright and injures author and public alike. "[T]o propose that fair use be imposed whenever the 'social value [of dissemination] . . . outweighs any detriment to the artist,' would be to propose depriving copyright owners of their right in the property precisely when they encounter those users who could afford to pay for it." Gordon, Fair Use as Market Failure: A Structural and Economic Analysis of the Betamax Case and its Predecessors, 82 Colum.L.Rev. 1600, 1615 (1982). And as one commentator has noted: "If every volume that was in the public interest could be pirated away by a competing publisher, . . . the public [soon] would have nothing worth reading." Sobel, Copyright and the First Amendment: A Gathering Storm?, 19 ASCAP Copyright Law Symposium 43, 78 (1971). See generally Comment, Copyright and the First Amendment; Where Lies the Public Interest?, 59 Tulane L.Rev. 135 (1984).

Moreover, freedom of thought and expression "includes both the right to speak freely and the right to refrain from speaking at all." Wooley v. Maynard, 430 U.S. 705, 714, 97 S.Ct. 1428, 1435, 51 L.Ed.2d 752 (1977) (BURGER, C.J.). We do not suggest this right not to speak would sanction abuse of the copyright owner's monopoly as an instrument to suppress facts. But in the words of New York's Chief Judge Fuld:

"The essential thrust of the First Amendment is to prohibit improper restraints on the voluntary public expression of ideas; it shields the man who wants to speak or publish when others wish him to be quiet. There is necessarily, and within suitably defined areas, a concomitant freedom not to speak publicly, one which serves the same ultimate end as freedom of speech in its affirmative aspect." Estate of Hemingway v. Random House, Inc., 23 N.Y.2d 341, 348, 296 N.Y.S.2d 771, 776, 244 N.E.2d 250, 255 (1968).

Courts and commentators have recognized that copyright, and the right of first publication in particular, serve this countervailing First Amendment value. See

Schnapper v. Foley, 215 U.S.App.D.C. 59, 667 F.2d 102 (1981), cert. denied, 455 U.S. 948, 102 S.Ct. 1448, 71 L.Ed.2d 661 (1982); 1 Nimmer § 1.10[B], at 1-70, n. 24; Patry 140-142.

In view of the First Amendment protections already embodied in the Copyright Act's distinction between copyrightable expression and uncopyrightable facts and ideas, and the latitude for scholarship and comment traditionally afforded by fair use, we see no warrant for expanding the doctrine of fair use to create what amounts to a public figure exception to copyright. Whether verbatim copying from a public figure's manuscript in a given case is or is not fair must be judged according to the traditional equities of fair use.

IV

Fair use is a mixed question of law and fact. Pacific & Southern Co. v. Duncan, 744 F.2d 1490, 1495, n. 8 (CA11 1984). Where the district court has found facts sufficient to evaluate each of the statutory factors, an appellate court "need not remand for further factfinding . . . [but] may conclude as a matter of law that [the challenged use] do[es] not qualify as a fair use of the copyrighted work." Id., at 1495. Thus whether The Nation article constitutes fair use under § 107 must be reviewed in light of the principles discussed above. The factors enumerated in the section are not meant to be exclusive: "[S]ince the doctrine is an equitable rule of reason, no generally applicable definition is possible, and each case raising the question must be decided on its own facts." House Report, at 65, U.S.Code Cong. & Admin.News 1976, p. 5678. The four factors identified by Congress as especially relevant in determining whether the use was fair are: (1) the purpose and character of the use; (2) the nature of the copyrighted work; (3) the substantiality of the portion used in relation to the copyrighted work as a whole; (4) the effect on the potential market for or value of the copyrighted work. We address each one separately.

Purpose of the Use. The Second Circuit correctly identified news reporting as the general purpose of The Nation's use. News reporting is one of the examples enumerated in § 107 to "give some idea of the sort of activities the courts might regard as fair use under the circumstances." Senate Report, at 61. This listing was not intended to be exhaustive, see ibid.; § 101 (definition of "including" and "such as"), or to single out any particular use as presumptively a "fair" use. The drafters resisted pressures from special interest groups to create presumptive categories of fair use, but structured the provision as an affirmative defense requiring a case-by-case analysis. See H.R.Rep. No. 83, 90th Cong., 1st Sess., 37 (1967); Patry 477, n. 4. "[W]hether a use referred to in the first sentence of section 107 is a fair use in a particular case will depend upon the application of the determinative factors, including those mentioned in the second sentence." Senate Report, at 62. The fact that an article arguably is "news" and therefore a productive use is simply one factor in a fair use analysis.

We agree with the Second Circuit that the trial court erred in fixing on whether the information contained in the memoirs was actually new to the public. As Judge

224

Meskill wisely noted, "[c]ourts should be chary of deciding what is and what is not news." 723 F.2d, at 215 (dissenting). Cf. Gertz v. Robert Welch, Inc., 418 U.S. 323, 345-346, 94 S.Ct. 2997, 3009-3010, 41 L.Ed.2d 789 (1974). "The issue is not what constitutes 'news,' but whether a claim of newsreporting is a valid fair use defense to an infringement of copyrightable expression." Patry 119. The Nation has every right to seek to be the first to publish information. But The Nation went beyond simply reporting uncopyrightable information and actively sought to exploit the headline value of its infringement, making a "news event" out of its unauthorized first publication of a noted figure's copyrighted expression.

The fact that a publication was commercial as opposed to nonprofit is a separate factor that tends to weigh against a finding of fair use. "[E]very commercial use of copyrighted material is presumptively an unfair exploitation of the monopoly privilege that belongs to the owner of the copyright." Sony Corp. of America v. Universal City Studios, Inc., 464 U.S., at 451, 104 S.Ct., at 793. In arguing that the purpose of news reporting is not purely commercial, The Nation misses the point entirely. The crux of the profit/nonprofit distinction is not whether the sole motive of the use is monetary gain but whether the user stands to profit from exploitation of the copyrighted material without paying the customary price. See Roy Export Co. Establishment v. Columbia Broadcasting System, Inc., 503 F.Supp., at 1144; 3 Nimmer § 13.05[A][1], at 13-71, n. 25.3.

In evaluating character and purpose we cannot ignore The Nation's stated purpose of scooping the forthcoming hardcover and Time abstracts. ... The Nation's use had not merely the incidental effect but the intended purpose of supplanting the copyright holder's commercially valuable right of first publication. See Meredith Corp. v. Harper & Row, Publishers, Inc., 378 F.Supp. 686, 690 (SDNY) (purpose of text was to compete with original), aff'd, 500 F.2d 1221 (CA2 1974). Also relevant to the "character" of the use is "the propriety of the defendant's conduct." 3 Nimmer § 13.05[A], at 13-72. "Fair use presupposes 'good faith' and 'fair dealing.'" Time Inc. v. Bernard Geis Associates, 293 F.Supp. 130, 146 (SDNY 1968), quoting [563] Schulman, Fair Use and the Revision of the Copyright Act, 53 Iowa L.Rev. 832 (1968). The trial court found that The Nation knowingly exploited a purloined manuscript. App. to Pet. for Cert. B-1, C-20 — C-21, C-28 — C-29. Unlike the typical claim of fair use, The Nation cannot offer up even the fiction of consent as justification. Like its competitor newsweekly, it was free to bid for the right of abstracting excerpts from "A Time to Heal." Fair use "distinguishes between 'a true scholar and a chiseler who infringes a work for personal profit.'" Wainwright Securities Inc. v. Wall Street Transcript Corp., 558 F.2d, at 94, quoting from Hearings on Bills for the General Revision of the Copyright Law before the House Committee on the Judiciary, 89th Cong., 1st Sess., ser. 8, pt. 3, p. 1706 (1966) (statement of John Schulman).

Nature of the Copyrighted Work Second, the Act directs attention to the nature of the copyrighted work. "A Time to Heal" may be characterized as an unpublished historical narrative or autobiography. The law generally recognizes a greater need to disseminate factual works than works of fiction or fantasy. See Gorman, Fact or Fancy? The Implications for Copyright, 29 J. Copyright Soc. 560, 561 (1982).

"[E]ven within the field of fact works, there are gradations as to the relative proportion of fact and fancy. One may move from sparsely embellished maps and directories to elegantly written biography. The extent to which one must permit expressive language to be copied, in order to assure dissemination of the underlying facts, will thus vary from case to case." Id., at 563.

Some of the briefer quotes from the memoirs are arguably necessary adequately to convey the facts; for example, Mr. Ford's characterization of the White House tapes as the "smoking gun" is perhaps so integral to the idea expressed as to be inseparable from it. Cf. 1 Nimmer § 1.10[C]. But The Nation did not stop at isolated phrases and instead excerpted subjective descriptions and portraits of public figures whose power lies in the author's individualized expression. Such [564] use, focusing on the most expressive elements of the work, exceeds that necessary to disseminate the facts.

The fact that a work is unpublished is a critical element of its "nature." 3 Nimmer § 13.05[A]; Comment, 58 St. John's L.Rev., at 613. Our prior discussion establishes that the scope of fair use is narrower with respect to unpublished works. While even substantial quotations might qualify as fair use in a review of a published work or a news account of a speech that had been delivered to the public or disseminated to the press, see House Report, at 65, the author's right to control the first public appearance of his expression weighs against such use of the work before its release. The right of first publication encompasses not only the choice whether to publish at all, but also the choices of when, where, and in what form first to publish a work.

In the case of Mr. Ford's manuscript, the copyright holders' interest in confidentiality is irrefutable; the copyright holders had entered into a contractual undertaking to "keep the manuscript confidential" and required that all those to whom the manuscript was shown also "sign an agreement to keep the manuscript confidential." App. to Pet. for Cert. C-19 — C-20. While the copyright holders' contract with Time required Time to submit its proposed article seven days before publication, The Nation's clandestine publication afforded no such opportunity for creative or quality control. Id., at C-18. It was hastily patched together and contained "a number of inaccuracies." App. 300b-300c (testimony of Victor Navasky). A use that so clearly infringes the copyright holder's interests in confidentiality and creative control is difficult to characterize as "fair."

Amount and Substantiality of the Portion Used. Next, the Act directs us to examine the amount and substantiality of the portion used in relation to the copyrighted work as a whole. In absolute terms, the words actually quoted were an insubstantial portion of "A Time to Heal." The District Court, however, found that "[T]he Nation took what was essentially the heart of the book." 557 F.Supp., at 1072. We believe the Court of Appeals erred in overruling the District Judge's evaluation of the qualitative nature of the taking. See, e.g., Roy Export Co. Establishment v. Columbia Broadcasting System, Inc., 503 F.Supp., at 1145 (taking of 55 seconds out of 1 hour and 29-minute film deemed qualitatively substantial). A Time editor described the chapters on the pardon as "the most interesting and moving parts of the entire manuscript." Reply Brief for Petitioners 16, n. 8. The portions actually quoted were selected by Mr. Navasky as among the most powerful passages in those chapters. He testified that he used verbatim excerpts because simply reciting the information could not adequately convey the "absolute certainty with which [Ford] expressed himself," App. 303; or show that "this comes from President Ford," id., at 305; or carry the "definitive quality" of the original, id., at 306. In short, he quoted these passages precisely because they qualitatively embodied Ford's distinctive expression.

As the statutory language indicates, a taking may not be excused merely because it is insubstantial with respect to the infringing work. As Judge Learned Hand cogently remarked, "no plagiarist can excuse the wrong by showing how much of his work he did not pirate." Sheldon v. Metro-Goldwyn Pictures Corp., 81 F.2d 49, 56 (CA2), cert. denied, 298 U.S. 669, 56 S.Ct. 835, 80 L.Ed. 1392 (1936). Conversely, the fact that a substantial portion of the infringing work was copied verbatim is evidence of the qualitative value of the copied material, both to the originator and to the plagiarist who seeks to profit from marketing someone else's copyrighted expression.

Stripped to the verbatim quotes,[8] the direct takings from the unpublished manuscript constitute at least 13% of the in [566] fringing article. See Meeropol v. Nizer, 560 F.2d 1061, 1071 (CA2 1977) (copyrighted letters constituted less than 1% of infringing work but were prominently featured). The Nation article is structured around the quoted excerpts which serve as its dramatic focal points. See Appendix to this opinion, post, p. 570. In view of the expressive value of the excerpts and their key role in the infringing work, we cannot agree with the Second Circuit that the "magazine took a meager, indeed an infinitesimal amount of Ford's original language." 723 F.2d, at 209.

Effect on the Market. Finally, the Act focuses on "the effect of the use upon the potential market for or value of the copyrighted work." This last factor is undoubtedly the single most important element of fair use.[9] See 3 Nimmer § 13.05[A], at 13-76, and cases cited therein. "Fair use, when properly applied, is limited to copying by others which does not materially impair the marketability of the work which is copied." 1 Nimmer § 1.10[D], at 1-87. The trial court found not merely a potential but an actual effect on the market. Time's cancellation of its projected serialization and its refusal to pay the $12,500 were the direct effect of the infringement. The Court of Appeals rejected this fact-finding as clearly erroneous, noting that the record did not establish a causal relation between Time's nonperformance and respondents' unauthorized publication of Mr. Ford's expression as opposed to the facts taken from the memoirs. We disagree. Rarely will a case of copyright infringement present such clear-cut evidence of actual damage. Petitioners assured Time that there would be no other authorized publication of any portion of the unpublished manuscript prior to April 23, 1979. Any publication of material from chapters 1 and 3 would permit Time to renegotiate its final payment. Time cited The Nation's article, which contained verbatim quotes from the unpublished manuscript, as a reason for its nonperformance. With respect to apportionment of profits flowing from a copyright infringement, this Court has held that an infringer who commingles infringing and noninfringing elements "must abide the consequences, unless he can make a separation of the profits so as to assure to the injured party all that justly belongs to him." Sheldon v. Metro-Goldwyn Pictures Corp., 309 U.S. 390, 406, 60 S.Ct. 681, 687, 84 L.Ed. 825 (1940). Cf. 17 U.S.C. § 504(b) (the infringer is required to prove elements of profits attributable to other than the infringed work). Similarly, once a copyright holder establishes with reasonable probability the existence of a causal connection between the infringement and a loss of revenue, the burden properly shifts to the infringer to show that this damage would have occurred had there been no taking of copyrighted expression. See 3 Nimmer § 14.02, at 14-7— 14-8.1. Petitioners established a prima facie case of actual damage that respondents failed to rebut. See Stevens Linen Associates, Inc. v. Mastercraft Corp., 656 F.2d 11, 15 (CA2 1981). The trial court properly awarded actual damages and accounting of profits. See 17 U.S.C. § 504(b).

More important, to negate fair use one need only show that if the challenged use "should become widespread, it would adversely affect the potential market for the copyrighted work." Sony Corp. of America v. Universal City Studios, Inc., 464 U.S., at 451, 104 S.Ct., at 793 (emphasis added); id., at 484, and n. 36, 104 S.Ct., at 810, and n. 36 (collecting cases) (dissenting opinion). This inquiry must take account not only of harm to the original but also of harm to the market for derivative works. See Iowa State University Research Foundation, Inc. v. American Broadcasting Cos., 621 F.2d 57 (CA2 1980); Meeropol v. Nizer, supra, at 1070; Roy Export v. Columbia Broadcasting System, Inc., 503 F.Supp., at 1146. "If the defendant's work adversely affects the value of any of the rights in the copyrighted work (in this case the adaptation [and serialization] right) the use is not fair." 3 Nimmer § 13.05[B], at 13-77—13-78 (footnote omitted).

It is undisputed that the factual material in the balance of The Nation's article, besides the verbatim quotes at issue here, was drawn exclusively from the chapters on the pardon. The excerpts were employed as featured episodes in a story about the Nixon pardon — precisely the use petitioners had licensed to Time. The borrowing of these verbatim quotes from the unpublished manuscript lent The Nation's piece a special air of authenticity as Navasky expressed it, the reader would know it was Ford speaking and not The Nation. App. 300c. Thus it directly competed for a share of the market for prepublication excerpts. The Senate Report states:

"With certain special exceptions . . . a use that supplants any part of the normal market for a copyrighted work would ordinarily be considered an infringement." Senate Report, at 65.

[569] Placed in a broader perspective, a fair use doctrine that permits extensive prepublication quotations from an unreleased manuscript without the copyright owner's consent poses substantial potential for damage to the marketability of first serialization rights in general. "Isolated instances of minor infringements, when multiplied many times, become in the aggregate a major inroad on copyright that must be prevented." Ibid.

The Court of Appeals erred in concluding that The Nation's use of the copyrighted material was excused by the public's interest in the subject matter. It erred, as well, in overlooking the unpublished nature of the work and the resulting impact on the potential market for first serial rights of permitting unauthorized prepublication excerpts under the rubric of fair use. Finally, in finding the taking "infinitesimal," the Court of Appeals accorded too little weight to the qualitative importance of the quoted passages of original expression. In sum, the traditional doctrine of fair use, as embodied in the Copyright Act, does not sanction the use made by The Nation of these copyrighted materials. Any copyright infringer may claim to benefit the public by increasing public access to the copyrighted work. See Pacific & Southern Co. v. Duncan, 744 F.2d, at 1499-1500. But Congress has not designed, and we see no warrant for judicially imposing, a "compulsory license" permitting unfettered access to the unpublished copyrighted expression of public figures.

The Nation conceded that its verbatim copying of some 300 words of direct quotation from the Ford manuscript would constitute an infringement unless excused as a fair use. Because we find that The Nation's use of these verbatim excerpts from the unpublished manuscript was not a fair use, the judgment of the Court of Appeals is reversed, and the case is remanded for further proceedings consistent with this opinion.

It is so ordered.

575 F.Supp.2d 513 (SDNY 2008)

WARNER BROS AND J.K. ROWLING

v.

RDR BOOKS

United States District Court, S.D. New York.

Robert P. Patterson, JR., District Judge.

On October 31, 2007, Plaintiffs Warner Bros. Entertainment Inc. and J.K. Rowling commenced this action against Defendant RDR Books, alleging copyright infringement pursuant to 17 U.S.C. §§ 101 et seq., as well as several other federal and state claims, and seeking both injunctive relief and damages. By order dated March 5, 2008, the Court consolidated the scheduled evidentiary hearing on Plaintiffs' motion for a preliminary injunction with a trial on the merits pursuant to Federal Rule of Civil Procedure 65(a)(2). By their pretrial orders, the parties narrowed the claims and defenses to be tried: Plaintiffs pursued only their claims for copyright infringement and statutory damages under 17 U.S.C. §§ 101 et seq. of the Copyright Act; Defendant pursued only its defenses and affirmative defenses of copyright fair use under 17 U.S.C. § 107, copyright misuse, and unclean hands. The Court held a bench trial on the merits from April 14, 2008 to April 17, 2008.

This opinion constitutes the Court's findings of fact and conclusions of law pursuant to Federal Rule of Civil Procedure 52(a).

FINDINGS OF FACT

I. The Copyrighted Works

Plaintiff J.K. Rowling ("Rowling") is the author of the highly acclaimed Harry Potter book series. (Tr. (Rowling) at 43:6-7, 47:17-20; Pl. Ex. 25 (Rowling Decl.) at ¶ 1.) Written for children but enjoyed by children and adults alike, the Harry Potter series chronicles the lives and adventures of Harry Potter and his friends as they come of age at the Hogwarts School of Witchcraft and Wizardry and face the evil Lord Voldemort. (Pl. Ex. 25 (Rowling Decl.) at ¶ 2.) It is a tale of a fictional world filled with magical spells, fantastical creatures, and imaginary places and things. (Tr. (Vander Ark) at 346:1-6; 371:1-22; id. (Sorensen) at 513:6-14.)

Rowling published the first of seven books in the series, Harry Potter and the Philosopher's Stone, in the United Kingdom in 1997. (Tr. (Rowling) at 46:12-16; id. (Vander Ark) at 363:19-20.) In 1998, the first book was published in the United States as Harry Potter and the Sorcerer's Stone. (Pl. Ex. 25 (Rowling Decl.) at ¶ 2.) Over the next ten years, Rowling wrote and published the remaining six books in the Harry Potter series (Id.): Harry Potter and the Chamber of Secrets (1998), Harry Potter and the Prisoner of Azkaban (1999), Harry Potter and the Goblet of Fire (2000), Harry Potter and the Order of the Phoenix (2003), and Harry Potter and the Half-Blood Prince (2005). (Pl. Exs. 5-9.) The seventh and final book, Harry Potter and the Deathly Hallows was released on July 21, 2007. (Pl. Ex. 10). Rowling owns a United States copyright in each of the Harry Potter books. (Pl. Ex. 12 (Blair Decl.) at ¶ 4; Pl. Ex. 12A; Tr. (Rowling) at 43:8-9.)

The Harry Potter series has achieved enormous popularity and phenomenal sales. (Tr. (Murphy) at 432:20-433:3; id. (Harris) at 443:16-18). The books have won numerous awards, including children's literary awards and the British Book Award. (Id. (Rowling) at 47:17-20). Most gratifying to Rowling is that the Harry Potter series has been credited with encouraging readership among children. (Id. (Rowling) at 103:8-22.)

As a result of the success of the Harry Potter books, Plaintiff Warner Bros. Entertainment Inc. ("Warner Brothers") obtained from Rowling the exclusive film rights to the entire seven-book Harry Potter series. (Pl. Ex. 26 (Williams Decl.) at ¶ 3.) Warner Brothers is the exclusive distributor for worldwide distribution of these films. (Id. at ¶ 4.) To date, Warner Brothers has released five Harry Potter films, and the sixth is scheduled for a worldwide release in November 2008. (Id. at ¶¶ 3, 4.) Each of the Harry Potter films is the subject of a copyright registration. (Id. at ¶ 3.) Warner Brothers licensed certain rights to Electronic Arts to create video games based on the Harry Potter books and films, which included a series of "Famous Wizard Cards" that Rowling created and which are the subject of U.S. copy-right registrations jointly owned by Warner Brothers and Electronic Arts. (Tr. (Rowling) at 76:15-17; Pl. Post-trial Br., Ex. B.)

Early on in the publication of the Harry Potter series, Rowling wrote a short series of fictional newspapers entitled "The Daily Prophet," which were published and distributed to fans in the United Kingdom. (Tr. (Rowling) at 73:17-74:1.) Rowling owns a U.K. copyright in "The Daily Prophet" newsletters. (Tr. (Rowling) at 74:6-7; see Pl. Post-trial Br., Ex. A.)

In addition, Rowling wrote two short companion books to the Harry Potter series (the "companion books"), the royalties from which she donated to the charity Comic Relief. (Tr. (Rowling) at 49:12-50:10.) The first, Quidditch Through the Ages (2001), recounts the history and development of "quidditch," an imaginary sport featured in the Harry Potter series that involves teams of witches and wizards on flying broomsticks. (Pl. Ex. 2.) The second, Fantastic Beasts & Where to Find Them (2001), is an A-to-Z encyclopedia of the imaginary beasts and beings that exist in Harry Potter's fictional world. (Pl. Ex. 3.) Both appear in the Harry Potter series as textbooks that the students at Hogwarts use in their studies, and the companion books are marketed as such. Neither of the companion books is written in narrative form; instead each book chronicles and expands on the fictional facts that unfold in the Harry Potter series. (Tr. (Vander Ark) at 396:21-25; see Pl. Exs. 2-3.) The companion books are both registered with the United States Copyright Office. (Pl. Ex. 12 (Blair Decl.) at ¶ 4.) Although the market for the companion books is not nearly as large as the market for the Harry Potter series, Rowling's companion books have earned more than $30 million to date. (Tr. (Rowling) at 49:25-50:10; Pl. Ex. 25 (Rowling Decl.) at ¶ 6; Pl. Ex. 12 (Blair Decl.) at ¶ 3.)

Rowling has stated on a number of occasions since 1998 that, in addition to the two companion books, she plans to publish a "Harry Potter encyclopedia" after the completion of the series and again donate the proceeds to charity. (Tr. (Rowling) at 50:25-51: 15,55: 1-5; Pl. Ex. 25 (Rowling Decl.) at ¶ 6; Pl. Ex. 12 (Blair Decl.) at ¶ 17.) Rowling intends that her encyclopedia contain alphabetical entries for the various people, places and things from the Harry Potter novels. (Tr. (Rowling) at 53:11-13.) While she intends to add new material as well, her encyclopedia is expected to reflect all of the information in the Harry Potter series. (Tr. (Vander Ark) at 387:20-388:16; Pl. Ex. 25 (Rowling Decl.) at ¶ 7; Pl. Ex. 32 (Suppl. Rowling Decl.) at ¶ 5.)

Rowling already has begun preparations for work on the encyclopedia by assembling her materials and requesting from her U.K. publisher its "bible" of Harry Potter materials. (Tr. (Rowling) at 52:1-24.) The publisher's "bible" is a catalogue of the people, places, and things from the Harry Potter books. (Pl. Ex. 23 (Odedina Decl.) ¶ 2; Pl. Ex. 23A.) Rowling's U.S. publisher has compiled a similar catalogue of elements from the Harry Potter books which Rowling has requested and intends to draw on in creating her encyclopedia. (Tr. (Rowling) at 52:25-53:10; Pl. Ex. 25 (Rowling Decl.) at ¶ 7; Pl. Ex. 18 (Klein Decl.) at ¶¶ 2-3; Pl. Ex. 18A.) Rowling plans on using an A-to-Z format for her encyclopedia. (Tr. (Rowling) at 53:11-13.)

II. The Allegedly Infringing Work

Defendant RDR Books is a Michigan-based publishing company that seeks to publish a book entitled "The Lexicon," the subject of this lawsuit. (Tr. (Rapoport) at 150:19-151:2.) Steven Vander Ark, a former library media specialist at a middle school in Michigan (Tr. (Vander Ark) at 248:4-6), is the attributed author of the

Lexicon (Def. Ex. 502 (Vander Ark Decl.) at ¶ 1). He is also the originator, owner, and operator of "The Harry Potter Lexicon" website (id.), a popular Harry Potter fan site from which the content of the Lexicon is drawn (id. at ¶ 30).

A. The Origins of the Lexicon

An immediate fan of the Harry Potter novels, Vander Ark began taking personal notes to keep track of the details and elements that unfold in the Harry Potter world while reading the second book in the series in 1999. (Tr. (Vander Ark) at 335:2-17.) After joining an online discussion group about the Harry Potter books, Vander Ark expanded his notes to include descriptive lists of the spells, characters, and fictional objects in Harry Potter to share with fellow fans. (Id. at 335:20-336:9.) These lists included brief descriptions or definitions of the terms. (Id. at 336:8-11.)

Vander Ark began work on his website, "The Harry Potter Lexicon" (the "website" or "Lexicon website"), in 1999 and opened the website in 2000. (Id. at 336:23.) His purpose in establishing the website was to create an encyclopedia that collected and organized information from the Harry Potter books in one central source for fans to use for reference. (Id. at 338:6-21; Def. Ex. 502 (Vander Ark Decl.) at ¶ 13.) At its launch, the website featured Vander Ark's descriptive lists of spells, characters, creatures, and magical items from Harry Potter with hyperlinks to cross-referenced entries. (Tr. (Vander Ark) at 337:7-10, 336:4-7.) In response to feedback from users of the website, Vander Ark developed an A-to-Z index to each list to allow users to search for entries alphabetically. (Id. at 343:2-21.)

The website presently features several indexed lists of people, places, and things from Harry Potter, including the "Encyclopedia of Spells," "Encyclopedia of Potions," "Wizards, Witches, and Beings," "The Bestiary," and "Gazetteer of the Wizarding World." (Pl. Exs. 14 (Bradley Decl.) at ¶ 5, 14C.) In addition to these reference features, the website contains a variety of supplemental material pertaining to Harry Potter, including fan art, commentary, essays, timelines, forums, and interactive data. (Pl. Exs. 14 (Bradley Decl.) at ¶ 3, 14A.) The website is currently run by a staff of seven or eight volunteers, including four primary editors (Tr. (Vander Ark) at 340:14-16), all of whom were recruited to help update and expand the website's content after the publication of the fifth book in the Harry Potter series. (Id. at 339:18-340:24.) The website uses minimal advertising to offset the costs of operation. (Id. at 349:24-350:10.) Use of the website is free and unrestricted. (Id. at 293:8-12; 351:25-352:4.)

The content of the encyclopedia entries on the Lexicon website is drawn primarily from the Harry Potter series, the companion books, "The Daily Prophet" newsletters, the "Famous Wizard Cards," and published interviews of Rowling. (Tr. (Vander Ark) at 348:7-13; Def. Ex. 502 (Vander Ark Decl.) at ¶ 14). According to Vander Ark, some additional content is drawn from outside reference sources, including Bullfinch's Mythology, Field Guide to Little People, New Shorter Oxford English Dictionary, and online encyclopedias such as Encyclopedia Mythica. (Tr. (Vander Ark) at 346:12-348:19; Def. Ex. 502 (Vander Ark Decl.) at ¶ 14.) Frequently, these sources are not cited in the website's encyclopedia entries. Vander Ark's purpose in including additional information from outside sources or from his own knowledge was to enrich the experience of readers of the Harry Potter series by illuminating "the incredibly rich world and hidden meanings" contained within them. (Tr. (Vander Ark) at 345:21-346:6.)

Vander Ark has received positive feedback, including from Rowling and her publishers, about the value of the Lexicon website as a reference source. In May 2004, Vander Ark read a remark by Rowling posted on her website praising his Lexicon website as follows: "This is such a great site that I have been known to sneak into an internet cafe while out writing and check a fact rather than go into a bookshop and buy a copy of Harry Potter (which is embarrassing). A website for the dangerously obsessive; my natural home." (Tr. (Rowling) at 118:2-119:2). In July 2005, Vander Ark received a note from Cheryl Klein, a Senior Editor at Scholastic Inc., American publisher of the Harry Potter series, thanking him and his staff "for the wonderful resource [his] site provides for fans, students, and indeed editors & copyeditors of the Harry Potter series," who "referred to the Lexicon countless times during the editing of [the sixth book in the series], whether to verify a fact, check a timeline, or get a chapter & book reference for a particular event." (Def. Ex. 502 (Vander Ark Decl.) at ¶ 39; Def. Ex. 502A.) In September 2006, Vander Ark was invited by Warner Brothers to the set of the film The Order of the Phoenix, where he met David Heyman, the producer of all the Harry Potter films. Heyman told Vander Ark that Warner Brothers used the Lexicon website almost every day. (Tr. 386:8-20; Def. Ex. 502 (Vander Ark Decl.) ¶ 39.) Finally, in July 2007, Vander Ark visited the studios of Electronic Arts, the licensed producer of the Harry Potter video games, where he observed printed pages from the Lexicon covering the walls of the studio. (Tr. at 387:3-13; Def. Ex. 502 (Vander Ark Decl.) ¶ 39.)

Prior to any discussions with RDR Books about publishing portions of the Lexicon website as a book, Vander Ark was aware of Rowling's public statements regarding her intention to write a Harry Potter encyclopedia upon completion of the seventh book in the series. (Tr. (Vander Ark) at 247:10-12, 250:21-251:13; Def. Ex. 502 at ¶ 37.) In June 2007, just before the release of the seventh book, Vander Ark emailed Christopher Little Literary Agency, Rowling's literary agent in the United Kingdom, and suggested that he would be "a good candidate for work as an editor, given [his] work on the Lexicon," should Rowling start working on an encyclopedia or other reference to the Harry Potter series. (Pl. Ex. 12C.) The literary agency advised him that Rowling intended to work alone and did not require a collaborator. (Tr. (Vander Ark) at 250:14-20; Pl. Ex. 12 (Blair Deck) at ¶ 12; Pl. Ex. 12C.)

B. RDR Books' Acquisition and Marketing of the Lexicon

Roger Rapoport is the president of Defendant RDR Books. Rapoport learned of Vander Ark and the Lexicon website when he read an article in his local newspaper dated July 23, 2007, profiling Vander Ark as a well known figure within the Harry Potter fan community and the proprietor of the Lexicon website who "holds the key to all things `Harry Potter.'" (Tr. (Rapoport) at 153:2-154:15; Pl. Ex. 77.) Recognizing a publishing opportunity, Rapoport contacted Vander Ark on August 6, 2007 about the possibility of publishing a Harry Potter encyclopedia based on some of the materials from the Lexicon website. (Tr. (Vander Ark) at 357:10-19.) Rapoport denies seeing any coverage by national news outlets of Rowling's appearance on NBC's Today Show on July 25, 2007 (Tr. (Rapoport) at 156:10-158:4), where Rowling stated that she intended to write a Harry Potter encyclopedia. (Def. Ex. 506a; Tr. (Rapoport) at 155:20-156:5.)

At his first meeting with Rapoport in August 2007, Vander Ark raised his concerns regarding the permissibility of publishing the Lexicon in view of Rowling's plan to publish an encyclopedia and her copyrights in the Harry Potter books. (Tr. (Vander Ark) at 251:14-22, 358:2-4). Prior to August 2007, Vander Ark had developed and circulated the opinion that publishing "any book that is a guide to [the Harry Potter] world" would be a violation of Rowling's intellectual property rights. (Pl. Ex. 20 (Lares Decl.) at ¶ 3, Pl. Ex. 21 (Lawliss Decl.) at ¶ 3); see also Tr. (Vander Ark) at 251:20-22. Vander Ark had even stated on a public internet newsgroup that he would not publish the Lexicon "in any form except online" without permission because Rowling, not he, was "entitled to that market." (Pl. Ex. 27 (Blumsack Corrected Supp. Decl.) at ¶ 12; Pl. Ex. 27G). Vander Ark changed his mind about publishing the Lexicon after Rapoport reassured him that he had looked into the legal issue and determined that publication of content from the Lexicon website in book form was legal. (Tr. (Vander Ark) at 357:10-359:5.) Rapoport agreed to stand by this opinion by adding an atypical clause to the publishing contract providing that RDR would defend and indemnify Vander Ark in the event of any lawsuits. (Tr. (Vander Ark) 359:6-10, 360:8-21; Def. Ex. 502 (Vander Ark Decl.) at ¶ 28; Pl. Ex. 14J.)

Rapoport and Vander Ark agreed that the content of the book would be limited to the encyclopedia sections of the Lexicon website that presented descriptions of the persons, places, spells, and creatures from the Harry Potter works. (Tr. (Vander Ark) at 359:14-21; Def. Ex. 502 (Vander Ark Decl.) at ¶ 28.) They conceived of the book as an encyclopedia organized in the A-to-Z format, rather than by topic as the Lexicon website is organized, to allow the user to find information as quickly as possible. (Tr. (Vander Ark) at 366:25-367:24.) The idea was to publish the first complete guide to the Harry Potter series that included information from the seventh and final Harry Potter novel. (Id. at 361:12-24.) Vander Ark believed that there was an advantage to being the first reference guide on the market to cover all seven Harry Potter books. (Id. at 255:7-14, 361:9-15). He also believed that by virtue of its completeness, the Lexicon would be most useful for the purpose it sought to serve, namely helping readers and fans to find information from the Harry Potter novels. (Id. at 361:17-362:6.)

RDR Books intended to have a manuscript of the Lexicon completed within two-to-three weeks of execution of the publishing contract. (Tr. (Vander Ark) at 255:15-18.) The plan was to rush the book to market by late-October 2007, in part, to capitalize on the interest generated by the last Harry Potter book and the surge in sales during the holiday season. (Tr. (Rapoport) at 165:14-165:21, 167:10-17.) RDR Books initially planned a print-run of 10,000 copies of the Lexicon, but would undertake subsequent print-runs if the book was successful. (Tr. at (Rapoport) 238:22-239:20.)

Even before his initial meeting with Vander Ark, Rapoport began working to secure foreign publishers for the proposed Lexicon project and had contacted Methuen Publishing in the United Kingdom to gauge their interest in doing such a project. (Tr. (Rapoport) at 160:18-161:18.) He marketed the Lexicon to foreign publishers, as well as to U.S. bookstores and book sellers, as the "definitive" Harry Potter encyclopedia. (Tr. (Rapoport) at 160:18-161:15, 213:5-214:4; Tr. (Vander Ark) at 361:9-16; see also Pl. Exs. 114, 117.) Some of Rapoport's marketing communications mischaracterized Rowling's statements about the Lexicon website, giving the impression that she supported the publication of the Lexicon book. (Tr. at (Rapoport) 175:2-176:5; Pl. Ex. 89.) One marketing flyer for the Lexicon prominently displayed Rowling's 2004 statement praising the Lexicon website. (Tr. (Rapoport) at 171:3-6; Pl. Ex. 14 (Bradley Decl.) at ¶ 17; Pl. Ex. 22 (Murphy Decl.) at ¶ 15; Pl. Ex. 22A). As a result of Rapoport's marketing efforts, RDR Books secured oral contracts with foreign publishers for rights to the Lexicon in England, Canada, France, Australia, New Zealand, and China, and an order from Borders bookstore in the United States. (Tr. (Rapoport) at 187:2-11; 240:15-241:4; Pl. Ex. 137).

...

D. The Content of the Lexicon

The Lexicon is an A-to-Z guide to the creatures, characters, objects, events, and places that exist in the world of Harry Potter. As received by the Court in evidence, the Lexicon manuscript is more than 400 type-written pages long and contains 2,437 entries organized alphabetically. The first few pages contain a list of abbreviations used throughout the Lexicon to cite to the original sources of the material.

The Lexicon manuscript was created using the encyclopedia entries from the Lexicon website. (Tr. (Vander Ark) at 365:1-5; Def. Ex. 502 (Vander Ark Decl.) ¶ 30.) Because of space limitations for the printed work, which seeks to be complete but also easy to use, about half of the material from the website was not included in the Lexicon manuscript. (Tr. 365:1-11, 366:9-18; Def. Ex. 502 (Vander Ark Decl.) ¶¶ 30, 31, 33.) The Lexicon itself makes clear that the only source of its content is the work of J.K. Rowling. The first page of the Lexicon manuscript states: "All the information in the Harry Potter Lexicon comes from J.K. Rowling, either in the novels, the `schoolbooks,' from her interviews, or from material which she developed or wrote herself." (Pl. Ex. 1 at 1). While Vander Ark claims that the Lexicon uses material from outside reference sources, such as Bullfinch's Mythology, Field Guide to Little People, New Shorter Oxford English Dictionary, and online encyclopedias (Tr. (Vander Ark) at 346:12-348:19; Def. Ex. 502 (Vander Ark Decl.) at ¶ 14), it is not possible to confirm this claim because, aside from four dictionary citations, no other citations to third-party works appear in the Lexicon. (Tr. (Vander Ark) at 295:13-296:13).

The Lexicon entries cull every item and character that appears in the Harry Potter works, no matter if it plays a significant or insignificant role in the story. The entries cover every spell (e.g., Expecto Patronum, Expelliarmus, and Incendio), potion (e.g., Love Potion, Felix Felicis, and Draught of Living Death), magical item or device (e.g., Deathly Hallows, Horcrux, Cloak of Invisibility), form of magic (e.g., Legilimency, Occlumency, and the Dark Arts), creature (e.g., Blast-Ended Skrewt, Dementors, and Blood-Sucking Bugbears), character (e.g., Harry Potter, Hagrid, and Lord Voldemort), group or force (e.g., Aurors, Dumbledore's Army, Death Eaters), invented game (e.g., Quidditch), and imaginary place (e.g., Hogwarts School of Witchcraft and Wizardry, Diagon Alley, and the Ministry of Magic) that appear in the Harry Potter works. The Lexicon also contains entries for items that are not explicitly named in the Harry Potter works but which Vander Ark has identified, such as medical magic, candle magic, wizard space, wizard clothing, and remorse. Some of the entries describe places or things that exist in the real world but also have a place in the Harry Potter works, such as moors, Greece, and Cornwall.

Each entry, with the exception of the shortest ones, gathers and synthesizes pieces of information relating to its subject that appear scattered across the Harry Potter novels, the companion books, The Daily Prophet newsletters, Famous Wizard Cards, and published interviews of Rowling. The types of information contained in the entries include descriptions of the subject's attributes, role in the story, relationship to other characters or things, and events involving the subject. Repositories of such information, the entries seek to give as complete a picture as possible of each item or character in the Harry Potter world, many of which appear only sporadically throughout the series or in various sources of Harry Potter material.

The snippets of information in the entries are generally followed by citations in parentheses that indicate where they were found within the corpus of the Harry Potter works. The thoroughness of the Lexicon's citation, however, is not consistent; some entries contain very few citations in relation to the amount material provided. (See, e.g., Pl. Ex. 1, entry for "Dumbledore, Albus Percival Wulfric Brian" (containing no citations in a five-page entry); entry for "Granger, Hermione Jean" (containing no citations in a three-page entry); entry for "Chamber of Secrets" (containing one citation for nearly two pages of material); entry for "Crouch, Bartemius `Barty', Sr." (containing one citation for nearly a full page of material).) When the Lexicon cites to one of the seven Harry Potter novels, the citation provides only the book and chapter number. Vander Ark explained that page numbers were excluded from the citations because the various editions of the Harry Potter books have different pagination, but the chapter numbers remain consistent. (Tr. (Vander Ark) at 277:19-278:1.) The Lexicon neither assigns a letter to each edition nor specifies a standard edition while providing a conversion table for other editions, practices which Plaintiffs' expert Jeri Johnson testified were common for reference guides. (Tr. (Johnson) at 594:11-16, 594:20-595:3.)

While not its primary purpose, the Lexicon includes commentary and background information from outside knowledge on occasion. For example, the Lexicon contains sporadic etymological references, (e.g., Pl. Ex. 1, entries for "Colloportus," "Lupin, Remus," "Alohamora," "Fidelius Charm"), analogies to characters outside the Harry Potter world such as Merlin, and observations of Rowling's allusions to other works of literature such as "the weird sisters" from Shakespeare's Macbeth. The Lexicon also points to the very few "flints," or errors in the continuity of the story, that appear in the Harry Potter series. (See Tr. (Vander Ark) at 297:15-298:4.)

While there was considerable opining at trial as to the type of reference work the Lexicon purports to be and whether it qualifies as such (no doubt in part due to its title), the Lexicon fits in the narrow genre of non-fiction reference guides to fictional works. As Defendant's expert testified, the Harry Potter series is a multi-volume work of fantasy literature, similar to the works of J.R.R. Tolkien and C.S. Lewis. Such works lend themselves to companion guides or reference works because they reveal an elaborate imaginary world over thousands of pages, involving many characters, creatures, and magical objects that appear and reappear across thousands of pages. (Tr. (Sorensen) at 504:16-23; id. at 507:1-5 (testifying that she found 19 or 20 companion guides to J.R.R. Tolkien's works, and about 15 guides to C.S. Lewis's works).) Fantasy literature spawns books having a wide variety of purposes and formats, as demonstrated by the books about Harry Potter that Plaintiffs entered into evidence. (Pl. Exs. 73, 74, 75, 192; 13E-13G.) The Lexicon, an A-to-Z guide which synthesizes information from the series and generally provides citations for location of that information rather than offering commentary, is most comparable to the comprehensive work of Paul F. Ford, Companion to Narnia: A Complete Guide to the Magical World of C.S. Lewis's The Chronicles of Narnia (Pl. Ex. 62), or the unauthorized A-to-Z guide by George W. Beahm, Fact, Fiction, and Folklore in Harry Potter's World: An Unofficial Guide (Pl. Ex. 192).

At trial, Rowling testified that the Lexicon took "all the highlights of [her] work, in other words [her] characters' secret history, the jokes certainly, certain exciting narrative twists, all the things that are the highlights of [her] stories." (Tr. (Rowling) at 647:6-10). She compared this taking of her work to plundering all of the "plums in [her] cake." (Tr. (Rowling) at 647:3-6). At trial, the testimony of Rowling and the expert opinion of Johnson focused at length on the Lexicon's verbatim copying of language from the Harry Potter works. Johnson testified that in particular, entries that deal with invented terms, creatures, places and things from the Harry Potter books use "again and again the specific, very colorful, idiosyncratic ... nouns and phrases of Ms. Rowling." (Tr. (Johnson) at 619:7-9.)

Although it is difficult to quantify how much of the language in the Lexicon is directly lifted from the Harry Potter novels and companion books,[5] the Lexicon indeed contains at least a troubling amount of direct quotation or close paraphrasing of Rowling's original language.[6] The Lexicon occasionally uses quotation marks to indicate Rowling's language, but more often the original language is copied without quotation marks, often making it difficult to know which words are Rowling's and which are Vander Ark's. (Tr. (Rowling) at 57:6-15, 58:24-59:12, 59:19-60:2; Tr. (Johnson) at 619:3-12.)

For example, in the entry for "armor, goblin made," the Lexicon uses Rowling's poetic language nearly verbatim without quotation marks. The original language from Harry Potter and the Deathly Hallows reads:

"Muggle-borns," he said. "Goblinmade armour does not require cleaning, simple girl. Goblins' silver repels mundane dirt, imbibing only that which strengthens it."

(Pl. Ex. 10 at 303.) The Lexicon entry for "armor, goblin made" reads in its entirety:

Some armor in the wizarding world is made by goblins, and it is quite valuable. (e.g., HBP20) According to Phineas Nigellus, goblin-made armor does not require cleaning, because goblins' silver repels mundane dirt, imbibing only that which strengthens it, such as basilisk venom. In this context, "armor" also includes blades such as swords.

Although the Lexicon entry introduces Rowling's language with the phrase, "According to Phineas Nigellus," it does not use quotation marks.

The Lexicon entry for "Dementors" reproduces Rowling's vivid description of this creature sometimes using quotation marks and sometimes quoting or closely paraphrasing without indicating which language is original expression. The original language appears in Chapters 5 and 10 of Harry Potter and the Prisoner of Azkaban as follows:

. . . Its face was completely hidden beneath its hood. . . . There was a hand protruding from the cloak and it was glistening, grayish, slimy-looking, and scabbed, like something dead that had decayed in water. . . .

And then the thing beneath the hood, whatever it was, drew a long, slow, rattling breath, as though it were trying to suck something more than air from its surroundings.

* * *

"Dementors are among the foulest creatures to walk this earth. They infest the darkest, filthiest places, they glory in decay and despair, they drain peace, hope, and happiness out of the air around them. Even Muggles feel their presence, though they can't see them. Get too near a dementor and every good feeling, every happy memory will be sucked out of you. If it can, the dementor will feed on you long enough to reduce you to something like itself . . . soulless and evil. . . ."

(Pl. Ex. 6 at 83, 187.) The Lexicon entry for "Dementors" reads in its entirety:

Dementors are some of the most terrible creatures on earth, flying tall black spectral humanoid things with flowing robes. They "infest the darkest, filthiest places, they glory in decay and despair, they drain peace, hope, and happiness out of the air around them," according to Lupin (PA10). Dementors affect even Muggles, although Muggles can't see the foul, black creatures. Dementors feed on positive human emotions; a large crowd is like a feast to them. They drain a wizard of his power if left with them too long. They were the guards at Azkaban and made that place horrible indeed. The Ministry used Dementors as guards in its courtrooms as well (GF30, DH13). There are certain defenses one can use against Dementors, specifically the Patronus Charm. A Dementor's breath sounds rattling and like it's trying to suck more than air out of a room. Its hands are "glistening, grayish, slimy-looking, and scabbed". It exudes a biting, soulfreezing cold (PA5).

Another example of verbatim copying and close paraphrase can be found in the Lexicon entry for "Mirror of Erised." The original language from Harry Potter and the Sorcerer's Stone reads:

It was a magnificent mirror, as high as the ceiling, with an ornate gold frame, standing on two clawed feet. There was an inscription carved around the top: Erised stra ehru oyt ube cafru oyt on wohsi.

* * *

. . . "It shows us nothing more or less than the deepest desire of our hearts. You [Harry Potter], who have never known your family, see them standing around you. Ronald Weasley, who has always been overshadowed by his brothers, sees himself standing alone, the best of all of them. However, this mirror will give us neither knowledge or truth. Men have wasted away before it, entranced by what they have seen, or been driven mad, not knowing if what it shows is real or even possible."

(Pl. Ex. 4 at 207, 213). The first paragraph of the Lexicon entry reads:

A magnificent mirror, as high as a classroom ceiling, with an ornate gold frame, standing on two clawed feet. The inscription carved around the top reads "Erised stra ehru oyt ube cafru oyt on wohsi," which is "I show you not your face but your heart's desire" written backwards (that is, in what is called `mirror writing'). When you look into the mirror you see the deepest, most desperate desire of your heart. The mirror has trapped people who can't bear to stop staring into it, unsure if what they see is going to actually happen. Harry sees his family in the Mirror; Ron sees himself as Head Boy and Quidditch champion (PS12).

The Lexicon entry for "Boggart" takes strands of dialogue from Harry Potter and the Prisoner of Azkaban and closely paraphrases it in the third person. The original work contains the following bits of dialogue:

"Boggarts like dark, enclosed spaces."

"It's a shape-shifter .... It can take the shape of whatever it thinks will frighten us most."

"Nobody knows what a boggart looks like when he is alone, but when I let him out, he will immediately become whatever each of us most fears."

(Pl. Ex. 6 at 133.) The Lexicon entry begins as follows:

A shape shifter that prefers to live in dark, confined spaces, taking the form of the thing most feared by the person it encounters; nobody knows what a boggart looks like in its natural state.

An example of particularly extensive direct quotation is found in the Lexicon entry for "Trelawney, Sibyll Patricia," the professor of Divination at the Hogwarts School who tells two important prophecies in the story. The Lexicon not only reproduces her prophecies word-for-word in their entirety, but in doing so, reveals dramatic plot twists and how they are resolved in the series. For example, the first prophecy reads:

"The one with the power to vanquish the Dark Lord approaches. . . . Born to those who have thrice defied him, born as the seventh month dies . . . and the Dark Lord will mark him as his equal, but he will have power the Dark Lord knows not . . . and either must die at the hand of the other for neither can live while the other survives. . . . The one with the power to vanquish the Dark Lord will be born as the seventh month dies. . . ."

(Pl. Ex. 8 at 841 (ellipses in original).) The Lexicon entry reproduces this prophecy exactly but in italics and indented. (Pl. Ex. 1, entry for "Trelawney, Sibyll Patricia.") The Lexicon entry continues by discussing what happens as a result of this prophecy: "Severus Snape was eavesdropping on this conversation and he reported the first part of the Prophecy to the Dark Lord. Voldemort immediately began searching for this threat, and centered his attention on the child of Lily and James Potter. (OP 37)." The entry then quotes the second prophecy, but without a citation to where it appears in the Harry Potter series.

A number of Lexicon entries copy Rowling's artistic literary devices that contribute to her distinctive craft as a writer. For example, the Lexicon entry for "brain room," uses Rowling's evocative literary device in a very close paraphrase. The original language from Harry Potter and the Order of the Phoenix reads:

For a moment it seemed suspended in midair, then it soared toward Ron, spinning as it came, and what looked like ribbons of moving images flew from it, unraveling like rolls of film.

(Pl. Ex. 8 at 798.) The Lexicon entry reads in part:

. . . When Summoned, the brains fly out of the tank, unspooling ribbons of thought like strips of film, which wrap themselves around the Summoner and cause quite a bit of damage (OP35). . . .

The Lexicon entry for "Clankers" copies a vivid simile created by Rowling and reproduces a thought in the mind of Harry Potter as a factual statement using nearly identical wording. The original language from Harry Potter and the Deathly Hallows reads:

Ron passed the bag to Griphook, and the goblin pulled out a number of small metal instruments that when shaken made a loud, ringing noise like miniature hammers on anvils. . . .

. . . Harry could see [the dragon] trembling, and as they drew nearer he saw the scars made by vicious slashes across its face, and guessed that it had been taught to fear hot swords when it heard the sound of the Clankers.

(Pl. Ex. 10 at 536). The Lexicon entry reads:

A number of small metal instruments, which when shaken make a loud, ringing noise like tiny hammers on anvil [sic]. Anyone visiting one of the high-security vaults at Gringotts must carry one of these, shaking it to make noise. The dragon guarding those vaults has been conditioned to back away at the sound, apparently by being taught to fear hot swords whenever it hears the Clankers (DH26).

Similarly, the Lexicon entry for "Marchbanks, Madam Griselda" uses an artful simile from the original works to describe this character. Rowling's language in Harry Potter and the Order of the Phoenix reads:

. . . Harry thought Professor Marchbanks must be the tiny, stooped witch with a face so lined it looked as though it had been draped in cobwebs; Umbridge was speaking to her very deferentially.. . .

(Pl. Ex. 8 at 710.) The Lexicon entry reads in part:

... Madam Marchbanks in June 1996 was tiny and stooped, her face so lined it appeared draped in cobwebs. . . .

The Lexicon's close paraphrasing is not limited to the seven Harry Potter novels, but can be found in entries drawn from the companion books as well. For example, the entry for "Montrose Magpies" uses language from Quidditch Through the Ages. The original language reads:

The Magpies are the most successful team in the history of the British and Irish League, which they have won thirty-two times. Twice European Champions . . . . The Magpies wear black and white robes with one magpie on the chest and another on the back.

(Pl. Ex. 2 at 35-36.) The Lexicon entry reads:

The most successful Quidditch team in history, which has won the British and Irish league thirty-two times and the European Cup twice. Their robes are black and white, with one magpie on the chest and another on the back (QA7).

(See also Pl. Ex. 1, entry for "Woollongong Shimmy.")

The same close paraphrasing takes place in the Lexicon entries drawing from Rowling's other companion book, Fantastic Beasts & Where to Find Them. For example, the entry for "Chinese Fireball" closely tracks the original language, which reads:

The only Oriental dragon. Scarlet and smooth-scaled, it has a fringe of golden spikes around its snub-snouted face and extremely protuberant eyes. The Fireball gained its name for the mushroom-shaped flame that bursts from its nostrils when it is angered. . . . Eggs are a vivid crimson speckled with gold....

(Pl. Ex. 3 at 11.) The Lexicon entry reads:

A species of dragon native to China. The Fireball is a scarlet dragon with golden spikes around its face and protruding eyes. The blast of flame from a fireball forms a distinctive mushroom shape. Eggs of a Fireball are vivid crimson, flecked with gold (FB).

(See also Pl. Ex. 1, entry for "Fire Crab.")

Instances of such verbatim copying or close paraphrasing of language in the Harry Potter works occur throughout the Lexicon. (See, e.g., Pl. Ex. 1, entries for "Apparition," "Bubtotuber," "Pince, Madam Irma," "Twycross, Wilkie," "Lovegood, Luna," "third-floor corridor," "Slytherin common room") Rowling provides numerous examples in Plaintiffs' Exhibit 47, "a chart [she] made to show what [she] felt was the constant pilfering of [her] work." (Tr. (Rowling) at 57:23-24.)

Aside from verbatim copying, another factual issue of contention at trial was the Lexicon entries that contain summaries of certain scenes or key events in the Harry

Potter series. Most frequently, these are the longer entries that describe important objects, such as the "Deathly Hallows," or momentous events, such as the "Triwizard Tournament," or that trace the development of an important character, such as Harry Potter, Lord Voldemort, Severus Snape, and Albus Dumbledore. Plaintiffs' expert testified at length that in her opinion these entries constitute "plot summaries," (Tr. (Johnson) at 592:14-22, 611:13-22, 623:4-624:11), while Defendant's expert characterized them as character studies or analysis.

Neither of these characterizations is exactly apt. Without endorsing one characterization or another, such entries in the Lexicon do encapsulate elements of the very elaborate and wide ranging plot (sometimes in chronological order, sometimes not) confined to the subject of the entry. In the entries for significant characters, these plot elements are occasionally used to support an observation about the character's nature or development. For instance, the three-and-a-half page entry for "Lovegood, Luna" contains the following paragraph:

Luna came into her own during her sixth year at Hogwarts. With Harry, Ron, and Hermione gone from school, she joined Ginny and Neville to revive the D.A. and resist the Death Eaters' influence at Hogwarts. She was kidnapped on the Hogwarts Express on her way home for the Christmas holidays (DH25) because of what Mr. Lovegood had been writing in The Quibbler, and imprisoned in the cellar at the Malfoy Mansion along with Ollivander. She was helpful in their efforts to escape the Malfoy Mansion, and then fought bravely, again, at the Battle of Hogwarts (DH31).

(See also, e.g., Pl. Ex. 1, entry for "Malfoy, Draco," ¶ ¶ 5, 6, 7.) But other times, the presentation of plot details, in effect, summarizes a vignette or portion of a scene. In the same entry for "Lovegood, Luna," the Lexicon summarizes a scene on the Hogwarts Express found on pages 185 to 188 of Chapter 10 of Harry Potter and the Order of the Phoenix:

Harry met Luna for the first time aboard the Hogwarts Express on September 1, 1995. He, Ginny, and Neville shared a compartment with her on the train (OP 10). She was reading a copy of The Quibbler magazine upside down. She informed the others that her father is the editor of The Quibbler, a magazine which most in the Wizarding World consider a joke. She laughed a little too loud; she stared at the other kids, and generally made an odd traveling companion. Harry privately thought, when Cho happened by their compartment to say hello, that he would much rather have been sitting with "cooler" kids than Luna and Neville.

(Compare Pl. Ex. 8 at 185-88.)

The entries for the hero and the villain of the Harry Potter series (Harry Potter and Lord Voldemort) present the closest thing to "plot summaries," but are more aptly characterized as synopses or outlines of the narrative revolving around those characters. Because Harry Potter and Lord Voldemort drive the narrative and because they appear in nearly every chapter of the series, an encapsulation of the events surrounding them ultimately yields a synopsis of the primary narrative thread in the Harry Potter series. The Lexicon entry for "Potter, Harry James" is eleven pages long and chronicles each year of Harry Potter's life at the fictional

Hogwarts School, providing the reader with all of the main events of the story through all seven of Rowling's novels, leading up to Harry Potter's final battle with Lord Voldemort. (Pl. Ex. 11 (Birchall Decl.) at ¶ 5). The nine-page entry for "Voldemort, Lord" begins by providing the pre-story for the character, which is included in the sixth Harry Potter novel, giving background into the character as a child. (Tr. (Rowling) at 146:10-13). The entry then proceeds to describe chronologically all of the events surrounding this character in the Harry Potter story from books one through seven, and also gives an account of this character's death in the last Harry Potter novel. (Tr. (Rowling) at 62: 12-20; Tr. (Johnson) at 623:6-624:11). Although the entries proceed chronologically and do not use the same plot structure as do the Harry Potter novels (which structure the plot so as to create an interesting drama), the entries do provide a skeleton of the plot elements that hold the story together.

Finally, Plaintiffs established the Lexicon's extensive copying from Rowling's companion books, Quidditch Through the Ages and Fantastic Beasts & Where to Find Them, the schoolbooks used by the students attending the Hogwarts School. These two books are very short, fifty-six and fifty-nine pages,[9] respectively. They are written in non-narrative form (Tr. (Vander Ark) at 396:21-25) and present fictional facts without commentary (id. (Rowling) at 63:18-20), in a similar way to the Lexicon. When questioned about his use of these books in creating the Lexicon, Vander Ark testified:

. . . Fantastic Beasts and Quidditch [Through] the Ages had sections of them which were essentially encyclopedias already which presented quite a problem. We wanted to be complete, but we certainly didn't want to replace Ms. Rowling's encyclopedia content which presented us with quite a challenge of how to do that, how to include information, but not to include all of it. And that was what we decided to do. We said we'll intentionally leave things out and put a very clear note, Please go read her books, which is what we did.

(Id. (Vander Ark) 287:20-288:4.) Although the Lexicon sporadically leaves out material, such as some material from the introductory chapters of Quidditch Through the Ages, it essentially takes wholesale from the companion books. (Tr. (Rowling) at 65:3-8, 62:25-63:1.) When questioned about the Lexicon entry for "Chudley Cannons" and whether there was anything about this quidditch team in Quidditch Through the Ages that he did not put in the Lexicon, Vander Ark admitted, "In that particular case, it looks like we pretty much caught it all." (Id. at 288:15-22.)[10] Vander Ark later admitted that although he left out some of the first half of Quidditch Through the Ages, "[w]hen it comes to descriptions of specific things, a Quidditch f[oul], for example, there's not a lot of information there to condense, and so there would be more of that included and referenced." (Id. at 290:3-6.)[11] Similarly, the Lexicon copies a large part of the descriptions of each beast in the A-to-Z section of Fantastic Beasts & Where to Find Them.

CONCLUSIONS OF LAW

I. Copyright Infringement

To establish a prima facie case of copyright infringement, a plaintiff must demonstrate "(1) ownership of a valid copyright, and (2) copying of constituent elements of the work that are original." Feist Publ'ns, Inc. v. Rural Tel. Serv. Co., 499 U.S. 340, 361, 111 S.Ct. 1282, 113 L.Ed.2d 358 (1991); Arica Institute. Inc. v. Palmer, 970 F.2d 1067, 1072 (2d Cir. 1992). The element of copying has two components: first, the plaintiff must establish actual copying by either direct or indirect evidence; then, the plaintiff must establish that the copying amounts to an improper or unlawful appropriation. Castle Rock Entm't, Inc. v. Carol Publ'g Group, Inc., 150 F.3d 132, 137 (2d Cir. 1998); Laureyssens v. Idea Group, Inc., 964 F.2d 131, 139-140 (2d Cir.1992). The plaintiff demonstrates that the copying is actionable "by showing that the second work bears a `substantial similarity' to protected expression in the earlier work." Castle Rock, 150 F.3d at 137 (citing Repp v. Webber, 132 F.3d 882, 889 (2d Cir.1997)); see Ringgold v. Black Entm't Television, Inc., 126 F.3d 70, 74-75 (2d Cir.1997) (explaining the distinction between actionable copying and factual copying); 4 Melville B. Nimmer & David Nimmer, Nimmer on Copyright § 13.03[A] (2007) [hereinafter Nimmer].

...

B. Copying

There is no dispute that the Lexicon actually copied from Rowling's copyrighted works. Vander Ark openly admitted that he created and updated the content of the Lexicon by taking notes while reading the Harry Potter books and by using without authorization scanned, electronic copies of the Harry Potter novels and companion books. (Tr. (Vander Ark) at 335:9-17, 259:5-9, 16-23.) While acknowledging actual copying, Defendant disputes that the copying amounts to an improper or unlawful appropriation of Rowling's works. Defendant argues that Plaintiffs fail to establish a prima facie case of infringement because they have not shown that the Lexicon is substantially similar to the Harry Potter works.

The appropriate inquiry under the substantial similarity test is whether "the copying is quantitatively and qualitatively sufficient to support the legal conclusion that infringement (actionable copying) has occurred."Ringgold, 126 F.3d at 75; accord Nihon Keizai Shimbun, Inc. v. Comline Bus. Data, Inc., 166 F.3d 65, 70 (2d Cir.1999); Castle Rock, 150 F.3d at 138. The quantitative component addresses the amount of the copyrighted work that is copied, while the qualitative component addresses the copying of protected expression, as opposed to unprotected ideas or facts. Ringgold, 126 F.3d at 75.

In evaluating the quantitative extent of copying in the substantial similarity analysis, the Court "considers the amount of copying not only of direct quotations and close paraphrasing, but also of all other protectable expression in the original work." Castle Rock, 150 F.3d at 140 n. 6. As the Second Circuit has instructed, "[i]t is not possible to determine infringement through a simple word count," which in this case would be an insuperable task; "the quantitative analysis of two works must always occur in the shadow of their qualitative nature." Nihon Keizai, 166

F.3d at 71. Where, as here, the copyrighted work is "wholly original," rather than mixed with unprotected elements, a lower quantity of copying will support a finding of substantial similarity. Nihon Keizai, 166 F.3d at 71.

Plaintiffs have shown that the Lexicon copies a sufficient quantity of the Harry Potter series to support a finding of substantial similarity between the Lexicon and Rowling's novels. The Lexicon draws 450 manuscript pages worth of material primarily from the 4,100-page Harry Potter series. Most of the Lexicon's 2,437 entries contain direct quotations or paraphrases, plot details, or summaries of scenes from' one or more of the Harry Potter novels. As Defendant admits, "the Lexicon reports thousands of fictional facts from the Harry Potter works." (Def's Post-trial Br. at 35). Although hundreds of pages or thousands of fictional facts may amount to only a fraction of the seven-book series, this quantum of copying is sufficient to support a finding of substantial similarity where the copied expression is entirely the product of the original author's imagination and creation. See Castle Rock, 150 F.3d at 138 (concluding that a Seinfeld trivia book that copied 643 fragments from 84 copyrighted Seinfeld episodes "plainly crossed the quantitative copying threshold under Ringgold"); Twin Peaks Prods., Inc. v. Publ'ns Int'l, Ltd., 996 F.2d 1366, 1372 (2d Cir.1993) (upholding the district court's conclusion that "the identity of 89 lines of dialogue" between Twin Peaks teleplays and a guide to the television series constituted substantial similarity); see also Harper & Row v. Nation Enterprises, 471 U.S. 539, 548-49, 105 S.Ct. 2218, 85 L.Ed.2d 588 (1985) (stating that "lifting verbatim quotes of the author's original language totaling between 300 and 400 words and constituting some 13% of [the defendant's] article" was sufficient to constitute copyright infringement).

The quantitative extent of the Lexicon's copying is even more substantial with respect to Fantastic Beasts and Quidditch Through the Ages. Rowling's companion books are only fifty-nine and fifty-six pages long, respectively. The Lexicon reproduces a substantial portion of their content, with only sporadic omissions, across hundreds of entries. (Tr. (Vander Ark) at 287:20-288:4) (testifying that to overcome the problem of copying the companion books, "which were essentially encyclopedias already," in their entirety, the Lexicon intentionally leaves some things out).

As to the qualitative component of the substantial similarity analysis, Plaintiffs have shown that the Lexicon draws its content from creative, original expression in the Harry Potter series and companion books. Each of the 2,437 entries in the Lexicon contains "fictional facts" created by Rowling, such as the attributes of imaginary creatures and objects, the traits and undertakings of major and minor characters, and the events surrounding them. The entry for "Boggart," for example, contains the fictional facts that a boggart is "[a] shape shifter that prefers to live in dark, confined spaces, taking the form of the thing most feared by the person it encounters; nobody knows what a boggart looks like in its natural state," and that "Lupin taught his third year Defence Against the Dark Arts class to fight [a boggart] with the Riddikulus spell (PA7), and used a boggart as a substitute for a Dementor in tutoring Harry (PA12)." (Pl. Ex. 1.) In Castle Rock Entertainment Inc. v. Carol Publishing Group, Inc., the Second Circuit explained that such invented facts constitute creative expression protected by copyright because "characters and events spring from the imagination of [the original] authors." 150 F.3d at 139; see also Paramount Pictures Corp. v. Carol Publ'g Group, 11 F.Supp.2d 329, 333 (S.D.N.Y.1998) (stating that "[t]he characters, plots and dramatic episodes" that comprise the story of the "fictitious history of Star Trek" are the story's "original elements," protected by copyright). The Castle Rock court held that a trivia book which tested the reader's knowledge of "facts" from the Seinfeld series copied protected expression because "each `fact' tested by [the trivia book] is in reality fictitious expression created by Seinfeld's authors." Id. It follows that the same qualitative conclusion should be drawn here, where each "fact" reported by the Lexicon is actually expression invented by Rowling.

Seeking to distinguish Castle Rock, Defendant argues that the qualitative similarity between the Lexicon and the Harry Potter works is significantly diminished because "the Lexicon uses fictional facts primarily in their factual capacity" to "report information and where to find it," unlike the Seinfeld trivia book, which used fictional facts "primarily in their fictional capacity to entertain and `satisfy' the reader's `craving' for the Seinfeld television series." (Def. Post-trial Br. at 36 (quoting Castle Rock, 150 F.3d at 142-43).) While this distinction is important, Defendant's argument goes to the fair use question of whether the Lexicon's use has a transformative purpose, not to the infringement question of whether the Lexicon, on its face, bears a substantial similarity to the Harry Potter works. The court in Castle Rock addressed these two inquires separately and found that the Seinfeld trivia book not only bore a substantial similarity to the Seinfeld series but also lacked a transformative purpose. See Castle Rock, 150 F.3d at 138-39, 141-43. What matters at the infringement stage of this case is that the copied text is expression original to Rowling, not fact or idea, and therefore is presumptively entitled to copyright protection. See Harper & Row, 471 U.S. at 547, 105 S.Ct. 2218; Feist, 499 U.S. at 344-46, 111 S.Ct. 1282. Even if expression is or can be used in its "factual capacity," it does not follow that expression thereby takes on the status of fact and loses its copyrightability.

Defendant also argues that while a substantial similarity may be found where invented facts are "reported and arranged in such a way as to tell essentially the same story" as the original, "the order in which the fictional facts are presented in the Lexicon bears almost no resemblance to the order in which the fictional facts are arranged to create the story of Harry Potter and the universe he inhabits." (Def. Post-trial Br. at 34, 36). Reproducing original expression in fragments or in a different order, however, does not preclude a finding of substantial similarity. See Castle Rock, 150 F.3d at 139 (finding a substantial similarity even though the allegedly infringing trivia book rearranged fragments of expression from Seinfeld in question-and-answer format); Paramount Pictures, 11 F.Supp.2d at 333-34 (finding that a book containing brief synopses of major plot lines, histories of major characters, and descriptions of fictional alien species in Star Trek was substantially similar to the Star Trek series even though "the fictitious history is presented in a different order than that in which it appeared in the [original works]"). Regardless of how the original expression is copied, "`the standard for determining copyright infringement is not whether the original could be recreated from the allegedly infringing copy, but whether the latter is "substantially similar" to the former.'"

Castle Rock, 150 F.3d at 141 (quoting Horgan v. Macmillan, Inc., 789 F.2d 157, 162 (2d Cir.1986)). Here, the Lexicon's rearrangement of Rowling's fictional facts does not alter the protected expression such that the Lexicon ceases to be substantially similar to the original works.

Furthermore, the law in this Circuit is clear that "the concept of similarity embraces not only global similarities in structure and sequence, but localized similarity in language." Twin Peaks, 996 F.2d at 1372 (endorsing the taxonomy of "comprehensive nonliteral similarity" and "fragmented literal similarity" from the Nimmer treatise, 4 Nimmer § 13.03[A][2]); see also Ringgold, 126 F.3d at 75 n. 3; Arica Institute, 970 F.2d at 1073. In evaluating fragmented literal similarity, or "localized similarity in language," the Court examines the copying of direct quotations or close paraphrasing of the original work. Castle Rock, 150 F.3d at 140; Paramount Pictures, 11 F.Supp.2d at 333 ("Fragmented similarity refers to exact copying of a portion of a work"). As determined in the Findings of Fact, the Lexicon contains a considerable number of direct quotations (often without quotation marks) and close paraphrases of vivid passages in the Harry Potter works. Although in these instances, the Lexicon often changes a few words from the original or rewrites original dialogue in the third person, the language is nonetheless substantially similar. See Salinger v. Random House, Inc., 811 F.2d 90, 97 (2d Cir.1987) (indicating that protected expression is infringed whether it is "quoted verbatim or only paraphrased"); Craft v. Kobler, 667 F.Supp. 120, 124 (S.D.N.Y. 1987) (stating that protected writing is infringed by "direct quotation" or "by paraphrase which remains sufficiently close that, in spite of changes, it appropriates the craft of authorship of the original"); see also 4 Nimmer § 13.03[A][1] ("The mere fact that the defendant has paraphrased rather than literally copied will not preclude a finding of substantial similarity. Copyright `cannot be limited literally to the text, else a plagiarist would escape by immaterial variations.'") (footnote omitted) (quoting Nichols v. Universal Pictures Corp., 45 F.2d 119, 121 (2d Cir.1930)).

Notwithstanding the dissimilarity in the overall structure of the Lexicon and the original works, some of the Lexicon entries contain summaries of certain scenes or key events in the Harry Potter series, as stated in the Findings of Fact. These passages, in effect, retell small portions of the novels, though without the same dramatic effect. In addition, the entries for Harry Potter and Lord Voldemort give a skeleton of the major plot elements of the Harry Potter series, again without the same dramatic effect or structure. Together these portions of the Lexicon support a finding of substantial similarity. To be sure, this case is different from Twin Peaks, where forty-six pages of the third chapter of a guidebook to the Twin Peaks television series were found to constitute "essentially a detailed recounting of the first eight episodes of the series. Every intricate plot twist and element of character development appear[ed] in the Book in the same sequence as in the teleplays." 996 F.2d at 1372-73 (supporting the Second Circuit's finding of comprehensive nonliteral similarity). Those "plot summaries" were far more detailed, comprehensive, and parallel to the original episodes than the so-called "plot summaries" in this case. Nonetheless, it is clear that the plotlines and scenes encapsulated in the Lexicon are appropriated from the original copyrighted works.

See Paramount Pictures, 11 F.Supp.2d at 334 (noting that Twin Peaks was distinguishable but nonetheless applying its broader holding that "a book which tells the story of a copyrighted television series infringes on its copyright"). Under these circumstances, Plaintiffs have established a prima facie case of infringement.

C. Derivative Work

Plaintiffs allege that the Lexicon not only violates their right of reproduction, but also their right to control the production of derivative works. The Copyright Act defines a "derivative work" as "a work based upon one or more preexisting works, such as a translation, musical arrangement, dramatization, fictionalization, motion picture version, sound recording, art reproduction, abridgment, condensation, or any other form in which a work may be recast, transformed, or adapted" 17 U.S.C. § 101 (emphasis added). A work "consisting of editorial revisions, annotations, elaborations, or other modifications which, as a whole, represents an original work of authorship" is also a derivative work. Id.

A work is not derivative, however, simply because it is "based upon" the preexisting works. If that were the standard, then parodies and book reviews would fall under the definition, and certainly "ownership of copyright does not confer a legal right to control public evaluation of the copyrighted work." Ty, Inc. v. Publ'ns Int'l Ltd., 292 F.3d 512, 521 (7th Cir.2002). The statutory language seeks to protect works that are "recast, transformed, or adapted" into another medium, mode, language, or revised version, while still representing the "original work of authorship." See Castle Rock, 150 F.3d at 143 n. 9 (stating that "derivative works that are subject to the author's copyright transform an original work into a new mode of presentation"); Twin Peaks, 996 F.2d at 1373 (finding a derivative work where a guidebook based on the Twin Peaks television series "contain[ed] a substantial amount of material from the teleplays, transformed from one medium to another"). Thus in Ty, Inc. v. Publications International Ltd., Judge Posner concluded, as the parties had stipulated, that a collectors' guide to Beanie Babies was not a derivative work because "guides don't recast, transform, or adapt the things to which they are guides." 292 F.3d at 520 (emphasis added).

Plaintiffs argue that based on the Twin Peaks decision "companion guides constitute derivative works where, as is the case here, they `contain a substantial amount of material from the underlying work.'" (Pl. Post-trial Br. ¶ 288, at 88-89.) This argument inaccurately states the holding of Twin Peaks and overlooks two important distinctions between the Lexicon and the guidebook in Twin Peaks. First, as mentioned earlier, the portions of the Lexicon that encapsulate plot elements or sketch plotlines bear no comparison with the guidebook in Twin Peaks, whose plot summaries giving "elaborate recounting of plot details" were found to constitute an "abridgement" of the original work. See Twin Peaks, 996 F.2d at 1373 n. 2 (reproducing an excerpt of the infringing book containing a high degree of detail). Given that the Lexicon's use of plot elements is far from an "elaborate recounting" and does not follow the same plot structure as the Harry Potter novels, Plaintiffs' suggestion that these portions of the Lexicon are "unauthorized abridgements" is unpersuasive. Second, and more importantly, although the Lexicon "contain[s] a substantial amount of material" from the Harry

Potter works, the material is not merely "transformed from one medium to another," as was the case in Twin Peaks. Id. at 1373. By condensing, synthesizing, and reorganizing the preexisting material in an A-to-Z reference guide, the Lexicon does not recast the material in another medium to retell the story of Harry Potter, but instead gives the copyrighted material another purpose. That purpose is to give the reader a ready understanding of individual elements in the elaborate world of Harry Potter that appear in voluminous and diverse sources. As a result, the Lexicon no longer "represents [the] original work[s] of authorship." 17 U.S.C. § 101. Under these circumstances, and because the Lexicon does not fall under any example of derivative works listed in the statute, Plaintiffs have failed to show that the Lexicon is a derivative work.

II. Fair Use

Defendant contends that even if Plaintiffs have shown a prima facie case of infringement, the Lexicon is nevertheless a fair use of the Harry Potter works. ...

A. Purpose and Character of the Use

Most critical to the inquiry under the first fair-use factor is "whether and to what extent the new work is transformative." Campbell, 510 U.S. at 579, 114 S.Ct. 1164; see also Bill Graham Archives v. Dorling Kindersley Ltd., 448 F.3d 605, 608 (2d Cir.2006); Elvis Presley Enters., Inc. v. Passport Video, 349 F.3d 622, 628 (9th Cir.2003). Specifically, the court asks "whether the new work merely `supersede[s] the objects' of the original creation, or instead adds something new, with a further purpose or different character, altering the first with new expression, meaning, or message." Campbell, 510 U.S. at 579, 114 S.Ct. 1164. The fair use doctrine seeks to protect a secondary work if it "adds value to the original—if [copyrightable expression in the original work] is used as raw material, transformed in the creation of new information, new aesthetics, new insights and understandings," because such a work contributes to the enrichment of society. Castle Rock, 150 F.3d at 141 (alteration in original) (quoting Leval, supra, at 1111). Courts have found a transformative purpose both where the defendant combines copyrighted expression with original expression to produce a new creative work, see, e.g., Campbell, 510 U.S. at 582-83, 114 S.Ct. 1164; Blanch, 467 F.3d at 251-51; Suntrust Bank v. Houghton Mifflin Co., 268 F.3d 1257 (11th Cir.2001), and where the defendant uses a copyrighted work in a different context to serve a different function than the original, see, e.g., Perfect 10, Inc. v. Amazon.com, Inc., 508 F.3d 1146 (9th Cir.2007); Bill Graham Archives v. Dorling Kindersley Ltd., 448 F.3d 605 (2d Cir.2006).

The purpose of the Lexicon's use of the Harry Potter series is transformative. Presumably, Rowling created the Harry Potter series for the expressive purpose of telling an entertaining and thought provoking story centered on the character Harry Potter and set in a magical world. The Lexicon, on the other hand, uses material from the series for the practical purpose of making information about the intricate world of Harry Potter readily accessible to readers in a reference guide. To fulfill this function, the Lexicon identifies more than 2,400 elements from the Harry Potter world, extracts and synthesizes fictional facts related to each element from all seven novels, and presents that information in a format that allows readers to access it quickly as they make their way through the series. Because it serves these reference purposes, rather than the entertainment or aesthetic purposes of the original works, the Lexicon's use is transformative and does not supplant the objects of the Harry Potter works. See Elvis Presley Enters., 349 F.3d at 629 (stating that new works are described as transformative "when the works use copyrighted materials for purposes distinct from the purpose of the original material"); see also Bill Graham Archives, 448 F.3d at 609 (concluding that the use of artistic images as historical artifacts is "transformatively different from the original expressive purpose").

The Lexicon's use of Rowling's companion books, however, is transformative to a much lesser extent. Although there is no supporting testimony, the companion books can be used for a reference purpose. Their packaging demonstrates an entertainment purpose: bringing to life the fictional schoolbooks they represent in the Harry Potter novels, the companion books have fictional authors, forewords written by Albus Dumbledore, handwritten notes to Harry from his friends, a game of tictac-toe sketched on one page, a library log and warning by the Hogwarts librarian, and a "Property of Hogwarts Library" stamp. In this regard, the companion books serve as playful accessories to the Harry Potter series. At the same time, the content of the companion books takes on the informational purpose of the schoolbooks they represent in the novels. As Vander Ark testified, the companion books are "essentially encyclopedias already." (Tr. (Vander Ark) at 287:21-22.) Fantastic Beasts describes the attributes and origins of each beast listed in the alphabetical guide, defines "beast," and explains the place of beasts in the "muggle" and wizard worlds. Quidditch Through the Ages describes the history and development of quidditch, the rules of the game, the teams, and the spread of quidditch internationally. Neither book, however, makes reference to where the beasts or quidditch facts appear in the Harry Potter novels. Although the Lexicon does not use the companion books for their entertainment purpose, it supplants the informational purpose of the original works by seeking to relate the same fictional facts in the same way. Even so, the Lexicon's use is slightly transformative in that it adds a productive purpose to the original material by synthesizing it within a complete reference guide that refers readers to where information can be found in a diversity of sources.

The best evidence of the Lexicon's transformative purpose is its demonstrated value as a reference source. See Am. Geophysical Union v. Texaco Inc., 60 F.3d 913, (2d Cir.1994) (stating that the "transformative use concept assesses the value generated by the secondary use and the means by which such value is generated"); Leval, supra, at 1111 (stating that for a use to be transformative, "[t]he use must be productive and must employ the quoted matter in a different manner or for a different purpose than the original"). The utility of the Lexicon, as a reference guide to a multi-volume work of fantasy literature, demonstrates a productive use for a different purpose than the original works. The Lexicon makes the elaborate imaginary world of Harry Potter searchable, item by item, and gives readers a complete picture of each item that cannot be gleaned by reading the voluminous series, since the material related to each item is scattered over thousands of pages of complex narrative and plot. The demand for and usefulness of this type of reference guide is evidenced by the publication of similar works such as Paul F. Ford's Companion to Narnia: A Complete Guide to the Magical World of C.S. Lewis's The Chronicles of Narnia. (Pl. Ex. 62; see also Def. Ex. 503 (Sorensen Decl. ¶ 12.)) The utility of the Lexicon as a reference guide has been demonstrated to Vander Ark by way of responses to his Lexicon website. This feedback included a remark by Rowling that she has "been known to sneak into an internet café while out writing and check a fact" on the Lexicon website, a remark by David Heyman of Warner Brothers that he used the Lexicon website almost every day while shooting the fifth Harry Potter film, and a glimpse of the walls of the Electronic Arts studios covered with printed pages from the Lexicon website. (Tr. 386:8-20, 387:3-13; Def. Ex. 502 (Vander Ark Decl.) ¶ 39.) This feedback supports Defendant's claim that it had good reason to believe that a print version of the Lexicon would serve as a valuable reference source to readers and fans of Harry Potter.

Its function as a reference guide distinguishes the Lexicon from the secondary work at issue in Castle Rock, a 132-page book of trivia about the events and characters depicted in Seinfeld. Despite its specious claims to critique and expose the Seinfeld series, the trivia book served no purpose but "to satiate Seinfeld fans' passion" for the series and simply "repackage[d] Seinfeld to entertain Seinfeld viewers." Castle Rock, 150 F.3d at 142. A statement by the book's creators on the back cover, urging readers to "open this book to satisfy [their] between-episode [Seinfeld] cravings," belied its transformative purpose. Id. By contrast, the Lexicon seeks not to entertain but to aid the reader or student of Harry Potter by providing references about the elements encountered in the series.[19]

The Lexicon's purpose as a reference guide also distinguishes it from the books at issue in Twin Peaks and Paramount Pictures. Those books sought to retell the fictional stories of the Twin Peaks series and the Star Trek series in abridged versions. See Twin Peaks, 996 F.2d at 1372-73, 1375-76 (finding that the book at issue was an "abridgment" because it recounted "precisely the plot details" of television episodes "in the same sequence" as they appeared in the original series); Paramount Pictures, 11 F.Supp.2d at 335 (finding that the work at issue "simply retells the story of Star Trek in a condensed version"). Because the books in those cases merely recast the originals in abridged versions, they were held to be derivative works. The Lexicon, on the other hand, has a "further purpose or different character," Campbell, 510 U.S. at 579, 114 S.Ct. 1164, that alters the original aesthetic of the Harry Potter series from an intricate narrative to an alphabetized catalogue of elements from the Harry Potter world.

Plaintiffs argue that the Lexicon's use of Rowling's works cannot be considered transformative because the Lexicon does not add significant analysis or commentary. In the opinion of Plaintiffs' expert, the Lexicon contributes nothing new other than occasional facetious phrases and facile jokes that are condescending to children (Pl. Ex. 28 (Suppl. Johnson Decl.) ¶ 9; Tr. (Johnson) at 633:8-634:7), sporadic and often wrong etymological references demonstrating "no real linguistic understanding" (Pl. Ex. 28, ¶ 11), and conclusions that would be obvious to any child reading Harry Potter (id. ¶ 7). The Lexicon, however, does not purport to be a work of literary criticism or to constitute a fair use on that basis;

and its lack of critical analysis, linguistic understanding, or clever humor is not determinative of whether or not its purpose is transformative.[20] Cf. Bill Graham Archives, 448 F.3d at 610 (concluding that the defendant's use of copyrighted images "is transformative both when accompanied by referencing commentary and when standing alone" because in either case the images are used as "historical artifacts" for the transformative purpose of "enhancing the biographical information" in the allegedly infringing book). Focusing on what the Lexicon fails to add by way of analysis misses the point that the Lexicon's chief contribution is the function it serves.

Nonetheless, despite Plaintiffs' criticisms, the Lexicon occasionally does offer "new information, new aesthetics, new insights and understandings," Castle Rock, 150 F.3d at 141 (internal quotation marks omitted), as to the themes and characters in the Harry Potter works. The Lexicon's discussion of certain characters, while perhaps not rigorous analysis, contain some reflections on the character, observations of his or her nature, and examples of how that nature is exhibited in the story. For example, the Lexicon observes that "Draco [Malfoy] was constantly frustrated by the attention given to Harry," and gives anecdotal examples from the novels to support this conclusion. (See also Pl. Ex. 1, entry for "Longbottom, Neville" (containing observations about the nature of his bravery and leadership); entry for "Lovegood, Luna" (containing observations about her social awkwardness and dignity)). Moreover, in some instances, the Lexicon yields insights about an element of the Harry Potter world simply by encapsulating all the fictional facts related to that element in a single entry. When all the fictional facts related to "Hallowe'en" are collected, for example, the entry reveals that this occasion is "an eventful day in Harry's life; on Hallowe'en 1981 his parents were killed (DH17) and his subsequent years included knocking out a troll (PS10), the opening of the Chamber of Secrets (CS8), Sirius Black's first break-in to Hogwarts (PA8), and Harry's name coming out of the Goblet of Fire (GF 16)." Finally, the Lexicon's etymological references, while occasionally inaccurate, offer one possible interpretation of the meaning and derivation of characters' names, even if not the meaning intended by Rowling. Thus, while not its primary purpose, the Lexicon does add some new insight, of whatever value, as to the Harry Potter works.

The transformative character of the Lexicon is diminished, however, because the Lexicon's use of the original Harry Potter works is not consistently transformative. The Lexicon's use lacks transformative character where the Lexicon entries fail to "minimize[] the expressive value" of the original expression. See Bill Graham Archives, 448 F.3d at 611 (finding evidence of transformative use where the defendant "minimized the expressive value of the reproduced images by combining them with a prominent timeline, textual material, and original graphical artwork to create a collage of text and images on each page of the book"). A finding of verbatim copying in excess of what is reasonably necessary diminishes a finding of a transformative use. See Campbell, 510 U.S. at 587, 114 S.Ct. 1164 (observing that "whether a substantial portion of the infringing work was copied verbatim from the copyrighted work . . . may reveal a dearth of transformative character" (internal quotation marks omitted)). As discussed more fully in analyzing the "amount and substantiality" factor, the Lexicon copies distinctive original language from the

Harry Potter works in excess of its otherwise legitimate purpose of creating a reference guide. Perhaps because Vander Ark is such a Harry Potter enthusiast, the Lexicon often lacks restraint in using Rowling's original expression for its inherent entertainment and aesthetic value. See Elvis Presley Enters., 349 F.3d at 629 (finding that where a film biography of Elvis Presley showed the plaintiffs' copyrighted clips of Elvis's television appearances without much interruption, "[t]he purpose of showing these clips likely goes beyond merely making a reference for a biography, but instead serves the same intrinsic entertainment value that is protected by Plaintiffs' copyrights").

The Lexicon also lacks transformative character where its value as a reference guide lapses. Although the Lexicon is generally useful, it cannot claim consistency in serving its purpose of pointing readers to information in the Harry Potter works. Some of the longest entries contain few or no citations to the Harry Potter works from which the material is taken. (See supra Findings of Fact; Pl. Ex. 28 (Suppl. Johnson Decl.) ¶ 16.) In these instances, the Lexicon's reference purposes are diminished.

While the transformative character of the secondary work is a central inquiry, the commercial or nonprofit nature of the secondary work is an explicit part of the first fair-use factor. 17 U.S.C. 107(1); Blanch, 467 F.3d at 253. Given that even the statutory examples of fair use are generally conducted for profit, courts often "do not make much of this point." Castle Rock, 150 F.3d at 141. The real concern behind the commercial nature inquiry is "the unfairness that arises when a secondary user makes unauthorized use of copyrighted material to capture significant revenues as a direct consequence of copying the original work." Blanch, 467 F.3d at 253. Courts will not find fair use when the secondary use "can fairly be characterized as a form of commercial exploitation," but "are more willing to find a secondary use fair when it produces a value that benefits the broader public interest." Id. In this case, Defendant's use of the copyrighted works is certainly for commercial gain. As the testimony of Rapoport and Vander Ark make clear, one of the Lexicon's greatest selling points is being the first companion guide to the Harry Potter series that will cover all seven novels. Seeking to capitalize on a market niche does not necessarily make Defendant's use non-transformative, but to the extent that Defendant seeks to "profit at least in part from the inherent entertainment value" of the original works, the commercial nature of the use weighs against a finding of fair use. Elvis Presley Enters., 349 F.3d at 628. To the extent that Defendant seeks to provide a useful reference guide to the Harry Potter novels that benefits the public, the use is fair, and its commercial nature only weighs slightly against a finding of fair use.

...

B. Amount and Substantiality of the Use

...

The Lexicon's use of copyrighted expression from Rowling's two companion books presents an easier determination. The Lexicon takes wholesale from these short books. See supra Findings of Fact. Depending on the purpose, using a substantial portion of a work, or even the whole thing, may be permissible. See, e.g., Perfect

10, 508 F.3d at 1167-68; Bill Graham Archives, 448 F.3d at 613; Nunez v. Caribbean Int'l News Corp., 235 F.3d 18, 24 (1st Cir.2000). In this case, however, the Lexicon's purpose is only slightly transformative of the companion books' original purpose. As a result, the amount and substantiality of the portion copied from the companion books weighs more heavily against a finding of fair use.

C. Nature of the Copyrighted Work

The second statutory fair use factor, the nature of the copyrighted work, recognizes that "some works are closer to the core of intended copyright protection than others." Campbell, 510 U.S. at 586, 114 S.Ct. 1164. It is well settled that creative and fictional works are generally more deserving of protection than factual works. Stewart v. Abend, d/b/a Authors Research Co., 495 U.S. 207, 237, 110 S.Ct. 1750, 109 L.Ed.2d 184 (1990) ("In general, fair use is more likely to be found in factual works than in fictional works."); Harper & Row, 471 U.S. at 563, 105 S.Ct. 2218 ("The law generally recognizes a greater need to disseminate factual works than works of fiction or fantasy."); Castle Rock, 150 F.3d at 143-144 (finding that the second factor favored plaintiff given the fictional nature of the copyrighted work); Twin Peaks, 996 F.2d at 1376 (stating that the second factor "must favor a creative and fictional work, no matter how successful"); Ty, Inc. v. Publ'ns Int'l, Ltd., 333 F.Supp.2d 705, 713 (N.D.Ill.2004) (recognizing that "creative works are deemed more deserving of protection than works that are more of diligence than of originality or inventiveness." (internal quotation marks omitted)). In creating the Harry Potter novels and the companion books, Rowling has given life to a wholly original universe of people, creatures, places, and things. (Tr. (Sorensen) at 504:7-15). Such highly imaginative and creative fictional works are close to the core of copyright protection, particularly where the character of the secondary work is not entirely transformative. See Castle Rock, 150 F.3d at 144; Twin Peaks, 996 F.2d at 1376; Paramount, 11 F.Supp.2d at 336. As a result, the second factor favors Plaintiffs.

D. Market Harm

The fourth statutory factor considers "the effect of the use upon the potential market for or value of the copyrighted work." 17 U.S.C. § 107(4). Courts must consider harm to "not only the primary market for the copyrighted work, but the current and potential market for derivative works" as well. Twin Peaks, 996 F.2d at 1377 (finding that fourth factor favored plaintiff where book about television series "may interfere with the primary market for the copyrighted works and almost certainly interferes with legitimate markets for derivative works"); see also Harper & Row, 471 U.S. at 568, 105 S.Ct. 2218. Potential derivative uses "include[] only those that creators of original works would in general develop or license others to develop." Campbell, 510 U.S. at 592, 114 S.Ct. 1164. The fourth factor will favor the copyright holder "if she can show a `traditional, reasonable, or likely to be developed' market for licensing her work." Ringgold, 126 F.3d at 81. In addition to evaluating the particular actions of the alleged infringer, the fourth factor examines "whether unrestricted and widespread conduct of the sort engaged in by the defendant. . . would result in a substantially adverse impact on the potential market for the original." Campbell, 510 U.S. at 590, 114 S.Ct. 1164 (omission in original) (internal quotation marks and citations omitted).

Plaintiffs presented expert testimony that the Lexicon would compete directly with, and impair the sales of, Rowling's planned encyclopedia by being first to market. (Tr. (Murphy) at 413:2-416:6, 417:21-418:9.) Defendant rebutted this evidence with its own expert who testified that publication of the Lexicon is "extremely unlikely" to affect the sales of any encyclopedia that Rowling might one day publish. (Id. (Harris) at 442:9-16.) This testimony does not bear on the determination of the fourth factor, however, because a reference guide to the Harry Potter works is not a derivative work; competing with Rowling's planned encyclopedia is therefore permissible. Notwithstanding Rowling's public statements of her intention to publish her own encyclopedia, the market for reference guides to the Harry Potter works is not exclusively hers to exploit or license, no matter the commercial success attributable to the popularity of the original works. See Twin Peaks, 996 F.2d at 1377 ("The author of `Twin Peaks' cannot preserve for itself the entire field of publishable works that wish to cash in on the `Twin Peaks' phenomenon"). The market for reference guides does not become derivative simply because the copyright holder seeks to produce or license one. Ty, Inc., 292 F.3d at 521; see also Castle Rock, 150 F.3d at 145 n. 11 ("[B]y developing or licensing a market for parody, news reporting, educational or other transformative uses of its own creative work, a copyrighted owner plainly cannot prevent others from entering those fair use markets"); Twin Peaks, 996 F.2d at 1377.

Furthermore, there is no plausible basis to conclude that publication of the Lexicon would impair sales of the Harry Potter novels. Plaintiffs' expert Suzanne Murphy, vice president and publisher of trade publishing and marketing at Scholastic, testified that in her opinion a child who read the Lexicon would be discouraged from reading the Harry Potter series because the Lexicon discloses key plot points and does not contain "spoiler alerts." (Tr. (Murphy) at 409:12-411:7.) Children may be an elusive market for book publishers, but it is hard to believe that a child, having read the Lexicon, would lose interest in reading (and thus his or her parents' interest in purchasing) the Harry Potter series. Because the Lexicon uses the Harry Potter series for a transformative purpose (though inconsistently), reading the Lexicon cannot serve as a substitute for reading the original novels; they are enjoyed for different purposes. The Lexicon is thus unlikely to serve as a market substitute for the Harry Potter series and cause market harm. Campbell, 510 U.S. at 591, 114 S.Ct. 1164 (stating that when "the second use is transformative, market substitution is at least less certain and market harm may not be so readily inferred"); see also Castle Rock, 150 F.3d at 145; Bill Graham Archives, 448 F.3d at 614-15. It seems unlikely that a publisher like HarperCollins would produce the Companion to Narnia (Pl. Ex. 62), which reveals storylines, plot twists, and the ultimate fates of the characters in C.S. Lewis's original works, if it expected the publication would reduce sales and enthusiasm for the original works. Accordingly, the Lexicon does not present any potential harm to the markets for the original Harry Potter works. See Bill Graham Archives, 448 F.3d at 614; Castle Rock, 150 F.3d at 145.

On the other hand, publication of the Lexicon could harm sales of Rowling's two companion books. Unless they sought to enjoy the companion books for their entertainment value alone, consumers who purchased the Lexicon would have scant incentive to purchase either of Rowling's companion books, as the information contained in these short works has been incorporated into the Lexicon almost wholesale. (Tr. (Murphy) at 419:10-19; id. (Rowling) at 104:2-11.) Because the Lexicon's use of the companion books is only marginally transformative, the Lexicon is likely to supplant the market for the companion books. See Campbell, 510 U.S. at 591, 114 S.Ct. 1164 (stating that "when a commercial use amounts to mere duplication of the entirety of an original, it clearly `supersede[s] the objects' of the original and serves as a market replacement for it, making it likely that cognizable harm to the original will occur" (citation omitted)). At trial, Vander Ark himself recognized that although "[t]here's no way that someone's going to take an encyclopedia of [the Harry Potter novels] and think of it as a replacement" (Tr. (Vander Ark) at 287:14-16), using the companion books without "replac[ing] Ms. Rowling's encyclopedia content" presents "quite a challenge" (id. at 287:22-25). In view of the market harm to Rowling's companion books, the fourth factor tips in favor of Plaintiffs.

Additionally, the fourth factor favors Plaintiffs if publication of the Lexicon would impair the market for derivative works that Rowling is entitled or likely to license. Ringgold, 126 F.3d at 81. Although there is no supporting testimony, one potential derivative market that would reasonably be developed or licensed by Plaintiffs is use of the songs and poems in the Harry Potter novels. Because Plaintiffs would reasonably license the musical production or print publication of those songs and poems, Defendant unfairly harms this derivative market by reproducing verbatim the songs and poems without a license.

* * *

The fair-use factors, weighed together in light of the purposes of copyright law, fail to support the defense of fair use in this case. The first factor does not completely weigh in favor of Defendant because although the Lexicon has a transformative purpose, its actual use of the copyrighted works is not consistently transformative. Without drawing a line at the amount of copyrighted material that is reasonably necessary to create an A-to-Z reference guide, many portions of the Lexicon take more of the copyrighted works than is reasonably necessary in relation to the Lexicon's purpose. Thus, in balancing the first and third factors, the balance is tipped against a finding of fair use. The creative nature of the copyrighted works and the harm to the market for Rowling's companion books weigh in favor of Plaintiffs. In striking the balance between the property rights of original authors and the freedom of expression of secondary authors, reference guides to works of literature should generally be encouraged by copyright law as they provide a benefit readers and students; but to borrow from Rowling's overstated views, they should not be permitted to "plunder" the works of original authors (Tr. (Rowling) at 62:25-63:3), "without paying the customary price" Harper & Row, 471 U.S. at 562, 105 S.Ct. 2218, lest original authors lose incentive to create new works that will also benefit the public interest (see Tr. (Rowling) at 93:20-94:13).

CONCLUSION

For the foregoing reasons, Plaintiffs have established copyright infringement of the Harry Potter series, Fantastic Beasts & Where to Find Them, and Quidditch Through the Ages by J.K. Rowling. Defendant has failed to establish its affirmative defense of fair use. Defendant's publication of the Lexicon (Doc. No. 22) is hereby permanently enjoined, and Plaintiffs are awarded statutory damages of $6,750.00.

IT IS SO ORDERED.

860 F. Supp. 158 (1994)

WILLIAMS v. CRICHTON

United States District Court, S.D. New York

McKENNA, District Judge.

On September 30, 1993, plaintiff Geoffrey T. Williams ("Plaintiff" or "Williams") brought suit against defendants Michael Crichton ("Crichton"), Alfred A. Knopf, Inc., Random House, Inc., Universal Studios, Inc., MCA, Inc., Amblin Entertainment, Inc., Steven Spielberg, and David Koepp (collectively "Defendants") alleging copyright infringement under the Copyright Act of 1976, as amended, 17 U.S.C. § 101, et seq., and related claims for an accounting. Plaintiff complains that Defendants' works, the Jurassic Park novel (the "Novel") and the Jurassic Park motion picture (the "Movie"), infringe upon Plaintiff's earlier copyrighted works. Presently before the Court is Defendants' motion for summary judgment. For the reasons set out below, Defendants' motion is granted.

...

II.

Construing the record in the light most favorable to Plaintiff, and drawing all inferences in Plaintiff's favor, Delaware & Hudson Ry. Co. v. Consolidated Rail Corp., 902 F.2d 174, 177 (2d Cir. 1990), cert. denied, 500 U.S. 928, 111 S. Ct. 2041, 114 L. Ed. 2d 125 (1991), the facts are as follows.

Plaintiff Geoffrey Williams is the author of books intended for children between the ages of six and eleven years old. In his books, Williams incorporates and presents natural and scientific phenomena in the context of fictional adventure stories.

During the years 1985 through 1988, Williams created and published a series of four original copyrighted works of fiction for children bearing the following titles: (i) "Dinosaur World," created and first published in 1985 ("Dinosaur World" or "Book I"); (ii) "Lost in Dinosaur World," created in 1986 and first published in 1987 ("Lost in Dinosaur World" or "Book II"); (iii) "Explorers in Dinosaur World," created in 1987 and first published in 1988 ("Explorers in Dinosaur World" or "Book III"); and (iv) "Saber Tooth: A Dinosaur World Adventure," created and first published in 1988 ("Saber Tooth" or "Book IV") (together, the "Dinosaur World books"). Plaintiff applied for and was issued a Certificate of Registration by the Register of Copyrights for Book I in December 1988 (registration number TX-1-966-153); Book II in August 1993 (number TX-3-598-943); Book III in March 1988 (number TX-2-294-611);[1] and Book IV in November 1988 (number TX-2-541-662).[2] Plaintiff represents that collectively the Dinosaur World books have sold over 800,000 copies in the United States and elsewhere.

The setting of each of Plaintiff's children's books is "Dinosaur World," a place where visitors can "tour and observe dinosaurs and other pre-historic animals in a presumably safe, man-made, controlled environment." Pl.'s Mem. Opp'n Defs.' Mot. Summ. J. ("Pl. Br.") at 7. Plaintiff's four children's books do not comprise a series of works in the sense of portraying the same characters or ongoing incidents and events in each book. Nonetheless, Plaintiff, citing Warner Bros., Inc. v. American Broadcasting Cos., Inc., 530 F. Supp. 1187, 1193 (S.D.N.Y.1982) ("Warner Bros. I"), aff'd, 720 F.2d 231 (2d Cir.1983), and Sid & Marty Krofft Television v. McDonald's Corp., 562 F.2d 1157 (9th Cir.1977), urges the Court to consider the works in their totality for the purpose of assessing his infringement claim against Defendants. The Court does not reach the issue of whether Plaintiff's works should be considered collectively, however, because, even so considered, the Court finds that there is no similarity between the parties respective works substantial enough to allow Plaintiff's claim to survive Defendants' motion.

Book I

Plaintiff's first book, Dinosaur World (29 pages), is a story about a visit by a young girl, Mary, and her father to Dinosaur World. When they arrive, they see many unfamiliar things: for example, plants that look like giant ferns, smoke rising from a volcano, and flying creatures that are not birds.

At the ticket booth, "Dad" pays the admission to a girl who hands him a small portable radio guide. The girl reads to Dad and Mary from the Official Dinosaur World Guide Book and tells them to observe all posted regulations, stay on the marked path, and for their own safety not to feed the dinosaurs.

As Mary and her father begin their tour, dozens of carnivorous dinosaurs "smaller than a chicken," Pl.'s Exh. A at 7, called compsognathus, run past Mary and her father. The radio guide informs them about these prehistoric animals.

Further down the path, Mary and her father hear waves as they approach a reproduction of the North American inland sea the park calls "Dinosaur Sea." They observe flying dinosaurs (pteranodons and pterodactyls), a "giant" turtle, and a predecessor of modern crocodiles (a tylosaurus). Continuing on the path, Mary and her father observe a series of other dinosaurs, with the radio guide supplying information. The two leave Dinosaur World soon after they observe, in a fenced pasture area, a tyrannosaurus rex stampede a group of triceratops dinosaurs.

In Book I, there is no menace or attack on humans by animals, and no fear of any danger to visitors. Plaintiff concedes that this book, viewed independently of the other Dinosaur World books, is not infringed by Defendants' works. Plaintiff asserts, however, the following, limited, assertedly protectible, similarities as indicative of infringement when the Dinosaur World books are viewed as a whole: (a) the first dinosaurs encountered by the reader are chicken-sized carnivorous animals (procompsognathus in the Jurassic Park novel) seen by a young girl on a beach, and (b) the stampede of a herd of dinosaurs chased by a tyrannosaurus rex.

Book II

Plaintiff's Lost in Dinosaur World (30 pages) was written for older children than the audience intended for Book I; consequently, Book II presents a somewhat more "sophisticated" and detailed setting for the Dinosaur World park. There is a Petting Zoo and next to it the Dinosaur World Nursery in a building where ten dinosaur eggs have hatched the week before the story begins. Visitors receive at the entrance gate a map of the park and a radio guide to answer questions about the animals. Visitors can tour the park either by walking on marked paths or by riding the "T-Rex Express" through the dinosaur time periods represented in the park, observing the animals from the safety of the train.

In Plaintiff's characterization, similar to the Dinosaur World books generally, the story of Lost in Dinosaur World "has as its theme a presumably safe place inhabited by dinosaurs in a controlled environment where adults and children can visit, tour about and safely observe dinosaurs." Pl. Br. at 11. The setting includes tall pines rising overhead, along with exotic ferns, gingko and monkey puzzle trees; giant pterosaurs and pteranodons circling in the blue sky, their eerie, high-pitched squeals carrying across the distance; roars, grunts and growls coming from deep in the forest, made by who-knows-what-kind of wild creatures....

Pl.'s Exh. B at 2. Despite the supposedly safe environment, Plaintiff asserts, "there is immediately a mood and feeling of mystery and menace surrounding the park." Pl. Br. at 11.

Book II begins with two children, Tim and Mary McDunn, and their parents readying to visit Dinosaur World for the first time. The boy's mother assures him: "We're just going to Dinosaur World, Tim. Not to the jungle or someplace dangerous." Pl.'s Exh. B at 1. Tim and his father discuss the first thing that Tim wants to do at Dinosaur World, which is to ride the T-Rex Express, and then to see an allosaur ("the scariest animal in the park," id.), a dinosaur assertedly similar to a tyrannosaurus rex.

After they arrive at Dinosaur World, the McDunn family receives their tickets, a map of the park and a small radio guide to answer any questions they may have about the animals. They discuss whether to first visit the nursery or to ride the T-Rex Express. Tim is impatient and wants to go directly to the train ride. His father, preferring to begin at the nursery, admonishes him: "Tim, it won't take but a few minutes, and I'm sure there'll be plenty of exciting things for you to do today." The narration continues: "Little did Mr. McDunn know how true that was." Id. at 4.

The story relates that the family then observes their first dinosaur, a brachiosaur, eating leaves from nearby trees. The radio guide explains that the brachiosaur is the largest land animal that ever lived. The family then enters the nursery, where the air is warm and humid, and views large proteceratop eggs.

Next, the family takes the T-Rex Express rail tour of Dinosaur World. Only Tim's ticket is for the "SuperTour," which covers all the geologic time periods during which dinosaurs lived (the Triassic, Jurassic, and Cretaceous eras); the rest of the family is to view only the Triassic period. "After that Tim would be on his own. He was very excited." Id. at 8.

During the ride through the Triassic period, the train passes by the shore of the Dinosaur Sea where it is approached by a shrieking, twenty-five foot sea reptile (a nothosaur) with "needle-sharp teeth" and a neck that moves "like a snake." Id. at 11. Tim is left "a little frightened and wondering how much excitement the rest of the trip would bring." Id.

As the Triassic tour ends, Tim's family leaves the train, and his father hands him the radio and warns:

"This is your first trip here, so be very careful not to lose your guide. Whatever you need to know, just ask. And remember, no matter what happens, don't get off the train."

Id. at 14. The narrative continues:

Then they all waved good-bye. Tim watched until they disappeared from sight around a curve. He couldn't help feeling just a little lonesome as he continued his adventure.

Id. As the train continues through the Jurassic landscape, Tim, now alone, doing "something that would change his whole day," id. at 15, accidentally bumps the radio off the train, where it falls under the tail of a stegosaur, a large, herbivorous dinosaur. When Tim retrieves the radio, the train leaves without him. Alone in the park, Tim is warned by the radio guide about the allosaur, an animal "that stood over twenty feet tall, had teeth like steak knives and a disposition like a bucket of rattlesnakes." Id. at 18. "[N]ow Dinosaur World seemed mysterious. Strange. Perhaps even ... dangerous." Id. at 20.

Walking on his own, Tim encounters a lost baby duckbill dinosaur (parasaurolophus). Tim feeds it, and the dinosaur follows him through the park. An allosaur soon emerges from the trees to chase Tim and the baby dinosaur. Closely pursued, Tim and the baby dinosaur escape into the Dinosaur Sea, just ahead of the allosaur that "was furious at seeing his dinner just out of reach." Id. at 14.[4]

After other incidents, the story ends when another roaring dinosaur turns out to be the T-Rex Express returning to take Tim back to his parents.

Book III

Plaintiff's Explorers in Dinosaur World (30 pages) is intended for audiences approximately eleven years old. The story centers on two children, Peter and his sister Wendy who, by virtue of Wendy's luck in a radio station contest, win the opportunity to preview the opening of "Dinosaur World's newest attraction Pangaea the island of mystery in the middle of Dinosaur Sea." Pl.'s Exh. C at 5.

Peter, a dinosaur enthusiast, and his sister Wendy are to spend a weekend at Pangaea exploring the jungles and beaches guided by Jake DuMel, a key figure in designing Pangaea. Jake greets the children as they arrive at Dinosaur World, and walks them past the Petting Zoo, the snack stands and the Nursery as they make their way to the boat dock. Uniformed Dinosaur World staff are also present: engineers for the T-Rex Express, keepers of the Nursery, gardeners, and staff scientists are mentioned in the text. On their way to the dock, Peter, Wendy and Jake see various types of dinosaurs, some of which are being monitored by staff taking notes.

Pangaea, about a half-mile from the mainland, appears "ghostly and mysterious." Id. at 10. Jake checks the children's backpacks and gear, including a radio. "We need it to call for help if we get into any trouble," Peter says to his sister. Jake adds, "Dinosaur World is full of surprises, not trouble. Still, you can't be too careful...." Id. at 11.

As they cross the water to the island, the party is pursued by an elasmosaur, a sea creature with a neck over 20 feet long. The serpent-like dinosaur arches over the boat with sharp teeth in view. The elasmosaur, however, is distracted by other prey, and the party escapes. Before they reach the island, the party also evades another sea dinosaur, a kronosaur, which roars "in frustration and anger" as it watches "its breakfast escape." Id. at 15.

Jake and the children then reach Pangaea, "a world impossibly old and, at the same time, wondrously new," id. at 16, where they are the first visitors. As they reach the shore, they first see an apetosaur "bigger than a moving van," id., and then a saltopus dinosaur, "no bigger than a cat," runs by "on its hind legs, bent over, balancing itself with its long tail." Id. at 17.

On Pangaea, Jake warns the children about deinonychus dinosaurs, carnivores "ten feet long [that] run like the wind, hunt in packs like wolves, are always hungry, and have extremely long, sharp claws." Id. at 18. "You can't see them from here," Jake says, "[b]ut there are special fences that keep dangerous dinosaurs from wandering into the areas where we'll be going." Id.

After an uneventful night camping on the island, Jake receives a warning on the portable radio:

"Security reports a break in the perimeter fencing on the east side of the lake."

"How bad is it, Main Base?"

"Bad enough. Tracking computers indicate a pack of deinonychus is on the loose, and Jake ... they're heading your way. Suggest you make for the chopper pad. We have a bird on its way now. You should have plenty of time to make it. Do you copy?"

"We're on our way. This is Pangaea Camp One over and out." Jake was all business now. "You heard him. Let's go, kids."Id. at 24.

As they seek to reach the helicopter pad, the party is confronted by a large dinosaur in their path, an ankylosaur, protected by bony plates, thick skin, spikes, and a club-like tail. As the deinonychus approach, the ankylosaur fights them off, enabling the characters to escape to the helicopter and depart from the island.

Book IV

Plaintiff's Saber Tooth (30 pages), written in 1988 for children of the approximate age of six, is set in a not yet opened area of Dinosaur World, "Prehistoria."

The story's children, Mimi and Barry, sneak into the new area and board an automated cable car and ride through landscape from the Cenozoic period, an era after dinosaurs became extinct. The cable car is equipped with an automated recorded guide which provides information about prehistoric animals when a button is pushed next to the animal's picture.

The children are the first outsiders to visit Prehistoria. On their tour, they observe and come into contact with sabertooth cats and other prehistoric animals.

The only elements of similarity Plaintiff asserts between Jurassic Park and Book IV is the setting of an animal park for prehistoric animals visited by children and the automated technology used in the cable cars. Plaintiff concedes that Book IV, considered alone, has not been infringed.

Jurassic Park

The Jurassic Park novel (400 pages), intended for an adult readership, was first published in 1990, and the two hour movie of the same title was released in 1993.

Like Plaintiff's works, Jurassic Park also centers around a type of dinosaur zoo. However, both the Movie and the Novel contain substantially more sophisticated plot and character development than Plaintiff's works. For instance, in Jurassic Park, the creation of the park involves issues of genetic engineering and financial intrigue that nowhere appear in Plaintiff's works. On the contrary, in all of Plaintiff's works, the establishment of the park is a given; in Jurassic Park, the issue of how the park was, and whether it should be, developed is a substantial aspect of, if not central to, engagement of audience interest. The respective tales also end in fundamentally different manners: in each of Plaintiff's stories, all the characters emerge unharmed indeed, in Plaintiff's works there is never any physical contact between a human and a dinosaur and, there being no serious permanent safety questions, the park exhibits remain open or scheduled to open to the general public. For instance, in Book II, the sum total of the effects of Tim's adventures is that they "change his whole day." Pl.'s Exh. B at 15. By the end of Jurassic Park, on the other hand, several characters have been killed or wounded, and the park is an obvious safety disaster, never to open.

III.

Copyright infringement may be established by "showing (a) that the defendant had access to the copyrighted work and (b) the substantial similarity of protectible material in the two works." Kregos v. Associated Press, 3 F.3d 656, 662 (2d

Cir.1993). cert. denied, ___ U.S. ___, 114 S. Ct. 1056, 127 L. Ed. 2d 376 (1994) (citations omitted). For purposes of the instant motion only, Defendants concede access to Plaintiff's works. Mem. Law Supp. Defs.' Mot. Summ. J. at 26. Thus, in order to decide Defendants' motion, the Court turns to the question of substantial similarity.

Traditionally, summary judgment was discouraged in copyright infringement cases because "substantial similarity" is customarily a close question of fact. Hoehling v. Universal City Studios, Inc., 618 F.2d 972, 977 (2d Cir.) (citing Arnstein v. Porter, 154 F.2d 464, 468 and 474 (2d Cir.1946)), cert. denied, 449 U.S. 841, 101 S. Ct. 121, 66 L. Ed. 2d 49 (1980). However, the Second Circuit has since "recognized that a district court may determine non-infringement as a matter of law on a motion for summary judgment, either because the similarity between two works concerns only `non-copyrightable elements of the plaintiff's work,' or because no reasonable jury, properly instructed, could find that the two works are substantially similar." Warner Bros. v. American Broadcasting Cos., 720 F.2d 231, 240 (2d Cir.1983) ("Warner Bros. II") (emphasis in original, citations omitted). See also Arica Inst., Inc. v. Palmer, 970 F.2d 1067, 1072 (2d Cir.1992).

"The basic issues concerning [a] copyright infringement claim are whether the ... works are substantially similar so as to support an inference of copying and whether the lack of substantial similarity is so clear as to fall outside the range of reasonably disputed fact questions requiring resolution by a jury." Warner Bros. II at 239. "The similarity to be assessed must concern the expression of ideas, not the ideas themselves," id. (citing Reyher v. Children's Television Workshop, 533 F.2d 87, 90 (2d Cir.), cert. denied, 429 U.S. 980, 97 S. Ct. 492, 50 L. Ed. 2d 588 (1976)), and Nichols v. Universal Picture Corp., 45 F.2d 119, 121 (2d. Cir.) (L. Hand, J.), cert. denied, 282 U.S. 902, 51 S. Ct. 216, 75 L. Ed. 795 (1931), "a distinction easier to assert than to apply," Warner Bros. II, 720 F.2d at 239, and necessarily an ad hoc enterprise. Durham Indus., Inc. v. Tomy Corp., 630 F.2d 905, 912 (2d Cir.1980) (quoting Peter Pan Fabrics, Inc. v. Martin Weiner Corp., 274 F.2d 487, 489 (2d Cir.1960)).

"The test for substantial similarity is most concretely stated as `whether an average lay observer would recognize the alleged copy as having been appropriated from the copyrighted work.'" Smith v. Weinstein, 578 F. Supp. 1297, 1302 (S.D.N.Y.) (quoting Ideal Toy Corp. v. Fab-Lu, Ltd., 360 F.2d 1021, 1022 (2d Cir.1966)), aff'd, 738 F.2d 419 (2d Cir.1984); see also Durham Indus., 630 F.2d at 911-12; Silverman v. CBS, Inc., 632 F. Supp. 1344, 1351-52 (S.D.N.Y.1986); Steinberg v. Columbia Pictures Industries, Inc., 663 F. Supp. 706, 711 (S.D.N.Y.1987). Only similarities of significance are to be considered, Durham, 630 F.2d at 912, and in comparing two works, a court must ignore a work's unprotectible aspects. Folio Impressions, Inc. v. Byer California, 937 F.2d 759, 765-66 (2d Cir.1991); Laureyssens v. Idea Group, Inc., 964 F.2d 131, 141 (2d Cir.1992); Novak v. National Broadcasting Co., Inc., 716 F. Supp. 745, 752 (S.D.N.Y.1989).

While Plaintiff concedes that the idea of a dinosaur zoo is unprotectible, Pl. Br. at 7, he nonetheless asserts that a factual issue regarding substantial similarity is to be found in a comparison of the following elements of the works at issue.

Total Concept and Feel

In comparing the "total concept and feel" of works, similarities in "mood, detail or characterization" must be considered. Reyher, 533 F.2d at 91-92. Consideration of "total concept and feel" is especially appropriate in an infringement claim involving inherently less complex children's works. Id. at 91. Where there is a marked difference in total concept and feel, summary judgment is appropriate. Id. at 92; see also Denker v. Uhry, 820 F. Supp. 722, 731 (S.D.N.Y.1992), aff'd, 996 F.2d 301 (2d Cir. 1993).

Plaintiff contends that the "total concept and feel" of his works is substantially similar to the menacing mood conveyed in Jurassic Park. The Court must disagree. Although Plaintiff's works contain certain chase scenes and "near misses," the overall tone and presentation of the work leaves the reader confident that the characters will emerge unharmed, as they indeed do. Instead of the real threat and actual incidents of violence found throughout Jurassic Park, the adventure park setting of Plaintiff's works functions to instill in the reader the feeling that, however exciting the adventures might become, no harm will come to the characters.[6] In fact, this confidence is only bolstered when the Dinosaur World books are read together: as the reader approaches each new story, the memory of the happy endings of the prior tales strongly suggests a similar result about to unfold.

Thus, although Plaintiff contends that his works, to a child, are menacing, terrifying and violent, there is in fact never violence done to any of Plaintiff's characters, and the underlying sense of security that pervades these works would preclude a reasonable jury from finding its mood substantially similar to that of Defendants' works.

Theme

Copyright protection does not extend to thematic concepts or scenes which must necessarily follow from similar plot situations. Smith, 578 F. Supp. at 1302 (quoting Reyher, 533 F.2d at 91). "In assessing claims of substantial similarity, courts ... must decide `whether the similarities shared by the works are something more than mere generalized idea or theme.'" Walker v. Time Life Films, Inc., 784 F.2d 44, 48-49 (2d Cir.1986) (quoting Warner Bros. v. American Broadcasting Co., Inc., 654 F.2d 204, 208) (2d Cir.1981). Themes commonly repeated in a certain genre are not protectible by copyright, American Direct Marketing, Inc. v. Azad Int'l, Inc., 783 F. Supp. 84, 95 (E.D.N.Y. 1992), as no one can own the basic idea for a story. Berkic v. Crichton, 761 F.2d 1289, 1293 (9th Cir.), cert. denied, 474 U.S. 826, 106 S. Ct. 85, 88 L. Ed. 2d 69 (1985). Rather, similarities must be found in plot, characters, dialogue, mood, setting and pace. Reyher, 533 F.2d at 91.

Although Plaintiff concedes that Jurassic Park "is a much more complex work than that of plaintiff's works for children," Pl.Br. at 32, he nonetheless contends that the works at issue are substantially similar with respect to theme. This common theme, Plaintiff asserts, "is that a visit to, and tour of, an animal park for prehistoric dinosaurs (if one were to exist) would not only be wondrous and exciting, but also very dangerous." Pl. Br. at 32.

The Court cannot agree that this description accurately portrays the theme of Jurassic Park, or even, necessarily, Plaintiff's works. Plaintiff's representation of Jurassic Park entirely abstracts the theme park adventure from its context and omits any reference to its fundamental story elements of genetic engineering, ego, and greed. See Jones v. CBS, Inc., 733 F. Supp. 748, 753 (S.D.N.Y.1990) ("[A]ll fictional plots, when abstracted to a sufficient level of generalization, can be described as similar to other *plots"). Indeed, a fairer representation of Jurassic Park's theme is that meddling with nature can be disastrous, and that such activities are only compounded when judgment is clouded by greed and other human shortcomings. No such theme is evident in any of Plaintiff's stories. Rather, the essence of Plaintiff's work is more fairly described as a simple vehicle to introduce the subject of dinosaurs and to satisfy childhood curiosity about the creatures. See also Reyher, 533 F.2d at 92-93 (different moral emphases may also distinguish works).

Setting

Similarity in the basic setting of a work of fiction is not by itself actionable, Burroughs v. Metro-Goldwyn-Mayer, Inc., 683 F.2d 610, 626 (2d Cir.1982); although it may be a factor in a determination of substantial similarity, setting alone can not constitute infringement. See also Alexander v. Haley, 460 F. Supp. 40, 45 (S.D.N.Y.1978) (setting and theme, "the skeleton of a creative work rather than the flesh, are not protected by the copyright laws").

Nonetheless, Plaintiff points to several similarities in the setting of the respective works. Indeed, the settings of the works are such that a reasonable jury could find them substantially similar.[10] These similarities, however, all flow from the concededly uncopyrightable concept of a dinosaur zoo. Pl. Br. at 7. As such, the corresponding scenic elements are scenes a faire that "follow naturally from the work's theme rather than the author's creativity." Computer Assocs. Int'l, Inc. v. Altai, Inc., 982 F.2d 693, 715 (2d Cir.1992) (quoting 3 M. & D. Nimmer, Nimmer on Copyright § 13.03[F][3], at 13-65), and are likewise unprotectible. See also Reyher, 533 F.2d at 91 ("Copyrights, then, do not protect thematic concepts or scenes which necessarily must follow from certain similar plot situations"); Burroughs, 683 F.2d at 627 ("[n]aturally there are certain similarities required by Tarzan's character and the jungle setting"); Walker, 784 F.2d at 50 (scenes a faire, i.e., "scenes that necessarily result from the choice of a setting or situation," and "`stock themes' commonly linked to a particular genre," are not protected by copyright); Berkic, 761 F.2d at 1293 ("all situations and incidents which flow naturally from a basic plot premise, so-called scenes a faire," are not protected against copying); Alexander, 460 F. Supp. at 45 ("[a]ttempted escapes, flights through the woods pursued by baying dogs, the sorrowful or happy singing of slaves, the atrocity of the buying and selling of human beings, and other miseries" are all scenes a faire, "indispensable, or at least standard, in the treatment of a given topic").

Thus, although there are certainly similarities to be found between the works' settings, as these all "flow naturally from the basic plot premises" of a dinosaur zoo, such similarities cannot support Plaintiff's infringement claim.

Time Sequence

Plaintiff argues that there is substantial similarity between the time sequences of the works at issue, arguing that "[a]ll of the action involving the children takes place within 24 hours at the dinosaur park." Pl. Br. at 35. Plaintiff, however, is able to truncate Jurassic Park to a single day's action only by restricting his consideration to action which involves the children, characters whom Plaintiff portrays as central to Defendants' works. Such a restriction, however, requires one to ignore not only important action contained in Jurassic Park that proceeds the park episodes, but also important implied and reported background concerning scientific research, park financing, recruitment of key park personnel, mining activity to provide dinosaur DNA, and so forth. Moreover, Plaintiff's characterization cuts off an implied time sequence trajectory concerning what the future will bring in a world for the first time inhabited simultaneously by humans and unconfined dinosaurs.

Pace

Viewed in a light most favorable to Plaintiff, the Court believes there is a basis to find similarity between the pace at which Jurassic Park and Plaintiff's Book III proceed. These works entail, at least in part, quick transitions from one dinosaur confrontation to another, punctuated by a hasty helicopter escape. Without more, however, such similarity is insufficient to create an issue of overall substantial similarity between the works.

Characters

With respect to their characters, the works are quite distinct. Plaintiff here again attempts to preserve the issue of substantial similarity by confining his consideration to the role of the children (Tim and Alexis in Jurassic Park, Peter and Wendy in Book III), along with their respective guides (Dr. Grant and Jake DuMel). Plaintiff asserts the following similarities:

Both boys are presented as dinosaur enthusiasts; in both works, the respective guides are knowledgeable about dinosaurs. Both boys are eager to talk about dinosaurs with the respective experts, and Dr. Grant's movie portrayal, Plaintiff asserts, dovetails with that of Jake DuMel: both are intelligent, rugged adventurers who are friendly and somewhat paternalistic toward the children.

The children in both works are brother and sister, and in both works camp out with their guide on the park island. They are together when threatened by dangerous dinosaurs, and at the end of both stories, both parties arrive safely at the helicopter pad as a result of the combined efforts of the children and their accompanying adult.

Even accepting Plaintiff's character descriptions as accurate, the characters of the works nonetheless fall far short of the substantial similarity required to preserve a factual question for trial. This shortcoming is twofold.

First, Plaintiff has artificially limited his claims to a select few of the Jurassic Park characters. Upon consideration of the many other characters in evidence in both the Novel and the Movie, it is apparent that Jurassic Park presents a universe of characters quantitatively far richer than anything attempted in any of the Dinosaur World stories.

Second, even considering only those characters Plaintiff discusses, the characters of the Dinosaur World books are much more thinly developed than those of Jurassic Park. No character infringement claim can succeed, however, unless Plaintiff's original work sufficiently developed the characters at issue. Smith, 578 F. Supp. at 1303 (quoting Warner Bros. I, 530 F.Supp. at 1193). See also Bevan v. Columbia Broadcasting System, 329 F. Supp. 601, 605-606 (S.D.N.Y.1971) (Hogan's Heroes does not infringe upon Stalag 17, though both feature a prison camp guard named Sergeant Schultz). Here, neither Wendy or Peter, nor any of Plaintiff's characters are well-developed enough to justify protection.

In the Jurassic Park novel, Tim and Alexis are brought to Jurassic Park as part of their grandfather Hammond's strategy to influence the decision about the park's safety, and their parents' divorce figures into the story as the pretext for their presence in the park during its inspection. Wendy and Peter, on the other hand, are at the park as contest winners, have no preexisting familial or personal relationship to anyone affiliated with the park and, other than Peter's enthusiasm for dinosaurs, they bring no helpful specialized skills or knowledge with them to the park. By contrast, in the Novel, Tim's knowledge of computers is key to keeping raptors from arriving on the mainland, while in the Movie, all the characters are benefited by Alexis' computer acumen in restoring park security systems.

Further, the children's relationship with their respective "guides" varies significantly. Although by the end of the works, the respective relationships could be described as "friendly," in Jurassic Park, the relationship in no way begins as such. In Jurassic Park, the children are thrown together with Dr. Grant solely as a result of the disasters that beset the park. Moreover, the association of Dr. Grant and the children in the Movie includes an ironic element, as Grant's discomfort with children has been foretold in prior discussions with his colleague and paramour, Dr. Ellie Sattler, about whether to have children. In Book III, on the other hand, Jake DuMel's relationship as the children's personal tour guide is planned, and DuMel's demeanor toward the children is appropriately polite and cordial from the outset. In contrast with Dr. Grant's extensive paleontology credentials, we know nothing of DuMel's professional training, romantic life, or feelings about raising children.

Thus, only three of Jurassic Park's major characters can be found to have any analog in the Dinosaur World stories. Moreover, even these three, beyond their superficial similarity to certain of Plaintiff's characters, are much more fully developed in Jurassic Park. As Learned Hand instructed, "the less developed the the characters, the less they can be copyrighted; that is the penalty an author must bear for marking them too indistinctly." Nichols, 45 F.2d at 121. Consequently, the Court concludes that no reasonable jury could find substantial similarity between the characters of the works at issue.

Sequence of Events

Plaintiff also claims that the sequence of events between his four works and the Jurassic Park movie and novel is "strikingly similar." Pl.Br. at 36. In support of this contention, Plaintiff cites the following events:

In Book III and Jurassic Park, two children have the opportunity to tour a dinosaur theme park prior to its opening for the general public. In Book I and in the Novel, the first dinosaurs encountered by the readers are small, and compared in size to a chicken, and in Book III and the Novel, Plaintiff asserts, the first dinosaur is described as walking "on its hind legs" and balancing itself on its large tail. Pl.s' Exh. C at 17; Defs.' Exh. 5 at 14.[12] In Book II and the Movie, the first dinosaur the visitors see in the park is a brachiosaur eating from a tree. Both Plaintiff's Book III and the Novel describe the respective characters' first arrival at the theme parks as entering a "new world." Pl.s' Exh. C at 16; Defs.' Exh. 5 at 85. Tours described in Book II and Jurassic Park are preceded by visits to humid nurseries, and where (in Book II and the Novel) one of the children expresses interest in lingering to play with the baby dinosaurs before proceeding with the rest of the tour.

In Books I and IV and Jurassic Park, visitors tour the park in trains, cable cars, and automated cars, respectively, and are informed by radio guides or prerecorded announcements; in both Book IV and the Movie, visitors can access information by touching a screen or button corresponding to an animal's picture.

In Books II and III and in Jurassic Park, the climactic action scenes begin after the tours are underway. In Book II, Tim's difficulties *170 begin when his radio falls and breaks; in Jurassic Park, trouble starts after the park-wide break-down of the two-way radio system. In both Book II and Jurassic Park, the stranded characters are without transportation when they first encounter a large dinosaur (an allosaur in Book II, and a tyrannosaur in Jurassic Park). While the children in all the works "escape being eaten," Pl.Br. at 40, in Jurassic Park, other members of the party are not so fortunate, and even the children do not escape physical trauma when their vehicle is destroyed.

In Book III and Jurassic Park, control fences break down, allowing dinosaurs to roam the parks unrestricted. Both the Novel and Book III contain scenes in which the children and their respective guides are in a boat and threatened by a large dinosaur which is ultimately distracted by other prey. Both Book I and the Movie contain scenes of smaller dinosaurs stampeded by a tyrannosaur. In Book III and Jurassic Park, parties comprised of children and their guides spend one night in the wild, the audience is initially startled by a dinosaur which turns out to be herbivorous. The next day, in both Book III and Jurassic Park, the visitors escape velociraptors in part due to the intervention of another dinosaur, and the parties reach safety when a helicopter takes them from the island. Only Book III's overnight, however, can fairly be characterized as "camping out," as Plaintiff does; in Jurassic Park, after a series of calamities, including the death and injury of fellow visitors, and the collapse of park safety features, the children and Dr. Grant spend the night hiding in a tree (Movie) or maintenance shed (Novel).

Plaintiff's comparison of these highly selective, scattered details, however, is not enough to warrant a finding of substantial similarity between the works. Walker, 784 F.2d at 50; Burroughs, 683 F.2d at 624 ("the few purported similarities either

268

are so general as to be meaningless, or are not similarities at all"); see also Litchfield v. Spielberg, 736 F.2d 1352, 1356 (9th Cir.1984), cert. denied, 470 U.S. 1052, 105 S. Ct. 1753, 84 L. Ed. 2d 817 (1985) (such lists of similarities are "inherently subjective and unreliable," particularly where "the list emphasizes random similarities scattered throughout the works").

For instance, Plaintiff cites incidents involving "chicken-sized" dinosaurs occurring in both authors' books as evidence of the respective works' similarity. These incidents, however, signal the works' fundamental differences: in Plaintiff's work (Book I), the chicken-sized dinosaurs are simply an amusing sight; in the Novel, the chicken allusion is part of an early scene culminating in a violent attack on a child, signalling to the audience danger at the outset. Moreover, in the Novel, this incident has occurred on the mainland outside the park's boundaries. Thus, the Jurassic Park audience is left with questions concerning compromised human safety even beyond the borders of the park itself. Nonetheless, in his attempt to assert substantial similarity, Plaintiff represents only the respective dinosaurs' size and how they use their tails in locomotion. Pl.Br. at 36-37. See, e.g., Bevan, 329 F. Supp. at 605 (rejecting "[q]uantitatively impressive" list of "apparent similarities" that "break down under the closer, detailed examination which the copyright law requires" because a comparison focusing "on the dramatic mood, the details and interplay of the characters, and the dynamic of events indicates such substantial dissimilarity" as to bar verdict for plaintiff).

Moreover, because Plaintiff effectively mixes and matches from six works, the opportunities for identifying similar details is greatly enhanced. Even considering the works together, the Court believes that such a comparison should focus on identifying important congruences only; to weight similar nonessential details discovered in such an exercise would seem as a general matter to allow a plaintiff to cast too wide a net.

Thus Plaintiff, although having sifted the works to produce a list of similarities, often not essential to the stories, has at the same time ignored major characters and events in Jurassic Park that do not comport with his theory of the case. Consequently, even assuming the accuracy of the various similarities in details as represented by Plaintiff, a finding of substantial similarity cannot be supported.

IV.

For the foregoing reasons, Defendants' motion for summary judgment is granted, and Defendants may have judgment dismissing the Complaint.

SO ORDERED.

7. Copyright on Music

No. 15-56880 (2018)

WILLIAMS V. GAYE

United States Court of Appeals of the Ninth Circuit

M. Smith, Circuit Judge:

After a seven-day trial and two days of deliberation, a jury found that Pharrell Williams, Robin Thicke, and Clifford Harris, Jr.'s song "Blurred Lines," the world's best-selling single in 2013, infringed Frankie Christian Gaye, Nona Marvisa Gaye, and Marvin Gaye III's copyright in Marvin Gaye's 1977 hit song "Got To Give It Up." Three consolidated appeals followed.

Appellants and Cross-Appellees Williams, Thicke, Harris, and More Water from Nazareth Publishing, Inc. (collectively, Thicke Parties) appeal from the district court's judgment. They urge us to reverse the district court's denial of their motion for summary judgment and direct the district court to enter judgment in their favor. In the alternative, they ask us to vacate the judgment and remand the case for a new trial, on grounds of instructional error, improper admission of expert testimony, and lack of evidence supporting the verdict. If a new trial is not ordered, they request that we reverse or vacate the jury's awards of actual damages and infringer's profits, and the district court's imposition of a running royalty. Finally, they seek reversal of the judgment against Harris, challenging the district court's decision to overturn the jury's general verdict finding in Harris's favor.

Appellants and Cross-Appellees Interscope Records, UMG Recordings, Inc., Universal Music Distribution, and Star Trak, LLC (collectively, Interscope Parties) appeal from the district court's judgment. They urge us to reverse the judgment against them, challenging the district court's decision to overturn the jury's general verdict finding in their favor.

Appellees and Cross-Appellants Frankie Christian Gaye, Nona Marvisa Gaye, and Marvin Gaye III (collectively, Gayes) appeal from the district court's order on attorney's fees and costs. They request that we vacate and remand for reconsideration the district court's denial of attorney's fees, and award them their costs in full. The Gayes also protectively cross-appeal the district court's ruling limiting the scope of the Gayes' compositional copyright to the four corners of the sheet music deposited with the United States Copyright Office. In the event a new trial is ordered, the Gayes urge us to hold that Marvin Gaye's studio recording of "Got To Give It Up," rather than the deposit copy, establishes the scope of the Gayes' copyright under the Copyright Act of 1909.

We have jurisdiction over this appeal pursuant to 28 U.S.C. § 1291. Our law requires that we review this case, which proceeded to a full trial on the merits in the district court, under deferential standards of review. We accordingly decide this case on narrow grounds, and affirm in part and reverse in part.

FACTUAL AND PROCEDURAL BACKGROUND

A. "Got To Give It Up"

In 1976, Marvin Gaye recorded the song "Got To Give It Up" in his studio. "Got To Give It Up" reached number one on Billboard's Hot 100 chart in 1977, and remains popular today.

In 1977, Jobete Music Company, Inc. registered "Got To Give It Up" with the United States Copyright Office and deposited six pages of handwritten sheet music attributing the song's words and music to Marvin Gaye. Marvin Gaye did not write or fluently read sheet music, and did not prepare the deposit copy. Instead, an unidentified transcriber notated the sheet music after Marvin Gaye recorded "Got To Give It Up."

The Gayes inherited the copyrights in Marvin Gaye's musical compositions.

B. "Blurred Lines"

In June 2012, Pharrell Williams and Robin Thicke wrote and recorded "Blurred Lines." Clifford Harris, Jr., known popularly as T.I., separately wrote and recorded a rap verse for "Blurred Lines" that was added to the track seven months later. "Blurred Lines" was the best-selling single in the world in 2013.

Thicke, Williams, and Harris co-own the musical composition copyright in "Blurred Lines." Star Trak and Interscope Records co-own the sound recording of "Blurred Lines." Universal Music Distribution manufactured and distributed "Blurred Lines."

C. The Action

The Gayes made an infringement demand on Williams and Thicke after hearing "Blurred Lines." Negotiations failed, prompting Williams, Thicke, and Harris to file suit for a declaratory judgment of non-infringement on August 15, 2013.

The Gayes counterclaimed against the Thicke Parties, alleging that "Blurred Lines" infringed their copyright in "Got To Give It Up,"1 and added the Interscope Parties as third-party defendants.

D. The District Court's Denial of Summary Judgment

The district court denied Williams and Thicke's motion for summary judgment on October 30, 2014.

1. The District Court's Interpretation of the Copyright Act of 1909

The district court ruled that the Gayes' compositional copyright, which is governed by the Copyright Act of 1909, did not extend to the commercial sound recording of "Got To Give It Up," and protected only the sheet music deposited with the

Copyright Office. The district court accordingly limited its review of the evidence to the deposit copy, and concluded there were genuine issues of material fact.

2. The Evidence

The Thicke Parties relied upon the opinion of musicologist Sandy Wilbur. The Gayes relied upon the opinions of Dr. Ingrid Monson, the Quincy Jones Professor of African American Music at Harvard University, and musicologist Judith Finell. The experts disagreed sharply in their opinions, which they articulated in lengthy reports.

Finell opined that there is a "constellation" of eight similarities between "Got To Give It Up" and "Blurred Lines," consisting of the signature phrase, hooks,2 hooks with backup vocals, "Theme X,"3 backup hooks, bass melodies, keyboard parts, and unusual percussion choices.

Wilbur opined that there are no substantial similarities between the melodies, rhythms, harmonies, structures, and lyrics of "Blurred Lines" and "Got To Give It Up," and disputed each area of similarity Finell identified. The district court compared Finell's testimony with Wilbur's and, pursuant to the extrinsic test under copyright law, meticulously filtered out elements Wilbur opined were not in the deposit copy, such as the backup vocals, "Theme X," descending bass line, keyboard rhythms, and percussion parts.

The district court also filtered out several unprotectable similarities Dr. Monson identified, including the use of a cowbell, hand percussion, drum set parts, background vocals, and keyboard parts. After filtering out those elements, the district court considered Dr. Monson's analysis of harmonic and melodic similarities between the songs, and noted differences between Wilbur's and Dr. Monson's opinions.

After performing its analytical dissection, as part of the extrinsic test, the district court summarized the remaining areas of dispute in the case. The district court identified disputes regarding the similarity of the songs' signature phrases, hooks, bass lines, keyboard chords, harmonic structures, and vocal melodies. Concluding that genuine issues of material fact existed, the district court denied Williams and Thicke's motion for summary judgment.

E. Trial

The case proceeded to a seven-day trial. The district court ruled before trial that the Gayes could present sound recordings of "Got To Give It Up" edited to capture only elements reflected in the deposit copy. Consequently, the commercial sound recording of "Got To Give It Up" was not played at trial.

Williams and Thicke testified, each acknowledging inspiration from Marvin Gaye and access to "Got To Give It Up."

Finell testified that "Blurred Lines" and "Got To Give It Up" share many similarities, including the bass lines, keyboard parts, signature phrases, hooks, "Theme X," bass melodies, word painting, and the placement of the rap and "parlando" sections in the two songs. She opined that nearly every bar of "Blurred Lines" contains an element similar to "Got To Give It Up." Although the district court had filtered out "Theme X," the descending bass line, and the keyboard rhythms as unprotectable at summary judgment, Finell testified that those elements were in the deposit copy.

Dr. Monson played three audio-engineered "mash-ups" she created to show the melodic and harmonic compatibility between "Blurred Lines" and "Got To Give It Up." She testified that the two songs shared structural similarities on a sectional and phrasing level.

Wilbur opined that the two songs are not substantially similar and disputed Finell and Dr. Monson's opinions. Wilbur prepared and played a sound recording containing her rendition of the deposit copy of "Got To Give It Up."

Neither the Thicke Parties nor the Gayes made a motion for judgment as a matter of law pursuant to Federal Rule of Civil Procedure 50(a) before the case was submitted to the jury.

On March 10, 2015, after two days of deliberation, the jury returned mixed general verdicts. The jury found that Williams, More Water from Nazareth Publishing,5 and Thicke infringed the Gayes' copyright in "Got To Give It Up." In contrast, the jury found that Harris and the Interscope Parties were not liable for infringement. The jury awarded the Gayes $4 million in actual damages, $1,610,455.31 in infringer's profits from Williams and More Water from Nazareth Publishing, and $1,768,191.88 in infringer's profits from Thicke.

F. The District Court's Order on Post–Trial Motions

The district court ruled on the parties' various post-trial motions in an omnibus order.

The Thicke Parties filed a motion for judgment as a matter of law, a new trial, or remittitur. The district court denied the Thicke Parties' motion for judgment as a matter of law and motion for a new trial, but remitted the award of actual damages and the award of Williams' profits.

The Gayes filed three motions, seeking (1) a declaration that Harris and the Interscope Parties were liable for infringement; (2) injunctive relief or, in the alternative, ongoing royalties; and (3) prejudgment interest. The district court construed the Gayes' motion for declaratory relief as a post-trial motion for judgment as a matter of law, and granted the motion, overturning the jury's general verdicts in favor of Harris and the Interscope Parties. The district court denied the Gayes' request for injunctive relief, but awarded them a running royalty of 50% of future songwriter and publishing revenues from "Blurred Lines." The district court granted in part the Gayes' motion for prejudgment interest.

G. The Judgment and Order on Attorney's Fees and Costs

The district court entered judgment on December 2, 2015. The court awarded the Gayes $3,188,527.50 in actual damages, profits of $1,768,191.88 against Thicke and $357,630.96 against Williams and More Water from Nazareth Publishing, and a running royalty of 50% of future songwriter and publishing revenues received by Williams, Thicke, and Harris.

On April 12, 2016, the district court denied the Gayes' motion for attorney's fees and apportioned costs between the parties. The parties timely appealed.

ANALYSIS

I. Governing Law

...

B. The Standard of Similarity for Musical Compositions

We have distinguished between "broad" and "thin" copyright protection based on the "range of expression" involved. Mattel, Inc. v. MGA Entm't, Inc., 616 F.3d 904, 913–14 (9th Cir. 2010). "If there's a wide range of expression ..., then copyright protection is 'broad' and a work will infringe if it's 'substantially similar' to the copyrighted work." Id. (citation omitted). On the other hand, "[i]f there's only a narrow range of expression ..., then copyright protection is 'thin' and a work must be 'virtually identical' to infringe." Id. at 914 (citation omitted). To illustrate, there are a myriad of ways to make an "aliens-attack movie," but "there are only so many ways to paint a red bouncy ball on blank canvas." Id. at 913–14. Whereas the former deserves broad copyright protection, the latter merits only thin copyright protection. See id.

17181920We reject the Thicke Parties' argument that the Gayes' copyright enjoys only thin protection. Musical compositions are not confined to a narrow range of expression.8 See Swirsky, 376 F.3d at 849 (noting that "[m]usic ... is not capable of ready classification into only five or six constituent elements," but "is comprised of a large array of elements"). They are unlike *1165 a page-shaped computer desktop icon, see Apple Computer, Inc. v. Microsoft Corp., 35 F.3d 1435, 1444 (9th Cir. 1994), or a "glass-in-glass jellyfish sculpture," Satava v. Lowry, 323 F.3d 805, 810 (9th Cir. 2003). Rather, as we have observed previously, "[m]usic ... is not capable of ready classification into only five or six constituent elements," but is instead "comprised of a large array of elements, some combination of which is protectable by copyright." Swirsky, 376 F.3d at 849. As "[t]here is no one magical combination of ... factors that will automatically substantiate a musical infringement suit," and as "each allegation of infringement will be unique," the extrinsic test is met, "[s]o long as the plaintiff can demonstrate, through expert testimony ..., that the similarity was 'substantial' and to 'protected elements' of the copyrighted work." Id. We have applied the substantial similarity standard to musical infringement suits before, see id.; Three Boys Music, 212 F.3d at 485, and see no reason to deviate from that standard now. Therefore, the Gayes' copyright is not limited to only thin copyright protection, and the Gayes need not prove virtual identity to substantiate their infringement action.

C. The Copyright Act of 1909

Marvin Gaye composed "Got To Give It Up" before January 1, 1978, the effective date of the Copyright Act of 1976. Accordingly, the Copyright Act of 1909 governs the Gayes' compositional copyright. See Twentieth Century Fox Film Corp. v. Entm't Distrib., 429 F.3d 869, 876 (9th Cir. 2005); Dolman v. Agee, 157 F.3d 708, 712 n.1 (9th Cir. 1998).

While the Copyright Act of 1976 protects "works of authorship" fixed in "sound recordings," 17 U.S.C. § 102, the 1909 Act did not protect sound recordings. It is well settled that "[s]ound recordings and musical compositions are separate works with their own distinct copyrights." See VMG Salsoul, LLC v. Ciccone, 824 F.3d 871, 877 (9th Cir. 2016) (quoting Erickson v. Blake, 839 F.Supp.2d 1132, 1135 n.3 (D. Or. 2012)). It remains unsettled, however, whether copyright protection for musical compositions under the 1909 Act extends only to the four corners of the sheet music deposited with the United States Copyright Office, or whether the commercial sound recordings of the compositions are admissible to shed light on the scope of the underlying copyright. Here, the district court ruled that the 1909 Act protected only the deposit copy of "Got To Give It Up," and excluded the sound recording from consideration.

The Gayes cross-appeal the district court's interpretation of the 1909 Act only in the event the case is remanded for a new trial. The parties have staked out mutually exclusive positions. The Gayes assert that Marvin Gaye's studio recording may establish the scope of a compositional copyright, despite the 1909 Act's lack of protection for sound recordings. The Thicke Parties, on the other hand, elevate the deposit copy as the quintessential measure of the scope of copyright protection. Nevertheless, because we do not remand the case for a new trial, we need not, and decline to, resolve this issue in this opinion. For purposes of this appeal, we accept, without deciding, the merits of the district court's ruling that the scope of the Gayes' copyright in "Got To Give It Up" is limited to the deposit copy.

...

III. The District Court Did Not Abuse its Discretion in Denying a New Trial.

We review the district court's denial of a motion for a new trial for abuse of discretion. Lam v. City of San Jose, 869 F.3d 1077, 1084 (9th Cir. 2017) (citing Molski v. M.J. Cable, Inc., 481 F.3d 724, 728 (9th Cir. 2007)). We may reverse the denial of a new trial only if the district court "reaches a result that is illogical, implausible, or without support in the inferences that may be drawn from the record." Id. (quoting Kode v. Carlson, 596 F.3d 608, 612 (9th Cir. 2010)). "The abuse of discretion standard requires us to uphold a district court's determination that falls within a broad range of permissible conclusions, provided the district court did not apply the law erroneously." Id. (quoting Kode, 596 F.3d at 612).

The Thicke Parties argue that a new trial is warranted on three grounds: (1) Jury Instructions 42 and 43 were erroneous; (2) the district court abused its discretion in admitting portions of Finell and Dr. Monson's testimony; and (3) the verdict is against the clear weight of the evidence. We disagree, and discuss each ground in turn.

A. Instructions 42 and 43 Were Not Erroneous.

2728We review de novo whether jury instructions state the law accurately, but review a district court's formulation of jury instructions for abuse of discretion. Id. at 1085 (citing Hunter v. County of Sacramento, 652 F.3d 1225, 1232 (9th Cir. 2011)). "In evaluating jury instructions, prejudicial error results when, looking to the instructions as a whole, the substance of the applicable law was [not] fairly and correctly covered." Dang v. Cross, 422 F.3d 800, 805 (9th Cir. 2005) (alteration in original) (quoting Swinton v. Potomac Corp., 270 F.3d 794, 802 (9th Cir. 2001)).

1. Jury Instruction 42

29The Thicke Parties argue that Instruction 42 allowed the jury to place undue weight on Williams and Thicke's statements claiming inspiration from "Got To Give It Up" and Marvin Gaye. The district court instructed the jurors:

In order to find that the Thicke Parties copied either or both of the Gaye Parties' songs, it is not necessary that you find that the Thicke Parties consciously or deliberately copied either or both of these songs. It is sufficient if you find that the Thicke Parties subconsciously copied either or both of the Gaye Parties' songs.

3031Because direct evidence is rare, copying is usually circumstantially proved by a combination of access and substantial similarity. See Swirsky, 376 F.3d at 844. As the Thicke Parties acknowledge, access may be "based on a theory of widespread dissemination and subconscious copying." Three Boys Music, 212 F.3d at 483. In short, there is no *1168 scienter requirement. See id. at 482–85. Instruction 42 stated as much.

32The Thicke Parties argue that Instruction 42 was nonetheless inappropriate, because the issue of access was not at issue. Not so. First, the fact that the Thicke Parties conceded access to "Got To Give It Up" does not diminish the importance of access to the case. To the contrary, access remains relevant. Our inverse ratio rule provides that the stronger the showing of access, the lesser the showing of substantial similarity is required. See id. at 485.

Second, and dispositive here, the instructions as a whole make plain that a circumstantial case of copying requires not just access, but also substantial similarity. Instructions 28 and 41 provide that copying may be proven by demonstrating access plus substantial similarity.12 Instruction 43 further underscores that the Gayes "must show that there is both substantial 'extrinsic similarity' and substantial 'intrinsic similarity' as to that pair of works." Looking to the jury instructions as a whole, see Dang, 422 F.3d at 805, it is clear that the district court properly instructed the jury to find both access and substantial similarity.

In light of the foregoing, we conclude that the district court did not err in giving Jury Instruction 42.

2. Jury Instruction 43

33The Thicke Parties argue that Instruction 43 erroneously instructed the jury to consider unprotectable elements. Specifically, they contend that the district court instructed the jury that it "must consider" elements that they contend are not present in the deposit copy: "Theme X," the descending bass line, and keyboard parts. Instruction 43 states, in pertinent part:

Extrinsic similarity is shown when two works have a similarity of ideas and expression as measured by external, objective criteria. To make this determination, you must consider the elements of each of the works and decide if they are substantially similar. This is not the same as "identical." There has been testimony and evidence presented by both sides on this issue, including by expert witnesses, as to such matters as: (a) for "Got to Give It Up" and "Blurred Lines," the so-called "Signature Phrase," hook, "Theme X," bass melodies, keyboard parts, word painting, lyrics, [and] rap v. parlando .... The Gaye Parties do not have to show that each of these individual elements is substantially similar, but rather that there is enough similarity between a work of the Gaye Parties and an allegedly infringing work of the Thicke Parties to comprise a substantial amount.

First, the Thicke Parties take the word "must" out of context. Instruction 43's use of the word "must" serves to underline the extrinsic test's requirement that the jury compare the objective elements of the works for substantial similarity.

Second, Finell testified that "Theme X," the descending bass line, and the keyboard parts are reflected in the deposit copy, while Wilbur testified to the contrary. The experts' quarrel over what was in the deposit copy was a factual dispute for the jury to decide. Even if Instruction 43's inclusion of contested elements could have led the jury to believe that the elements were in the deposit copy, and to consider them as protectable elements for purposes of the substantial similarity analysis, we cannot view Instruction 43 in isolation. In light of the jury instructions as a whole, we do not conclude that the district court's listing of elements in Instruction 43 prevented the jury from making a factual determination of what was in the deposit copy.

The instructions on whole make clear that the jury could consider only elements in the deposit copy. Instruction 28 states that the Gayes bear "the burden of proving that the Thicke Parties copied original elements from the Gaye[s'] copyrighted work." Instruction 35, in turn, defines the Gayes' copyrighted work. Instruction 35 informed jurors that at the time the copyright in "Got To Give It Up" was registered, "only written music could be filed by a copyright owner with the Copyright Office as the deposit copy of the copyrighted work." In contrast, "[r]ecordings of musical compositions could not be filed with the Copyright Office at that time." The district court cautioned the jurors to distinguish between the commercial sound recording of "Got To Give It Up" and the deposit copy, noting that "although [a] sound recording[ ] of 'Got to Give It Up' ... w[as] made and released commercially, th[e] particular recording[ ] [is] not at issue in this case, w[as] not produced into evidence, and w[as] not played for you during the trial." What was at issue was "testimony from one or more witnesses from each side about what each thinks is shown on the deposit copy for each composition," as well as "recorded versions of each work that each side has prepared based on what each side contends is shown in the deposit copy that was filed with the Copyright Office." In short, the district court instructed the jurors that the deposit copy, not the commercial sound recording, was the copyrighted work in the case.

Harper House, Inc. v. Thomas Nelson, Inc., 889 F.2d 197 (9th Cir. 1989), is not helpful to the Thicke Parties. In Harper House, we held that the district court erred in failing to give jury instructions that "adequately distinguish[ed] between protectable and unprotectable material." 889 F.2d at 207–08. The copyrighted works at issue in Harper House were organizers, which receive "extremely limited protection" and are "compilations consisting largely of uncopyrightable elements," such as "blank forms, common property, or utilitarian aspects." Id. at 205, 207–08.

Suffice to say, musical compositions are not like organizers, and this case is easily distinguishable. The jury never heard the commercial sound recording. Elements indisputably present only in the sound recording, such as the use of cowbell and party noises, were never played at trial. Had that been the case, the district court would have had to instruct the jury to distinguish between elements in the commercial recording and elements in the deposit copy. Instead, the jury heard sound clips edited to capture elements that the experts testified were in the deposit copy. The question of which expert to believe was properly confided to the jury.

*The district court did not err in giving Instruction 43.

B. The District Court Did Not Abuse its Discretion in Admitting Portions of Finell and Dr. Monson's Testimony.

We review the district court's evidentiary rulings for abuse of discretion. Wagner v. County of Maricopa, 747 F.3d 1048, 1052 (9th Cir. 2013). The Thicke Parties contend that the district court abused its discretion in admitting portions of Finell and Dr. Monson's expert testimony, arguing that they based their testimony on unprotectable elements. We disagree.

1. Finell's Testimony

The Thicke Parties object only to three portions of Finell's testimony: her testimony regarding "Theme X," the descending bass line, and the keyboard parts. Finell testified that "Theme X," the descending bass line, and the keyboard rhythms were in the deposit copy.

Finell was cross-examined for four hours. During cross-examination, Finell conceded that the notes of "Theme X" were not written on the sheet music, and she was questioned about her testimony that the notes of "Theme X" were implied in the deposit copy. She also acknowledged that the bass melody she presented at trial differed from that notated in the deposit copy. She was impeached with her deposition testimony, in which she admitted that the rhythm of the keyboard parts in the sound recording of "Got To Give It Up" is not notated in the deposit copy.

Wilbur disputed her testimony, opining that "Theme X," the descending bass line, and the keyboard rhythms are not contained in the deposit copy. The dispute boiled down to a question of whose testimony to believe. Both experts referenced the sound recording.13 Both experts agreed that sheet music requires interpretation.14 The question of whose interpretation of the deposit copy to credit was a question properly left for the jury to resolve. See Three Boys Music, 212 F.3d at 485–86 ("We refuse to interfere with the jury's credibility determination[.]"). Therefore, the district court did not abuse its discretion by permitting Finell's testimony.

2. Dr. Monson's Testimony

The Thicke Parties argue that the district court abused its discretion in allowing Dr. Monson to play audio "mash-ups" superimposing Marvin Gaye's vocals from "Got To Give It Up" onto the accompaniment in "Blurred Lines," and vice versa. They argue that the "mash-ups" contained unprotectable elements, such as the keyboard parts, bass melodies, and Marvin Gaye's vocals.15

*1171 This argument faces the same hurdle as the Thicke Parties' objection to Finell's testimony. Dr. Monson testified that there were structural similarities between the two songs at a sectional level and at a phrasing level, and used the "mash-ups" to demonstrate the songs' shared harmonic and melodic compatibility. We have permitted similar expert testimony in the past. Cf. Swirsky, 376 F.3d at 845–47 (holding that district court erred in discounting expert's testimony regarding structural similarities between two choruses). Dr. Monson was cross-examined on her opinion, and the jury was free to weigh her testimony as it saw fit.

Our decision in Three Boys Music confirms that the district court acted within its discretion. Three Boys Music was a 1909 Act copyright infringement case in which the jury heard not only a rendition of the deposit copy, see 212 F.3d at 486, but the complete commercial sound recording of the copyrighted song. Although the sufficiency of the deposit copy arose in the context of subject matter jurisdiction in Three Boys Music, our treatment of the issue lends support for our present conclusion. In Three Boys Music, the defendants argued that there were "inaccuracies in the deposit copy." 212 F.3d at 486–87. While the plaintiffs' expert testified that "the song's essential elements" were in the deposit copy, the defendants argued that "the majority of the musical elements that were part of the infringement claim" were not in the deposit copy. Id. at 486. Despite the fact that the jury heard the complete sound recording, which differed from the deposit copy, we still upheld the jury's verdict finding for the plaintiffs. Id. at 486–87.

Here, the district court excluded the commercial sound recording of "Got To Give It Up" from trial, and vigilantly policed the admission of testimony throughout trial, repeatedly instructing counsel to ensure that the experts tethered their testimony to the sheet music. The district court did not abuse its discretion in admitting portions of the Gayes' experts' testimony.

...

IV. The Awards of Actual Damages and Profits and the District Court's Running Royalty Were Proper.

A. The Award of Damages Was Not Based on Undue Speculation.

We afford "great deference" to a jury's award of damages and will uphold the award "unless it is 'clearly not supported by the evidence' or 'only based on speculation or guesswork.' " In re First All. Mortg. Co., 471 F.3d 977, 1001 (9th Cir. 2006) (quoting L.A. Mem'l Coliseum Comm'n v. Nat'l Football League, 791 F.2d 1356, 1360 (9th Cir. 1986)). We will uphold an award of hypothetical-license damages "provided the amount is not based on 'undue speculation.' " Oracle Corp. v. SAP AG, 765 F.3d 1081, 1088 (9th Cir. 2014) (quoting Polar Bear Prods., Inc. v. Timex Corp., 384 F.3d 700, 709 (9th Cir. 2004)). "The touchstone for hypothetical-license damages is 'the range of [the license's] reasonable market value.' " Id. (alteration in original) (quoting Polar Bear Prods., Inc., 384 F.3d at 709)).

43Here, the jury awarded the Gayes actual damages in the amount of 50% of the publishing revenues for "Blurred Lines." The Thicke Parties ask us to vacate the award of $3,188,527.50 (remitted by the district court from the jury's original award of $4 million),18 because it was based upon an unduly speculative hypothetical license rate of 50%. We disagree.

The Gayes called Nancie Stern, an industry expert with over twenty years of experience in negotiating and assigning valuations for the use of portions of older musical compositions in new compositions. Stern has performed such valuations thousands of times. Major labels, as well as renowned artists, have retained her services. Few other people or businesses perform her line of work.

Stern testified that the prototypical negotiation centers on the percentage of the new musical composition that the owner of the older composition should receive for the use. The industry standard assigns 50% for the music and 50% for the lyrics. Turning to the two songs at hand, Stern opined that the value of the use of "Got To Give It Up" in "Blurred Lines" would have been 50% had the Thicke Parties sought a license pre-release. Had the Thicke Parties sought a license post-release, the valuation would range between 75% to 100% percent. Stern arrived at her conclusion by reviewing "snippets" of the two songs and "A-B'ing" them, or playing them back and forth.19 Stern's methodology and opinion were not unduly speculative, but tethered to her deep industry expertise.

In an attempt to buttress their position, the Thicke Parties cite to two decisions which are distinguishable. In Oracle, we held the jury's award of $1.3 billion in hypothetical-license damages to be unduly speculative because "the evidence presented at trial failed to provide 'the range of the reasonable market value' " underlying the actual damages award. 765 F.3d at 1089 (quoting Polar Bear Prods., Inc., 384 F.3d at 709)). Oracle's evidence was based on projected benefits and costs, and Oracle lacked a history of granting comparable licenses and provided no evidence of "benchmark" licenses in the industry. See id. at 1091–93. "Although a copyright plaintiff need not demonstrate that it would have reached a licensing agreement with the infringer or present evidence of 'benchmark' agreements in order to recover hypothetical-license damages," we observed that "it may be difficult for a plaintiff to establish the amount of such damages without undue speculation in the absence of such evidence." Id. at 1093.

Here, as in Oracle, there is no evidence of a prior benchmark license agreement between the Thicke Parties and the Gayes. However, in contrast to Oracle, the Gayes tethered their hypothetical license damages to evidence of a benchmark license in the industry. Instead of relying on undue speculation, the Gayes presented an expert who had extensive and specialized knowledge regarding the type of hypothetical license at issue. Stern opined, based on an industry standard and her evaluation of the songs involved, that the reasonable market value of a license would range between 50% pre-release and 75% to 100% post-release.

In Uniloc USA, Inc. v. Microsoft Corp., 632 F.3d 1292 (Fed. Cir. 2011), the Federal Circuit held that the "25 percent rule of thumb," used in patent cases "to approximate the reasonable royalty rate that the manufacturer of a patented product would be willing to offer to pay to the patentee during a hypothetical negotiation," is a "fundamentally flawed tool." 632 F.3d at 1312, 1315. The Federal Circuit observed that the 25% rule is "an abstract and largely theoretical construct" that "does not say anything about a particular hypothetical negotiation or reasonable royalty involving any particular technology, industry, or party." Id. at 1317. The 50% standard Stern identified does not extend without bounds across art forms or different copyrightable media in the same way the 25% rule of thumb applied without regard to the industry or technology involved. Stern's opinion was not based on abstraction, but on an industry standard and her expert assessment of the two songs. Her testimony was not unduly speculative, and did not render the damages award improper.

B. The Award of Profits Is Not Clearly Erroneous.

We review an apportionment of infringer's profits for clear error. Cream Records, Inc. v. Joseph Schlitz Brewing Co., 864 F.2d 668, 669 (9th Cir. 1989) (per curiam); see also Three Boys Music, 212 F.3d at 487 (upholding jury's apportionment of profits for lack of clear error). The burden is on the defendant to prove what percentage of its profits is not attributable to infringement. Three Boys Music, 212 F.3d at 487.

The Thicke Parties contend that the award of $1,768,191.88 in profits against Thicke and $357,630.96 (remitted by the district court from the jury's original award of $1,610,455.31) against Williams, which amounted to approximately 40% of their non-publishing profits from "Blurred Lines," is excessive. They assert that the evidence supports a profits award of only 5%, citing Wilbur's opinion that less than 5% of "Blurred Lines" contains elements allegedly similar to ones in "Got To Give It Up."

We affirmed a similar profits award in Three Boys Music. See id. In Three Boys Music, the defendant presented evidence that only 10% to 15% of profits were attributable to the song's infringing elements. Id. Despite the evidence, the jury attributed 66% of profits to the song's infringing elements. Id. Here, the Thicke Parties bore the burden of proof. The jury was free to accept Wilbur's testimony or instead credit Finell's testimony that nearly every measure of "Blurred Lines" contains an element similar to "Got To Give It Up." The jury's choice to "apportion[ ] less than 100% of the profits but more than the percentage estimates of [the Thicke Parties'] expert[ ] does not represent clear error." Id.

C. The District Court Did Not Abuse its Discretion in Awarding the Gayes a Running Royalty at the Rate of 50%.

We review a district court's decision to award equitable relief for abuse of discretion. Traxler v. Multnomah County, 596 F.3d 1007, 1014 n.4 (9th Cir. 2010); see also Presidio Components, Inc. v. Am. Tech. Ceramics Corp., 702 F.3d 1351, 1363 (Fed. Cir. 2012) (reviewing district court's imposition of an ongoing royalty for abuse of discretion). Findings of fact are reviewed for clear error. See Traxler, 596 F.3d at 1014 n.4.

The district court based the royalty rate on Stern's testimony. For the same reasons set forth above, see supra Part VI.A, we conclude that the district court did not abuse its discretion in awarding the Gayes a running royalty at the rate of 50%.

...

510 U.S. 569 (1994)

CAMPBELL aka LUKE SKYYWALKER v. ACUFF ROSE MUSIC

United States Supreme Court

Justice Souter:

In 1964, Roy Orbison and William Dees wrote a rock ballad called "Oh, Pretty Woman" and assigned their rights in it to respondent Acuff Rose Music, Inc. See Appendix A, infra, at 26. Acuff Rose registered the song for copyright protection.

Petitioners Luther R. Campbell, Christopher Wongwon, Mark Ross, and David Hobbs, are collectively known as2 Live Crew, a popular rap music group. In 1989, Campbell wrote a song entitled "Pretty Woman," which he later described in an affidavit as intended, "through comical lyrics, to satirize the original work . . . ." App. to Pet. for Cert. 80a. On July 5, 1989, 2 Live Crew's manager informed Acuff Rose that 2 Live Crew had written a parody of "Oh, Pretty Woman," that they would afford all credit for ownership and authorship of the original song to Acuff Rose, Dees, and Orbison, and that they were willing to pay a fee for the use they wished to make of it. Enclosed with the letter were a copy of the lyrics and a recording of 2 Live Crew's song. See Appendix B, infra, at 27. Acuff Rose's agent refused permission, stating that "I am aware of the success enjoyed by `The 2 Live Crews', but I must inform you that we cannot permit the use of a parody of `Oh, Pretty

Woman.' " App. to Pet. for Cert. 85a. Nonetheless, in June or July 1989, 2 Live Crew released records, cassette tapes, and compact discs of "Pretty Woman" in a collection of songs entitled "As Clean As They Wanna Be." The albums and compact discs identify the authors of "Pretty Woman" as Orbison and Dees and its publisher as Acuff Rose.

Almost a year later, after nearly a quarter of a millioncopies of the recording had been sold, Acuff Rose sued 2 Live Crew and its record company, Luke Skyywalker Records, for copyright infringement. The District Court granted summary judgment for 2 Live Crew, reasoning that the commercial purpose of 2 Live Crew's song was no bar to fair use; that 2 Live Crew's version was a parody, which "quickly degenerates into a play on words, substituting predictable lyrics with shocking ones" to show "how bland and banal the Orbison song" is; that 2 Live Crew had taken no more than was necessary to "conjure up" the original in order to parody it; and that it was "extremely unlikely that 2 Live Crew's song could adversely affect the market for the original." 754 F. Supp. 1150, 1154-1155, 1157-1158 (MD Tenn. 1991). The District Court weighed these factors and held that 2 Live Crew's song made fair use of Orbison's original. Id., at 1158-1159.

The Court of Appeals for the Sixth Circuit reversed and remanded. 972 F. 2d 1429, 1439 (1992). Although it assumed for the purpose of its opinion that 2 Live Crew's song was a parody of the Orbison original, the Court of Appeals thought the District Court had put too little emphasis on the fact that "every commercial use . . . is presumptively . . . unfair," Sony Corp. of America v. Universal City Studios, Inc., 464 U.S. 417, 451 (1984), and it held that "the admittedly commercial nature" of the parody "requires the conclusion" that the first of four factors relevant under the statute weighs against a finding of fair use. 972 F. 2d, at 1435, 1437. Next, the Court of Appeals determined that, by "taking the heart of the original and making it the heart of a new work," 2 Live Crew had, qualitatively, taken too much. Id., at 1438. Finally, after noting that the effecton the potential market for the original (and the market for derivative works) is "undoubtedly the single most important element of fair use," Harper & Row, Publishers, Inc. v. Nation Enterprises, 471 U.S. 539, 566 (1985), the Court of Appeals faulted the District Court for "refus[ing] to indulge the presumption" that "harm for purposes of the fair use analysis has been established by the presumption attaching to commercial uses." 972 F. 2d, at 1438-1439. In sum, the court concluded that its "blatantly commercial purpose . . . prevents this parody from being a fair use." Id., at 1439.

We granted certiorari, 507 U. S. ____ (1993), to determine whether 2 Live Crew's commercial parody could be a fair use.

It is uncontested here that 2 Live Crew's song would be an infringement of Acuff Rose's rights in "Oh, Pretty Woman," under the Copyright Act of 1976, 17 U.S.C. § 106 (1988 ed. and Supp. IV), but for a finding of fair use through parody. From the infancy of copyrightprotection, some opportunity for fair use of copyrighted materials has been thought necessary to fulfill copyright's very purpose, "[t]o promote the Progress of Science and useful Arts . . . ." U. S. Const., Art. I, § 8, cl. 8. For as Justice Story explained, "[i]n truth, in literature, in science and in art, there are, and can be, few, if any, things which in an abstract sense, are strictly new and original throughout. Every book in literature, science and art, borrows, and must necessarily borrow, and use much which was well known and used before." Emerson v. Davies, 8 F. Cas. 615, 619 (No. 4,436) (CCD Mass. 1845). Similarly, Lord Ellenborough expressed the inherent tension in the need simultaneously to protect copyrighted material and to allow others to build upon it when he wrote, "while I shall think myself bound to secure every man in the enjoyment of his copy right, one must not put manacles upon science." Carey v. Kearsley, 4 Esp. 168, 170, 170 Eng. Rep. 679, 681 (K.B. 1803). In copyright cases brought under the Statute of Anne of 1710, English courts held that in some instances "fair abridgements" would not infringe an author's rights, see W. Patry, The Fair Use Privilege in Copyright Law 6-17 (1985) (hereinafter Patry); Leval, Toward a Fair Use Standard, 103 Harv. L. Rev. 1105, 1105 (1990) (hereinafter Leval),and although the First Congress enacted our initial copyright statute, Act of May 31, 1790, 1 Stat. 124, without any explicit reference to "fair use," as it later came to be known, the doctrine was recognized by the American courts nonetheless.

In Folsom v. Marsh, Justice Story distilled the essence of law and methodology from the earlier cases: "look to the nature and objects of the selections made, the quantity and value of the materials used, and the degree in which the use may prejudice the sale, or diminish the profits, or supersede the objects, of the original work." 9 F. Cas. 342, 348 (No. 4,901) (CCD Mass. 1841). Thus expressed, fair use remained exclusively judge made doctrine until the passage of the 1976 Copyright Act, in which Story's summary is discernible:

"§ 107. Limitations on exclusive rights: Fair use

%Notwithstanding the provisions of sections 106 and 106A, the fair use of a copyrighted work, including such use by reproduction in copies or phonorecords or by any other means specified by that section, for purposes such as criticism, comment, news reporting, teaching (including multiple copies for classroom use), scholarship, or research, is not an infringement of copyright. In determining whether the use made of a work in any particular case is a fair use the factors to be considered shall include--

%(1) the purpose and character of the use, including whether such use is of a commercial nature or is for nonprofit educational purposes;

%(2) the nature of the copyrighted work;

%(3) the amount and substantiality of the portionused in relation to the copyrighted work as a whole; and

%(4) the effect of the use upon the potential market for or value of the copyrighted work.

%The fact that a work is unpublished shall not itself bar a finding of fair use if such finding is made upon consideration of all the above factors." 17 U.S.C. § 107 (1988 ed. and Supp. IV).

Congress meant § 107 "to restate the present judicial doctrine of fair use, not to change, narrow, or enlarge it in any way" and intended that courts continue the common law tradition of fair use adjudication. H. R. Rep. No. 94-1476, p. 66 (1976)

(hereinafter House Report); S. Rep. No. 94-473, p. 62 (1975) (hereinafter Senate Report). The fair use doctrine thus "permits [and requires] courts to avoid rigid application of the copyright statute when, on occasion, it would stifle the very creativity which that law is designed to foster." Stewart v. Abend, 495 U.S. 207, 236 (1990) (internal quotation marks and citation omitted).

The task is not to be simplified with bright line rules, for the statute, like the doctrine it recognizes, calls for case-by-case analysis. Harper & Row, 471 U. S., at 560; Sony, 464 U. S., at 448, and n. 31; House Report, pp. 65-66; Senate Report, p. 62. The text employs the terms "including" and "such as" in the preamble paragraph to indicate the "illustrative and not limitative" function of the examples given, § 101; see Harper & Row, supra, at 561, which thus provide only general guidance about the sorts of copying that courts and Congress most commonly had found to be fair uses. Nor may the four statutory factors be treated in isolation, one from another. All are to be explored, and the results weighed together, in light of the purposes of copyright. See Leval 1110-1111; Patry & Perlmutter, Fair Use Misconstrued: Profit, Presumptions, and Parody, 11 Cardozo Arts & Ent. L. J. 667, 685-687 (1993) (hereinafter Patry & Perlmutter).

The first factor in a fair use enquiry is "the purpose and character of the use, including whether such use is of a commercial nature or is for nonprofit educational purposes." § 107(1). This factor draws on Justice Story's formulation, "the nature and objects of the selections made." Folsom v. Marsh, 9 F. Cas., at 348. The enquiry here may be guided by the examples given in the preamble to § 107, looking to whether the use is for criticism, or comment, or news reporting, and the like, see § 107. The central purpose of this investigation is to see, in Justice Story's words, whether the new work merely "supersede[s] the objects" of the original creation, Folsom v. Marsh, supra, at 348; accord, Harper & Row, supra, at 562 ("supplanting" the original), or instead adds something new, with a further purpose or different character, altering the first with new expression, meaning, or message; it asks, in other words, whether and to what extent the new work is "transformative." Leval 1111. Although such transformative use is not absolutely necessary for a finding of fair use, Sony, supra, at 455, n. 40, the goal of copyright, to promote science and the arts, is generally furthered by the creation of transformative works. Such works thus lie at the heart of the fair use doctrine's guarantee of breathing space within the confines of copyright, see, e. g., Sony, supra, at 478-480 (Blackmun, J., dissenting), and the more transformative the new work, the less will be the significance of other factors, like commercialism, that may weigh against a finding of fair use.

This Court has only once before even considered whether parody may be fair use, and that time issued no opinion because of the Court's equal division. Benny v. Loew's Inc., 239 F. 2d 532 (CA9 1956), aff'd sub nom. Columbia Broadcasting System, Inc. v. Loew's Inc., 356 U.S. 43 (1958). Suffice it to say now that parody has an obvious claim to transformative value, as Acuff Rose itself does not deny. Like less ostensibly humorous forms of criticism, it can provide social benefit, by shedding light on an earlier work, and, in the process, creating a new one. We thus line up with the courts that have held that parody, like other comment or criticism, may claim fair use under § 107. See, e. g., Fisher v. Dees, 794 F. 2d 432 (CA9 1986)

("When Sonny Sniffs Glue," a parody of "When Sunny Gets Blue," isfair use); Elsmere Music, Inc. v. National Broadcasting Co., 482 F. Supp. 741 (SDNY), aff'd, 623 F. 2d 252 (CA2 1980) ("I Love Sodom," a "Saturday Night Live" television parody of "I Love New York" is fair use); see also House Report, p. 65; Senate Report, p. 61 ("[U]se in a parody of some of the content of the work parodied" may be fair use).

The germ of parody lies in the definition of the Greek parodeia, quoted in Judge Nelson's Court of Appeals dissent, as "a song sung alongside another." 972 F. 2d, at 1440, quoting 7 Encyclopedia Britannica 768 (15th ed. 1975). Modern dictionaries accordingly describe a parody as a "literary or artistic work that imitates the characteristic style of an author or a work for comic effect or ridicule," or as a "composition in prose or verse in which the characteristic turns of thought and phrase in an author or class of authors are imitated in such a way as to make them appear ridiculous." For the purposes of copyright law, the nub of the definitions, and the heart of any parodist's claim to quote from existing material, is the use of some elements of a prior author's composition to create a new one that, at least in part, comments on that author's works. See, e. g., Fisher v. Dees, supra, at 437; MCA, Inc. v. Wilson, 677 F. 2d 180, 185 (CA2 1981). If, on the contrary, the commentary has no critical bearing on the substance or style of the original composition, which the alleged infringer merely uses to get attention or to avoid the drudgery in working up something fresh, the claim to fairness in borrowing from another's work diminishes accordingly (if it does not vanish), and other factors, like the extent of its commerciality, loom larger. Parodyneeds to mimic an original to make its point, and so has some claim to use the creation of its victim's (or collective victims') imagination, whereas satire can stand on its own two feet and so requires justification for the very act of borrowing. See Ibid.; Bisceglia, Parody and Copyright Protection: Turning the Balancing Act Into a Juggling Act, in ASCAP, Copyright Law Symposium, No. 34, p. 25 (1987).

The fact that parody can claim legitimacy for some appropriation does not, of course, tell either parodist or judge much about where to draw the line. Like a book review quoting the copyrighted material criticized, parody may or may not be fair use, and petitioner's suggestion that any parodic use is presumptively fair has no more justification in law or fact than the equally hopeful claim that any use for news reporting should be presumed fair, see Harper & Row, 471 U. S., at 561. The Act has no hint of an evidentiary preference for parodists over their victims, and no workable presumption for parody could take account of the fact that parody often shades into satire when society is lampooned through its creative artifacts, or that a work may contain both parodic and non parodic elements. Accordingly, parody, like any other use, has to work its way through the relevant factors, and be judged case by case, in light of the ends of the copyright law.

Here, the District Court held, and the Court of Appeals assumed, that 2 Live Crew's "Pretty Woman" contains parody, commenting on and criticizing the original work, whatever it may have to say about society at large. As the District Court remarked, the words of 2 Live Crew's song copy the original's first line, but then "quickly degenerat[e] into a play on words, substituting predictable lyrics with shocking ones . . . [that] derisively demonstrat[e] how bland and banal the Orbison song seems to them." 754 F. Supp., at 1155 (footnote omitted). Judge Nelson, dissenting below, came to the same conclusion, that the 2 Live Crew song "was clearly intended to ridicule the white bread original" and "reminds us that sexual congress with nameless streetwalkers is not necessarily the stuff of romance and is not necessarily without its consequences. The singers (there are several) have the same thing on their minds as did the lonely man with the nasal voice, but here there is no hint of wine and roses." 972 F. 2d, at 1442. Although the majority below had difficulty discerning any criticism of the original in 2 Live Crew's song, it assumed for purposes of its opinion that there was some. Id., at 1435-1436, and n. 8.

We have less difficulty in finding that critical element in 2 Live Crew's song than the Court of Appeals did, although having found it we will not take the further step of evaluating its quality. The threshold question when fair use is raised in defense of parody is whether a parodic character may reasonably be perceived. Whether, going beyond that, parody is in good taste or bad does not and should not matter to fair use. As Justice Holmes explained, "[i]t would be a dangerous undertaking for persons trained only to the law to constitute themselves final judges of the worth of [a work], outside of the narrowest and most obvious limits. At the one extreme some works of genius would be sure to miss appreciation. Their very novelty would make them repulsive until the public had learned the new language in which their author spoke." Bleistein v. Donaldson Lithographing Co., 188 U.S. 239, 251 (1903) (circus posters have copyright protection); cf. Yankee Publishing Inc. v. News America Publishing, Inc., 809 F. Supp. 267, 280 (SDNY 1992) (Leval, J.) ("First Amendment protections do not apply only to those who speak clearly, whose jokes are funny, and whose parodies succeed") (trademark case).

While we might not assign a high rank to the parodic element here, we think it fair to say that 2 Live Crew's song reasonably could be perceived as commenting on the original or criticizing it, to some degree. 2 Live Crew juxtaposes the romantic musings of a man whose fantasy comes true, with degrading taunts, a bawdy demand for sex, and a sigh of relief from paternal responsibility. The later words can be taken as a comment on the naivete of the original of an earlier day, as a rejection of its sentiment that ignores the ugliness of street life and the debasement that it signifies. It is this joinder of reference and ridicule that marks off the author's choice of parody from the other types of comment and criticism that traditionally have had aclaim to fair use protection as transformative works.

The Court of Appeals, however, immediately cut short the enquiry into 2 Live Crew's fair use claim by confining its treatment of the first factor essentially to one relevant fact, the commercial nature of the use. The court then inflated the significance of this fact by applying a presumption ostensibly culled from Sony, that "every commercial use of copyrighted material is presumptively . . . unfair . . . ." Sony, 464 U. S., at 451. In giving virtually dispositive weight to the commercial nature of the parody, the Court of Appeals erred.

The language of the statute makes clear that the commercial or nonprofit educational purpose of a work is only one element of the first factor enquiry into its purpose and character. Section 107(1) uses the term "including" to begin the dependent clause referring to commercial use, and the main clause speaks of a broader investigation into "purpose and character." As we explained in Harper & Row, Congress resisted attempts to narrow the ambit of this traditional enquiry by adopting categories of presumptively fair use, and it urged courts to preserve the breadth of their traditionally ample view of the universe of relevant evidence. 471 U. S., at 561; House Report, p. 66. Accordingly, the mere fact that a use is educational and not for profit does not insulate it from a finding of infringement, any more than the commercial character of a use bars a finding of fairness. If, indeed, commerciality carried presumptive force against a finding of fairness, the presumption would swallow nearly all of the illustrativeuses listed in the preamble paragraph of § 107, including news reporting, comment, criticism, teaching, scholarship, and research, since these activities "are generally conducted for profit in this country." Harper & Row, supra, at 592 (Brennan, J., dissenting). Congress could not have intended such a rule, which certainly is not inferable from the common law cases, arising as they did from the world of letters in which Samuel Johnson could pronounce that "[n]o man but a blockhead ever wrote, except for money." 3 Boswell's Life of Johnson 19 (G. Hill ed. 1934).

Sony itself called for no hard evidentiary presumption. There, we emphasized the need for a "sensitive balancing of interests," 464 U. S., at 455, n. 40, noted that Congress had "eschewed a rigid, bright line approach to fair use," id., at 449, n. 31, and stated that the commercial or nonprofit educational character of a work is "not conclusive," id., at 448-449, but rather a fact to be "weighed along with other[s] in fair use decisions." Id., at 449, n. 32 (quoting House Report, p. 66). The Court of Appeals's elevation of one sentence from Sony to a per se rule thus runs as much counter to Sony itself as to the long common law tradition of fair use adjudication. Rather, as we explained in Harper & Row, Sony stands for the proposition that the "fact that a publication was commercial as opposed to nonprofit is a separate factor that tends to weigh against a finding of fair use." 471 U. S., at 562. But that is all, and the fact that even the force of that tendency will vary with the context is a further reason against elevating commerciality to hard presumptive significance. The use, for example, of a copyrighted work to advertise a product, even in a parody, will be entitled to less indulgence under the first factor of the fair use enquiry, than the sale of a parody for its own sake, let alone one performed a single time by students in school. See generally Patry & Perlmutter 679-680; Fisher v. Dees, 794 F. 2d, at 437; Maxtone Graham v. Burtchaell, 803 F. 2d 1253, 1262 (CA2 1986); Sega Enterprises Ltd. v. Accolade, Inc., 977 F. 2d 1510, 1522 (CA9 1992).

The second statutory factor, 'the nature of the copyrighted work,' § 107(2), draws on Justice Story's expression, the "value of the materials used." Folsom v. Marsh, 9 F. Cas., at 348. This factor calls for recognition that some works are closer to the core of intended copyright protection than others, with the consequence that fair use is more difficult to establish when the former works are copied. See, e. g., Stewart v. Abend, 495 U. S., at 237-238 (contrasting fictional short story with factual works); Harper & Row, 471 U. S., at 563-564 (contrasting soon to be published memoir with published speech); Sony, 464 U. S., at 455, n. 40 (contrasting motion pictures with news broadcasts); Feist, 499 U. S., 348-351 (contrasting creative works with bare factual compilations); 3 M. Nimmer & D. Nimmer, Nimmer on Copyright § 13.05[A][2] (1993) (hereinafter Nimmer); Leval

1116. We agree with both the District Court and the Court of Appeals that the Orbison original's creative expression for public dissemination falls within the core of the copyright's protective purposes. 754 F. Supp., at 1155-1156; 972 F. 2d, at 1437. This fact, however, is not much help in this case, or ever likely to help much in separating the fair use sheep from the infringing goats in a parody case, since parodies almost invariably copy publicly known, expressive works.

The third factor asks whether "the amount and substantiality of the portion used in relation to the copyrighted work as a whole," § 107(3) (or, in Justice Story's words, "the quantity and value of the materials used," Folsom v. Marsh, supra, at 348) are reasonable in relation to the purpose of the copying. Here, attention turns to the persuasiveness of a parodist's justification for the particular copying done, and the enquiry will harken back to the first of the statutory factors, for, as in prior cases, we recognize that the extent of permissible copying varies with the purpose and character of the use. See Sony, 464 U. S., at 449-450 (reproduction of entire work "does not have its ordinary effect of militating against a finding of fair use" as to home videotaping of television programs); Harper & Row, 471 U. S., at 564 ("[E]ven substantial quotations might qualify as fair use in a review of a published work or a news account of a speech" but not in a scoop of a soon to be published memoir). The facts bearing on this factor will also tend to address the fourth, by revealing the degree to which the parody may serve as a market substitute for the original or potentially licensed derivatives. See Leval 1123.

The District Court considered the song's parodic purpose in finding that 2 Live Crew had not helped themselves overmuch. 754 F. Supp., at 1156-1157. The Court of Appeals disagreed, stating that "[w]hile it may not be inappropriate to find that no more was takenthan necessary, the copying was qualitatively substantial. . . . We conclude that taking the heart of the original and making it the heart of a new work was to purloin a substantial portion of the essence of the original." 972 F. 2d, at 1438.

The Court of Appeals is of course correct that this factor calls for thought not only about the quantity of the materials used, but about their quality and importance, too. In Harper & Row, for example, the Nation had taken only some 300 words out of President Ford's memoirs, but we signalled the significance of the quotations in finding them to amount to "the heart of the book," the part most likely to be newsworthy and important in licensing serialization. 471 U. S., at 564-566, 568 (internal quotation marks omitted). We also agree with the Court of Appeals that whether "a substantial portion of the infringing work was copied verbatim" from the copyrighted work is a relevant question, see id., at 565, for it may reveal a dearth of transformative character or purpose under the first factor, or a greater likelihood of market harm under the fourth; a work composed primarily of an original, particularly its heart, with little added or changed, is more likely to be a merely superseding use, fulfilling demand for the original.

Where we part company with the court below is in applying these guides to parody, and in particular to parody in the song before us. Parody presents a difficult case. Parody's humor, or in any event its comment, necessarily springs from recognizable allusion to its object through distorted imitation. Its art lies in the tension between a known original and its parodic twin. When parody takes aim at a particular original work, the parody must be able to "conjure up" at least enough of that original to make the object of its critical wit recognizable. See, e. g., Elsmere Music, 623 F. 2d, at 253, n. 1; Fisher v. Dees, 794 F. 2d, at 438-439. What makes for this recognition is quotation of the original's most distinctive or memorable features, which the parodist can be sure the audience will know. Once enough has been taken to assure identification, how much more is reasonable will depend, say, on the extent to which the song's overriding purpose and character is to parody the original or, in contrast, the likelihood that the parody may serve as a market substitute for the original. But using some characteristic features cannot be avoided.

We think the Court of Appeals was insufficiently appreciative of parody's need for the recognizable sight or sound when it ruled 2 Live Crew's use unreasonable as a matter of law. It is true, of course, that 2 Live Crew copied the characteristic opening bass riff (or musical phrase) of the original, and true that the words of the first line copy the Orbison lyrics. But if quotation of the opening riff and the first line may be said to go to the "heart" of the original, the heart is also what most readily conjures up the song for parody, and it is the heart at which parody takes aim. Copying does not become excessive in relation to parodic purpose merely because the portion taken was the original's heart. If 2 Live Crew had copied a significantly less memorable part of the original, it is difficult to see how its parodic character would have come through. See Fisher v. Dees, 794 F. 2d, at 439.

This is not, of course, to say that anyone who calls himself a parodist can skim the cream and get away scot free. In parody, as in news reporting, see Harper & Row, supra, context is everything, and the question of fairness asks what else the parodist did besides go to the heart of the original. It is significant that 2 Live Crew not only copied the first line of the original, but thereafter departed markedly from the Orbison lyrics for its own ends. 2 Live Crew not only copied the bass riff and repeated it, but also produced otherwise distinctive sounds, interposing "scraper" noise, overlaying the music with solos in different keys, and altering the drum beat. See 754 F. Supp., at 1155. This is not a case, then, where "a substantial portion" of the parody itself is composed of a "verbatim" copying of the original. It is not, that is, a case where the parody is so insubstantial, as compared to the copying, that the third factor must be resolved as a matter of law against the parodists.

Suffice it to say here that, as to the lyrics, we think the Court of Appeals correctly suggested that "no more was taken than necessary," 972 F. 2d, at 1438, but just for that reason, we fail to see how the copying can be excessive in relation to its parodic purpose, even if the portion taken is the original's "heart." As to the music, we express no opinion whether repetition of the bass riff is excessive copying, and we remand to permit evaluation of the amount taken, in light of the song's parodic purpose and character, its transformative elements, and considerations of the potential for market substitution sketched more fully below.

The fourth fair use factor is "the effect of the use upon the potential market for or value of the copyrighted work." § 107(4). It requires courts to consider not only the extent of market harm caused by the particular actions of the alleged infringer, but also "whether unrestricted and widespread conduct of the sort engaged in by the defendant . . . would result in a substantially adverse impact on the potential market" for the original. Nimmer § 13.05[A][4], p. 13-102.61 (footnote omitted); accord Harper & Row, 471 U. S., at 569; Senate Report, p. 65; Folsom v. Marsh, 9 F. Cas., at 349. The enquiry "must take account not only of harm to the original but also of harm to the market for derivative works." Harper & Row, supra, at 568.

Since fair use is an affirmative defense, its proponent would have difficulty carrying the burden of demonstrating fair use without favorable evidence about relevant markets. In moving for summary judgment, 2 Live Crew left themselves at just such a disadvantage when they failed to address the effect on the market for rap derivatives, and confined themselves to uncontroverted submissions that there was no likely effect on the market for the original. They did not, however, thereby subject themselves to the evidentiary presumption applied by the Court of Appeals. In assessing the likelihood of significant market harm, the Court of Appeals quoted from language in Sony that " `[i]f the intended use is for commercial gain, that likelihood may be presumed. But if it is for a noncommercial purpose, the likelihood must be demonstrated.' " 972 F. 2d, at 1438, quoting Sony, 464 U. S., at 451. The court reasoned that because "the use of the copyrighted work is wholly commercial, . . . we presume a likelihood of future harm to Acuff Rose exists." 972 F. 2d, at 1438. In so doing, the court resolved the fourth factor against 2 Live Crew, just as it had the first, by applying a presumption about the effect of commercial use, a presumption which as applied here we hold to be error.

No "presumption" or inference of market harm that might find support in Sony is applicable to a case involving something beyond mere duplication for commercial purposes. Sony's discussion of a presumption contrasts a context of verbatim copying of the original in its entirety for commercial purposes, with the non commercial context of Sony itself (home copying of television programming). In the former circumstances, what Sony said simply makes common sense: when a commercial use amounts to mere duplication of the entirety of an original, it clearly "supersede[s] the objects," Folsom v. Marsh, 9 F. Cas., at 348, of the original and serves as a market replacement for it, making it likely that cognizable market harm to the original will occur. Sony, 464 U. S., at 451. But when, on the contrary, the second use is transformative, market substitution is at least less certain, and market harm may not be so readily inferred. Indeed, as to parody pure and simple, it is more likely that the new work will not affect the market for the original in a way cognizable under this factor, that is, by acting as a substitute for it ("supersed[ing] [its] objects"). See Leval 1125; Patry & Perlmutter 692, 697-698. This is so because the parody and the original usually serve different market functions. Bisceglia, ASCAP, Copyright Law Symposium, No. 34, p. 23.

We do not, of course, suggest that a parody may not harm the market at all, but when a lethal parody, like a scathing theater review, kills demand for the original, it does not produce a harm cognizable under the Copyright Act. Because "parody may quite legitimately aim at garroting the original, destroying it commercially as well as artistically," B. Kaplan, An Unhurried View of Copyright 69 (1967), the role of the courts is to distinguish between "[b]iting criticism [that merely] suppresses demand [and] copyright infringement[, which] usurps it." Fisher v. Dees, 794 F. 2d, at 438.

This distinction between potentially remediable displacement and unremediable disparagement is reflected in the rule that there is no protectable derivative market for criticism. The market for potential derivative uses includes only those that creators of original works would in general develop or license others to develop. Yet the unlikelihood that creators of imaginative works will license critical reviews or lampoons of their own productions removes such uses from the very notion of a potential licensing market. "People ask . . . for criticism, but they only want praise." S. Maugham, Of Human Bondage 241 (Penguin ed. 1992). Thus, to the extent that the opinion below may be read to have considered harm to the market for parodies of "Oh, Pretty Woman," see 972 F. 2d, at 1439, the court erred. Accord, Fisher v. Dees, 794 F. 2d, at 437; Leval 1125; Patry & Perlmutter 688-691.

In explaining why the law recognizes no derivative market for critical works, including parody, we have, of course, been speaking of the later work as if it had nothing but a critical aspect (i.e., "parody pure and simple," supra, at 22). But the later work may have a more complex character, with effects not only in the arena of criticism but also in protectable markets for derivative works, too. In that sort of case, the law looks beyond the criticism to the other elements of the work, as it does here. 2 Live Crew's song comprises not only parody but also rap music, and the derivative market forrap music is a proper focus of enquiry, see Harper & Row, 471 U. S., at 568; Nimmer § 13.05[B]. Evidence of substantial harm to it would weigh against a finding of fair use, because the licensing of derivatives is an important economic incentive to the creation of originals. See 17 U.S.C. § 106(2) (copyright owner has rights to derivative works). Of course, the only harm to derivatives that need concern us, as discussed above, is the harm of market substitution. The fact that a parody may impair the market for derivative uses by the very effectiveness of its critical commentary is no more relevant under copyright than the like threat to the original market. [n.24]

Although 2 Live Crew submitted uncontroverted affidavits on the question of market harm to the original, neither they, nor Acuff Rose, introduced evidence or affidavits addressing the likely effect of 2 Live Crew's parodic rap song on the market for a non parody, rap version of "Oh, Pretty Woman." And while Acuff Rose would have us find evidence of a rap market in the very facts that 2 Live Crew recorded a rap parody of "Oh, Pretty Woman" and another rap group sought a license to record a rap derivative, there was no evidence that a potential rap market was harmed in any way by 2 Live Crew's parody, rap version. The fact that 2 Live Crew's parody sold as part of a collection of rap songs says very little about the parody's effect on a market for a rap version of the original, either of the music alone or ofthe music with its lyrics. The District Court essentially passed on this issue, observing that Acuff Rose is free to record "whatever version of the original it desires," 754 F. Supp., at 1158; the Court of Appeals went the other way by erroneous presumption. Contrary to each treatment, it is impossible to deal with the fourth factor except by recognizing that a silent record on an important factor bearing on fair use disentitled the proponent of the defense, 2 Live Crew, to summary judgment. The evidentiary hole will doubtless be plugged on remand.

It was error for the Court of Appeals to conclude that the commercial nature of 2 Live Crew's parody of "Oh, Pretty Woman" rendered it presumptively unfair. No such evidentiary presumption is available to address either the first factor, the character and purpose of the use, or the fourth, market harm, in determining whether a transformative use, such as parody, is a fair one. The court also erred in holding that 2 Live Crew had necessarily copied excessively from the Orbison original, considering the parodic purpose of the use. We therefore reverse the judgment of the Court of Appeals and remand for further proceedings consistent with this opinion.

It is so ordered.

Appendix A

"Oh, Pretty Woman" by Roy Orbison and William Dees

Pretty Woman, walking down the street,

Pretty Woman, the kind I like to meet,

Pretty Woman, I don't believe you,

you're not the truth,

No one could look as good as you

Mercy

Pretty Woman, won't you pardon me,

Pretty Woman, I couldn't help but see,

Pretty Woman, that you look lovely as can be

Are you lonely just like me?

Pretty Woman, stop a while,

Pretty Woman, talk a while,

Pretty Woman give your smile to me

Pretty woman, yeah, yeah, yeah

Pretty Woman, look my way,

Pretty Woman, say you'll stay with me

`Cause I need you, I'll treat you right

Come to me baby, Be mine tonight

Pretty Woman, don't walk on by,

Pretty Woman, don't make me cry,

Pretty Woman, don't walk away,

Hey, O. K.

If that's the way it must be, O. K.

I guess I'll go on home, it's late

There'll be tomorrow night, but wait!

What do I see

Is she walking back to me?

Yeah, she's walking back to me!

Oh, Pretty Woman.

Appendix B

%Pretty Woman" as Recorded by 2 Live Crew

Pretty woman walkin' down the street

Pretty woman girl you look so sweet

Pretty woman you bring me down to that knee

Pretty woman you make me wanna beg please

Oh, pretty woman

Big hairy woman you need to shave that stuff

Big hairy woman you know I bet it's tough

Big hairy woman all that hair it ain't legit

`Cause you look like `Cousin It'

Big hairy woman

Bald headed woman girl your hair won't grow

Bald headed woman you got a teeny weeny afro

Bald headed woman you know your hair could look nice

Bald headed woman first you got to roll it with rice

Bald headed woman here, let me get this hunk of biz for ya

Ya know what I'm saying you look better than rice a roni

Oh bald headed woman

Big hairy woman come on in

And don't forget your bald headed friend

Hey pretty woman let the boys

Jump in

Two timin' woman girl you know you ain't right

Two timin' woman you's out with my boy last night

Two timin' woman that takes a load off my mind

Two timin' woman now I know the baby ain't mine

Oh, two timin' woman

Oh pretty woman

388 F.3d 1189 (2003)

NEWTON v DIAMOND

NINTH CIRCUIT COURT OF APPEALS

SCHROEDER, Chief Judge:

This appeal raises the difficult and important issue of whether the incorporation of a short segment of a musical recording into a new musical recording, i.e., the practice of "sampling," requires a license to use both the performance and the composition of the original recording. The particular sample in this case consists of a six-second, three-note segment of a performance of one of his own compositions by plaintiff, and accomplished jazz flutist, James W. Newton. The defendants, the performers who did the sampling, are the members of the musical group Beastie Boys. They obtained a license to sample the sound recording of Newton's copyrighted performance, but they did not obtain a license to use Newton's underlying composition, which is also copyrighted.

The district court granted summary judgment to the defendants. In a scholarly opinion, it held that no license to the underlying composition was required because, as a matter of law, the notes in question -- C - D flat - C, over a held C note -- lacked sufficient originality to merit copyright protection. The district court also held that even if the sampled segment of the composition were original, Beastie Boys' use of a brief segment of the sound recording of "Choir" was a de minimis use of the "Choir" composition and therefore was not actionable. We affirm on the ground that the use was de minimis.

Background and Procedural History

The plaintiff and appellant in this case, James W. Newton, is an accomplished avant-garde jazz flutist and composer. In 1978, he composed the song "Choir," a piece for flute and voice intended to incorporate elements of African-American gospel music, Japanese ceremonial court music, tradi- tional African music, and classical music, among others. According to Newton, the song was in- spired by his earliest memory of music, watching four women singing in a church in rural Arkansas. In 1981, Newton performed and recorded "Choir" and licensed all rights in the sound recording to ECM Records for $ 5000.1 The license covered only the sound recording, and it is undisputed that Newton retained all rights to the composition of "Choir." Sound recordings and their underlying compositions are separate works with their own distinct copyrights. 17 U.S.C. ß 102(a)(2), (7).

The defendants and appellees include the members of the rap and hip-hop group Beastie Boys, and their business associates. In 1992, Beastie Boys obtained a license from ECM Records to use portions of the sound recording of "Choir" in various renditions of their song "Pass the Mic" in exchange for a one-time fee of $

1000. Beastie Boys did not obtain a license from Newton to use the underlying composition.

The portion of the composition at issue consists of three notes, C -- D flat -- C, sung over a background C note played on the flute. The score to "Choir" also indicates that the entire song should be played in a "largo/senza-misura" tempo, meaning "slowly/without-measure." The parties disagree about whether two additional elements appear in the score. First, Newton argues that the score contains an instruction that requires overblowing the background C note that is played on the flute. Second, Newton argues that multiphonics are part of the composition because they are neces- sarily created when a performer follows the instructions on the score to simultaneously play the flute note and sing the vocal notes. Because we review the district court's grant of summary judg- ment to the Beastie Boys, we must construe the evidence in Newton's favor. We therefore assume that these two elements are part of the "Choir" composition. As we will discuss more fully below, there are other elements that are part of Newton's performance that was captured in the sound recording, but that do not appear in the score.

The dispute between Newton and Beastie Boys centers around the copyright implications of the practice of sampling, a practice now common to many types of popular music. Sampling entails the incorporation of short segments of prior sound recordings into new recordings. The practice originated in Jamaica in the 1960s, when disc jockeys (DJs) used portable sound systems to mix segments of prior recordings into new mixes, which they would overlay with chanted or 'scatted' vocals. Sampling migrated to the United States and developed throughout the 1970s, using the analog technologies of the time. The digital sampling involved here developed in the early 1980s with the advent of digital synthesizers having MIDI (Musical Instrument Digital Interface) keyboard con- trols. These digital instruments allowed artists digitally to manipulate and combine sampled sounds, expanding the range of possibilities for the use of prerecorded music. Whereas analog devices lim- ited artists to "scratching" vinyl records and "cutting" back and forth between different sound re- cordings, digital technology allowed artists to slow down, speed up, combine, and otherwise alter the samples.

Pursuant to their license from ECM Records, Beastie Boys digitally sampled the opening six seconds of Newton's sound recording of "Choir." Beastie Boys repeated or "looped" this six-second sample as a background element throughout "Pass the Mic," so that it appears over forty times in various renditions of the song. In addition to the version of "Pass the Mic" released on their 1992 album, "Check Your Head," Beastie Boys included the "Choir" sample in two remixes, "Dub the Mic" and "Pass the Mic (Pt. 2, Skills to Pay the Bills)." It is unclear whether the sample was altered or manipulated, though Beastie Boys' sound engineer stated that alterations of tone, pitch, and rhythm are commonplace, and Newton maintains that the pitch was lowered slightly.

Newton filed the instant action in federal court on May 9, 2000, alleging violations of his copy- right in the underlying composition, as well as Lanham Act violations for misappropriation and re- verse passing off. The district court dismissed Newton's Lanham Act claims on September 12, 2000, and granted summary judgment in favor of Beastie Boys on the copyright claims on May 21, 2002. The district court held that the three-note segment of the "Choir" composition could not be copyrighted because, as a matter of law, it lacked the requisite originality. The court also concluded that even if the segment were copyrightable, Beastie Boys' use of the work was de minimis and therefore not actionable. Newton appealed.

Whether Defendants' Use was De Minimis

We may affirm the grant of summary judgment on any basis supported by the record and need not reach each ground relied upon by the district court. Assuming that the sampled segment of the composition was sufficiently original to merit copyright protection, we nevertheless affirm on the ground that Beastie Boys' use was de minimis and therefore not actionable.

For an unauthorized use of a copyrighted work to be actionable, the use must be significant enough to constitute infringement. See Ringgold v. Black Entertainment TV, 126 F.3d 70, 74-75 (2d Cir. 1997). This means that even where the fact of copying is conceded, no legal consequences will follow from that fact unless the copying is substantial. The principle that trivial copy- ing does not constitute actionable infringement has long been a part of copyright law. Indeed, as Judge Learned Hand observed over 80 years ago: "Even where there is some copying, that fact is not conclusive of infringement. Some copying is permitted. In addition to copying, it must be shown that this has been done to an unfair extent." This principle reflects the legal maxim, de mini- mis non curat lex (often rendered as, "the law does not concern itself with trifles"). See Ringgold, 126 F.3d at 74-75.

A leading case on de minimis infringement in our circuit is Fisher v. Dees, 794 F.2d 432 (9th Cir. 1986), where we observed that a use is de minimis only if the average audience would not recognize the appropriation. See id. at 434 n.2 ("[A] taking is considered de minimis only if it is so meager and fragmentary that the average audience would not recognize the appropriation."). This observation reflects the relationship between the de minimis maxim and the general test for substan- tial similarity, which also looks to the response of the average audience, or ordinary observer, to determine whether a use is infringing. See, e.g., Cavalier v. Random House, Inc., 297 F.3d 815, 822 (9th Cir. 2002); Castle Rock Entm't, Inc. v. Carol Publ'g Group, Inc., 150 F.3d 132 (2d Cir. 1998) ("Two works are substantially similar where 'the ordinary observer, unless he set out to detect the disparities, would be disposed to overlook them, and regard [the] aesthetic appeal [of the two works] as the same.'" To say that a use is de minimis because no audience would recognize the ap- propriation is thus to say that the use is not sufficiently significant.

On the facts of Fisher, this court rejected the de minimis defense because the copying was substantial: the defendant had appropriated the main theme and lyrics of the plaintiff's song, both of which were easily recognizable in the defendant's parody. Specifically, the defendant copied six of the thirty-eight bars to the 1950s standard, "When Sunny Gets Blue," to make the parody, "When Sonny Sniffs Glue," and paralleled the original lyrics with only minor variations. However, despite the works' substantial similarities, we held that the use was nevertheless non-infringing because, as a parody, it was "fair use" under 17 U.S.C.

ß 107. We explained that the defendant's successful fair use defense precluded a finding that the use was insubstantial or unrecognizable because "the parodist must appropriate a substantial enough portion of [the original] to evoke recognition."

This case involves not only use of a composition, as was the case in Fisher, but also use of a sound recording of a particular performance of that composition. Because the defendants were authorized to use the sound recording, our inquiry is confined to whether the unauthorized use of the composition itself was substantial enough to sustain an infringement claim. Therefore, we may consider only Beastie Boys' appropriation of the song's compositional elements and must remove from consideration all the elements unique to Newton's performance. Stated another way, we must "filter out" the licensed elements of the sound recording to get down to the unlicensed elements of the composition, as the composition is the sole basis for Newton's infringement claim. See Cavalier, 297 F.3d at 822; Apple Computer, Inc. v. Microsoft Corp., 35 F.3d 1435, 1446 (9th Cir. 1994).

In filtering out the unique performance elements from consideration, and separating them from those found in the composition, we find substantial assistance in the testimony of Newton's own experts. Because we are reviewing a grant of summary judgment in favor of the Beastie Boys, we must view the evidence in the light most favorable to Newton and affirm only if there is no genuine issue of material fact. Newton's experts, however, reveal the extent to which the sound recording of "Choir" is the product of Newton's highly developed performance techniques, rather than the result of a generic rendition of the composition. As a general matter, according to Newton's expert Dr. Christopher Dobrian, "the contribution of the performer is often so great that s/he in fact provides as much musical content as the composer." This is particularly true with works like "Choir," given the improvisational nature of jazz performance and the minimal scoring of the composition. Indeed, as Newton's expert Dr. Oliver Wilson explained:

The copyrighted score of "Choir", as is the custom in scores written in the jazz tradi- tion, does not contain indications for all of the musical subtleties that it is assumed the performer-composer of the work will make in the work's performance. The function of the score is more mnemonic in intention than prescriptive.

And it is clear that Newton goes beyond the score in his performance. For example, Dr. Dobrian declared that "Mr. Newton blows and sings in such a way as to emphasize the upper partials of the flute's complex harmonic tone, [although] such a modification of tone color is not explicitly re- quested in the score." Dr. Dobrian also concludes that Newton "uses breath control to modify the timbre of the sustained flute note rather extremely" and "uses portamento to glide expressively from one pitch to another in the vocal part." Dr. Dobrian concedes that these elements do not appear in the score, and that they are part of Newton's performance of the piece.

A crucial problem with the testimony of Newton's experts is that they continually refer to the "sound" produced by the "Newton technique." A sound is protected by copyright law only when it is "fixed in a tangible medium." 17 U.S.C. ß 102(a). Here, the only time any sound was fixed in a tangible medium was when a particular performance was recorded. Newton licensed the recording at issue to ECM Records over twenty years ago, and ECM Records in turn licensed the interest in the recording to the Beastie Boys. Newton's copyright extends only to the elements that he fixed in a tangible medium -- those that he wrote on the score. Thus, regardless of whether the average audience might recognize the "Newton technique" at work in the sampled sound recording, those performance elements are beyond consideration in Newton's claim for infringement of his copyright in the underlying composition.

Once we have isolated the basis of Newton's infringement action -- the "Choir" composition, devoid of the unique performance elements found only in the sound recording -- we turn to the nub of our inquiry: whether Beastie Boys' unauthorized use of the composition, as opposed to their authorized use of the sound recording, was substantial enough to sustain an infringement action. In answering that question, we must distinguish between whether there is a high enough degree of similarity [*1195] between the works to establish copying, and whether that copying is substantial enough to constitute infringement. The practice of music sampling will often present cases where the degree of similarity is high. Indeed, unless the sample has been altered or digitally manipulated, it will be identical to the sampled portion of the original recording. Yet as Nimmer explains, "[if] the similarity is only as to nonessential matters, then a finding of no substantial similarity should result." This reflects the principle that the substantiality requirement applies throughout the law of copyright, including cases of music sampling, even where there is a high degree of similarity.

The high degree of similarity between the works here (i.e., "Pass the Mic" and "Choir"), but the limited scope of the copying, place Newton's claim for infringement into the class of cases that al- lege what Nimmer refers to as "fragmented literal similarity." Fragmented literal similarity exists where the defendant copies a portion of the plaintiff's work exactly or nearly exactly, without ap- propriating the work's overall essence or structure. Because the degree of similarity is high in such cases, the dispositive question is whether the copying goes to trivial or substantial elements. Sub- stantiality is measured by considering the qualitative and quantitative significance of the copied por- tion in relation to the plaintiff's work as a whole. See, e.g., Worth v. Selchow & Righter Co., 827 F.2d 569, 570 n. 1 (9th Cir. 1987) ("The relevant inquiry is whether a substantial portion of the pro- tectible material in the plaintiff's work was appropriated -- not whether a substantial portion of de- fendant's work was derived from plaintiff's work."). This focus on the sample's relation to the plain- tiff's work as a whole embodies the fundamental question in any infringement action, as expressed more than 150 years ago by Justice Story: whether "so much is taken[] that the value of the original is sensibly diminished, or the labors of the original author are substantially to an injurious extent appropriated by another." Folsom v. Marsh, 9 F. Cas. 342, 348, F. Cas. No. 4901 (C.C. Mass. 1841) (No. 4901). Courts also focus on the relationship to the plaintiff's work because a contrary rule that measured the significance of the copied segment in the defendant's work would allow an unscrupu- lous defendant to copy large or qualitatively significant portions of another's work and escape liabil- ity by burying them beneath non-infringing material in the defendant's own work, even where the average audience might recognize the appropriation. Cf. Sheldon v. Metro-Goldwyn Pictures Corp., 81 F.2d 49, 56 (2d Cir. 1936) ("It is enough that substantial parts were lifted; no plagiarist can ex- cuse the wrong by showing how much of his work he did not pirate."). Thus, as the district court properly concluded, the fact that Beastie Boys "looped" the sample throughout "Pass the Mic" is irrelevant in weighing the sample's qualitative and quantitative significance.

On the undisputed facts of this record, no reasonable juror could find the sampled portion of the composition to be a quantitatively or qualitatively significant portion of the composition as a whole. Quantitatively, the three-note sequence appears only once in Newton's composition. It is difficult to measure the precise relationship between this segment and the composition as a whole, because the score calls for between 180 and 270 seconds of improvisation. When played, however, the segment [*1196] lasts six seconds and is roughly two percent of the four-and-a-half-minute "Choir" sound recording licensed by Beastie Boys. Qualitatively, this section of the composition is no more significant than any other section. Indeed, with the exception of two notes, the entirety of the scored portions of "Choir" consist of notes separated by whole- and half-steps from their neighbors and is played with the same technique of singing and playing the flute simultaneously; the remainder of the composition calls for sections of improvisation that range between 90 and 180 seconds in length.

The Beastie Boys' expert, Dr. Lawrence Ferrara, concludes that the compositional elements of the sampled section do not represent the heart or the hook of the "Choir" composition, but rather are "simple, minimal and insignificant." The sampled section may be representative of the scored por- tions of the composition as Newton's expert's contend. Newton has failed to offer any evidence, however, to rebut Dr. Ferrara's testimony and to create a triable issue of fact on the key question, which is whether the sampled section is a qualitatively significant portion of the "Choir" composi- tion as a whole. Instead, Newton's experts emphasize the uniqueness of the "Newton technique," which is found throughout the "Choir" composition and in Newton's other work.

Newton nevertheless maintains that the testimony of his experts creates a genuine issue of mate- rial fact on the substantiality of the copying. To the extent the expert testimony is relevant, it is not helpful to Newton. On the key question of whether the sample is quantitatively or qualitatively sig- nificant in relation to the composition as a whole, his experts are either silent or fail to distinguish between the sound recording, which was licensed, and the composition, which was not. Moreover, their testimony on the composition does not contain anything from which a reasonable jury could infer the segment's significance in relation to the composition as a whole. In contrast, Dr. Ferrara stated that the sampled excerpt from the "Choir" composition "is merely a common, trite, and ge- neric three-note sequence, which lacks any distinct melodic, harmonic, rhythmic or structural ele- ments." He described the sequence as "a common building block tool" that "has been used over and over again by major composers in the 20th century, particularly in the '60s and '70s, just prior to James Newton's usage."

Because Newton conceded that "Choir" and "Pass the Mic" "are substantially dissimilar in con- cept and feel, that is, in [their] overall thrust and meaning" and failed to offer any evidence to rebut Dr. Ferrara's testimony that the sampled section is not a quantitatively or qualitatively significant portion of the "Choir" composition, the Beastie Boys are entitled to prevail on summary judgment. On the undisputed facts of this case, we conclude that an average audience would not discern New- ton's hand as a composer, apart from his talent as a performer, from Beastie Boys' use of the sample. The copying was not significant enough to constitute infringement. Beastie Boys' use of the "Choir" composition was de minimis. There is no genuine issue of material fact, and the grant of summary judgment was appropriate.

Conclusion

Because Beastie Boys' use of the sound recording was authorized, the sole basis of Newton's in- fringement action is his remaining copyright interest in the "Choir" composition. We hold that Beastie Boys' use of a brief segment of that composition, consisting of three notes separated by a half-step over a background C note, is not sufficient to sustain a claim for infringement of Newton's copyright in the composition "Choir". We affirm the district court's grant of summary judgment on the ground that Beastie Boys' use of the composition was de minimis and therefore not actionable.

410 F.3d 792 (2005)

BRIDGEPORT V. DIMENSION FILMS

US Court of Appeals for the Sixth Circuit

RALPH B. GUY, JR., Circuit Judge.

The court issued an initial opinion in these consolidated cases on September 7, 2004. Bridgeport Music, Inc. v. Dimension Films, 383 F.3d 390 (6th Cir. 2004). Through an Order entered December 20, 2004, the full court denied the petition for rehearing en banc filed by No Limit Films and a panel rehearing was granted only with respect to the issues discussed in Section II of the opinion as amended. Bridgeport Music, Inc. v. Dimension Films, 401 F.3d 647 (6th Cir. 2004). After additional briefing and argument on rehearing, we adhere to our conclusions and amend the opinion to further clarify our reasoning.

Plaintiffs, Bridgeport Music, Inc., Westbound Records, Inc., Southfield Music, Inc., and Nine Records, Inc., appeal from several of the district court's findings with respect to the copyright infringement claims asserted against No Limit Films. This action arises out of the use of a sample from the composition and sound recording "Get Off Your Ass and Jam" ("Get Off") in the rap song "100 Miles and Runnin'" ("100 Miles"), which was included in the sound track of the movie I Got the Hook Up (Hook Up). Specifically, Westbound appeals from the district court's decision to grant summary judgment to defendant on the grounds that the alleged infringement was de minimis and therefore not actionable. Bridgeport, while not appealing from the summary judgment order, challenges instead the denial of its motion to amend the complaint to assert new claims of infringement based on a different song included in the sound track of Hook Up. Finally, Bridgeport, Southfield, and Nine Records appeal from the decision to award attorney fees and costs totaling $41,813.30 to No Limit Films under 17 U.S.C. § 505. For the reasons that follow, we reverse the district court's grant of summary judgment to No Limit on Westbound's claim of infringement of its sound recording copyright, but affirm the decision of the district court as to the award of attorney fees and the denial of Bridgeport's motion to amend.

The claims at issue in this appeal were originally asserted in an action filed on May 4, 2001, by the related entities Bridgeport Music, Southfield Music, Westbound Records, and Nine Records, alleging nearly 500 counts against approximately 800 defendants for copyright infringement and various state law claims relating to the use of samples without permission in new rap recordings. In August 2001, the district court severed that original complaint into 476 separate actions, this being one of them, based on the allegedly infringing work and ordered that amended complaints be filed.

The claims in this case were brought by all four plaintiffs: Bridgeport and Southfield, which are in the business of music publishing and exploiting musical composition copyrights, and Westbound Records and Nine Records, which are in the business of recording and distributing sound recordings. It was conceded at the time of summary judgment, however, that neither Southfield Music nor Nine Records had any ownership interest in the copyrights at issue in this case. As a result, the district court ordered that they be jointly and severally liable for 10% of the attorney fees and costs awarded to No Limit Films.

Bridgeport and Westbound claim to own the musical composition and sound recording copyrights in "Get Off Your Ass and Jam" by George Clinton, Jr. and the Funkadelics. We assume, as did the district court, that plaintiffs would be able to establish ownership in the copyrights they claim. There seems to be no dispute either that "Get Off" was digitally sampled or that the recording "100 Miles" was included on the sound track of I Got the Hook Up. Defendant No Limit Films, in conjunction with Priority Records, released the movie to theaters on May 27, 1998. The movie was apparently also released on VHS, DVD, and cable television. Fatal to Bridgeport's claims of infringement was the Release and Agreement it entered into with two of the original owners of the composition "100 Miles," Ruthless Attack Muzick (RAM) and Dollarz N Sense Music (DNSM), in December 1998, granting a sample use license to RAM, DNSM, and their licensees. Finding that No Limit Films had previously been granted an oral synchronization license to use the composition "100 Miles" in the sound track of Hook Up, the district court concluded Bridgeport's claims against No Limit Films were barred by the unambiguous terms of the Release and Agreement. Bridgeport Music, Inc. v. Dimension Films, 230 F. Supp. 2d 830, 833-38 (M.D. Tenn. 2002). Although Bridgeport does not appeal from this determination, it is relevant to the district court's later decision to award attorney fees to No Limit Films.

Westbound's claims are for infringement of the sound recording "Get Off."3 Because defendant does not deny it, we assume that the sound track of Hook Up used portions of "100 Miles" that included the allegedly infringing sample from "Get Off." The recording "Get Off" opens with a three-note combination solo guitar "riff" that lasts four seconds. According to one of plaintiffs' experts, Randy Kling, the recording "100 Miles" contains a sample from that guitar solo. Specifically, a two-second sample from the guitar solo was copied, the pitch was lowered, and the copied piece was "looped" and extended to 16 beats. Kling states that this sample appears in the sound recording "100 Miles" in five places; specifically, at 0:49, 1:52, 2:29, 3:20 and 3:46. By the district court's estimation, each looped segment lasted approximately 7 seconds. As for the segment copied from "Get Off," the district court described it as follows:

The portion of the song at issue here is an arpeggiated chord—that is, three notes that, if struck together, comprise a chord but instead are played one at a time in very quick succession—that is repeated several times at the opening of "Get Off." The arpeggiated chord is played on an unaccompanied electric guitar. The rapidity of the notes and the way they are played produce a high-pitched, whirling sound that captures the listener's attention and creates anticipation of what is to follow.

Bridgeport, 230 F. Supp. 2d at 839. No Limit Films moved for summary judgment, arguing (1) that the sample was not protected by copyright law because it was not "original"; and (2) that the sample was legally insubstantial and therefore does not amount to actionable copying under copyright law.

Mindful of the limited number of notes and chords available to composers, the district court explained that the question turned not on the originality of the chord but, rather, on "the use of and the aural effect produced by the way the notes and the chord are played, especially here where copying of the sound recording is at issue." Id. (citations omitted). The district court found, after carefully listening to the recording of "Get Off," "that a jury could reasonably conclude that the way the arpeggiated chord is used and memorialized in the `Get Off' sound recording is original and creative and therefore entitled to copyright protection." Id. (citing Newton v. Diamond, 204 F. Supp. 2d 1244, 1249-59 (C.D. Cal. 2002)) (later affirmed on other grounds at 349 F.3d 591 (9th Cir. 2003)). No Limit Films does not appeal from this determination.

Turning then to the question of de minimis copying in the context of digital sampling, the district court concluded that, whether the sampling is examined under a qualitative/quantitative de minimis analysis or under the so-called "fragmented literal similarity" test, the sampling in this case did not "rise to the level of a legally cognizable appropriation." 230 F. Supp. 2d at 841. Westbound argues that the district court erred both in its articulation of the applicable standards and its determination that there was no genuine issue of fact precluding summary judgment on this issue.

On October 11, 2002, the district court granted summary judgment to No Limit Films on the claims of Bridgeport and Westbound; dismissed with prejudice the claims of Southfield and Nine Records; denied as moot the motion of Bridgeport and Westbound for partial summary judgment on the issue of copyright ownership; and entered final judgment accordingly. Bridgeport and Westbound appealed. The facts relevant to the earlier denial of Bridgeport's motion to amend the complaint will be discussed below. No Limit Films filed a post-judgment motion for attorney fees and costs, which the district court granted for the reasons set forth in its memorandum opinion and order of April 24, 2003. Bridgeport, Southfield Music, and Nine Records appealed from that award.

The district court's decision granting summary judgment is reviewed de novo. Smith v. Ameritech, 129 F.3d 857, 863 (6th Cir. 1997). In deciding a motion for summary judgment, the court must view the evidence and reasonable inferences in the light most favorable to the nonmoving party. Matsushita Elec. Indus. Co. v. Zenith Radio Corp., 475 U.S. 574, 587, 106 S. Ct. 1348, 89 L. Ed. 2d 538 (1986). Summary judgment is appropriate when there are no genuine issues of material fact in dispute and the moving party is entitled to judgment as a matter of law. Fed. R. Civ. P. 56(c).

In granting summary judgment to defendant, the district court looked to general de minimis principles and emphasized the paucity of case law on the issue of whether digital sampling amounts to copyright infringement. Drawing on both the quantitative/qualitative and "fragmented literal similarity" approaches, the district court found the de minimis analysis was a derivation of the substantial similarity element when a defendant claims that the literal copying of a small and insignificant portion of the copyrighted work should be allowed. After listening to the copied segment, the sample, and both songs, the district court found that no reasonable juror, even one familiar with the works of George Clinton, would recognize the source of the sample without having been told of its source. This finding, coupled with findings concerning the quantitatively small amount of copying involved and the lack of qualitative similarity between the works, led the district court to conclude that Westbound could not prevail on its claims for copyright infringement of the sound recording.4

Westbound does not challenge the district court's characterization of either the segment copied from "Get Off" or the sample that appears in "100 Miles." Nor does Westbound argue that there is some genuine dispute as to any material fact concerning the nature of the protected material in the two works. The heart of Westbound's arguments is the claim that no substantial similarity or de minimis inquiry should be undertaken at all when the defendant has not disputed that it digitally sampled a copyrighted sound recording. We agree and accordingly must reverse the grant of summary judgment.

A. Digital Sampling of Copyrighted Sound Recordings

At the outset it is important to make clear the precise nature of our decision. Our conclusions are as follows:

1. The analysis that is appropriate for determining infringement of a musical composition copyright, is not the analysis that is to be applied to determine infringement of a sound recording. We address this issue only as it pertains to sound recording copyrights.

2. Since the district court decision essentially tracked the analysis that is made if a musical composition copyright were at issue, we depart from that analysis.

3. We agree with the district court's analysis on the question of originality. On remand, we assume that Westbound will be able to establish it has a copyright in the sound recording and that a digital sample from the copyrighted sound recording was used in this case.

4. This case involves "digital sampling" which is a term of art well understood by the parties to this litigation and the music industry in general. Accordingly, we adopt the definition commonly accepted within the industry.

5. Because of the court's limited technological knowledge in this specialized field, our opinion is limited to an instance of digital sampling of a sound recording protected by a valid copyright. If by analogy it is possible to extend our analysis to other forms of sampling, we leave it to others to do so.

6. Advances in technology coupled with the advent of the popularity of hip hop or rap music have made instances of digital sampling extremely common and have spawned a plethora of copyright disputes and litigation.

7. The music industry, as well as the courts, are best served if something approximating a bright-line test can be established. Not necessarily a "one size fits all" test, but one that, at least, adds clarity to what constitutes actionable infringement with regard to the digital sampling of copyrighted sound recordings.

We do not set forth the arguments made by Westbound since our analysis differs somewhat from that offered by the plaintiff. Our analysis begins and largely ends with the applicable statute. Section 114(a) of Title 17 of the United States Code provides:

The exclusive rights of the owner of copyright in a sound recording are limited to the rights specified by clauses (1), (2), (3) and (6) of section 106, and do not include any right of performance under section 106(4).

Section 106 provides:

Subject to sections 107 through 122, the owner of copyright under this title has the exclusive rights to do and to authorize any of the following:

(1) to reproduce the copyrighted work in copies or phonorecords;

(2) to prepare derivative works based upon the copyrighted work;

(3) to distribute copies or phonorecords of the copyrighted work to the public by sale or other transfer of ownership, or by rental, lease, or lending;

(4) in the case of literary, musical, dramatic, and choreographic works, pantomimes, and motion pictures and other audiovisual works to perform the copyrighted work publicly;

(5) in the case of literary, musical, dramatic, and choreographic works, pantomimes, and pictorial, graphic, or sculptural works, including the individual images of a motion picture or other audiovisual work, to display the copyrighted work publicly; and

(6) in the case of sound recordings, to perform the copyrighted work publicly by means of a digital audio transmission.

Section 114(b) states:

(b) The exclusive right of the owner of copyright in a sound recording under clause (1) of section 106 is limited to the right to duplicate the sound recording in the form of phonorecords or copies that directly or indirectly recapture the actual sounds fixed in the recording. The exclusive right of the owner of copyright in a sound recording under clause (2) of section 106 is limited to the right to prepare a derivative work in which the actual sounds fixed in the sound recording are rearranged, remixed, or otherwise altered in sequence or quality. The exclusive rights of the owner of copyright in a sound recording under clauses (1) and (2) of section 106 do not extend to the making or duplication of another sound recording that consists entirely of an independent fixation of other sounds, even though such sounds imitate or simulate those in the copyrighted sound recording. The exclusive rights of the owner of copyright in a sound recording under clauses (1), (2), and (3) of section 106 do not apply to sound recordings included in educational television and radio programs (as defined in section 397 of title 47) distributed or transmitted by or through public broadcasting entities (as defined by section 118(g)): Provided, That copies or phonorecords of said programs are not commercially distributed by or through public broadcasting entities to the general public.

Before discussing what we believe to be the import of the above quoted provisions of the statute, a little history is necessary. The copyright laws attempt to strike a balance between protecting original works and stifling further creativity. The provisions, for example, for compulsory licensing make it possible for "creators" to enjoy the fruits of their creations, but not to fence them off from the world at large. 17 U.S.C. § 115. Although musical compositions have always enjoyed copyright protection, it was not until 1971 that sound recordings were subject to a separate copyright. If one were to analogize to a book, it is not the book, i.e., the paper and binding, that is copyrightable, but its contents. There are probably any number of reasons why the decision was made by Congress to treat a sound recording differently from a book even though both are the medium in which an original work is fixed rather than the creation itself. None the least of them certainly were advances in technology which made the "pirating" of sound recordings an easy task. The balance that was struck was to give sound recording copyright holders the exclusive right "to duplicate the sound recording in the form of phonorecords or copies that directly or indirectly recapture the actual sounds fixed in the recording." 17 U.S.C. § 114(b). This means that the world at large is free to imitate or simulate the creative work fixed in the recording so long as an actual copy of the sound recording itself is not made. That leads us directly to the issue in this case. If you cannot pirate the whole sound recording, can you "lift" or "sample" something less than the whole. Our answer to that question is in the negative.9

Section 114(b) provides that " [t]he exclusive right of the owner of copyright in a sound recording under clause (2) of section 106 is limited to the right to prepare a derivative work in which the actual sounds fixed in the sound recording are rearranged, remixed, or otherwise altered in sequence or quality." Further, the rights of sound recording copyright holders under clauses (1) and (2) of section 106 "do not extend to the making or duplication of another sound recording that consists entirely of an independent fixation of other sounds, even though such sounds imitate or simulate those in the copyrighted sound recording." 17 U.S.C. § 114(b) (emphasis added). The significance of this provision is amplified by the fact that the Copyright Act of 1976 added the word "entirely" to this language. Compare Sound Recording Act of 1971, Pub. L. 92-140, 85 Stat. 391 (Oct. 15, 1971) (adding subsection (f) to former 17 U.S.C. § 1) ("does not extend to the making or duplication of another sound recording that is an independent fixation of other sounds"). In other words, a sound recording owner has the exclusive right to "sample" his own recording. We find much to recommend this interpretation.10

To begin with, there is ease of enforcement. Get a license or do not sample. We do not see this as stifling creativity in any significant way. It must be remembered that if an artist wants to incorporate a "riff" from another work in his or her recording, he is free to duplicate the sound of that "riff" in the studio. Second, the market will control the license price and keep it within bounds. The sound recording copyright holder cannot exact a license fee greater than what it would cost the person seeking the license to just duplicate the sample in the course of making the new recording. Third, sampling is never accidental. It is not like the case of a composer who has a melody in his head, perhaps not even realizing that the reason he hears this melody is that it is the work of another which he had heard before. When you sample a sound recording you know you are taking another's work product.

This analysis admittedly raises the question of why one should, without infringing, be able to take three notes from a musical composition, for example, but not three notes by way of sampling from a sound recording. Why is there no de minimis taking or why should substantial similarity not enter the equation. Our first answer to this question is what we have earlier indicated. We think this result is dictated by the applicable statute. Second, even when a small part of a sound recording is sampled, the part taken is something of value. No further proof of that is necessary than the fact that the producer of the record or the artist on the record intentionally sampled because it would (1) save costs, or (2) add something to the new recording, or (3) both. For the sound recording copyright holder, it is not the "song" but the sounds that are fixed in the medium of his choice. When those sounds are sampled they are taken directly from that fixed medium. It is a physical taking rather than an intellectual one.

This case also illustrates the kind of mental, musicological, and technological gymnastics that would have to be employed if one were to adopt a de minimis or substantial similarity analysis. The district judge did an excellent job of navigating these troubled waters, but not without dint of great effort. When one considers that he has hundreds of other cases all involving different samples from different songs, the value of a principled bright-line rule becomes apparent. We would want to emphasize, however, that considerations of judicial economy are not what drives this opinion. If any consideration of economy is involved it is that of the music industry. As this case and other companion cases make clear, it would appear to be cheaper to license than to litigate.

Since our holding arguably sets forth a new rule, several other observations are in order. First, although there were no existing sound recording judicial precedents to follow, we did not pull this interpretation out of thin air. Several law review and text writers, some of whom have been referenced in this opinion, have suggested that this is the proper interpretation of the copyright statute as it pertains to sound recordings. Since digital sampling has become so commonplace and rap music has become such a significant part of the record industry, it is not surprising that there are probably a hundred articles dealing with sampling and its ramifications. It is also not surprising that the viewpoint expressed in a number of these articles appears driven by whose ox is being gored. As is so often the case, where one stands depends on where one sits. For example, the sound recording copyright holders favor this interpretation as do the studio musicians and their labor organization. On the other hand, many of the hip hop artists may view this rule as stifling creativity. The record companies and performing artists are not all of one mind, however, since in many instances, today's sampler is tomorrow's samplee. The incidence of "live and let live" has been relatively high, which explains why so many instances of sampling go unprotested and why so many sampling controversies have been settled.

Second, to pursue further the subject of stifling creativity, many artists and record companies have sought licenses as a matter of course. Since there is no record of those instances of sampling that either go unnoticed or are ignored, one cannot come up with precise figures, but it is clear that a significant number of persons and companies have elected to go the licensing route. Also there is a large body of pre-1972 sound recordings that is not subject to federal copyright protection. Additionally, just as many artists and companies choose to sample and take their chances, it is likely that will continue to be the case.

Third, the record industry, including the recording artists, has the ability and know-how to work out guidelines, including a fixed schedule of license fees, if they so choose.

Fourth, we realize we are announcing a new rule and because it is new, it should not play any role in the assessment of concepts such as "willful" or "intentional" in cases that are currently before the courts or had their genesis before this decision was announced.

Finally, and unfortunately, there is no Rosetta stone for the interpretation of the copyright statute. We have taken a "literal reading" approach. The legislative history is of little help because digital sampling wasn't being done in 1971. If this is not what Congress intended or is not what they would intend now, it is easy enough for the record industry, as they have done in the past, to go back to Congress for a clarification or change in the law. This is the best place for the change to be made, rather than in the courts, because as this case demonstrates, the court is never aware of much more than the tip of the iceberg. To properly sort out this type of problem with its complex technical and business overtones, one needs the type of investigative resources as well as the ability to hold hearings that is possessed by Congress.

These conclusions require us to reverse the entry of summary judgment entered in favor of No Limit Films on Westbound's claims of copyright infringement. Since the district judge found no infringement, there was no necessity to consider the affirmative defense of "fair use." On remand, the trial judge is free to consider this defense and we express no opinion on its applicability to these facts.

...

AFFIRMED in part, REVERSED in part, and REMANDED for further proceedings

Nos. 13-57104 (2016)

SALSOUL v. MADONNA LOUISE CICCONE

United States Court of Appeals, Ninth Circuit

GRABER, Circuit Judge:

In the early 1990s, pop star Madonna Louise Ciccone, commonly known by her first name only, released the song Vogue to great commercial success. In this copyright infringement action, Plaintiff VMG Salsoul, LLC, alleges that the producer of Vogue, Shep Pettibone, copied a 0.23-second segment of horns from an earlier song, known as Love Break, and used a modified version of that snippet when recording Vogue. Plaintiff asserts that Defendants Madonna, Pettibone, and others thereby violated Plaintiff's copyrights to Love Break. The district court applied the longstanding legal rule that "de minimis" copying does not constitute infringement and held that, even if Plaintiff proved its allegations of actual copying, the claim failed because the copying (if it occurred) was trivial. The district court granted summary judgment to Defendants and awarded them attorney's fees under 17 U.S.C. § 505. Plaintiff timely appeals.

Reviewing the summary judgment de novo, Alcantar v. Hobart Serv., 800 F.3d 1047, 1051 (9th Cir. 2015), we agree with the district court that, as a matter of law, a general audience would not recognize the brief snippet in Vogue as originating from Love Break. We also reject Plaintiff's argument that Congress eliminated the "de minimis" exception to claims alleging infringement of a sound recording. We recognize that the Sixth Circuit held to the contrary in Bridgeport Music, Inc. v. Dimension Films, 410 F.3d 792 (6th Cir. 2005), but—like the leading copyright treatise and several district courts—we find Bridgeport's reasoning unpersuasive. We hold that the "de minimis" exception applies to infringement actions concerning copyrighted sound recordings, just as it applies to all other copyright infringement actions. Accordingly, we affirm the summary judgment in favor of Defendants.

But we conclude that the district court abused its discretion in granting attorney's fees to Defendants under 17 U.S.C. § 505. See Seltzer v. Green Day, Inc., 725 F.3d 1170, 1180 (9th Cir. 2013) (holding that we review for abuse of discretion the district court's award of attorney's fees under § 505). A claim premised on a legal theory adopted by the only circuit court to have addressed the issue is, as a matter of law, objectively reasonable. The district court's conclusion to the contrary constitutes legal error. We therefore vacate the award of fees and remand for reconsideration.

FACTUAL AND PROCEDURAL HISTORY

Because this case comes to us on appeal from a grant of summary judgment to Defendants, we recount the facts in the light most favorable to Plaintiff. Alcantar, 800 F.3d at 1051.

In the early 1980s, Pettibone recorded the song Ooh I Love It (Love Break), which we refer to as Love Break. In 1990, Madonna and Pettibone recorded the song Vogue, which would become a mega-hit dance song after its release on Madonna's albums. Plaintiff alleges that, when recording Vogue, Pettibone "sampled" certain sounds from the recording of Love Break and added those sounds to Vogue. "Sampling" in this context means the actual physical copying of sounds from an existing recording for use in a new recording, even if accomplished with slight modifications such as changes to pitch or tempo. See Newton v. Diamond, 388 F.3d 1189, 1192 (9th Cir. 2004) (discussing the term "sampling").

Plaintiff asserts that it holds copyrights to the composition and to the sound recording of Love Break. Plaintiff argues that, because Vogue contains sampled material from Love Break, Defendants have violated both copyrights. Although Plaintiff originally asserted improper sampling of strings, vocals, congas, "vibraslap," and horns from Love Break as well as another song, Plaintiff now asserts a sole theory of infringement: When creating two commercial versions of Vogue, Pettibone sampled a "horn hit"[1] from Love Break, violating Plaintiff's copyrights to both the composition and the sound recording of Love Break.

The horn hit appears in Love Break in two forms. A "single" horn hit in Love Break consists of a quarter-note chord comprised of four notes—E-flat, A, D, and F—in the key of B-flat. The single horn hit lasts for 0.23 seconds. A "double" horn hit in Love Break consists of an eighth-note chord of those same notes, followed immediately by a quarter-note chord of the same notes. Plaintiff's expert identified the instruments as "predominantly" trombones and trumpets.

The alleged source of the sampling is the "instrumental" version of Love Break,[2] which lasts 7 minutes and 46 seconds. The single horn hit occurs 27 times, and the double horn hit occurs 23 times. The horn hits occur at intervals of approximately 2 to 4 seconds in two different segments: between 3:11 and 4:38, and from 7:01 to the end, at 7:46. The general pattern is single-double repeated, double-single repeated, single-single-double repeated, and double-single repeated. Many other instruments are playing at the same time as the horns.

The horn hit in Vogue appears in the same two forms as in Love Break: single and double. A "single" horn hit in Vogue consists of a quarter-note chord comprised of four notes—E, A-sharp, D-sharp, and F-sharp—in the key of B-natural.[3] A double horn hit in Vogue consists of an eighth-note chord of those same notes, followed immediately by a quarter-note chord of the same notes.

The two commercial versions of Vogue that Plaintiff challenges are known as the "radio edit" version and the "compilation" version. The radio edit version of Vogue lasts 4 minutes and 53 seconds. The single horn hit occurs once, the double horn hit occurs three times, and a "breakdown" version of the horn hit occurs once.4 They occur at 0:56, 1:02, 3:41, 4:05, and 4:18. The pattern is single-double-double-double-breakdown. As with Love Break, many other instruments are playing at the same time as the horns.

The compilation version of Vogue lasts 5 minutes and 17 seconds. The single horn hit occurs once, and the double horn hit occurs five times. They occur at 1:14, 1:20, 3:59, 4:24, 4:40, and 4:57. The pattern is single-double-double-double-double-double. Again, many other instruments are playing as well.

One of Plaintiff's experts transcribed the composition of the horn hits in the two songs as follows. Love Break's single horn hit:

Tabular or graphical material not displayable at this time.

Vogue's single horn hit:

Tabular or graphical material not displayable at this time.

Love Break's double horn hit:

Tabular or graphical material not displayable at this time.

Vogue's double horn hit:

Tabular or graphical material not displayable at this time.

In a written order, the district court granted summary judgment to Defendants on two alternative grounds. First, neither the composition nor the sound recording of the horn hit was "original" for purposes of copyright law. Second, the court ruled that, even if the horn hit was original, any sampling of the horn hit was "de minimis or trivial." In a separate order, the district court awarded attorney's fees to Defendants under 17 U.S.C. § 505. Plaintiff timely appeals both orders.

DISCUSSION

Plaintiff has submitted evidence of actual copying. In particular, Tony Shimkin has sworn that he, as Pettibone's personal assistant, helped with the creation of Vogue and that, in Shimkin's presence, Pettibone directed an engineer to introduce sounds from Love Break into the recording of Vogue. Additionally, Plaintiff submitted reports from music experts who concluded that the horn hits in Vogue were sampled from Love Break. Defendants do not concede that sampling occurred, and they have introduced much evidence to the contrary.5 But for purposes of summary judgment, Plaintiff has introduced sufficient evidence (including direct evidence) to create a genuine issue of material fact as to whether copying in fact occurred. Taking the facts in the light most favorable to Plaintiff, Plaintiff has demonstrated actual copying. Accordingly, our analysis proceeds to the next step.

Our leading authority on actual copying is Newton, 388 F.3d 1189. We explained in Newton that proof of actual copying is insufficient to establish copyright infringement:

For an unauthorized use of a copyrighted work to be actionable, the use must be significant enough to constitute infringement. See Ringgold v. Black Entm't Television, Inc., 126 F.3d 70, 74–75 (2d Cir. 1997). This means that even where the fact of copying is conceded, no legal consequences will follow from that fact unless the copying is substantial. See Laureyssens v. Idea Group, Inc., 964 F.2d 131, 140 (2d Cir. 1992); 4 Melville B. Nimmer & David Nimmer, Nimmer on Copyright § 13.03[A], at 13-30.2. The principle that trivial copying does not constitute actionable infringement has long been a part of copyright law. Indeed, as [a judge] observed over 80 years ago: "Even where there is some copying, that fact is not conclusive of infringement. Some copying is permitted. In addition to copying, it must be shown that this has been done to an unfair extent." West Publ'g Co. v. Edward Thompson Co., 169 F. 833, 861 (E.D.N.Y. 1909). This principle reflects the legal maxim, de minimis non curatlex (often rendered as, "the law does not concern itself with trifles"). See Ringgold, 126 F.3d at 74–75.

Newton, 388 F.3d at 1192–93. In other words, to establish its infringement claim, Plaintiff must show that the copying was greater than de minimis.

Plaintiff's claim encompasses two distinct alleged infringements: infringement of the copyright to the composition of Love Break and infringement of the copyright to the sound recording of Love Break. Compare 17 U.S.C. § 102(a)(2) (protecting "musical works") with id. § 102(a)(7) (protecting "sound recordings"); see Erickson v. Blake, 839 F. Supp. 2d 1132, 1135 n.3 (D. Or. 2012) ("Sound recordings and musical compositions are separate works with their own distinct copyrights."); see also Newton, 388 F.3d at 1193–94 (noting the distinction). We squarely held in Newton, 388 F.3d at 1193, that the de minimis exception applies to claims of infringement of a copyrighted composition. But it is an open question in this circuit whether the exception applies to claims of infringement of a copyrighted sound recording.

Below, we address (A) whether the alleged copying of the composition or the sound recording was de minimis, (B) whether the de minimis exception applies to alleged infringement of copyrighted sound recordings, and (C) whether the district court abused its discretion in awarding attorney's fees to Defendants under 17 U.S.C. § 505.6

A. Application of the De Minimis Exception

A "use is de minimis only if the average audience would not recognize the appropriation." Newton, 388 F.3d at 1193; see id. at 1196 (affirming the grant of summary judgment because "an average audience would not discern Newton's hand as a composer . from Beastie Boys' use of the sample"); Fisher v. Dees, 794 F.2d 432, 435 n.2 (9th Cir. 1986) ("As a rule, a taking is considered de minimis only if it is so meager and fragmentary that the average audience would not recognize the appropriation."); see also Dymow v. Bolton, 11 F.2d 690, 692 (2d Cir. 1926) ("[C]opying which is infringement must be something which ordinary observations would cause to be recognized as having been taken from the work of another." (internal quotation marks omitted)). Accordingly, we must determine whether a reasonable juror could conclude that the average audience would recognize the appropriation. We will consider the composition and the sound recording copyrights in turn.7

1. Alleged Infringement of the Composition Copyright

When considering an infringement claim of a copyrighted musical composition, what matters is not how the musicians actually played the notes but, rather, a "generic rendition of the composition." Newton, 388 F.3d at 1194; see id. at 1193 (holding that, when considering infringement of the composition copyright, one "must remove from consideration all the elements unique to [the musician's] performance"). That is, we must compare the written compositions of the two pieces.

Viewing the evidence in the light most favorable to Plaintiff, Defendants copied two distinct passages in the horn part of the score for Love Break. First, Defendants copied the quarter-note single horn hit. But no additional part of the score concerning the single horn hit is the same, because the single horn hit appears at a different place in the measure. In Love Break, the notes for the measure are: half-note rest, quarter-note rest, single horn hit. In Vogue, however, the notes for the measure are: half-note rest, eighth-note rest, single horn hit, eighth-note rest. Second, Defendants copied a full measure that contains the double horn hit. In both songs, the notes for the measure are: half-note rest, eighth-note rest, eighth-note horn hit, quarter-note horn hit. In sum, Defendants copied, at most, a quarter-note single horn hit and a full measure containing rests and a double horn hit.

After listening to the recordings, we conclude that a reasonable jury could not conclude that an average audience would recognize the appropriation of the composition. Our decision in Newton is instructive. That case involved a copyrighted composition of "a piece for flute and voice." Newton, 388 F.3d at 1191. The defendants used a six-second sample that "consist[ed] of three notes, C–D flat–C, sung over a background C note played on the flute." Id. The composition also "require[d] overblowing the background C note that is played on the flute." Id. The defendants repeated a six-second sample "throughout [the song], so that it appears over forty times in various renditions of the song." Id. at 1192. After listening to the recordings, we affirmed the grant of summary judgment because "an average audience would not discern [the composer's] hand as a composer." Id. at 1196.

The snippets of the composition that were (as we must assume) taken here are much smaller than the sample at issue in Newton. The copied elements from the Love Break composition are very short, much shorter than the six-second sample in Newton. The single horn hit lasts less than a quarter-second, and the double horn hit lasts—even counting the rests at the beginning of the measure—less than a second. Similarly, the horn hits appear only five or six times in Vogue, rather than the dozens of times that the sampled material in Newton occurred in the challenged song in that case. Moreover, unlike in Newton, in which the challenged song copied the entire composition of the original work for the given temporal segment, the sampling at issue here involves only one instrument group out of many. As noted above, listening to the audio recordings confirms what the foregoing analysis of the composition strongly suggests: A reasonable jury could not conclude that an average audience would recognize an appropriation of the Love Break composition.

2. Alleged Infringement of the Sound Recording Copyright

When considering a claimed infringement of a copyrighted sound recording, what matters is how the musicians played the notes, that is, how their rendition distinguishes the recording from a generic rendition of the same composition. See Newton, 388 F.3d at 1193 (describing the protected elements of a copyrighted sound recording as "the elements unique to [the musician's] performance"). Viewing the evidence in the light most favorable to Plaintiff, by accepting its experts' reports, Pettibone sampled one single horn hit, which occurred at 3:35 in Love Break. Pettibone then used that sampled single horn hit to create the double horn hit used in Vogue.

The horn hit itself was not copied precisely. According to Plaintiff's expert, the chord "was modified by transposing it upward, cleaning up the attack slightly in order to make it punchier [by truncating the horn hit] and overlaying it with other sounds and effects. One such effect mimicked the reverse cymbal crash. . The reverb/delay 'tail' . was prolonged and heightened." Moreover, as with the composition, the horn hits are not isolated sounds. Many other instruments are playing at the same time in both Love Break and Vogue.

In sum, viewing the evidence in the light most favorable to Plaintiff, Pettibone copied one quarter-note of a four-note chord, lasting 0.23 seconds; he isolated the horns by filtering out the other instruments playing at the same time; he transposed it to a different key; he truncated it; and he added effects and other sounds to the chord itself.8 For the double horn hit, he used the same process, except that he duplicated the single horn hit and shortened one of the duplicates to create the eighth-note chord from the quarter-note chord. Finally, he overlaid the resulting horn hits with sounds from many other instruments to create the song Vogue.

After listening to the audio recordings submitted by the parties, we conclude that a reasonable juror could not conclude that an average audience would recognize the appropriation of the horn hit. That common-sense conclusion is borne out by dry analysis. The horn hit is very short—less than a second. The horn hit occurs only a few times in Vogue. Without careful attention, the horn hits are easy to miss. Moreover, the horn hits in Vogue do not sound identical to the horn hits from Love Break. As noted above, assuming that the sampling occurred, Pettibone truncated the horn hit, transposed it to a different key, and added other sounds and effects to the horn hit itself. The horn hit then was added to Vogue along with many other instrument tracks. Even if one grants the dubious proposition that a listener recognized some similarities between the horn hits in the two songs, it is hard to imagine that he or she would conclude that sampling had occurred.

A quirk in the procedural history of this case is illuminating on this point. Plaintiff's primary expert originally misidentified the source of the sampled double horn hit. In his original report, the expert concluded that both a single horn hit and a double horn hit were sampled from Love Break. The parties later discovered the original tracks to Vogue and were able to listen to the horn hits without interference from the many other instruments. After listening to those tracks, the expert decided that he had erred in opining that a double horn hit was sampled. He concluded instead that only a single horn hit was sampled, which was used to create the double horn hit in Vogue. In other words, a highly qualified and trained musician listened to the recordings with the express aim of discerning which parts of the song had been copied, and he could not do so accurately. An average audience would not do a better job.

In sum, the district court correctly held that summary judgment to Defendants was appropriate on the issue of de minimis copying.

B. The De Minimis Exception and Sound Recordings

Plaintiff argues, in the alternative, that even if the copying here is trivial, that fact is irrelevant because the de minimis exception does not apply to infringements of copyrighted sound recordings. Plaintiff urges us to follow the Sixth Circuit's decision in Bridgeport Music, Inc. v. Dimension Films, 410 F.3d 792 (6th Cir. 2005), which adopted a bright-line rule: For copyrighted sound recordings, any unauthorized copying—no matter how trivial—constitutes infringement.

The rule that infringement occurs only when a substantial portion is copied is firmly established in the law. The leading copyright treatise traces the rule to the mid-1800s. 4 Melville B. Nimmer & David Nimmer, Nimmer on Copyright § 13.03[A][2][a], at 13-56 to 13-57, 13-57 n.102 (2013) (citing Folsom v. Marsh, 9 F. Cas. 342, No. 4901 (C.C. Mass. 1841)); id. § 13.03[E][2], at 13-100 & n.208 (citing Daly v. Palmer, 6 F. Cas. 1132, No. 3,552 (C.C.S.D.N.Y. 1868)); see also Perris v. Hexamer, 99 U.S. (9 Otto) 674, 675–76 (1878) (stating that a "copyright gives the author or the publisher the exclusive right of multiplying copies of what he has written or printed. It follows that to infringe this right a substantial copy of the whole or of a material part must be produced."); Dymow, 11 F.2d 690 (applying the rule in 1926). We recognized the rule as early as 1977: "If copying is established, then only does there arise the second issue, that of illicit copying (unlawful appropriation). On that issue the test is the response of the ordinary lay hearer ." Sid & Marty Krofft Television Prods., Inc. v. McDonald's Corp., 562 F.2d 1157, 1164 (9th Cir. 1977) (alteration and internal quotation marks omitted), superseded in other part by 17 U.S.C. § 504(b); see Fisher, 794 F.2d at 434 n.2 (using the term "de minimis" to describe the concept). The reason for the rule is that the "plaintiff's legally protected interest [is] the potential financial return from his compositions which derive from the lay public's approbation of his efforts." Krofft, 562 F.2d at 1165 (quoting Arnstein v. Porter, 154 F.2d 464, 473 (2d Cir. 1946)). If the public does not recognize the appropriation, then the copier has not benefitted from the original artist's expressive content. Accordingly, there is no infringement.

Other than Bridgeport and the district courts following that decision, we are aware of no case that has held that the de minimis doctrine does not apply in a copyright infringement case. Instead, courts consistently have applied the rule in all cases alleging copyright infringement. Indeed, we stated in dictum in Newton that the rule "applies throughout the law of copyright, including cases of music sampling."9 388 F.3d at 1195 (emphasis added).

Plaintiff nevertheless argues that Congress intended to create a special rule for copyrighted sound recordings, eliminating the de minimis exception. We begin our analysis with the statutory text.

Title 17 U.S.C. § 102, titled "Subject matter of copyright: In general," states, in relevant part:

(a) Copyright protection subsists, in accordance with this title, in original works of authorship fixed in any tangible medium of expression, now known or later developed, from which they can be perceived, reproduced, or otherwise communicated, either directly or with the aid of a machine or device. Works of authorship include the following categories:

(1) literary works;

(2) musical works, including any accompanying words;

(3) dramatic works, including any accompanying music;

(4) pantomimes and choreographic works;

(5) pictorial, graphic, and sculptural works;

(6) motion pictures and other audiovisual works;

(7) sound recordings; and

(8) architectural works.

(Emphasis added.) That provision treats sound recordings identically to all other types of protected works; nothing in the text suggests differential treatment, for any purpose, of sound recordings compared to, say, literary works. Similarly, nothing in the neutrally worded statutory definition of "sound recordings" suggests that Congress intended to eliminate the de minimis exception. See id. § 101 (" 'Sound recordings' are works that result from the fixation of a series of musical, spoken, or other sounds, but not including the sounds accompanying a motion picture or other audiovisual work, regardless of the nature of the material objects, such as disks, tapes, or other phonorecords, in which they are embodied.").

Title 17 U.S.C. § 106, titled "Exclusive rights in copyrighted works," states:

Subject to sections 107 through 122, the owner of copyright under this title has the exclusive rights to do and to authorize any of the following:

(1) to reproduce the copyrighted work in copies or phonorecords;

(2) to prepare derivative works based upon the copyrighted work;

(3) to distribute copies or phonorecords of the copyrighted work to the public by sale or other transfer of ownership, or by rental, lease, or lending;

(4) in the case of literary, musical, dramatic, and choreographic works, pantomimes, and motion pictures and other audiovisual works, to perform the copyrighted work publicly;

(5) in the case of literary, musical, dramatic, and choreographic works, pantomimes, and pictorial, graphic, or sculptural works, including the individual images of a motion picture or other audiovisual work, to display the copyrighted work publicly; and

(6) in the case of sound recordings, to perform the copyrighted work publicly by means of a digital audio transmission.

Again, nothing in that provision suggests differential treatment of de minimis copying of sound recordings compared to, say, sculptures. Although subsection (6) deals exclusively with sound recordings, that subsection concerns public performances; nothing in its text bears on de minimis copying.

Instead, Plaintiff's statutory argument hinges on the third sentence of 17 U.S.C. § 114(b), which states:10

The exclusive rights of the owner of copyright in a sound recording under clauses (1) and (2) of section 106 do not extend to the making or duplication of another sound recording that consists entirely of an independent fixation of other sounds, even though such sounds imitate or simulate those in the copyrighted sound recording.

Like all the other sentences in § 114(b), the third sentence imposes an express limitation on the rights of a copyright holder: "The exclusive rights of the owner of a copyright in a sound recording . do not extend to the making or duplication of another sound recording [with certain qualities]." Id. (emphasis added); see id. (first sentence: "exclusive rights . do not extend" to certain circumstances; second sentence: "exclusive rights . do not extend" to certain circumstances; fourth sentence: "exclusive rights . do not apply" in certain circumstances). We ordinarily would hesitate to read an implicit expansion of rights into Congress' statement of an express limitation on rights. Given the considerable background of consistent application of the de minimis exception across centuries of jurisprudence, we are particularly hesitant to read the statutory text as an unstated, implicit elimination of that steadfast rule.

A straightforward reading of the third sentence in § 114(b) reveals Congress' intended limitation on the rights of a sound recording copyright holder: A new recording that mimics the copyrighted recording is not an infringement, even if the mimicking is very well done, so long as there was no actual copying. That is, if a band played and recorded its own version of Love Break in a way that sounded very similar to the copyrighted recording of Love Break, then there would be no infringement so long as there was no actual copying of the recorded Love Break. But the quoted passage does not speak to the question that we face: whether Congress intended to eliminate the longstanding de minimis exception for sound recordings in all circumstances even where, as here, the new sound recording as a whole sounds nothing like the original.

Even if there were some ambiguity as to congressional intent with respect to § 114(b), the legislative history clearly confirms our analysis on each of the above points. Congress intended § 114 to limit, not to expand, the rights of copyright holders: "The approach of the bill is to set forth the copyright owner's exclusive rights in broad terms in section 106, and then to provide various limitations, qualifications, or exemptions in the 12 sections that follow. Thus, everything in section 106 is made 'subject to sections 107 through 118,' and must be read in conjunction with those provisions." H.R. Rep. No. 94-1476, at 61 (1976), reprinted in 1976 U.S.C.C.A.N. 5659, 5674.

With respect to § 114(b) specifically, a House Report stated:

Subsection (b) of section 114 makes clear that statutory protection for sound recordings extends only to the particular sounds of which the recording consists, and would not prevent a separate recording of another performance in which those sounds are imitated. Thus, infringement takes place whenever all or any substantial portion of the actual sounds that go to make up a copyrighted sound recording are reproduced in phonorecords by repressing, transcribing, recapturing off the air, or any other method, or by reproducing them in the soundtrack or audio portion of a motion picture or other audiovisual work. Mere imitation of a recorded performance would not constitute a copyright infringement even where one performer deliberately sets out to simulate another's performance as exactly as possible.

Id. at 106, reprinted in 1976 U.S.C.C.A.N. at 5721 (emphasis added). That passage strongly supports the natural reading of § 114(b), discussed above. Congress intended to make clear that imitation of a recorded performance cannot be infringement so long as no actual copying is done. There is no indication that Congress intended, through § 114(b), to expand the rights of a copyright holder to a sound recording.

Perhaps more importantly, the quoted passage articulates the principle that "infringement takes place whenever all or any substantial portion of the actual sounds . are reproduced." Id. (emphasis added). That is, when enacting this specific statutory provision, Congress clearly understood that the de minimis exception applies to copyrighted sound recordings, just as it applies to all other copyrighted works. In sum, the statutory text, confirmed by the legislative history, reveals that Congress intended to maintain the de minimis exception for copyrighted sound recordings.

In coming to a different conclusion, the Sixth Circuit reasoned as follows:

[T]he rights of sound recording copyright holders under clauses (1) and (2) of section 106 "do not extend to the making or duplication of another sound recording that consists entirely of an independent fixation of other sounds, even though such sounds imitate or simulate those in the copyrighted sound recording." 17 U.S.C. § 114(b) (emphasis added). The significance of this provision is amplified by the fact that the Copyright Act of 1976 added the word "entirely" to this language. Compare Sound Recording Act of 1971, Pub. L. 92-140, 85 Stat. 391 (Oct. 15, 1971) (adding subsection (f) to former 17 U.S.C. § 1) ("does not extend to the making or duplication of another sound recording that is an independent fixation of other sounds"). In other words, a sound recording owner has the exclusive right to "sample" his own recording. Bridgeport, 410 F.3d at 800–01.

We reject that interpretation of § 114(b). Bridgeport ignored the statutory structure and § 114(b)'s express limitation on the rights of a copyright holder. Bridgeport also declined to consider legislative history on the ground that "digital sampling wasn't being done in 1971." 410 F.3d at 805. But the state of technology is irrelevant to interpreting Congress' intent as to statutory structure. Moreover, as Nimmer points out, Bridgeport's reasoning fails on its own terms because contemporary technology plainly allowed the copying of small portions of a protected sound recording. Nimmer § 13.03[A][2][b], at 13-62 n.114.16.

Close examination of Bridgeport's interpretive method further exposes its illogic. In effect, Bridgeport inferred from the fact that "exclusive rights . do not extend to the making or duplication of another sound recording that consists entirely of an independent fixation of other sounds," 17 U.S.C. § 114(b) (emphases added), the conclusion that exclusive rights do extend to the making of another sound recording that does not consist entirely of an independent fixation of other sounds. As pointed out by Nimmer, Bridgeport's interpretive method "rests on a logical fallacy." Nimmer § 13.03 [A][2][b], at 13-61; see also Saregama India Ltd. v. Mosley, 687 F. Supp. 2d 1325, 1340–41 (S.D. Fla. 2009) (critiquing Bridgeport's interpretive method for a similar reason). A statement that rights do not extend to a particular circumstance does not automatically mean that the rights extend to all other circumstances. In logical terms, it is a fallacy to infer the inverse of a conditional from the conditional. E.g., Joseph G. Brennan, A Handbook of Logic 79–80 (2d ed. 1961).

For example, take as a given the proposition that "if it has rained, then the grass is not dry." It does not necessarily follow that "if it has not rained, then the grass is dry." Someone may have watered the lawn, for instance. We cannot infer the second if-then statement from the first. The first if-then statement does not tell us anything about the condition of the grass if it has not rained. Accordingly, even though it is true that, "if the recording consists entirely of independent sounds, then the copyright does not extend to it," that statement does not necessarily mean that "if the recording does not consist entirely of independent sounds, then the copyright does extend to it."

The Sixth Circuit also looked beyond the statutory text, to the nature of a sound recording, and reasoned:

[E]ven when a small part of a sound recording is sampled, the part taken is something of value. No further proof of that is necessary than the fact that the producer of the record or the artist on the record intentionally sampled because it would (1) save costs, or (2) add something to the new recording, or (3) both. For the sound recording copyright holder, it is not the "song" but the sounds that are fixed in the medium of his choice. When those sounds are sampled they are taken directly from that fixed medium. It is a physical taking rather than an intellectual one. Bridgeport, 410 F.3d at 801–02 (footnote omitted).

We disagree for three reasons. First, the possibility of a "physical taking" exists with respect to other kinds of artistic works as well, such as photographs, as to which the usual de minimis rule applies. See, e.g., Sandoval v. New Line Cinema Corp., 147 F.3d 215, 216 (2d Cir. 1998) (affirming summary judgment to the defendant because the defendant's use of the plaintiff's photographs in a movie was de minimis). A computer program can, for instance, "sample" a piece of one photograph and insert it into another photograph or work of art. We are aware of no copyright case carving out an exception to the de minimis requirement in that context, and we can think of no principled reason to differentiate one kind of "physical taking" from another. Second, even accepting the premise that sound recordings differ qualitatively from other copyrighted works and therefore could warrant a different infringement rule, that theoretical difference does not mean that Congress actually adopted a different rule. Third, the distinction between a "physical taking" and an "intellectual one," premised in part on "sav[ing] costs" by not having to hire musicians, does not advance the Sixth Circuit's view. The Supreme Court has held unequivocally that the Copyright Act protects only the expressive aspects of a copyrighted work, and not the "fruit of the [author's] labor." Feist Publ'ns, Inc. v. Rural Tel. Serv. Co., 499 U.S. 340, 349 (1991). Indeed, the Supreme Court in Feist explained at length why, though that result may seem unfair, protecting only the expressive aspects of a copyrighted work is actually a key part of the design of the copyright laws. Id. at 349–54 (explaining how "the 'sweat of the brow' doctrine flouted basic copyright principles"). Accordingly, all that remains of Bridgeport's argument is that the second artist has taken some expressive content from the original artist. But that is always true, regardless of the nature of the work, and the de minimis test nevertheless applies. See Nimmer § 13.03[A][2][b], at 13-63 to 13-64 (providing a similar critique of Bridgeport's physical/intellectual distinction and concluding that it "seems to be built on air").

Because we conclude that Congress intended to maintain the "de minimis" exception for copyrights to sound recordings, we take the unusual step of creating a circuit split by disagreeing with the Sixth Circuit's contrary holding in Bridgeport. We do so only after careful reflection because, as we noted in Seven Arts Filmed Entertainment Ltd. v. Content Media Corp., 733 F.3d 1251, 1256 (9th Cir. 2013), "the creation of a circuit split would be particularly troublesome in the realm of copyright. Creating inconsistent rules among the circuits would lead to different levels of protection in different areas of the country, even if the same alleged infringement is occurring nationwide." (Citation, internal quotations marks, and brackets omitted.) We acknowledge that our decision has consequences. But the goal of avoiding a circuit split cannot override our independent duty to determine congressional intent. Otherwise, we would have no choice but to blindly follow the rule announced by whichever circuit court decided an issue first, even if we were convinced, as we are here, that our sister circuit erred.

Moreover, other considerations suggest that the "troublesome" consequences ordinarily attendant to the creation of a circuit split are diminished here. In declining to create a circuit split in Seven Arts, we noted that "the leading copyright treatise," Nimmer, agreed with the view of our sister circuits. 733 F.3d at 1255. As to the issue before us, by contrast, Nimmer devotes many pages to explaining why the Sixth Circuit's opinion is, in no uncertain terms, wrong. Nimmer § 13.03[A][2][b], at 13-59 to 13-66.

Additionally, as a practical matter, a deep split among the federal courts already exists. Since the Sixth Circuit decided Bridgeport, almost every district court not bound by that decision has declined to apply Bridgeport's rule. See, e.g., Saregama, 687 F. Supp. 2d at 1340–41 (rejecting Bridgeport's rule after analysis); Steward v. West, No. 13-02449, Docket No. 179 at 14 n.8 (C.D. Cal. 2014) (unpublished civil minutes) ("declin[ing] to follow the per se infringment analysis from Bridgeport" because Bridgeport "has been criticized by courts and commentators alike"); Batiste v. Najm, 28 F. Supp. 3d 595, 625 (E.D. La. 2014) (noting that, because some courts have declined to apply Bridgeport's rule, "it is far from clear" that Bridgeport's rule should apply); Pryor v. Warner/Chappell Music, Inc., No. CV13-04344, 2014 WL 2812309, at *7 n.3 (C.D. Cal. June 20, 2014) (unpublished) (declining to apply Bridgeport's rule because it has not been adopted by the Ninth Circuit); Zany Toys, LLC v. Pearl Enters., LLC, No. 13-5262, 2014 WL 2168415, at *11 n.7 (D.N.J. May 23, 2014) (unpublished) (stating Bridgeport's rule without discussion); see also EMI Records Ltd v. Premise Media Corp., No. 601209, 2008 WL 5027245 (N.Y. Sup. Ct. Aug. 8, 2008) (unpublished) (expressly rejecting Bridgeport's analysis). Although we are the first circuit court to follow a different path than Bridgeport's, we are in well-charted territory.

Plaintiff next argues that, because Congress has not amended the copyright statute in response to Bridgeport, we should conclude that Bridgeport correctly divined congressional intent. We disagree. The Supreme Court has held that congressional inaction in the face of a judicial statutory interpretation, even with respect to the Supreme Court's own decisions affecting the entire nation, carries almost no weight. See Alexander v. Sandoval, 532 U.S. 275, 292 (2001) ("It is impossible to assert with any degree of assurance that congressional failure to act represents affirmative congressional approval of the Court's statutory interpretation." (internal quotation marks omitted)). Here, Congress' inaction with respect to a decision by one circuit court has even less import, especially considering that many other courts have declined to apply Bridgeport's rule.

Finally, Plaintiff advances several reasons why Bridgeport's rule is superior as a matter of policy. For example, the Sixth Circuit opined that its bright-line rule was easy to enforce; that "the market will control the license price and keep it within bounds"; and that "sampling is never accidental" and is therefore easy to avoid. Bridgeport, 410 F.3d at 801. Those arguments are for a legislature, not a court. They speak to what Congress could decide; they do not inform what Congress actually decided.11

We hold that the "de minimis" exception applies to actions alleging infringement of a copyright to sound recordings.

...

Judgment AFFIRMED; award of fees VACATED and REMANDED for reconsideration. The parties shall bear their own costs on appeal.

Dissent:

The plaintiff is the owner of a copyright in a fixed sound recording. This is a valuable property right, the stock-in-trade of artists who make their living recording music and selling records. The plaintiff alleges that the defendants, without a license or any sort of permission, physically copied a small part of the plaintiff's sound recording – which, to repeat, is property belonging to the plaintiff – and, having appropriated it, inserted into their own recording. If the plaintiff's allegations are to be believed, the defendants deemed this maneuver preferable to paying for a license to use the material, or to hiring their own musicians to record it. In any other context, this would be called theft. It is no defense to theft that the thief made off with only a "de minimis" part of the victim's property.

The majority chooses to follow the views of a popular treatise instead of an on-point decision of the Sixth Circuit, a decision that has governed the music industry in Nashville – "Music City"1 – and elsewhere for over a decade without causing either the sky to fall in, or Congress to step in. And just exactly what is the Sixth Circuit's radical holding in Bridgeport Music, Inc. v. Dimension Films that the majority finds so distasteful? It's this: if you want to use an identical copy of a portion of a copyrighted fixed sound recording – we're not talking about "substantially similar" tunes or rhythms, but an actual identical copy of a sound that has already been recorded in a fixed medium – get a license. You can't just take it. 410 F.3d 792, 800–01 (6th Cir. 2005).

As the majority acknowledges, after Newton v. Diamond, 388 F.3d 1189 (9th Cir. 2003), it is an "open question" in the Ninth Circuit whether a de minimis defense applies to fixed sound recordings as it does to less tangible works. The Bridgeport court explained why it should not.

First, by statute, sound recording copyright holders have an exclusive right to sample their own recordings. It's an exclusive right; the statute does not give that right to others. 410 F.3d at 800–01. Under 17 U.S.C. §§ 106 and 114, the holder of a copyright in a sound recording (but not others) has the exclusive right to reproduce the work in copies or records "that directly or indirectly recapture the actual sounds fixed in the recording," as well as the exclusive right to prepare derivative works "in which the actual sounds fixed in the sound recording are rearranged, remixed, or otherwise altered in sequence or quality." 17 U.S.C. §§ 106(1) and (2); 114(b). Congress clearly qualified these exclusive rights, writing that "another sound recording that consists entirely of an independent fixation of other sounds, even though such sounds imitate or simulate those in the copyrighted sound recording" are not within the scope of the copyright holder's exclusive rights. 17 U.S.C. § 114(b). In other words, the world at large is free to imitate or simulate the creative work fixed in the recording (like a tribute band, for example) so long as an actual copy of the sound recording itself is not made. 410 F.3d at 800.

The majority rejects this straightforward reading, explaining by way of a rhetorical exercise that Bridgeport's reading of § 114(b) is a logical fallacy, expanding the rights of copyright holders beyond that allowed under the judicial de minimis rule. As I see it, it is the majority that tortures the natural reading of these provisions. Bear in mind that § 114(b) simply explains the scope of exclusive rights already granted to copyright holders under § 106. These two provisions must be read together, as the Sixth Circuit did. 410 F.3d at 799–801. When read together, their message is clear: copyright holders have exclusive rights to their recordings, but cannot be heard to complain (i.e., there can be no infringement of those exclusive rights) where a new recording consists entirely of independently created sounds, such as might be found in a very good imitation. By the same token, if a new recording includes something other than independently created sounds, such as a blatant copy, the copyright holder whose work was sampled has a legitimate gripe. That right was not invented by the Sixth Circuit: it already exists in the statutes. And these statutes say nothing about the de minimis exception.

The second reason the Sixth Circuit gave for not adopting the de minimis rule is that sound recordings are different than their compositional counterparts: when a defendant copies a recording, he or she takes not the song but the sounds as they are fixed in the medium of the copyright holders' choice. Id. at 801–02. In other words, the very nature of digital sampling makes a de minimis analysis inapplicable, since sampling or pirating necessarily involves copying a fixed performance. See id. at 801 n.13. The defendants wanted horns to punctuate their song, so they took the plaintiff's copyrighted recording of horns. The horn hit is brief, but clearly perceptible and does its job. This is unlike indiscernible photographs used, not for their content (which cannot be made out), but to dress a movie set. See Sandoval v. New Line Cinema Corp., 147 F.2d 215, 218 (2d Cir. 1998).

This is a physical taking, not an intellectual one. Id. at 802. Sampling is never accidental. Id. at 801. As the Sixth Circuit observed, it is not like the case of a composer who has a melody in his head, perhaps not even realizing that the reason he hears this melody is that it is the work of another that he has heard before. Id. When you sample a sound recording you know you are taking another's work product. Id. Accordingly, the pertinent inquiry in a sampling case is not whether a defendant sampled a little or a lot, but whether a defendant sampled at all. Id. at 798 n.6, 801–02 and n.13.

Again, the majority disagrees, rejecting Bridgeport's characterization of a sample as a "physical taking" on the basis that copyright protection extends only to expressive aspects of a work, not the fruit of the author's labor. According to the majority, copyright protection doesn't extend to the sweat of an author's brow. Feist Publ'ns, Inc. v. Rural Tel. Serv. Co., 499 U.S. 340, 349 (1991) (discussing originality as applied to factual compilations, such as telephone directories). But that's irrelevant here, since there is no question that the underlying sound recording can be copyrighted, and it is the taking of that protectable work that is at issue.

I find Bridgeport's arguments well-reasoned and persuasive. Equally compelling is, I think, Congress's silence in the wake of Bridgeport, especially in light of the fact that the Sixth Circuit explicitly invited Congress to clarify or change the law if Bridgeport's bright-line rule was not what Congress intended. 410 F.3d at 805. While it's true that congressional inaction in the face of judicial interpretation is not ironclad evidence of Congressional approval, see Alexander v. Sandoval, 532 U.S. 275, 292 (2001), it's not chopped liver either. In this case Bridgeport has not been hiding out in the woods, waiting to be found: it has been governing the music industry in Nashville and elsewhere for eleven years. The majority now proposes to introduce a different rule for this circuit, creating a circuit split, and providing a lower level of protection for copyright holders in a different area of the country. See Seven Arts Filmed Entertainment Ltd. v. Content Media Corp. PLC, 733 F.3d 1251, 1256 (9th Cir. 2013). This inconsistent approach is plainly in contravention of Congressional intent that copyright laws be predictable and uniform, yet the majority defends its rogue path on the ground that Congress must have intended something other than what the Sixth Circuit has concluded, even though we've heard not a peep from Congress, or for that matter the Supreme Court, in the eleven years since Bridgeport has been on the books.

In short, the majority's fuzzy approach would require a factual and largely visceral inquiry into whether each and every instance of sampling was "substantial," whereas Bridgeport provides in the case of a fixed sound recording a bright-line rule, and I quote: "Get a license or do not sample." 410 F.3d at 801. True, Get a license or do not sample doesn't carry the same divine force as Thou Shalt Not Steal, but it's the same basic idea. I would hold that the de minimis exception does not apply to the sampling, copying, stealing, pirating, misappropriation – call it what you will – of copyrighted fixed sound recordings. Once the sound is fixed, it is tangible property belonging to the copyright holder, and no one else has the right to take even a little of it without permission. I therefore respectfully dissent.

No. 06-55102

LEADSINGER INC v. BMG MUSIC PUBLISHING

United States Court of Appeals, Ninth Circuit

MILAN D. SMITH, JR., Circuit Judge:

This case requires us to determine how the Copyright Act, 17 U.S.C. §§ 101-1332, applies to karaoke devices that enable individuals to sing along to recordings of musical compositions, which is a matter of first impression in this circuit. In the district court, Plaintiff-Appellant Leadsinger, Inc., a karaoke device manufacturer, filed a complaint for declaratory judgment against music publishers, Defendants-Appellees BMG Music Publishing and Zomba Enterprises, Inc. ("BMG"). Leadsinger sought a declaration that it is entitled to print or display song lyrics in real time with song recordings as long as it obtains a compulsory mechanical license under 17 U.S.C. § 115, or that it is entitled to do so under the fair use doctrine, 17 U.S.C. § 107. The district court dismissed the complaint without leave to amend for failure to state a claim. We affirm.

I. FACTUAL AND PROCEDURAL BACKGROUND

Karaoke devices necessarily involve copyrighted works because both musical compositions and their accompanying song lyrics are essential to their operation. BMG owns or administers copyrights in musical compositions and through its licensing agent, the Harry Fox Agency, has issued to Leadsinger compulsory mechanical licenses to copyrighted musical compositions under § 115 of the

Copyright Act. In addition to the mechanical fee required to secure a compulsory license, BMG has demanded that Leadsinger and other karaoke companies pay a "lyric reprint" fee and a "synchronization fee." Leadsinger has refused to pay these additional fees and filed for declaratory judgment to resolve whether it has the right to visually display song lyrics in real time with song recordings, as well as print song lyrics, without holding anything more than the § 115 compulsory licenses it already possesses.

In its complaint, Leadsinger describes the karaoke device it manufactures as "an all-in-one microphone player" that has recorded songs imbedded in a microchip in the microphone. When the microphone is plugged into a television, the lyrics of the song appear on the television screen in real time as the song is playing, enabling the consumer to sing along with the lyrics. Though most karaoke companies put their recordings on cassettes, compact discs, or use a compact disc + graphic ("CD+G") or DVD format, these other karaoke devices, much like Leadsinger's, display lyrics visually when played in a device that is connected to a television.

Leadsinger's device sometimes displays licensed reproductions of still photographs as a background for the onscreen lyrics. And, on occasion, Leadsinger includes with the device a printed copy of the lyrics to the songs recorded on the microchip. According to Leadsinger's complaint, the purpose of both the printed and visually displayed song lyrics is to "facilitate the customer's ability to read the lyrics and/or sing along with the recorded music." Leadsinger further claims that both in and outside the karaoke context, the inclusion of printed lyrics assists buyers in understanding song lyrics and enables parents to control "the lyrical content that children are exposed to."

The district court concluded that a § 115 compulsory license does not grant Leadsinger the right to display visual images and lyrics in real time with music, and that the allegations in Leadsinger's complaint do not support its fair use claim. Leadsinger, Inc. v. BMG Music Publ'g, 429 F.Supp.2d 1190, 1193-97 (C.D.Cal.2005). The district court dismissed Leadsinger's complaint without leave to amend, concluding that amendment would be futile. Id. at 1197. This appeal followed.

II. STANDARD OF REVIEW AND JURISDICTION

We review a district court's grant of a motion to dismiss de novo. Silvers v. Sony Pictures Entm't, Inc., 402 F.3d 881, 883 (9th Cir.2005) (citation omitted). Dismissal for failure to state a claim is proper only "if it appears beyond doubt" that the non-moving party "can prove no set of facts which would entitle him to relief." Vasquez v. L.A. County, 487 F.3d 1246, 1249 (9th Cir.2007) (internal quotations and citation omitted). In making this determination, we accept all allegations of fact as true and construe the complaint in the light most favorable to the non-moving party. Id. We have jurisdiction under 28 U.S.C. § 1291.

III. DISCUSSION

A. The Copyright Act

In deciding whether the district court properly dismissed Leadsinger's complaint, we are guided by the language of the Copyright Act. Section 102 of the Copyright

Act extends copyright protection to, among other original works of authorship, literary works, musical works (including any accompanying words), and sound recordings. 17 U.S.C. § 102. Though 17 U.S.C. § 106 grants copyright owners the exclusive right to reproduce copyrighted works "in copies or phonorecords" and to "distribute copies or phonorecords of the copyrighted work to the public by sale," 17 U.S.C. § 115 limits copyright owners' exclusive rights with respect to phonorecords.

Phonorecords are defined as:

[M]aterial objects in which sounds, other than those accompanying a motion picture or other audiovisual work, are fixed by any method now known or later developed, and from which the sounds can be perceived, reproduced, or otherwise communicated, either directly or with the aid of a machine or device. The term "phonorecords" includes the material object in which the sounds are first fixed.

17 U.S.C. § 101 (emphasis added). Section 115 subjects phonorecords to a compulsory licensing scheme that authorizes any person who complies with its provisions to obtain a license to make and distribute phonorecords of a nondramatic musical work if: (1) the work has "been distributed to the public in the United States under the authority of the copyright owner"; and (2) the person's "primary purpose in making phonorecords is to distribute them to the public for private use." Id. § 115(a)(1). As the definition of phonorecords indicates, audiovisual works are not phonorecords. See id. § 101. Thus, § 115's compulsory licensing scheme does not apply to audiovisual works.

The Copyright Act defines audiovisual works as:

[W]orks that consist of a series of related images which are intrinsically intended to be shown by the use of machines, or devices such as projectors, viewers, or electronic equipment, together with accompanying sounds, if any, regardless of the nature of the material objects, such as films or tapes, in which the works are embodied.

Id.; see 1 Melville B. Nimmer & David Nimmer, Nimmer on Copyright § 2.09 [A] (2007)[hereinafter Nimmer on Copyright]. Though it is not explicit in the Copyright Act, courts have recognized a copyright holder's right to control the synchronization of musical compositions with the content of audiovisual works and have required parties to obtain synchronization licenses from copyright holders. See Maljack Prods., Inc. v. GoodTimes Home Video Corp., 81 F.3d 881, 884-85 (9th Cir.1996) (recognizing the concept of synchronization rights); ABKCO Music, Inc. v. Stellar Records, Inc., 96 F.3d 60, 63 n. 4 (2d Cir.1996) ("A synchronization license is required if a copyrighted musical composition is to be used in 'timed-relation' or synchronization with an audiovisual work.") (citation omitted); see also 6 Nimmer on Copyright § 30.02 [F][3] ("A license is necessary if an existing musical composition is to be used in synchronization or 'timed-relation' with an audiovisual work.").

The Copyright Act defines literary works as "works, other than audiovisual works, expressed in words, numbers, or other verbal or numerical symbols or indicia, regardless of the nature of the material objects, such as books, periodicals, manuscripts, phonorecords, film, tapes, disks, or cards, in which they are embodied." 17 U.S.C. § 101. Song lyrics are copyrightable as a literary work and, therefore, enjoy separate protection under the Copyright Act. See id. § 102(a)(1) (extending copyright protection to "literary works"); Zomba Enters., Inc. v. Panorama Records, Inc., 491 F.3d 574, 578 n. 1 (6th Cir.2007); ABKCO Music, 96 F.3d at 64; 1 Nimmer on Copyright § 2.05[B] (lyrics "alone are nevertheless copyrightable as a literary work").

B.   Karaoke Devices As "Audiovisual Works"

The district court concluded that Leadsinger would not be entitled, under any set of facts, to a declaration that a § 115 compulsory license to make and distribute phonorecords authorizes it to display song lyrics in real time with song recordings. While our reasoning differs slightly from that of the district court, we agree with the district court's conclusion.

The district court reasoned that Leadsinger's device falls outside of the definition of phonorecord because the device contains more than sounds. Leadsinger, Inc. v. BMG Music Publ'g, 429 F.Supp.2d 1190, 1194-95 (C.D.Cal.2005); see 17 U.S.C. § 101 ("Phonorecords are material objects in which sounds, other than those accompanying a motion picture or other audiovisual work, are fixed."). While it is true that the microchip in Leadsinger's device stores visual images and visual representations of lyrics in addition to sounds, the plain language of the Copyright Act does not expressly preclude a finding that devices on which sounds and visual images are fixed fall within the definition of phonorecords. 17 U.S.C. § 101. The definition of phonorecords is explicit, however, that audiovisual works are not phonorecords and are excluded from § 115's compulsory licensing scheme. Id. § 101. We need not settle upon a precise interpretation of § 101's definition of phonorecords in this case because Leadsinger's karaoke device meets each element of the statutory definition of audiovisual works and, therefore, cannot be a phonorecord.

As stated above, § 101 of the Copyright Act defines audiovisual works as works consisting of "a series of related images" that are "intrinsically intended to be shown by the use of machines." First, the visual representation of successive portions of song lyrics that Leadsinger's device projects onto a television screen constitutes "a series of related images." Though Leadsinger suggests that its images of song lyrics are not related, the images bear a significant relationship when examined in context. In its complaint, Leadsinger explained that the purpose of karaoke is for the consumer to sing the lyrics to a song "in real time" as the song is playing. To accomplish this purpose, it is necessary that the images of song lyrics be "presented sequentially" so as to match the accompanying music and make the lyrics readable. See 1 Nimmer on Copyright § 2.09[B] ("[A] series of slides . if presented sequentially (or in a 'related sequence') will constitute an audiovisual work.").

The fact that the related images are comprised of song lyrics, which constitute a literary work, does not preclude us from concluding that Leadsinger's device is an audiovisual work. The definition of literary works is clear that the categories of literary works and audiovisual works are not mutually exclusive. The Copyright Act defines literary works as "works, other than audiovisual works, expressed in words regardless of the nature of the material objects, such as phonorecords, film, tapes, disks, or cards, in which they are embodied." 17 U.S.C. § 101. That the definition of literary works includes the phrase "other than audiovisual works," confirms that a literary work may constitute an audiovisual work if it also fulfills the definition of an audiovisual work.

Second, though § 101 does not require that an audiovisual work have sound, in the case of Leadsinger's karaoke device, its images of successive portions of song lyrics are "intrinsically intended to be shown by the use of machine together with accompanying sounds." Id. § 101. An essential function of Leadsinger's device is its ability to indicate to the consumer exactly when to sing each lyric. Leadsinger's device is able to do so only because it utilizes a machine to project the song lyrics "in real time" with the accompanying music.

In ABKCO Music, the Second Circuit similarly concluded that the karaoke device in that case was an audiovisual work. 96 F.3d at 65. Though the ABKCO Music court failed to discuss the importance of a machine to the functioning of the karaoke device at issue, it held that the device constituted an audiovisual work, "since [it] 'consist[s] of a series of related images'-the lyrics-'together with accompanying sounds'-the music." Id. (quoting 17 U.S.C. § 101).

To the extent it is requested, Leadsinger also is not entitled to a declaration that compulsory mechanical licenses under § 115 allow it to reprint lyrics in booklets that accompany its karaoke products. As stated above, lyrics are separately copyrightable as literary works. See Zomba Enters., 491 F.3d at 578 n. 1; ABKCO Music, 96 F.3d at 64. Section 115 covers only the right to "make and distribute phonorecords." Though these phonorecords may include oral renditions of song lyrics, the reproduction of song lyrics on paper is not within the scope of § 115. See ABKCO Music, Inc., 96 F.3d at 64; cf. EMI Entm't World, 505 F.Supp.2d at 1223 (noting that the defendants had "reprint licenses" entitling them to reprint lyrics of copyrighted songs).

We hold that Leadsinger's device falls within the definition of an audiovisual work. As a result, in addition to any § 115 compulsory licenses necessary to make and distribute phonorecords and reprint licenses necessary to reprint song lyrics, Leadsinger is also required to secure synchronization licenses to display images of song lyrics in timed relation with recorded music.

...

CONCLUSION

For the foregoing reasons, we AFFIRM the district court's dismissal of Leadsinger's complaint without leave to amend.

8. Copyright on Audiovisual Works

Docket No. 13–3865 (2015)

16 CASA DUSE v. MERKIN

United States Court of Appeals, Second Circuit

KATZMANN, Chief Judge

This is an appeal from a judgment of the United States District Court for the Southern District of New York (Richard J. Sullivan, Judge) granting summary judgment to the plaintiff on its copyright and state-law claims, dismissing the defendant's copyright counterclaims, and awarding the plaintiff costs and attorney's fees. Because we agree with the district court that the plaintiff owns the copyright to all versions of the work in question, a film entitled Heads Up, and that copyright does not subsist in individual contributions to that film, we conclude that the district court properly granted summary judgment to the plaintiff on its copyright claims and did not abuse its discretion in enjoining the defendant from interfering with the plaintiff's use of the film. We also conclude, however, that the defendant, not the plaintiff, was entitled to summary judgment on the plaintiff's claim for tortious interference with business relations under New York law. We therefore affirm in part, reverse in part, and remand the case to the district court with instructions for it to grant the defendant's motion for summary judgment on the tortious interference claim and for such further proceedings as are warranted.

BACKGROUND

Appellee 16 Casa Duse, LLC, ("Casa Duse") is a film-production company based in Brooklyn, New York. The company is owned and operated by Robert Krakovski. Appellant Alex Merkin is a film director, producer, and editor. Appellant Maurice Reichman is an attorney who represented Merkin in some of his dealings with Casa Duse.

In September 2010, Krakovski, acting at all relevant times as the principal of Casa Duse, purchased the rights to a screenplay entitled Heads Up from the work's author, Ben Carlin. Krakovski, who planned to finance and produce a short film based on the screenplay, asked Merkin whether he would be willing to direct the film. Merkin agreed, and the two settled informally on a fee of $1,500 for Merkin's services.

In the ensuing months, Krakovski assembled a cast and crew for the film, also entitled Heads Up. He hired additional producers, a script supervisor, a photography director, camera operators, various designers and technicians, and actors, creating an ensemble of about thirty members. Although Merkin recommended that Krakovski employ some persons as crew members, Krakovski made the ultimate hiring decisions. In the meantime, Krakovski, Merkin, and others involved with the project planned various aspects of the production, including props, locations, and scheduling.

Each cast and crew member other than Merkin entered into an "Independent Contractor [ ] Agreement" with Casa Duse. The agreements contained statements that Casa Duse would "engage the services [of the cast or crew member] as 'work for hire' of an independent contractor," J.A. 485, and set out terms for compensation, performance standards, and other matters. The work-for-hire agreements also stated that Casa Duse would retain "complete control" of the film's production and "own all of the results and proceeds of [the cast and crew's] services in connection with the [film] . including, but not limited to, all rights throughout the world of . copyright." J.A. 487.

In February 2011, Krakovski sent Merkin a draft work-for-hire agreement entitled "Director Employment Agreement." Its terms were similar to those in the agreements signed by other cast and crew. It provided, inter alia, that Casa Duse would own all rights in the film. Merkin acknowledged his receipt of the draft by e-mail, noting that he would ask his lawyer to review it.

Some two-and-a-half months later, on May 9, 2011, Krakovski sent Merkin an e-mail reminding him to execute the agreement. Merkin did not respond.

Krakovski contacted Merkin again on May 16, a week before production was scheduled to start, reminding him again of the importance of completing the agreement before work on the film began. Merkin again failed to reply. On May 18, Krakovski e-mailed again asking for a completed agreement, to no avail.

Despite the lack of a completed agreement, production began later that month. During production, which included three days of filming, Merkin performed his role as director by advising and instructing the film's cast and crew on matters ranging from camera angles and lighting to wardrobe and makeup to the actors' dialogue and movement. Merkin completed his direction of the film by the end of May.

In June 2011, Krakovski gave Merkin a hard drive containing the raw film footage in the hope that Merkin would be able to edit the footage. In the absence of a work-for-hire agreement, the parties entered into a "Media Agreement" under which Merkin would edit but not license, sell, or copy the footage for any purpose without the permission of Casa Duse.

On June 16, Krakovski sent an e-mail to Merkin proposing changes to the Media Agreement in order to "clarify," first, that Casa Duse and not Merkin owned the footage and hard drive, and, second, that Casa Duse's entry into the Media Agreement had not relinquished "any directorial/editorial terms [or] rights" that would be finally allocated by a work-for-hire agreement. J.A. 580. Merkin replied, saying that the proposed changes seemed acceptable but also "clarify [ing]," for his part, that he was "not giving up any creative or artistic rights" he had in the project and "all of [his] creative work is still [his] work and not the property of 16 Casa Duse, LLC." J.A. 581. Krakovski responded, asserting that he had never intended the film to be "a 'Joint Venture'" and instead had intended to obtain Merkin's services pursuant to a work-for-hire agreement. J.A. 521.

From July to October 2011, Krakovski and Merkin continued to negotiate the terms of the Media Agreement and a work-for-hire agreement. The parties communicated directly—via e-mail—and through their attorneys. From time to time, they appeared to reach agreement on some key terms, including Casa Duse's ownership of the film, Merkin's authority to make a "director's cut," and Merkin's ability to remove his name from the final product if he so desired, but negotiations ultimately collapsed. Krakovski demanded the return of the hard drive containing the raw film footage. Merkin refused and warned Krakovski that, without an agreement in place, Casa Duse could not, in his view, release the film.

In November 2011, Merkin sent Krakovski a letter "putting [Krakovski] on notice that [Merkin] forb[ade] any use whatsoever of the raw footage." J.A. 400. The letter conceded that Krakovski owned the screenplay but insisted that Merkin owned the "raw footage." Id. In December 2011, Krakovski responded through counsel, who, by e-mail, proposed that Casa Duse pay Merkin the agreed-upon $1,500 for his directorial services, allow him to complete his desired "director's cut," and ensure his opportunity to remove his name from the finished product if he wished. In exchange, Merkin would agree to deem his directorial services a "work for hire" for Casa Duse. The e-mail also advised that Casa Duse had, by then, retained a different editor. Merkin responded and reiterated his position that Casa Duse was "not permitted to use [his] work in any edit without [his] involvement." J.A. 403. Merkin threatened to contact film festivals to inform them that Casa Duse lacked rights to the film in the event Krakovski did not assent. Krakovski's attorney responded by sending an e-mail to Merkin's attorney, disputing Merkin's position and warning that any interference with screening of the film would potentially subject Merkin to liability.

In January 2012, as the dispute continued to simmer, Merkin registered a copyright in the film with the United States Copyright Office. The title of the registration was "Raw footage for film 'Heads Up' Disks 1–4," reflecting the fact that Merkin had copied the footage from the hard drive onto four DVDs. J.A. 71. The registration listed the type of work as "Motion Picture" and asserted that Merkin was its sole author. Merkin did not obtain Casa Duse's permission to register the copyright, and Krakovski was unaware of the registration.

In March 2012, Krakovski began submitting Heads Up to film festivals and making plans to publicize the film. To that end, he scheduled an invitation-only screening for approximately seventy persons at the New York Film Academy ("NYFA") on April 18, 2012. Krakovski also organized a reception to follow at a nearby restaurant, City Crab, for which he paid a non-refundable deposit of $1,956.58.

On the date of the event, the NYFA chairperson contacted Krakovski to tell him that Merkin's attorney (Reichman) had threatened the NYFA with a ceaseand-desist order to prevent the screening from proceeding. According to Reichman, it was Merkin—not Reichman—who contacted the NYFA and mentioned a cease and desist "notice," not an order, at which point the NYFA contacted Reichman. In any event, the NYFA cancelled the screening in response to these threats, and Casa Duse lost its restaurant deposit. Casa Duse subsequently missed at least four film festival submission deadlines as a result of the dispute. Merkin did not return the hard drive, the DVDs, or the raw footage in any form.

Casa Duse brought suit against Merkin and his limited liability company, A. Merkin Entertainment, LLC, ("AME") in May 2012 seeking, inter alia, a temporary restraining order and injunction enjoining Merkin from interfering with its use of the film. The district court granted the temporary restraining order and issued an order to show cause why a preliminary injunction should not issue. After briefing, on May 18, 2012, the court issued the preliminary injunction that Casa Duse sought.

Some two months later, in July 2012, Casa Duse filed an amended complaint requesting a judgment declaring that (1) Casa Duse was not liable to Merkin or AME for copyright infringement; (2) Neither Merkin nor AME owned a copyright interest in the film; and (3) Merkin's copyright registration was invalid. Casa Duse also asserted claims for breach of contract, tortious interference with business relations, and conversion. It sought relief in the form of compensatory damages; an order requiring Merkin to withdraw his copyright registration, return all forms of the footage, and refrain from interfering with Casa Duse's use of the film; and costs and attorney's fees as a sanction under 28 U.S.C. § 1927 and pursuant to the Copyright Act's fees provision, U.S.C. § 505.

..

DISCUSSION

This case requires us to answer a question of first impression in this Circuit: May a contributor to a creative work whose contributions are inseparable from, and integrated into, the work maintain a copyright interest in his or her contributions alone? We conclude that, at least on the facts of the present case, he or she may not.

...

III. Copyright Claims

Merkin argues that the district court erred in concluding, first, that Merkin could not copyright his creative contributions to the film, and, second, that he lacks copyright ownership of the "raw film footage." Casa Duse responds that individual contributions to a film, such as direction, are not themselves subject to copyright protection and that Casa Duse retains sole copyright ownership of the film and the "raw footage," to the extent the two are distinguishable for copyright purposes.

Two points merit mention at the outset.

First, the parties agree that Merkin is not a "joint author" or "co-author" of the film under the 1976 Copyright Act. See 17 U .S.C. § 101 ("A 'joint work' is a work prepared by two or more authors with the intention that their contributions be merged into inseparable or interdependent parts of a unitary whole."). If he were, that fact would likely prohibit his interference with Casa Duse's use and display of the film, because "[o]ne joint owner cannot be liable for copyright infringement to another joint owner." 1 Melville B. Nimmer & David Nimmer, Nimmer on Copyright § 6.10[A] (2015). A co-authorship claimant in our Circuit generally must show that "each of the putative co-authors (1) made independently copyrightable contributions to the work; and (2) fully intended to be co-authors." Thomson v. Larson, 147 F .3d 195,200 (2d Cir.1998) (citing Childress v. Taylor, 945 F.2d 500, 507–08 (2d Cir.1991)). Even assuming the first prong3 is met here, we agree with the district court that "the record uniformly establishes that [Casa Duse], through its principal, Krakovski, never intended to share authorship of the film with Merkin or anyone else," and "[t]here is also considerable evidence that Merkin never intended to be [Casa Duse's] co-author." 16 Casa Duse, LLC, 2013 WL 5510770, at *8–9,2013 U.S. Dist. LEXIS 143958, at *23–25.

Second, the parties also agree that Merkin's efforts cannot be deemed a "work made for hire." See 17 U.S.C. § 201(b) ("[T]he . person for whom the work [-for-hire] was prepared is considered the author . and, unless the parties have expressly agreed otherwise in a written instrument signed by them, owns all of the rights comprised in the copyright."). A work-for-hire arrangement requires:

(1) a work prepared by an employee within the scope of his or her employment; or (2) a work specially ordered or commissioned for use as a contribution to a collective work, as a part of a motion picture[, or for other specified purposes] . if the parties expressly agree in a written instrument signed by them that the work shall be considered a work made for hire.

Id. § 101. Merkin was not Casa Duse's employee, see Cmty. for Creative Non–Violence v. Reid, 490 U.S. 730, 740–41 (1989) ("[T]he term 'employee' [in section 101] should be understood in light of the general common law of agency."), and the parties failed to execute a written agreement.

A. Copyright in Creative Contributions to a Work

"Copyright protection subsists . in original works of authorship fixed in any tangible medium of expression, now known or later developed, from which they can be perceived, reproduced, or otherwise communicated, either directly or with the aid of a machine or device." 17 U.S.C. § 102(a). We have never decided whether an individual's non-de minimis creative contributions to a work in which copyright protection subsists, such as a film, fall within the subject matter of copyright, when the contributions are inseparable from the work and the individual is neither the sole nor a joint author of the work and is not a party to a work-for-hire arrangement. See Thomson, 147 F.3d at 206 (acknowledging open question and resolving case on alternative grounds). We answer that question in the negative on the facts of the present case, finding that the Copyright Act's terms, structure, and history support the conclusion that Merkin's contributions to the film do not themselves constitute a "work of authorship" amenable to copyright protection.

The Copyright Act does not define the term "works of authorship." Section 102 of the Act, however, lists examples of categories of "works of authorship," including "literary works," 17 U.S.C. § 102(a)(1), "musical works," id. § 102(a)(2), and—most relevant here—"motion pictures and other audiovisual works," id. § 102(a)(6). This list is not exhaustive, but as we have previously observed, categories of creative efforts that are not "similar [ ] or analogous to any of the listed categories" are unlikely to fall within the subject matter of federal copyright protection. Nat'l

Basketball Ass'n v. Motorola, Inc., 105 F.3d 841, 846 (2d Cir.1997) (concluding that "basketball games do not fall within the subject matter of federal copyright protection because they do not constitute 'original works of authorship' under 17 U.S.C. § 102(a)."). Motion pictures, like "pantomimes," 17 U.S.C. § 102(a)(4), and "dramatic works," id. § 102(a)(3), are works that may be expected to contain contributions from multiple individuals. See Richlin v. Metro–Goldwyn–Mayer Pictures, Inc., 531 F.3d 962, 975 (9th Cir.2008) ("A motion picture is a work to which many contribute; however, those contributions ultimately merge to create a unitary whole."). But the Act lists none of the constituent parts of any of these kinds of works as "works of authorship." This uniform absence of explicit protection suggests that non-freestanding contributions to works of authorship are not ordinarily themselves works of authorship.

Other provisions of the Act support this conclusion. The Act's definition of "joint work," a work prepared by multiple authors "with the intention that their contributions be merged into inseparable or interdependent parts of a unitary whole," 17 U.S.C. § 101 (emphasis added), suggests that such inseparable contributions are not themselves "works of authorship." Copyright may subsist in contributions to a collective work, see id. § 201(c) ("Copyright in each separate contribution to a collective work is distinct from copyright in the collective work as a whole."), but only when such contributions constitute "separate and independent" works. Id. § 101 ("A 'collective work' is a work, such as a periodical issue, anthology, or encyclopedia, in which a number of contributions, constituting separate and independent works in themselves, are assembled into a collective whole." (emphasis added)). The requirement that contributions be "separate and independent" in order to obtain their own copyright protection also indicates that inseparable contributions integrated into a single work cannot separately obtain such protection.

The legislative history of the Copyright Act further supports this reading. According to the House Report on the 1976 Act:

[A] motion picture would normally be a joint rather than a collective work with respect to those authors who actually work on the film, although their usual status as employees for hire would keep the question of coownership from coming up. On the other hand, although a novelist, playwright, or songwriter may write a work with the hope or expectation that it will be used in a motion picture, this is clearly a case of separate or independent authorship rather than one where the basic intention behind the writing of the work was for motion picture use.

H.R.Rep. No. 94–1476, at 120 (1976), reprinted in 1976 U.S.C.C.A.N. 5659, 5736. While issues of "coownership" of a copyright may arise in the motion picture context, the question of separate contributions meriting separate copyrights as "works" ordinarily would not, unless the motion picture incorporates separate, freestanding pieces that independently constitute "works of authorship." In a joint work, "the separate elements [comprising the work] merge into a unified whole," whereas in a collective work, individuals' contributions "remain unintegrated and disparate." Id., H.R.Rep. No. 94–1476, at 122, 1976 U.S.C .C.A.N., at 5738.

As Casa Duse observes, the Copyright Office has, in an unrelated case, suggested a similar interpretation of the Act. The Office has stated that an individual who lacks a work-for-hire agreement but who "intend[s] her contribution or performance to 'be merged into inseparable or interdependent parts of a unitary whole[,]' 17 U.S.C. § 101[,] . may assert a claim in joint authorship in the motion picture, but not sole authorship of her performance in a portion of the work." Letter from Robert J. Kasunic, Assoc. Register of 10 Copyrights and Dir. of Registration Policy and Practices, U.S. Copyright Office, 11 to M. Cris Armenta, The Armenta Law Firm (Mar. 6, 2014) (attached as appendix 12 to Brief in Response to Suggestion of Rehearing En Banc [Dkt. 54] at ADD47, Garcia v. Google, No. 12–57302 (9th Cir. Mar. 12, 2014)). We need not defer to the Copyright Office's interpretation as a general matter, see Carol Barnhart Inc. v. Econ. Cover Corp., 773 F.2d 411, 414 (2d Cir.1985), or under the factually distinct circumstances of the present case. We find its analysis persuasive nonetheless.

There was, until recently, some authority apparently to the contrary. The majority of a three-judge panel of the Ninth Circuit concluded that copyright protection may subsist in an actor's performance in a motion picture. See Garcia v. Google, Inc., 766 F.3d 929, 933–36 (9th Cir.), rev'd en banc, ––– F.3d ––––, No. 12–57302, 2015 WL 2343586, 2015 U.S.App. LEXIS 8105 (9th Cir. May 18, 2015) ("Garcia (en banc)"). In Garcia, as in the present case, an individual who made a contribution to a finished film—in that case, an actor—claimed ownership of a copyright interest in her contribution. The court reasoned that the actor's performance exhibited at least a "minimal degree of creativity" such that the actor had probably engaged in an original act of authorship. Id. at 934 (quoting Feist Publ'ns, Inc. v. Rural Tel. Serv. Co., 499 U.S. 340, 345 (1991)). And the performance was, in the court's view, "fixed" in a tangible medium as part of the finished film. Id.

An en banc panel reversed, however, adhering to the Copyright Office's view and, based thereon, concluding that the actor's "theory of copyright law would result in [a] legal morass[,] . [making] Swiss cheese of copyrights." Garcia (en banc), ––– F.3d at ––––, 2015 WL 2343586, at *6,2015 U.S.App. LEXIS 8105, at *23 (internal quotation marks omitted). We agree. Filmmaking is a collaborative process typically involving artistic contributions from large numbers of people, including—in addition to producers, directors, and screenwriters—actors, designers, cinematographers, camera operators, and a host of skilled technical contributors. If copyright subsisted separately in each of their contributions to the completed film, the copyright in the film itself, which is recognized by statute as a work of authorship, could be undermined by any number of individual claims. These various contributors may make original artistic expressions, which are arguably fixed in the medium of film footage. But while originality and fixation are necessary prerequisites to obtaining copyright protection, see 17 U.S.C. § 102(a), they are not alone sufficient: Authors are not entitled to copyright protection except for the "works of authorship" they create and fix. See id.; see also Garcia, 766 F.3d at 941 (N.R.Smith, J., dissenting).

Our conclusion in the present case does not suggest that motion picture directors such as Merkin may never achieve copyright protection for their creative efforts.

The director of a film may, of course, be the sole or joint author of that film, such that she or he can secure copyright protection for the work. See Cmty. for Creative Non–Violence, 490 U.S. at 737 ("As a general rule, the author is the party who actually creates the work, that is, the person who translates an idea into a fixed, tangible expression entitled to copyright protection."); see also F. Jay Dougherty, Not A Spike Lee Joint? Issues in the Authorship of Motion Pictures Under U.S. Copyright Law, 49 UCLA L.Rev. 225, 312 (2001) ("[T]he director of the film is certainly potentially one of its most important authors."). And authors of freestanding works that are incorporated into a film, such as dance performances or songs, may copyright these "separate and independent work[s]." 17 U.S.C. § 101 (defining "collective work"). But a director's contribution to an integrated "work of authorship" such as a film is not itself a "work of authorship" subject to its own copyright protection.

A final observation: A conclusion other than the one we adopt would grant contributors like Merkin greater rights than joint authors, who, as we have noted, have no right to interfere with a co-author's use of the copyrighted work. See Childress, 945 F.2d at 508("Joint authorship entitles the co-authors to equal undivided interests in the work."). We doubt that Congress intended for contributors who are not joint authors to have greater rights enabling them to hamstring authors' use of copyrighted works, as apparently occurred in the case at bar. We agree with the en banc Ninth Circuit, then, that the creation of "thousands of standalone copyrights" in a given work was likely not intended. Garcia (en banc), ––– F.3d at ––––, 2015 WL 2343586, at *7, 2015 U.S.App. LEXIS 8105, at * 26.

We conclude that Merkin did not obtain and does not possess a copyright in his directorial contributions to the finished film.

B. Copyright in Raw Film Footage

Merkin also contends that he and not Casa Duse owns all copyright interests in the "raw film footage" which was contained on the hard drive and DVDs and from which the final film Heads Up was or will be produced.

Unlike Merkin's creative contributions to the film, the film footage is subject to copyright protection. An original motion picture is surely a "work of authorship" in which copyright protection "subsists" under the Copyright Act. See 17 U.S.C. § 102(a)(6). And "where a work is prepared over a period of time, the portion of it that has been fixed at any particular time constitutes the work as of that time." Id. § 101. The unedited film footage at issue in this case seems to us to be an early version of the finished product, constituting the film "as of that time." Because "the Copyright Act [ ] affords protection to each work at the moment of its creation," Weissmann v. Freeman, 868 F.2d 1313, 1317 (2d Cir.1989), copyright subsists even in such an unfinished work.

With respect to the ownership of any such copyright, "[c]opyright in a work protected under this title vests initially in the author or authors of the work." 17 U.S.C. § 201(a). The Copyright Act contemplates instances in which multiple authors of a single work may maintain some form of copyright ownership in that work, but the parties agree that Heads Up fits into none of those categories. In cases in which none of the multiple-author scenarios specifically identified by the Copyright Act applies, but multiple individuals lay claim to the copyright in a single work, the dispositive inquiry is which of the putative authors is the "dominant author." See Childress, 945 F.2d at 508.

The district court concluded, and we agree, that Casa Duse was that 4 "dominant author." See 16 Casa Duse, 2013 WL 5510770 at *10,2013 U.S. Dist. LEXIS 143958 at *29. Our Circuit has not proffered rules for determining which of multiple authors is "dominant." See Childress, 945 F.2d at 508 (discussing joint authorship inquiry "where one person [ ] is indisputably the dominant author of the work and the only issue is whether that person is the sole author or she and another [ ] are joint authors"). We have, however, identified "factual indicia of ownership and authorship" relevant to the joint-author inquiry. Thomson, 147 F.3d at 202. These factors—including decisionmaking authority, billing, and written agreements with third parties, see id. at 202–04—are also relevant to our dominant-author inquiry.

As to decisionmaking authority, which refers to the parties' relative control "over what changes are made and what is included in a work," id. at 202, the parties agree that Merkin exercised a significant degree of control over many of the creative decisions underlying both the raw film footage and the finished product. As director, Merkin made a variety of creative decisions related to camera work, lighting, blocking, and actors' wardrobe, makeup, and dialogue delivery, particularly during the three days of filming. But in the context of the project as a whole, Casa Duse exercised far more decisionmaking authority. Cf. id. at 198 n. 10 (putative co-author's claim to have "developed [a play's] plot and theme, contributed extensively to the story, created many character elements, [and written] a significant portion of the dialogue and song lyrics" did not render her a joint, let alone dominant, author of play). Casa Duse initiated the project; acquired the rights to the screenplay; selected the cast, crew and director; controlled the production schedule; and coordinated (or attempted to coordinate) the film's publicity and release. Cf. Aalmuhammed v. Lee, 202 F .3d 1227, 1234 (9th Cir.2000) ("[A]n author superintend[s] the work by exercising control. This will likely be . the inventive or master mind who creates, or gives effect to the idea." (second alteration in original) (footnotes and internal quotation marks omitted)).

The second factor is "the way in which the parties bill or credit themselves," which provides evidence of intent of authorship. Thomson, 147 F.3d at 203. Although Merkin evidently sought to retain the right to remove his name from the finished film, both parties initially intended to take some credit for the final product. The billing inquiry as to the raw footage, then, appears to us to be essentially neutral, as we understand will often be the case in the context of a motion picture. See Dougherty, supra at 264 (explaining that this factor "is less helpful in evidencing the contributors' intent for works such as motion pictures").

The third factor, "the parties' agreements with outsiders," Thomson, 147 F.3d at 204, points decisively in Casa Duse's favor. Casa Duse obtained written work-for-hire agreements from every cast and crew member other than Merkin. Merkin did not, so far as the record shows, enter into any third party agreements. Indeed, nothing in the record suggests he had any intention to do so. Casa Duse also entered into an agreement with the screenwriter, authorizing the very creation of the film as a derivative work. See 17 U.S.C. § 101 ("A 'derivative work' is a work based upon one or more preexisting works."). Thus Casa Duse executed all of the relevant third-party agreements.

We agree with the district court that in this case, Casa Duse was the dominant author of the film. The record does not reflect any developments that occurred between the creation of the raw film footage and Casa Duse's attempts to create a finished product that would alter this analysis as to the raw footage. We thus conclude that Casa Duse, not Merkin, owns the copyright in the finished film and its prior versions, including the disputed "raw film footage."

...

CONCLUSION

For the foregoing reasons, we AFFIRM the district court's grant of summary judgment to Casa Duse on its copyright claims and thus the court's entry of a permanent injunction against Merkin, REVERSE the district court's grant of summary judgment to Casa Duse on its tortious interference with business relations claim, and REMAND to the district court with instructions to enter summary judgment in favor of Merkin on that claim, based thereon to reexamine its award of costs and attorney's fees, and for such other proceedings as are warranted.

1:17-cv-05867 (2018)

GAYLE v HOME BOX OFFICE

United States Southern District Of New York

JESSE M. FURMAN, United States District Judge

Plaintiff Itoffee R. Gayle, proceeding pro se, brings this action against Home Box Office, Inc. ("HBO") alleging copyright and trademark infringement. Gayle's claims derive from the brief depiction of graffiti in the background of one scene in an episode of the HBO television series Vinyl. (Docket No. 19 ("Am. Compl."), at ¶ 1). In the scene, a woman is shown walking down a New York City street and passing a dumpster tagged with graffiti stating "art we all" that Gayle claims is his intellectual property. (Id. ¶¶ 1-2). Gayle alleges that HBO depicted the graffiti "without permission, compensation, or attribution" and thus infringed his copyright and trademark rights. (Id. ¶ 1). He contends that HBO's infringement was "calculated & coordinated" and occurred without the company's ever "attempt[ing] to contact [him], hire [him] or pay the licensing fee(s) to [him]." (Id. ¶¶ 2-3). Gayle also maintains that HBO "exploited & capitalized" on the "brand name recognition" of his trademark "art we all" in order to make their television show seem "more authentic to viewers." (Id. ¶ 4). On the basis of these allegations, he brings claims of copyright infringement; unfair competition under the Lanham

Act, 15 U.S.C. § 1125(a); and unspecified "unfair competition & trademark infringement under related state laws." (Am. Compl. ¶ 5). He seeks $1,500,000 plus fees. (Id. ¶ 7).

...

To prevail on his claim of copyright infringement, Gayle "must prove that (1) unauthorized copying of the copyrighted work occurred, and (2) the infringing work is substantially similar." Gottlieb Dev. LLC v. Paramount Pictures Corp., 590 F. Supp. 2d 625, 631 (S.D.N.Y. 2008) (citing Tufenkian Import/Export Ventures, Inc. v. Einstein Moomjy, Inc., 338 F.3d 127, 131 (2d Cir. 2003)). Significantly, demonstrating substantial similarity requires showing both that work copied was "protected expression" and "that the amount that was copied is more than de minimis." Tufenkian, 338 F.3d at 131 (internal quotation marks omitted) . In the copyright arena, de minimis can "mean[] what it means in most legal contexts: a technical violation of a right so trivial that the law will not impose legal consequences," or it can mean "that copying has occurred to such a trivial extent as to fall below the quantitative threshold of substantial similarity, which is always a required element of actionable copying." Ringgold v. Black Entm't Television, Inc., 126 F.3d 70, 74 (2d Cir. 1997). In analyzing similarity, courts assess "the extent to which the copyrighted work is copied in the allegedly infringing work," with a work's "observability" being paramount. Gottlieb, 590 F. Supp. 2d at 632. Observability turns on "the length of time the copyrighted work is observable as well as factors such as focus, lighting, camera angles, and prominence." Id. (citing Sandoval v. New Line Cinema Corp., 147 F.3d 215, 217 (2d Cir. 1998); Ringgold, 126 F.3d at 75)). The assessment is to be made from the viewpoint of an "average lay observer." Sandoval, 147 F.3d at 218.

...

Then-District Judge Chin's decision in Gottlieb provides a helpful illustration of how these principles apply to claims of the sort at issue here. In that case, the plaintiff claimed that the defendant had infringed his copyright and trademark in a pinball machine by depicting it in the movie What Women Want starring Mel Gibson. Judge Chin dismissed the copyright claim on the ground that the defendant's use of the pinball machine "was de minimis as a matter of law." 590 F. Supp. 2d at 630-32. He explained:

The scene in question lasts only three-and-a-half minutes, and the [machine] appears in the scene sporadically, for no more than a few seconds at a time. More importantly, the pinball machine is always in the background; it is never seen in the foreground. It never appears by itself or in a close-up. It is never mentioned and plays no role in the plot. It is almost always partially obscured (by Gibson and pieces of furniture), and is fully visible for only a few seconds during the entire scene. The Designs (on the backglass and playfield of the pinball machine) are never fully visible and are either out of focus or obscured. Indeed, an average observer would not recognize the Designs as anything other than generic designs in a pinball machine.

...

If Gottlieb's claims were implausible, Gayle's border on frivolous. Whereas Gottlieb's claims were based on three-and-a-half minutes of film, Gayle's claims are premised on a fleeting shot of barely visible graffiti painted on what appears to be a dumpster in the background of a single scene. The overall scene is brief, and the graffiti at issue appears on screen for no more than two to three seconds. (See Video at 46:21-46:24). Moreover, the graffiti is never pictured "by itself or in a close-up," and it plays absolutely no "role in the plot." Gottlieb, 590 F. Supp. 2d at 632. Instead, the camera is focused on the actress in the foreground, who is well-lit and depicted in an eye-catching bright-red dress. By contrast, the graffiti is, at best, shown in the background at an oblique angle and in low, uneven light such that it is "never fully visible," let alone legible. Id. In fact, the graffiti is hard enough to notice when the video is paused at the critical moment. (See Am. Compl. 8). It is next to impossible to notice when viewing the episode in real time. In short, the graffiti "was filmed in such a manner and appears so fleetingly that . . . there is no plausible claim for copyright infringement here." Gottlieb, 590 F. Supp. 2d at 634; see also Sandoval, 147 F.3d at 218 ("Because [the plaintiff's] photographs appear fleetingly and are obscured, severely out of focus, and virtually unidentifiable, we find the use of those photographs to be de minimis."). And given how "difficult" it would be "for even a keen observer to pick out" Gayle's trademark (if, indeed, it even qualifies as such), "no viewer" of the episode "would consider whether [HBO] sponsored the [graffiti] or [Gayle] sponsored the [episode]." Gottlieb, 590 F. Supp. 2d at 635-36; see also Louis Vuitton Malletier S.A. v. Warner Bros. Enter. Inc., 868 F. Supp. 2d 172, 184 n.19 (S.D.N.Y. 2012) (finding "the possibility of sponsorship confusion" was "unlikely").

As evidence that his graffiti was "visible & observable to average lay viewers," Gayle points to an Instagram message from a user named "Goldpoo_" congratulating him on the appearance of the graffiti in the episode of Vinyl. (See Docket No. 26 ("Gayle Decl."), ¶ 4; see also Am. Compl. 9). But the anonymous "Goldpoo_" is hardly a stand-in for the "average lay observer" relevant to the copyright inquiry, Sandoval, 147 F.3d at 218, or the "ordinary prudent purchasers" relevant to the trademark inquiry, Star Indus., Inc., 412 F.3d at 383 (internal quotation marks omitted). Citing a YouTube video featuring "members of the series' [sic] production team detailing the importance of graffiti" in "recreat[ing] . . . the 1970s New York City theme," Gayle also asserts that HBO's use of his graffiti cannot be deemed de minimis because it was "certainly deliberate" and "very much consequential." (Gayle Decl. ¶ 4). But putting aside whether the Court can even consider such extrinsic evidence at this stage of the litigation, HBO's motive in depicting the graffiti is irrelevant to the de minimis inquiry. "[W]here the use is de minimis," as here, "the copying will not be actionable, even where the work was chosen to be in the background for some thematic relevance." Gottlieb, 590 F. Supp. 2d at 634; see id. (dismissing a copyright claim as de minimis even though the copied work was "undoubtedly . . . chosen by the production staff because it fit in with the 'sporty' theme of the background in the scene"); see also Sandoval, 147 F.3d at 218 (deeming the use of copyrighted photographs in the background of a film set de minimis because, "though selected by production staff for thematic relevance, or at least for [their] decorative value, [the photographs were] filmed at such distance and so out of focus that a typical program viewer would not discern any decorative effect that the work of art contributes to the set" (citation omitted)).

...

973 F. Supp. 409 (1997)

SANDOVAL v. NEW LINE CINEMA CORP.

United States District Court, S.D. New York

STEIN, District Judge.

Plaintiff Jorge Antonio Sandoval brought this action alleging that defendants infringed his copyrights in several photographs when they were shown in the background of a scene in the motion picture Seven. Defendants have moved for summary judgment dismissing the complaint pursuant to Fed. R.Civ.P. 56 and plaintiff has cross-moved for summary judgment in his favor. Defendants' motion is granted and plaintiff's motion is denied on the grounds that the display of the photographs constituted a fair use of them within the terms and intendment of the Copyright Act.

Background

Sandoval is the author of, and owns valid copyrights in, a series of ten photographs of himself which depict his body or face in a variety of unusual poses ("the Photographs"). Sandoval's Statement Pursuant to Local Rule 3(g) ("Sandoval Rule 3(g) Statement") ¶¶ 2-3. Sandoval created the Photographs between 1991 and 1994 "for his own artistic satisfaction" and has never publicly exhibited or commercially exploited them, nor does he have any current plans to do so. Compl. ¶ 9; Sandoval Rule 3(g) Statement ¶ 4.

Defendants are the producers and distributors of the motion picture Seven, a murder mystery which chronicles the pursuit by two detectives of a serial killer whose murders are each connected to one of the seven deadly sins. Seven, whose gross receipts totaled approximately $100 million,[1] has been variously described by critics as "a dark, grisly, horrifying and intelligent thriller, ... film-making of a high order"[2] and "the equivalent of a forced tour of a morgue."[3] In one of the film's scenes the detectives, after a hermeneutical discussion of Fourth Amendment jurisprudence, agree that probable cause does not exist to justify seeking a warrant to enter and search the killer's apartment. They then immediately kick the apartment door down, suborn a witness to testify to probable cause, and enter. The apartment is filled with artifacts suggestive of the killer's mental derangement. Included in the background of the scene is a light box turned on by one of the detectives upon which hangs a series of black and white translucent forms, including certain of Sandoval's Photographs. New Line Cinema's Statement Pursuant to Local Rule 3(g) ¶ 5.

The scene in which the Photographs appear is approximately 1½ minutes in length. The light box which holds the Photographs is only visible in the background in approximately ten camera shots that range in duration from one to six seconds each, totaling at most thirty seconds. In the majority of those shots, the Photographs are obstructed by other objects in the scene such as actors or furniture and in no instance does the camera focus exclusively on the light box or the Photographs. Moreover, the light box images are out of focus for much of the time, since the camera is focused on the foreground. For these reasons, it is not surprising that plaintiff can state only that he and one or two unnamed acquaintances were able to identify the Photographs as his work, and only after careful scrutiny. Sandoval himself not only returned to the theater "at least twice," but also viewed enlarged still frames from the scene before he was able to conclude with certainty that ten of the images on the light box were the Photographs. Sandoval Aff. ¶¶ 7-13. The Court was only able to identify one of the Photographs as Sandoval's, and only after repeated viewings of the scene in connection with this motion for summary judgment.

After plaintiff concluded that the Photographs used were his, he commenced this action. The complaint alleges copyright infringement, intentional infliction of emotional distress, and invasion of privacy pursuant to both New York's Civil Rights Law § 51 and California common law. Plaintiff seeks inter alia to enjoin the further distribution and display of the film and to collect actual and statutory damages pursuant to 17 U.S.C. § 504(c). Defendants concede for purposes of this motion that plaintiff's Photographs are in the subject scene, see Defs.' Mem. in Supp. of Defs.' Mot. for Summ. J., dated November 18, 1996 ("Defs.' Mem.") at 9, but contend principally that the fleeting and insignificant use of the Photographs constitutes fair use of the copyrighted works pursuant to section 107 of the Copyright Act.

Discussion

...

II. Copyright Infringement

To establish a claim of copyright infringement, the plaintiff must establish (1) ownership of a valid copyright and (2) unauthorized copying or a violation of one of the other exclusive rights afforded copyright owners pursuant to the Copyright Act. See Twin Peaks Productions v. Publications Int'l. Ltd., 996 F.2d 1366, 1372 (2d Cir.1993). Among these rights are the rights to reproduce and display publicly the copyrighted work. See 29 U.S.C. §§ 106(1), (5) (1996).

In this case, defendants do not contest the validity of plaintiff's copyrights in the Photographs at issue. See Defs.' Mem. at 9. Moreover, defendants concede, for purposes of its summary judgment motion only, that plaintiff's copyrighted work is in the subject scene. See id. However, defendants argue that the light box images do not constitute "legally cognizable copies" because they are: (1) severely out of focus; (2) obscured by the scene's action and set dressing; and (3) substantially reduced in size. Similarly, defendants contend that their use of the Photographs cannot constitute a "public display" of plaintiff's Photographs because they are not recognizable to the public. Plaintiff counters that defendants did, in fact, make transparencies, or copies, of the Photographs, and that defendants also violated plaintiff's copyrights by "displaying" his copyrighted works by means of film.

For the reasons set forth below, plaintiff's copyrights have not been infringed because defendants' use of the Photographs was a fair use. Because this finding of fair use negates any liability stemming from defendants' use of the Photographs, this Court need not decide whether plaintiff has established the two elements of a copyright infringement claim.

III. Fair Use

17 U.S.C. § 107 provides that "the fair use of a copyrighted work ... is not an infringement of copyright." "This doctrine recognizes that there are circumstances in which the Copyright Act's goals of encouraging creative and original work is better served by allowing a use of a copyrighted work than prohibiting its use." Robinson, 877 F. Supp. at 839 (citing Arica Institute, Inc. v. Palmer, 970 F.2d 1067, 1077 (2d Cir.1992)). Section 107 goes on to provide that "[i]n determining whether the use made of a work in any particular case is a fair use the factors to be considered shall include (1) the purpose and character of the use ... (2) the nature of the copyrighted work, (3) the amount and substantiality of the portion used in relation to the copyrighted work as a whole, and (4) the effect of the use on the potential market for or value of the copyrighted work." The inquiry requires a case-by-case analysis and the four factors are to be "weighed together in light of the purposes of copyright." Campbell v. Acuff-Rose Music, Inc., 510 U.S. 569, 578, 114 S. Ct. 1164, 1171, 127 L. Ed. 2d 500 (1994) (citations omitted).

Importantly, the factors enumerated in Section 107 are nonexclusive, and unenumerated factors may have bearing on the fair use determination. See American Geophysical Union v. Texaco, Inc., 60 F.3d 913, 931 (2d Cir.1994); 4 MELVILLE B. NIMMER & DAVID NIMMER, NIMMER ON COPYRIGHT § 13.05[A], at 13-155 to 156 (1997). The defendant bears the burden of proof with respect to all issues in dispute concerning whether a particular use of a copyrighted work is a "fair use" for purposes of 17 U.S.C. § 107. See American Geophysical Union, 60 F.3d at 918.

A. The Purpose and Character of the Use

The first factor listed in section 107 is "the purpose and character of the use, including whether such use is of a commercial nature or is for nonprofit educational purposes." Uses of a copyrighted work for purposes such as "criticism, comment, news reporting, teaching ..., scholarship, or research," are more likely to be found to be fair uses than uses for commercial purposes. See id.; Twin Peaks Productions v. Publications Int'l. Ltd., 996 F.2d 1366, 1374-75 (2d Cir.1993). However, the Second Circuit has recently explained that courts should be wary of placing too much emphasis on whether or not a given use is commercial in nature, "[s]ince many, if not most, secondary users seek at least some measure of commercial gain from their use." American Geophysical Union, 60 F.3d at 921. A second consideration under this factor is whether the secondary use might be said to be a "transformative use" in the sense that it "adds something new, with a further purpose or different character" than the copyrighted work. Id. at 922-23 (citing Campbell, 510 U.S. at 579, 114 S.Ct. at 1171).

In this case, defendants surely produced and distributed the film Seven with a commercial purpose. However, it is also true that defendants do much more than "merely supersede the [copyrighted work]" by exhibiting them, however obscurely, for the first time in the film. See Campbell, 510 U.S. at 579, 114 S. Ct. at 1171. The use of plaintiff's Photographs was transformative, in the sense that defendants used the visual images created in plaintiff's work in furtherance of the creation of a distinct visual aesthetic and overall mood for the moviegoer watching the scene in the killer's apartment. Defendants did not use the Photographs to promote Seven, nor is there any indication that defendants were trying to exploit directly the theoretical market for Sandoval's previously unexhibited photography. See Ringgold v. Black Entertainment Television, Inc., 1996 WL 535547, at 3. This case is thus unlike Woods v. Universal City Studios, Inc., 920 F. Supp. 62 (S.D.N.Y.1996), which is unavailingly relied upon by plaintiff. In that case, the court found that the movie set created by the defendant film studio was essentially a recreation of plaintiff's copyrighted drawing. Id. at 64-65.

While the commercial purpose of Seven weighs in favor of plaintiff on this first factor, the transformative nature of the use of the Photographs means that factor one will not weigh heavily in the overall fair use analysis. See Campbell, 510 U.S. at 579, 114 S. Ct. at 1171 ("the more transformative the new work, the less will be the significance of other factors, like commercialism, that may weigh against a finding of fair use").

B. Nature of the Copyrighted Work

There is no dispute that Sandoval's Photographs are creative and original works of art. Thus, this factor favors plaintiff. This finding is buttressed by the fact that Sandoval has yet to exhibit publicly his Photographs, since the unpublished nature of a copyrighted work weighs against a finding of fair use under this factor. See Harper & Row, Publishers, Inc. v. Nation Enterprises, 471 U.S. 539, 563, 105 S. Ct. 2218, 2232, 85 L. Ed. 2d 588 (1985).

C. Amount and Substantiality of the Portion Used

The third factor listed in section 107 is "the amount and substantiality of the portion used in relation to the copyrighted work as a whole." The Court must take into account the quantity and value of the material used in relation to the work as a whole. See Campbell, 510 U.S. at 586-87, 114 S. Ct. at 1175.

Though defendant included in the scene's background plaintiff's ten copyrighted works in their entirety, at most a single one of the Photographs is recognizable as Sandoval's work, and that only after careful scrutiny and repeated viewings. For the vast majority of the thirty seconds in which the light box appears, the Photographs are not discernible to even an individual viewing the scene with an eye toward identifying the copyrighted works; they are even less identifiable to the average viewer concentrating on the foreground action. This fleeting and obscured use of plaintiff's work did not and cannot capture the essence or value of the plaintiff's work. See Ringgold, supra, 1996 WL 535547 at 4 (holding that obstructed, unfocused view of copyrighted poster in television episode for a total of less than twenty-seven seconds was insubstantial, and that factor favored finding of fair use); Amsinck, 862 F. Supp. at 1050 (finding that defendant's display of copyrighted mobile in its entirety in defendant's film for periods of a few seconds and over a total of ninety-six seconds at some points in close-ups did not preclude a finding of fair use); Mura v. Columbia Broadcasting System, Inc., 245 F. Supp. 587, 590 (S.D.N.Y.1965) (use of copyrighted puppets *414 for approximately thirty-five seconds in children's television program was fair use, in part, because the puppets were not a principal attraction but were used in an "incidental" manner).

Although the use of the Photographs in their entirety leads the Court to find that this fair use factor favors plaintiff, the Court declines to hold that the obscured and fleeting nature of the use precludes a finding of fair use. See Amsinck, 862 F. Supp. at 1050.

D. The Effect upon the Potential Market for the Copyrighted Work

The fourth factor listed in section 107 instructs the court to examine the effect that the infringing work will have on the market for the original work. 17 U.S.C. § 107(4). This factor is arguably the most important of the four enumerated factors of the fair use analysis. See Harper & Row, 471 U.S. at 566, 105 S. Ct. at 2233 (this factor is "undoubtedly the single most important element of fair use"); accord 4 NIMMER ON COPYRIGHT § 13.05[A][4], 13-186 to 187 ("this [factor] emerges as the most important, and indeed, central fair use factor"); but see American Geophysical Union, 37 F.3d at 889 (noting that the Supreme Court's discussion of the fourth factor in its most recent fair use decision, Campbell v. Acuff-Rose Music, Inc., 510 U.S. 569, 114 S. Ct. 1164, 127 L. Ed. 2d 500 (1994), omits that this factor is the most important element). This factor requires courts to consider not only the extent of market harm caused by the specific use in question, but the effect that would occur if that type of use became widespread. See Harper & Row, 471 U.S. at 568, 105 S. Ct. at 2234.

Here, the defendant's fleeting and obscured use of the Photographs as part of the background to a movie scene cannot be considered a substitute for the Photographs by any stretch of the imagination. Sandoval's work is virtually undetectable in the scene at issue. Thus, the value of and market potential for his work is in no way usurped, since the public is not even aware after viewing Seven that they have had a glimpse of Sandoval's work. Even widespread uses of Sandoval's Photographs in such a fleeting, obscured, and out-of-focus manner could not begin to encroach on the potential market for his work. In short, this important factor weighs decidedly in defendants' favor.

Conclusion

After weighing the above factors, the Court concludes that the use defendants have made of the Photographs is a "fair use" of them pursuant to 17 U.S.C. § 107. The fleeting, obscured, and virtually undetectable use of Sandoval's Photographs in Seven for at most thirty seconds could not have adversely effected the potential market for Sandoval's work. As a matter of law, this finding is not outweighed by those fair use factors which favor plaintiff. See Wright v. Warner Books, Inc., 953 F.2d 731, 740 (2d Cir.1991).

For the reasons set forth above, defendants' motion for summary judgment is granted and plaintiff's cross-motion for summary judgment is denied.

SO ORDERED

9. Copyright on Architectural Works

14 F. Supp. 2d 154 (1998)

THE YANKEE CANDLE COMPANY v.

NEW ENGLAND CANDLE COMPANY

U.S. District Court for the District of Massachusetts

FREEDMAN, Senior District Judge.

I. INTRODUCTION

This dispute lit up when the plaintiff, The Yankee Candle Company, Inc. ("Yankee"), noticed that the defendants, New England Candle Company, Inc., and its owners Henry and Kristine Komosa (hereinafter collectively referred to as "New England"), had opened a retail candle store that possessed strikingly similar characteristics to its own stores. Yankee turned directly to this Court with a seven-count complaint alleging federal and state trademark infringement, federal copyright infringement, and state deceptive trade practices against New England.

After extensive hearings, the Court granted Yankee's motion for a preliminary injunction on the copyright infringement claim. Despite some initial difficulty, New England complied with the terms of the Court's order by making structural changes to its store. Seeking a permanent injunction, Yankee now moves for summary judgment only on the copyright claim. In response, New England seeks summary judgment on all claims and a dissolution of the preliminary injunction.

II. FACTS

...

Founded in bucolic western Massachusetts a quarter century ago, Yankee manufactures and sells candles and related products in its numerous retail stores throughout the northeastern and midwestern United States. During a recent expansion of stores situated in shopping malls, Yankee engaged architect John Wood Kuhn ("Kuhn") to design an archetypal colonial candle shop whose look Yankee could replicate. In crafting the Natick Mall store that opened in October 1994 in Natick, Massachusetts, Kuhn combined several common design elements, including dark, wooden display cases lining the interior walls, multi-paned glass windows framed by dark wood on the exterior storefront, and a brass letter sign placed above French doors in a recessed entrance. Yankee and Kuhn patterned its subsequent shopping mall stores after the Natick store's composition of elements.

The shop at the heart of this dispute, the Holyoke Mall store in Holyoke, Massachusetts, opened in October 1995. Prior to the opening, Yankee acquired ownership interest in the architectural blueprints for the Holyoke store from Kuhn and his architectural firm. On September 4, 1996, Yankee registered those blueprints with the United States Copyright Office as a "Technical drawing." Well after the commencement of this litigation, on February 2, 1998, Yankee also registered the "Yankee Candle at Holyoke Mall" store with the U.S. Copyright Office as an "Architectural work," describing it as the "Design of a Building as Embodied in Architectural Plans."

Around the time Yankee debuted its Holyoke store, the defendants Henry and Kristine Komosa hatched a plan to compete with Yankee in the retail candle business. In due time, the Komosas incorporated the New England Candle Company, Inc. and planned to open a colonial style candle store at the Enfield Square Mall in Enfield, Connecticut. The New England store opened on September 4, 1996, looking remarkably similar to its Yankee competitor just north of the Massachusetts border in Holyoke. In fact, the New England store employed many of the same design elements the Yankee's Holyoke store used.

None too happy with these resemblances, Yankee filed suit on September 9, 1996, seeking to enjoin New England from copying the look of its store. The Court found the plaintiff likely to succeed on the merits of its copyright claim, but not its trademark infringement claims. Accordingly, the Court issued an injunction ordering New England to make various structural changes to its Enfield Mall store and to refrain from constructing another retail candle shop that looked similar to Yankee's Holyoke store. New England complied with the injunction, but now rejects the merits of Yankee's copyright and trademark allegations and seeks summary judgment.

III. STANDARD OF REVIEW

The essential purpose of summary judgment is "to pierce the boilerplate of the pleadings" and appraise the proof to determine whether a trial is necessary. See Wynne v. Tufts Univ. Sch. of Med., 976 F.2d 791, 794 (1st Cir. 1992), cert. denied, 507 U.S. 1030, 113 S.Ct. 1845, 123 L.Ed.2d 470 (1993). When summary judgment is at stake, the Court must scrutinize the record in the light most favorable to the nonmoving party, "indulging all reasonable inferences in that party's favor," Griggs-Ryan v. Smith, 904 F.2d 112, 115 (1st Cir.1990), yet disregarding unsupported allegations, unreasonable inferences, and conclusory speculation. See Smith v. F.W. Morse & Co., 76 F.3d 413, 428 (1st Cir.1996); Medina-Munoz v. R.J. Reynolds Tobacco Co., 896 F.2d 5, 8 (1st Cir.1990). If no genuine issue of material fact percolates through the record and the movant is entitled to judgment as a matter of law, then summary judgment is proper because a trial would serve no useful purpose. See Fed. R.Civ.P. 56(c); Anderson v. Liberty Lobby, Inc., 477 U.S. 242, 247-48, 106 S.Ct. 2505, 91 L.Ed.2d 202 (1986); Wynne, 976 F.2d at 794.

IV. DISCUSSION

Yankee's motion for partial summary judgment seeks brevis disposition only on count seven of its complaint, an alleged violation of the federal Copyright Act of 1976. See 17 U.S.C. § 101 et seq. New England seeks summary judgment on all counts of the complaint. The Court will consider the copyright claim first as it presents a novel question of law.

A. Copyright Infringement

In Count Seven of its Second Amended Complaint, Yankee alleges that New England infringed on its registered copyrights to both the architectural blueprints of the Holyoke store and the architectural work that the store itself represents. To sustain a claim of copyright infringement, Yankee has the burden of demonstrating that it owns a valid copyright in the architectural blueprints and architectural work alleged to have been copied, and that New England copied constituent elements of the blueprints that are original. See Feist Publications, Inc. v. Rural Tel. Serv. Co., 499 U.S. 340, 361, 111 S.Ct. 1282, 113 L.Ed.2d 358 (1991); Grubb v. KMS Patriots, L.P., 88 F.3d 1, 3 (1st Cir.1996); Concrete Mach. Co. v. Classic Lawn Ornaments, Inc., 843 F.2d 600, 605 (1st Cir.1988). In this case, New England contests Yankee's ownership of a valid copyright and denies that it copied Yankee's designs. New England argues that the Holyoke store does not merit copyright protection as an architectural work and that the plaintiff has not alleged or offered evidence of infringement of its architectural plans. Yankee responds that its retail shopping mall store qualifies for copyright protection and that the substantial similarities between the stores demonstrate the copying of its protected works.

...

2. Protection of Architectural Works

In passing the Copyright Act of 1976, Congress expressly indicated that architectural plans and drawings deserved copyright protection as "pictorial, graphic and sculptural works" under 17 U .S.C. § 101. See H.R.Rep. No. 94-1476, reprinted in 1976 U.S.C.C.A.N. 5659, 5668 ("An architect's plans and drawings would, of course, be protected by copyright [law]"). Congress, however, also indicated that architectural structures built from plans possessed only minimal copyright protection:

[T]he extent to which ... protection would extend to the structure depicted would depend on the circumstances. Purely non-functional or monumental structures would be subject to full copyright protection under the bill, and the same would be true of artistic sculpture or decorative ornamentation or embellishment added to a structure. On the other hand, where the only elements of shape in an architectural design are conceptually inseparable from the utilitarian aspects of the structure, copyright protection for the design would not be available.

After the passage of the 1976 Act, courts extended federal copyright protection to architectural plans, but not to buildings constructed from those plans. See Robert R. Jones Assoc. v. Nino Homes, 858 F.2d 274, 280 (6th Cir.1988) ("one may construct a house which is identical to a house depicted in copyrighted architectural plans, but one may not directly copy those plans and then use the infringing copy to construct the house"); Donald Frederick Evans v. Continental Homes, Inc., 785 F.2d 897, 901 n. 7 (11th Cir.1986) ("A builder who constructs a home substantially similar to a dwelling already constructed is not liable for copyright infringement merely based on the substantial similarity if he or she did not engage in an unauthorized copying or use of the copyrighted architectural drawings"); Demetriades v. Kaufmann, 680 F.Supp. 658, 665-66 (S.D.N.Y.1988) (enjoining defendant from copying plaintiff's architectural plans or relying on infringing copies in construction, but declining to enjoin construction of defendant's substantially similar house); see also Imperial Homes Corp. v. Lamont, 458 F.2d 895, 899 (5th Cir.1972) (holding that copying floor plans from copyrighted brochure constitutes infringement, yet building substantially identical house not prohibited by existence of copyrighted architectural drawings for original house); Herman Frankel Org. v. Tegman, 367 F.Supp. 1051, 1053 (E.D.Mich.1973) ("A person cannot, by copyrighting plans, prevent the building of a house similar to that taught by the copyrighted plans.... A person should, however, be able to prevent another from copying copyrighted house plans and using them to build the house.").

In 1990, the Architectural Works Copyright Protection Act ("AWCPA") codified the copyright prophylaxis of architectural plans and architectural works. See Pub.L. No. 101-650, Tit. VII, 104 Stat. 5133 (1990) (codified in scattered sections of 17 U.S.C.). The AWCPA makes an "architectural work" an "original work of authorship" eligible for copyright protection. 17 U.S.C. § 102(a) (8). The Copyright Act defines an architectural work as "the design of a building as embodied in any tangible medium of expression, including a building, architectural plans, or drawings. The work includes the overall form as well as the arrangement and composition of spaces and elements in the design, but does not include individual standard features." 17 U.S.C. § 101.

With the passage of the AWCPA, a copyright owner may claim infringement of both the architectural plans and the structure based on such plans. See H.R.Rep. 101-735, reprinted in 1990 U.S.C.C.A.N. 6935, 6950 ("Either or both of these copyrights may be infringed and eligible separately for damages"). Courts have routinely protected modern architectural structures, such as commercial homes, that possess the minimal amount of originality that copyright law requires, as well as the plans from which owners built them. See Johnson v. Jones, 921 F.Supp. 1573, 1583 (E.D.Mich.1996) (protecting residential home as architectural work); Richmond Homes Management v. Raintree, Inc., 862 F.Supp. 1517, 1523-26 (W.D.Va.1994) (finding residential home built from plans qualified as protected architectural work), aff'd in part and rev'd in part, 66 F.3d 316, 1995 WL 551274 (4th Cir.1995); Value Group, Inc. v. Mendham Lake Estates, L.P., 800 F.Supp. 1228, 1232-35 (D.N.J. 1992) (enjoining construction of house that would infringe on developer's copyrighted single family luxury home).

This case, however, presents a different situation than a residential home. The Court cannot find, nor can plaintiff cite, a case where copyright law protected a structure-within-a-structure similar to the candle store within a mall in this case. New England argues that Yankee's store does not deserve copyright protection because it does not constitute a "building" under 17 U.S.C. § 101.

As in any case where the Court considers certain contours of a Congressional creation, the first rule of thumb is to read statutory terms, including any provided definitions, according to their plain meaning. See Bailey v. United States, 516 U.S. 137, 144-45, 116 S.Ct. 501, 133 L.Ed.2d 472 (1995); United States v. Missouri Pac. R.R. Co., 278 U.S. 269, 278, 49 S.Ct. 133, 73 L.Ed. 322 (1929). When those terms are clear and unambiguous, the Court assigns them their "ordinary and natural" meaning. Bailey, 516 U.S. at 145, 116 S.Ct. 501. If, and only if, "the literal words of the statute create ambiguity or lead to an unreasonable result," then the Court will look to other principles of statutory construction and the underlying legislative history. ...

The Copyright Act does not define the term "building." An oft-quoted authority on plain meaning defines a building as a "[s]tructure designed for habitation, shelter, storage, trade, manufacture, religion, business, education, and the like. A structure or edifice inclosing a space within its walls, and usually, but not necessarily, covered with a roof." Black's Law Dictionary 194-95 (6th ed.1990). Further inquiry yields a slightly different definition: "anything that is built with walls and a roof, as a house, factory, etc." Webster's New World Dictionary 185 (2d ed.1984). By these definitions, the term "building" is susceptible to numerous interpretations. A host of structures could fall within the scope of the term, as long as they have walls and a roof. The term's ambiguous nature might leave a structure like Fenway Park, one of the greatest architectural works ever designed, undeserving of copyright protection as a building without a roof over its baseball diamond (a space used for recreation, business, and, some would say, religion). See Raphael Winick, Copyright Protection for Architecture After the Architectural Works Copyright Protection Act of 1990, 41 Duke L.J. 1598, 1613 (1992) ("Golf courses, gardens, tunnels, bridges, overpasses, fences, and walls are only a few of the structures designed by architects that would not fit the common definition of `building.' Unless courts interpreting the AWCPA contort the definition of `building' well beyond its generally accepted limits, architects designing these other structures will not find copyright protection under the new subject matter category for architectural works.").

Surveying the AWCPA's legislative landscape, see North Haven Bd. of Educ. v. Bell, 456 U.S. 512, 522, 102 S.Ct. 1912, 72 L.Ed.2d 299 (1982), adds some clarity. The House Report accompanying the AWCPA states that "the term encompassed habitable structures such as houses and office buildings. It also covers structures that are used, but not inhabited, by human beings, such as churches, pergolas, gazebos, and garden pavilions." See H.R.Rep. 101-735, reprinted in 1990 U.S.C.C.A.N. 6935, 6951. From this language, Yankee argues that its retail mall store qualifies as a copyrightable building because it constitutes a habitable three-dimensional structure and more closely resembles a "traditional or conventional building structure" than a pergola or gazebo. See Plaintiff's Memorandum in

Opposition to Defendant's Cross Motion for Summary Judgment and Motion to Vacate the Preliminary Injunction at 8-10.

This argument misses the mark. The Court has difficulty concluding that constructing an empty room in a large shopping mall into a candle shop with a colonial motif transforms that room into a "building" within the meaning of the Copyright Act. The entire mall itself, with its interior walled off and divided into separate spaces for stores, easily qualifies as a building, but an individual store does not. Yankee did not design or construct the walls and ceiling in its store; it built within an existing structure. Had Yankee designed a church to fit into that mall space, certainly it would not become a "building" just because the AWCPA's legislative history lists a "church" as an example of a "building." Holding that the mall store constitutes a "building" would distort the plain meaning of the term. The Court believes that protection extends to free standing structures, like Yankee's "stand alone" flagship candle store in South Deerfield, not individual units comprising a larger structure. Surely Congress did not intend for individual offices in an office building, though elaborately designed, to qualify as "buildings" themselves.

In addition to historical guidance, the Court accords deference to the interpretation of the agency charged with the statute's administration, the Copyright Office. See Chevron U.S.A. Inc. v. Natural Resources Defense Council, Inc., 467 U.S. 837, 844, 104 S.Ct. 2778, 81 L.Ed.2d 694 (1984); 17 U.S.C. § 702. The regulations pertinent to architectural work registration provide a similar understanding of the term "building" as the statute:

The term building means humanly habitable structures that are intended to be both permanent and stationary, such as house and office buildings, and other permanent and stationary structures designed for human occupancy, including but not limited to churches, museums, gazebos, and garden pavilions. 37 C.F.R. § 202.11(b) (2) (1997).

The regulations exclude from copyright protection "[s]tructures other than buildings, such as bridges, cloverleafs, dams, walkways, tents, recreational vehicles, mobile homes, and boats." 37 C.F.R. § 202.11(d) (1) (1997). The Court concludes that although Yankee may have intended its Holyoke store to offer a structure habitable by employees and shoppers alike, its proper characterization lies as a structure other than a building, or a structure in a building, not as a "building" in and of itself.

The Court concludes that New England has successfully rebutted the presumption of copyright validity that Yankee's registration raises. Yankee does not have a valid copyright in the Holyoke store as an architectural work. By contrast, Yankee does have a valid copyright in the architectural blueprints, which New England does not contest.

New England claims, however, that Yankee's complaint does not allege blueprint infringement, and that Yankee has offered no evidence of infringement, thereby entitling New England to summary judgment. The Court disagrees with this disingenuous contention. Construing the complaint liberally, see McIntosh v.

Antonino, 71 F.3d 29, 35 (1st Cir.1995), both the Court and the parties focused on the issue of New England's factual copying of Yankee's blueprints during two days of preliminary injunction hearings, after which New England requested a ruling that Yankee had not proven factual copying.

2. Blueprint Infringement

To demonstrate actionable copying, Yankee must first prove that New England copied the copyrighted Holyoke store blueprints as a factual matter. Yankee has endeavored to accomplish this task with evidence that Henry Komosa, who designed New England's allegedly infringing store, had access to Yankee's blueprints and that the offending and copyrighted blueprints are so similar that the Court may infer that factual copying occurred. See Lotus, 49 F.3d at 813; Concrete Mach., 843 F.2d at 606. Yankee must still prove that the copying of the blueprints was so extensive that it rendered the two sets of plans substantially similar. See CMM Cable Rep, Inc. v. Ocean Coast Properties, Inc., 97 F.3d 1504, 1513 (1st Cir.1996); Lotus, 49 F.3d at 813. The Court may conclude that two works are "substantially similar" if, in the words of Judge Learned Hand, "the ordinary observer, unless he set out to detect the disparities, would be disposed to overlook them, and regard their aesthetic appeal as the same." Peter Pan Fabrics, Inc. v. Martin Weiner Corp., 274 F.2d 487, 489 (2d Cir.1960) (quoted with approval in Concrete Mach., 843 F.2d at 607).

In this case, the points of similarity between the plans overwhelmingly exceed the points of dissimilarity. Nothing the defendants have presented has caused the Court to stray from the conclusion made in the Court's order granting a preliminary injunction: "[A] reasonable person observing the two stores would conclude that [New England] had copied the design of the Holyoke store." The Yankee Candle Co. v. New England Candle Co., C.A. No. 96-30165-FHF, slip op. at 11-12 (D.Mass. June 26, 1997).

Dissecting the plans, the Court finds that five of the six elements expressed in New England's plans remarkably resemble designs found in its competitor's blueprints. The designs for New England's storefront windows and framing, the display units depicted from the front and the side, and the overhead layout of the store, including its French doors and recessed entrance, could pass for replicas of the designs for the same elements in Yankee's Holyoke store plans. Only the "light cove detail" that illuminates the New England store's sign does not have a twin in the Yankee plans. Nevertheless, given Komosa's access to the copyrighted blueprints and the similarities between the two sets of plans, the Court concludes that copying has occurred.

Further, careful comparison of Yankee's six-page store layout designs and the New England one-page blueprint reveal striking, illuminating, and unmistakable similarities. Independent creation cannot explain away the similarity between the plans. The manner in which an architect can express the idea of a colonial era store varies immeasurably. A drive from West Stockbridge, Massachusetts to Caribou, Maine will yield as many different colonial style stores as the mind can imagine.

But a reasonable observer in this case, viewing these blueprints, could only conclude that New England's design and arrangement of the elements in its store plan well surpasses coincidental resemblance to Yankee's blueprints. As a result, because of substantial similarity in the plans, the Court concludes that defendants infringed upon Yankee's valid copyright on the Holyoke Mall store blueprints.

Although Yankee has waived damages in this case, under copyright law, this Court may grant a final injunction on reasonable terms to prevent or restrain infringement of a copyrighted work. 17 U.S.C. § 502. To prevent the suspected infringement, the Court previously ordered New England to make physical changes to its Enfield Square Mall store. The Court now makes that preliminary injunction permanent, ordering the defendants to keep the requisite structural changes and prohibitions in place, and to refrain from constructing future stores that incorporate the same combination of interior and exterior elements that rendered its Enfield store blueprints substantially similar to Yankee's Holyoke store.

...

V. CONCLUSION

The Court permanently enjoins New England from infringing on Yankee's copyrighted blueprints and orders it to comply with the terms of the Court's preliminary injunction. Each party to bear its own costs.

No. Civ.B-98-2226, Feb. 16, 2001.

NELSON-SALABES v. MORNINGSIDE HOLDINGS

United States District Court, D. Maryland.

BLACK, Senior J.:

Plaintiff, Nelson-Salabes, Inc. brings this action against defendants Morningside Holdings of Satyr Hill, L.L.C., Morningside Development, LLC, and G. Nevill Turner for copyright infringement. More specifically, Nelson-Salabes alleges that the defendants copied the footprint and front exterior elevation from architectural designs and plans created by Nelson-Salabes for the development of an assisted living facility. ...

Nelson-Salabes' proposed design   Satyr Hill as built

I.

Nelson-Salabes is an architectural firm based in Maryland. In the spring of 1996, Nelson-Salabes was hired by a local real estate development and construction company, The Strutt Group, to provide architectural work for a proposed assisted living facility, Satyr Hill Catered Living ("Satyr Hill"), located in Baltimore County, Maryland. On June 5, 1996, John Hollick, Vice President of Nelson-Salabes, sent Kim Strutt a letter agreement pursuant to which Nelson-Salabes agreed to develop a schematic building footprint on an hourly basis. Strutt never signed the agreement. Nonetheless, both parties performed fully under the contract.

The following month, Strutt retained Nelson-Salabes to perform the architectural work for the next phase of the project, the Design Phase. On July 24, 1996, Hollick sent Strutt another letter agreement outlining the services that Nelson-Salabes would perform for the Design Phase. Among other things, Nelson-Salabes agreed to develop the exterior elevations and attend the zoning exception hearing. All assisted living facilities in Baltimore County, such as the Satyr Hill site, require a special exception to the zoning laws. The special exception process entails submitting development plans prepared by the architect and civil engineer, attending meetings with community members, and attending a hearing on the matter. Again, Strutt did not sign the letter agreement. Nonetheless, Nelson-Salabes performed the services outlined in the Design Phase letter agreement, and in consideration Strutt paid Nelson-Salabes $18,250.

Pursuant to the Design Phase letter agreement, Nelson-Salabes created four drawings depicting the footprint, floor plans, and elevations of the Satyr Hill site. As designed by Nelson-Salabes, the Satyr Hill site has a three-story building configured in "Y" shape. The front elevation features an octagonal shaped silo in the center, where two arms of the "Y" intersect. The first floor of the silo serves as an entrance. A porte-cochere extends from the entrance to a traffic circle in front of the building. The second and third floors of the silo serve as common areas and contain large windows. The first floor of the vertical element is brick, and the remainder of the building is vinyl siding. Both ends of the front elevation contain a vertical element protruding from the building with bay windows and a gable roof. There are also vertical elements with gable roofs located between the silo and the ends of the building. These elements protrude from the building and aesthetically break up the length of the building.

The Strutt Group's civil engineer, Colbert Matz Rosenfelt, Inc. ("Colbert Matz"), incorporated Nelson-Salabes's drawings into its development plan. The development plan was then submitted to Baltimore County as part of Strutt's application for a special exception. Baltimore County granted the exception on April 7, 1997.

On February 14, 1997, Nelson-Salabes sent Strutt a third letter proposal offering to provide the design and working drawings for the remaining phases of the project. The letter agreement sets forth the services to be performed by Nelson-Salabes and concludes with the statement, "If the above is acceptable, we will prepare a Standard AIA Agreement." The letter agreement was signed only by Hollick and was revised on September 29, 1997, to exclude mechanical and electrical engineering from the scope of work.

On September 29, Nelson-Salabes also sent Strutt a revised AIA contract. The AIA contract is a form created by the American Institute of Architects which contains standard terms and conditions between architects and their clients. Architects then tailor the document to specific projects. Article 6 of the AIA Agreement provides, in relevant part:

The Architect's Drawings, Specifications or other documents shall not be used by the Owner or others on other projects, for additions to this Project, or for completion of this Project by others unless the Architect is adjudged to be in default under this Agreement, except by agreement in writing and with appropriate compensation to the Architect.

On October 7, 1997, Strutt instructed Nelson-Salabes to stop working on the project. Strutt's potential partner for the project, Gary Raffel, had backed out. Raffel was the only one with expertise operating assisted living facilities and his absence created too great a risk for Strutt. Strutt then asked Hollick if he knew of anyone who might be interested in purchasing the project.

Hollick solicited potential purchasers for the Satyr Hill site, including defendant G. Nevill Turner. Turner is the managing agent for defendant Morningside Development, LLC and defendant Morningside Holdings of Satyr Hill, L.L.C. Turner was particularly interested in the Satyr Hill site because it had an approved development plan.

On November 18, 1997, Turner sent Strutt a letter of intent to purchase two sites, including the Satyr Hill site. Turner was aware that Nelson-Salabes created the development plans for Strutt. In fact, Nelson-Salabes sent Turner its Design Development proposal for the Satyr Hill project as well as its latest billing for the project. Turner eventually decided to purchase the Satyr Hill site for $900,000. Morningside Holdings of Satyr Hill would actually own the property and Morningside Development would develop it. The closing occurred on December 22, 1997.

In January 1998, Turner and Salabes then met to discuss Nelson-Salabes's continued involvement in the project. Turner testified that he wanted the Satyr Hill site to conform with the Morningside prototype for assisted living centers, specifically the Morningside at Friendship assisted living center. According to Turner, this would require a massive redrawing. Turner informed Salabes of his various concerns at the meeting, and Salabes indicated that Nelson-Salabes would make any desired changes in the plans. After the meeting, however, Salabes was concerned that Turner did not want to proceed with Nelson-Salabes as the architect. Shortly thereafter, Salabes called Turner, and Turner confirmed Salabes's suspicions. Salabes testified that he instructed Turner that Turner could proceed with another architect, but if he did so, he could not use Nelson-Salabes's design, including the footprint and elevations. Further, Nelson-Salabes's attorney subsequently wrote Turner a letter to inform him that none of the design concepts or design documents prepared by Nelson-Salabes should be used without the express written consent of Nelson-Salabes. On February 13, 1998, Nelson-Salabes submitted its certificate of registration of a copyright for its schematic designs of the Satyr Hill project.

Instead of retaining Nelson-Salabes as the architect, Turner entered into a design build contract with Hamil Commercial, Inc. ("Hamil"). Hamil then employed EDG Architects ("EDG") to perform the architectural work for the project. Turner had previously used Hamil and EDG to design and build the Morningside at Friendship assisted living center. Turner gave Hamil a copy of Nelson-Salabes's plans and the approved development plan, which Hamil then gave to EDG. Turner also met with Phillip Gibbs, a contractor from Hamil, and Donald Tucker, an architect from EDG, to discuss the Satyr Hill plans. Turner asked EDG to design Satyr Hill to conform with Morningside's model and the Friendship assisted living facility. Importantly, however, Turner also instructed EDG not to change the plans to such a degree that EDG's design did not fit within the approved plan. Turner knew that substantial changes would require a new special exception, which would be time-consuming and costly. According, to Turner, EDG rolled up the Nelson-Salabes plans after the meeting and never used them again.

EDG designed the building according to Turner's instructions. EDG's design was then incorporated by Colbert Matz into a First Amended Development Plan and a Second Amended Development Plan, which were submitted to Baltimore County for approval. As stated on the amended development plans, the reasons for the amendments included "minor footprint revisions" and "minor changes to architectural elevations of buildings." Both of the amended plans were approved and the building was constructed.

On July 13, 1998, Nelson-Salabes filed a one-count complaint, alleging that the defendants infringed Nelson-Salabes's copyright by copying the footprint and exterior elevations from the architectural designs and plans created by Nelson-Salabes.

II.

A. Copyright Infringement

The owner of a copyright has the exclusive right to reproduce the copyrighted work and prepare derivative works. See 17 U.S.C. § 106. When the copyright owner's exclusive rights are violated, 17 U.S.C. § 501 provides a cause of action for copyright infringement. To prevail in a copyright infringement action, a plaintiff must establish: (1) ownership of a valid copyright, and (2) unauthorized copying of the protected work by the defendant. Towler v. Sayles, 76 F.3d 579, 581 (4th Cir.1996).

1. Ownership of a Valid Copyright

Architectural works, including buildings and architectural plans or drawings, are subject to copyright protection. See 17 U.S.C. §§ 101, 102(a)(5) and (8). Further, the production of a registration certificate made with the United States Copyright Office constitutes prima facie evidence of the validity of the copyright. 17 U.S.C. § 410(c); see M. Kramer Mfg. Co. v. Andrews, 783 F.2d 421, 434, (4th Cir.1986). Here, Nelson-Salabes presented a certificate of registration for its architectural work for the Satyr Hill site. Consequently, the burden shifts to the defendants to rebut plaintiff's prima facie case of validity. See 4 Melville B. Nimmer & David Nimmer, Nimmer on Copyright § 13.01 [A], at 13-7; M. Kramer Mfg. Co., 783 F.2d at 434.

The defendants assert that neither the footprint of the building, nor the elevations are copyrightable. More specifically, defendants assert that the Y-shaped footprint is neither original nor an expression of artistic merit. Rather, they argue that it is utilitarian and within the public domain. According to the defendants, the "Y" shape is commonly used for architectural structures and, in this case, was dictated by zoning regulations, building codes, and physical attributes of the site. Similarly, the defendants assert that the various elements of the front elevation, such as brick, siding, gables, the octagonal entrance, and bay windows are common features of similar buildings in the area. Defendants further assert that the height of the building and the elevations were dictated by the Baltimore County zoning ordinance.

The Court agrees that Nelson-Salabes's use of certain individual features, such as the bay windows or the octagonal entrance, is neither original nor an expression of artistic merit. Nonetheless, "[t]he mere fact that component parts of a collective work are neither original to the plaintiff nor copyrightable by the plaintiff does not preclude a determination that the combination of such component parts as a separate entity is both original and copyrightable." Id. at 438. Moreover, 17 U.S.C.

§ 101 provides that an "architectural work" includes "the overall form as well as the arrangement and composition of spaces and elements in the design, but does not include individual standard features." 17 U.S.C. § 101.

Here, the Court finds that Nelson-Salabes's combination of common features such as a Y-shaped footprint, bay windows, the octagonal silo entrance, and gables created a unique design. To be sure, Paul Seiben, plaintiff's expert in architecture, testified that he had never seen the same combination of elements used by Nelson-Salabes on any other building. Further, the footprint and front elevation used by Nelson-Salabes were not the only feasible designs. Consequently, the Court further finds that the defendants have failed to rebut the prima facie validity of plaintiff's copyright, and that Nelson-Salabes's selection and arrangement of common architectural features is unique and exhibits artistic expression. Therefore, the Court further finds that Nelson-Salabes owns a valid copyright in its architectural work for the Satyr Hill site.

2. Copying

The second prong of an infringement action requires the plaintiff to prove copying. See Towler, 76 F.3d at 581. As is typically the case, the Court finds that the plaintiff has failed to offer sufficient evidence of direct copying. Nonetheless, the plaintiff may raise a presumption of copying by proving through circumstantial evidence (1) that the defendants had access to the copyrighted work and (2) that the alleged copy is substantially similar to the original work. See Keeler Brass Co., 862 F.2d 1063, 1065 (4 th Cir.1988). Access to the copyrighted designs in this case is not disputed. The Strutt Group provided Turner with a copy of Nelson-Salabes's plans for the Satyr Hill site as well as a copy of the approved development plan incorporating Nelson-Salabes's design. Turner even discussed the plans with Hamil and EDG.

With respect to the second element, substantial similarity, the Fourth Circuit uses a two-prong test to assist the trier of fact in determining whether both works contain the same ideas and express those ideas in a substantially similar manner. See Towler v. Sayles, 76 F.3d 579, 583-84 (4 th Cir.1996). "First, a plaintiff must show--typically with the aid of expert testimony--that the works in question are extrinsically similar because they contain substantially similar ideas that are subject to copyright protection." Towler, 76 F.3d at 583. Here, the plaintiff's experts testified that the defendants' design contained numerous design elements that were substantially similar to the design elements in plaintiff's design. For example, both designs contained an octagonal silo as the main entrance, bay windows, protruding gables, and sun porches. Further, the design elements were the same dimensions. And, plaintiff's expert had not seen such close similarities without both buildings being designed by the same architect. In response, the defendants assert that they made substantial changes to Nelson-Salabes's design, including changes to the footprint and front elevation. In particular, the defendants assert that the changes to the interior of the building caused the footprint and elevations to change. Specific differences cited by the defendants include: the use of metal roofing instead of fiberglass roofing, windows of a different size and in different locations, elimination of the porte-cochere, different gable vents, different roofs on the bay windows, different brick elevation, and the elimination of shutters.

The Court finds that the plaintiff has proved that extrinsically the two designs are substantially similar. In particular, the Court finds that both works contain the same unique combination of design elements including the use of an octagonal entrance, protruding gables, and bay windows on the ends of the building. The Court recognizes that differences do exist between the two designs. Nonetheless, "[i]t is entirely immaterial that, in many respects, plaintiff's and defendant's works are dissimilar, if in other respects, similarity as to a substantial element of plaintiff's work can be shown." 4 Nimmer, supra, § 13.03[B][1][a], at 13-53. Further supporting the Court's conclusion is the fact that Turner told his architect that he wanted the design to fit within the approved plan. It is also undisputed that only minor changes could be made to the plan or it would require a new special exception. Moreover, the defendants noted on their amended development plans that they only made "minor" changes to the footprint and elevations. Accordingly, the Court finds that the plaintiff has satisfied the first prong of the test.

The second prong of the substantial similarity test requires the plaintiff to prove that the work's intended audience could conclude that the ideas are expressed in a substantially similar manner. Towler, 76 F.3d at 583-84. In other words, whether both works have the same "total concept and feel." See id. at 584. Comparing a photograph of the defendants' design, as constructed, to a computer generated depiction of the plaintiff's design, the Court finds that the two designs are strikingly similar in total concept and feel. Again, certain differences between the designs slightly affect the feel, such as the use of different windows, the use of brick instead of siding in certain areas, and different roofs on the bay windows. Despite these differences, however, the two designs still have the same overall feel based on the same combination of the unique features, including the octagonal silo entrance, the bay windows on the ends, and the protruding gables. Although the defendants purport to base their design on Morningside's prototype, the total concept of the Satyr Hill site much more closely resembles the plaintiff's design than any of its own, including the defendants' assisted living center at Friendship. Accordingly, the Court finds that the plaintiff has satisfied the second prong and have established a prima facie case of copying. ...

To rebut the presumption of copying raised by the plaintiff's prima facie case, defendants assert the defense of independent creation. To support its contention, the defendants point to testimony of Donald Tucker, a principal in EDG, who stated that he did not use Nelson-Salabes's plans when designing the building. Rather, Tucker asserted that he based the design of the Satyr Hill site on Morningside's model and its assisted living center at Friendship. The Court, however, is not persuaded by the defendants' argument. It is simply unbelievable that the defendants could look at plaintiff's design and then independently design a substantially similar building containing the same combination of features and in the same proportions. The Court recognizes that the defendants may have incorporated many of the individual features in its other buildings. Nonetheless, the evidence demonstrates that the Satyr Hill design clearly resembles Nelson-Salabes's design more closely than any of the defendants' own designs.

B. Implied Nonexclusive License

Notwithstanding the Court's finding that the defendants copied plaintiff's architectural designs, the defendants nonetheless assert that they are not liable for infringement because Nelson-Salabes granted them a nonexclusive license to use the plans. According to the defendants, such a license is implied based upon Nelson-Salabes's failure to contractually prohibit the use of the designs despite its knowledge that Strutt intended to sell the approved development plan containing plaintiff's designs if he could not obtain financing. In response, Nelson-Salabes asserts that there is no implied nonexclusive license because it never acknowledged that Strutt could use the drawings without Nelson-Salabes's involvement as the architect, and that Nelson-Salabes tendered an AIA document to Strutt expressly prohibiting such conduct. Nelson-Salabes further asserts that even if it granted Strutt a nonexclusive license, he could not transfer the license to the defendants.

A nonexclusive license permits the licensee to use the copyrighted work in a particular manner and creates an affirmative defense to copyright infringement. See I.A.E., Inc. v. Shaver, 74 F.3d 768, 775 (7 th Cir.1996). A nonexclusive license may "be granted orally, or may even be implied ... [w]hen the totality of the parties' conduct indicates an intent to grant such permission." 3 Nimmer, supra, § 10.03[A][7], at 10-42.

In I.A.E., Inc. v. Shaver, a case that is factually similar to the present case, the Seventh Circuit set forth several factors to guide the judicial inquiry as to whether an implied nonexclusive license exists. 74 F.3d at 776. In Shaver, an architect, Paul Shaver, created schematic design drawings for an air cargo/hanger building pursuant to a letter agreement entered into by Shaver and a joint venture ("Joint Venture"). Id. at 770. Shaver delivered the drawings to the Joint Venture with notice of copyright and under the belief that, once the drawings were approved, he would perform the architectural work for the remaining phases of the project. Id . at 771. The Joint Venture, however, employed another architect to perform the remaining work. Id. Shaver then wrote a letter to the Airport's Executive Director indicating that he was no longer involved in the project and stating "[w]e trust that our ideas and knowledge exhibited in our work will assist the Airport in realizing a credible and flexible use Cargo/Hanger facility." Id. Shaver enclosed copies of his drawings with the letter. Id. I.A.E, a member of the Joint Venture, then sought a declaratory judgment that it had a right to use the drawings and that it did not infringe Shaver's copyright. Shaver, 74 F.3d at 771. To determine whether Shaver granted I.A.E an implied nonexclusive license, the court considered various factors, including: the language of the copyright registration certificate, the letter agreement, the deposition testimony, and the delivery of the copyrighted material without warning that its further use would constitute copyright infringement. Id.

at 776 (citation omitted). Applying these factors, the court held that the evidence supported the existence of a license to use Shaver's drawings to construct the air cargo building. Id. at 777.

Here, the defendants assert that the evidence similarly supports a finding that an implied nonexclusive license was granted. More specifically, the defendants point out that here, like in Shaver, the architectural work was completed in components, and that Nelson-Salabes did not have a contractual right to remain the architect through the completion of the project. The defendants further assert that, despite Nelson-Salabes's knowledge that Strutt would sell the development plan if he could not obtain financing, neither contract contained language prohibiting the transfer of the development plan or completion of the project using another architect. In fact, the defendants contend that Nelson-Salabes did not assert a copyright claim on the designs until after the defendants purchased the property. According to the defendants, these facts are sufficient to support a finding that Nelson-Salabes intended to grant Strutt and Morningside a nonexclusive license.

The Court, however, disagrees. While the facts of this case are similar to the facts in Shaver, there is a critical difference. In Shaver, after the architect ended his involvement, he sent a copy of the plans to the Airport Executive Director and expressed his intent regarding the continued use of the plans. 74 F.3d at 771. Here, by contrast, there is no such expression of intent by Nelson-Salabes. Rather, the Court is left to infer Nelson-Salabes's intent based on its silence regarding its copyright protection. The Court is satisfied that these facts do not support a finding that Nelson-Salabes granted Strutt a nonexclusive license. The Court further finds that because Nelson-Salabes never granted Strutt a nonexclusive license, Strutt obviously could not assign such a right to the defendants. Nor is there any evidence suggesting that Nelson-Salabes granted a nonexclusive license directly to any of the defendants. [FN3] Accordingly, the Court finds that the defendants did not have an implied nonexclusive license to use Nelson-Salabes's designs.

FN3. Prior to purchasing the Satyr Hill site, Turner received a copy of the most recent proposal between Strutt and Nelson-Salabes which referenced an AIA agreement. Turner testified that he was familiar with AIA agreements, which provide, among other things, that an architect's work cannot be used without written permission. Turner further testified that Strutt told him that he never signed the AIA agreement. Nonetheless, Turner's knowledge was sufficient to put him on notice that Nelson-Salabes was asserting copyright protection for its designs. ...

VI.

For all of the foregoing reasons, the Court will enter Judgment in favor of plaintiff, Nelson-Salabes, Inc. in the amount of $736,037.45, with costs. Judgment will be entered in accordance with this Opinion.

D.Md.,2001.

495 F.3d 344 (2007)

TISEO ARCHITECTS v. B & B POOLS

United States Court of Appeals, Sixth Circuit

ROGERS, Circuit Judge.

Tiseo Architects, Inc., alleged that another architect, Gary Olson, copied a design and site plan drawings that Tiseo Architects had prepared for B & B Pools Service and Supply Company. After a bench trial, the district court ruled in favor of the defendants, B & B Pools and Olson. Tiseo Architects now appeals, arguing that the district court applied the wrong legal standard in reaching its conclusion that Olson's design and construction drawings were not substantially similar to Tiseo Architects' design and site plan drawings. Because the district court properly analyzed the similarity of the works after filtering out the unprotectable elements of Tiseo Architects' drawings, the judgment of the district court is affirmed.

In the summer of 2003, John Juntunen, president and CEO of B & B Pools, first asked Gary Olson to prepare the plans for the renovation and expansion of B & B Pools' commercial building in Livonia, Michigan. After receiving a sketch of the proposed building plan, Olson determined that he was unable to work on the project at that time. On June 18, 2003, B & B Pools entered into a contract with Tiseo Architects for the preparation of a design and site plan for the proposed addition. The contract left open the possibility that B & B Pools might later retain Tiseo Architects for the "Construction Documents Phase" of the project.

Benedito Tiseo, president of Tiseo Architects, testified that when he first met with B & B Pools, they may have given him "some rough, crude sketch" illustrating what B & B Pools wanted the new offices to look like. Tiseo Architects was also provided with various requirements for the plans based upon zoning requirements and B & B Pools' preferences. Additionally, Benedito Tiseo testified that he revised his drafts of the site plan in response to specific changes requested by Juntunen.

B & B Pools used the site plan prepared by Tiseo Architects to obtain site plan approval from the city zoning board, but did not retain Tiseo Architects to draw the construction plans. Tiseo Architects was paid in full according to the terms of the parties' contract for the initial design and site plan documents. Later, B & B Pools hired Olson to prepare the construction documents. Juntunen provided Olson with photographs of the existing building, sketches of the existing layout, and "some ideas about what [Juntunen] wanted to accomplish in the form of an addition." Olson also had access to Tiseo Architects' drawings, though he testified that he did not copy Tiseo Architects' design. As he had done with Tiseo Architects' site plan, Juntunen requested multiple revisions of the architectural plans prepared by Olson.

In November, 2004, Tiseo Architects discovered that B & B Pools had completed the addition. Tiseo Architects then filed its drawings of the site plan with the Copyright Office and initiated this action against B & B Pools, John Juntunen, and

Gary Olson, alleging that the creation of the construction plans for the addition violated Tiseo Architects' copyright in the site plan drawings. Tiseo Architects' complaint also alleged violations of the Lanham Act and civil conspiracy.

The district court conducted a bench trial. At the close of the evidence the court ruled for B & B Pools and Olson on the Lanham Act and civil conspiracy counts because "no proof" was presented to support those claims. As to the alleged copyright violation, the parties agreed that the sole issue was whether Olson's construction plans were substantially similar to Tiseo Architects' site plan drawings. In an oral opinion, the district court held that the plaintiff, Tiseo Architects, "did not carry the burden of proving substantial similarity by a preponderance of the evidence" and granted judgment in favor of the defendants. Tiseo Architects filed a motion for reconsideration, which the district court denied. Tiseo Architects now appeals the district court's judgment with respect to its copyright and Lanham Act claims.

The district court applied the correct legal standard in finding that the architectural drawings at issue were not substantially similar. Tiseo Architects' argument on appeal is based on a misinterpretation of the district court's opinion, and is therefore without merit.

"Since direct evidence of copying is rarely available, a plaintiff may establish an inference of copying by showing (1) access to the allegedly-infringed work by the defendant(s) and (2) a substantial similarity between the two works at issue." Stromback v. New Line Cinema, 384 F.3d 283, 293 (6th Cir. 2004) (internal quotation marks and citation omitted). The district court began its opinion by observing that Tiseo Architects, as plaintiff, had the burden of proof. The court then stated that of the two elements of a prima facie copyright claim in the absence of evidence of direct copying, access was admitted, and therefore the only disputed matter before the court was "the issue of substantial similarity." In addressing the merits of the substantial similarity issue, the district court noted that "the floor plan[s] [of both Tiseo Architects' and Olson's designs are] very, very similar . . . you can just look at the two drawings and see that they are substantially similar." The court then continued, "[h]owever, there is an explanation for that offered by the defendant that I think balances the fact of the similarity of the two works."

The district court explained that both drawings were based on Juntunen's original sketches, that both incorporated Juntunen's suggestions for various features of the floor plan, and that the options for how to design the addition "were extremely limited" by zoning requirements and the presence of a load-bearing wall that the plans had to accommodate. The court concluded that "there weren't a lot of ways to lay out these offices." The court also found that the floor plan was "at least as much Mr. Juntunen's concept as it was Mr. Tiseo's" and that "there are very few ways that this idea can be expressed consistent with the specific requests made by Mr. Juntunen, and I think that balances, if not outweighs the substantial similarity between the floor plans." The district court then concluded its analysis with a discussion of the differences between the plans. These included "differences in materials used, [ ] differences in the roof line . . ., [and] differences in the windows."

Based on this analysis, the district court concluded that Tiseo Architects failed to prove that the drawings were substantially similar.

Tiseo Architects contends that the district court's analysis was improper because the court first made a factual finding of substantial similarity and then proceeded to "engage[] in a 'balancing' test to address how [the court] believed those documents came to be substantially similar." Tiseo Architects argues that, since no such balancing test is called for by the law of copyrights, the district court applied the wrong legal standard and should be reversed.

It is well established that "originality is a constitutionally mandated prerequisite for copyright protection." Feist Publ'ns, Inc. v. Rural Telephone Serv. Co., Inc., 499 U.S. 340, 351, 111 S.Ct. 1282, 113 L.Ed.2d 358 (1991). Accordingly, the substantial similarity analysis of a copyright infringement claim is divided into two steps: "the first step requires identifying which aspects of the artist's work, if any, are protectible by copyright; the second involves determining whether the allegedly infringing work is 'substantially similar' to protectible elements of the artist's work." Kohus v. Mariol, 328 F.3d 848, 855 (6th Cir. 2003) (internal quotation marks and citations omitted). "The essence of the first step is to filter out the unoriginal, unprotectible elements—elements that were not independently created by the inventor, and that possess no minimal degree of creativity—through a variety of analyses." Id. (citation omitted). The district court's discussion of the "explanation" for the "substantial similarity" between the floor plans merely identifies those unoriginal and uncreative parts of Tiseo Architects' work that are not protectable by copyright. Then, after extracting those unprotectable aspects of Tiseo Architects' drawings, the district court compared the remaining protectable elements to Olson's work, and found that they were not substantially similar.

The portion of the district court's opinion that Tiseo Architects labels a "balancing test" reflects the court's application of the first step described in Kohus. The court "filtered out" many elements of Tiseo Architects' site plan drawings because they were "unoriginal," having been based on Juntunen's sketch; and the court identified several elements of the site plan that "possess[ed] no minimal degree of creativity" because they were dictated by zoning regulations or the realities of the existing physical structure. The district court then turned to the second step, comparing the allegedly infringing building plans to the protectable elements of Tiseo Architects' site plan drawings. In so doing, the district court found "a lot of differences" and no substantial similarity.

Because the district court applied the correct legal analysis in determining that Olson's work did not infringe on Tiseo Architects' copyright, this court reviews the district court's factual finding that there is no substantial similarity between the works for clear error. Ellis v. Diffie, 177 F.3d 503, 505 (6th Cir. 1999). Tiseo Architects offers no argument on appeal to refute the district court's factual finding that the protectable aspects of the drawings are not substantially similar. Therefore this court has no basis for disturbing the district court's judgment that Olson's construction drawings did not violate Tiseo Architects' copyright in the site plan drawings. See Dillery v. City of Sandusky, 398 F.3d 562, 569 (6th Cir. 2005)

("Because [appellant] wholly fails to address this issue in her appellate brief, we conclude that she has waived her right to appeal the district court's [ruling].").

Finally, Tiseo Architects' Lanham Act claim fails because it parallels its copyright claim. "Where a plaintiff's Lanham Act claim parallels his copyright infringement claim, a finding of no substantial similarity on the copyright claim precludes the Lanham Act claim." Stromback, 384 F.3d at 300. Like the plaintiff in Stromback, Tiseo Architects "makes no attempt to distinguish his Lanham Act claim from his copyright infringement claim or to explain how there could be a likelihood of confusion when the two works are not substantially similar." Id. Accordingly, the district court correctly denied this claim as well.

For the foregoing reasons, the judgment of the district court is AFFIRMED.

10. Copyright & the Arts

536 F.2d 486 (2d Cir. 1976)

L. BATLIN & SON V. SNYDER

US Court of Appeals for the Second Circuit

OAKES, Circuit Judge:

Appellants Jeffrey Snyder and Etna Products Co., Inc., his licensee, appeal from a preliminary injunction granted L. Batlin & Son, Inc. (Batlin), compelling appellants to cancel a recordation of a copyright with the United States Customs Service and restraining them from enforcing that copyright. The district court held, 394 F. Supp. 1389 (S.D.N.Y. 1975), as it had previously in Etna Products Co. v. E. Mishan & Sons, 75 Civ. 428 (S.D.N.Y. Feb. 13, 1975), that there was "little probability" that appellants' copyright "will be found valid in the trial on the merits" on the basis that any variations between appellants' copyrighted plastic bank and a cast iron bank in the public domain were merely "trivial," and hence appellants' bank insufficiently "original" to support a copyright. 394 F. Supp. at 1390, citing Alfred Bell & Co. v. Catalda Fine Arts, Inc., 191 F.2d 99 (2d Cir. 1951). We agree with the district court and therefore affirm the judgment granting the preliminary injunction.

Uncle Sam mechanical banks have been on the American scene at least since June 8, 1886, when Design Patent No. 16,728, issued on a toy savings bank of its type. The basic delightful design has long since been in the public domain. The banks are well documented in collectors' books and known to the average person interested in Americana. A description of the bank is that Uncle Sam, dressed in his usual stove pipe hat, blue full dress coat, starred vest and red and white striped trousers, and leaning on his umbrella, stands on a four- or five-inch wide base, on which sits his carpetbag. A coin may be placed in Uncle Sam's extended hand. When a lever is pressed, the arm lowers, and the coin falls into the bag, while Uncle

Sam's whiskers move up and down. The base has an embossed American eagle on it with the words "Uncle Sam" on streamers above it, as well as the word "Bank" on each side. Such a bank is listed in a number of collectors' books, the most recent of which may be F. H. Griffith, Mechanical Banks (1972 ed.) where it was listed as No. 280, and is said to be not particularly rare.

Appellant Jeffrey Snyder doing business as "J.S.N.Y." obtained a registration of copyright on a plastic "Uncle Sam bank" in Class G ("Works of Art") as "sculpture" on January 23, 1975. According to Snyder's affidavit, in January, 1974, he had seen a cast metal antique Uncle Sam bank with an overall height of the figure and base of 11 inches. In April, 1974, he flew to Hong Kong to arrange for the design and eventual manufacture of replicas of the bank as Bicentennial items, taking the cast metal Uncle Sam bank with him. His Hong Kong buying agent selected a firm, "Unitoy," to make the plastic "prototype" because of its price and the quality of its work. Snyder wanted his bank to be made of plastic and to be shorter than the cast metal sample "in order to fit into the required price range and quality and quantity of material to be used." The figure of Uncle Sam was thus shortened from 11 to nine inches, and the base shortened and narrowed. It was also decided, Snyder averred, to change the shape of the carpetbag and to include the umbrella in a one-piece mold for the Uncle Sam figure, "so as not to have a problem with a loose umbrella or a separate molding process." The Unitoy representative made his sketches while looking at the cast metal bank. After a "clay model" was made, a plastic "prototype" was approved by Snyder and his order placed in May, 1974. The plastic bank carried the legend "CR Copyright J.S.N.Y." and was assertedly first "published" on October 15, 1974, before being filed with the Register of Copyrights in January, 1975.

Appellee Batlin is also in the novelty business and as early as August 9, 1974, ordered 30 cartons of cast iron Uncle Sam mechanical banks from Taiwan where its president had seen the bank made. When he became aware of the existence of a plastic bank, which he considered "an almost identical copy" of the cast iron bank, Batlin's trading company in Hong Kong procured a manufacturer and the president of Batlin ordered plastic copies also. Beginning in April, 1975, Batlin was notified by the United States Customs Service that the plastic banks it was receiving were covered by appellants' copyright. In addition the Customs Service was also refusing entry to cast iron banks previously ordered, according to the Batlin affidavit. Thus Batlin instituted suit for a judgment declaring appellants' copyright void and for damages for unfair competition and restraint of trade. The sole question on this appeal is whether Judge Metzner abused his discretion in granting Batlin a preliminary injunction. We find that he did not.

This court has examined both the appellants' plastic Uncle Sam bank made under Snyder's copyright and the uncopyrighted model cast iron mechanical bank which is itself a reproduction of the original public domain Uncle Sam bank. Appellant Snyder claims differences not only of size but also in a number of other very minute details: the carpetbag shape of the plastic bank is smooth, the iron bank rough; the metal bank bag is fatter at its base; the eagle on the front of the platform in the metal bank is holding arrows in his talons while in the plastic bank he clutches leaves, this change concededly having been made, however, because "the arrows did not reproduce well in plastic on a smaller size." The shape of Uncle Sam's face is supposedly different, as is the shape and texture of the hats, according to the Snyder affidavit. In the metal version the umbrella is hanging loose while in the plastic item it is included in the single mold. The texture of the clothing, the hairline, shape of the bow ties and of the shirt collar and left arm as well as the flag carrying the name on the base of the statue are all claimed to be different, along with the shape and texture of the eagles on the side. Many of these differences are not perceptible to the casual observer. Appellants make no claim for any difference based on the plastic mold lines in the Uncle Sam figure which are perceptible.

Our examination of the banks results in the same conclusion as that of Judge Metzner in Etna Products, the earlier case enjoining Snyder's copyright, that the Snyder bank is "extremely similar to the cast iron bank, save in size and material" with the only other differences, such as the shape of the satchel and the leaves in the eagle's talons being "by all appearances, minor." Similarities include, more importantly, the appearance and number of stripes on the trousers, buttons on the coat, and stars on the vest and hat, the attire and pose of Uncle Sam, the decor on his base and bag, the overall color scheme, the method of carpetbag opening, to name but a few. After seeing the banks and hearing conflicting testimony from opposing expert witnesses as to the substantiality or triviality of the variations and as to the skill necessary to make the plastic model, the court below stated:

I am making a finding of fact that as far as I'm concerned, it is practically an exact copy and whatever you point to in this (sic) differences are so infinitesimal they make no difference. All you have proved here by the testimony today is that if you give a man a seven-inch model and you say I want this to come out in a five-inch model, and he copies it, the fact that he has to have some artistic ability to make a model by reducing the seven to the five adds something to it. That is the only issue in this case.

Mr. Faber: No, sir.

The Court: That is the only issue. I have given you my finding of fact.

As Judge Metzner went on to say in his opinion, the appellants' plastic version "reproduces" the cast iron bank "except that it proportionately reduces the height from approximately eleven inches to approximately nine inches with trivial variations." 394 F. Supp. at 1390. The court noted that appellants "went to great pains on the hearing to prove that there were substantial differences between the iron and the plastic articles," id. at 1391, and found that there had been no "level of input" such as in Alva Studios, Inc. v. Winninger, 177 F. Supp. 265, 267 (S.D.N.Y. 1959) ("great skill and originality" called for in producing an exact scale reduction of Rodin's famous "Hand of God," to museum specifications). The substance of appellee's expert's testimony on which the district judge evidently relied was that the variations found in appellants' plastic bank were merely "trivial" and that it was a reproduction of the metal bank made as simply as possible for the purposes of manufacture. In other words, there were no elements of difference that amounted to significant alteration or that had any purpose other than the functional one of making a more suitable (and probably less expensive) figure in the plastic medium.

What the leading authority has called "the one pervading element prerequisite to copyright protection regardless of the form of the work" is the requirement of originality that the work be the original product of the claimant. 1 M. Nimmer, The Law of Copyright § 10, at 32 (1975). This derives from the fact that, constitutionally, copyright protection may be claimed only by "authors." U.S.Const., art. I, § 8; Burrow-Giles Lithographic Co. v. Sarony, 111 U.S. 53, 58, 4 S. Ct. 279, 281, 28 L. Ed. 349, 351 (1884). Thus, "(o)ne who has slavishly or mechanically copied from others may not claim to be an author." 1 M. Nimmer, supra, § 6, at 10.2. Since the constitutional requirement must be read into the Copyright Act, 17 U.S.C. § 1 et seq., the requirement of originality is also a statutory one. Chamberlin v. Uris Sales Corp., 150 F.2d 512 (2d Cir. 1945). It has been the law of this circuit for at least 30 years that in order to obtain a copyright upon a reproduction of a work of art under 17 U.S.C. § 5(h) that the work "contain some substantial, not merely trivial originality . . . ." Chamberlin v. Uris Sales Corp., supra, 150 F.2d at 513.

Originality is, however, distinguished from novelty; there must be independent creation, but it need not be invention in the sense of striking uniqueness, ingeniousness, or novelty, since the Constitution differentiates " authors" and their "writings" from "inventors" and their "discoveries." Alfred Bell & Co. v. Catalda Fine Arts, Inc., supra, 191 F.2d at 100; Runge v. Lee, 441 F.2d 579, 581 (9th Cir.), cert. denied, 404 U.S. 887, 92 S. Ct. 197, 30 L. Ed. 2d 169 (1971). Originality means that the work owes its creation to the author and this in turn means that the work must not consist of actual copying. Alfred Bell & Co. v. Catalda Fine Arts, Inc., supra, 191 F.2d at 102-03; Sheldon v. Metro-Goldwyn Pictures Corp., 81 F.2d 49, 54 (2d Cir. 1936), aff'd, 309 U.S. 390, 60 S. Ct. 681, 84 L. Ed. 825 (1940).3

The test of originality is concededly one with a low threshold in that "(a)ll that is needed . . . is that the 'author' contributed something more than a 'merely trivial' variation, something recognizably 'his own.' " Alfred Bell & Co. v. Catalda Fine Arts, Inc., 191 F.2d at 103. But as this court said many years ago, "(w)hile a copy of something in the public domain will not, if it be merely a copy, support a copyright, a distinguishable variation will. . . . " Gerlach-Barklow Co. v. Morris & Bendien, Inc., 23 F.2d 159, 161 (2d Cir. 1927).

Necessarily, none of these underlying principles is different in the case of "(r)eproductions of a work of art," 17 U.S.C. § 5(h), from the case of "(w) orks of art . . .," 17 U.S.C. § 5(g). The requirement of substantial as opposed to trivial variation and the prohibition of mechanical copying, both of which are inherent in and subsumed by the concept of originality, apply to both statutory categories. There is implicit in that concept a "minimal element of creativity over and above the requirement of independent effort." 1 M. Nimmer, supra, § 10.2, at 36. While the quantum of originality that is required may be modest indeed, Herbert Rosenthal Jewelry Corp. v. Grossbardt, 436 F.2d 315, 316 (2d Cir. 1970), we are not inclined to abandon that requirement, even if in the light of the constitutional and statutory bases therefor and our precedents we could do so.

A reproduction of a work of art obviously presupposes an underlying work of art. Since Mazer v. Stein, 347 U.S. 201, 218, 74 S. Ct. 460, 470, 98 L. Ed. 630, 642 (1954) (statuette of Balinese dancer copyrightable despite intended use as lamp base), it has been established that mass-produced commercial objects with a minimal element of artistic craftsmanship may satisfy the statutory requirement of such a work. See also Puddu v. Buonamici Statuary, Inc., 450 F.2d 401, 402 (2d Cir. 1971). So, too, a toy which qualifies as a work of art such as the original Uncle Sam mechanical bank may qualify as a "work of art" under Section 5(g). See Rushton v. Vitale, 218 F.2d 434, 435-36 (2d Cir. 1955); Ideal Toy Corp. v. Sayco Doll Corp., 302 F.2d 623, 624 (2d Cir. 1962). The underlying work of art may as here be in the public domain. But even to claim the more limited protection given to a reproduction of a work of art (that to the distinctive features contributed by the reproducer), the reproduction must contain "an original contribution not present in the underlying work of art" and be "more than a mere copy." 1 M. Nimmer, supra, § 20.2, at 93.

According to Professor Nimmer, moreover, "the mere reproduction of a work of art in a different medium should not constitute the required originality for the reason that no one can claim to have independently evolved any particular medium." Id. at 94. See Millworth Converting Corp. v. Slifka,276 F.2d 443, 444-45 (2d Cir. 1960). Cf. Gardenia Flowers, Inc. v. Joseph Markovitz, Inc., 280 F. Supp. 776, 781 (S.D.N.Y. 1968). Professor Nimmer refers to Doran v. Sunset House Distributing Corp., 197 F. Supp. 940 (S.D. Cal. 1961), aff'd, 304 F.2d 251 (9th Cir. 1962), as suggesting "the ludicrous result that the first person to execute a public domain work of art in a different medium thereafter obtains a monopoly on such work in such medium, at least as to those persons aware of the first such effort." 1 M. Nimmer, supra, § 20.2, at 94. We do not follow the Doran case. We do follow the school of cases in this circuit and elsewhere supporting the proposition that to support a copyright there must be at least some substantial variation, not merely a trivial variation such as might occur in the translation to a different medium.

Nor can the requirement of originality be satisfied simply by the demonstration of "physical skill" or "special training" which, to be sure, Judge Metzner found was required for the production of the plastic molds that furnished the basis for appellants' plastic bank. A considerably higher degree of skill is required, true artistic skill, to make the reproduction copyrightable. Thus in Alfred Bell & Co. v. Catalda Fine Arts, Inc., supra, 191 F.2d at 104-05 n.22, Judge Frank pointed out that the mezzotint engraver's art there concerned required "great labour and talent" to effectuate the "management of light and shade . . . produced by different lines and dots . . .," means "very different from those employed by the painter or draughtsman from whom he copies. . . . " See also Millworth Converting Corp. v. Slifka, supra (fabric designer required one month of work to give three-dimensional color effect to flat surface). Here on the basis of appellants' own expert's testimony it took the Unitoy representative "(a)bout a day and a half, two days work" to produce the plastic mold sculpture from the metal Uncle Sam bank. If there be a point in the copyright law pertaining to reproductions at which sheer artistic skill and effort can act as a substitute for the requirement of substantial variation, it was not reached here.

Appellants rely heavily upon Alva Studios, Inc. v. Winninger, supra, the "Hand of God" case, where the court held that "great skill and originality (were required) to produce a scale reduction of a great work with exactitude." 177 F. Supp. at 267.

There, the original sculpture was, "one of the most intricate pieces of sculpture ever created" with "(i)nnumerable planes, lines and geometric patterns ... interdependent in (a) multi-dimensional work." Id. Originality was found by the district court to consist primarily in the fact that "(i)t takes 'an extremely skilled sculptor' many hours working directly in front of the original" to effectuate a scale reduction. Id. at 266. The court, indeed, found the exact replica to be so original, distinct, and creative as to constitute a work of art in itself. The complexity and exactitude there involved distinguishes that case amply from the one at bar. As appellants themselves have pointed out, there are a number of trivial differences or deviations from the original public domain cast iron bank in their plastic reproduction. Thus concededly the plastic version is not, and was scarcely meticulously produced to be, an exactly faithful reproduction. Nor is the creativity in the underlying work of art of the same order of magnitude as in the case of the "Hand of God." Rodin's sculpture is, furthermore, so unique and rare, and adequate public access to it such a problem that a significant public benefit accrues from its precise, artistic reproduction. No such benefit can be imagined to accrue here from the "knock-off" reproduction of the cast iron Uncle Sam bank. Thus appellants' plastic bank is neither in the category of exactitude required by Alva Studios nor in a category of substantial originality; it falls within what has been suggested by the amicus curiae is a copyright no-man's land.

Absent a genuine difference between the underlying work of art and the copy of it for which protection is sought, the public interest in promoting progress in the arts indeed, the constitutional demand, Chamberlin v. Uris Sales Corp., supra could hardly be served. To extend copyrightability to minuscule variations would simply put a weapon for harassment in the hands of mischievous copiers intent on appropriating and monopolizing public domain work. Even in Mazer v. Stein, supra, which held that the statutory terms "works of art" and "reproduction of works of art" (terms which are clearly broader than the earlier term "works of the fine arts") permit copyright of quite ordinary mass-produced items, the Court expressly held that the objects to be copyrightable, "must be original, that is, the author's tangible expression of his ideas." 347 U.S. at 214, 74 S. Ct. at 468, 98 L. Ed. at 640. No such originality, no such expression, no such ideas here appear.

To be sure, the test of "originality" may leave a lot to be desired, although it is the only one we have, in that as one scholar has said, the originality requirement does not perform the function of excluding commonplace matters in the public domain from copyright status very effectively. See Comment, Copyright Protection for Mass Produced Commercial Products: A Review of the Developments Following Mazer v. Stein, 38 U. Chi. L. Rev. 807 (1971). In any event, however, the articles should be judged on their own merits, id. at 823, and on these merits appellants' claim must fail. Here as elsewhere in the copyright law there are lines that must be drawn even though reasonable men may differ where.

Judgment affirmed.

MESKILL, Circuit Judge (dissenting) (with whom TIMBERS and VAN GRAAFEILAND, Circuit Judges, concur):

I respectfully dissent.

In the instant case the author has contributed substantially more than a merely trivial variation. "Any 'distinguishable variation' of a prior work will constitute sufficient originality to support a copyright if such variation is the product of the author's independent efforts, and is more than merely trivial." 1 Nimmer on Copyright § 10.1 at 34.2. In accord with the purposes of the copyright law to promote progress by encouraging individual effort through copyright protection, we should require only minimal variations to find copyrightability. The independent sculpting of the mold for the plastic bank and the aggregated differences in size and conformation of the figurine should satisfy this standard.

The plastic bank in question admittedly is based on a work now in the public domain. This does not render it uncopyrightable since "(i)t is hornbook that a new and original plan or combination of existing materials in the public domain is sufficiently original to come within the copyright protection . . . ." Alva Studios, Inc. v. Winninger, 177 F. Supp. 265, 267 (S.D.N.Y. 1959). The courts have repeatedly emphasized that only a modest level of originality is necessary to be eligible for a copyright. Alfred Bell & Co. v. Catalda Fine Arts, Inc., 191 F.2d 99, 102-103 (2 Cir. 1951). See also, Thomas Wilson & Co. v. Irving J. Dorfman Co., 433 F.2d 409, 411 (2 Cir. 1970) and Dan Kasoff, Inc. v. Novelty Jewelry Co., Inc., 309 F.2d 745, 746 (2 Cir. 1962), where this Court required only a "faint trace of originality" to support a copyright.

Looking first to copyright cases involving sculptures, in Puddu v. Buonamici Statuary, Inc., 450 F.2d 401, 402 (2 Cir. 1971), this Court found that where plaintiff's employee had sculpted statuettes from scratch, even though there was a "strong family resemblance between the copyrighted and the uncopyrighted models, the differences suffice to satisfy the modest requirement of originality. . . . Originality sufficient for copyright protection exists if the 'author' has introduced any element of novelty as contrasted with the material previously known to him." Similarly, in Blazon, Inc. v. DeLuxe Game Corp., 268 F. Supp. 416, 422 (S.D.N.Y. 1965) the court assumed a hobby horse could be copyrightable since plaintiff could have added "unique features to the horse, enlarged it and made it sufficiently dissimilar from defendant's horse as to render it copyrightable . . . ." See also Royalty Designs, Inc. v. Thrifticheck Service Corp., 204 F. Supp. 702 (S.D.N.Y. 1962) (banks in shape of dogs); F. W. Woolworth Co. v. Contemporary Arts, 193 F.2d 162 (1 Cir. 1951) (originality in shape of dog figurine). The fabric cases likewise have found designs copyrightable with only a "very modest grade of originality." Peter Pan Fabrics, Inc. v. Dan River Mills, Inc., 295 F. Supp. 1366, 1368 (S.D.N.Y. 1969). In the latter case, the embellishment and expansion of purchased designs before being rolled onto fabric constituted the "slight addition" sufficient to qualify as originality. Finally, there are also cases where no changes were required because the process of reproduction itself required great skill. See Alva Studios, Inc. v. Winninger, supra, where originality was found in a detailed scaled reproduction differing only in the treatment of the rear side of the base; see also Millworth Converting Corp. v. Slifka, 276 F.2d 443 (2 Cir. 1960) (creation of a three dimensional effect on a flat fabric required effort and skill).

...

The most obvious differences between the two exhibits in this case are size and medium. While these factors alone may not be sufficient to render a work copyrightable, they surely may be considered along with the other variations. On the other hand, the author's reasons for making changes should be irrelevant to a determination of whether the differences are trivial. As noted in Alfred Bell, supra, 191 F.2d at 105, even an inadvertent variation can form the basis of a valid copyright. After the fact speculation as to whether Snyder made changes for aesthetic or functional reasons should not be the basis of decision.

The primary variations between the two banks involve height; medium; anatomical proportions of the Uncle Sam figure, including shape and expression of face; design of the clothing (hat, tie, shirt, collar, trousers); detail around the eagle figure on the platform; placement of the umbrella; and the shape and texture of the satchel. Granting Snyder a copyright protecting these variations would ensure only that no one could copy his particular version of the bank now in the public domain, i. e., protection from someone using Snyder's figurine to slavishly copy and make a mold. In Alva Studios, supra, 177 F. Supp. at 267, where the author produced no distinctive variations of his own in reproducing the Rodin sculpture, the court still found that the reproduction was copyrightable and that infringement was possible; although mere resemblance would not justify a finding of infringement where the principal elements of a design were taken from the public domain, evidence of actual copying would support such a finding.

This approach seems quite in accord with the purpose of the copyright statute to promote progress by encouraging individual effort through copyright protection. The relatively low standard of originality required for copyrightability is derived from this purpose. The objective is to progress first and, if necessary, litigate the question of infringement later. In the meantime, the public culture benefits from progress; the issue of who is entitled to the profits should not induce rigidity and slowness in industries and fields naturally subject to great flux.

Accordingly, I would reverse the district court decision.

853 F. Supp. 319 (1994)

ENTERTAINMENT RESEARCH GROUP v. GENESIS

United States District Court, N.D. California

LANGFORD, United States Magistrate Judge.

I. INTRODUCTION

This case unites together old adversaries in the arena of advertising to pit them collectively against a common foe in an arena to which they are not accustomed; the federal courtroom. Creatures which are normally docile and pleasant as they hawk their wares have now turned hostile and litigious. The Pillsbury "Doughboy", "Toucan Sam", "Dino the Dinosaur", "Geoffrey the Giraffe", "Oatis Oat Square", "Little Sprout" and yes, even that smiling old salt "Cap'n Crunch" have abandoned their jocular demeanor, joined forces and donned their battle garb in order to engage an enemy far more dangerous than any competitor encountered on the commercial airwaves: the derivative copyrighter.

Their common foe is Plaintiff Entertainment Research Group (ERG). ERG (with authorization from the original copyright holders), manufactures three-dimensional, inflatable costumes of the above named characters for use in grocery stores, shopping malls and other appropriate venues. In an attempt to protect its work, ERG attached copyright notices to the derivative costumes. Defendant Aerostar (another costume manufacturer), is accused of copying these costumes and infringing upon ERG's copyrights. As a defense, Aerostar has brought a summary judgment motion asserting that ERG has not created anything entitled to copyright protection and therefore Aerostar cannot be guilty of copyright infringement. Although not parties to this action at the time of the hearing, Hanna-Barbera, Quaker Oats, Toys "R" Us (some of the owners of the original copyrights), were present by their counsel and voiced disapproval of Plaintiff's derivative copyright assertion. They stand poised to intervene, pending the outcome of this motion.

II. COPYRIGHT VALIDITY

Defendant Aerostar brings this motion for summary judgment claiming ERG's copyright is not valid. To establish copyright infringement, the holder of the copyright must prove both valid ownership of copyright and infringement of that copyright by the alleged infringer. The registration of a copyright certificate itself establishes a prima facie presumption of validity, which may be rebutted by a showing on the part of the alleged infringer that the copyright holder's work is not original. Since Aerostar has put ERG's copyrights in dispute, ERG must prove the validity of its copyright as a threshold issue. Without proper copyright protection any infringement claim is moot and summary judgment rejecting the alleged infringement claim is appropriate.

Plaintiff ERG contends they are entitled to copyright protection for their creation of inflatable derivative works which are based on previously copyrighted characters (i.e., ERG is claiming a derivative copyright in their inflatable "Doughboy", where Pillsbury obviously owns the underlying copyright for the "Doughboy").

The first issue to be decided is whether or not ERG is entitled to a derivative copyright. This requires the court to determine the scope of derivative copyrights and decide whether ERG's inflatable derivative costumes fall within the boundaries delineated by copyright law.

Section 101 of the Copyright Act defines a derivative work as:

a work based upon one or more pre-existing works, such as a translation, fictionalization, motion picture version, sound recording, art reproduction, abridgment, condensation, or any other form in which a work may be recast, transformed, or adapted. A work consisting of editorial revisions, annotations, elaborations, or other modifications which, as a whole, represent an original work of authorship, is a "derivative work". 17 U.S.C.A. § 101.

Although there is relatively little guidance from the Ninth Circuit on derivative copyrights where the underlying work is not in the public domain, the Court of Appeals for the Second Circuit has considerable experience with the question of derivative copyrights and we now turn to that circuit for guidance.

The Second Circuit has held that in order to constitute a separately protectable derivative work, an adaptation of a preexisting work must contain "some substantial, not merely trivial, originality." L. Batlin & Son v. Snyder, 536 F.2d 486 (2d Cir. 1976), cert. denied, 429 U.S. 857, 97 S. Ct. 156, 50 L. Ed. 2d 135 (1976).

The Second Circuit further refined this test in Durham Industries, Inc. v. Tomy Corp, 630 F.2d 905 (2d Cir.1980), where they *322 formulated a two pronged test: "First, to support a copyright the original aspects of a derivative work must be more than trivial. Second, the original aspects of a derivative work must reflect the degree to which it relies on preexisting material and must not in any way affect the scope of any copyright protection in that preexisting material." Id. at 909 (emphasis added).

The basis for the second prong of the Durham test is § 103(b) of the Copyright Act which provides:

The copyright in a compilation or derivative work extends only to the material contributed by the author of such work, as distinguished from the preexisting material employed in the work, and does not imply any exclusive right in the preexisting material. The copyright in such work is independent of, and does not affect or enlarge the scope, duration, ownership, or subsistence of, any copyright protection in the preexisting material. 17 U.S.C.A. § 103(b) (emphasis added).

For the purposes of summary judgment however, this court feels constrained by the Ninth Circuit's decision in North Coast Industries v. Jason Maxwell Inc., 972 F.2d 1031 (9th Cir.1992). In that case, the Ninth Circuit overturned a summary judgment ruling by the district court. The district court had held that the minimum changes in design made by the plaintiff over a work already existing in the public domain were insufficient to warrant copyright protection. In reversing the trial court, the Ninth Circuit stated that summary judgment is appropriate when "... no reasonable trier-of-fact could find even trivial differences in the designs...." Id. at 1034.

Although this court is prepared to adopt the language of North Coast, an important distinction needs to be drawn between North Coast and the case at bar. North Coast dealt exclusively with a pattern design imprinted on a dress. There was no aspect of the North Coast designs which was functional or useful (or to use language from § 102 of the Copyright Act, there was no aspect of those designs which had a "mechanical or utilitarian aspect").

Unlike the designs in North Coast, the costumes at issue in this case are a necessary hybrid of form and function. Unlike North Coast, this court must determine the scope of copyright protection and the propriety of summary judgment when elements of artistry and function are intertwined.

Section 102 of the Copyright Act defines the subject matter of copyright. Subsection (a) lists 7 categories of works which are copyrightable including "pictorial, graphic and sculptural works." This court feels that any copyright protection afforded ERG would fall under this category. A quick look at the definition of "sculptural works" under § 101 leads us to relevant, useful language.

The definition states that sculptural works, including works of artistic craftsmanship are entitled to copyright protection "insofar as their form but not their mechanical or utilitarian aspects are concerned." 17 U.S.C.A. § 101. It further states that "the design of a useful ... article shall be considered a ... sculptural work only if, and only to the extent that, such design incorporates ... sculptural features that can be identified separately from and are capable of existing independently of, the utilitarian aspects of the article." 17 U.S.C.A. § 101 (emphasis added).

Based on this, this court finds that any aspect of a "sculptural work" which is driven primarily by a functional, utilitarian or mechanical consideration will not merit copyright protection. Any differences in appearance between a derivative work and the preexisting work which are driven primarily by a functional, utilitarian or mechanical purpose cannot be considered when seeking artistic differences for the purpose of originality.

This court is certain that ERG's clients would request costumes which are completely identical to their preexisting characters. Any minimal differences in appearance are therefore a result of functional costume considerations, i.e., the costume must be worn by a human.

A quick look at ERG's "Toucan Sam" costume illustrates this point. In the preexisting work, "Toucan Sam" has rather short, skinny, rubbery legs placed far apart on "Sam's" torso. In the derivative costume work, "Toucan Sam" has thick, bulky, tall legs which are placed close together on "Sam's" torso. Are these differences the result of an "artistic" decision on the part of ERG? No, they are due to the limitations of the human body. The legs need to be thicker, and narrowly spaced. ERG was forced to make an alteration in appearance based on mechanical, functional and utilitarian considerations. No reasonable trier-of-fact could find that these differences were the result of "artistic" decision making.

With this in mind, this court will adopt and apply the two part Durham test in light of what the Ninth Circuit has held in North Coast. After careful review of photos of the costumes in question this court finds that no reasonable trier-of-fact could find even trivial artistic differences in design between the preexisting work and the underlying work. Adopting the language of the Durham Court to this case, this court finds that:

[o]ne look at [ERG's costumes] reveals that, in each, the element of originality that is necessary to support a valid copyright is totally lacking. For [some time these characters] have peered at us from [television sets, product labels, newspapers] and a variety of other media, and it would be safe to say that they have a recognition factor that any politician or celebrity would envy. The [ERG costumes] are instantly identifiable as embodiments of the [advertising] characters in yet another form: [Toucan Sam, Dino the Dinosaur, Doughboy, Little Sprout, Cap'n Crunch, Oatis Oat Square and Geoffrey the Giraffe] are now represented as [three-dimensional walk-around costumes]. Durham, 630 F.2d at 909 (citations omitted).

The linchpin of this derivative copyright claim is originality in appearance. It fails because ERG's clients do not want original looking costumes. On the contrary, what ERG's customers ask for is exact replication. Pillsbury necessarily wants a costume which people recognize as their "Doughboy", not an artistic derivation or interpretation of it. Replications which do not include trivial differences in appearance are not entitled to copyright protection. Ironically, the very thing which precludes ERG from obtaining derivative copyright protection in their costumes is what makes them successful in the business of costume making: the ability to manufacture walk-around life-sized replicas of these characters with what appears to be relative precision and accuracy.

Furthermore, Federal Courts have not been inclined to extend derivative copyright protection for conversion of a two-dimensional design into a three-dimensional object,[5] where the three-dimensional object lacks the requisite originality. "The mere reproduction of the underlying characters in plastic, even though ... [it] undoubtedly involved some degree of manufacturing skill, does not constitute originality as this Court has defined the term." Durham, 630 F.2d at 911. In Gallery House, Inc. v. Yi, 582 F. Supp. 1294 (N.D.Ill.1984), the court refused to grant a derivative copyright to a moldmaker stating that "[the moldmaker] did not add any artistic effort. It simply converted a two-dimensional design to a three-dimensional object, which, without sufficient original artistic contribution does not constitute a copyrightable effort." Id. at 1297.

ERG also fails the second prong of the Durham test in that any granting of derivative copyrights in an inflatable "Doughboy" would "simply put a weapon for harassment in the hands of mischievous copiers." Durham, 630 F.2d at 910. This court does not intend to characterize ERG as a "mischievous copier". However, the fear of the Durham Court and this court as well, is that ERG would have a pseudo-monopoly on all inflatable "Doughboys". Any subsequent costume makers and the original copyright holders themselves (Pillsbury, for example) would be limited by the granting of a derivative copyright in this situation or at the very least be vulnerable to harassment. One need only look at the procedure for registering a copyright to see that this fear is well-founded. Copyright Office procedure requires only that an image of the copyrighted article be submitted along with a registration form for the work. In order to substantiate a prima facie case of infringement, a company such as ERG would need only to submit their copyright registration along with a photograph of the infringing costume which would necessarily look like Plaintiff's.

To avoid this potential harassment liability, a subsequent costume-maker would need to make significant changes in the "Doughboy's" appearance, which would detract from the original character, in which ERG has no copyright. As a result, Pillsbury's right to copy (or to permit others to copy) its own creation would, in effect, be circumscribed. See Durham, 630 F.2d at 911.

III. CONCLUSION

This court holds that ERG's derivative walk-around costume figures do not merit copyright protection. They lack even a modest degree of artistic originality and the grant of a derivative copyright would affect the scope of the copyright protection in the preexisting material. Therefore, as to "Toucan Sam", "Dino the Dinosaur", "Doughboy", "Little Sprout", "Cap'n Crunch", "Oatis Oat Square" and "Geoffrey Giraffe", we need not consider the question of copyright infringement by Aerostar.

This court suspects ERG is attempting to gain copyright protection in the ideas of structure, methods and function which support and make up the internal workings of the inflatable walk-around costumes. Unfortunately, this is not the realm or jurisdiction of Copyright law. Protection for the "useful arts" (if warranted in this case), is found in the patent system. Defendant's motion for partial summary judgment is hereby GRANTED.

...

273 F.3d 262 (2d Cir. 2001)
BOISSON v. BANIAN
US Court of Appeals for the Second Circuit

CARDAMONE, Circuit Judge:

Plaintiffs Judi Boisson and her wholly-owned company, American Country Quilts and Linens, Inc., d/b/a Judi Boisson American Country, brought suit in the United States District Court for the Eastern District of New York (Platt, J.), alleging that defendants Vijay Rao and his wholly-owned company Banian Ltd., illegally copied two quilt designs for which plaintiffs had obtained copyright registrations. Following a bench trial, the trial court, in denying the claims of copyright infringement, ruled that defendants' quilts were not substantially similar to what it deemed were the protectible elements of plaintiffs' works. Plaintiffs have appealed this ruling. ...

BACKGROUND

Judi Boisson has been in the quilt trade for over 20 years, beginning her career by selling an- tique American quilts -- in particular, Amish quilts -- she purchased in various states throughout the country. By the late 1980s, having difficulty finding antique quilts, she decided to design and manu- facture her own and began selling them in 1991 through her company. Boisson published catalogs in 1993 and 1996 to advertise and sell her quilts. Her works are also sold to linen, gift, antique, and children's stores and high-end catalog companies. Various home furnishing magazines have pub- lished articles featuring Boisson and her quilts.

In 1991 plaintiff designed and produced two alphabet quilts entitled "School Days I" and "School Days II. "Although we later describe the quilts in greater detail, we note each consists of square blocks containing the capital letters of the alphabet, displayed in order. The blocks are set in horizontal rows and vertical columns, with the last row filled by blocks containing various pictures or icons. The letters and blocks are made up of different colors, set off by a white border and col- ored edging.

Boisson testified at trial that she worked on these quilts at home where she drew the letters by hand, decided on their placement in the quilts, picked out the color combinations and chose the quilting patterns. She obtained certificates of copyright registration for each quilt on December 9, 1991. All of her quilts, as well as the catalogs advertising them, include a copyright notice.

...

DISCUSSION

...

Ruling of the Trial Court

Following the bench trial, the district court found some elements of plaintiffs' quilts were unpro- tectible (i.e., not original) because they were in the public domain: (1) the alphabet, (2) formation of the alphabet using six rows of five blocks across and four icons in the last row, and (3) color. Although that court expressed doubt as to whether copyright protection would extend to the shapes of the letters used in the quilts, it did not rule on that issue. These determinations as to originality may be overturned only if clearly erroneous. A finding is clearly erroneous if, upon reviewing the entire record, we are left with "the definite and firm conviction" that a mistake was made.

1. Use of Alphabet

Passing now to the court's ruling, it correctly determined that the alphabet is in the public do- main, a finding plaintiffs do not dispute. Nor could they object, considering the applicable regulations provide no copyright protection for "familiar symbols or designs" or "mere variations of . . . lettering."

2. Layouts of Alphabet

To support its finding that the layouts of plaintiffs' quilts were not protected by copyright, the district court relied upon evidence submitted by defendants showing that alphabet quilts have been in existence for over a century, suggesting that such layouts were also in the public domain. One circa 1900 quilt displayed letters and icons in blocks arranged in the same format used in "School Days I." From this evidence the court reasoned that such formation belonged to the public domain. Although it made specific findings only as to the block formation in "School Days I, " we presume for purposes of our discussion that, in the absence of a specific finding as to the "School Days II" format, the trial court intended its findings on unprotectibility to extend to the layouts of both of plaintiffs' quilts.

These findings are clearly erroneous. Not only did plaintiffs obtain valid certificates of copyright registration, but also the alphabetical arrangement of the letters in the five-by-six block format required some minimum degree of creativity, which is all that is required for copyrightability. Moreover, unlike the use of letters, no federal regulation establishes that the use of this layout is un- protectible. These factors create a presumption that the layout is original and therefore a protectible element. Therefore, if defendants want to contest this presumption, they bear the burden of proving that this particular layout is not original. At trial, defendants asserted that the particular layout of plaintiffs' quilts was copied from the public domain, but they presented insufficient proof to establish that proposition.

As noted earlier, a plaintiff attempting to prove actual copying on the part of a defendant is enti- tled to use direct or indirect evidence. Indirect evidence of access and substantial similarity to the plaintiff's work can "support an inference" that copying took place. Scholars disagree as to whether a defendant may also rely upon circumstantial evidence to show that a plaintiff copied from the public domain. Compare Jessica Litman, The Public Domain, 39 Emory L.J. 965, 1002-03 (1990) (explaining that a defendant is not entitled to any inference that a plaintiff copied from the public domain simply by showing access and substantial similarity to the public domain work), with Russ VerSteeg, Rethinking Originality, 34 Wm. & Mary L. Rev. 801, 874-75 & n.328 (1993) (permitting a defendant to show copying on the part of the plaintiff through circumstantial evidence that the plaintiff had access and created a work substantially similar to a public domain work). Assuming arguendo that an inference is allowable, defendants in the case at hand nevertheless fall short of proving Boisson copied from the public domain.

Access may be established directly or inferred from the fact that a work was widely dissemi-nated or that a party had a reasonable possibility of viewing the prior work. Defendants proffered no evidence that Boisson owned an alphabet quilt prior to designing "School Days I" or "School Days II." Instead they point to Boisson's affirmative answer when asked at her deposition whether she had "seen an alphabet design in any other quilts." Boisson was not asked what these quilts looked like or when she saw them relative to designing her own quilts, or whether they bore any resemblance to her own designs.

Moreover, having seen an alphabet design would not conclusively establish that Boisson saw one from which she copied the arrangement of letters for her "School

Days" quilts. As defendants' own proof reveals, alphabet quilts are not limited to the formations found in either the 1900 quilt or plaintiffs' quilts. Some quilts display letters out of order; some display three letters in the first and last rows with five letters in each of the middle rows; one has six letters in rows with icons placed in the border; another has varying numbers of letters in each row with icons or quilting designs in the remaining blocks; while still others have five rows of five letters with the "Z" by itself in a corner or followed by numbers representing the year the quilt was made. Nor are all letters of the alphabet always displayed or even displayed with each letter in its own block.

Defendants also failed to show that quilts with layouts similar to the "School Days" quilts were so widely disseminated or known as to infer that Boisson reasonably would have seen one before designing her own works. In particular, bearing in mind that Boisson testified as to her specialty in Amish quilts, among the books submitted by defendants into evidence for purposes of showing copying on the part of plaintiffs, only two pertained specifically to Amish designs -- Rachel & Ken- neth Pellman, The World of Amish Quilts (1998) and Rachel & Kenneth Pellman, A Treasury of Amish Quilts (1998). Neither book, however, contains an alphabet quilt, although they do contain photographs of other quilts owned by Boisson. Further, Boisson testified at her deposition that she was unaware of any Amish alphabet quilts and had never seen one.

Absent evidence of copying, an author is entitled to copyright protection for an independently produced original work despite its identical nature to a prior work, because it is independent creation, and not novelty that is required. Judge Jerome Frank said that an "'author' is entitled to a copy- right if he independently [*271] contrived a work completely identical with what went before." Al- fred Bell & Co. v. Catalda Fine Arts, Inc., 191 F.2d 99, 103 (2d Cir. 1951).

3. Shapes of Letters

The trial judge made no explicit finding with respect to the shapes of the letters of the alphabet. Instead, the court stated it was "questionable" whether plaintiffs could copyright the shapes of the letters used, and it cited the regulation that provides "mere variations of typographic ornamentation" are not copyrightable. 37 C.F.R. § 202.1(a). At this juncture, we hesitate to say that letter shapes are unprotectible in this context, but in the absence of a trial court finding, it is not necessary for us to reach this issue.

4. Color

Color by itself is not subject to copyright protection. See 37 C.F.R. § 202.1(a). Nevertheless, "an original combination or arrangement of colors should be regarded as an artistic creation capable of copyright protection." 1 Nimmer & Nimmer, supra, § 2.14, at 2-178.4. We have previously declined to single out color as an individual element when conducting a copyright infringement analysis. In Streetwise Maps, 159 F.3d at 748, we determined that "instead of examining the [plaintiff's and defendants'] maps feature-by-feature, viewing the individual colors chosen by [plaintiff] as the protected elements upon which defendants encroached, we focus on the overall manner in which [plaintiff] selected, coordinated, and arranged the expressive elements in its map, including color, to depict the map's factual content" (emphasis added). We reached this conclusion after considering the following two Circuit precedents.

Knitwaves, Inc. v. Lollytogs Ltd., 71 F.3d 996 (2d Cir. 1995), involved the copyrightability of children's sweater designs. In finding copyright violations, we considered the plaintiff's original contributions to include: "(1) selecting leaves and squirrels as its dominant design elements; (2) co- ordinating these design elements with a 'fall' palette of colors and with a 'shadow-striped' . . . or a four-paneled . . . background; and (3) arranging all the design elements and colors into an original pattern for each sweater." Similarly, in Novelty Textile Mills, Inc. v. Joan Fabrics Corp., 558 F.2d 1090, 1093 n.5 (2d Cir. 1977), we viewed color in conjunction with the plaid fabric designs utilized by the parties.

Taken together, these cases teach that even though a particular color is not copyrightable, the author's choice in incorporating color with other elements may be copyrighted. This lesson is in ac- cord with the holding of Feist Publications. See 499 U.S. at 348 ("Choices as to selection and arrangement, so long as they are made independently by the compiler and entail a minimal degree of creativity, are sufficiently original that Congress may protect such compilations through the copy- right laws."). Boisson testified that she selected on a trial-and-error basis what colors to use, without reference to any existing work. This approach, combined with Boisson's other creative choices, leads us to conclude it was clear error for the district court to find that plaintiffs' choice of colors in the "School Days" quilts was an unprotectible element.

IV Substantial Similarity Ordinary Observer v. More Discerning Observer

Having found that plaintiffs' quilts are entitled to copyright protection and that defendants actually copied at least some elements of plaintiffs' quilts, we turn our analysis to defendants' contention that its quilts were not substantially similar to plaintiffs'. We review de novo the district court's determination with respect to substantial similarity because credibility is not at stake and all that is required is a visual comparison of the products -- a task we may perform as well as the district court.

Generally, an allegedly infringing work is considered substantially similar to a copyrighted work if "the ordinary observer, unless he set out to detect the disparities, would be disposed to over- look them, and regard their aesthetic appeal as the same." Folio Impressions, 937 F.2d at 765. Yet in Folio Impressions, the evidence at trial showed the plaintiff designer had copied the background for its fabric from a public domain document and "contributed nothing, not even a trivial variation." Thus, part of the plaintiff's fabric was not original and therefore not protectible. We articulated the need for an ordinary observer to be "more discerning" in such circumstances.

The ordinary observer would compare the finished product that the fabric designs were intended to grace (women's dresses), and would be inclined to view the entire dress -- consisting of protectible and unprotectible elements -- as one whole. Here, since only some of the design enjoys copyright protection, the observer's inspection must be more discerning.

Shortly after Folio Impressions was decided, we reiterated that a "more refined analysis" is required where a plaintiff's work is not "wholly original," but rather incorporates elements from the public domain. Key Publ'ns, Inc. v. Chinatown Today Publ'g Enters., Inc., 945 F.2d 509, 514 (2d Cir. 1991). In these instances, "what must be shown is substantial similarity between those elements, and only those elements, that provide copyrightability to the allegedly infringed compilation." In contrast, where the plaintiff's work contains no material imported from the public domain, the "more discerning" test is unnecessary. Hamil Am., Inc. v. GFI, 193 F.3d 92, 101-02 (2d Cir. 1999), cert. denied, 528 U.S. 1160, 145 L. Ed. 2d 1080, 120 S. Ct. 1171 (2000). In the case at hand, be- cause the alphabet was taken from the public domain, we must apply the "more discerning" ordinary observer test.

In applying this test, a court is not to dissect the works at issue into separate components and compare only the copyrightable elements. To do so would be to take the "more discerning" test to an extreme, which would result in almost nothing being copyrightable because original works bro- ken down into their composite parts would usually be little more than basic unprotectible elements like letters, colors and symbols. This outcome -- affording no copyright protection to an original compilation of unprotectible elements -- would be contrary to the Supreme Court's holding in Feist Publications.

Although the "more discerning" test has not always been identified by name in our case law, we have nevertheless always recognized that the test is guided by comparing the "total concept and feel" of the contested works. For example, in Streetwise Maps, 159 F.3d at 748, we found no infringement -- not because the plaintiff's map consisted of public domain facts such as street locations, landmasses, bodies of water and landmarks, as well as color -- but rather "because the total concept and overall feel created by the two works may not be said to be substantially similar."

Likewise, when evaluating claims of infringement involving literary works, we have noted that while liability would result only if the protectible elements were substantially similar, our examina- tion would encompass "the similarities in such aspects as the total concept and feel, theme, charac- ters, plot, sequence, pace, and setting of the [plaintiff's] books and the [defendants'] works." Wil- liams v. Crichton, 84 F.3d 581, 588; see also id. 84 F.3d at 590 ("[A] scattershot approach cannot support a finding of substantial similarity because it fails to address the underlying issue: whether a lay observer would consider the works as a whole substantially similar to one another."). But see Fisher-Price, Inc. v. Well-Made Toy Mfg. Corp., 25 F.3d 119, 123-24 (2d Cir. 1994) (pre-dating Knitwaves and comparing feature-by-feature only the protectible elements of copyrighted dolls).

In the present case, while use of the alphabet may not provide a basis for infringement, we must compare defendants' quilts and plaintiffs' quilts on the basis of the arrangement and shapes of the letters, the colors chosen to represent the letters and other parts of the quilts, the quilting patterns, the particular icons chosen and their placement. Our analysis of the "total concept and feel" of these works should be instructed by common sense. Cf. Hamil Am., 193 F.3d at 102 (noting that the or- dinary observer test involves an examination of "total concept and feel," which in turn can be guided by "good eyes and common sense"). It is at this juncture that we part from the district court, which never considered the arrangement of the whole when comparing plaintiffs' works with defen- dants'. With this concept in mind, we pass to a comparison of the quilts at issue.

V. Comparison

A. "School Days I" v. "ABC Green" Versions

"School Days I" consists of six horizontal rows, each row containing five blocks, with a capital letter or an icon in each block. The groupings of blocks in each row are as follows: A-E; F-J; K-O; P-T; U-Y; and Z with four icons following in the last row. The four icons are a cat, a house, a sin- gle-starred American flag and a basket. "ABC Green Version I" displays the capital letters of the alphabet in the same formation. The four icons in the last row are a cow jumping over the moon, a sailboat, a bear and a star. "ABC Green Version II" is identical to "ABC Green Version I," except that the picture of the cow jumping over the moon is somewhat altered, the bear is replaced by a teddy bear sitting up and wearing a vest that looks like a single-starred American flag, and the star in the last block is represented in a different color.

All three quilts use a combination of contrasting solid color fabrics or a combination of solid and polka-dotted fabrics to represent the blocks and letters. The following similarities are observed in plaintiffs' and defendants' designs: "A" is dark blue on a light blue background; "B" is red on a white background; "D" is made of polka-dot fabric on a light blue background; "F" on plaintiffs' "School Days I" is white on a pink background, while the "F" on defendants' "ABC Green" versions is pink on a white background; "G" has a green background; "H" and "L" are each a shade of blue on a white background; "M" in each quilt is a shade of yellow on a white background. "N" is green on a white background; "O" is blue on a polka-dot background; "P" is polka-dot fabric on a yellow background; "Q" is brown on a light background; "R" is pink on a gray/purple background. "S" is white on a red background; "T" is blue on a white background; "U" is gray on a white back- ground; "V" is white on a gray background; "W" is pink on a white background; "X" is purple in all quilts, albeit in different shades, on a light background; "Y" is a shade of yellow on the same light background; and "Z" is navy blue or black, in all the quilts.

Boisson also testified that defendants utilized the same unique shapes as she had given to the letters "J," "M," "N," "P," "R" and "W." With respect to the quilting patterns, "School Days I" and the "ABC Green" versions feature diamond-shaped quilting within the blocks and a "wavy" pattern in the plain white border that surrounds the blocks. The quilts are also edged with a 3/8" green bind- ing.

From this enormous amount of sameness, we think defendants' quilts sufficiently similar to plaintiffs' design as to demonstrate illegal copying. In particular, the overwhelming similarities in color choices lean toward a finding of infringement. Although the icons chosen for each quilt are different and defendants added a green rectangular border around their rows of blocks, these differences are not sufficient to cause even the "more discerning" observer to think the quilts are other than substantially similar insofar as the protectible elements of plaintiffs' quilt are concerned. See Williams, 84 F.3d at 588 ("[HN22] Dissimilarity between some aspects of the works will not automatically relieve the infringer of liability." (emphasis removed)); Sheldon v. Metro-Goldwyn Pictures Corp., 81 F.2d 49, 56 (2d Cir. 1936) ("It is enough that substantial parts were lifted; no plagiarist can excuse the wrong by showing how much of his work he did not pirate."). Moreover, the substitution in "ABC Green Version II" of the teddy bear wearing a flag vest as the third icon causes this version of defendants' quilt to look even more like plaintiffs' quilt that [**29] uses a single- starred American flag as its third icon. Consequently, both of defendants' "ABC Green" quilts in- fringed plaintiffs' copyright on its "School Days I" quilt.

B. "School Days I" v. "ABC Navy"

We agree with the district court, however, that Rao did not infringe on plaintiffs' design in "School Days I" when he created "ABC Navy." While both quilts utilize an arrangement of six horizontal rows of five blocks each, "ABC Navy" does not have its four icons in the last row. Rather, the teddy bear with the flag vest is placed after the "A" in the first row, the cow jumping over the moon is placed after the "L" in the third row, the star is placed after the "S" in the fifth row, and the sailboat is placed after the "Z" in the last row. Further, the colors chosen to represent the letters and the blocks in "ABC Navy" are, for the most part, entirely different from "School Days I." Defendants dropped the use of polka-dot fabric, and plaintiffs did not even offer a color comparison in their proposed findings of fact to the district court, as they had with each of the "ABC Green" versions. The quilting pattern in the plain white border is changed to a "zig-zag" in "ABC Navy," as opposed to plaintiffs' "wavy" design. Finally, although defendants use a binding around the edge of their quilt, in this instance it is blue instead of green.

Looking at these quilts side-by-side, we conclude they are not substantially similar to one an- other. Just as we rejected defendants' earlier argument and held that what few differences existed between "School Days I" and the "ABC Green" quilts could not preclude a finding of infringement, plaintiffs' emphasis on the similarity in style between some of the letters between "School Days I" and "ABC Navy" cannot support a finding of infringement. See Williams, 84 F.3d at 588 ("When the similarities between the protected elements of plaintiff's work and the allegedly infringing work are of 'small import quantitatively or qualitatively[,]' the defendant will be found innocent of in- fringement."). Because no observer, let alone a "more discerning" observer, would likely find the two works to be substantially similar, no copyright violation could properly be found.

C. "School Days II" v. "ABC Green" Versions

Boisson modified her design in "School Days II" in that she utilized seven horizontal rows of four blocks each. The capital letters are displayed A-D, E-H, I-L, M-P, Q-T, U-X, and Y-Z followed by two blocks showing a single-starred American flag and a house. In addition, she framed the rows of blocks with a red rectangular border and vertical blue stripes located off to the left and right sides. The remainder of the quilt is white, with a blue binding on the edge.

The quilting patterns and the colors used to display the letters and the blocks are substantially the same as those used in "School Days I," as are the shapes of the letters. These similarities be- tween "School Days II" and "School Days I" mean the same similarities are shared with both of de- fendants' "ABC Green" quilts. Nevertheless, the "total concept and feel" of the quilts are not sub- stantially similar. As in Streetwise Maps, where the maps at issue each depicted geographical facts pertaining to New York City but were found to do so in ways that were not alike, defendants' "ABC Green" quilts depict the alphabet in a manner different from "School Days II." Beyond the difference in how the letters are arranged, this version of plaintiffs' quilt uses the colors red, white and blue to depict a look and feel of American patriotism, while defendants' predominant use of green in their borders and edging do not create the same impression.

D. "School Days II" v. "ABC Navy"

As has been explained, although "School Days II" shares the same color combinations in its display of letters and blocks as in "School Days I," defendants' "ABC Navy" quilt does not share the same color combinations as "School Days I." Defendants' quilt is therefore different from "School Days II" in this regard as well. Combined with the varying number of rows and blocks, the placement of icons, the different use and color of rectangular borders around the blocks and the choice of quilting patterns, we agree with the district court that defendants have committed no copyright in- fringement in their design of "ABC Navy" when compared to plaintiffs' "School Days II." The similarity in letter design and the use of a blue edge are so trivial in the overall look of the two quilts that defendants did not infringe on plaintiffs' copyright.

...

CONCLUSION

For the reasons stated above, we affirm the judgment of the district court insofar as it found no infringement on the part of defendants with respect to their "ABC Navy" quilt as compared to plain- tiffs' "School Days I" and "School Days II" quilts and their "ABC Green Version I" and "ABC Green Version II" quilts as compared to plaintiffs' "School Days II" quilt. We reverse the judgment of the district court with respect to plaintiffs' remaining claims, and find defendants' versions I and II of their "ABC Green" quilts infringed on plaintiffs' "School Days I" quilt. Accordingly, we remand the case to the district court for it to determine the appropriate remedies.

"School Days I" by Judi Boisson

The Second Circuit described School Days as follows: "'School Days I' consists of six horizontal rows, each row containing five blocks, with a capital letter or an icon in each block. The groupings of blocks in each row are as follows: A-E; F-J; K-O; P-T; U-Y; and Z with four icons following in the last row. The four icons are a cat, a house, a single-starred American flag and a basket."

"ABC Green II" by Banian Ltd.

The Second Circuit described "ABC Green II" as follows: ABC Green Version II "displays the capital letters of the alphabet in the same formation [as "School Days I"]. The four icons in the last row are a cow jumping over the moon, a sailboat, . . . a teddy bear sitting up and wearing a vest that looks like a single-starred American flag, and [a] star."

"ABC Navy" by Banian Ltd.

The Second Circuit described "ABC Navy" in comparison to "School Days I" as follows: "While both quilts utilize an arrangement of six horizontal rows of five blocks each, 'ABC Navy' does not have its four icons in the last row. Rather, the teddy bear with the flag vest is placed after the 'A' in the first row, the cow jumping over the moon is placed after the 'L' in the third row, the star is placed after the 'S' in the fifth row, and the sailboat is placed after the 'Z' in the last row."

[source: https://guides.lib.umich.edu/substantial-similarity/boisson]

856 F.2d 1341 (1998)

MIRAGE EDITIONS v. ALBUQUERQUE A.R.T.

United States Court of Appeals, Ninth Circuit

BRUNETTI, Circuit Judge:

Albuquerque A.R.T. (appellant or A.R.T.) appeals the district court's granting of summary judgment in favor of appellees Mirage, Dumas, and Van Der Marck (Mirage). The district court, in granting summary judgment, found that appellant had infringed Mirage's copyright and issued an order enjoining appellant from further infringing Mirage's copyright.

Patrick Nagel was an artist whose works appeared in many media including lithographs, posters, serigraphs, and as graphic art in many magazines, most notably Playboy. Nagel died in 1984. His widow Jennifer Dumas owns the copyrights to the Nagel art works which Nagel owned at the time of his death. Mirage is the exclusive publisher of Nagel's works and also owns the copyrights to many of those works. Dumas and Mirage own all of the copyrights to Nagel's works. No one else holds a copyright in any Nagel work. Appellee Alfred Van Der Marck Editions, Inc. is the licensee of Dumas and Mirage and the publisher of the commemorative book entitled NAGEL: The Art of Patrick Nagel ("the book"), which is a compilation of selected copyrighted individual art works and personal commentaries.

Since 1984, the primary business of appellant has consisted of: 1) purchasing artwork prints or books including good quality artwork page prints therein; 2) gluing each individual print or page print onto a rectangular sheet of black plastic material exposing a narrow black margin around the print; 3) gluing the black sheet with print onto a major surface of a rectangular white ceramic tile; 4) applying a transparent plastic film over the print, black sheet and ceramic tile surface; and 5) offering the tile with artwork mounted thereon for sale in the retail market.

It is undisputed, in this action, that appellant did the above process with the Nagel book. The appellant removed selected pages from the book, mounted them individually onto ceramic tiles and sold the tiles at retail.

Mirage, Dumas and Van Der Marck brought an action alleging infringement of registered copyrights in the artwork of Nagel and in the book. Mirage also alleged trademark infringement and unfair competition under the Lanham Act, 15 U.S.C. Sec. 1051 et seq. and the state law of unfair competition, Cal.Bus. & Prof.Code Secs. 17200 et seq.

Appellant moved for summary judgment on the Lanham Act and Copyright Act causes of action. The district court granted summary judgment as to the Lanham Act cause of action but denied summary judgment on the copyright cause of action. Mirage then moved for summary judgment on the copyright claim which was granted. The court also enjoined appellants from removing individual art images from the book, mounting each individual image onto a separate tile and advertising for sale and/or selling the tiles with the images mounted thereon.

The Copyright Act of 1976, 17 U.S.C. Sec. 101 et seq., confers upon the copyright holder exclusive rights to make several uses of his copyright. Among those rights are: (1) the right to reproduce the copyrighted work in copies, 17 U.S.C. Sec. 106(1); (2) the right to prepare derivative works based upon the copyrighted work, 17 U.S.C. Sec. 106(2); (3) the right to distribute copies of the copyrighted work to the public by sale or other transfer of ownership, or by rental, lease or lending, 17 U.S.C. Sec. 106(3); and (4) in the case of literary, pictorial, graphic and sculptural works, including individual images, the right to display the copyrighted work publicly.

...

The district court concluded appellant infringed the copyrights in the individual images through its tile-preparing process and also concluded that the resulting products comprised derivative works.

Appellant contends that there has been no copyright infringement because (1) its tiles are not derivative works, and (2) the "first sale" doctrine precludes a finding of infringement

The Copyright Act of 1976, 17 U.S.C. Sec. 101 defines a derivative work as:

[A] work based upon one or more preexisting works such as a translation, musical arrangement, dramatization, fictionalization, motion picture version, sound recording, art reproduction, abridgment, condensation or any other form in which a work may be recast, transformed, or adapted. A work consisting of editorial revisions, annotations, elaborations, or other modifications which, as a whole, represent an original work of authorship is a "derivative work."(Emphasis added).

The protection of derivative rights extends beyond mere protection against unauthorized copying to include the right to make other versions of, perform, or exhibit the work. Lone Ranger Television v. Program Radio Corp., 740 F.2d 718, 722 (9th Cir.1984); Russell v. Price, 612 F.2d 1123, 1128 n. 16 (9th Cir.1979).

Melvin Nimmer in his treatise on copyright law wrote: [A] work will be considered a derivative work only if it would be considered an infringing work if the material which it has derived from a preexisting work had been taken without the consent of a copyright proprietor of such preexisting work. 1 Nimmer on Copyright Sec. 3.01 (1986) cited in Litchfield v. Spielberg, 736 F.2d 1352, 1357 (9th Cir.1984), cert. denied, 470 U.S. 1052, 105 S.Ct. 1753, 84 L.Ed.2d 817 (1985); United States v. Taxe, 540 F.2d 961, 965 n. 2 (9th Cir.1976), cert. denied, 429 U.S. 1040, 97 S.Ct. 737, 50 L.Ed.2d 751 (1977).

What appellant has clearly done here is to make another version of Nagel's art works, Lone Ranger, supra, and that amounts to preparation of a derivative work. By borrowing and mounting the preexisting, copyrighted individual art images without the consent of the copyright proprietors--Mirage and Dumas as to the art works and Van Der Marck as to the book--appellant has prepared a derivative work and infringed the subject copyrights. Nimmer, supra.

Appellant's contention that since it has not engaged in "art reproduction" and therefore its tiles are not derivative works is not fully dispositive of this issue. Appellant has ignored the disjunctive phrase "or any other form in which a work may be recast, transformed or adapted." The legislative history of the Copyright Act of 1976 indicates that Congress intended that for a violation of the right to prepare derivative works to occur "the infringing work must incorporate a portion of the copyrighted work in some form." 1976 U.S.Code Cong. & Admin.News 5659, 5675. (emphasis added). The language "recast, transformed or adapted" seems to encompass other alternatives besides simple art reproduction. By removing the individual images from the book and placing them on the tiles, perhaps the appellant has not accomplished reproduction. We conclude, though, that appellant has certainly recast or transformed the individual images by incorporating them into its tile-preparing process.

The "first sale" doctrine, which appellant also relies on in its contention that no copyright infringement has occurred, appears at 17 U.S.C. Sec. 109(a). That section provides: Notwithstanding the provisions of Section 106(3), the owner of a particular copy or phonorecord lawfully made under this title, or any person authorized by such owner, is entitled, without the authority of the copyright owner, to sell or otherwise dispose of the possession of that copy or phonorecord.

In United States v. Wise, 550 F.2d 1180 (9th Cir.1977), which concerned a criminal prosecution under the pre-1976 Copyright Act, this court held that:

[T]he "first sale" doctrine provides that where a copyright owner parts with title to a particular copy of his copyrighted work, he divests himself of his exclusive right to vend that particular copy. While the proprietor's other copyright rights (reprinting, copying, etc.) remain unimpaired, the exclusive right to vend the transferred copy rests with the vendee, who is not restricted by statute from further transfers of that copy. 550 F.2d at 1187.

We recognize that, under the "first sale" doctrine as enunciated at 17 U.S.C. Sec. 109(a) and as discussed in Wise, appellant can purchase a copy of the Nagel book and subsequently alienate its ownership in that book. However, the right to transfer applies only to the particular copy of the book which appellant has purchased and nothing else. The mere sale of the book to the appellant without a specific transfer by the copyright holder of its exclusive right to prepare derivative works, does not transfer that right to appellant. The derivative works right, remains unimpaired and with the copyright proprietors--Mirage, Dumas and Van Der Marck. As we have previously concluded that appellant's tile-preparing process results in derivative works and as the exclusive right to prepare derivative works belongs to the copyright holder, the "first sale" doctrine does not bar the appellees' copyright infringement claims.

We AFFIRM.

125 F.3d 580 (1997)

LEE v. A.R.T. COMPANY

United States Court of Appeals of the Seventh Circuit

Easterbrook, Circuit Judge.

Annie Lee creates works of art, which she sells through her firm Annie Lee & Friends. Deck the Walls, a chain of outlets for modestly priced art, is among the buyers of her works, which have been registered with the Register of Copyrights. One Deck the Walls store sold some of Lee's notecards and small lithographs to A.R.T. Company, which mounted the works on ceramic tiles (covering the art with transparent epoxy resin in the process) and resold the tiles. Lee contends that these tiles are derivative works, which under 17 U.S.C. § 106(2) may not be prepared without the permission of the copyright proprietor. She seeks both monetary and injunctive relief. Her position has the support of two cases holding that A.R.T.'s business violates the copyright laws. Muoz v. Albuquerque A.R.T. Co., 38 F.3d 1218 (9th Cir. 1994), affirming without published opinion 829 F. Supp. 309 (D. Alaska 1993); Mirage Editions, Inc. v. Albuquerque A.R.T. Co., 856 F.2d 1341 (9th Cir. 1988). Mirage Editions, the only full appellate discussion, dealt with pages cut from books and mounted on tiles; the court of appeals' brief order in Muoz concludes that the reasoning of Mirage Editions is equally applicable to works of art that were sold loose. Our district court disagreed with these decisions and entered summary judgment for the defendant. 925 F. Supp. 576 (N.D. Ill. 1996).

Now one might suppose that this is an open and shut case under the doctrine of first sale, codified at 17 U.S.C. § 109(a). A.R.T. bought the work legitimately, mounted it on a tile, and resold what it had purchased. Because the artist could capture the value of her art's contribution to the finished product as part of the price for the original transaction, the economic rationale for protecting an adaptation as "derivative" is absent. See William M. Landes & Richard A. Posner, An Economic Analysis of Copyright Law, 17 J. Legal Studies 325, 353-57 (1989). An alteration that includes (or consumes) a complete copy of the original lacks economic significance. One work changes hands multiple times, exactly what § 109(a) permits, so it may lack legal significance too. But § 106(2) creates a separate exclusive right, to "prepare derivative works", and Lee believes that affixing the art to the tile is "preparation," so that A.R.T. would have violated § 106(2) even if it had dumped the finished tiles into the Marianas Trench. For the sake of argument we assume that this is so and ask whether card-on-a-tile is a "derivative work" in the first place.

"Derivative work" is a defined term:

A "derivative work" is a work based upon one or more preexisting works, such as a translation, musical arrangement, dramatization, fictionalization, motion picture version, sound recording, art reproduction, abridgment, condensation, or any other form in which a work may be recast, transformed, or adapted. A work consisting of editorial revisions, annotations, elaborations, or other modifications which, as a whole, represent an original work of authorship, is a "derivative work".17 U.S.C. § 101. The district court concluded that A.R.T.'s mounting of Lee's works on tile is not an "original work of authorship" because it is no different in form or function from displaying a painting in a frame or placing a medallion in a velvet case. No one believes that a museum violates § 106(2) every time it changes the frame of a painting that is still under copyright, although the choice of frame or glazing affects the impression the art conveys, and many artists specify frames (or pedestals for sculptures) in detail. Muoz and Mirage Editions acknowledge that framing and other traditional means of mounting and displaying art do not infringe authors' exclusive right to make derivative works. Nonetheless, the ninth circuit held, what A.R.T. does creates a derivative work because the epoxy resin bonds the art to the tile. Our district judge thought this a distinction without a difference, and we agree. If changing the way in which a work of art will be displayed creates a derivative work, and if Lee is right about what "prepared" means, then the derivative work is "prepared" when the art is mounted; what happens later is not relevant, because the violation of the § 106(2) right has already occurred. If the framing process does not create a derivative work, then mounting art on a tile, which serves as a flush frame, does not create a derivative work. What is more, the ninth circuit erred in assuming that normal means of mounting and displaying art are easily reversible. A painting is placed in a wooden "stretcher" as part of the framing process; this leads to some punctures (commonly tacks or staples), may entail trimming the edges of the canvas, and may affect the surface of the painting as well. Works by Jackson Pollock are notoriously hard to mount without damage, given the thickness of their paint. As a prelude to framing, photographs, prints, and posters may be mounted on stiff boards using wax sheets, but sometimes glue or another more durable substance is employed to create the bond.

Lee wages a vigorous attack on the district court's conclusion that A.R.T.'s mounting process cannot create a derivative work because the change to the work "as a whole" is not sufficiently original to support a copyright. Cases such as Gracen v. The Bradford Exchange, Inc., 698 F.2d 300 (7th Cir. 1983), show that neither A.R.T. nor Lee herself could have obtained a copyright in the card-on-a-tile, thereby not only extending the period of protection for the images but also eliminating competition in one medium of display. After the ninth circuit held that its mounting process created derivative works, A.R.T. tried to obtain a copyright in one of its products; the Register of Copyrights sensibly informed A.R.T. that the card-on-a-tile could not be copyrighted independently of the note card itself. But Lee says that this is irrelevant - that a change in a work's appearance may infringe the exclusive right under § 106(2) even if the alteration is too trivial to support an independent copyright. Pointing to the word "original" in the second sentence of the statutory definition, the district judge held that "originality" is essential to a derivative work. This understanding has the support of both cases and respected commentators. E.g., L. Batlin & Son, Inc. v. Snyder, 536 F.2d 486 (2d Cir. 1976); Melville B. Nimmer & David Nimmer, 1 Nimmer on Copyrights § 3.03 (1997). Pointing to the fact that the first sentence in the statutory definition omits any reference to originality, Lee insists that a work may be derivative despite the mechanical nature of the transformation. This view, too, has the support of both cases and respected commentators. E.g., Lone Ranger Television, Inc. v. Program Radio Corp., 740 F.2d 718, 722 (9th Cir. 1984); Paul Goldstein, Copyright: Principles, Law and Practice § 5.3.1 (2d ed. 1996) (suggesting that a transformation is covered by § 106(2) whenever it creates a "new work for a different market").

Fortunately, it is not necessary for us to choose sides. Assume for the moment that the first sentence recognizes a set of non-original derivative works. To prevail, then, Lee must show that A.R.T. altered her works in one of the ways mentioned in the first sentence. The tile is not an "art reproduction"; A.R.T. purchased and mounted Lee's original works. That leaves the residual clause: "any other form in which a work may be recast, transformed, or adapted." None of these words fits what A.R.T. did. Lee's works were not "recast" or "adapted". "Transformed" comes closer and gives the ninth circuit some purchase for its view that the permanence of the bond between art and base matters. Yet the copyrighted note cards and lithographs were not "transformed" in the slightest. The art was bonded to a slab of ceramic, but it was not changed in the process. It still depicts exactly what it depicted when it left Lee's studio. See William F. Patry, Copyright Law and Practice

823-24 (1994) (disapproving Mirage Editions on this ground).[n1] If mounting works a "transformation," then changing a painting's frame or a photograph's mat equally produces a derivative work. Indeed, if Lee is right about the meaning of the definition's first sentence, then any alteration of a work, however slight, requires the author's permission. We asked at oral argument what would happen if a purchaser jotted a note on one of the note cards, or used it as a coaster for a drink, or cut it in half, or if a collector applied his seal (as is common in Japan); Lee's counsel replied that such changes prepare derivative works, but that as a practical matter artists would not file suit. A definition of derivative work that makes criminals out of art collectors and tourists is jarring despite Lee's gracious offer not to commence civil litigation.

If Lee (and the ninth circuit) are right about what counts as a derivative work, then the United States has established through the back door an extraordinarily broad version of authors' moral rights, under which artists may block any modification of their works of which they disapprove. No European version of droit moral goes this far. Until recently it was accepted wisdom that the United States did not enforce any claim of moral rights; even bowdlerization of a work was permitted unless the modifications produced a new work so different that it infringed the exclusive right under § 106(2). Compare WGN Continental Broadcasting Co. v. United Video, Inc., 693 F.2d 622 (7th Cir. 1982), with Gilliam v. American Broadcasting Companies, Inc., 538 F.2d 14, 24 (2d Cir. 1976). The Visual Artists Rights Act of 1990, Pub. L. 101-650, 104 Stat. 5089, 5123-33, moves federal law in the direction of moral rights, but the cornerstone of the new statute, 17 U.S.C. § 106A, does not assist Lee. Section 106A(a)(3)(A) gives an artist the right to "prevent any intentional distortion, mutilation, or other modification of that work which would be prejudicial to his or her honor or reputation". At oral argument Lee's lawyer disclaimed any contention that the sale of her works on tile has damaged her honor or reputation. What is more, § 106A applies only to a "work of visual art", a new term defined in § 101 to mean either a unique work or part of a limited edition (200 copies or fewer) that has been "signed and consecutively numbered by the author". Lee's note cards and lithographs are not works of visual art under this definition, so she could not invoke § 106A even if A.R.T.'s use of her works to produce kitsch had damaged her reputation. It would not be sound to use § 106(2) to provide artists with exclusive rights deliberately omitted from the Visual Artists Rights Act. We therefore decline to follow Muoz and Mirage Editions.[n2]

Affirmed

[Footnotes: 1. Scholarly disapproval of Mirage Editions has been widespread. Goldstein § 5.3 at 5:81-82; Nimmer & Nimmer § 3.03; Wendy J. Gordon, On Owning Information: Intellectual Property and the Restitutionary Impulse, 78 Va. L. Rev. 149, 255 n.401 (1992) 2. Because this opinion creates a conflict among the circuits, it has been circulated to all judges in active service. See Circuit Rule 40(e). No judge requested a hearing en banc.

PATRICK CARIOU V. RICHARD PRINCE

United States Court of Appeals, Second Circuit

[edited by Fisher, Copyright Law (2014)]

BARRINGTON D. PARKER, Circuit Judge:[...]

BACKGROUND

21 The relevant facts, drawn primarily from the parties' submissions in connection with their cross-motions for summary judgment, are undisputed. Cariou is a professional photographer who, over the course of six years in the mid-1990s, lived and worked among Rastafarians in Jamaica. The relationships that Cariou developed with them allowed him to take a series of portraits and landscape photographs that Cariou published in 2000 in a book titled Yes Rasta. As Cariou testified, Yes Rasta is "extreme classical photography [and] portraiture," and he did not "want that book to look pop culture at all." [...]

22 Cariou's publisher, PowerHouse Books, Inc., printed 7,000 copies of Yes Rasta, in a single printing. Like many, if not most, such works, the book enjoyed limited commercial success. The book is currently out of print. As of January 2010, PowerHouse had sold 5,791 copies, over sixty percent of which sold below the suggested retail price of sixty dollars. PowerHouse has paid Cariou, who holds the copyrights to the Yes Rasta photographs, just over $8,000 from sales of the book. Except for a handful of private sales to personal acquaintances, he has never sold or licensed the individual photographs.

23 Prince is a well-known appropriation artist. The Tate Gallery has defined appropriation art as "the more or less direct taking over into a work of art a real object or even an existing work of art." [...] Prince's work, going back to the mid-1970s, has involved taking photographs and other images that others have produced and incorporating them into paintings and collages that he then presents, in a different context, as his own. He is a leading exponent of this genre and his work has been displayed in museums around the world, including New York's Solomon R. Guggenheim Museum and Whitney Museum, San Francisco's Museum of Modern Art, Rotterdam's Museum Boijmans van Beuningen, and Basel's Museum fur Gegenwartskunst. As Prince has described his work, he "completely tr[ies] to change [another artist's work] into something that's completely different." [...]

24 Prince first came across a copy of Yes Rasta in a bookstore in St. Barth's in 2005. Between December 2007 and February 2008, Prince had a show at the Eden Rock hotel in St. Barth's that included a collage, titled Canal Zone (2007), comprising 35 photographs torn out of Yes Rasta and pinned to a piece of plywood. Prince altered those photographs significantly, by among other things painting "lozenges" over their subjects' facial features and using only portions of some of the images. In June 2008, Prince purchased three additional copies of Yes Rasta. He went on to create thirty additional artworks in the Canal Zone series, twenty-nine of which incorporated partial or whole images from Yes Rasta.[4] The

portions of Yes Rasta [...] photographs used, and the amount of each artwork that they constitute, vary significantly from piece to piece. In certain works, such as James Brown Disco Ball, Prince affixed headshots from Yes Rasta onto other appropriated images, all of which Prince placed on a canvas that he had painted. In these, Cariou's work is almost entirely obscured. The Prince artworks also incorporate photographs that have been enlarged or tinted, and incorporate photographs appropriated from artists other than Cariou as well. Yes Rasta is a book of photographs measuring approximately 9.5″ × 12″. Prince's artworks, in contrast, comprise inkjet printing and acrylic paint, as well as pasted-on elements, and are several times that size. For instance, Graduation measures 72 3/4″ × 52 1/2″ and James Brown Disco Ball 100 1/2″ × 104 1/2″. The smallest of the Prince artworks measures 40″ × 30″, or approximately ten times as large as each page of Yes Rasta.

25 Patrick Cariou, Photographs from Yes Rasta, pp. 11, 59 [...]

27 Richard Prince, James Brown Disco Ball

28 In other works, such as Graduation, Cariou's original work is readily apparent: Prince did little more than paint blue lozenges over the subject's eyes and mouth, and paste a picture of a guitar over the subject's body.[...]

30 Patrick Cariou, Photograph from Yes Rasta, p. 118 [...]

32 Richard Prince, Graduation

33 Between November 8 and December 20, 2008, the Gallery put on a show featuring twenty-two of Prince's Canal Zone artworks, and also published and sold an exhibition catalog from the show. The catalog included all of the Canal Zone artworks (including those not in the Gagosian show) except for one, as well as, among other things, photographs showing Yes Rasta photographs in Prince's studio. Prince never sought or received permission from Cariou to use his photographs.

34 Prior to the Gagosian show, in late August, 2008, a gallery owner named Cristiane Celle contacted Cariou and asked if he would be interested in discussing the possibility of an exhibit in New York City. Celle did not mention Yes Rasta, but did express interest in photographs Cariou took of surfers, which he published in 1998 in the aptly titled Surfers. Cariou responded that Surfers would be republished in 2008, and inquired whether Celle might also be interested in a book Cariou had recently completed on gypsies. The two subsequently met and discussed Cariou's exhibiting work in Celle's gallery, including prints from Yes Rasta. They did not select a date or photographs to exhibit, nor [...] did they finalize any other details about the possible future show.

35 At some point during the Canal Zone show at Gagosian, Celle learned that Cariou's photographs were "in the show with Richard Prince." Celle then phoned Cariou and, when he did not respond, Celle mistakenly concluded that he was "doing something with Richard Prince.... [Maybe] he's not pursuing me because he's doing something better, bigger with this person.... [H]e didn't want to tell the French girl I'm not doing it with you, you know, because we had started a relation and that would have been bad." [...] At that point, Celle decided that she would not put on a "Rasta show" because it had been "done already," and that any future Cariou exhibition she put on would be of photographs from Surfers. Celle remained interested in exhibiting prints from Surfers, but Cariou never followed through.

36 According to Cariou, he learned about the Gagosian Canal Zone show from Celle in December 2008. On December 30, 2008, he sued Prince, the Gagosian Gallery, and Lawrence Gagosian, raising claims of copyright infringement. [...] The defendants asserted a fair use defense, arguing that Prince's artworks are transformative of Cariou's photographs and, accordingly, do not violate Cariou's copyrights. [...] Ruling on the parties' subsequently-filed cross-motions for summary judgment, the district court (Batts, J.) "impose[d] a requirement that the new work in some way comment on, relate to the historical context of, or critically refer back to the original works" in order to be qualify as fair use, and stated that "Prince's Paintings are transformative only to the extent that they comment on the Photos." [...] The court concluded that "Prince did not intend to comment on Cariou, on Cariou's Photos, or on aspects of popular culture closely associated with Cariou or the Photos when he appropriated the Photos," [...] and for that reason rejected the defendants' fair use defense and granted summary judgment to Cariou. The district court also granted sweeping injunctive relief, ordering the defendants to "deliver up for impounding, destruction, or other disposition, as [Cariou] determines, all infringing copies of the Photographs, including the Paintings and unsold copies of the Canal Zone exhibition book, in their possession." [...][5] This appeal followed.

DISCUSSION

I.

39 We review a grant of summary judgment de novo. [...] The well known standards for summary judgment set forth in Rule 56(c) apply. [...] "Although fair

use is a mixed question of law and fact, this court has on numerous occasions resolved fair use determinations at the summary judgment stage where ... there are no genuine issues of material fact." [...] This case lends itself to that approach.

II.

41 The purpose of the copyright law is "[t]o promote the Progress of Science and useful Arts...." U.S. Const., Art. I, § 8, cl. 8. As Judge Pierre Leval of this court has explained, "[t]he copyright is not an inevitable, divine, or natural right that confers on authors the absolute ownership of their creations. It is designed rather to stimulate activity and progress in the arts for the intellectual enrichment of the public." Pierre N. Leval, Toward a Fair Use Standard, 103 Harv. L.Rev. 1105, 1107 (1990) (hereinafter "Leval"). Fair use is "necessary to fulfill [that] very purpose." Campbell, 510 U.S. at 575[...]. Because " `excessively broad protection would stifle, rather than advance, the law's objective,'" fair use doctrine "mediates between" "the property rights [copyright law] establishes in creative works, which must be protected up to a point, and the ability of authors, artists, and the rest of us to express them — or ourselves by reference to the works of others, which must be protected up to a point." [...]

42 The doctrine was codified in the Copyright Act of 1976, which lists four non-exclusive factors that must be considered in determining fair use. Under the statute,

43 [T]he fair use of a copyrighted work ... for purposes such as criticism, comment, news reporting, teaching (including multiple copies for classroom use), scholarship, or research, is not an infringement of copyright. In determining whether the use made of a work in any particular case is a fair use the factors to be considered shall include —

44 (1) the purpose and character of the use, including whether such use is of a commercial nature or is for nonprofit educational purposes;

45 (2) the nature of the copyrighted work;

46 (3) the amount and substantiality of the portion used in relation to the copyrighted

work as a whole; and

47 (4) the effect of the use upon the potential market for or value of the copyrighted work.

48 17 U.S.C. § 107. As the statute indicates, and as the Supreme Court and our court have recognized, the fair use determination is an open-ended and context-sensitive inquiry. [...] The statute "employs the terms `including' and `such as' in the preamble paragraph to indicate the illustrative and not limitative function of the examples given, which thus

Copyright Law (Fisher 2014) Cariou v. Prince

provide only general guidance about the sorts of copying that courts and Congress most commonly had found to be fair uses." [...] The "ultimate test of fair use ... is whether the copyright law's goal of `promoting the Progress of Science and useful Arts' ... would be better served by allowing the use than by preventing it." [...]

49 The first statutory factor to consider, which addresses the manner in which the copied work is used, is "[t]he heart of the fair use inquiry." [...] We ask

50 whether the new work merely `supersedes the objects' of the original creation, or instead adds something new, with a further purpose or different character, altering the first with new expression, meaning, or message[,] ... in other words, whether and to what extent the new work is transformative.... [T]ransformative works ... lie at the heart of [706] the fair use doctrine's guarantee of breathing space....

51 Campbell, 510 U.S. at 579[...]. "If `the secondary use adds value to the original — if [the original work] is used as raw material, transformed in the creation of new information, new aesthetics, new insights and understandings — this is the very type of activity that the fair use doctrine intends to protect for the enrichment of society.'" [...] For a use to be fair, it "must be productive and must employ the quoted matter in a different manner or for a different purpose from the original." [...]

52 The district court imposed a requirement that, to qualify for a fair use defense, a secondary use must "comment on, relate to the historical context of, or critically refer back to the original works." [...] Certainly, many types of fair use, such as satire and parody, invariably comment on an original work and/or on popular culture. For example, the rap group 2 Live Crew's parody of Roy Orbison's "Oh, Pretty Woman" "was clearly intended to ridicule the white-bread original." [...] Much of Andy Warhol's work, including work incorporating appropriated images of Campbell's soup cans or of Marilyn Monroe, comments on consumer culture and explores the relationship between celebrity culture and advertising. As even Cariou concedes, however, the district court's legal premise was not correct. The law imposes no requirement that a work comment on the original or its author in order to be considered transformative, and a secondary work may constitute a fair use even if it serves some purpose other than those (criticism, comment, news reporting, teaching, scholarship, and research) identified in the preamble to the statute. [...] Instead, as the Supreme Court as well as decisions from our court have emphasized, to qualify as a fair use, a new work generally must alter the original with "new expression, meaning, or message." Campbell, 510 U.S. at 579, 114 S.Ct. 1164; see also Blanch, 467 F.3d at 253 (original must be employed "in the creation of new information, new aesthetics, new insights and understandings" [...]); Castle Rock, 150 F.3d at 142.

53 Here, our observation of Prince's artworks themselves convinces us of the transformative nature of all but five, which we discuss separately below. These twenty-five of Prince's artworks manifest an entirely different aesthetic from Cariou's photographs. Where Cariou's serene and deliberately composed portraits and landscape photographs depict the natural beauty of Rastafarians and their surrounding environs, Prince's crude and jarring works, on the other hand, are

hectic and provocative. Cariou's black-and-white photographs were printed in a 9 1/2″ × 12″ book. Prince has created collages on canvas that incorporate color, feature distorted human and other forms and settings, and measure between ten and nearly a hundred times the size of the photographs. Prince's composition, presentation, scale, color palette, and media are fundamentally different and new compared to the photographs, as is the expressive nature of Prince's work. [...]

54 Prince's deposition testimony further demonstrates his drastically different approach and aesthetic from Cariou's. Prince testified that he "[doesn't] have any really interest in what [another artist's] [...] original intent is because ... what I do is I completely try to change it into something that's completely different.... I'm trying to make a kind of fantastic, absolutely hip, up to date, contemporary take on the music scene." [...] As the district court determined, Prince's Canal Zone artworks relate to a "post-apocalyptic screenplay" Prince had planned, and "emphasize themes [of Prince's planned screenplay] of equality of the sexes; highlight `the three relationships in the world, which are men and women, men and men, and women and women'; and portray a contemporary take on the music scene." [...]

55 The district court based its conclusion that Prince's work is not transformative in large part on Prince's deposition testimony that he "do[es]n't really have a message," that he was not "trying to create anything with a new meaning or a new message," and that he "do[es]n't have any ... interest in [Cariou's] original intent." [...] On appeal, Cariou argues that we must hold Prince to his testimony and that we are not to consider how Prince's works may reasonably be perceived unless Prince claims that they were satire or parody. No such rule exists, and we do not analyze satire or parody differently from any other transformative use.

56 It is not surprising that, when transformative use is at issue, the alleged infringer would go to great lengths to explain and defend his use as transformative. Prince did not do so here. However, the fact that Prince did not provide those sorts of explanations in his deposition — which might have lent strong support to his defense — is not dispositive. What is critical is how the work in question appears to the reasonable observer, not simply what an artist might say about a particular piece or body of work. Prince's work could be transformative even without commenting on Cariou's work or on culture, and even without Prince's stated intention to do so. Rather than confining our inquiry to Prince's explanations of his artworks, we instead examine how the artworks may "reasonably be perceived" in order to assess their transformative nature. Campbell, 510 U.S. at 582[...]; Leibovitz v. Paramount Pictures Corp., 137 F.3d 109, 113-14 (2d Cir.1998) (evaluating parodic nature of advertisement in light of how it "may reasonably be perceived"). The focus of our infringement analysis is primarily on the Prince artworks themselves, and we see twenty-five of them as transformative as a matter of law.[...]

58 Here, looking at the artworks and the photographs side-by-side, we conclude [...] that Prince's images, except for those we discuss separately below, have a different character, give Cariou's photographs a new expression, and employ new aesthetics with creative and communicative results distinct from Cariou's. Our

conclusion should not be taken to suggest, however, that any cosmetic changes to the photographs would necessarily constitute fair use. A secondary work may modify the original without being transformative. For instance, a derivative work that merely presents the same material but in a new form, such as a book of synopses of televisions shows, is not transformative. See Castle Rock, 150 F.3d at 143; Twin Peaks Prods., Inc. v. Publ'ns Int'l, Ltd., 996 F.2d 1366, 1378 (2d Cir.1993). In twenty-five of his artworks, Prince has not presented the same material as Cariou in a different manner, but instead has "add[ed] something new" and presented images with a fundamentally different aesthetic. [...]

59 The first fair use factor — the purpose and character of the use — also requires that we consider whether the allegedly infringing work has a commercial or nonprofit educational purpose. [...] That being said, "nearly all of the illustrative uses listed in the preamble paragraph of § 107, including news reporting, comment, criticism, teaching, scholarship, and research... are generally conducted for profit." [...] "The commercial/nonprofit dichotomy concerns the unfairness that arises when a secondary user makes unauthorized use of copyrighted material to capture significant revenues as a direct consequence of copying the original work." [...] This factor must be applied with caution because, as the Supreme Court has recognized, Congress "could not have intended" a rule that commercial uses are presumptively unfair. [...] Instead, "[t]he more transformative the new work, the less will be the significance of other factors, like commercialism, that may weigh against a finding of fair use." [...] Although there is no question that Prince's artworks are commercial, we do not place much significance on that fact due to the transformative nature of the work.

60 We turn next to the fourth statutory factor, the effect of the secondary use upon the potential market for the value of the copyrighted work, because such discussion further demonstrates the significant differences between Prince's work, generally, and Cariou's. Much of the district court's conclusion that Prince and Gagosian infringed on Cariou's copyrights was apparently driven by the fact that Celle decided not to host a Yes Rasta show at her gallery once she learned of the Gagosian Canal Zone show. The district court determined that this factor weighs against Prince because he "has unfairly damaged both the actual and potential markets for Cariou's original work and the potential market for derivative use licenses for Cariou's original work." [...]

61 Contrary to the district court's conclusion, the application of this factor does not focus principally on the question of damage to Cariou's derivative market. We have made clear that "our concern is not whether the secondary use suppresses or even destroys the market for the original work or its potential derivatives, but whether the secondary use usurps the market of the original work." Blanch, 467 F.3d at 258 (quotation marks omitted) (emphasis added); NXIVM Corp. v. Ross Inst., 364 F.3d 471, 481-82 (2d Cir.2004). "The market for potential derivative uses [...] includes only those that creators of original works would in general develop or license others to develop." [...] Our court has concluded that an accused infringer has usurped the market for copyrighted works, including the derivative market, where the infringer's target audience and the nature of the infringing content is the same as the original. For instance, a book of trivia about the television show

Seinfeld usurped the show's market because the trivia book "substitute[d] for a derivative market that a television program copyright owner ... would in general develop or license others to develop." [...] Conducting this analysis, we are mindful that "[t]he more transformative the secondary use, the less likelihood that the secondary use substitutes for the original," even though "the fair use, being transformative, might well harm, or even destroy, the market for the original." [...]

62 As discussed above, Celle did not decide against putting on a Yes Rasta show because it had already been done at Gagosian, but rather because she mistakenly believed that Cariou had collaborated with Prince on the Gagosian show. Although certain of Prince's artworks contain significant portions of certain of Cariou's photographs, neither Prince nor the Canal Zone show usurped the market for those photographs. Prince's audience is very different from Cariou's, and there is no evidence that Prince's work ever touched — much less usurped — either the primary or derivative market for Cariou's work. There is nothing in the record to suggest that Cariou would ever develop or license secondary uses of his work in the vein of Prince's artworks. Nor does anything in the record suggest that Prince's artworks had any impact on the marketing of the photographs. Indeed, Cariou has not aggressively marketed his work, and has earned just over $8,000 in royalties from Yes Rasta since its publication. He has sold four prints from the book, and only to personal acquaintances.

63 Prince's work appeals to an entirely different sort of collector than Cariou's. Certain of the Canal Zone artworks have sold for two million or more dollars. The invitation list for a dinner that Gagosian hosted in conjunction with the opening of the Canal Zone show included a number of the wealthy and famous such as the musicians Jay-Z and Beyonce Knowles, artists Damien Hirst and Jeff Koons, professional football player Tom Brady, model Gisele Bundchen, Vanity Fair editor Graydon Carter, Vogue editor Anna Wintour, authors Jonathan Franzen and Candace Bushnell, and actors Robert DeNiro, Angelina Jolie, and Brad Pitt. Prince sold eight artworks for a total of $10,480,000, and exchanged seven others for works by painter Larry Rivers and by sculptor Richard Serra. Cariou on the other hand has not actively marketed his work or sold work for significant sums, and nothing in the record suggests that anyone will not now purchase Cariou's work, or derivative non-transformative works (whether Cariou's own or licensed by him) as a result of the market space that Prince's work has taken up. This fair use factor therefore weighs in Prince's favor.

64 The next statutory factor that we consider, the nature of the copyrighted work, "calls for recognition that some works are closer to the core of intended copyright protection than others, with the consequence that fair use is more difficult to establish when the former works are copied." [...] We consider "`(1) whether the work is expressive or creative, ... with a greater leeway being allowed to a claim of fair use where the work is factual or informational, [...] and (2) whether the work is published or unpublished, with the scope for fair use involving unpublished works being considerably narrower.'" [...]

65 Here, there is no dispute that Cariou's work is creative and published. Accordingly, this factor weighs against a fair use determination. However, just as

with the commercial character of Prince's work, this factor "may be of limited usefulness where," as here, "the creative work of art is being used for a transformative purpose." [...]

66 The final factor that we consider in our fair use inquiry is "the amount and substantiality of the portion used in relation to the copyrighted work as a whole." 17 U.S.C. § 107(3). We ask "whether the quantity and value of the materials used[] are reasonable in relation to the purpose of the copying." [...] In other words, we consider the proportion of the original work used, and not how much of the secondary work comprises the original.

67 Many of Prince's works use Cariou's photographs, in particular the portrait of the dreadlocked Rastafarian at page 118 of Yes Rasta, the Rastafarian on a burro at pages 83 to 84, and the dreadlocked and bearded Rastafarian at page 108, in whole or substantial part. In some works, such as Charlie Company, Prince did not alter the source photograph very much at all. In others, such as Djuana Barnes, Natalie Barney, Renee Vivien and Romaine Brooks take over the Guanahani, the entire source photograph is used but is also heavily obscured and altered to the point that Cariou's original is barely recognizable. Although "[n]either our court nor any of our sister circuits has ever ruled that the copying of an entire work favors fair use[,].... courts have concluded that such copying does not necessarily weigh against fair use because copying the entirety of a work is sometimes necessary to make a fair use of the image." [...] "[T]he third-factor inquiry must take into account that the extent of permissible copying varies with the purpose and character of the use." [...]

68 The district court determined that Prince's "taking was substantially greater than necessary." [...] We are not clear as to how the district court could arrive at such a conclusion. In any event, the law does not require that the secondary artist may take no more than is necessary. [...] We consider not only the quantity of the materials taken but also "their quality and importance" to the original work. [...] The secondary use "must be [permitted] to `conjure up' at least enough of the original" to fulfill its transformative purpose. [...] Prince used key portions of certain of Cariou's photographs. In doing that, however, we determine that in twenty-five of his artworks, Prince transformed those photographs into something new and different and, as a result, this factor weighs heavily in Prince's favor.

69 As indicated above, there are five artworks that, upon our review, present closer questions. Specifically, Graduation, Meditation, Canal Zone (2008), Canal Zone (2007), and Charlie Company do not sufficiently differ from the photographs of Cariou's that they incorporate for us confidently to make a determination about their [...] transformative nature as a matter of law. Although the minimal alterations that Prince made in those instances moved the work in a different direction from Cariou's classical portraiture and landscape photos, we can not say with certainty at this point whether those artworks present a "new expression, meaning, or message." [...]

70 Certainly, there are key differences in those artworks compared to the photographs they incorporate. Graduation, for instance, is tinted blue, and the jungle background is in softer focus than in Cariou's original. Lozenges painted

over the subject's eyes and mouth — an alteration that appears frequently throughout the Canal Zone artworks — make the subject appear anonymous, rather than as the strong individual who appears in the original. Along with the enlarged hands and electric guitar that Prince pasted onto his canvas, those alterations create the impression that the subject is not quite human. Cariou's photograph, on the other hand, presents a human being in his natural habitat, looking intently ahead. Where the photograph presents someone comfortably at home in nature, Graduation combines divergent elements to create a sense of discomfort. However, we cannot say for sure whether Graduation constitutes fair use or whether Prince has transformed Cariou's work enough to render it transformative.

71 We have the same concerns with Meditation, Canal Zone (2007), Canal Zone (2008), and Charlie Company. Each of those artworks differs from, but is still similar in key aesthetic ways, to Cariou's photographs. In Meditation, Prince again added lozenges and a guitar to the same photograph that he incorporated into Graduation, this time cutting the subject out of his background, switching the direction he is facing, and taping that image onto a blank canvas. In Canal Zone (2007), Prince created a gridded collage using 31 different photographs of Cariou's, many of them in whole or significant part, with alterations of some of those photographs limited to lozenges or cartoonish appendages painted or drawn on. Canal Zone (2008) incorporates six photographs of Cariou's in whole or in part, including the same subject as Meditation and Graduation. Prince placed the subject, with lozenges and guitar, on a background comprising components of various landscape photographs, taped together. The cumulative effect is of the subject in a habitat replete with lush greenery, not dissimilar from many of Cariou's Yes Rasta photographs. And Charlie Company prominently displays four copies of Cariou's photograph of a Rastafarian riding a donkey, substantially unaltered, as well as two copies of a seated nude woman with lozenges covering all six faces. Like the other works just discussed, Charlie Company is aesthetically similar to Cariou's original work because it maintains the pastoral background and individual focal point of the original photograph — in this case, the man on the burro. While the lozenges, repetition of the images, and addition of the nude female unarguably change the tenor of the piece, it is unclear whether these alterations amount to a sufficient transformation of the original work of art such that the new work is transformative.

72 We believe the district court is best situated to determine, in the first instance, whether such relatively minimal alterations render Graduation, Meditation, Canal Zone (2007), Canal Zone (2008), and Charlie Company fair uses (including whether the artworks are transformative) or whether any impermissibly infringes on Cariou's copyrights in his original photographs. We remand for that determination.[...]

III.

74 In addition to its conclusion that Prince is liable for infringing on Cariou's copyrights, the district court determined that the Gagosian defendants are liable

as vicarious and contributory infringers. [...] With regard to the twenty-five of Prince's artworks, which, as we have held, do not infringe on Cariou's copyrights, neither Lawrence Gagosian nor the Gallery may be liable as a vicarious or contributory infringer. [...] If the district court concludes on remand that Prince is liable as a direct infringer with regard to any of the remaining five works, the district court should determine whether the Gagosian defendants should be held liable, directly or secondarily, as a consequence of their actions with regard to those works. [...]

CONCLUSION

76 For the reasons discussed, we hold that all except five (Graduation, Meditation, Canal Zone (2007), Canal Zone (2008), and Charlie Company) of Prince's artworks make fair use of Cariou's photographs. We express no view as to whether the five are also entitled to a fair use defense. We REMAND with respect to those five so that the district court, applying the proper standard, can determine in the first instance whether any of them infringes on Cariou's copyrights or whether Prince is entitled to a fair use defense with regard to those artworks as well. The judgment of the district court is REVERSED in part and VACATED in part.[6] The case is REMANDED for further proceedings consistent with this opinion.

[Notes:]

89 [4] Images of the Prince artworks, along with the Yes Rasta photographs incorporated therein, appear in the Appendix to this opinion. The Appendix is available at http://www.ca2.uscourts.gov/11-1197apx.htm.

90 [5] At oral argument, counsel for Cariou indicated that he opposes the destruction of any of the works of art that are the subject of this litigation.

91 [6] Because we reverse the district court with regard to the twenty-five of the artworks, and leave open the question of fair use with regard to the remaining five, we vacate the district court's injunction. In the event that Prince and Gagosian are ultimately held liable for copyright infringement, and in light of all parties' agreement at oral argument that the destruction of Prince's artwork would be improper and against the public interest, a position with which we agree, the district court should revisit what injunctive relief, if any, is appropriate. See eBay, Inc. v. MercExchange, L.L.C., 547 U.S. 388, 391, 126 S.Ct. 1837, 164 L.Ed.2d 641 (2006); Salinger v. Colting, 607 F.3d 68, 77 (2d Cir.2010).

11. Copyright in Characters

11.1. Basics

900 F. Supp. 1287 (1995)

METRO-GOLDWYN-MAYER v. AMERICAN HONDA

United States District Court, C.D. California

KENYON, District Judge.

Based on the papers submitted and the brief arguments presented at the March 13, 1995 hearing, the Court GRANTS Plaintiffs' motion for a preliminary injunction and DENIES Defendants' motion for summary judgment for the reasons set forth below. Plaintiffs are ORDERED to post a bond in the amount of $6,000,000 for this preliminary injunction to issue.

The Court ORDERS that Defendants, their agents, employees, representatives, and all others purporting to work, or working, on their behalf, be, and by this order are, enjoined from continuing to infringe on Plaintiffs' copyrighted works by displaying or exhibiting in any manner, or causing to be displayed or exhibited in any manner, the Honda del Sol commercial which is the subject of this action, in any medium, including network or cable television or movie theaters.

I. Introduction

This case arises out of Plaintiffs Metro-Goldwyn-Mayer's and Danjaq's claim that Defendants American Honda Motor Co. and its advertising agency Rubin Postaer and Associates, violated Plaintiffs' "copyrights to sixteen James Bond films and the exclusive intellectual property rights to the James Bond character and the James Bond films" through Defendants' recent commercial for its Honda del Sol automobile. Plaintiffs' Opening Memo re: Preliminary Injunction Motion, at 3.

Premiering last October 1994, Defendants' "Escape" commercial features a young, well-dressed couple in a Honda del Sol being chased by a high-tech helicopter. A grotesque villain with metal-encased arms jumps out of the helicopter onto the car's roof, threatening harm. With a flirtatious turn to his companion, the male driver deftly releases the Honda's detachable roof (which Defendants claim is the main feature allegedly highlighted by the commercial), sending the villain into space and effecting the couple's speedy get-away.

Plaintiffs move to enjoin Defendants' commercial pending a final trial on the merits, and Defendants move for summary judgment.

II. Factual Background

In 1992, Honda's advertising agency Rubin Postaer came up with a new concept to sell the Honda del Sol convertible with its detachable rooftop. For what was to become the commercial at issue, Rubin Postaer vice-president Gary Yoshida claims that he was initially inspired by the climax scene in "Aliens," wherein the alien is ejected from a spaceship still clinging onto the spacecraft's door. From there, Yoshida and coworker Robert Coburn began working on the story-boards for the "Escape" commercial. As the concept evolved into the helicopter chase scene, it acquired various project names, one of which was "James Bob," which Yoshida understood to be a play on words for James Bond. Yoshida Depo. at 45. In addition, David Spyra, Honda's National Advertising Manager, testified the same way, gingerly agreeing that he understood "James Bob to be a pun on the name James Bond." Spyra Depo. at 91.

While the commercial was initially approved by Honda in May 1992, it was put on hold because of financing difficulties. Actual production for the commercial did not begin until after July 8, 1994, when Honda reapproved the concept. Defendants claim that, after the initial May 1992 approval, they abandoned the "James Bob" concept, whiting out "James" from the title on the commercial's storyboards because of the implied reference to "James Bond." However, Plaintiffs dispute this assertion, pointing to the fact that when casting began on the project in the summer of 1994, the casting director specifically sent requests to talent agencies for "James Bond"-type actors and actresses to star in what conceptually could be "the next James Bond film."

With the assistance of the same special effects team that worked on Arnold Schwarzenegger's "True Lies," Defendants proceeded to create a sixty- and thirty-second version of the Honda del Sol commercial at issue: a fast-paced helicopter chase scene featuring a suave hero and an attractive heroine, as well as a menacing and grotesque villain.

The commercial first aired on October 24, 1994, but was apparently still not cleared for major network airing as late as December 21, 1994. Plaintiffs first viewed the film during the weekend of December 17 and 18, 1994; they demanded that Defendants pull the commercial off the air on December 22; Defendants refused on December 23; and Plaintiffs filed this action on December 30, 1994. After a brief telephone conference with this Court on January 4, 1995, the Court allowed Plaintiffs to conduct expedited discovery in this matter.

On January 15, 1995, in an effort to accommodate Plaintiffs' demands without purportedly conceding liability, Defendants changed their commercial by: (1) altering the protagonists' accents from British to American; and (2) by changing the music to make it less like the horn-driven James Bond theme. This version of the commercial was shown during the Superbowl, allegedly the most widely viewed TV event of the year.

Plaintiffs filed the instant motion for preliminary injunction on January 23, 1995, and Defendants filed their summary judgment motion on February 21, 1995.

III. Legal Analysis

...

2. Merits Of Plaintiff's Copyright Infringement Claim

...

a. Plaintiffs' Ownership Of The Copyrights

Plaintiffs claim that the Honda commercial: (1) "infringes [P]laintiffs' copyrights in the James Bond films by intentionally copying numerous specific scenes from the films;" and (2) "independently infringes [P]laintiffs' copyright in the James Bond character as expressed and delineated in those films." Plaintiffs' Opening Memo, at 14.

Neither side disputes that Plaintiffs own registered copyrights to each of the sixteen films which Plaintiffs claim "define and delineate the James Bond character." Plaintiffs' Opening Memo re: Preliminary Injunction Motion, at 14. However, Defendants argue that because Plaintiffs have not shown that they own the copyright to the James Bond character in particular, Plaintiffs cannot prevail. Defendants' Opposition Memo re: Preliminary Injunction Motion, at 22 (citing Warner Bros. Pictures, Inc. v. Columbia Broadcasting System, Inc., 216 F.2d 945, 949-50 (9th Cir.1954), cert. denied, 348 U.S. 971, 75 S. Ct. 532, 99 L. Ed. 756 (1955) (evidence at bar suggesting that assignment from author to plaintiffs did not include copyrights to author's characters) [the Sam Spade case]). Specifically, Defendants claim that James Bond has appeared in two films in which Plaintiffs hold no copyright "Casino Royale" and "Never Say Never Again" and therefore, Plaintiffs cannot have exclusive rights to the James Bond character.

It appears that Defendants misconstrue Plaintiffs' claim. First, Plaintiffs do not allege that Defendants have violated Plaintiffs' copyright in the James Bond character itself, but rather in the James Bond character as expressed and delineated in Plaintiffs' sixteen films. To the extent that copyright law only protects original expression, not ideas,[4] Plaintiffs' argument is that the James Bond character as developed in the sixteen films is the copyrighted work at issue, not the James Bond character generally. See, e.g., Anderson v. Stallone, 11 U.S.P.Q.2d 1161, 1989 WL 206431, *6 (C.D.Cal.1989) (holding that Rocky characters as developed in three "Rocky" movies "constitute expression protected by copyright independent from the story in which they are contained"). Second, there is sufficient authority for the proposition that a plaintiff who holds copyrights in a film series acquires copyright protection as well for the expression of any significant characters portrayed therein. See, e.g., New Line Cinema Corp. v. Bertlesman Music Group, 693 F. Supp. 1517, 1521 n. 5 (S.D.N.Y.1988) ("Because New Line has valid copyrights in the Nightmare [on Elm Street film] series, it is clear that it has acquired copyright protection as well for the character of Freddy.") (emphasis added); Warner Bros. Inc. v. American Broadcasting Cos., 720 F.2d 231, 235 (2d Cir.1983) (same). And third, the Sam Spade case, 216 F.2d at 949-50, on which Defendants' rely, is distinguishable on its facts because Sam Spade dealt specifically with the transfer of rights from author to film producer rather than the copyrightability of a character as developed and expressed in a series of films.

Accordingly, Plaintiffs will likely satisfy the "ownership" prong of the test. See also infra discussion re: Plaintiffs' copyright ownership in context of summary judgment discussion, at 27-29.

b. What Elements Of Plaintiffs' Work Are Protectable Under Copyright Law

Plaintiffs contend that Defendants' commercial infringes in two independent ways: (1) by reflecting specific scenes from the 16 films; and (2) by the male protagonist's possessing James Bond's unique character traits as developed in the films.

Defendants respond that Plaintiffs are simply trying to gain a monopoly over the "action/spy/police hero" genre which is contrary to the purposes of copyright law. Specifically, Defendants argue that the allegedly infringed elements identified by Plaintiffs are not protectable because: (1) the helicopter *1294 chase scene in the Honda commercial is a common theme that naturally flows from most action genre films, and the woman and villain in the film are but stock characters that are not protectable; and (2) under the Ninth Circuit's Sam Spade decision, the James Bond character does not constitute the "story being told," but is rather an unprotected dramatic character.

(1) Whether Film Scenes Are Copyrightable

In their opening brief, Plaintiffs contend that each of their sixteen films contains distinctive scenes that together comprise the classic James Bond adventure: "a high-thrill chase of the ultra-cool British charmer and his beautiful and alarming sidekick by a grotesque villain in which the hero escapes through wit aided by high-tech gadgetry." Plaintiffs' Opening Memo re: Preliminary Injunction Motion, at 20. Defendants argue that these elements are naturally found in any action film and are therefore unprotected "scenes-a-faire."[5]

Both sides provide expert testimony to support their claims that such scenes are distinctive or generic, and both sides question the qualifications and hence, the testimony of the others' experts.[6] Indeed, there is a notable difference in the backgrounds of the parties' experts. Plaintiffs' impressive array of James Bond experts includes: (1) Lee Pfeiffer, a writer and James Bond expert whose 1992 book is entitled "The Incredible World of 007" he has appeared on many radio and television programs as a James Bond expert; (2) Richard B. Jewell, a professor at the USC School of Cinema-Television who recently taught a course on James Bond films in the Spring of 1994; (3) Mark Cerulli, a writer/producer at HBO who has written articles and film reviews of many of the Bond films; (4) Drew Casper, a professor and film historian at the USC School of Cinema-Television; and (5) Irwin Coster, president of Coster Music Research Enterprises, Inc. Defendants' less-impressive expert list includes: (1) Arnold Margolin, a writer and producer, who considers himself to be "conversant with the genre to which James Bond and his films belong," because he has been a fan of Bond films since 1959 and has written several screenplays in the "spy film" genre; and (2) Hal Needham, a movie director responsible for the "Cannonball Run" and "Smokey and the Bandit" comedy film series.

410

Plaintiffs' experts describe in a fair amount of detail how James Bond films are the source of a genre rather than imitators of a broad "action/spy film" genre as Defendants contend. Specifically, film historian Casper explains how the James Bond films represented a fresh and novel approach because they "hybridize[d] the spy thriller with the genres of adventure, comedy (particularly, social satire and slapstick), and fantasy. This amalgam ... was also a departure from the series' literary source, namely writer Ian Fleming's novels." Casper Decl., ¶ 9. Casper also states: "I also believe that this distinct melange of genres, which was also seminal ... created a protagonist, antagonist, sexual consort, type of mission, type of *1295 exotic setting, type of mood, type of dialogue, type of music, etc. that was not there in the subtype of the spy thriller films of that ilk hitherto." Id., ¶ 11. In addition, Professor Jewell and Lee Pfeiffer describe the aforementioned elements in more detail and how these are in essence copied by the Honda commercial.[7]

Based on Plaintiffs' experts' greater familiarity with the James Bond films, as well as a review of Plaintiffs' James Bond montage and defense expert Needham's video montage of the "action/spy" genre films, it is clear that James Bond films are unique in their expression of the spy thriller idea. A filmmaker could produce a helicopter chase scene in practically an indefinite number of ways, but only James Bond films bring the various elements Casper describes together in a unique and original way.

Thus, the Court believes that Plaintiffs will likely succeed on their claim that their expression of the action film sequences in the James Bond films is copyrightable as a matter of law.[8]

(2) Whether James Bond Character Is Copyrightable

The law in the Ninth Circuit is unclear as to when visually-depicted characters such as James Bond can be afforded copyright protection. In the landmark Sam Spade case, Warner Bros., 216 F.2d at 950, the Ninth Circuit held that the literary character Sam Spade was not copyrightable because he did not constitute "the story being told." The court opined: "It is conceivable that the character really constitutes the story being told, but if the character is only the chessman in the game of telling the story he is not within the area of the protection afforded by the copyright." Id.

Two subsequent Ninth Circuit decisions have cast doubt on the continued viability of the Sam Spade holding as applied to graphic characters. In Walt Disney Productions v. Air Pirates, 581 F.2d 751, 755 (9th Cir.1978), cert. denied, 439 U.S. 1132, 99 S. Ct. 1054, 59 L. Ed. 2d 94 (1979), the circuit panel held that several Disney comic book characters were protected by copyright. In acknowledging the Sam Spade opinion, the court reasoned that because "comic book characters ... are distinguishable from literary characters, the [Sam Spade] language does not preclude protection of Disney's characters." Id. The Air Pirates decision may be viewed as either: (1) following Sam Spade by implicitly holding that Disney's graphic characters constituted the story being told; or (2) applying a less stringent test for the protectability of graphic characters. See Anderson, 1989 WL 206431, at

*6-7 (identifying two views and citing 1 M. Nimmer, The Law of Copyright, § 2-12, at 2-176 (1988) (interpreting Air Pirates as limiting the "story being told" test to word portraits, not graphic depictions)). One rationale for adopting the second view is that, "[a]s a practical matter, a graphically depicted character is much more likely than a literary character to be fleshed out in sufficient detail so as to warrant copyright protection." Anderson, 1989 WL 206431, at *7. However, as one district court warned, "this fact does not warrant the creation of separate analytical paradigms for protection of characters in the two mediums." Id.

A second Ninth Circuit opinion issued in 1988 did little to clarify Air Pirates' impact on the Sam Spade test. In Olson v. National Broadcasting Co., 855 F.2d 1446, 1451-52 n. 6 (9th Cir.1988), the court cited with approval the Sam Spade "story being told" test and declined to characterize this language as *1296 dicta. Later in the opinion, the court cited the Air Pirates decision along with Second Circuit precedent,[9] recognizing that "cases subsequent to [the Sam Spade decision] have allowed copyright protection for characters who are especially distinctive." Id. at 1452. Olson also noted that "copyright protection may be afforded to characters visually delineation in a television series or in a movie." Id. However, later in the opinion, the court distanced itself from the character delineation test applied by these other cases, referring to it as "the more lenient standard[] adopted elsewhere." Id.

There have been no Ninth Circuit cases on the protectability of visually-depicted characters since Olson, and therefore, it behooves this Court to analyze James Bond's status under the Sam Spade/Olson/Ninth Circuit "story being told" test, as well as under the Air Pirates/Second Circuit "character delineation" test.

Predictably, Plaintiffs claim that under either test, James Bond's character as developed in the sixteen films is sufficiently unique and deserves copyright protection, just as Judge Keller ruled that Rocky and his cohorts were sufficiently unique. See Anderson, 1989 WL 206431, at *7-8. Plaintiffs point to various character traits that are specific to Bond i.e. his cold-bloodedness; his overt sexuality; his love of martinis "shaken, not stirred;" his marksmanship; his "license to kill" and use of guns; his physical strength; his sophistication some of which, Plaintiffs' claim, appear in the Honda commercial's hero.

On the other hand, Defendants assert that, like Sam Spade, James Bond is not the "story being told," but instead "has changed enormously from film to film, from actor to actor, and from year to year." Defendants' Opp. Memo re: Preliminary Injunction Motion, at 22. Moreover, Defendants contend that even if Bond's character is sufficiently delineated, there is so little character development in the Honda commercial's hero that Plaintiffs cannot claim that Defendants copied more than the broader outlines of Bond's personality. See, e.g., Smith v. Weinstein, 578 F. Supp. 1297, 1303 (S.D.N.Y.), aff'd, 738 F.2d 419 (2d Cir.1984) ("no character infringement claim can succeed unless plaintiff's original conception sufficiently developed the character, and defendants have copied this development and not merely the broader outlines").

Reviewing the evidence and arguments, the Court believes that James Bond is more like Rocky than Sam Spade in essence, that James Bond is a copyrightable character under either the Sam Spade "story being told test" or the Second Circuit's "character delineation" test. Like Rocky, Sherlock Holmes, Tarzan, and Superman, James Bond has certain character traits that have been developed over time through the sixteen films in which he appears. Contrary to Defendants' assertions, because many actors can play Bond is a testament to the fact that Bond is a unique character whose specific qualities remain constant despite the change in actors. See Pfeiffer and Lisa, The Incredible World of 007, at 8 ("[Despite the different actors who have played the part] James Bond is like an old reliable friend."). Indeed, audiences do not watch Tarzan, Superman, Sherlock Holmes, or James Bond for the story, they watch these films to see their heroes at work. A James Bond film without James Bond is not a James Bond film. Moreover, as discussed more specifically below, the Honda Man's character, from his appearance to his grace under pressure, is substantially similar to Plaintiffs' Bond.

Accordingly, the Court concludes that Plaintiffs will probably succeed on their claim that James Bond is a copyrightable character under either the "story being told" or the "character delineation" test.

...

The "extrinsic" test compares specific, objective criteria of two works on the basis of an analytic dissection of the following elements of each work plot, theme, dialogue, mood, setting, pace, characters, and sequence of events. Shaw, 919 F.2d at 1359. Evidence is usually supplied by expert testimony comparing the works at issue. Because the extrinsic test relies on objective analytical criteria, "this question may often be decided as a matter of law." Krofft, 562 F.2d at 1164.

Here, both Plaintiffs' and Defendants' experts go through specific analyses of the similarities in ideas between the James Bond films and the Honda commercial. Plaintiffs contend that the commercial illegally copies specific protected portions of the James Bond films and the James Bond character itself. Defendants claim that the commercial depicts a generic action scene with a generic hero, all of which is not protected by *1298 copyright. Alternatively, Defendants argue that they did not copy a substantial portion of any one James Bond work to be liable for infringement as a matter of law.

Viewing Plaintiffs' and Defendants' videotapes and examining the experts' statements, Plaintiffs will likely prevail on this issue because there is substantial similarity between the specific protected elements of the James Bond films and the Honda commercial: (1) the theme, plot, and sequence both involve the idea of a handsome hero who, along with a beautiful woman, lead a grotesque villain on a high-speed chase, the male appears calm and unruffled, there are hints of romance between the male and female, and the protagonists escape with the aid of intelligence and gadgetry; (2) the settings both involve the idea of a high-speed chase with the villain in hot pursuit; (3) the mood and pace of both works are fast-paced and involve hi-tech effects, with loud, exciting horn music in the background;[12] (4) both the James Bond and Honda commercial dialogues are laced with dry wit and subtle humor; (5) the characters of Bond and the Honda man are very similar in the way they look and act both heros are young, tuxedo-clad, British-looking men with beautiful women in tow and grotesque villains close at hand; moreover, both men exude uncanny calm under pressure, exhibit a dry sense of humor and wit, and are attracted to, and are attractive to, their female companions.

In addition, several specific aspects of the Honda commercial appear to have been lifted from the James Bond films:

(1) In "The Spy Who Loved Me," James Bond is in a white sports car, a beautiful woman passenger at his side, driving away down a deserted road from some almost deadly adventure, when he is suddenly attacked by a chasing helicopter whose bullets he narrowly avoids by skillfully weaving the car down the road at high speed. At the beginning of the Honda commercial, the Honda man turns to his companion and says, "That wasn't so bad"; to which the woman replies, "Well, I wouldn't congratulate yourself quite yet" implying that they had just escaped some prior danger. Suddenly, a helicopter appears from out of nowhere and the adventure begins.

(2) In "Dr. No.," the villain has metal hands. In the Honda commercial, the villain uses his metal-encased hands to cling onto the roof of the car after he jumps onto it.

(3) In "Goldfinger," Bond's sports car has a roof which Bond can cause to detach with the flick of a lever. In the Honda commercial, the Honda del Sol has a detachable roof which the Honda man uses to eject the villain.

(4) In "Moonraker," the villainous henchman, Jaws, sporting a broad grin revealing metallic teeth and wearing a pair of oversized goggles, jumps out of an airplane. In the Honda commercial, the villain, wearing similar goggles and revealing metallic teeth, jumps out of a helicopter.

(5) In "The Spy Who Loved Me," Jaws assaults a vehicle in which Bond and his female sidekick are trying to make their escape. In the Honda commercial, the villain jumps onto the roof of the Honda del Sol and scrapes at the roof, attempting to hold on and possibly get inside the vehicle.

(6) In "You Only Live Twice," a chasing helicopter drops a magnetic line down to snag a speeding car. In the Honda commercial, the villain is dropped down to the moving car and is suspended from the helicopter by a cable.

In sum, the extrinsic ideas that are inherent parts of the James Bond films appear to be substantially similar to those in the Honda commercial.

(b) Intrinsic Test

The "intrinsic" test asks whether the "total concept and feel" of the two works is also substantially similar. Litchfield v. Spielberg, 736 F.2d 1352, 1357 (9th Cir.1984), cert. denied, 470 U.S. 1052, 105 S. Ct. 1753, 84 L. Ed. 2d 817 (1985). This is a subjective test that requires a determination of whether the ordinary reasonable audience could recognize the Defendants' commercial as a picturization of Plaintiffs' copyrighted work. See Berkic v. Crichton, 761 F.2d 1289, 1292 (9th Cir.), cert. denied, 474 U.S. 826, 106 S. Ct. 85, 88 L. Ed. 2d 69 (1985).

Because this is a subjective determination, the comparison during the intrinsic test is left for the trier of fact. This would involve showing the Honda commercial to the members of the jury so that they may compare the same with the sixteen Bond films at issue. Viewing the evidence, it appears likely that the average viewer would immediately think of James Bond when viewing the Honda commercial, even with the subtle changes in accent and music.

As in this Court's Jaws opinion, Universal, 543 F. Supp. at 1141, the Court finds that Defendants' attempt to characterize all of the alleged similarities between the works as scenes-a-faire to be unavailing. There are many ways to express a helicopter chase scene, but only Plaintiffs' Bond films would do it the way the Honda commercial did with these very similar characters, music, pace, and mood. Plaintiffs are therefore likely to prevail on the "intrinsic test."

...

802 F.3d 1012 (2015)

DC COMICS v. TOWLE

United States Court of Appeals, Ninth Circuit

IKUTA, Circuit Judge:

We are asked to decide whether defendant Mark Towle infringed DC Comics' exclusive rights under a copyright when he built and sold replicas of the Batmobile, as it appeared in the 1966 television show Batman and the 1989 film BATMAN. Holy copyright law, Batman!

I

DC Comics (DC) is the publisher and copyright owner of comic books featuring the story of the world-famous character, Batman. Since his first comic book appearance in 1939, the Caped Crusader has protected Gotham City from villains with the help of his sidekick Robin the Boy Wonder, his utility belt, and of course, the Batmobile.

Originally introduced in the Batman comic books in 1941, the Batmobile is a fictional, high-tech automobile that Batman employs as his primary mode of transportation. The Batmobile has varied in appearance over the years, but its name and key characteristics as Batman's personal crime-fighting vehicle have remained consistent. Over the past eight decades, the comic books have continually depicted the Batmobile as possessing bat-like external features, ready to leap into action to assist Batman in his fight against Gotham's most dangerous villains, and equipped with futuristic weaponry and technology that is "years ahead of anything else on wheels."

Since its creation in the comic books, the Batmobile has also been depicted in numerous television programs and motion pictures. Two of these depictions are relevant to this case: the 1966 television series Batman, starring Adam West, and the 1989 motion picture BATMAN, starring Michael Keaton.

The 1966 Batman television series was the product of a licensing agreement between DC's predecessor, National Periodical Publications, Inc. (National Periodical) and the American Broadcasting Company (ABC). In 1965, National Periodical entered into a licensing agreement with ABC (the 1965 ABC Agreement) in which it granted ABC "an exclusive license to produce a series of half-hour television programs . based upon the literary property consisting of the comic book and comic strip stories entitled 'Batman' . including the characters therein." This exclusive right included the right to "translate, adapt, [or] arrange" the Batman literary property "to such extent as ABC may desire" in the making of the television programs, and the right to secure copyrights in the television programs produced. The agreement also provided that "[a]ll rights in the property not specifically granted to ABC are hereby reserved to and may be exercised by National at all times during the term of this agreement" except as otherwise expressly stated in the agreement. National Periodical's reserved rights included "[a]ll rights of publication," and the exclusive merchandising rights to all products manufactured or distributed under the name of any character in the Batman comic books.

Under this agreement, ABC (through a series of sub-licensing agreements) produced the 1966 television show starring Adam West as Batman. In addition to Batman, Robin, and the use of visual onomatopoeia that flashed on screen during fight scenes—Pow! Boff! Thwack!—the television series featured the Batmobile. The design of the Batmobile did not directly copy any iterations of the Batmobile as it appeared in the comic books. As in the comic books, however, the Batmobile in the 1966 television show maintained a bat-like appearance and was equipped with state-of-the-art weaponry and technology.1

In 1979, DC again licensed its rights in the Batman literary property, this time to Batman Productions, Inc. (BPI). In the agreement (the 1979 BPI Agreement), DC granted BPI the exclusive right to create a motion picture based on the "Property," which was defined to include "[t]he names, titles, fictional locations and fictional conveyances as depicted and contained in the comic magazines [published by DC], which are identifiable with or associated with the fictional character known as 'Batman,' such as . that certain conveyance known as the 'Batmobile.' " The 1979 BPI Agreement also granted BPI the right to "adapt, use, modify, [or] alter the Property" for the purpose of producing the motion picture. Like the 1965 ABC Agreement, the 1979 BPI Agreement provided that "[a]ll rights in the Property not specifically granted to" BPI under the agreement "are reserved to DC and may be exercised by DC at all times without any limitation or restriction whatsover except as specifically set forth herein." These reserved rights included "[a]ll rights of publication in and to the Property," as well as "[a]ll 'merchandising rights' " in "products manufactured or distributed under the name of or using a representation of 'Batman' or any other character or thing included in the Property or under a name which incorporates any phrase, clause or expression used in DC's comic strips or comic magazines. "

BPI subsequently sub-licensed its rights to Warner Bros., Inc., who eventually (through a number of additional sub-licensing agreements) produced the 1989 motion picture BATMAN, starring Michael Keaton as Batman. Like the 1966 television series, the 1989 motion picture featured a Batmobile that was physically distinct from the Batmobile portrayed in the comic books and the 1966 television series. Nonetheless, the Batmobile as portrayed in the motion picture retained a bat-like physical appearance and was again equipped with futuristic technology and crime-fighting weaponry.

Defendant Mark Towle produces replicas of the Batmobile as it appeared in both the 1966 television show and 1989 motion picture as part of his business at Gotham Garage, where he manufactures and sells replicas of automobiles featured in motion pictures or television programs. Towle concedes that these replicas copy the designs of the Batmobile as depicted on television and in the motion picture, though they do not copy every feature. Towle then sells these vehicles for approximately $90,000 to "avid car collectors" who "know the entire history of the Batmobile." Towle also sells kits that allow customers to modify their cars to look like the Batmobile, as it appeared in the 1966 television show and the 1989 motion picture.

Before DC brought this lawsuit, Towle advertised each replica as the "Batmobile," and used the domain name batmobilereplicas.com to market his business. He also advertised that the replicas included such features as "custom bat insignias, wheel bats, [and a] bat steering wheel," and would attract attention due to the fame of the Batmobile. By his own admission, Towle is not authorized by DC to manufacture or sell any products bearing DC's copyright or trademark.

In May 2011, DC filed this action against Towle, alleging among other things, causes of action for copyright infringement, trademark infringement, and unfair competition arising from Towle's manufacture and sale of the Batmobile replicas.3 Towle denied that he had infringed upon DC's copyright. He claimed that the Batmobile as it appeared in the 1966 television show and 1989 motion picture was not subject to copyright protection. Alternatively, Towle argued that DC did not own the copyright in the Batmobile as it appeared in either production. Towle also asserted the affirmative defense of laches. The parties subsequently filed cross motions for partial summary judgment as to DC's trademark, copyright, and unfair competition claims, and as to Towle's laches defense.

In a published order, the district court granted in part and denied in part DC's motion for summary judgment, and denied Towle's cross motion for summary judgment. DC Comics v. Towle, 989 F.Supp.2d 948 (C.D.Cal.2013). First, the district court held that the Batmobile was a character entitled to copyright protection. In reaching this conclusion, the district court made a number of findings. Among other things, it found that the Batmobile "is known by one consistent name that identifies it as Batman's personal vehicle," and, although some of its physical traits have changed over time, several have remained consistent, including its "high-tech gadgets and weaponry," "bat-like motifs," and its jet black color. Additionally, the district court found that the Batmobile is always "depicted as being swift, cunning, strong and elusive," and is even portrayed as a "superhero" and "Batman's sidekick, if not an extension of Batman's own persona."

Second, the district court held that DC maintained a copyright in the Batmobile as it appeared in both the 1966 television show and the 1989 motion picture based on its ownership of the merchandising rights. Alternatively, the district court concluded that DC owns a copyright in the Batmobile as it appeared in each production because the appearance of the Batmobile in each production was derived from the Batmobile depicted in DC's comic books. Finally, the district court concluded that Towle infringed upon DC's copyright because he copied the Batmobile as it appeared in the 1966 and 1989 productions in his replicas. Accordingly, the district court granted summary judgment on the copyright infringement claim to DC.

The district court also granted summary judgment to DC on Towle's affirmative laches defense to the trademark infringement claim. The court found that Towle admitted that he knew of the Batman property and the various bat emblems and symbols, and did not dispute "that he intentionally copied the designs" of the Batmobile as it appeared in the 1966 television show and 1989 motion picture, which included DC's Batman trademarks. He also intentionally referred to his replicas as "Batmobiles." Therefore, the court concluded that Towle acted in bad faith and intentionally copied DC's trademarks "so as to associate his products with the Batman films and television show."

Finally, the court denied DC's summary judgment motion on Towle's laches defense to the copyright infringement claim because it determined that there was a genuine dispute of fact as to whether Towle was aware that copying the Batmobile as it appeared in the 1966 television show and 1989 motion picture constituted copyright infringement.

After the district court issued its decision, the parties entered into a joint stipulation in which they agreed that the district court would enter a judgment against Towle on DC's copyright infringement and other claims. They also agreed that, except as provided in the stipulation, all claims were to be dismissed with prejudice. The district court entered a judgment consistent with this stipulation on February 22, 2013, and Towle timely appealed.

Because the parties entered into a stipulation that finalized the district court order, we have jurisdiction over this appeal under 28 U.S.C. § 1291. See Dannenberg v. Software Toolworks Inc., 16 F.3d 1073, 1074–75 (9th Cir.1994).

II

In order to prevail on its claim for copyright infringement, DC must prove that it owns a copyright in the Batmobile as it appeared in the 1966 television series and 1989 movie, and that Towle infringed that copyright by creating unauthorized replicas. See Entm't Research Grp., Inc. v. Genesis Creative Grp., Inc., 122 F.3d 1211, 1217 (9th Cir.1997).

To the Batmobile!

A

We begin with the question whether the Batmobile, as it appears in the comic books, television series, and motion picture, is entitled to copyright protection. See Ets–Hokin v. Skyy Spirits, Inc., 225 F.3d 1068, 1073 (9th Cir.2000). In the context of copyright law, where, as here, "the question requires us to consider legal concepts in the mix of fact and law and to exercise judgment about the values that animate legal principles, . the question should be classified as one of law and reviewed de novo." Harper House, Inc. v. Thomas Nelson, Inc., 889 F.2d 197, 201 (9th Cir.1989).

Courts have recognized that copyright protection extends not only to an original work as a whole, but also to "sufficiently distinctive" elements, like comic book characters, contained within the work. Halicki Films, LLC v. Sanderson Sales & Mktg., 547 F.3d 1213, 1224 (9th Cir.2008). Although comic book characters are not listed in the Copyright Act, we have long held that such characters are afforded copyright protection. See Walt Disney Productions v. Air Pirates, 581 F.2d 751 (9th Cir.1978). In Air Pirates, for instance, we considered a number of subversive comic books that portrayed well-known Disney characters as being active participants in "a free thinking, promiscuous, drug ingesting counterculture." Id. at 753. In holding that the Disney characters were copyrightable (and that Disney's copyright in those characters had been infringed), we distinguished a prior decision suggesting that literary "characters ordinarily are not copyrightable," id. at 755 (citing Warner Bros. Pictures, Inc. v. Columbia Broad. Sys., Inc., 216 F.2d 945 (9th Cir.1954)), on the grounds that a comic book character "has physical as well as conceptual qualities" and "is more likely to contain some unique elements of expression" than a purely literary character. Id. (citing Detective Comics, Inc. v. Bruns Publications Inc., 111 F.2d 432 (2d Cir.1940) (holding that comic book characters are copyrightable); Fleischer Studios v. Freundlich, 73 F.3d 276 (2d Cir.1934) (same); King Features Syndicate v. Fleischer, 299 F. 533 (2d Cir.1924) (same)). We subsequently held that characters in a television series or a motion picture may also be entitled to copyright protection. See Olson v. National Broadcasting Co., 855 F.2d 1446 (9th Cir.1988).

Not every comic book, television, or motion picture character is entitled to copyright protection. We have held that copyright protection is available only "for characters that are especially distinctive." Halicki, 547 F.3d at 1224. To meet this standard, a character must be "sufficiently delineated" and display "consistent, widely identifiable traits." Rice v. Fox Broadcasting Co., 330 F.3d 1170 (9th Cir.2003) (citing Toho Co., Ltd. v. William Morrow & Co., Inc., 33 F.Supp.2d 1206, 1215 (C.D. Cal.1998) (Godzilla)). A masked magician "dressed in standard magician garb" whose role "is limited to performing and revealing the magic tricks," for example, is not "an 'especially distinct' character differing from an ordinary magician in a manner that warrants copyright protection." Id. Further, characters that have been "lightly sketched" and lack descriptions may not merit copyright protection. Olson, 855 F.2d at 1452–53.

We have previously determined that an automotive character can be copyrightable. See Halicki, 547 F.3d at 1224. In Halicki, we considered whether "Eleanor," a car that appeared in both the original 1971 and 2000 remake motion picture Gone in 60 Seconds, could be entitled to copyright protection as a character. Id. at 1224–25. Considering Eleanor's persistent attributes in both the original and remake of Gone in 60 Seconds, we concluded that Eleanor met some of the key factors necessary to qualify for copyright protection. Id. at 1225. We first noted that Eleanor was more like a comic book character than a literary character given Eleanor's "physical as well as conceptual qualities." Id. We also stated that Eleanor "displays consistent, widely identifiable traits and is especially distinctive." Id. (alteration, citation, and internal quotation marks omitted). We gave several examples of these traits. First, we noted that "[i]n both films, the thefts of the other cars go largely as planned, but whenever the main human character tries to steal Eleanor, circumstances invariably become complicated." Id. Second, we noted that in the original, "the main character says 'I'm getting tired of stealing this Eleanor car,' " and in the remake "the main character refers to his history with Eleanor." Id. Despite this evidence of distinctive traits, we were sensitive to the fact that the district court had implied that Eleanor was deserving of copyright protection, but had not directly examined this "fact-intensive issue." Id. Therefore, we remanded the issue to the district court to decide in the first instance. Id.

As indicated in Halicki, a character may be protectable if it has distinctive character traits and attributes, even if the character does not maintain the same physical appearance in every context. As the Eighth Circuit has recognized, "the presence of distinctive qualities apart from visual appearance can diminish or even negate the need for consistent visual appearance." Warner Bros. Entm't, Inc. v. X One X Prods., 644 F.3d 584, 599 n. 8 (8th Cir.2011). For example, in Halicki, Eleanor's ability to consistently disrupt heists by her presence was more pertinent to our analysis of whether the car should qualify as a sufficiently distinctive character than Eleanor's make and model. 547 F.3d at 1225. Indeed, Halicki put no weight on the fact that Eleanor was a customized yellow 1971 Fastback Ford Mustang in one film, and a silver 1967 Shelby GT–500 in another.

Similarly, district courts have determined that James Bond, Batman, and Godzilla are characters protected by copyright, despite their changes in appearance. See Metro–Goldwyn–Mayer, Inc. v. Am. Honda Motor Co., 900 F.Supp. 1287, 1295–96 (C.D.Cal.1995) (James Bond) (cited with approval in Rice); Toho Co. v. William Morrow & Co., 33 F.Supp.2d 1206, 1216 (C.D.Cal.1998) (Godzilla) (cited with approval in Rice); Sapon v. DC Comics, No. 00 CIV. 8992(WHP), 2002 WL 485730, at *3–4 (S.D.N.Y. Mar. 29, 2002) (Batman). In each instance, courts have deemed the persistence of a character's traits and attributes to be key to determining whether the character qualifies for copyright protection. The character "James Bond" qualifies for copyright protection because, no matter what the actor who portrays this character looks like, James Bond always maintains his "cold-bloodedness; his overt sexuality; his love of martinis 'shaken, not stirred;' his marksmanship; his 'license to kill' and use of guns; his physical strength; [and] his sophistication." Metro–Goldwyn–Mayer, 900 F.Supp. at 1296. Similarly, while the character "Godzilla" may have a different appearance from time to time, it is entitled to copyright protection because it "is always a pre-historic, fire-breathing, gigantic dinosaur alive and well in the modern world." Toho Co., 33 F.Supp.2d at

1216. In short, although James Bond's, Godzilla's, and Batman's "costume and character have evolved over the years, [they have] retained unique, protectable characteristics" and are therefore entitled to copyright protection as characters. Sapon, 2002 WL 485730, at *3–4.

We read these precedents as establishing a three-part test for determining whether a character in a comic book, television program, or motion picture is entitled to copyright protection. First, the character must generally have "physical as well as conceptual qualities." Air Pirates, 581 F.2d at 755. Second, the character must be "sufficiently delineated" to be recognizable as the same character whenever it appears. See Rice, 330 F.3d at 1175. Considering the character as it has appeared in different productions, it must display consistent, identifiable character traits and attributes, although the character need not have a consistent appearance. See Halicki, 547 F.3d at 1224. Third, the character must be "especially distinctive" and "contain some unique elements of expression." Halicki, 547 F.3d at 1224. It cannot be a stock character such as a magician in standard magician garb. Rice, 330 F.3d at 1175. Even when a character lacks sentient attributes and does not speak (like a car), it can be a protectable character if it meets this standard. Halicki, 547 F.3d at 1224.

We now apply this framework to this case. Because (unlike in Halicki) the district court here addressed this question in detail, we consider its factual findings in analyzing this issue. Cf. Halicki, 547 F.3d at 1225. First, because the Batmobile has appeared graphically in comic books, and as a three-dimensional car in television series and motion pictures, it has "physical as well as conceptual qualities," and is thus not a mere literary character. Air Pirates, 581 F.2d at 755.

Second, the Batmobile is "sufficiently delineated" to be recognizable as the same character whenever it appears. See Rice, 330 F.3d at 1175. As the district court determined, the Batmobile has maintained distinct physical and conceptual qualities since its first appearance in the comic books in 1941. In addition to its status as "a highly-interactive vehicle, equipped with high-tech gadgets and weaponry used to aid Batman in fighting crime," the Batmobile is almost always bat-like in appearance, with a bat-themed front end, bat wings extending from the top or back of the car, exaggerated fenders, a curved windshield, and bat emblems on the vehicle. This bat-like appearance has been a consistent theme throughout the comic books, television series, and motion picture, even though the precise nature of the bat-like characteristics have changed from time to time.

The Batmobile also has consistent character traits and attributes. No matter its specific physical appearance, the Batmobile is a "crime-fighting" car with sleek and powerful characteristics that allow Batman to maneuver quickly while he fights villains. In the comic books, the Batmobile is described as waiting "[l]ike an impatient steed straining at the reins . shiver[ing] as its super-charged motor throbs with energy" before it "tears after the fleeing hoodlums" an instant later. Elsewhere, the Batmobile "leaps away and tears up the street like a cyclone," and at one point "twin jets of flame flash out with thunderclap force, and the miracle car of the dynamic duo literally flies through the air!"6 Like its comic book counterpart, the Batmobile depicted in both the 1966 television series and the 1989

421

motion picture possesses "jet engine[s]" and flame-shooting tubes that undoubtedly give the Batmobile far more power than an ordinary car. Furthermore, the Batmobile has an ability to maneuver that far exceeds that of an ordinary car. In the 1966 television series, the Batmobile can perform an "emergency bat turn" via reverse thrust rockets. Likewise, in the 1989 motion picture, the Batmobile can enter "Batmissile" mode, in which the Batmobile sheds "all material outside [the] central fuselage" and reconfigures its "wheels and axles to fit through narrow openings."

Equally important, the Batmobile always contains the most up-to-date weaponry and technology. At various points in the comic book, the Batmobile contains a "hot-line phone . directly to Commissioner Gordon's office" maintained within the dashboard compartment, a "special alarm" that foils the Joker's attempt to steal the Batmobile, and even a complete "mobile crime lab" within the vehicle. Likewise, the Batmobile in the 1966 television series possesses a "Bing–Bong warning bell," a mobile Bat-phone, a "Batscope, complete with [a] TV-like viewing screen on the dash," and a "Bat-ray." Similarly, the Batmobile in the 1989 motion picture is equipped with a "pair of forward-facing Browning machine guns," "spherical bombs," "chassis-mounted shinbreakers," and "side-mounted disc launchers."

Because the Batmobile, as it appears in the comic books as well as in the 1966 television show and 1989 motion picture, displays "consistent, identifiable character traits and attributes," the second prong of the character analysis is met here.

Third, the Batmobile is "especially distinctive" and contains unique elements of expression. In addition to its status as Batman's loyal bat-themed sidekick complete with the character traits and physical characteristics described above, the Batmobile also has its unique and highly recognizable name. It is not merely a stock character.

Accordingly, applying our three-part test, we conclude that the Batmobile is a character that qualifies for copyright protection.

Towle raises two arguments against this conclusion. First, he points out that the Batmobile has at times appeared without its signature sleek "bat-like" features. He notes that in a 1988 comic book rendition, the Batmobile appears as a heavily armored tank with large tires and a rocket launcher. The Batmobile portrayed in the 1989 motion picture could also transform into a Batmissile. As we have noted, however, a consistent appearance is not as significant in our analysis as consistent character traits and attributes. The changes in appearance cited by Towle resemble costume changes that do not alter the Batmobile's innate characteristics, any more than James Bond's change from blue swimming trunks (in Casino Royale) to his classic tuxedo affects his iconic character. In context, the depictions of the Batmobile as a tank or missile promote its character as Batman's crime-fighting super car that can adapt to new situations as may be necessary to help Batman vanquish Gotham City's most notorious evildoers. See Halicki, 547 F.3d at 1224–25.

Second, Towle argues that a jury should decide the question whether the Batmobile displayed unique elements of expression and consistent, widely identifiable traits. We disagree. We have previously recognized that "[w]hether a particular work is subject to copyright protection is a mixed question of fact and law subject to de novo review." Societe Civile Succession Guino v. Renoir, 549 F.3d 1182, 1185 (9th Cir.2008). Neither party disputes the relevant facts regarding the Batmobile here. Accordingly, we are well-equipped to determine whether, as a matter of law, these undisputed facts establish that the Batmobile is an "especially distinctive" character entitled to copyright protection.

B

Having concluded that the Batmobile is a copyrightable character, we next consider whether Towle's copies of the Batmobile as it appeared in the 1966 and 1989 productions infringed on DC's copyright. Here, Towle does not contest that his replicas copy the Batmobile as it appeared in the 1966 and 1989 productions, even if they do not copy every feature. Rather, Towle's main argument is that DC does not own any copyright interest in the 1966 and 1989 productions and therefore lacks standing to pursue its copyright infringement claim against Towle.

To analyze Towle's argument, we begin with the applicable legal framework. Under the Copyright Act, "copyright ownership 'vests initially in the author or authors of the work,' which is generally the creator of the copyrighted work." U.S. Auto Parts Network, Inc. v. Parts Geek, LLC, 692 F.3d 1009, 1015 (9th Cir.2012) (quoting 17 U.S.C. § 201(a)). The owner of a copyright has a number of exclusive rights, including the right "to prepare derivative works" based on its original work of authorship, 17 U.S.C. § 106. A derivative work is a "work based upon one or more preexisting works that recasts, transforms, or adapts the preexisting work." Parts Geek, 692 F.3d at 1015–16 (alterations omitted) (quoting 17 U.S.C. § 101), such as a motion picture that is based on a literary work, see, e.g., Stewart v. Abend, 495 U.S. 207, 212–14 (1990), a three-dimensional costume based upon two-dimensional cartoon characters, see Entm't Research Grp., 122 F.3d at 1218, or three-dimensional figurines based on cartoon characters, Durham Indus., Inc. v. Tomy Corp., 630 F.2d 905, 909 (9th Cir.1980). If an unauthorized third party prepares a derivative work, the copyright owner of the underlying work can sue for infringement. See Silvers v. Sony Pictures Entm't, Inc., 402 F.3d 881, 885 (9th Cir.2005) (en banc) (citing 17 U.S.C. § 501(b)); see also, e.g., Air Pirates, 581 F.2d at 754–55; Durham Indus., 630 F.2d at 909.

A copyright owner also has the exclusive right to "authorize others to prepare derivative works based on their copyrighted works." Lewis Galoob Toys, Inc. v. Nintendo of Am., Inc., 964 F.2d 965, 967 (9th Cir.1992). When a copyright owner authorizes a third party to prepare a derivative work, the owner of the underlying work retains a copyright in that derivative work with respect to all of the elements that the derivative creator drew from the underlying work and employed in the derivative work. See Stewart, 495 U.S. at 223. By contrast, the creator of the derivative work has a copyright only as to those original aspects of the work that the derivative creator contributed, and only to the extent the derivative creator's contributions are "more than trivial." Parts Geek, 692 F.3d at 1016; see also

derivative rights

423

Stewart, 495 U.S. at 223. Moreover, a copyright in a derivative work "must not in any way affect the scope of any copyright protection in that preexisting material." Id.; see 17 U.S.C. § 103(a) ("The copyright in a . derivative work . is independent of, and does not affect or enlarge the scope, duration, ownership, or subsistence of, any copyright protection in the preexisting material."). Logically, therefore, if a third party copies a derivative work without authorization, it infringes the original copyright owner's copyright in the underlying work to the extent the unauthorized copy of the derivative work also copies the underlying work.

...

Towle argues that his replicas of the Batmobile as it appeared in the 1966 and 1989 productions do not infringe on DC's underlying work because those versions of the Batmobile look substantially different from any particular depiction of the Batmobile in the comic books. We reject this argument. As a copyrightable character, the Batmobile need not have a consistent appearance in every context, so long as the character has distinctive character traits and attributes. See, e.g., Warner Bros. Entm't, Inc., 644 F.3d at 599 n. 8. For instance, as we explained above, an automotive character may be copyrightable even if it appears as a yellow Fastback Ford Mustang in one film, and a silver 1967 Shelby GT–500 in another. Halicki, 547 F.3d at 1218, 1224. Here, DC retained its copyright in the Batmobile character even though its appearance in the 1966 and 1989 productions did not directly copy any comic book depiction. Because Towle produced a three-dimensional expression of the entire Batmobile character as it appeared in the 1966 and 1989 productions, and the Batmobile character in each of those productions was derived from DC's underlying work, we conclude that Towle's replicas necessarily copied some aspects of DC's underlying works. See e.g., Durham Indus., 630 F.2d at 909 (noting that three-dimensional "small, plastic, wind-up toys" of Disney characters Mickey, Donald, and Pluto were derivative works of these characters). Therefore, while we question whether a derivative work based on a character could ever have any independently copyrightable elements that would not "affect the scope of any copyright protection in that preexisting material," Parts Geek, 692 F.3d at 1016, we need not address that issue here.

For the same reason, we reject Towle's argument that his replicas of the Batmobile as it appeared in the 1966 television series and 1989 movie did not infringe DC's underlying work because the series and movies were produced by third parties, pursuant to sub-licensing agreements with ABC and BPI. Towle argues that while DC had an agreement with ABC and BPI to retain certain rights, DC failed to show that the agreements between ABC and BPI and the sublicensees also protected DC's interests. This argument fails because DC retained its rights to the underlying Batmobile character, and the creation of derivative works by sublicensees cannot deprive DC of such rights. DC may sue any third party who infringes on that work, even if the third party copies "indirectly via the derivative work." Nimmer on Copyright § 3.05.

C

Having established that the Batmobile character is entitled to copyright protection, and that DC owns a copyright to this character as it appears in the 1966 television series and 1989 motion picture, we conclude that Towle infringed upon these copyrights when he produced replicas of the Batmobile. While we ordinarily apply a two-part "substantial similarity" test to determine whether a plaintiff has established "copying of constituent elements of the work that are original," Funky Films, Inc. v. Time Warner Entm't Co., L.P., 462 F.3d 1072, 1076–77 (9th Cir.2006) (internal quotation marks omitted), we need not do so where, as here, "the copying of the substance of the entire work" is admitted, Narell v. Freeman, 872 F.2d 907, 910 (9th Cir.1989). Based on the undisputed facts, Towle's production and sale of replicas of the Batmobile, as it appeared in the 1966 and 1989 productions, infringed DC's exclusive right to produce derivative works of this character. Therefore, there is no genuine issue of material fact as to whether he infringed DC's copyrighted material. DC is entitled to judgment, and we affirm.

...

As Batman so sagely told Robin, "In our well-ordered society, protection of private property is essential." Batman: The Penguin Goes Straight, (Greenway Productions television broadcast March 23, 1966). Here, we conclude that the Batmobile character is the property of DC, and Towle infringed upon DC's property rights when he produced unauthorized derivative works of the Batmobile as it appeared in the 1966 television show and the 1989 motion picture. Accordingly, we affirm the district court.

AFFIRMED.

APPENDIX A

Batmobile Depicted in the 1966 Television Series

Towle Replica

APPENDIX B

Batmobile Depicted in the 1989 Motion Picture

Towle Replica

11.2. Friction with the Right of Publicity

849 F.2d 460 (1988)

BETTE MIDLER V. FORD MOTOR COMPANY

United States Court of Appeals for The Ninth Circuit

JOHN T. NOONAN, Circuit Judge:

This case centers on the protectibility of the voice of a celebrated chanteuse from commercial exploitation without her consent. Ford Motor Company and its advertising agency, Young & Rubi- cam, Inc., in 1985 advertised the Ford Lincoln

Mercury with a series of nineteen 30 or 60 second television commercials in what the agency called "The Yuppie Campaign." The aim was to make an emotional connection with Yuppies, bringing back memories of when they were in college. Differ- ent popular songs of the seventies were sung on each commercial. The agency tried to get "the original people," that is, the singers who had popularized the songs, to sing them. Failing in that endeavor in ten cases the agency had the songs sung by "sound alikes." Bette Midler, the plaintiff and appellant here, was done by a sound alike.

Midler is a nationally known actress and singer. She won a Grammy as early as 1973 as the Best New Artist of that year. Records made by her since then have gone Platinum and Gold. She was nominated in 1979 for an Academy award for Best Female Actress in The Rose, in which she por- trayed a pop singer. Newsweek in its June 30, 1986 issue described her as an "outrageously original singer/comedian." Time hailed her in its March 2, 1987 issue as "a legend" and "the most dynamic and poignant singer-actress of her time."

When Young & Rubicam was preparing the Yuppie Campaign it presented the commercial to its client by playing an edited version of Midler singing "Do You Want To Dance," taken from the 1973 Midler album, "The Divine Miss M." After the client accepted the idea and form of the com- mercial, the agency contacted Midler's manager, Jerry Edelstein. The conversation went as follows: "Hello, I am Craig Hazen from Young and Rubicam. I am calling you to find out if Bette Midler would be interested in doing . . .? Edelstein: "Is it a commercial?" "Yes." "We are not interested."

Undeterred, Young & Rubicam sought out Ula Hedwig whom it knew to have been one of "the Harlettes" a backup singer for Midler for ten years. Hedwig was told by Young & Rubicam that "they wanted someone who could sound like Bette Midler's recording of [Do You Want To Dance]." She was asked to make a "demo" tape of the song if she was interested. She made an a capella demo and got the job.

At the direction of Young & Rubicam, Hedwig then made a record for the commercial. The Midler record of "Do You Want To Dance" was first played to her. She was told to "sound as much as possible like the Bette Midler record," leaving out only a few "aahs" unsuitable for the commercial. Hedwig imitated Midler to the best of her ability.

After the commercial was aired Midler was told by "a number of people" that it "sounded exactly" like her record of "Do You Want To Dance." Hedwig was told by "many per- sonal friends" that they thought it was Midler singing the commercial. Ken Fritz, a personal man- ager in the entertainment business not associated with Midler, declares by affidavit that he heard the commercial on more than one occasion and thought Midler was doing the singing.

Neither the name nor the picture of Midler was used in the commercial; Young & Rubicam had a license from the copyright holder to use the song. At issue in this case is only the protec- tion of Midler's voice. The district court described the defendants' conduct as that "of the average thief." They decided, "If we can't buy it, we'll take it." The court nonetheless believed there was no legal principle preventing imitation of Midler's voice and so gave summary judgment for the defen- dants. Midler appeals.

The First Amendment protects much of what the media do in the reproduction of likenesses or sounds. A primary value is freedom of speech and press. Time, Inc. v. Hill, 385 U.S. 374, 388, 17 L. Ed. 2d 456, 87 S. Ct. 534 (1967). The purpose of the media's use of a person's identity is central. If the purpose is "informative or cultural" the use is immune; "if it serves no such function but merely exploits the individual portrayed, immunity will not be granted." Felcher and Rubin, "Pri- vacy, Publicity and the Portrayal of Real People by the Media," 88 Yale L.J. 1577, 1596 (1979). Moreover, federal copyright law preempts much of the area. "Mere imitation of a recorded per- formance would not constitute a copyright infringement even where one performer deliberately sets out to simulate another's performance as exactly as possible." Notes of Committee on the Judiciary, 17 U.S.C.A. ß 114(b). It is in the context of these First Amendment and federal copyright distinctions that we address the present appeal.

Nancy Sinatra once sued Goodyear Tire and Rubber Company on the basis of an advertising campaign by Young & Rubicam featuring "These Boots Are Made For Walkin'," a song closely identified with her; the female singers of the commercial were alleged to have imitated her voice and style and to have dressed and looked like her. The basis of Nancy Sinatra's complaint was un- fair competition; she claimed that the song and the arrangement had acquired "a secondary mean- ing" which, under California law, was protectible. This court noted that the defendants "had paid a very substantial sum to the copyright proprietor to obtain the license for the use of the song and all of its arrangements." To give Sinatra damages for their use of the song would clash with federal copyright law. Summary judgment for the defendants was affirmed. Sinatra v. Goodyear Tire & Rubber Co., 435 F.2d 711, 717-718 (9th Cir. 1970), cert. denied, 402 U.S. 906, 28 L. Ed. 2d 646, 91 S. Ct. 1376 (1971). If Midler were claiming a secondary meaning to "Do You Want To Dance" or seeking to prevent the defendants from using that song, she would fail like Sinatra. But that is not this case. Midler does not seek damages for Ford's use of "Do You Want To Dance," and thus her claim is not preempted by federal copyright law. Copyright protects "original works of authorship fixed in any tangible medium of expression." 17 U.S.C. ß 102(a). A voice is not copy- rightable. The sounds are not "fixed." What is put forward as protectible here is more personal than any work of authorship.

Bert Lahr once sued Adell Chemical Co. for selling Lestoil by means of a commercial in which an imitation of Lahr's voice accompanied a cartoon of a duck. Lahr alleged that his style of vocal delivery was distinctive in pitch, accent, inflection, and sounds. The First Circuit held that Lahr had stated a cause of action for unfair competition, that it could be found "that defendant's conduct saturated plaintiff's audience, curtailing his market." Lahr v. Adell Chemical Co., 300 F.2d 256, 259 (1st Cir. 1962). That case is more like this one. But we do not find unfair competition here. One-minute commercials of the sort the defendants put on would not have saturatedMidler's audience and curtailed her market. Midler did not do television commercials. The defen- dants were not in competition with her. See Halicki v. United Artists Communications, Inc., 812 F.2d 1213 (9th Cir. 1987).

California Civil Code section 3344 is also of no aid to Midler. The statute affords damages to a person injured by another who uses the person's "name, voice, signature, photograph or likeness, in any manner." The defendants did not use Midler's name or anything else whose use is prohibited by the statute. The voice they used was Hedwig's, not hers. The term "likeness" refers to a visual image not a vocal imitation. The statute, however, does not preclude Midler from pursuing any cause of action she may have at common law; the statute itself implies that such common law causes of ac- tion do exist because it says its remedies are merely "cumulative." Id. ß 3344(g).

The companion statute protecting the use of a deceased person's name, voice, signature, photo- graph or likeness states that the rights it recognizes are "property rights." Id. ß 990(b). By analogy the common law rights are also property rights. Appropriation of such common law rights is a tort in [**8] California. Motschenbacher v. R.J. Reynolds Tobacco Co., 498 F.2d 821 (9th Cir. 1974). In that case what the defendants used in their television commercial for Winston cigarettes was a photograph of a famous professional racing driver's racing car. The number of the car was changed and a wing-like device known as a "spoiler" was attached to the car; the car's features of white pinpointing, an oval medallion, and solid red coloring were retained. The driver, Lothar Motschenbacher, was in the car but his features were not visible. Some persons, viewing the com- mercial, correctly inferred that the car was his and that he was in the car and was therefore endors- ing the product. The defendants were held to have invaded a "proprietary interest" of Motschen- bacher in his own identity. Id. at 825.

Midler's case is different from Motschenbacher's. He and his car were physically used by the tobacco company's ad; he made part of his living out of giving commercial endorsements. But, as Judge Koelsch expressed it in Motschenbacher, California will recognize an injury from "an appro- priation of the attributes of one's identity." Id. at 824. It was irrelevant that Motschenbacher could not be identified in the ad. The ad suggested that it was he. The ad did so by emphasizing signs or symbols associated with him. In the same way the defendants here used an imitation to convey the impression that Midler was singing for them.

Why did the defendants ask Midler to sing if her voice was not of value to them? Why did they studiously acquire the services of a sound-alike and instruct her to imitate Midler if Midler's voice was not of value to them? What they sought was an attribute of Midler's identity. Its value was what the market would have paid for Midler to have sung the commercial in person.

A voice is more distinctive and more personal than the automobile accouterments protected in Motschenbacher. A voice is as distinctive and personal as a face. The human voice is one of the most palpable ways identity is manifested. We are all aware that a friend is at once known by a few words on the phone. At a philosophical level it has been observed that with the sound of a voice, "the other stands before me." D. Ihde, Listening and Voice 77 (1976). A fortiori, these observations hold true of singing, especially singing by a singer of renown. The singer manifests herself in the song. To impersonate her voice is to pirate her identity. See W. Keeton, D. Dobbs, R. Keeton, D. Owen, Prosser & Keeton on Torts 852 (5th ed. 1984).

We need not and do not go so far as to hold that every imitation of a voice to advertise mer- chandise is actionable. We hold only that when a distinctive voice of a professional singer is widely known and is deliberately imitated in order to sell a product, the sellers have appropriated what is not theirs and have committed a tort in California. Midler has made a showing, sufficient to defeat summary judgment, that the defendants here for their own profit in selling their product did appropriate part of her identity.

REVERSED AND REMANDED FOR TRIAL.

971 F.2d 1395 (1992)

WHITE v. SAMSUNG ELECTRONICS

United States Court of Appeals, Ninth Circuit

GOODWIN, Senior Circuit Judge:

This case involves a promotional "fame and fortune" dispute. In running a particular advertisement without Vanna White's permission, defendants Samsung Electronics America, Inc. (Samsung) and David Deutsch Associates, Inc. (Deutsch) attempted to capitalize on White's fame to enhance their fortune. White sued, alleging infringement of various intellectual property rights, but the district court granted summary judgment in favor of the defendants. We affirm in part, reverse in part, and remand.

Plaintiff Vanna White is the hostess of "Wheel of Fortune," one of the most popular game shows in television history. An estimated forty million people watch the program daily. Capitalizing on the fame which her participation in the show has bestowed on her, White markets her identity to various advertisers.

The dispute in this case arose out of a series of advertisements prepared for Samsung by Deutsch. The series ran in at least half a dozen publications with widespread, and in some cases national, circulation. Each of the advertisements in the series followed the same theme. Each depicted a current item from popular culture and a Samsung electronic product. Each was set in the twenty-first century and conveyed the message that the Samsung product would still be in use by that time. By hypothesizing outrageous future outcomes for the cultural items, the ads created humorous effects. For example, one lampooned current popular notions of an unhealthy diet by depicting a raw steak with the caption: "Revealed to be health food. 2010 A.D." Another depicted irreverent "news"-show host Morton Downey Jr. in front of an American flag with the caption: "Presidential candidate. 2008 A.D."

The advertisement which prompted the current dispute was for Samsung videocassette recorders (VCRs). The ad depicted a robot, dressed in a wig, gown, and jewelry which Deutsch consciously selected to resemble White's hair and dress. The robot was posed next to a game board which is instantly recognizable as the Wheel of Fortune game show set, in a stance for which White is famous. The caption of the ad read: "Longest-running game show. 2012 A.D." Defendants referred to the ad as the "Vanna White" ad. Unlike the other celebrities used in the campaign, White neither consented to the ads nor was she paid.

Following the circulation of the robot ad, White sued Samsung and Deutsch in federal district court under: (1) California Civil Code § 3344; (2) the California common law right of publicity; and (3) § 43(a) of the Lanham Act, 15 U.S.C. § 1125(a). The district court granted summary judgment [1397] against White on each of her claims. White now appeals.

I. Section 3344

White first argues that the district court erred in rejecting her claim under section 3344. Section 3344(a) provides, in pertinent part, that "[a]ny person who knowingly uses another's name, voice, signature, photograph, or likeness, in any manner, ... for purposes of advertising or selling, ... without such person's prior consent ... shall be liable for any damages sustained by the person or persons injured as a result thereof."

White argues that the Samsung advertisement used her "likeness" in contravention of section 3344. In Midler v. Ford Motor Co., 849 F.2d 460 (9th Cir.1988), this court rejected Bette Midler's section 3344 claim concerning a Ford television commercial in which a Midler "sound-alike" sang a song which Midler had made famous. In rejecting Midler's claim, this court noted that "[t]he defendants did not use Midler's name or anything else whose use is prohibited by the statute. The voice they used was [another person's], not hers. The term `likeness' refers to a visual image not a vocal imitation." Id. at 463.

In this case, Samsung and Deutsch used a robot with mechanical features, and not, for example, a manikin molded to White's precise features. Without deciding for all purposes when a caricature or impressionistic resemblance might become a "likeness," we agree with the district court that the robot at issue here was not White's "likeness" within the meaning of section 3344. Accordingly, we affirm the court's dismissal of White's section 3344 claim.

II. Right of Publicity

White next argues that the district court erred in granting summary judgment to defendants on White's common law right of publicity claim. In Eastwood v. Superior Court, 149 Cal.App.3d 409, 198 Cal. Rptr. 342 (1983), the California court of appeal stated that the common law right of publicity cause of action "may be pleaded by alleging (1) the defendant's use of the plaintiff's identity; (2) the appropriation of plaintiff's name or likeness to defendant's advantage, commercially or otherwise; (3) lack of consent; and (4) resulting injury." Id. at 417, 198 Cal.Rptr. 342 (citing Prosser, Law of Torts (4th ed. 1971) § 117, pp. 804-807). The district court dismissed White's claim for failure to satisfy Eastwood's second prong, reasoning that defendants had not appropriated White's "name or likeness" with their robot ad. We agree that the robot ad did not make use of White's name or likeness. However, the common law right of publicity is not so confined.

The Eastwood court did not hold that the right of publicity cause of action could be pleaded only by alleging an appropriation of name or likeness. Eastwood involved an unauthorized use of photographs of Clint Eastwood and of his name. Accordingly, the Eastwood court had no occasion to consider the extent beyond the use of name or likeness to which the right of publicity reaches. That court held only that the right of publicity cause of action "may be" pleaded by alleging, inter alia, appropriation of name or likeness, not that the action may be pleaded only in those terms.

The "name or likeness" formulation referred to in Eastwood originated not as an element of the right of publicity cause of action, but as a description of the types of cases in which the cause of action had been recognized. The source of this formulation is Prosser, Privacy, 48 Cal.L.Rev. 383, 401-07 (1960), one of the earliest and most enduring articulations of the common law right of publicity cause of action. In looking at the case law to that point, Prosser recognized that right of publicity cases involved one of two basic factual scenarios: name appropriation, and picture or other likeness appropriation. Id. at 401-02, nn. 156-57.

Even though Prosser focused on appropriations of name or likeness in discussing the right of publicity, he noted that "[i]t is not impossible that there might be appropriation of the plaintiff's identity, as by impersonation, without the use of either his name or his likeness, and that this would [1398] be an invasion of his right of privacy." Id. at 401, n. 155.[1] At the time Prosser wrote, he noted however, that "[n]o such case appears to have arisen." Id.

Since Prosser's early formulation, the case law has borne out his insight that the right of publicity is not limited to the appropriation of name or likeness. In Motschenbacher v. R.J. Reynolds Tobacco Co., 498 F.2d 821 (9th Cir.1974), the defendant had used a photograph of the plaintiff's race car in a television commercial. Although the plaintiff appeared driving the car in the photograph, his features were not visible. Even though the defendant had not appropriated the plaintiff's name or likeness, this court held that plaintiff's California right of publicity claim should reach the jury.

In Midler, this court held that, even though the defendants had not used Midler's name or likeness, Midler had stated a claim for violation of her California common law right of publicity because "the defendants ... for their own profit in selling their product did appropriate part of her identity" by using a Midler sound-alike. Id. at 463-64.

In Carson v. Here's Johnny Portable Toilets, Inc., 698 F.2d 831 (6th Cir.1983), the defendant had marketed portable toilets under the brand name "Here's Johnny" — Johnny Carson's signature "Tonight Show" introduction — without Carson's permission. The district court had dismissed Carson's Michigan common law right of publicity claim because the defendants had not used Carson's "name or likeness." Id. at 835. In reversing the district court, the sixth circuit found "the district court's conception of the right of publicity ... too narrow" and held that the right was implicated because the defendant had appropriated Carson's identity by using, inter alia, the phrase "Here's Johnny." Id. at 835-37.

These cases teach not only that the common law right of publicity reaches means of appropriation other than name or likeness, but that the specific means of appropriation are relevant only for determining whether the defendant has in fact appropriated the plaintiff's identity. The right of publicity does not require that appropriations of identity be accomplished through particular means to be actionable. It is noteworthy that the Midler and Carson defendants not only avoided using the plaintiff's name or likeness, but they also avoided appropriating the celebrity's voice, signature, and photograph. The photograph in Motschenbacher did include the plaintiff, but because the plaintiff was not visible the driver could have been an actor or dummy and the analysis in the case would have been the same.

Although the defendants in these cases avoided the most obvious means of appropriating the plaintiffs' identities, each of their actions directly implicated the commercial interests which the right of publicity is designed to protect. As the Carson court explained:

[t]he right of publicity has developed to protect the commercial interest of celebrities in their identities. The theory of the right is that a celebrity's identity can be valuable in the promotion of products, and the celebrity has an interest that may be protected from the unauthorized commercial exploitation of that identity.... If the celebrity's identity is commercially exploited, there has been an invasion of his right whether or not his "name or likeness" is used.

Carson, 698 F.2d at 835. It is not important how the defendant has appropriated the plaintiff's identity, but whether the defendant has done so. Motschenbacher, Midler, and Carson teach the impossibility of treating the right of publicity as guarding only against a laundry list of specific means of appropriating identity. A rule which says that the right of publicity can be infringed only through the use of nine different methods of appropriating identity merely challenges the clever advertising strategist to come up with the tenth.

Indeed, if we treated the means of appropriation as dispositive in our analysis of the right of publicity, we would not only weaken the right but effectively eviscerate it. The right would fail to protect those plaintiffs most in need of its protection. Advertisers use celebrities to promote their products. The more popular the celebrity, the greater the number of people who recognize her, and the greater the visibility for the product. The identities of the most popular celebrities are not only the most attractive for advertisers, but also the easiest to evoke without resorting to obvious means such as name, likeness, or voice.

Consider a hypothetical advertisement which depicts a mechanical robot with male features, an African-American complexion, and a bald head. The robot is wearing black hightop Air Jordan basketball sneakers, and a red basketball uniform with black trim, baggy shorts, and the number 23 (though not revealing "Bulls" or "Jordan" lettering). The ad depicts the robot dunking a basketball one-handed, stiff-armed, legs extended like open scissors, and tongue hanging out. Now envision that this ad is run on television during professional basketball games. Considered individually, the robot's physical attributes, its dress, and its stance tell us little. Taken together, they lead to the only conclusion that any sports viewer who has registered a discernible pulse in the past five years would reach: the ad is about Michael Jordan.

Viewed separately, the individual aspects of the advertisement in the present case say little. Viewed together, they leave little doubt about the celebrity the ad is meant to depict. The female-shaped robot is wearing a long gown, blond wig, and large jewelry. Vanna White dresses exactly like this at times, but so do many other women. The robot is in the process of turning a block letter on a game-board. Vanna White dresses like this while turning letters on a game-board but perhaps similarly attired Scrabble-playing women do this as well. The robot is standing on what looks to be the Wheel of Fortune game show set. Vanna White dresses like this, turns letters, and does this on the Wheel of Fortune game show. She is the only one. Indeed, defendants themselves referred to their ad as the "Vanna White" ad. We are not surprised.

Television and other media create marketable celebrity identity value. Considerable energy and ingenuity are expended by those who have achieved celebrity value to exploit it for profit. The law protects the celebrity's sole right to exploit this value whether the celebrity has achieved her fame out of rare ability, dumb luck, or a combination thereof. We decline Samsung and Deutch's invitation to permit the evisceration of the common law right of publicity through means as facile as those in this case. Because White has alleged facts showing that Samsung and Deutsch had appropriated her identity, the district court erred by rejecting, on summary judgment, White's common law right of publicity claim.

...

IV. The Parody Defense

In defense, defendants cite a number of cases for the proposition that their robot ad constituted protected speech. The only cases they cite which are even remotely relevant to this case are Hustler Magazine v. Falwell, 485 U.S. 46, 108 S.Ct. 876, 99 L.Ed.2d 41 (1988) and L.L. Bean, Inc. v. Drake Publishers, Inc., 811 F.2d 26 (1st Cir.1987). Those cases involved parodies of advertisements run for the purpose of poking fun at Jerry Falwell and L.L. Bean, respectively. This case involves a true advertisement run for the purpose of selling Samsung VCRs. The ad's spoof of Vanna White and Wheel of Fortune is subservient and only tangentially related to the ad's primary message: "buy Samsung VCRs." Defendants' parody arguments are better addressed to non-commercial parodies.[3] The difference between a "parody" and a "knock-off" is the difference between fun and profit.

V. Conclusion

In remanding this case, we hold only that White has pleaded claims which can go to the jury for its decision.

AFFIRMED IN PART, REVERSED IN PART, and REMANDED.

KOZINSKI, Circuit Judge, with whom Circuit Judges O'SCANNLAIN and KLEINFELD join, dissenting from the order rejecting the suggestion for rehearing en banc.

I

Saddam Hussein wants to keep advertisers from using his picture in unflattering contexts. Clint Eastwood doesn't want tabloids to write about him. Rudolf Valentino's heirs want to control his film biography. The Girl Scouts don't want their image soiled by association with certain activities. George Lucas wants to keep Strategic Defense Initiative fans from calling it "Star Wars." Pepsico doesn't want singers to use the word "Pepsi" in their songs. Guy Lombardo wants an exclusive property right to ads that show big bands playing on New Year's Eve. Uri Geller thinks he should be paid for ads showing psychics bending metal through telekinesis. Paul Prudhomme, that household name, thinks the same about ads featuring corpulent bearded chefs. And scads of copyright holders see purple when their creations are made fun of.

Something very dangerous is going on here. Private property, including intellectual property, is essential to our way of life. It provides an incentive for investment and innovation; it stimulates the flourishing of our culture; it protects the moral entitlements of people to the fruits of their labors. But reducing too much to private property can be bad medicine. Private land, for instance, is far more useful if separated from other private land by public streets, roads and highways. Public parks, utility rights-of- way and sewers reduce the amount of land in private hands, but vastly enhance the value of the property that remains.

So too it is with intellectual property. Overprotecting intellectual property is as harmful as underprotecting it. Creativity is impossible without a rich public domain. Nothing today, likely nothing since we tamed fire, is genuinely new: Culture, like science and technology, grows by accretion, each new creator building on the works of those who came before. Overprotection stifles the very creative forces it's supposed to nurture.

The panel's opinion is a classic case of overprotection. Concerned about what it sees as a wrong done to Vanna White, the panel majority erects a property right of remarkable and dangerous breadth: Under the majority's opinion, it's now a tort for advertisers to remind the public of a celebrity. Not to use a celebrity's name, voice, signature or likeness; not to imply the celebrity endorses a product; but simply to evoke the celebrity's image in the public's mind. This Orwellian notion withdraws far more from the public domain than prudence and common sense allow. It conflicts with the Copyright Act and the Copyright Clause. It raises serious First Amendment problems. It's bad law, and it deserves a long, hard second look.

II

Samsung ran an ad campaign promoting its consumer electronics. Each ad depicted a Samsung product and a humorous prediction: One showed a raw steak with the caption "Revealed to be health food. 2010 A.D." Another showed Morton Downey, Jr. in front of an American flag with the caption "Presidential candidate.

2008 A.D." The ads were meant to convey—humorously—that Samsung products would still be in use twenty years from now.

The ad that spawned this litigation starred a robot dressed in a wig, gown and jewelry reminiscent of Vanna White's hair and dress; the robot was posed next to a Wheel-of-Fortune-like game board. See Appendix. The caption read "Longest-running game show. 2012 A.D." The gag here, I take it, was that Samsung would still be around when White had been replaced by a robot.

Perhaps failing to see the humor, White sued, alleging Samsung infringed her right of publicity by "appropriating" her "identity." Under California law, White has the exclusive right to use her name, likeness, signature and voice for commercial purposes. Cal. Civ. Code § 3344(a); Eastwood v. Superior Court, 149 Cal. App. 3d 409, 417, 198 Cal. Rptr. 342, 347 (1983). But Samsung didn't use her name, voice or signature, and it certainly didn't use her likeness. The ad just wouldn't have been funny had it depicted White or someone who resembled her—the whole joke was that the game show host(ess) was a robot, not a real person. No one seeing the ad could have thought this was supposed to be White in 2012.

The district judge quite reasonably held that, because Samsung didn't use White's name, likeness, voice or signature, it didn't violate her right of publicity. 971 F.2d at 1396–97. Not so, says the panel majority: The California right of publicity can't possibly be limited to name and likeness. If it were, the majority reasons, a "clever advertising strategist" could avoid using White's name or likeness but nevertheless remind people of her with impunity, "effectively eviscerat[ing]" her rights. To prevent this "evisceration," the panel majority holds that the right of publicity must extend beyond name and likeness, to any "appropriation" of White's "identity"—anything that "evoke[s]" her personality. Id. at 1398–99.

III

But what does "evisceration" mean in intellectual property law? Intellectual property rights aren't like some constitutional rights, absolute guarantees protected against all kinds of interference, subtle as well as blatant. They cast no penumbras, emit no emanations: The very point of intellectual property laws is that they protect only against certain specific kinds of appropriation. I can't publish unauthorized copies of, say, Presumed Innocent; I can't make a movie out of it. But I'm perfectly free to write a book about an idealistic young prosecutor on trial for a crime he didn't commit. So what if I got the idea from Presumed Innocent? So what if it reminds readers of the original? Have I "eviscerated" Scott Turow's intellectual property rights? Certainly not. All creators draw in part on the work of those who came before, referring to it, building on it, poking fun at it; we call this creativity, not piracy.

The majority isn't, in fact, preventing the "evisceration" of Vanna White's existing rights; it's creating a new and much broader property right, a right unknown in California law. It's replacing the existing balance between the interests of the celebrity and those of the public by a different balance, one substantially more favorable to the celebrity. Instead of having an exclusive right in her name, likeness, signature or voice, every famous person now has an exclusive right to anything that reminds the viewer of her. After all, that's all Samsung did: It used an inanimate object to remind people of White, to "evoke [her identity]." 971 F.2d at 1399.

Consider how sweeping this new right is. What is it about the ad that makes people think of White? It's not the robot's wig, clothes or jewelry; there must be ten million blond women (many of them quasi-famous) who wear dresses and jewelry like White's. It's that the robot is posed near the "Wheel of Fortune" game board. Remove the game board from the ad, and no one would think of Vanna White. See Appendix. But once you include the game board, anybody standing beside it—a brunette woman, a man wearing women's clothes, a monkey in a wig and gown— would evoke White's image, precisely the way the robot did. It's the "Wheel of Fortune" set, not the robot's face or dress or jewelry that evokes White's image. The panel is giving White an exclusive right not in what she looks like or who she is, but in what she does for a living.

This is entirely the wrong place to strike the balance. Intellectual property rights aren't free: They're imposed at the expense of future creators and of the public at large. Where would we be if Charles Lindbergh had an exclusive right in the concept of a heroic solo aviator? If Arthur Conan Doyle had gotten a copyright in the idea of the detective story, or Albert Einstein had patented the theory of relativity? If every author and celebrity had been given the right to keep people from mocking them or their work? Surely this would have made the world poorer, not richer, culturally as well as economically.

This is why intellectual property law is full of careful balances between what's set aside for the owner and what's left in the public domain for the rest of us: The relatively short life of patents; the longer, but finite, life of copyrights; copyright's idea-expression dichotomy; the fair use doctrine; the prohibition on copyrighting facts; the compulsory license of television broadcasts and musical compositions; federal preemption of overbroad state intellectual property laws; the nominative use doctrine in trademark law; the right to make soundalike recordings. All of these diminish an intellectual property owner's rights. All let the public use something created by someone else. But all are necessary to maintain a free environment in which creative genius can flourish.

The intellectual property right created by the panel here has none of these essential limitations: No fair use exception; no right to parody; no idea-expression dichotomy. It impoverishes the public domain, to the detriment of future creators and the public at large. Instead of well-defined, limited characteristics such as name, likeness or voice, advertisers will now have to cope with vague claims of "appropriation of identity," claims often made by people with a wholly exaggerated sense of their own fame and significance. See pp. 1512–13 & notes 1-10 supra. Future Vanna Whites might not get the chance to create their personae, because their employers may fear some celebrity will claim the persona is too similar to her own. The public will be robbed of parodies of celebrities, and our culture will be deprived of the valuable safety valve that parody and mockery create.

Moreover, consider the moral dimension, about which the panel majority seems to have gotten so exercised. Saying Samsung "appropriated" something of White's begs the question: Should White have the exclusive right to something as broad and amorphous as her "identity"? Samsung's ad didn't simply copy White's schtick—like all parody, it created something new. True, Samsung did it to make money, but White does whatever she does to make money, too; the majority talks of "the difference between fun and profit," 971 F.2d at 1401, but in the entertainment industry fun is profit. Why is Vanna White's right to exclusive for-profit use of her persona—a persona that might not even be her own creation, but that of a writer, director or producer—superior to Samsung's right to profit by creating its own inventions? Why should she have such absolute rights to control the conduct of others, unlimited by the idea-expression dichotomy or by the fair use doctrine?

To paraphrase only slightly Feist Publications, Inc. v. Rural Telephone Service Co., 499 U.S. 340, — – —, 111 S. Ct. 1282, 1289–90, 113 L. Ed. 2d 358 (1991), it may seem unfair that much of the fruit of a creator's labor may be used by others without compensation. But this is not some unforeseen byproduct of our intellectual property system; it is the system's very essence. Intellectual property law assures authors the right to their original expression, but encourages others to build freely on the ideas that underlie it. This result is neither unfair nor unfortunate: It is the means by which intellectual property law advances the progress of science and art. We give authors certain exclusive rights, but in exchange we get a richer public domain. The majority ignores this wise teaching, and all of us are the poorer for it.

IV

The panel, however, does more than misinterpret California law: By refusing to recognize a parody exception to the right of publicity, the panel directly contradicts the federal Copyright Act. Samsung didn't merely parody Vanna White. It parodied Vanna White appearing in "Wheel of Fortune," a copyrighted television show, and parodies of copyrighted works are governed by federal copyright law.

Copyright law specifically gives the world at large the right to make "fair use" parodies, parodies that don't borrow too much of the original. Fisher v. Dees, 794 F.2d 432, 435 (9th Cir. 1986). Federal copyright law also gives the copyright owner the exclusive right to create (or license the creation of) derivative works, which include parodies that borrow too much to qualify as "fair use." See Acuff-Rose Music, Inc. v. Campbell, 972 F.2d 1429, 1434–35 (6th Cir. 1992). When Mel Brooks, for instance, decided to parody Star Wars, he had two options: He could have stuck with his fair use rights under 17 U.S.C. § 107, or he could have gotten a license to make a derivative work under 17 U.S.C. § 106(b) from the holder of the Star Wars copyright. To be safe, he probably did the latter, but once he did, he was guaranteed a perfect right to make his movie.

The majority's decision decimates this federal scheme. It's impossible to parody a movie or a TV show without at the same time "evok[ing]" the "identit[ies]" of the actors. You can't have a mock Star Wars without a mock Luke Skywalker, Han Solo and Princess Leia, which in turn means a mock Mark Hamill, Harrison Ford and Carrie Fisher. You can't have a mock Batman commercial without a mock Batman, which means someone emulating the mannerisms of Adam West or Michael

Keaton. See Carlos V. Lozano, West Loses Lawsuit over Batman TV Commercial, L.A. Times, Jan. 18, 1990, at B3 (describing Adam West's right of publicity lawsuit over a commercial produced under license from DC Comics, owner of the Batman copyright). The public's right to make a fair use parody and the copyright owner's right to license a derivative work are useless if the parodist is held hostage by every actor whose "identity" he might need to "appropriate."

Our court is in a unique position here. State courts are unlikely to be particularly sensitive to federal preemption, which, after all, is a matter of first concern to the federal courts. The Supreme Court is unlikely to consider the issue because the right of publicity seems so much a matter of state law. That leaves us. It's our responsibility to keep the right of publicity from taking away federally granted rights, either from the public at large or from a copyright owner. We must make sure state law doesn't give the Vanna Whites and Adam Wests of the world a veto over fair use parodies of the shows in which they appear, or over copyright holders' exclusive right to license derivative works of those shows. In a case where the copyright owner isn't even a party—where no one has the interests of copyright owners at heart—the majority creates a rule that greatly diminishes the rights of copyright holders in this circuit.

V

The majority's decision also conflicts with the federal copyright system in another, more insidious way. Under the dormant Copyright Clause, state intellectual property laws can stand only so long as they don't "prejudice the interests of other States." Goldstein v. California, 412 U.S. 546, 558, 93 S. Ct. 2303, 2310, 37 L. Ed. 2d 163 (1973). A state law criminalizing record piracy, for instance, is permissible because citizens of other states would "remain free to copy within their borders those works which may be protected elsewhere." Id. But the right of publicity isn't geographically limited. A right of publicity created by one state applies to conduct everywhere, so long as it involves a celebrity domiciled in that state. If a Wyoming resident creates an ad that features a California domiciliary's name or likeness, he'll be subject to California right of publicity law even if he's careful to keep the ad from being shown in California. See Acme Circus Operating Co. v. Kuperstock, 711 F.2d 1538, 1540 (11th Cir. 1983); Groucho Marx Prods. v. Day and Night Co., 689 F.2d 317, 320 (2d Cir. 1982); see also Factors Etc. v. Pro Arts, 652 F.2d 278, 281 (2d Cir. 1981).

The broader and more ill-defined one state's right of publicity, the more it interferes with the legitimate interests of other states. A limited right that applies to unauthorized use of name and likeness probably does not run afoul of the Copyright Clause, but the majority's protection of "identity" is quite another story. Under the majority's approach, any time anybody in the United States—even somebody who lives in a state with a very narrow right of publicity—creates an ad, he takes the risk that it might remind some segment of the public of somebody, perhaps somebody with only a local reputation, somebody the advertiser has never heard of. See note 17 supra (right of publicity is infringed by unintentional appropriations). So you made a commercial in Florida and one of the characters reminds Reno residents of their favorite local TV anchor (a California domiciliary)? Pay up.

This is an intolerable result, as it gives each state far too much control over artists in other states. No California statute, no California court has actually tried to reach this far. It is ironic that it is we who plant this kudzu in the fertile soil of our federal system.

VI

Finally, I can't see how giving White the power to keep others from evoking her image in the public's mind can be squared with the First Amendment. Where does White get this right to control our thoughts? The majority's creation goes way beyond the protection given a trademark or a copyrighted work, or a person's name or likeness. All those things control one particular way of expressing an idea, one way of referring to an object or a person. But not allowing any means of reminding people of someone? That's a speech restriction unparalleled in First Amendment law.

What's more, I doubt even a name-and-likeness-only right of publicity can stand without a parody exception. The First Amendment isn't just about religion or politics—it's also about protecting the free development of our national culture. Parody, humor, irreverence are all vital components of the marketplace of ideas. The last thing we need, the last thing the First Amendment will tolerate, is a law that lets public figures keep people from mocking them, or from "evok[ing]" their images in the mind of the public. 971 F.2d at 1399.

The majority dismisses the First Amendment issue out of hand because Samsung's ad was commercial speech. Id. at 1401 & n.3. So what? Commercial speech may be less protected by the First Amendment than noncommercial speech, but less protected means protected nonetheless. Central Hudson Gas & Elec. Corp. v. Public Serv. Comm'n, 447 U.S. 557, 100 S. Ct. 2343, 65 L. Ed. 2d 341 (1980). And there are very good reasons for this. Commercial speech has a profound effect on our culture and our attitudes. Neutral-seeming ads influence people's social and political attitudes, and themselves arouse political controversy. "Where's the Beef?" turned from an advertising catchphrase into the only really memorable thing about the 1984 presidential campaign. Four years later, Michael Dukakis called George Bush "the Joe Isuzu of American politics."

In our pop culture, where salesmanship must be entertaining and entertainment must sell, the line between the commercial and noncommercial has not merely blurred; it has disappeared. Is the Samsung parody any different from a parody on Saturday Night Live or in Spy Magazine? Both are equally profit-motivated. Both use a celebrity's identity to sell things—one to sell VCRs, the other to sell advertising. Both mock their subjects. Both try to make people laugh. Both add something, perhaps something worthwhile and memorable, perhaps not, to our culture. Both are things that the people being portrayed might dearly want to suppress. See notes 1 & 29 supra.

Commercial speech is a significant, valuable part of our national discourse. The Supreme Court has recognized as much, and has insisted that lower courts carefully scrutinize commercial speech restrictions, but the panel totally fails to do this. The panel majority doesn't even purport to apply the Central Hudson test, which the Supreme Court devised specifically for determining whether a commercial speech restriction is valid. The majority doesn't ask, as Central Hudson requires, whether the speech restriction is justified by a substantial state interest. It doesn't ask whether the restriction directly advances the interest. It doesn't ask whether the restriction is narrowly tailored to the interest. See id. at 566, 100 S.Ct. at 2351. These are all things the Supreme Court told us—in no uncertain terms—we must consider; the majority opinion doesn't even mention them.

...

VII

For better or worse, we are the Court of Appeals for the Hollywood Circuit. Millions of people toil in the shadow of the law we make, and much of their livelihood is made possible by the existence of intellectual property rights. But much of their livelihood—and much of the vibrancy of our culture—also depends on the existence of other intangible rights: The right to draw ideas from a rich and varied public domain, and the right to mock, for profit as well as fun, the cultural icons of our time.

In the name of avoiding the "evisceration" of a celebrity's rights in her image, the majority diminishes the rights of copyright holders and the public at large. In the name of fostering creativity, the majority suppresses it. Vanna White and those like her have been given something they never had before, and they've been given it at our expense. I cannot agree.

12. Copyright on Software

714 F.2d 1240 (1983)

APPLE COMPUTER, INC. V. FRANKLIN COMPUTER CORPORATION

U.S. Court of Appeals Third Circuit

Sloviter, Circuit Judge.

I. Introduction

Apple Computer, Inc. appeals from the district court's denial of a motion to preliminarily enjoin Franklin Computer Corp. from infringing the copyrights Apple holds on fourteen computer programs.

The decision to grant or refuse to grant a preliminary injunction is within the discretion of the district court. See A.O. Smith Corp. v. FTC, 530 F.2d 515, 525 (3d Cir. 1976). Although the scope of our review of the action of the district court in ruling on a motion for preliminary injunction is narrow, reversal is warranted if the trial court has abused its discretion or committed error in applying the law.

Kennecott Corp. v. Smith, 637 F.2d 181, 187 (3d Cir. 1980). As the Second Circuit has stated recently, "Despite oft repeated statements that the issuance of a preliminary injunction rests in the discretion of the trial judge whose decisions will be reversed only for 'abuse', a court of appeals must reverse if the district court has proceeded on the basis of an erroneous view of the applicable law." Donovan v. Bierwirth, 680 F.2d 263, 269 (2d Cir.), cert. denied, 103 S.Ct. 488 (1982).

In this case the district court denied the preliminary injunction, inter alia, because it had "some doubt as to the copyrightability of the programs." Apple Computer, Inc. v. Franklin Computer Corp., 545 F. Supp. 812(E.D. Pa. 1982). This legal ruling is fundamental to all future proceedings in this action and, as the parties and amici curiae seem to agree, has considerable significance to the computer services industry.1 Because we conclude that the district court proceeded under an erroneous view of the applicable law, we reverse the denial of the preliminary injunction and remand.

II. Facts and Procedural History

Apple, one of the computer industry leaders, manufactures and markets personal computers (micro-computers), related peripheral equipment such as disk drives (peripherals), and computer programs (software). It presently manufactures Apple II computers and distributes over 150 programs. Apple has sold over 400,000 Apple II computers, employs approximately 3,000 people, and had annual sales of $335,000,000 for fiscal year 1981. One of the byproducts of Apple's success is the independent development by third parties of numerous computer programs which are designed to run on the Apple II computer.

Franklin, the defendant below, manufactures and sells the ACE 100 personal computer and at the time of the hearing employed about 75 people and had sold fewer than 1,000 computers. The ACE 100 was designed to be "Apple compatible," so that peripheral equipment and software developed for use with the Apple II computer could be used in conjunction with the ACE 100. Franklin's copying of Apple's operating system computer programs in an effort to achieve such compatibility precipitated this suit.

Like all computers both the Apple II and ACE 100 have a central processing unit (CPU) which is the integrated circuit that executes programs. In lay terms, the CPU does the work it is instructed to do. Those instructions are contained on computer programs.

There are three levels of computer language in which computer programs may be written. High level language, such as the commonly used BASIC or FORTRAN, uses English words and symbols, and is relatively easy to learn and understand (e.g., "GO TO 40" tells the computer to skip intervening steps and go to the step at line 40). A somewhat lower level language is assembly language, which consists of alphanumeric labels (e.g., "ADC" means "add with carry"). Statements in high level language, and apparently also statements in assembly language, are referred to as written in "source code." The third, or lowest level computer language, is machine language, a binary language using two symbols, 0 and 1, to indicate an open or closed switch (e.g., "01101001" means, to the Apple, add two numbers and save the result). Statements in machine language are referred to as written in "object code."

The CPU can only follow instructions written in object code. However, programs are usually written in source code which is more intelligible to humans. Programs written in source code can be converted or translated by a "compiler" program into object code for use by the computer. Programs are generally distributed only in their object code version stored on a memory device.

A computer program can be stored or fixed on a variety of memory devices, two of which are of particular relevance for this case. The ROM (Read Only Memory) is an internal permanent memory device consisting of a semi-conductor "chip" which is incorporated into the circuitry of the computer. A program in object code is embedded on a ROM before it is incorporated in the computer. Information stored on a ROM can only be read, not erased or rewritten. The ACE 100 apparently contains EPROMS (Erasable Programmable Read Only Memory) on which the stored information can be erased and the chip reprogrammed, but the district court found that for purposes of this proceeding, the difference between ROMs and EPROMs is inconsequential. 545 F. Supp. at 813 n.3, 215 USPQ 935, 938 n.3. The other device used for storing the programs at issue is a diskette or "floppy disk", an auxiliary memory device consisting of a flexible magnetic disk resembling a phonograph record, which can be inserted into the computer and from which data or instructions can be read.

Computer programs can be categorized by function as either application programs or operating system programs. Application programs usually perform a specific task for the computer user, such as word processing, checkbook balancing, or playing a game. In contrast, operating system programs generally manage the internal functions of the computer or facilitate use of application programs. The parties agree that the fourteen computer programs at issue in this suit are operating system programs.

Apple filed suit in the United States District Court for the Eastern District of Pennsylvania pursuant to 28 U.S.C. §1338 on May 12, 1982, alleging that Franklin was liable for copyright infringement of the fourteen computer programs, patent infringement, unfair competition, and misappropriation. Franklin's answer in respect to the copyright counts included the affirmative defense that the programs contained no copyrightable subject matter. Franklin counterclaimed for declaratory judgment that the copyright registrations were invalid and unenforceable, and sought affirmative relief on the basis of Apple's alleged misuse. Franklin also moved to dismiss eleven of the fourteen copyright infringement counts on the ground that Apple failed to comply with the procedural requirements for suit under 17 U.S.C. §§410, 411.

After expedited discovery, Apple moved for a preliminary injunction to restrain Franklin from using, copying, selling, or infringing Apple's copyrights. The district court held a three day evidentiary hearing limited to the copyright infringement claims. Apple produced evidence at the hearing in the form of affidavits and testimony that programs sold by Franklin in conjunction with its ACE 100 computer were virtually identical with those covered by the fourteen Apple copyrights. The variations that did exist were minor, consisting merely of such things as deletion of reference to Apple or its copyright notice. James Huston, an Apple systems programmer, concluded that the Franklin programs were "unquestionably copied from Apple and could not have been independently created." He reached this conclusion not only because it is "almost impossible for so many lines of code" to be identically written, but also because his name, which he had embedded in one program (Master Create), and the word "Applesoft", which was embedded in another (DOS 3.3), appeared on the Franklin master disk. Apple estimated the "works in suit" took 46 man-months to produce at a cost of over $740,000, not including the time or cost of creating or acquiring earlier versions of the programs or the expense of marketing the programs.

Franklin did not dispute that it copied the Apple programs. Its witness admitted copying each of the works in suit from the Apple programs. Its factual defense was directed to its contention that it was not feasible for Franklin to write its own operating system programs. David McWherter, now Franklin's vice-president of engineering, testified he spent 30-40 hours in November 1981 making a study to determine if it was feasible for Franklin to write its own autostart ROM program and concluded it was not because "there were just too many entry points in relationship to the number of instructions in the program." Entry points at specific locations in the program can be used by programmers to mesh their application programs with the operating system program. McWherter concluded that use of the identical signals was necessary in order to ensure 100% compatibility with application programs created to run on the Apple computer. He admitted that he never attempted to rewrite Autostart ROM and conceded that some of the works in suit (i.e., Copy, Copy A, Master Create, and Hello) probably could have been rewritten by Franklin. Franklin made no attempt to rewrite any of the programs prior to the lawsuit except for Copy, although McWherter testified that Franklin was "in the process of redesigning" some of the Apple programs and that "[w]e had a fair degree of certainty that that would probably work." Apple introduced evidence that Franklin could have rewritten programs, including the Autostart ROM program, and that there are in existence operating programs written by third parties which are compatible with Apple II.

Franklin's principal defense at the preliminary injunction hearing and before us is primarily a legal one, directed to its contention that the Apple operating system programs are not capable of copyright protection.

The district court denied the motion for preliminary injunction by order and opinion dated July 30, 1982. Apple moved for reconsideration in light of this court's decision in Williams Electronics, Inc. v. Artic International, Inc., 685 F.2d 870, 215 USPQ 405 (3d Cir. 1982), which was decided August 2, 1982, three days after the district court decision. The district court denied the motion for reconsideration. We have jurisdiction of Apple's appeal pursuant to 28 U.S.C. §1292(a)(1).

...

IV. Discussion

A. Copyrightability of a Computer Program Expressed in Object Code

Certain statements by the district court suggest that programs expressed in object code, as distinguished from source code, may not be the proper subject of copyright. We find no basis in the statute for any such concern. Furthermore, our decision in Williams Electronics, Inc. v. Artic International, Inc., supra, laid to rest many of the doubts expressed by the district court.

In 1976, after considerable study, Congress enacted a new copyright law to replace that which had governed since 1909. Act of October 19, 1976, Pub. L. No. 94-553, 90 Stat. 2541 (codified at 17 U.S.C. §§101 et seq.). Under the law, two primary requirements must be satisfied in order for a work to constitute copyrightable subject matter – it must be an "original wor[k] of authorship" and must be "fixed in [a] tangible medium of expression." 17 U.S.C. §102(a). The statute provides:

(a) Copyright protection subsists, in accordance with this title, in original works of authorship fixed in any tangible medium of expression, now known or later developed, from which they can be perceived, reproduced, or otherwise communicated, either directly or with the aid of a machine or device.

Id. The statute enumerates seven categories under "works of authorship" including "literary works", defined as follows:

"Literary works" are works, other than audiovisual works, expressed in words, numbers, or other verbal or numerical symbols or indicia, regardless of the nature of the material objects, such as books, periodicals, manuscripts, phonorecords, film, tapes, disks, or cards, in which they are embodied.

17 U.S.C. §101. A work is "fixed" in a tangible medium of expression when:

its embodiment in a copy or phonorecord, by or under the authority of the author, is sufficiently permanent or stable to permit it to be perceived, reproduced, or otherwise communicated for a period of more than transitory duration. A work consisting of sounds, images, or both, that are being transmitted, is "fixed" for purposes of this title if a fixation of the work is being made simultaneously with its transmission. Id.

Although section 102(a) does not expressly list computer programs as works of authorship, the legislative history suggests that programs were considered copyrightable as literary works. See H.R. Rep. No. 1476, 94th Cong., 2d Sess. 54, reprinted in 1976 U.S. Code Cong. & Ad. News 5659, 5667 ("literary works' includes computer programs"). Because a Commission on New Technological Uses ("CONTU") had been created by Congress to study, inter alia, computer uses of copyrighted works, Pub. L. No. 93-573, §201, 88 Stat. 1873 (1974), Congress enacted a status quo provision, section 117, in the 1976 Act concerning such computer uses pending the CONTU report and recommendations.

The CONTU Final Report recommended that the copyright law be amended, inter alia, "to make it explicit that computer programs, to the extent that they embody an author's original creation, are proper subject matter of copyright." National

Commission on New Technological Uses of Copyrighted Works, Final Report 1 (1979) [hereinafter CONTU Report]. CONTU recommended two changes relevant here: that section 117, the status quo provision, be repealed and replaced with a section limiting exclusive rights in computer programs so as "to ensure that rightful possessors of copies of computer programs may use or adapt these copies for their use," id.; and that a definition of computer program be added to section 101. Id. at 12. Congress adopted both changes. Act of Dec. 12, 1980, Pub. L. No. 96-517, §10, 94 Stat. 3015, 3028. The revisions embodied CONTU's recommendations to clarify the law of copyright of computer software. H.R. Rep. No. 1307, 96th Cong., 2d Sess. 23, reprinted in 1980 U.S. Code Cong. & Ad. News 6460, 6482.

The 1980 amendments added a definition of a computer program: A "computer program" is a set of statements or instructions to be used directly or indirectly in a computer in order to bring about a certain result.

17 U.S.C. §101. The amendments also substituted a new section 117 which provides that "it is not an infringement for the owner of a copy of a computer program to make or authorize the making of another copy or adaptation of that computer program" when necessary to "the utilization of the computer program" or "for archival purposes only." 17 U.S.C. §117. The parties agree that this section is not implicated in the instant law suit. The language of the provision, however, by carving out an exception to the normal proscriptions against copying, clearly indicates that programs are copyrightable and are otherwise afforded copyright protection.

We considered the issue of copyright protection for a computer program in Williams Electronics, Inc. v. Artic International, Inc., and concluded that "the copyrightability of computer programs is firmly established after the 1980 amendment to the Copyright Act." 685 F.2d at 875, 215 USPQ at 409. At issue in Williams were not only two audiovisual copyrights to the "attract" and "play" modes of a video game, but also the computer program which was expressed in object code embodied in ROM and which controlled the sights and sounds of the game. Defendant there had argued "that when the issue is the copyright on a computer program, a distinction must be drawn between the 'source code' version of a computer program, which can be afforded copyright protection, and the 'object code' stage, which cannot be so protected," an argument we rejected. Id. at 876, 215 USPQ at 409.

The district court here questioned whether copyright was to be limited to works "designed to be 'read' by a human reader [as distinguished from] read by an expert with a microscope and patience", 545 F. Supp. at 821, 215 USPQ at 944. The suggestion that copyrightability depends on a communicative function to individuals stems from the early decision of White-Smith Music Publishing Co. v. Apollo Co., 209 U.S. 1 (1908), which held a piano roll was not a copy of the musical composition because it was not in a form others, except perhaps for a very expert few, could perceive. See 1 Nimmer on Copyright §2.03[B][1] (1983). However, it is clear from the language of the 1976 Act and its legislative history that it was intended to obliterate distinctions engendered by White-Smith. H.R. Rep. No. 1476, supra, at 52, reprinted in 1976 U.S. Code Cong. & Ad. News at 5665.

Under the statute, copyright extends to works in any tangible means of expression " from which they can be perceived, reproduced, or otherwise communicated, either directly or with the aid of a machine or device.'" 17 U.S.C. §102(a) (emphasis added). Further, the definition of "computer program" adopted by Congress in the 1980 amendments is "sets of statements or instructions to be used directly or indirectly in a computer in order to bring about a certain result." 17 U.S.C. §101 (emphasis added). As source code instructions must be translated into object code before the computer can act upon them, only instructions expressed in object code can be used "directly" by the computer. See Midway Manufacturing Co. v. Strohon, No. 82 C 1305, slip op. at 25-26, 219 USPQ 42, 50 (N.D. Ill. June 1, 1983). This definition was adopted following the CONTU Report in which the majority clearly took the position that object codes are proper subjects of copyright. See CONTU Report at 21. The majority's conclusion was reached although confronted by a dissent based upon the theory that the "machine-control phase" of a program is not directed at a human audience. See CONTU Report at 28-30 (dissent of Commissioner Hersey).

The defendant in Williams had also argued that a copyrightable work "must be intelligible to human beings and must be intended as a medium of communication to human beings," id. at 876-77, 215 USPQ at 409. We reiterate the statement we made in Williams when we rejected that argument: "[t]he answer to defendant's contention is in the words of the statute itself." 685 F.2d at 877, 215 USPQ at 410.

The district court also expressed uncertainty as to whether a computer program in object code could be classified as a "literary work."7 However, the category of "literary works", one of the seven copyrightable categories, is not confined to literature in the nature of Hemingway's For Whom the Bell Tolls. The definition of "literary works" in section 101 includes expression not only in words but also "numbers, or other numerical symbols or indicia", thereby expanding the common usage of "literary works." Cf. Harcourt, Brace & World, Inc. v. Graphic Controls Corp., 329 F. Supp. 517, 523-24, 171 USPQ 219, 223-224 (S.D.N.Y. 1971) (the symbols designating questions or response spaces on exam answer sheets held to be copyrightable "writings" under 1909 Act); Reiss v. National Quotation Bureau, Inc., 276 F. 717 (S.D.N.Y. 1921) (code book of coined words designed for cable use copyrightable). Thus a computer program, whether in object code or source code, is a "literary work" and is protected from unauthorized copying, whether from its object or source code version. Accord Midway Mfg. Co. v. Strohon, slip op. at 25-27, 219 USPQ at 50; see also GCA Corp. v. Chance, 217 USPQ at 719.

B. Copyrightability of a Computer Program Embedded on a ROM

Just as the district court's suggestion of a distinction between source code and object code was rejected by our opinion in Williams issued three days after the district court opinion, so also was its suggestion that embodiment of a computer program on a ROM, as distinguished from in a traditional writing, detracts from its copyrightability. In Williams we rejected the argument that "a computer program is not infringed when the program is loaded into electronic memory devices (ROMs) and used to control the activity of machines." 685 F.2d at 876, 215 USPQ at 409. Defendant there had argued that there can be no copyright protection for the ROMs because they are utilitarian objects or machine parts. We held that the statutory requirement of "fixation", the manner in which the issue arises, is satisfied through the embodiment of the expression in the ROM devices. Id. at 874, 876, 215 USPQ at 408; See also Midway Mfg. Co. v. Strohon, slip op. at 27-30, 219 USPQ at 51; Tandy Corp. v. Personal Micro Computers, Inc., 524 F. Supp. at 173, 214 USPQ at 179; cf. Stern Electronics, Inc. v. Kaufman, 669 F.2d 852, 855-56, 213 USPQ 443, 445-446 (2d Cir. 1982) (audiovisual display of video game "fixed" in ROM). Therefore we reaffirm that a computer program in object code embedded in a ROM chip is an appropriate subject of copyright. See also Note, Copyright Protection of Computer Program Object Code, 96 Harv. L. Rev. 1723 (1983); Note, Copyright Protection for Computer Programs in Read Only Memory Chips, 11 Hofstra L. Rev. 329 (1982).

C. Copyrightability of Computer Operating System Programs

We turn to the heart of Franklin's position on appeal which is that computer operating system programs, as distinguished from application programs, are not the proper subject of copyright "regardless of the language or medium in which they are fixed." Brief of Appellee at 15 (emphasis deleted). Apple suggests that this issue too is foreclosed by our Williams decision because some portion of the program at issue there was in effect an operating system program. Franklin is correct that this was not an issue raised by the parties in Williams and it was not considered by the court. Thus we consider it as a matter of first impression.

Franklin contends that operating system programs are per se excluded from copyright protection under the express terms of section 102(b) of the Copyright Act, and under the precedent and underlying principles of Baker v. Selden, 101 U.S. 99 (1879). These separate grounds have substantial analytic overlap.

In Baker v. Selden, plaintiff's testator held a copyright on a book explaining a bookkeeping system which included blank forms with ruled lines and headings designed for use with that system. Plaintiff sued for copyright infringement on the basis of defendant's publication of a book containing a different arrangement of the columns and different headings, but which used a similar plan so far as results were concerned. The Court, in reversing the decree for the plaintiff, concluded that blank account-books were not the subject of copyright and that "the mere copyright of Selden's book did not confer upon him the exclusive right to make and use account-books, ruled and arranged as designated by him and described and illustrated in said book." Id. at 107. The Court stated that copyright of the books did not give the plaintiff the exclusive right to use the system explained in the books, noting, for example, that "copyright of a work on mathematical science cannot give to the author an exclusive right to the methods of operation which he propounds." Id. at 103.

Franklin reads Baker v. Selden as "stand[ing] for several fundamental principles, each presenting an insuperable obstacle to the copyrightability of Apple's operating systems." It states:

First, Baker teaches that use of a system itself does not infringe a copyright on the description of the system. Second, Baker enunciates the rule that copyright does not extend to purely utilitarian works. Finally, Baker emphasizes that the copyright laws may not be used to obtain and hold a monopoly over an idea. In so doing, Baker highlights the principal difference between the copyright and patent laws – a difference that is highly pertinent in this case. Brief of Appellee at 22.

Section 102(b) of the Copyright Act, the other ground on which Franklin relies, appeared first in the 1976 version, long after the decision in Baker v. Selden. It provides:

In no case does copyright protection for an original work of authorship extend to any idea, procedure, process, system, method of operation, concept, principle, or discovery, regardless of the form in which it is described, explained, illustrated, or embodied in such work.

It is apparent that section 102(b) codifies a substantial part of the holding and dictum of Baker v. Selden. See 1 Nimmer on Copyright §2.18[D], at 2-207.

We turn to consider the two principal points of Franklin's argument.

1. "Process", "System" or "Method of Operation"

Franklin argues that an operating system program is either a "process", "system", or "method of operation" and hence uncopyrightable. Franklin correctly notes that underlying section 102(b) and many of the statements for which Baker v. Selden is cited is the distinction which must be made between property subject to the patent law, which protects discoveries, and that subject to copyright law, which protects the writings describing such discoveries. However, Franklin's argument misapplies that distinction in this case. Apple does not seek to copyright the method which instructs the computer to perform its operating functions but only the instructions themselves. The method would be protected, if at all, by the patent law, an issue as yet unresolved. See Diamond v. Diehr, 450 U.S. 175 (1981).

Franklin's attack on operating system programs as "methods" or "processes" seems inconsistent with its concession that application programs are an appropriate subject of copyright. Both types of programs instruct the computer to do something. Therefore, it should make no difference for purposes of section 102(b) whether these instructions tell the computer to help prepare an income tax return (the task of an application program) or to translate a high level language program from source code into its binary language object code form (the task of an operating system program such as "Applesoft", see note 4 supra). Since it is only the instructions which are protected, a "process" is no more involved because the instructions in an operating system program may be used to activate the operation of the computer than it would be if instructions were written in ordinary English in a manual which described the necessary steps to activate an intricate complicated machine. There is, therefore, no reason to afford any less copyright protection to the instructions in an operating system program than to the instructions in an application program.

Franklin's argument, receptively treated by the district court, that an operating system program is part of a machine mistakenly focuses on the physical characteristics of the instructions. But the medium is not the message. We have already considered and rejected aspects of this contention in the discussion of object code and ROM. The mere fact that the operating system program may be etched on a ROM does not make the program either a machine, part of a machine or its equivalent. Furthermore, as one of Franklin's witnesses testified, an operating system does not have to be permanently in the machine in ROM, but it may be on some other medium, such as a diskette or magnetic tape, where it could be readily transferred into the temporary memory space of the computer. In fact, some of the operating systems at issue were on diskette. As the CONTU majority stated.

Programs should no more be considered machine parts than videotapes should be considered parts of projectors or phonorecords parts of sound reproduction equipment. That the words of a program are used ultimately in the implementation of a process should in no way affect their copyrightability. CONTU Report at 21.

Franklin also argues that the operating systems cannot be copyrighted because they are "purely utilitarian works" and that Apple is seeking to block the use of the art embodied in its operating systems. This argument stems from the following dictum in Baker v. Selden:

The very object of publishing a book on science or the useful arts is to communicate to the world the useful knowledge which it contains. But this object would be frustrated if the knowledge could not be used without incurring the guilt of piracy of the book. And where the art it teaches cannot be used without employing the methods and diagrams used to illustrate the book, or such as are similar to them, such methods and diagrams are to be considered as necessary incidents to the art, and given therewith to the public; not given for the purpose of publication in other works explanatory of the art, but for the purpose of practical application.

101 U.S. at 103. We cannot accept the expansive reading given to this language by some courts, see, e.g., Taylor Instrument Companies v. Fawley-Brost Co., 139 F.2d 989, 59 USPQ 384 (7th Cir. 1943), cert. denied, 321 U.S. 785, 60 USPQ 579 (1944). In this respect we agree with the views expressed by Professor Nimmer in his treatise. See 1 Nimmer on Copyright §2.18[C].

Although a literal construction of this language could support Franklin's reading that precludes copyrightability if the copyright work is put to a utilitarian use, that interpretation has been rejected by a later Supreme Court decision. In Mazer v. Stein, 347 U.S. 201, 218, 100 USPQ 325 (1954), the Court stated: "We find nothing in the copyright statute to support the argument that the intended use or use in industry of an article eligible for copyright bars or invalidates its registration. We do not read such a limitation into the copyright law." Id. at 218, 100 USPQ at 333. The CONTU majority also rejected the expansive view some courts have given Baker v. Selden, and stated, "That the words of program are used ultimately in the implementation of a process should in no way affect their copyrightability." Id. at 21. It referred to "copyright practice past and present, which recognizes copyright protection for a work of authorship regardless of the uses to which it may be put." Id. The Commission continued: "The copyright status of the written rules for a game or a system for the operation of a machine is unaffected by the fact that those rules direct the actions of those who play the game or carry out the process.'" Id. (emphasis added). As we previously noted, we can consider the CONTU Report as accepted by Congress since Congress wrote into the law the majority's recommendations almost verbatim. See 18 Cong. Rec. H10767 (daily ed. Nov. 17, 1980) (Rep. Kastenmeier: Bill "eliminates confusion about the legal status of computer software by enacting the recommendations of [CONTU] clarifying the law of copyright of computer software"); 18 Cong. Rec. S14766 (daily ed. Nov. 20, 1980) (Sen. Bayh: "[t]his language reflects that proposed by [CONTU"]).

Perhaps the most convincing item leading us to reject Franklin's argument is that the statutory definition of a computer program as a set of instructions to be used in a computer in order to bring about a certain result, 17 U.S.C. §101, makes no distinction between application programs and operating programs. Franklin can point to no decision which adopts the distinction it seeks to make. In the one other reported case to have considered it, Apple Computer, Inc. v. Formula International, Inc., 562 F. Supp. 775, 218 USPQ 47 (C.D. Cal. 1983), the court reached the same conclusion which we do, i.e. that an operating system program is not per se precluded from copyright. It stated, "There is nothing in any of the statutory terms which suggest a different result for different types of computer programs based upon the function they serve within the machine." Id. at 780, 218 at 51. Other courts have also upheld the copyrightability of operating programs without discussion of this issue. See Tandy Corp. v. Personal Micro Computers, INc., 524 F. Supp. at 173, 214 USPQ at 179 (input-output routine stored in ROM which translated input into machine language in a similar fashion as Applesoft and Apple Integer Basic proper subject of copyright); GCA Corp. v. Chance, 217 USPQ at 719 (object code version of registered source code version of operating programs is the same work and protected).

2. Idea/Expression Dichotomy

Franklin's other challenge to copyright of operating system programs relies on the line which is drawn between ideas and their expression. Baker v. Selden remains a benchmark in the law of copyright for the reading given it in Mazer v. Stein, supra, where the Court stated, "Unlike a patent, a copyright gives no exclusive right to the art disclosed; protection is given only to the expression of the idea – not the idea itself." 347 U.S. at 217, 100 USPQ 333 (footnote omitted).

The expression/idea dichotomy is now expressly recognized in section 102(b) which precludes copyright for "any idea." This provision was not intended to enlarge or contract the scope of copyright protection but "to restate that the basic dichotomy between expression and idea remains unchanged." H.R. Rep. No. 1476, supra, at 57, reprinted in 1976 U.S. Code Cong. & Ad. News at 5670. The legislative history indicates that section 102(b) was intended "to make clear that the expression adopted by the programmer is the copyrightable element <714 F.2d 1253> in a computer program, and that the actual processes or methods embodied in the program are not within the scope of the copyright law." Id.

Many of the courts which have sought to draw the line between an idea and expression have found difficulty in articulating where it falls. See, e.g., Nichols v. Universal Pictures Corp., 45 F.2d 119, 121, 7 USPQ 84, 86 (2d Cir. 1930) (L. Hand, J.); see discussion in 3 Nimmer on Copyright §13.03[A]. We believe that in the context before us, a program for an operating system, the line must be a pragmatic one, which also keeps in consideration "the preservation of the balance between competition and protection reflected in the patent and copyright laws". Herbert Rosenthal Jewelry Corp. v. Kalpakian, 446 F.2d 738, 742, 170 USPQ 557, 559 (9th Cir. 1971). As we stated in Franklin Mint Corp. v. National Wildlife Art Exchange, Inc., 575 F.2d 62, 64, 197 USPQ 721, 723 (3d Cir.), cert. denied, 439 U.S. 880, 199 USPQ 57 (1978), "Unlike a patent, a copyright protects originality rather than novelty or invention." In that opinion, we quoted approvingly the following passage from Dymow v. Bolton, 11 F.2d 690, 691 (2d Cir. 1926).

Just as a patent affords protection only to the means of reducing an inventive idea to practice, so the copyright law protects the means of expressing an idea; and it is as near the whole truth as generalization can usually reach that, if the same idea can be expressed in a plurality of totally different manners, a plurality of copyrights may result, and no infringement will exist. (emphasis added).

We adopt the suggestion in the above language and thus focus on whether the idea is capable of various modes of expression. If other programs can be written or created which perform the same function as an Apple's operating system program, then that program is an expression of the idea and hence copyrightable. In essence, this inquiry is no different than that made to determine whether the expression and idea have merged, which has been stated to occur where there are no or few other ways of expressing a particular idea. See, e.g., Morrissey v. Procter & Gamble Co., 379 F.2d 675, 678-79, 154 USPQ 193, 194-95 (1st Cir. 1967); Freedman v. Grolier Enterprises, Inc., 179 USPQ 476, 478 (S.D.N.Y. 1973) ("[c]opyright protection will not be given to a form of expression necessarily dictated by the underlying subject matter"); CONTU Report at 20.

The district court made no findings as to whether some or all of Apple's operating programs represent the only means of expression of the idea underlying them. Although there seems to be a concession by Franklin that at least some of the programs can be rewritten, we do not believe that the record on that issue is so clear that it can be decided at the appellate level. Therefore, if the issue is pressed on remand, the necessary finding can be made at that time.

Franklin claims that whether or not the programs can be rewritten, there are a limited "number of ways to arrange operating systems to enable a computer to run the vast body of Apple-compatible software," Brief of Appellee at 20. This claim has no pertinence to either the idea/expression dichotomy or merger. The idea which may merge with the expression, thus making the copyright unavailable, is the idea which is the subject of the expression. The idea of one of the operating system programs is, for example, how to translate source code into object code. If other methods of expressing that idea are not foreclosed as a practical matter, then there is no merger. Franklin may wish to achieve total compatibility with independently developed application programs written for the Apple II, but that is a commercial and competitive objective which does not enter into the somewhat metaphysical issue of whether particular ideas and expressions have merged.

In summary, Franklin's contentions that operating system programs are per se not copyrightable is unpersuasive. The other courts before whom this issue has been raised have rejected the distinction. Neither the CONTU majority nor Congress made a distinction between operating and application programs. We believe that the 1980 amendments reflect Congress' receptivity to new technology and its desire to encourage, through the copyright laws, continued imagination and creativity in computer programming. Since we believe that the district court's decision on the preliminary injunction was, to a large part, influenced by an erroneous view of the availability of copyright for operating system programs and unnecessary concerns about object code and ROMs, we must reverse the denial of the preliminary injunction and remand for reconsideration.

...

V.

For the reasons set forth in this opinion, we will reverse the denial of the preliminary injunction and remand to the district court for further proceedings in accordance herewith.

982 F.2d 693

COMPUTER ASSOCIATES INTERNATIONAL v. ALTAI

United States Court of Appeals for The Second Circuit

WALKER, Circuit Judge:

In recent years, the growth of computer science has spawned a number of challenging legal questions, particularly in the field of copyright law. As scientific knowledge advances, courts en- deavor to keep pace, and sometimes--as in the area of computer technology--they are required to venture into less than familiar waters. This is not a new development, though. "From its beginning, the law of copyright has developed in response to significant changes in technology." Sony Corp. v. Universal City Studios, Inc., 464 U.S. 417, 430, 78 L. Ed. 2d 574, 104 S. Ct. 774 (1984).

Article I, section 8 of the Constitution authorizes Congress "to promote the Progress of Science and useful Arts, by securing for limited Times to Authors and Inventors the exclusive Right to their respective Writings and Discoveries." The Supreme Court has stated that "the economic philosophy behind the clause . . . is the conviction that encouragement of individual effort by personal gain is the best way to advance public welfare . . . ." Mazer v. Stein, 347 U.S. 201, 219, 98 L. Ed. 630, 74 S. Ct. 460 (1954). The author's benefit, however, is clearly a "secondary" consideration. See United States v. Paramount Pictures, Inc., 334 U.S. 131, 158, 92 L. Ed. 1260, 68 S. Ct. 915 (1948). "The ultimate aim is, by this incentive, to stimulate artistic creativity for the general public good." Twen- tieth Century Music Corp. v. Aiken, 422 U.S. 151, 156, 45 L. Ed. 2d 84, 95 S. Ct. 2040 (1975).

Thus, the copyright law seeks to establish a delicate equilibrium. On the one hand, it affords protection to authors as an incentive to create, and, on the other, it must appropriately limit the ex- tent of that protection so as to avoid the effects of monopolistic stagnation. In applying the federal act to new types of cases, courts must always keep this symmetry in mind. Id.

Among other things, this case deals with the challenging question of whether and to what extent the "non-literal" aspects of a computer program, that is, those aspects that are not reduced to written code, are protected by copyright. While a few other courts have already grappled with this issue, this case is one of first impression in this circuit. As we shall discuss, we find the results reached by other courts to be less than satisfactory. Drawing upon long-standing doctrines of copyright law, we take an approach that we think better addresses the practical difficulties embedded in these types of cases. In so doing, we have kept in mind the necessary balance between creative incentive and in- dustrial competition.

This appeal comes to us from the United States District Court for the Eastern District of New York, the Honorable George C. Pratt, Circuit Judge, sitting by designation. By Memorandum and Order entered August 12, 1991, Judge Pratt found that defendant Altai, Inc.'s ("Altai"), OSCAR 3.4 computer program had infringed plaintiff Computer Associates' ("CA"), copyrighted computer pro- gram entitled CA-SCHEDULER. Accordingly, the district court awarded CA $ 364,444 in actual damages and apportioned profits. Altai has abandoned its appeal from this award. With respect to CA's second claim for copyright infringement, Judge Pratt found that Altai's OSCAR 3.5 program was not substantially similar to a portion of CA-SCHEDULER called ADAPTER, and thus denied relief. Finally, the district court concluded that CA's state law trade secret misappropriation claim against Altai had been preempted by the federal copyright act. CA appealed from these findings.

Because we are in full agreement with Judge Pratt's decision and in substantial agreement with his careful reasoning regarding CA's copyright infringement claim, we affirm the district court's judgment on that issue. However, we vacate the district court's preemption ruling with respect to CA's trade secret claim, and remand the case to the district court for further proceedings.

BACKGROUND

We assume familiarity with the facts set forth in the district court's comprehensive and scholarly opinion. See Computer Assocs. Int'l, Inc. v. Altai, Inc., 775 F. Supp. 544, 549-55 (E.D.N.Y. 1991). Thus, we summarize only those facts necessary to resolve this appeal.

I. COMPUTER PROGRAM DESIGN

Certain elementary facts concerning the nature of computer programs are vital to the following discussion. The Copyright Act defines a computer program as "a set of statements or instructions to be used directly or indirectly in a computer in order to bring about a certain result." 17 U.S.C. § 101. In writing these directions, the programmer works "from the general to the specific." Whelan Assoc., Inc. v. Jaslow Dental Lab., Inc., 797 F.2d 1222, 1229 (3d Cir. 1986), cert. denied, 479 U.S. 1031, 93 L. Ed. 2d 831, 107 S. Ct. 877 (1987). See generally Steven R. Englund, Note, Idea, Proc- ess, or Protected Expression?: Determining the Scope of Copyright Protection of the Structure of Computer Programs, 88 MICH. L. REV. 866, 867-73

(1990) (hereinafter "Englund"); Peter S. Menell, An Analysis of the Scope of Copyright Protection for Application Programs, 41 STAN. L. REV. 1045, 1051-57 (1989) (hereinafter "Menell"); Mark T. Kretschmer, Note, Copyright Protec- tion For Software Architecture: Just Say No!, 1988 COLUM. BUS. L. REV. 823, 824-27 (1988) (hereinafter "Kretschmer"); Peter G. Spivack, Comment, Does Form Follow Function? The Idea/Expression Dichotomy In Copyright Protection of Computer Software, 35 U.C.L.A. L. REV. 723, 729-31 (1988) (hereinafter "Spivack").

The first step in this procedure is to identify a program's ultimate function or purpose. An ex- ample of such an ultimate purpose might be the creation and maintenance of a business ledger. Once this goal has been achieved, a programmer breaks down or "decomposes" the program's ulti- mate function into "simpler constituent problems or subtasks,'" Englund, at 870, which are also known as subroutines or modules. See Spivack, at 729. In the context of a business ledger program, a module or subroutine might be responsible for the task of updating a list of outstanding accounts receivable. Sometimes, depending upon the complexity of its task, a subroutine may be broken down further into sub-subroutines.

Having sufficiently decomposed the program's ultimate function into its component elements, a programmer will then arrange the subroutines or modules into what are known as organizational or flow charts. Flow charts map the interactions between modules that achieve the program's end goal. See Kretschmer, at 826.

In order to accomplish these intra-program interactions, a programmer must carefully design each module's parameter list. A parameter list, according to the expert appointed and fully credited by the district court, Dr. Randall Davis, is "the information sent to and received from a subroutine." See Report of Dr. Randall Davis, at 12. The term "parameter list" refers to the form in which infor- mation is passed between modules (e.g. for accounts receivable, the designated time frame and par- ticular customer identifying number) and the information's actual content (e.g. 8/91-7/92; customer No. 3). Id. With respect to form, interacting modules must share similar parameter lists so that they are capable of exchanging information.

"The functions of the modules in a program together with each module's relationships to other modules constitute the 'structure' of the program." Englund, at 871. Additionally, the term structure may include the category of modules referred to as "macros." A macro is a single instruction that initiates a sequence of operations or module interactions within the program. Very often the user will accompany a macro with an instruction from the parameter list to refine the instruction (e.g. current total of accounts receivable (macro), but limited to those for 8/91 to 7/92 from customer No. 3 (parameters)).

In fashioning the structure, a programmer will normally attempt to maximize the program's speed, efficiency, as well as simplicity for user operation, while taking into consideration certain externalities such as the memory constraints of the computer upon which the program will be run. See id.; Kretschmer, at 826; Menell, at 1052. "This stage of program design often requires the most time and investment." Kretschmer, at 826.

Once each necessary module has been identified, designed, and its relationship to the other modules has been laid out conceptually, the resulting program structure must be embodied in a writ- ten language that the computer can read. This process is called "coding," and requires two steps. Whelan, 797 F.2d at 1230. First, the programmer must transpose the program's structural blue-print into a source code. This step has been described as "comparable to the novelist fleshing out the broad outline of his plot by crafting from words and sentences the paragraphs that convey the ideas." Kretschmer, at 826. The source code may be written in any one of several computer languages, such as COBAL, FORTRAN, BASIC, EDL, etc., depending upon the type of computer for which the program is intended. Whelan, 797 F.2d at 1230. Once the source code has been com- pleted, the second step is to translate or "compile" it into object code. Object code is the binary lan- guage comprised of zeros and ones through which the computer directly receives its instructions. Id., at 1230-31; Englund, at 868 & n.13.

After the coding is finished, the programmer will run the program on the computer in order to find and correct any logical and syntactical errors. This is known as "debugging" and, once done, the program is complete. See Kretschmer, at 826-27.

II. FACTS

CA is a Delaware corporation, with its principal place of business in Garden City, New York. Altai is a Texas corporation, doing business primarily in Arlington, Texas. Both companies are in the computer software industry--designing, developing and marketing various types of computer programs.

The subject of this litigation originates with one of CA's marketed programs entitled CA- SCHEDULER. CA-SCHEDULER is a job scheduling program designed for IBM mainframe com- puters. Its primary functions are straightforward: to create a schedule specifying when the computer should run various tasks, and then to control the computer as it executes the schedule. CA-SCHEDULER contains a sub-program entitled ADAPTER, also developed by CA. ADAPTER is not an independently marketed product of CA; it is a wholly integrated component of CA- SCHEDULER and has no capacity for independent use.

Nevertheless, ADAPTER plays an extremely important role. It is an "operating system compati- bility component," which means, roughly speaking, it serves as a translator. An "operating system" is itself a program that manages the resources of the computer, allocating those resources to other programs as needed. The IBM System 370 family of computers, for which CA-SCHEDULER was created, is, depending upon the computer's size, designed to contain one of three operating systems: DOS/VSE, MVS, or CMS. As the district court noted, the general rule is that "a program written for one operating system, e.g., DOS/VSE, will not, without modification, run under another operat- ing system such as MVS." Computer Assocs., 775 F. Supp. at 550. ADAPTER's function is to trans- late the language of a given program into the particular language that the computer's own operating system can understand.

The district court succinctly outlined the manner in which ADAPTER works within the context of the larger program. In order to enable CA-SCHEDULER to function on different operating sys- tems, CA divided the CA-SCHEDULER into two components:

--a first component that contains only the task-specific portions of the program, independent of all operating system issues, and

--a second component that contains all the interconnections between the first component and the operating system.

In a program constructed in this way, whenever the first, task-specific, component needs to ask the operating system for some resource through a "system call", it calls the second component in- stead of calling the operating system directly.

The second component serves as an "interface" or "compatibility component" between the task- specific portion of the program and the operating system. It receives the request from the first component and translates it into the appropriate system call that will be recognized by whatever op- erating system is installed on the computer, e.g., DOS/VSE, MVS, or CMS. Since the first, task- specific component calls the adapter component rather than the operating system, the first compo- nent need not be customized to use any specific operating system. The second, interface, component insures that all the system calls are performed properly for the particular operating system in use. Id. at 551. ADAPTER serves as the second, "common system interface" component referred to above.

A program like ADAPTER, which allows a computer user to change or use multiple operating systems while maintaining the same software, is highly desirable. It saves the user the costs, both in time and money, that otherwise would be expended in purchasing new programs, modifying exist- ing systems to run them, and gaining familiarity with their operation. The benefits run both ways. The increased compatibility afforded by an ADAPTER-like component, and its resulting popularity among consumers, makes whatever software in which it is incorporated significantly more market- able.

Starting in 1982, Altai began marketing its own job scheduling program entitled ZEKE. The original version of ZEKE was designed for use in conjunction with a VSE operating system. By late 1983, in response to customer demand, Altai decided to rewrite ZEKE so that it could be run in con- junction with an MVS operating system.

At that time, James P. Williams ("Williams"), then an employee of Altai and now its President, approached Claude F. Arney, III ("Arney"), a computer programmer who worked for CA. Williams and Arney were longstanding friends, and had in fact been co-workers at CA for some time before Williams left CA to work for Altai's predecessor. Williams wanted to recruit Arney to assist Altai in designing an MVS version of ZEKE.

At the time he first spoke with Arney, Williams was aware of both the CA-SCHEDULER and ADAPTER programs. However, Williams was not involved in their development and had never seen the codes of either program. When he asked Arney to come work for Altai, Williams did not know that ADAPTER was a component of CA-SCHEDULER.

Arney, on the other hand, was intimately familiar with various aspects of ADAPTER. While working for CA, he helped improve the VSE version of ADAPTER, and was permitted to take home a copy of ADAPTER'S source code. This apparently developed into an irresistible habit, for when Arney left CA to work for Altai in January, 1984, he took with him copies of the source code for both the VSE and MVS versions of ADAPTER. He did this in knowing violation of the CA em- ployee agreements that he had signed.

Once at Altai, Arney and Williams discussed design possibilities for adapting ZEKE to run on MVS operating systems. Williams, who had created the VSE version of ZEKE, thought that ap- proximately 30% of his original program would have to be modified in order to accommodate MVS. Arney persuaded Williams that the best way to make the needed modifications was to intro- duce a "common system interface" component into ZEKE. He did not tell Williams that his idea stemmed from his familiarity with ADAPTER. They decided to name this new component-program OSCAR.

Arney went to work creating OSCAR at Altai's offices using the ADAPTER source code. The district court accepted Williams' testimony that no one at Altai, with the exception of Arney, af- firmatively knew that Arney had the ADAPTER code, or that he was using it to create OS- CAR/VSE. However, during this time period, Williams' office was adjacent to Arney's. Williams testified that he and Arney "conversed quite frequently" while Arney was "investigating the source code of ZEKE" and that Arney was in his office "a number of times daily, asking questions." In three months, Arney successfully completed the OSCAR/VSE project. In an additional month he developed an OSCAR/MVS version. When the dust finally settled, Arney had copied approximately 30% of OSCAR's code from CA's ADAPTER program.

The first generation of OSCAR programs was known as OSCAR 3.4. From 1985 to August 1988, Altai used OSCAR 3.4 in its ZEKE product, as well as in programs entitled ZACK and ZEBB. In late July 1988, CA first learned that Altai may have appropriated parts of ADAPTER. After confirming its suspicions, CA secured copyrights on its 2.1 and 7.0 versions of CA- SCHEDULER. CA then brought this copyright and trade secret misappropriation action against Al- tai.

Apparently, it was upon receipt of the summons and complaint that Altai first learned that Ar- ney had copied much of the OSCAR code from ADAPTER. After Arney confirmed to Williams that CA's accusations of copying were true, Williams immediately set out to survey the damage. Without ever looking at the ADAPTER code himself, Williams learned from Arney exactly which sections of code Arney had taken from ADAPTER.

Upon advice of counsel, Williams initiated OSCAR's rewrite. The project's goal was to save as much of OSCAR 3.4 as legitimately could be used, and to excise those portions which had been copied from ADAPTER. Arney was entirely excluded from the process, and his copy of the ADAPTER code was locked away. Williams put eight other programmers on the project, none of whom had been involved in any way in the development of OSCAR 3.4. Williams provided the programmers with a description of the ZEKE operating system services so that they could rewrite the appropriate code. The rewrite project took about six months to complete and was finished in mid-November 1989. The resulting program was entitled OSCAR 3.5.

From that point on, Altai shipped only OSCAR 3.5 to its new customers. Altai also shipped OSCAR 3.5 as a "free upgrade" to all customers that had previously purchased OSCAR 3.4. While Altai and Williams acted responsibly to correct Arney's literal copying of the ADAPTER program, copyright infringement had occurred.

After CA originally instituted this action in the United States District Court for the District of New Jersey, the parties stipulated its transfer in March, 1989, to the Eastern District of New York where it was assigned to Judge Jacob Mishler. On October 26, 1989, Judge Mishler transferred the case to Judge Pratt who was sitting in the district court by designation. Judge Pratt conducted a six day trial from March 28 through April 6, 1990. He entered judgment on August 12, 1991, and this appeal followed.

DISCUSSION

While both parties originally appealed from different aspects of the district court's judgment, Al- tai has now abandoned its appellate claims. In particular, Altai has conceded liability for the copy ing of ADAPTER into OSCAR 3.4 and raises no challenge to the award of $ 364,444 in damages on that score. Thus, we address only CA's appeal from the district court's rulings that: (1) Altai was not liable for copyright infringement in developing OSCAR 3.5; and (2) in developing both OSCAR 3.4 and 3.5, Altai was not liable for misappropriating CA's trade secrets.

CA makes two arguments. First, CA contends that the district court applied an erroneous method for determining whether there exists substantial similarity between computer programs, and thus, erred in determining that OSCAR 3.5 did not infringe the copyrights held on the different ver- sions of its CA-SCHEDULER program. CA asserts that the test applied by the district court failed to account sufficiently for a computer program's non-literal elements. ...

I. COPYRIGHT INFRINGEMENT

In any suit for copyright infringement, the plaintiff must establish its ownership of a valid copy- right, and that the defendant copied the copyrighted work. See Novelty Textile Mills, Inc. v. Joan Fabrics Corp., 558 F.2d 1090, 1092 (2d Cir. 1977); see also 3 Melville B. Nimmer & David Nim- mer, Nimmer on Copyright § 13.01, at 13-4 (1991) (hereinafter "Nimmer"). The plaintiff may prove defendant's copying either by direct evidence or, as is most often the case, by showing that (1) the defendant had access to the plaintiff's copyrighted work and (2) that defendant's work is substan- tially similar to the plaintiff's copyrightable material.

See Walker v. Time Life Films, Inc., 784 F.2d 44, 48 (2d Cir.), cert. denied, 476 U.S. 1159, 90 L. Ed. 2d 721, 106 S. Ct. 2278 (1986).

For the purpose of analysis, the district court assumed that Altai had access to the ADAPTER code when creating OSCAR 3.5. See Computer Assocs., 775 F. Supp. at 558. Thus, in determining whether Altai had unlawfully copied protected aspects of CA's ADAPTER, the district court nar- rowed its focus of inquiry to ascertaining whether Altai's OSCAR 3.5 was substantially similar to ADAPTER. Because we approve Judge Pratt's conclusions regarding substantial similarity, our analysis will proceed along the same assumption.

As a general matter, and to varying degrees, copyright protection extends beyond a literary work's strictly textual form to its non-literal components. As we have said, "it is of course essential to any protection of literary property . . . that the right cannot be limited literally to the text, else a plagiarist would escape by immaterial variations." Nichols v. Universal Pictures Co., 45 F.2d 119, 121 (2d Cir. 1930) (L. Hand, J.), cert. denied, 282 U.S. 902, 75 L. Ed. 795, 51 S. Ct. 216 (1931). Thus, where "the fundamental essence or structure of one work is duplicated in another," 3 Nimmer, § 13.03[A][1], at 13-24, courts have found copyright infringement. See, e.g., Horgan v. Macmillan, 789 F.2d 157, 162 (2d Cir. 1986) (recognizing that a book of photographs might infringe ballet cho- reography); Twentieth Century-Fox Film Corp. v. MCA, Inc., 715 F.2d 1327, 1329 (9th Cir. 1983) (motion picture and television series); Sid & Marty Krofft Television Prods., Inc. v. McDonald's Corp., 562 F.2d 1157, 1167 (9th Cir. 1977) (television commercial and television series); Sheldon v. Metro-Goldwyn Pictures Corp., 81 F.2d 49, 55 (2d Cir.), cert. denied, 298 U.S. 669, 80 L. Ed. 1392, 56 S. Ct. 835 (1936) (play and motion picture); accord Stewart v. Abend, 495 U.S. 207, 238, 109 L. Ed. 2d 184, 110 S. Ct. 1750 (1990) (recognizing that motion picture may infringe copyright in book by using its "unique setting, characters, plot, and sequence of events"). This black letter proposition is the springboard for our discussion.

A. Copyright Protection for the Non-literal Elements of Computer Programs

It is now well settled that the literal elements of computer programs, i.e., their source and object codes, are the subject of copyright protection. See Whelan, 797 F.2d at 1233 (source and object code); CMS Software Design Sys., Inc. v. Info Designs, Inc., 785 F.2d 1246, 1247 (5th Cir. 1986) (source code); Apple Computer, Inc. v. Franklin Computer Corp., 714 F.2d 1240, 1249 (3d Cir. 1983), cert. dismissed, 464 U.S. 1033, 104 S. Ct. 690, 79 L. Ed. 2d 158 (1984) (source and object code); Williams Electronics, Inc. v. Artic Int'l, Inc., 685 F.2d 870, 876-77 (3d Cir. 1982) (object code). Here, as noted earlier, Altai admits having copied approximately 30% of the OSCAR 3.4 program from CA's ADAPTER source code, and does not challenge the district court's related find- ing of infringement.

In this case, the hotly contested issues surround OSCAR 3.5. As recounted above, OSCAR 3.5 is the product of Altai's carefully orchestrated rewrite of OSCAR 3.4. After the purge, none of the ADAPTER source code remained in the 3.5 version; thus, Altai made sure that the literal elements of its revamped OSCAR program were no longer substantially similar to the literal elements of CA's ADAPTER.

According to CA, the district court erroneously concluded that Altai's OSCAR 3.5 was not sub- stantially similar to its own ADAPTER program. CA argues that this occurred because the district court "committed legal error in analyzing [its] claims of copyright infringement by failing to find that copyright protects expression contained in the non-literal elements of computer software." We disagree.

CA argues that, despite Altai's rewrite of the OSCAR code, the resulting program remained sub- stantially similar to the structure of its ADAPTER program. As discussed above, a program's struc- ture includes its nonliteral components such as general flow charts as well as the more specific or- ganization of inter-modular relationships, parameter lists, and macros. In addition to these aspects, CA contends that OSCAR 3.5 is also substantially similar to ADAPTER with respect to the list of services that both ADAPTER and OSCAR obtain from their respective operating systems. We must decide whether and to what extent these elements of computer programs are protected by copyright law.

The statutory terrain in this area has been well explored. See Lotus Dev. Corp. v. Paperback Software Int'l, 740 F. Supp. 37, 47-51 (D. Mass. 1990); see also Whelan, 797 F.2d at 1240-42; Englund, at 885-90; Spivack, at 731-37. The Copyright Act affords protection to "original works of authorship fixed in any tangible medium of expression...." 17 U.S.C. § 102(a). This broad cate- gory of protected "works" includes "literary works," id. at § 102(a)(1), which are defined by the Act as

works, other than audiovisual works, expressed in words, numbers, or other verbal or numerical symbols or indicia, regardless of the nature of the material objects, such as books, periodicals, manuscripts, phonorecords, film tapes, disks, or cards, in which they are embodied. 17 U.S.C. § 101. While computer programs are not specifically listed as part of the above statutory definition, the legislative history leaves no doubt that Congress intended them to be considered lit- erary works. See H.R.Rep. No. 1476, 94th Cong., 2d Sess. 54, reprinted in 1976 U.S.C.C.A.N. 5659, 5667 (hereinafter "House Report"); Whelan, 797 F.2d at 1234; Apple Computer, 714 F.2d at 1247.

The syllogism that follows from the foregoing premises is a powerful one: if the non-literal structures of literary works are protected by copyright; and if computer programs are literary works, as we are told by the legislature; then the non-literal structures of computer programs are protected by copyright. See Whelan, 797 F.2d at 1234 ("By analogy to other literary works, it would thus appear that the copyrights of computer programs can be infringed even absent copying of the literal elements of the program."). We have no reservation in joining the company of those courts that have already ascribed to this logic. See, e.g., Johnson Controls, Inc. v. Phoenix Control Sys., Inc., 886 F.2d 1173, 1175 (9th Cir. 1989); Lotus Dev. Corp., 740 F. Supp. at 54; Digital Communications Assocs., Inc. v. Softklone Distrib. Corp., 659 F. Supp. 449, 455-56 (N.D.Ga. 1987); Q-Co Indus., Inc. v. Hoffman, 625 F. Supp. 608, 615 (S.D.N.Y. 1985); SAS Inst., Inc. v. S & H Computer Sys., Inc., 605 F. Supp. 816, 829-30 (M.D.Tenn. 1985). However, that conclusion does not end our analysis. We must determine the scope of copyright protection that extends to a computer program's non-literal structure.

As a caveat, we note that our decision here does not control infringement actions regarding categorically distinct works, such as certain types of screen displays. These items represent products of computer programs, rather than the programs themselves, and fall under the copyright rubric of audiovisual works. If a computer audiovisual display is copyrighted separately as an audiovisual work, apart from the literary work that generates it (i.e., the program), the display may be protectable regardless of the underlying program's copyright status. See Stern Elecs., Inc. v. Kaufman, 669 F.2d 852, 855 (2d Cir. 1982) (explaining that an audiovisual works copyright, rather than a copy- right on the underlying program, extended greater protection to the sights and sounds generated by a computer video game because the same audiovisual display could be generated by different pro- grams). Of course, the copyright protection that these displays enjoy extends only so far as their ex- pression is protectable. See Data East USA, Inc. v. Epyx, Inc., 862 F.2d 204, 209 (9th Cir. 1988). In this case, however, we are concerned not with a program's display, but the program itself, and then with only its non-literal components. In considering the copyrightability of these components, we must refer to venerable doctrines of copyright law.

1) Idea vs. Expression Dichotomy

It is a fundamental principle of copyright law that a copyright does not protect an idea, but only the expression of the idea. See Baker v. Selden, 101 U.S. 99, 25 L. Ed. 841 (1879); Mazer v. Stein, 347 U.S. 201, 217, 98 L. Ed. 630, 74 S. Ct. 460 (1954). This axiom of common law has been incor- porated into the governing statute. Section 102(b) of the Act provides:

In no case does copyright protection for an original work of authorship extend to any idea, procedure, process, system, method of operation, concept, principle, or discovery, regardless of the form in which it is described, explained, illustrated, or embodied in such work. 17 U.S.C. § 102(b). See also House Report, at 5670 ("Copyright does not preclude others from us- ing ideas or information revealed by the author's work.").

Congress made no special exception for computer programs. To the contrary, the legislative his- tory explicitly states that copyright protects computer programs only "to the extent that they incor- porate authorship in programmer's expression of original ideas, as distinguished from the ideas themselves." Id. at 5667; see also id. at 5670 ("Section 102(b) is intended . . . to make clear that the expression adopted by the programmer is the copyrightable element in a computer program, and that the actual processes or methods embodied in the program are not within the scope of copyright law.").

Similarly, the National Commission on New Technological Uses of Copyrighted Works ("CONTU") established by Congress to survey the issues generated by the interrelationship of ad- vancing technology and copyright law, see Pub.L. No. 93- 573, § 201, 88 Stat. 1873 (1974), recommended, inter alia, that the 1976 Copyright Act "be amended . . . to make it explicit that computer programs, to the extent that they embody the author's original creation, are proper subject matter for copyright." See National Commission on New Technological Uses of Copyrighted Works, Final Report 1 (1979) (hereinafter "CONTU Report"). To that end, Congress adopted CONTU's sugges- tions and amended the Copyright Act by adding, among other things, a provision to 17 U.S.C. § 101 which defined the term "computer program." See Pub.L. No. 96-517, § 10(a), 94 Stat. 3028 (1980). CONTU also "concluded that the idea-expression distinction should be used to determine which aspects of computer programs are copyrightable." Lotus Dev. Corp., 740 F. Supp. at 54 (citing CONTU Report, at 44).

Drawing the line between idea and expression is a tricky business. Judge Learned Hand noted that "nobody has ever been able to fix that boundary, and nobody ever can." Nichols, 45 F.2d at 121. Thirty years later his convictions remained firm. "Obviously, no principle can be stated as to when an imitator has gone beyond copying the 'idea,' and has borrowed its 'expression,'" Judge Hand concluded. "Decisions must therefore inevitably be ad hoc." Peter Pan Fabrics, Inc. v. Martin Weiner Corp., 274 F.2d 487, 489 (2d Cir. 1960).

The essentially utilitarian nature of a computer program further complicates the task of distilling its idea from its expression. See SAS Inst., 605 F. Supp. at 829; cf. Englund, at 893. In order to de-scribe both computational processes and abstract ideas, its content "combines creative and technical expression." See Spivack, at 755. The variations of expression found in purely creative composi- tions, as opposed to those contained in utilitarian works, are not directed towards practical applica- tion. For example, a narration of Humpty Dumpty's demise, which would clearly be a creative com-position, does not serve the same ends as, say, a recipe for scrambled eggs--which is a more process-oriented text. Thus, compared to aesthetic works, computer programs hover even more closely to the elusive boundary line described in § 102(b).

...

The line between idea and expression may be drawn with reference to the end sought to be achieved by the work in question. In other words, the purpose or function of a utilitarian work would be the work's idea, and everything that is not necessary to that purpose or function would be part of the expression of the idea.... Where there are various means of achieving the desired purpose, then the particular means chosen is not necessary to the purpose; hence, there is expression, not idea.

797 F.2d at 1236 (citations omitted). The "idea" of the program at issue in Whelan was identified by the court as simply "the efficient management of a dental laboratory." Id. at n.28.

So far, in the courts, the Whelan rule has received a mixed reception. While some decisions have adopted its reasoning, see, e.g., Bull HN Info. Sys., Inc. v. American Express Bank, Ltd., 1990 Copyright Law Dec. (CCH) P 26,555 at 23,278 (S.D.N.Y. 1990); Dynamic Solutions, Inc. v. Plan- ning & Control, Inc., 1987 Copyright Law Dec. (CCH) P 26,062 at 20,912 (S.D.N.Y. 1987); Brod- erbund Software Inc. v. Unison World, Inc., 648 F. Supp. 1127, 1133 (N.D.Cal. 1986), others have rejected it. See Plains Cotton Co-op v. Goodpasture Computer Serv, Inc., 807 F.2d 1256, 1262 (5th Cir.), cert. denied, 484 U.S. 821, 108 S. Ct. 80, 98 L. Ed. 2d 42 (1987); cf. Synercom Technology, Inc. v. University Computing Co., 462 F. Supp. 1003, 1014

(N.D.Tex. 1978) (concluding that order and sequence of data on computer input formats was idea not expression).

Whelan has fared even more poorly in the academic community, where its standard for distin- guishing idea from expression has been widely criticized for being conceptually overbroad. See, e.g., Englund, at 881; Menell, at 1074, 1082; Kretschmer, at 837-39; Spivack, at 747-55; Thomas M. Gage, Note, Whelan Associates v. Jaslow Dental Laboratories: Copyright Protection for Com- puter Software Structure--What's the Purpose?, 1987 WIS. L. REV. 859, 860-61 (1987). The lead- ing commentator in the field has stated that, "the crucial flaw in [Whelan's] reasoning is that it as- sumes that only one 'idea,' in copyright law terms, underlies any computer program, and that once a separable idea can be identified, everything else must be expression." 3 Nimmer § 13.03[F], at 13- 62.34. This criticism focuses not upon the program's ultimate purpose but upon the reality of its structural design. As we have already noted, a computer program's ultimate function or purpose is the composite result of interacting subroutines. Since each subroutine is itself a program, and thus, may be said to have its own "idea," Whelan's general formulation that a program's overall purpose equates with the program's idea is descriptively inadequate.

Accordingly, we think that Judge Pratt wisely declined to follow Whelan. See Computer As- socs., 775 F. Supp. at 558-60. In addition to noting the weakness in the Whelan definition of "pro- gram-idea," mentioned above, Judge Pratt found that Whelan's synonymous use of the terms "struc- ture, sequence, and organization," see Whelan, 797 F.2d at 1224 n.1, demonstrated a flawed under- standing of a computer program's method of operation. See Computer Assocs., 775 F. Supp. at 559- 60 (discussing the distinction between a program's "static structure" and "dynamic structure"). Rightly, the district court found Whelan's rationale suspect because it is so closely tied to what can now be seen--with the passage of time--as the opinion's somewhat outdated appreciation of com- puter science.

2) Substantial Similarity Test for Computer Program Structure: Abstraction- Filtration- Comparison

We think that Whelan's approach to separating idea from expression in computer programs re- lies too heavily on metaphysical distinctions and does not place enough emphasis on practical con- siderations. Cf. Apple Computer, 714 F.2d at 1253 (rejecting certain commercial constraints on programming as a helpful means of distinguishing idea from expression because they did "not enter into the somewhat metaphysical issue of whether particular ideas and expressions have merged"). As the cases that we shall discuss demonstrate, a satisfactory answer to this problem cannot be reached by resorting, a priori, to philosophical first principals.

As discussed herein, we think that district courts would be well-advised to undertake a three- step procedure, based on the abstractions test utilized by the district court, in order to determine whether the non-literal elements of two or more computer programs are substantially similar. This approach breaks no new ground; rather, it draws on such familiar copyright doctrines as merger, scenes a faire, and public domain. In taking this approach, however, we are cognizant that computer technology is a dynamic field which can quickly outpace judicial decisionmaking. Thus, in cases where the technology in question does not allow for a literal application of the procedure we outline below, our opinion should not be read to foreclose the district courts of our circuit from utilizing a modified version.

In ascertaining substantial similarity under this approach, a court would first break down the al- legedly infringed program into its constituent structural parts. Then, by examining each of these parts for such things as incorporated ideas, expression that is necessarily incidental to those ideas, and elements that are taken from the public domain, a court would then be able to sift out all non- protectable material. Left with a kernel, or possibly kernels, of creative expression after following this process of elimination, the court's last step would be to compare this material with the structure of an allegedly infringing program. The result of this comparison will determine whether the protectable elements of the programs at issue are substantially similar so as to warrant a finding of in- fringement. It will be helpful to elaborate a bit further.

Step One: Abstraction

As the district court appreciated, see Computer Assocs., 775 F. Supp. at 560, the theoretic framework for analyzing substantial similarity expounded by Learned Hand in the Nichols case is helpful in the present context. In Nichols, we enunciated what has now become known as the "ab- stractions" test for separating idea from expression:

Upon any work . . . a great number of patterns of increasing generality will fit equally well, as more and more of the incident is left out. The last may perhaps be no more than the most general state- ment of what the [work] is about, and at times might consist only of its title; but there is a point in this series of abstractions where they are no longer protected, since otherwise the [author] could prevent the use of his "ideas," to which, apart from their expression, his property is never extended. Nichols, 45 F.2d at 121.

While the abstractions test was originally applied in relation to literary works such as novels and plays, it is adaptable to computer programs. In contrast to the Whelan approach, the abstractions test "implicitly recognizes that any given work may consist of a mixture of numerous ideas and expres- sions." 3 Nimmer § 13.03[F] at 13-62.34-63.

As applied to computer programs, the abstractions test will comprise the first step in the exami- nation for substantial similarity. Initially, in a manner that resembles reverse engineering on a theo- retical plane, a court should dissect the allegedly copied program's structure and isolate each level of abstraction contained within it. This process begins with the code and ends with an articulation of the program's ultimate function. Along the way, it is necessary essentially to retrace and map each of the designer's steps--in the opposite order in which they were taken during the program's crea- tion. See Background: Computer Program Design, supra.

As an anatomical guide to this procedure, the following description is helpful:

At the lowest level of abstraction, a computer program may be thought of in its entirety as a set of individual instructions organized into a hierarchy of modules. At a higher level of abstraction, the instructions in the lowest-level modules may be replaced conceptually by the functions of those modules. At progressively higher levels of abstraction, the functions of higher-level modules con- ceptually replace the implementations of those modules in terms of lower-level modules and in- structions, until finally, one is left with nothing but the ultimate function of the program.... A program has structure at every level of abstraction at which it is viewed. At low levels of abstraction, a program's structure may be quite complex; at the highest level it is trivial. Englund, at 897-98. Cf. Spivack, at 774.

Step Two: Filtration

Once the program's abstraction levels have been discovered, the substantial similarity inquiry moves from the conceptual to the concrete. Professor Nimmer suggests, and we endorse, a "successive filtering method" for separating protectable expression from non-protectable material. See gen- erally 3 Nimmer § 13.03[F]. This process entails examining the structural components at each level of abstraction to determine whether their particular inclusion at that level was "idea" or was dictated by considerations of efficiency, so as to be necessarily incidental to that idea; required by factors external to the program itself; or taken from the public domain and hence is nonprotectable expres- sion. See also Kretschmer, at 844-45 (arguing that program features dictated by market externalities or efficiency concerns are unprotectable). The structure of any given program may reflect some, all, or none of these considerations. Each case requires its own fact specific investigation.

Strictly speaking, this filtration serves "the purpose of defining the scope of plaintiff's copy- right." Brown Bag Software v. Symantec Corp., 960 F.2d 1465, 1475 (9th Cir.) (endorsing "analytic dissection" of computer programs in order to isolate protectable expression), cert. denied, 113 S. Ct. 198, 121 L. Ed. 2d 141 (1992). By applying well developed doctrines of copyright law, it may ulti- mately leave behind a "core of protectable material." 3 Nimmer § 13.03[F][5], at 13-72. Further ex- plication of this second step may be helpful.

(a) Elements Dictated by Efficiency

The portion of Baker v. Selden, discussed earlier, which denies copyright protection to expres- sion necessarily incidental to the idea being expressed, appears to be the cornerstone for what has developed into the doctrine of merger. See Morrissey v. Procter & Gamble Co., 379 F.2d 675, 678- 79 (1st Cir. 1967) (relying on Baker for the proposition that expression embodying the rules of a sweepstakes contest was inseparable from the idea of the contest itself, and therefore were not pro- tectable by copyright); see also Digital Communications, 659 F. Supp. at 457. The doctrine's under- lying principle is that "when there is essentially only one way to express an idea, the idea and its expression are inseparable and copyright is no bar to copying that expression." Concrete Machinery Co. v. Classic Lawn Ornaments, Inc., 843 F.2d 600, 606 (1st Cir. 1988). Under these circumstances, the expression is said to have "merged" with the idea itself. In order not to confer a monopoly of the idea upon the copyright owner, such expression should not be protected. See Herbert Rosenthal Jewelry Corp. v. Kalpakian, 446 F.2d 738, 742 (9th Cir. 1971).

CONTU recognized the applicability of the merger doctrine to computer programs. In its report to Congress it stated that:

Copyrighted language may be copied without infringing when there is but a limited number of ways to express a given idea.... In the computer context, this means that when specific instruc- tions, even though previously copyrighted, are the only and essential means of accomplishing a given task, their later use by another will not amount to infringement. CONTU Report at 20. While this statement directly concerns only the application of merger to program code, that is, the textual aspect of the program, it reasonably suggests that the doctrine fits comfortably within the general context of computer programs.

Furthermore, when one considers the fact that programmers generally strive to create programs "that meet the user's needs in the most efficient manner," Menell, at 1052, the applicability of the merger doctrine to computer programs becomes compelling. In the context of computer program design, the concept of efficiency is akin to deriving the most concise logical proof or formulating the most succinct mathematical computation. Thus, the more efficient a set of modules are, the more closely they approximate the idea or process embodied in that particular aspect of the pro- gram's structure.

While, hypothetically, there might be a myriad of ways in which a programmer may effectuate certain functions within a program,--i.e., express the idea embodied in a given subroutine-- efficiency concerns may so narrow the practical range of choice as to make only one or two forms of expression workable options. See 3 Nimmer § 13.03[F][2], at 13-63; see also Wholon, 797 F.2d at 1243 n.43 ("It is true that for certain tasks there are only a very limited number of file structures available, and in such cases the structures might not be copyrightable...."). Of course, not all program structure is informed by efficiency concerns. See Menell, at 1052 (besides efficiency, sim- plicity related to user accommodation has become a programming priority). It follows that in order to determine whether the merger doctrine precludes copyright protection to an aspect of a program's structure that is so oriented, a court must inquire "whether the use of this particular set of modules is necessary efficiently to implement that part of the program's process" being implemented. Englund, at 902. If the answer is yes, then the expression represented by the programmer's choice of a specific module or group of modules has merged with their underlying idea and is unprotected. Id. at 902-03.

Another justification for linking structural economy with the application of the merger doctrine stems from a program's essentially utilitarian nature and the competitive forces that exist in the software marketplace. See Kretschmer, at 842. Working in tandem, these factors give rise to a prob- lem of proof which merger helps to eliminate.

Efficiency is an industry-wide goal. Since, as we have already noted, there may be only a limited number of efficient implementations for any given program task, it is quite possible that multi- ple programmers, working independently, will design the identical method employed in the alleg- edly infringed work. Of course, if this is the case, there is no copyright infringement. See Roth Greeting Cards v. United Card Co., 429 F.2d 1106, 1110 (9th Cir. 1970); Sheldon, 81 F.2d at 54.

Under these circumstances, the fact that two programs contain the same efficient structure may as likely lead to an inference of independent creation as it does to one of copying. See 3 Nimmer § 13.03[F][2], at 13-65; cf. Herbert Rosenthal Jewelry Corp., 446 F.2d at 741 (evidence of independ- ent creation may stem from defendant's standing as a designer of previous similar works). Thus, since evidence of similarly efficient structure is not particularly probative of copying, it should be disregarded in the overall substantial similarity analysis. See 3 Nimmer § 13.03[F][2], at 13-65.

We find support for applying the merger doctrine in cases that have already addressed the ques- tion of substantial similarity in the context of computer program structure. Most recently, in Lotus Dev. Corp., 740 F. Supp. at 66, the district court had before it a claim of copyright infringement relating to the structure of a computer spreadsheet program. The court observed that "the basic spreadsheet screen display that resembles a rotated 'L'. . ., if not present in every expression of such a program, is present in most expressions." Id. Similarly, the court found that "an essential detail present in most if not all expressions of an electronic spreadsheet--is the designation of a particular key that, when pressed, will invoke the menu command system." Id. Applying the merger doctrine, the court denied copyright protection to both program elements.

In Manufacturers Technologies, Inc. v. Cams, Inc., 706 F. Supp. 984, 995-99 (D. Conn. 1989), the infringement claims stemmed from various alleged program similarities "as indicated in their screen displays." Id. at 990. Stressing efficiency concerns in the context of a merger analysis, the court determined that the program's method of allowing the user to navigate within the screen dis- plays was not protectable because, in part, "the process or manner of navigating internally on any specific screen displays . . . is limited in the number of ways it may be simply achieved to facilitate user comfort." Id. at 995.

The court also found that expression contained in various screen displays (in the form of alphabetical and numerical columns), was not the proper subject of copyright protection because it was "necessarily incident to the ideas" embodied in the displays. Id. at 996-97. Cf. Digital Communications, 659 F. Supp. at 460 (finding no merger and affording copyright protection to program's status screen display because "modes of expression chosen . . . are clearly not necessary to the idea of the status screen").

We agree with the approach taken in these decisions, and conclude that application of the merger doctrine in this setting is an effective way to eliminate non-protectable expression contained in computer programs.

(b) Elements Dictated By External Factors

We have stated that where "it is virtually impossible to write about a particular historical era or fictional theme without employing certain 'stock' or standard literary devices," such expression is not copyrightable. Hoehling v. Universal City

Studios, Inc., 618 F.2d 972, 979 (2d Cir.), cert. de- nied, 449 U.S. 841, 66 L. Ed. 2d 49, 101 S. Ct. 121 (1980). For example, the Hoehling case was an infringement suit stemming from several works on the Hindenberg disaster. There we concluded that similarities in representations of German beer halls, scenes depicting German greetings such as "Heil Hitler," or the singing of certain German songs would not lead to a finding of infringement because they were "'indispensable, or at least standard, in the treatment of'" life in Nazi Germany. Id. (quoting Alexander v. Haley, 460 F. Supp. 40, 45 (S.D.N.Y. 1978)). This is known as the scenes a faire doctrine, and like "merger," it has its analogous application to computer programs. Cf. Data East USA, 862 F.2d at 208 (applying scenes a faire to a home computer video game).

Professor Nimmer points out that "in many instances it is virtually impossible to write a pro- gram to perform particular functions in a specific computing environment without employing stan- dard techniques." 3 Nimmer § 13.03[F][3], at 13-65. This is a result of the fact that a programmer's freedom of design choice is often circumscribed by extrinsic considerations such as (1) the me- chanical specifications of the computer on which a particular program [*710] is intended to run; (2) compatibility requirements of other programs with which a program is designed to operate in conjunction; (3) computer manufacturers' design standards; (4) demands of the industry being serv- iced; and (5) widely accepted programming practices within the computer industry. Id. at 13-66-71.

Courts have already considered some of these factors in denying copyright protection to various elements of computer programs. In the Plains Cotton case, the Fifth Circuit refused to reverse the district court's denial of a preliminary injunction against an alleged program infringer because, in part, "many of the similarities between the programs [were] dictated by the externalities of the cotton market." 807 F.2d at 1262.

In Manufacturers Technologies, the district court noted that the program's method of screen navigation "is influenced by the type of hardware that the software is designed to be used on." 706 F. Supp. at 995. Because, in part, "the functioning of the hardware package impacted and con- strained the type of navigational tools used in plaintiff's screen displays," the court denied copyright protection to that aspect of the program. Cf. Data East USA, 862 F.2d at 209 (reversing a district court's finding of audiovisual work infringement because, inter alia, "the use of the Commodore computer for a karate game intended for home consumption is subject to various constraints inher- ent in the use of that computer").

Finally, the district court in Q-Co Industries rested its holding on what, perhaps, most closely approximates a traditional scenes a faire rationale. There, the court denied copyright protection to four program modules employed in a teleprompter program. This decision was ultimately based upon the court's finding that "the same modules would be an inherent part of any prompting pro- gram." 625 F. Supp. at 616.

Building upon this existing case law, we conclude that a court must also examine the structural content of an allegedly infringed program for elements that might have been dictated by external factors.

(c) Elements taken From the Public Domain

Closely related to the non-protectability of scenes a faire, is material found in the public do- main. Such material is free for the taking and cannot be appropriated by a single author even though it is included in a copyrighted work. See E.F. Johnson Co. v. Uniden Corp. of America, 623 F. Supp. 1485, 1499 (D. Minn. 1985); see also Sheldon, 81 F.2d at 54. We see no reason to make an exception to this rule for elements of a computer program that have entered the public domain by virtue of freely accessible program exchanges and the like. See 3 Nimmer § 13.03[F][4]; see also Brown Bag Software, 960 F.2d at 1473 (affirming the district court's finding that "'plaintiffs may not claim copyright protection of an . . . expression that is, if not standard, then commonplace in the computer software industry.'"). Thus, a court must also filter out this material from the allegedly infringed program before it makes the final inquiry in its substantial similarity analysis.

Step Three: Comparison

The third and final step of the test for substantial similarity that we believe appropriate for non- literal program components entails a comparison. Once a court has sifted out all elements of the al- legedly infringed program which are "ideas" or are dictated by efficiency or external factors, or taken from the public domain, there may remain a core of protectable expression. In terms of a work's copyright value, this is the golden nugget. See Brown Bag Software, 960 F.2d at 1475. At this point, the court's substantial similarity inquiry focuses on whether the defendant copied any as- pect of this protected expression, as well as an assessment of the copied portion's relative impor- tance with respect to the plaintiff's overall program. See 3 Nimmer § 13.03[F][5]; Data East USA, 862 F.2d at 208 ("To determine whether similarities result from unprotectable expression, analytic dissection of similarities may be performed. If . . . all similarities in expression arise from use of common ideas, then no substantial similarity can be found.").

3) Policy Considerations

We are satisfied that the three step approach we have just outlined not only comports with, but advances the constitutional policies underlying the Copyright Act. Since any method that tries to distinguish idea from expression ultimately impacts on the scope of copyright protection afforded to a particular type of work, "the line [it draws] must be a pragmatic one, which also keeps in consid- eration 'the preservation of the balance between competition and protection... .'" Apple Computer, 714 F.2d at 1253 (citation omitted).

CA and some amici argue against the type of approach that we have set forth on the grounds that it will be a disincentive for future computer program research and development. At bottom, they claim that if programmers are not guaranteed broad copyright protection for their work, they will not invest the extensive time, energy and funds required to design and improve program struc- tures. While they have a point, their argument cannot carry the day. The interest of the copyright law is not in simply conferring a monopoly on industrious persons, but in advancing the public welfare through rewarding artistic creativity, in a manner that permits the free use and development of non-protectable ideas and processes.

In this respect, our conclusion is informed by Justice Stewart's concise discussion of the principles that correctly govern the adaptation of the copyright law to new circumstances. In Twentieth Century Music Corp. v. Aiken, he wrote:

The limited scope of the copyright holder's statutory monopoly, like the limited copyright dura- tion required by the Constitution, reflects a balance of competing claims upon the public interest: Creative work is to be encouraged and rewarded, but private motivation must ultimately serve the cause of promoting broad public availability of literature, music, and the other arts.

The immediate effect of our copyright law is to secure a fair return for an "author's" creative la- bor. But the ultimate aim is, by this incentive, to stimulate artistic creativity for the general public good... . When technological change has rendered its literal terms ambiguous, the Copyright Act must be construed in light of this basic purpose. 422 U.S. 151, 156, 95 S. Ct. 2040, 45 L. Ed. 2d 84 (1975) (citations and footnotes omitted).

Recently, the Supreme Court has emphatically reiterated that "the primary objective of copyright is not to reward the labor of authors...." Feist Publications, Inc. v. Rural Tel. Serv. Co., 113 L. Ed. 2d 358, 111 S. Ct. 1282, 1290 (1991) (emphasis added). While the Feist decision deals pri- marily with the copyrightability of purely factual compilations, its underlying tenets apply to much of the work involved in computer programming. Feist put to rest the "sweat of the brow" doctrine in copyright law. Id. at 1295. The rationale of that doctrine "was that copyright was a reward for the hard work that went into compiling facts." Id. at 1291. The Court flatly rejected this justification for extending copyright protection, noting that it "eschewed the most fundamental axiom of copyright law--that no one may copyright facts or ideas." Id.

Feist teaches that substantial effort alone cannot confer copyright status on an otherwise uncopyrightable work. As we have discussed, despite the fact that significant labor and expense often goes into computer program flow-charting and debugging, that process does not always result in inherently protectable expression. Thus, Feist implicitly undercuts the Whelan rationale, "which al- lowed copyright protection beyond the literal computer code ... . [in order to] provide the proper incentive for programmers by protecting their most valuable efforts... ." Whelan, 797 F.2d at 1237 (footnote omitted). We note that Whelan was decided prior to Feist when the "sweat of the brow" doctrine still had vitality. In view of the Supreme Court's recent holding, however, we must reject the legal basis of CA's disincentive argument.

Furthermore, we are unpersuaded that the test we approve today will lead to the dire consequences for the computer program industry that plaintiff and some amici predict. To the contrary, serious students of the industry have been highly critical of the sweeping scope of copyright protec- tion engendered by the Whelan rule, in that it "enables first comers to 'lock up' basic programming techniques as implemented in programs to perform particular tasks." Menell, at 1087; see also Spivack, at 765 (Whelan "results in an inhibition of creation by virtue of the copyright owner's quasi-monopoly power").

To be frank, the exact contours of copyright protection for non-literal program structure are not completely clear. We trust that as future cases are decided, those limits will become better defined. Indeed, it may well be that the Copyright Act serves as a relatively weak barrier against public access to the theoretical interstices behind a program's source and object codes. This results from the hybrid nature of a computer program, which, while it is literary expression, is also a highly func- tional, utilitarian component in the larger process of computing.

Generally, we think that copyright registration--with its indiscriminating availability--is not ide- ally suited to deal with the highly dynamic technology of computer science. Thus far, many of the decisions in this area reflect the courts' attempt to fit the proverbial square peg in a round hole. The district court, see Computer Assocs., 775 F. Supp. at 560, and at least one commentator have suggested that patent registration, with its exacting up-front novelty and non-obviousness requirements, might be the more appropriate rubric of protection for intellectual property of this kind. See Randell M. Whitmeyer, Comment, A Plea for Due Processes: Defining the Proper Scope of Patent Protec- tion for Computer Software, 85 NW. U. L. REV. 1103, 1123-25 (1991); see also Lotus Dev. Corp. v. Borland Int'l, Inc., 788 F. Supp. 78, 91 (D. Mass. 1992) (discussing the potentially supplemental relationship between patent and copyright protection in the context of computer programs). In any event, now that more than 12 years have passed since CONTU issued its final report, the resolution of this specific issue could benefit from further legislative investigation--perhaps a CONTU II.

In the meantime, Congress has made clear that computer programs are literary works entitled to copyright protection. Of course, we shall abide by these instructions, but in so doing we must not impair the overall integrity of copyright law. While incentive based arguments in favor of broad copyright protection are perhaps attractive from a pure policy perspective, see Lotus Dev. Corp., 740 F. Supp. at 58, ultimately, they have a corrosive effect on certain fundamental tenets of copyright doctrine. If the test we have outlined results in narrowing the scope of protection, as we ex- pect it will, that result flows from applying, in accordance with Congressional intent, long-standing principles of copyright law to computer programs. Of course, our decision is also informed by our concern that these fundamental principles remain undistorted.

...

49 F.3d 807 (1995)

LOTUS DEVELOPMENT CORP. v. BORLAND

United States Court of Appeals First Circuit

STAHL, Circuit Judge.

[1] This appeal requires us to decide whether a computer menu command hierarchy is copyrightable subject matter. In particular, we must decide whether, as the district court held, plaintiff-appellee Lotus Development Corporation's

copyright in Lotus 1-2-3, a computer spreadsheet program, was infringed by defendant-appellant Borland International, Inc., when Borland copied the Lotus 1-2-3 menu command hierarchy into its Quattro and Quattro Pro computer spreadsheet programs. ...

I.

[2] Background

[3] Lotus 1-2-3 is a spreadsheet program that enables users to perform accounting functions electronically on a computer. Users manipulate and control the program via a series of menu commands, such as "Copy," "Print," and "Quit." Users choose commands either by highlighting them on the screen or by typing their first letter. In all, Lotus 1-2-3 has 469 commands arranged into more than 50 menus and submenus.

[4] Lotus 1-2-3, like many computer programs, allows users to write what are called "macros." By writing a macro, a user can designate a series of command choices with a single macro keystroke. Then, to execute that series of commands in multiple parts of the spreadsheet, rather than typing the whole series each time, the user only needs to type the single pre-programmed macro keystroke, causing the program to recall and perform the designated series of commands automatically. Thus, Lotus 1-2-3 macros shorten the time needed to set up and operate the program.

[5] Borland released its first Quattro program to the public in 1987, after Borland's engineers had labored over its development for nearly three years. Borland's objective was to develop a spreadsheet program far superior to existing programs, including Lotus 1-2-3. In Borland's words, "[f]rom the time of its initial release . . . Quattro included enormous innovations over competing spreadsheet products."

[6] The district court found, and Borland does not now contest, that Borland included in its Quattro and Quattro Pro version 1.0 programs "a virtually identical copy of the entire 1-2-3 menu tree." Borland III, 831 F. Supp. at 212 (emphasis in original). In so doing, Borland did not copy any of Lotus's underlying computer code; it copied only the words and structure of Lotus's menu command hierarchy. Borland included the Lotus menu command hierarchy in its programs to make them compatible with Lotus 1-2-3 so that spreadsheet users who were already familiar with Lotus 1-2-3 would be able to switch to the Borland programs without having to learn new commands or rewrite their Lotus macros.

[7] In its Quattro and Quattro Pro version 1.0 programs, Borland achieved compatibility with Lotus 1-2-3 by offering its users an alternate user interface, the "Lotus Emulation Interface." By activating the Emulation Interface, Borland users would see the Lotus menu commands on their screens and could interact with Quattro or Quattro Pro as if using Lotus 1-2-3, albeit with a slightly different looking screen and with many Borland options not available on Lotus 1-2-3. In effect, Borland allowed users to choose how they wanted to communicate with Borland's spreadsheet programs: either by using menu commands designed by Borland, or by using the commands and command structure used in Lotus 1-2-3 augmented by Borland-added commands.

...

[19] This appeal concerns only Borland's copying of the Lotus menu command hierarchy into its Quattro programs and Borland's affirmative defenses to such copying. Lotus has not cross-appealed; in other words, Lotus does not contend on appeal that the district court erred in finding that Borland had not copied other elements of Lotus 1-2-3, such as its screen displays.

II.

[20] Discussion

[21] On appeal, Borland does not dispute that it factually copied the words and arrangement of the Lotus menu command hierarchy. Rather, Borland argues that it "lawfully copied the unprotectable menus of Lotus 1-2-3." Borland contends that the Lotus menu command hierarchy is not copyrightable because it is a system, method of operation, process, or procedure foreclosed from protection by 17 U.S.C. 102(b). Borland also raises a number of affirmative defenses.

...

[25] In this appeal, we are faced only with whether the Lotus menu command hierarchy is copyrightable subject matter in the first instance, for Borland concedes that Lotus has a valid copyright in Lotus 1-2-3 as a wholeand admits to factually copying the Lotus menu command hierarchy. As a result, this appeal is in a very different posture from most copyright-infringement cases, for copyright infringement generally turns on whether the defendant has copied protected expression as a factual matter. Because of this different posture, most copyright-infringement cases provide only limited help to us in deciding this appeal. This is true even with respect to those copyright-infringement cases that deal with computers and computer software.

...

[31] C. Altai

[32] Before we analyze whether the Lotus menu command hierarchy is a system, method of operation, process, or procedure, we first consider the applicability of the test the Second Circuit set forth in Computer Assoc. Int'l, Inc. v. Altai, Inc., 982 F.2d 693 (2d Cir. 1992). The Second Circuit designed its Altai test to deal with the fact that computer programs, copyrighted as "literary works," can be infringed by what is known as "nonliteral" copying, which is copying that is paraphrased or loosely paraphrased rather than word for word. See id. at 701 (citing nonliteral-copying cases); see also 3 Melville B. Nimmer & David Nimmer, Nimmer on Copyright § 13.03[A][1] (1993). When faced with nonliteral-copying cases, courts must determine whether similarities are due merely to the fact that the two works share the same underlying idea or whether they instead indicated that the second author copied the first author's expression. The Second Circuit designed its Altai test to deal with this situation in the computer context, specifically with whether one computer program copied nonliteral expression from another program's code.

...

[34] In the instant appeal, we are not confronted with alleged nonliteral copying of computer code. Rather, we are faced with Borland's deliberate, literal copying of the Lotus menu command hierarchy. Thus, we must determine not whether nonliteral copying occurred in some amorphous sense, but rather whether the literal copying of the Lotus menu command hierarchy constitutes copyright infringement.

[35] While the Altai test may provide a useful framework for assessing the alleged nonliteral copying of computer code, we find it to be of little help in assessing whether the literal copying of a menu command hierarchy constitutes copyright infringement. In fact, we think that the Altai test in this context may actually be misleading because, in instructing courts to abstract the various levels, it seems to encourage them to find a base level that includes copyrightable subject matter that, if literally copied, would make the copier liable for copyright infringement. While that base (or literal) level would not be at issue in a nonliteral-copying case like Altai, it is precisely what is at issue in this appeal. We think that abstracting menu command hierarchies down to their individual word and menu levels and then filtering idea from expression at that stage, as both the Altai and the district court tests require, obscures the more fundamental question of whether a menu command hierarchy can be copyrighted at all. The initial inquiry should not be whether individual components of a menu command hierarchy are expressive, but rather whether the menu command hierarchy as a whole can be copyrighted. But see Gates Rubber Co. v. Bando Chem. Indus., Ltd., 9 F.3d 823 (10th Cir. 1993) (endorsing Altai's abstraction-filtration-comparison test as a way of determining whether "menus and sorting criteria" are copyrightable).

[36] D. The Lotus Menu Command Hierarchy: A "Method of Operation"

[37] Borland argues that the Lotus menu command hierarchy is uncopyrightable because it is a system, method of operation, process, or procedure foreclosed from copyright protection by 17 U.S.C. 102(b). Section 102(b) states: "In no case does copyright protection for an original work of authorship extend to any idea, procedure, process, system, method of operation, concept, principle, or discovery, regardless of the form in which it is described, explained, illustrated, or embodied in such work." Because we conclude that the Lotus menu command hierarchy is a method of operation, we do not consider whether it could also be a system, process, or procedure.

[38] We think that "method of operation," as that term is used in 102(b), refers to the means by which a person operates something, whether it be a car, a food processor, or a computer. Thus a text describing how to operate something would not extend copyright protection to the method of operation itself; other people would be free to employ that method and to describe it in their own words. Similarly, if a new method of operation is used rather than described, other people would still be free to employ or describe that method.

[39] We hold that the Lotus menu command hierarchy is an uncopyrightable "method of operation." The Lotus menu command hierarchy provides the means

by which users control and operate Lotus 1-2-3. If users wish to copy material, for example, they use the "Copy" command. If users wish to print material, they use the "Print" command. Users must use the command terms to tell the computer what to do. Without the menu command hierarchy, users would not be able to access and control, or indeed make use of, Lotus 1-2-3's functional capabilities.

[40] The Lotus menu command hierarchy does not merely explain and present Lotus 1-2-3's functional capabilities to the user; it also serves as the method by which the program is operated and controlled. The Lotus menu command hierarchy is different from the Lotus long prompts, for the long prompts are not necessary to the operation of the program; users could operate Lotus 1-2-3 even if there were no long prompts. The Lotus menu command hierarchy is also different from the Lotus screen displays, for users need not "use" any expressive aspects of the screen displays in order to operate Lotus 1-2-3; because the way the screens look has little bearing on how users control the program, the screen displays are not part of Lotus 1-2-3's "method of operation." The Lotus menu command hierarchy is also different from the underlying computer code, because while code is necessary for the program to work, its precise formulation is not. In other words, to offer the same capabilities as Lotus 1-2-3, Borland did not have to copy Lotus's underlying code (and indeed it did not); to allow users to operate its programs in substantially the same way, however, Borland had to copy the Lotus menu command hierarchy. Thus the Lotus 1-2-3 code is not a uncopyrightable "method of operation."

[41] The district court held that the Lotus menu command hierarchy, with its specific choice and arrangement of command terms, constituted an "expression" of the "idea" of operating a computer program with commands arranged hierarchically into menus and submenus. Borland II, 799 F. Supp. at 216. Under the district court's reasoning, Lotus's decision to employ hierarchically arranged command terms to operate its program could not foreclose its competitors from also employing hierarchically arranged command terms to operate their programs, but it did foreclose them from employing the specific command terms and arrangement that Lotus had used. In effect, the district court limited Lotus 1-2-3's "method of operation" to an abstraction.

[42] Accepting the district court's finding that the Lotus developers made some expressive choices in choosing and arranging the Lotus command terms, we nonetheless hold that that expression is not copyrightable because it is part of Lotus 1-2-3's "method of operation." We do not think that "methods of operation" are limited to abstractions; rather, they are the means by which a user operates something. If specific words are essential to operating something, then they are part of a "method of operation" and, as such, are unprotectable. This is so whether they must be highlighted, typed in, or even spoken, as computer programs no doubt will soon be controlled by spoken words.

[43] The fact that Lotus developers could have designed the Lotus menu command hierarchy differently is immaterial to the question of whether it is a "method of operation." In other words, our initial inquiry is not whether the Lotus menu command hierarchy incorporates any expression. Rather, our initial inquiry is

whether the Lotus menu command hierarchy is a "method of operation." Concluding, as we do, that users operate Lotus 1-2-3 by using the Lotus menu command hierarchy, and that the entire Lotus menu command hierarchy is essential to operating Lotus 1-2-3, we do not inquire further whether that method of operation could have been designed differently. The "expressive" choices of what to name the command terms and how to arrange them do not magically change the uncopyrightable menu command hierarchy into copyrightable subject matter.

... Lotus wrote its menu command hierarchy so that people could learn it and use it. Accordingly, it falls squarely within the prohibition on copyright protection established in Baker v. Selden and codified by Congress in 102(b).

[46] In many ways, the Lotus menu command hierarchy is like the buttons used to control, say, a video cassette recorder ("VCR"). A VCR is a machine that enables one to watch and record video tapes. Users operate VCRs by pressing a series of buttons that are typically labelled "Record, Play, Reverse, Fast Forward, Pause, Stop/Eject." That the buttons are arranged and labeled does not make them a "literary work," nor does it make them an "expression" of the abstract "method of operating" a VCR via a set of labeled buttons. Instead, the buttons are themselves the "method of operating" the VCR.

[47] When a Lotus 1-2-3 user chooses a command, either by highlighting it on the screen or by typing its first letter, he or she effectively pushes a button. Highlighting the "Print" command on the screen, or typing the letter "P," is analogous to pressing a VCR button labeled "Play."

[48] Just as one could not operate a buttonless VCR, it would be impossible to operate Lotus 1-2-3 without employing its menu command hierarchy. Thus the Lotus command terms are not equivalent to the labels on the VCR's buttons, but are instead equivalent to the buttons themselves. Unlike the labels on a VCR's buttons, which merely make operating a VCR easier by indicating the buttons' functions, the Lotus menu commands are essential to operating Lotus 1-2-3. Without the menu commands, there would be no way to "push" the Lotus buttons, as one could push unlabeled VCR buttons. While Lotus could probably have designed a user interface for which the command terms were mere labels, it did not do so here. Lotus 1-2-3 depends for its operation on use of the precise command terms that make up the Lotus menu command hierarchy.

[49] One might argue that the buttons for operating a VCR are not analogous to the commands for operating a computer program because VCRs are not copyrightable, whereas computer programs are. VCR's may not be copyrighted because they do not fit within any of the 102(a) categories of copyrightable works; the closest they come is "sculptural work." Sculptural works, however, are subject to a "useful-article" exception whereby "the design of a useful article . . . shall be considered a pictorial, graphic, or sculptural work only if, and only to the extent that, such design incorporates pictorial, graphic, or sculptural features that can be identified separately from, and are capable of existing independently of, the utilitarian aspects of the article." 17 U.S.C. 101. A "useful article" is "an article having an intrinsic utilitarian function that is not merely to portray the appearance of the article or to convey information." Id. Whatever expression there may be in

the arrangement of the parts of a VCR is not capable of existing separately from the VCR itself, so an ordinary VCR would not be copyrightable.

[50] Computer programs, unlike VCRs, are copyrightable as "literary works." 17 U.S.C. 102(a). Accordingly, one might argue, the "buttons" used to operate a computer program are not like the buttons used to operate a VCR, for they are not subject to a useful-article exception. The response, of course, is that the arrangement of buttons on a VCR would not be copyrightable even without a useful-article exception, because the buttons are an uncopyrightable "method of operation." Similarly, the "buttons" of a computer program are also an uncopyrightable "method of operation."

[51] That the Lotus menu command hierarchy is a "method of operation" becomes clearer when one considers program compatibility. Under Lotus's theory, if a user uses several different programs, he or she must learn how to perform the same operation in a different way for each program used. For example, if the user wanted the computer to print material, then the user would have to learn not just one method of operating the computer such that it prints, but many different methods. We find this absurd. The fact that there may be many different ways to operate a computer program, or even many different ways to operate a computer program using a set of hierarchically arranged command terms, does not make the actual method of operation chosen copyrightable; it still functions as a method for operating the computer and as such is uncopyrightable.

[52] Consider also that users employ the Lotus menu command hierarchy in writing macros. Under the district court's holding, if the user wrote a macro to shorten the time needed to perform a certain operation in Lotus 1-2-3, the user would be unable to use that macro to shorten the time needed to perform that same operation in another program. Rather, the user would have to rewrite his or her macro using that other program's menu command hierarchy. This is despite the fact that the macro is clearly the user's own work product. We think that forcing the user to cause the computer to perform the same operation in a different way ignores Congress's direction in   102(b) that "methods of operation" are not copyrightable. That programs can offer users the ability to write macros in many different ways does not change the fact that, once written, the macro allows the user to perform an operation automatically. As the Lotus menu command hierarchy serves as the basis for Lotus 1-2-3 macros, the Lotus menu command hierarchy is a "method of operation."

...

III.

[57] Conclusion

[58] Because we hold that the Lotus menu command hierarchy is uncopyrightable subject matter, we further hold that Borland did not infringe Lotus's copyright by copying it. Accordingly, we need not consider any of Borland's affirmative defenses. The judgment of the district court is

[59] Reversed.

ORACLE v. GOOGLE (I)
United States Court of Appeals, Federal Circuit

O'MALLEY, Circuit Judge:

This copyright dispute involves 37 packages of computer source code. The parties have often referred to these groups of computer programs, individually or collectively, as "application programming interfaces," or API packages, but it is their content, not their name, that matters. The predecessor of Oracle America, Inc. ("Oracle") wrote these and other API packages in the Java programming language, and Oracle licenses them on various terms for others to use. Many software developers use the Java language, as well as Oracle's API packages, to write applications (commonly referred to as "apps") for desktop and laptop computers, tablets, smartphones, and other devices.

Oracle filed suit against Google Inc. ("Google") in the United States District Court for the Northern District of California, alleging that Google's Android mobile operating system infringed Oracle's patents and copyrights. The jury found no patent infringement, and the patent claims are not at issue in this appeal. As to the copyright claims, the parties agreed that the jury would decide infringement, fair use, and whether any copying was de minimis, while the district judge would decide copyrightability and Google's equitable defenses. The jury found that Google infringed Oracle's copyrights in the 37 Java packages and a specific computer routine called "rangeCheck," but returned a noninfringement verdict as to eight decompiled security files. The jury deadlocked on Google's fair use defense.

After the jury verdict, the district court denied Oracle's motion for judgment as a matter of law ("JMOL") regarding fair use as well as Google's motion for JMOL with respect to the rangeCheck files. Order on Motions for Judgment as a Matter of Law, Oracle Am., Inc. v. Google Inc., No. 3:10−cv−3561 (N.D.Cal. May 10, 2012), ECF No. 1119. Oracle also moved for JMOL of infringement with respect to the eight decompiled security files. In granting that motion, the court found that: (1) Google admitted to copying the eight files; and (2) no reasonable jury could find that the copying was de minimis. Oracle Am., Inc. v. Google Inc., No. C 10−3561, 2012 U.S. Dist. LEXIS 66417 (N.D.Cal. May 11, 2012) ("Order Granting JMOL on Decompiled Files ").

Shortly thereafter, the district court issued its decision on copyrightability, finding that the replicated elements of the 37 API packages-including the declaring code and the structure, sequence, and organization-were not subject to copyright protection. Oracle Am., Inc. v. Google Inc., 872 F.Supp.2d 974 (N.D.Cal.2012) ("Copyrightability Decision"). Accordingly, the district court entered final judgment in favor of Google on Oracle's copyright infringement claims, except with respect to the rangeCheck code and the eight decompiled files. Final Judgment,

Oracle Am., Inc. v. Google Inc., No. 3:10–cv3561 (N.D. Cal. June 20, 2012), ECF No. 1211. Oracle appeals from the portion of the final judgment entered against it, and Google cross-appeals from the portion of that same judgment entered in favor of Oracle as to the rangeCheck code and eight decompiled files.

Because we conclude that the declaring code and the structure, sequence, and organization of the API packages are entitled to copyright protection, we reverse the district court's copyrightability determination with instructions to reinstate the jury's infringement finding as to the 37 Java packages. Because the jury deadlocked on fair use, we remand for further consideration of Google's fair use defense in light of this decision. With respect to Google's cross-appeal, we affirm the district court's decisions: (1) granting Oracle's motion for JMOL as to the eight decompiled Java files that Google copied into Android; and (2) denying Google's motion for JMOL with respect to the rangeCheck function. Accordingly, we affirm-in-part, reverse-in-part, and remand for further proceedings.

Background

A. The Technology

Sun Microsystems, Inc. ("Sun") developed the Java "platform" for computer programming and released it in 1996. The aim was to relieve programmers from the burden of writing different versions of their computer programs for different operating systems or devices. "The Java platform, through the use of a virtual machine, enable[d] software developers to write programs that [we]re able to run on different types of computer hardware without having to rewrite them for each different type." Copyrightability Decision, 872 F.Supp.2d at 977. With Java, a software programmer could "write once, run anywhere."

The Java virtual machine ("JVM") plays a central role in the overall Java platform. The Java programming language itself-which includes words, symbols, and other units, together with syntax rules for using them to create instructions-is the language in which a Java programmer writes source code, the version of a program that is "in a human-readable language." Id. For the instructions to be executed, they must be converted (or compiled) into binary machine code (object code) consisting of 0s and 1s understandable by the particular computing device. In the Java system, "source code is first converted into 'bytecode,' an intermediate form, before it is then converted into binary machine code by the Java virtual machine" that has been designed for that device. Id. The Java platform includes the "Java development kit (JDK), javac compiler, tools and utilities, runtime programs, class libraries (API packages), and the Java virtual machine." Id. at 977 n.2.

Sun wrote a number of ready-to-use Java programs to perform common computer functions and organized those programs into groups it called "packages." These packages, which are the application programming interfaces at issue in this appeal, allow programmers to use the pre-written code to build certain functions into their own programs, rather than write their own code to perform those functions from scratch. They are shortcuts. Sun called the code for a specific operation (function) a "method." It defined "classes" so that each class consists of specified methods plus variables and other elements on which the methods operate. To organize the classes for users, then, it grouped classes (along with certain related "interfaces") into "packages." See id. at 982 (describing organization: "[e]ach package [i]s broken into classes and those in turn [are] broken into methods"). The parties have not disputed the district court's analogy: Oracle's collection of API packages is like a library, each package is like a bookshelf in the library, each class is like a book on the shelf, and each method is like a how-to chapter in a book. Id. at 977.

The original Java Standard Edition Platform ("Java SE") included "eight packages of pre-written programs." Id. at 982. The district court found, and Oracle concedes to some extent, that three of those packages—java.lang, java.io, and java.util—were "core" packages, meaning that programmers using the Java language had to use them "in order to make any worthwhile use of the language." Id. By 2008, the Java platform had more than 6,000 methods making up more than 600 classes grouped into 166 API packages. There are 37 Java API packages at issue in this appeal, three of which are the core packages identified by the district court. These packages contain thousands of individual elements, including classes, subclasses, methods, and interfaces.

Every package consists of two types of source code—what the parties call (1) declaring code; and (2) implementing code. Declaring code is the expression that identifies the prewritten function and is sometimes referred to as the "declaration" or "header." As the district court explained, the "main point is that this header line of code introduces the method body and specifies very precisely the inputs, name and other functionality." Id. at 979–80. The expressions used by the programmer from the declaring code command the computer to execute the associated implementing code, which gives the computer the step-by-step instructions for carrying out the declared function.

To use the district court's example, one of the Java API packages at issue is "java.lang." Within that package is a class called "math," and within "math" there are several methods, including one that is designed to find the larger of two numbers: "max." The declaration for the "max" method, as defined for integers, is: "public static int max(int x, int y)," where the word "public" means that the method is generally accessible, "static" means that no specific instance of the class is needed to call the method, the first "int" indicates that the method returns an integer, and "int x" and "int y" are the two numbers (inputs) being compared. Copyrightability Decision, 872 F.Supp.2d at 980–82. A programmer calls the "max" method by typing the name of the method stated in the declaring code and providing unique inputs for the variables "x" and "y." The expressions used command the computer to execute the implementing code that carries out the operation of returning the larger number.

Although Oracle owns the copyright on Java SE and the API packages, it offers three different licenses to those who want to make use of them. The first is the General Public License, which is free of charge and provides that the licensee can use the packages—both the declaring and implementing code—but must "contribute back" its innovations to the public. This arrangement is referred to as an "open source" license. The second option is the Specification License, which provides that the licensee can use the declaring code and organization of Oracle's

API packages but must write its own implementing code. The third option is the Commercial License, which is for businesses that "want to use and customize the full Java code in their commercial products and keep their code secret." Appellant Br. 14. Oracle offers the Commercial License in exchange for royalties. To maintain Java's "write once, run anywhere" motto, the Specification and Commercial Licenses require that the licensees' programs pass certain tests to ensure compatibility with the Java platform.

The testimony at trial also revealed that Sun was licensing a derivative version of the Java platform for use on mobile devices: the Java Micro Edition ("Java ME"). Oracle licensed Java ME for use on feature phones and smartphones. Sun/Oracle has never successfully developed its own smartphone platform using Java.

B. Google's Accused Product: Android

The accused product is Android, a software platform that was designed for mobile devices and competes with Java in that market. Google acquired Android, Inc. in 2005 as part of a plan to develop a smartphone platform. Later that same year, Google and Sun began discussing the possibility of Google "taking a license to use and to adapt the entire Java platform for mobile devices." Copyrightability Decision, 872 F.Supp.2d at 978. They also discussed a "possible co-development partnership deal with Sun under which Java technology would become an open-source part of the Android platform, adapted for mobile devices." Id. The parties negotiated for months but were unable to reach an agreement. The point of contention between the parties was Google's refusal to make the implementation of its programs compatible with the Java virtual machine or interoperable with other Java programs. Because Sun/Oracle found that position to be anathema to the "write once, run anywhere" philosophy, it did not grant Google a license to use the Java API packages.

When the parties' negotiations reached an impasse, Google decided to use the Java programming language to design its own virtual machine—the Dalvik virtual machine ("Dalvik VM")—and "to write its own implementations for the functions in the Java API that were key to mobile devices." Id. Google developed the Android platform, which grew to include 168 API packages—37 of which correspond to the Java API packages at issue in this appeal.

With respect to the 37 packages at issue, "Google believed Java application programmers would want to find the same 37 sets of functionalities in the new Android system callable by the same names as used in Java." Id. To achieve this result, Google copied the declaring source code from the 37 Java API packages verbatim, inserting that code into parts of its Android software. In doing so, Google copied the elaborately organized taxonomy of all the names of methods, classes, interfaces, and packages—the "overall system of organized names-covering 37 packages, with over six hundred classes, with over six thousand methods." Copyrightability Decision, 872 F.Supp.2d at 999. The parties and district court referred to this taxonomy of expressions as the "structure, sequence, and organization" or "SSO" of the 37 packages. It is undisputed, however, that Google wrote its own implementing code, except with respect to: (1) the rangeCheck function, which consisted of nine lines of code; and (2) eight decompiled security files.

As to rangeCheck, the court found that the Sun engineer who wrote it later worked for Google and contributed two files he created containing the rangeCheck function—"Timsort.java" and "ComparableTimsort"—to the Android platform. In doing so, the nine-line rangeCheck function was copied directly into Android. As to the eight decompiled files, the district court found that they were copied and used as test files but "never found their way into Android or any handset." Id. at 983.

Google released the Android platform in 2007, and the first Android phones went on sale the following year. Although it is undisputed that certain Android software contains copies of the 37 API packages' declaring code at issue, neither the district court nor the parties specify in which programs those copies appear. Oracle indicated at oral argument, however, that all Android phones contain copies of the accused portions of the Android software. Oral Argument at 1:35, available at http://www. cafc.uscourts.gov/oral–argument–recordings/2013–1021/all. Android smartphones "rapidly grew in popularity and now comprise a large share of the United States market." Copyrightability Decision, 872 F.Supp.2d at 978. Google provides the Android platform free of charge to smartphone manufacturers and receives revenue when customers use particular functions on the Android phone. Although Android uses the Java programming language, it is undisputed that Android is not generally Java compatible. As Oracle explains, "Google ultimately designed Android to be incompatible with the Java platform, so that apps written for one will not work on the other." Appellant Br. 29.

...

Discussion

I. Oracle's Appeal

It is undisputed that the Java programming language is open and free for anyone to use. Except to the limited extent noted below regarding three of the API packages, it is also undisputed that Google could have written its own API packages using the Java language. Google chose not to do that. Instead, it is undisputed that Google copied 7,000 lines of declaring code and generally replicated the overall structure, sequence, and organization of Oracle's 37 Java API packages. The central question before us is whether these elements of the Java platform are entitled to copyright protection. The district court concluded that they are not, and Oracle challenges that determination on appeal. Oracle also argues that the district court should have dismissed Google's fair use defense as a matter of law.

According to Google, however, the district court correctly determined that: (1) there was only one way to write the Java method declarations and remain "interoperable" with Java; and (2) the organization and structure of the 37 Java API packages is a "command structure" excluded from copyright protection under Section 102(b). Google also argues that, if we reverse the district court's copyrightability determination, we should direct the district court to retry its fair use defense.

"When the questions on appeal involve law and precedent on subjects not exclusively assigned to the Federal Circuit, the court applies the law which would be applied by the regional circuit." Atari Games Corp. v. Nintendo of Am., Inc., 897 F.2d 1572, 1575 (Fed.Cir.1990). Copyright issues are not exclusively assigned to the Federal Circuit. See 28 U.S.C. § 1295. The parties agree that Ninth Circuit law applies and that, in the Ninth Circuit, whether particular expression is protected by copyright law is "subject to de novo review." Ets–Hokin v. Skyy Spirits, Inc., 225 F.3d 1068, 1073 (9th Cir.2000).3

We are mindful that the application of copyright law in the computer context is often a difficult task. See Lotus Dev. Corp. v. Borland Int'l, Inc., 49 F.3d 807, 820 (1st Cir.1995) (Boudin, J ., concurring) ("Applying copyright law to computer programs is like assembling a jigsaw puzzle whose pieces do not quite fit."). On this record, however, we find that the district court failed to distinguish between the threshold question of what is copyrightable—which presents a low bar—and the scope of conduct that constitutes infringing activity. The court also erred by importing fair use principles, including interoperability concerns, into its copyrightability analysis.

For the reasons that follow, we conclude that the declaring code and the structure, sequence, and organization of the 37 Java API packages are entitled to copyright protection. Because there is an insufficient record as to the relevant fair use factors, we remand for further proceedings on Google's fair use defense.

A. Copyrightability

...

It is well established that copyright protection can extend to both literal and non-literal elements of a computer program. See Altai, 982 F.2d at 702. The literal elements of a computer program are the source code and object code. See Johnson Controls, Inc. v. Phoenix Control Sys., Inc., 886 F.2d 1173, 1175 (9th Cir.1989). Courts have defined source code as "the spelled-out program commands that humans can read." Lexmark Int'l, Inc. v. Static Control Components, Inc., 387 F.3d 522, 533 (6th Cir.2004). Object code refers to "the binary language comprised of zeros and ones through which the computer directly receives its instructions." Altai, 982 F.2d at 698. Both source and object code "are consistently held protected by a copyright on the program." Johnson Controls, 886 F.2d at 1175; see also Altai, 982 F.2d at 702 ("It is now well settled that the literal elements of computer programs, i.e., their source and object codes, are the subject of copyright protection."). Google nowhere disputes that premise. See, e.g., Oral Argument at 57:38.

The non-literal components of a computer program include, among other things, the program's sequence, structure, and organization, as well as the program's user interface. Johnson Controls, 886 F.2d at 1175. As discussed below, whether the non-literal elements of a program "are protected depends on whether, on the particular facts of each case, the component in question qualifies as an expression of an idea, or an idea itself." Id.

In this case, Oracle claims copyright protection with respect to both: (1) literal elements of its API packages—the 7,000 lines of declaring source code; and (2) non-literal elements—the structure, sequence, and organization of each of the 37 Java API packages.

The distinction between literal and non-literal aspects of a computer program is separate from the distinction between literal and non-literal copying. See Altai, 982 F.2d at 701–02. "Literal" copying is verbatim copying of original expression. "Non-literal" copying is "paraphrased or loosely paraphrased rather than word for word." Lotus Dev. Corp. v. Borland Int'l, 49 F.3d 807, 814 (1st Cir.1995). Here, Google concedes that it copied the declaring code verbatim. Oracle explains that the lines of declaring code "embody the structure of each [API] package, just as the chapter titles and topic sentences represent the structure of a novel." Appellant Br. 45. As Oracle explains, when Google copied the declaring code in these packages "it also copied the 'sequence and organization' of the packages (i.e., the three-dimensional structure with all the chutes and ladders)" employed by Sun/Oracle in the packages. Appellant Br. 27. Oracle also argues that the nonliteral elements of the API packages—the structure, sequence, and organization that led naturally to the implementing code Google created—are entitled to protection. Oracle does not assert "literal" copying of the entire SSO, but, rather, that Google literally copied the declaring code and then paraphrased the remainder of the SSO by writing its own implementing code. It therefore asserts non-literal copying with respect to the entirety of the SSO.

At this stage, it is undisputed that the declaring code and the structure and organization of the Java API packages are original. The testimony at trial revealed that designing the Java API packages was a creative process and that the Sun/Oracle developers had a vast range of options for the structure and organization. In its copyrightability decision, the district court specifically found that the API packages are both creative and original, and Google concedes on appeal that the originality requirements are met. See Copyrightability Decision, 872 F.Supp.2d at 976 ("The overall name tree, of course, has creative elements."); Id. at 999 ("Yes, it is creative. Yes, it is original."); Appellee Br. 5 ("Google does not dispute" the district court's finding that "the Java API clears the low originality threshold."). The court found, however, that neither the declaring code nor the SSO was entitled to copyright protection under the Copyright Act.

Although the parties agree that Oracle's API packages meet the originality requirement under Section 102(a), they disagree as to the proper interpretation and application of Section 102(b). For its part, Google suggests that there is a two-step copyrightability analysis, wherein Section 102(a) grants copyright protection to original works, while Section 102(b) takes it away if the work has a functional component. To the contrary, however, Congress emphasized that Section 102(b) "in no way enlarges or contracts the scope of copyright protection" and that its "purpose is to restate . that the basic dichotomy between expression and idea remains unchanged." Feist, 499 U.S. at 356 (quoting H.R.Rep. No. 1476, 94th Cong., 2d Sess. 54, reprinted in 1976 U.S.C.C.A.N. 5659, 5670). "Section 102(b) does not extinguish the protection accorded a particular expression of an idea merely because that expression is embodied in a method of operation." Mitel, Inc. v. Iqtel, Inc., 124 F.3d 1366, 1372 (10th Cir.1997). Section 102(a) and 102(b) are to be considered collectively so that certain expressions are subject to greater scrutiny. Id. In assessing copyrightability, the district court is required to ferret out apparent expressive aspects of a work and then separate protectable expression from "unprotectable ideas, facts, processes, and methods of operation." See Atari, 975 F.2d at 839.

Of course, as with many things, in defining this task, the devil is in the details. Circuit courts have struggled with, and disagree over, the tests to be employed when attempting to draw the line between what is protectable expression and what is not. Compare Whelan Assocs., Inc. v. Jaslow Dental Lab., Inc., 797 F.2d 1222, 1236 (3d Cir.1986) (everything not necessary to the purpose or function of a work is expression), with Lotus, 49 F.3d at 815 (methods of operation are means by which a user operates something and any words used to effectuate that operation are unprotected expression). When assessing whether the non-literal elements of a computer program constitute protectable expression, the Ninth Circuit has endorsed an "abstraction-filtration-comparison" test formulated by the Second Circuit and expressly adopted by several other circuits. Sega Enters. Ltd. v. Accolade, Inc., 977 F.2d 1510, 1525 (9th Cir.1992) ("In our view, in light of the essentially utilitarian nature of computer programs, the Second Circuit's approach is an appropriate one."). This test rejects the notion that anything that performs a function is necessarily uncopyrightable. See Mitel, 124 F.3d at 1372 (rejecting the Lotus court's formulation, and concluding that, "although an element of a work may be characterized as a method of operation, that element may nevertheless contain expression that is eligible for copyright protection."). And it also rejects as flawed the Whelan assumption that, once any separable idea can be identified in a computer program everything else must be protectable expression, on grounds that more than one idea may be embodied in any particular program. Altai, 982 F.2d at 705–06.

Thus, this test eschews bright line approaches and requires a more nuanced assessment of the particular program at issue in order to determine what expression is protectable and infringed. As the Second Circuit explains, this test has three steps. In the abstraction step, the court "first break[s] down the allegedly infringed program into its constituent structural parts." Id. at 706. In the filtration step, the court "sift[s] out all non-protectable material," including ideas and "expression that is necessarily incidental to those ideas." Id. In the final step, the court compares the remaining creative expression with the allegedly infringing program.

In the second step, the court is first to assess whether the expression is original to the programmer or author. Atari, 975 F.2d at 839. The court must then determine whether the particular inclusion of any level of abstraction is dictated by considerations of efficiency, required by factors already external to the program itself, or taken from the public domain—all of which would render the expression unprotectable. Id. These conclusions are to be informed by traditional copyright principles of originality, merger, and scenes a faire. See Mitel, 124 F.3d at 1372 ("Although this core of expression is eligible for copyright protection, it is subject to the rigors of filtration analysis which excludes from protection expression that is in the public domain, otherwise unoriginal, or subject to the doctrines of merger and scenes a faire.").

In all circuits, it is clear that the first step is part of the copyrightability analysis and that the third is an infringement question. It is at the second step of this analysis where the circuits are in less accord. Some treat all aspects of this second step as part of the copyrightability analysis, while others divide questions of originality from the other inquiries, treating the former as a question of copyrightability and the latter as part of the infringement inquiry. Compare Lexmark, 387 F.3d at 537–38 (finding that the district court erred in assessing principles of merger and scenes a faire in the infringement analysis, rather than as a component of copyrightability), with Kregos, 937 F.2d at 705 (noting that the Second Circuit has considered the merger doctrine "in determining whether actionable infringement has occurred, rather than whether a copyright is valid"); see also Lexmark, 387 F.3d at 557 (Feikens, J., dissenting-in-part) (noting the circuit split and concluding that, where a court is assessing merger of an expression with a method of operation, "I would find the merger doctrine can operate only as a defense to infringement in that context, and as such has no bearing on the question of copyrightability."). We need not assess the wisdom of these respective views because there is no doubt on which side of this circuit split the Ninth Circuit falls.

In the Ninth Circuit, while questions regarding originality are considered questions of copyrightability, concepts of merger and scenes a faire are affirmative defenses to claims of infringement. Ets–Hokin, 225 F.3d at 1082; Satava v. Lowry, 323 F.3d 805, 810 n.3 (9th Cir.2003) ("The Ninth Circuit treats scenes a faire as a defense to infringement rather than as a barrier to copyrightability."). The Ninth Circuit has acknowledged that "there is some disagreement among courts as to whether these two doctrines figure into the issue of copyrightability or are more properly defenses to infringement." EtsHokin, 225 F.3d at 1082 (citations omitted). It, nonetheless, has made clear that, in that circuit, these concepts are to be treated as defenses to infringement. Id. (citing Kregos, 937 F.2d at 705 (holding that the merger doctrine relates to infringement, not copyrightability); Reed–Union Corp. v. Turtle Wax, Inc., 77 F.3d 909, 914 (7th Cir.1996) (explaining why the doctrine of scenes a faire is separate from the validity of a copyright)).

With these principles in mind, we turn to the trial court's analysis and judgment and to Oracle's objections thereto. While the trial court mentioned the abstractionfiltration-comparison test when describing the development of relevant law, it did not purport to actually apply that test. Instead, it moved directly to application of familiar principles of copyright law when assessing the copyrightability of the declaring code and interpreted Section 102(b) to preclude copyrightability for any functional element "essential for interoperability" "regardless of its form." Copyrightability Decision, 872 F.Supp.2d at 997.

Oracle asserts that all of the trial court's conclusions regarding copyrightability are erroneous. Oracle argues that its Java API packages are entitled to protection under the Copyright Act because they are expressive and could have been written and organized in any number of ways to achieve the same functions. Specifically, Oracle argues that the district court erred when it: (1) concluded that each line of declaring code is uncopyrightable because the idea and expression have merged; (2) found the declaring code uncopyrightable because it employs short phrases; (3) found all aspects of the SSO devoid of protection as a "method of operation" under 17 U.S.C. § 102(b); and (4) invoked Google's "interoperability" concerns in the copyrightability analysis. For the reasons explained below, we agree with Oracle on each point.

1. Declaring Source Code

First, Oracle argues that the district court erred in concluding that each line of declaring source code is completely unprotected under the merger and short phrases doctrines. Google responds that Oracle waived its right to assert copyrightability based on the 7,000 lines of declaring code by failing "to object to instructions and a verdict form that effectively eliminated that theory from the case." Appellee Br. 67. Even if not waived, moreover, Google argues that, because there is only one way to write the names and declarations, the merger doctrine bars copyright protection.

We find that Oracle did not waive arguments based on Google's literal copying of the declaring code. Prior to trial, both parties informed the court that Oracle's copyright infringement claims included the declarations of the API elements in the Android class library source code. See Oracle's Statement of Issues Regarding Copyright, Oracle Am., Inc. v. Google Inc., No. 3:10–cv–3561 (N.D.Cal. Apr. 12, 2012), ECF No. 899–1, at 3 (Oracle accuses the "declarations of the API elements in the Android class library source code and object code that implements the 37 API packages" of copyright infringement.); see also Google's Proposed Statement of Issues Regarding Copyright, Oracle Am., Inc. v. Google Inc., No. 3:10–cv–3561 (N.D.Cal. Apr. 12, 2012), ECF No. 901, at 2 (Oracle accuses the "declarations of the API elements in Android class library source code and object code that implements the 37 API packages.").

While Google is correct that the jury instructions and verdict form focused on the structure and organization of the packages, we agree with Oracle that there was no need for the jury to address copying of the declaring code because Google conceded that it copied it verbatim. Indeed, the district court specifically instructed the jury that "Google agrees that it uses the same names and declarations" in Android. Final Charge to the Jury at 10.

That the district court addressed the declaring code in its post-jury verdict copyrightability decision further confirms that the verbatim copying of declaring code remained in the case. The court explained that the "identical lines" that Google copied into Android "are those lines that specify the names, parameters and functionality of the methods and classes, lines called 'declarations' or 'headers.' " Copyrightability Decision, 872 F.Supp.2d at 979. The court specifically found that the declaring code was not entitled to copyright protection under the merger and short phrases doctrines. We address each in turn.

a. Merger

The merger doctrine functions as an exception to the idea/expression dichotomy. It provides that, when there are a limited number of ways to express an idea, the idea is said to "merge" with its expression, and the expression becomes unprotected. Altai, 982 F.2d at 707–08. As noted, the Ninth Circuit treats this concept as an affirmative defense to infringement. Ets–Hokin, 225 F.3d at 1082. Accordingly, it appears that the district court's merger analysis is irrelevant to the question of whether Oracle's API packages are copyrightable in the first instance. Regardless of when the analysis occurs, we conclude that merger does not apply on the record before us.

Under the merger doctrine, a court will not protect a copyrighted work from infringement if the idea contained therein can be expressed in only one way. Satava v. Lowry, 323 F.3d 805, 812 n .5 (9th Cir.2003). For computer programs, "this means that when specific [parts of the code], even though previously copyrighted, are the only and essential means of accomplishing a given task, their later use by another will not amount to infringement." Altai, 982 F.2d at 708 (citation omitted). We have recognized, however, applying Ninth Circuit law, that the "unique arrangement of computer program expression . does not merge with the process so long as alternate expressions are available." Atari, 975 F.2d at 840.

In Atari, for example, Nintendo designed a program—the 10NES—to prevent its video game system from accepting unauthorized game cartridges. 975 F.2d at 836. Nintendo "chose arbitrary programming instructions and arranged them in a unique sequence to create a purely arbitrary data stream" which "serves as the key to unlock the NES." Id. at 840. Because Nintendo produced expert testimony "showing a multitude of different ways to generate a data stream which unlocks the NES console," we concluded that Nintendo's specific choice of code did not merge with the process. Id.

Here, the district court found that, "no matter how creative or imaginative a Java method specification may be, the entire world is entitled to use the same method specification (inputs, outputs, parameters) so long as the line-by-line implementations are different." Copyrightability Decision, 872 F.Supp.2d at 998. In its analysis, the court identified the method declaration as the idea and found that the implementation is the expression. Id. ("The method specification is the idea. The method implementation is the expression. No one may monopolize the idea.") (emphases in original). The court explained that, under the rules of Java, a programmer must use the identical "declaration or method header lines" to "declare a method specifying the same functionality." Id. at 976. Because the district court found that there was only one way to write the declaring code for each of the Java packages, it concluded that "the merger doctrine bars anyone from claiming exclusive copyright ownership" of it. Id. at 998. Accordingly, the court held there could be "no copyright violation in using the identical declarations." Id.

Google agrees with the district court that the implementing code is the expression entitled to protection—not the declaring code. Indeed, at oral argument, counsel for Google explained that, "it is not our position that none of Java is copyrightable. Obviously, Google spent two and a half years . to write from scratch all of the implementing code." Oral Argument at 33:16.5 Because it is undisputed that Google wrote its own implementing code, the copyrightability of the precise language of that code is not at issue on appeal. Instead, our focus is on the declaring code and structure of the API packages.

On appeal, Oracle argues that the district court: (1) misapplied the merger doctrine; and (2) failed to focus its analysis on the options available to the original author. We agree with Oracle on both points. First, we agree that merger cannot bar copyright protection for any lines of declaring source code unless Sun/Oracle had only one way, or a limited number of ways, to write them. See Satava, 323 F.3d at 812 n.5 ("Under the merger doctrine, courts will not protect a copyrighted work from infringement if the idea underlying the copyrighted work can be expressed in only one way, lest there be a monopoly on the underlying idea."). The evidence showed that Oracle had "unlimited options as to the selection and arrangement of the 7000 lines Google copied." Appellant Br. 50. Using the district court's "java.lang.Math.max" example, Oracle explains that the developers could have called it any number of things, including "Math. maximum" or "Arith.larger." This was not a situation where Oracle was selecting among preordained names and phrases to create its packages. As the district court recognized, moreover, "the Android method and class names could have been different from the names of their counterparts in Java and still have worked." Copyrightability Decision, 872 F.Supp.2d at 976. Because "alternative expressions [we]re available," there is no merger. See Atari, 975 F.2d at 840.

We further find that the district court erred in focusing its merger analysis on the options available to Google at the time of copying. It is well-established that copyrightability and the scope of protectable activity are to be evaluated at the time of creation, not at the time of infringement. See Apple Computer, Inc. v. Formula Int'l, Inc., 725 F.2d 521, 524 (9th Cir.1984) (quoting National Commission on New Technological Uses of Copyrighted Works, Final Report at 21 (1979) ("CONTU Report") (recognizing that the Copyright Act was designed "to protect all works of authorship from the moment of their fixation in any tangible medium of expression")). The focus is, therefore, on the options that were available to Sun/Oracle at the time it created the API packages. Of course, once Sun/Oracle created "j ava.lang.Math. max," programmers who want to use that particular package have to call it by that name. But, as the court acknowledged, nothing prevented Google from writing its own declaring code, along with its own implementing code, to achieve the same result. In such circumstances, the chosen expression simply does not merge with the idea being expressed.7

It seems possible that the merger doctrine, when properly analyzed, would exclude the three packages identified by the district court as core packages from the scope of actionable infringing conduct. This would be so if the Java authors, at the time these packages were created, had only a limited number of ways to express the methods and classes therein if they wanted to write in the Java language. In that instance, the idea may well be merged with the expression in these three packages.8 Google did not present its merger argument in this way below and does not do so here, however. Indeed, Google does not try to differentiate among the packages for purposes of its copyrightability analysis and does not appeal the infringement verdict as to the packages. For these reasons, we reject the trial court's merger analysis.

b. Short Phrases

The district court also found that Oracle's declaring code consists of uncopyrightable short phrases. Specifically, the court concluded that, "while the Android method and class names could have been different from the names of their counterparts in Java and still have worked, copyright protection never extends to names or short phrases as a matter of law." Copyrightability Decision, 872 F.Supp.2d at 976.

The district court is correct that "[w]ords and short phrases such as names, titles, and slogans" are not subject to copyright protection. 37 C.F.R. § 202.1(a). The court failed to recognize, however, that the relevant question for copyrightability purposes is not whether the work at issue contains short phrases-as literary works often do-but, rather, whether those phrases are creative. See Soc'y of Holy Transfiguration Monastery, Inc. v. Gregory, 689 F.3d 29, 52 (1st Cir.2012) (noting that "not all short phrases will automatically be deemed uncopyrightable"); see also 1 Melville B. Nimmer & David Nimmer, Nimmer on Copyright § 2.01[B] (2013) ("[E]ven a short phrase may command copyright protection if it exhibits sufficient creativity."). And, by dissecting the individual lines of declaring code at issue into short phrases, the district court further failed to recognize that an original combination of elements can be copyrightable. See Softel, Inc. v. Dragon Med. & Scientific Commc'ns, 118 F.3d 955, 964 (2d Cir.1997) (noting that, in Feist, "the Court made quite clear that a compilation of nonprotectible elements can enjoy copyright protection even though its constituent elements do not").

By analogy, the opening of Charles Dickens' A Tale of Two Cities is nothing but a string of short phrases. Yet no one could contend that this portion of Dickens' work is unworthy of copyright protection because it can be broken into those shorter constituent components. The question is not whether a short phrase or series of short phrases can be extracted from the work, but whether the manner in which they are used or strung together exhibits creativity.

Although the district court apparently focused on individual lines of code, Oracle is not seeking copyright protection for a specific short phrase or word. Instead, the portion of declaring code at issue is 7,000 lines, and Google's own "Java guru" conceded that there can be "creativity and artistry even in a single method declaration." Joint Appendix ("J.A.") 20,970. Because Oracle "exercised creativity in the selection and arrangement" of the method declarations when it created the API packages and wrote the relevant declaring code, they contain protectable expression that is entitled to copyright protection. See Atari, 975 F.2d at 840; see also 17 U.S.C. §§ 101, 103 (recognizing copyright protection for "compilations" which are defined as work that is "selected, coordinated, or arranged in such a way that the resulting work as a whole constitutes an original work of authorship"). Accordingly, we conclude that the district court erred in applying the short phrases doctrine to find the declaring code not copyrightable.

c. Scenes a Faire

The scenes a faire doctrine, which is related to the merger doctrine, operates to bar certain otherwise creative expression from copyright protection. Apple Computer, Inc. v. Microsoft Corp., 35 F.3d 1435, 1444 (9th Cir.1994). It provides that "expressive elements of a work of authorship are not entitled to protection against infringement if they are standard, stock, or common to a topic, or if they necessarily follow from a common theme or setting." Mitel, 124 F.3d at 1374. Under this doctrine, "when certain commonplace expressions are indispensable and naturally associated with the treatment of a given idea, those expressions are treated like ideas and therefore [are] not protected by copyright." Swirsky v. Carey, 376 F.3d 841, 850 (9th Cir.2004). In the computer context, "the scene a faire doctrine denies protection to program elements that are dictated by external factors such as 'the mechanical specifications of the computer on which a particular program is intended to run' or 'widely accepted programming practices within the computer industry.' " Softel, 118 F.3d at 963 (citation omitted).

The trial court rejected Google's reliance on the scenes a faire doctrine. It did so in a footnote, finding that Google had failed to present evidence to support the claim that either the grouping of methods within the classes or the code chosen for them "would be so expected and customary as to be permissible under the scenes a faire doctrine." Copyrightability Decision, 872 F.Supp.2d at 999 n.9. Specifically, the trial court found that "it is impossible to say on this record that all of the classes and their contents are typical of such classes and, on this record, this order rejects Google's global argument based on scenes a faire." Id.

On appeal, Google refers to scenes a faire concepts briefly, as do some amici, apparently contending that, because programmers have become accustomed to and comfortable using the groupings in the Java API packages, those groupings are so commonplace as to be indispensable to the expression of an acceptable programming platform. As such, the argument goes, they are so associated with the "idea" of what the packages are accomplishing that they should be treated as ideas rather than expression. See Br. of Amici Curiae Rackspace US, Inc., et al. at 19–22.

Google cannot rely on the scenes a faire doctrine as an alternative ground upon which we might affirm the copyrightability judgment of the district court. This is so for several reasons. First, as noted, like merger, in the Ninth Circuit, the scenes a faire doctrine is a component of the infringement analysis. "[S]imilarity of expression, whether literal or non-literal, which necessarily results from the fact that the common idea is only capable of expression in more or less stereotyped form, will preclude a finding of actionable similarity." 4 Nimmer on Copyright § 13.03[B][3]. Thus, the expression is not excluded from copyright protection; it is just that certain copying is forgiven as a necessary incident of any expression of the underlying idea. See Satava, 323 F.3d at 810 n.3 ("The Ninth Circuit treats scenes a faire as a defense to infringement rather than as a barrier to copyrightability.").

...

Finally, Google's reliance on the doctrine below and the amici reference to it here are premised on a fundamental misunderstanding of the doctrine. Like merger, the focus of the scenes a faire doctrine is on the circumstances presented to the creator, not the copier. See Mitel, 124 F.3d at 1375 (finding error to the extent the trial court discussed "whether external factors such as market forces and efficiency considerations justified Iqtel's copying of the command codes"). The court's analytical focus must be upon the external factors that dictated Sun's selection of classes, methods, and code—not upon what Google encountered at the time it chose to copy those groupings and that code. See id. "[T]he scenes a faire doctrine identifies and excludes from protection against infringement expression whose creation 'flowed naturally from considerations external to the author's creativity.' " Id. (quoting Nimmer § 13.03[F][3], at 13–131 (1997)). It is this showing the trial court found Google failed to make, and Google cites to nothing in the record which indicates otherwise.

For these reasons, the trial court was correct to conclude that the scenes a faire doctrine does not affect the copyrightability of either the declaring code in, or the SSO of, the Java API packages at issue.

2. The Structure, Sequence, and Organization of the API Packages

The district court found that the SSO of the Java API packages is creative and original, but nevertheless held that it is a "system or method of operation . and, therefore, cannot be copyrighted" under 17 U.S.C. § 102(b). Copyrightability Decision, 872 F.Supp.2d at 976–77. In reaching this conclusion, the district court seems to have relied upon language contained in a First Circuit decision: Lotus Development Corp. v. Borland International, Inc., 49 F.3d 807 (1st Cir.1995), aff'd without opinion by equally divided court, 516 U.C. 233 (1996).

In Lotus, it was undisputed that the defendant copied the menu command hierarchy and interface from Lotus 1–2–3, a computer spreadsheet program "that enables users to perform accounting functions electronically on a computer." 49 F.3d at 809. The menu command hierarchy referred to a series of commands— such as "Copy," "Print," and "Quit"—which were arranged into more than 50 menus and submenus. Id. Although the defendant did not copy any Lotus source code, it copied the menu command hierarchy into its rival program. The question before the court was "whether a computer menu command hierarchy is copyrightable subject matter." Id.

Although it accepted the district court's finding that Lotus developers made some expressive choices in selecting and arranging the command terms, the First Circuit found that the command hierarchy was not copyrightable because, among other things, it was a "method of operation" under Section 102(b). In reaching this conclusion, the court defined a "method of operation" as "the means by which a person operates something, whether it be a car, a food processor, or a computer." Id. at 815. ecause the Lotus menu command hierarchy provided "the means by which users control and operate Lotus 1–2–3," it was deemed unprotectable. Id. For example, if users wanted to copy material, they would use the "Copy" command and the command terms would tell the computer what to do. According to the Lotus court, the "fact that Lotus developers could have designed the Lotus menu command hierarchy differently is immaterial to the question of whether it is a 'method of operation.' " Id. at 816. (noting that "our initial inquiry is not whether the Lotus menu command hierarchy incorporates any expression"). The court further indicated that, "[i]f specific words are essential to operating something, then they are part of a 'method of operation' and, as such, are unprotectable." Id.

On appeal, Oracle argues that the district court's reliance on Lotus is misplaced because it is distinguishable on its facts and is inconsistent with Ninth Circuit law. We agree. First, while the defendant in Lotus did not copy any of the underlying code, Google concedes that it copied portions of Oracle's declaring source code verbatim. Second, the Lotus court found that the commands at issue there (copy, print, etc.) were not creative, but it is undisputed here that the declaring code and the structure and organization of the API packages are both creative and original. Finally, while the court in Lotus found the commands at issue were "essential to operating" the system, it is undisputed that—other than perhaps as to the three core packages—Google did not need to copy the structure, sequence, and organization of the Java API packages to write programs in the Java language.

More importantly, however, the Ninth Circuit has not adopted the court's "method of operation" reasoning in Lotus, and we conclude that it is inconsistent with binding precedent. Specifically, we find that Lotus is inconsistent with Ninth Circuit case law recognizing that the structure, sequence, and organization of a computer program is eligible for copyright protection where it qualifies as an expression of an idea, rather than the idea itself. See Johnson Controls, 886 F.2d at 1175–76. And, while the court in Lotus held "that expression that is part of a 'method of operation' cannot be copyrighted," 49 F.3d at 818, this court—applying Ninth Circuit law—reached the exact opposite conclusion, finding that copyright protects "the expression of [a] process or method," Atari, 975 F.2d at 839.

We find, moreover, that the hard and fast rule set down in Lotus and employed by the district court here—i.e., that elements which perform a function can never be copyrightable—is at odds with the Ninth Circuit's endorsement of the abstraction-filtration-comparison analysis discussed earlier. As the Tenth Circuit concluded in expressly rejecting the Lotus "method of operation" analysis, in favor of the Second Circuit's abstraction-filtrationcomparison test, "although an element of a work may be characterized as a method of operation, that element may nevertheless contain expression that is eligible for copyright protection." Mitel, 124 F.3d at 1372. Specifically, the court found that Section 102(b) "does not extinguish the protection accorded a particular expression of an idea merely because that expression is embodied in a method of operation at a higher level of abstraction." Id.

Other courts agree that components of a program that can be characterized as a "method of operation" may nevertheless be copyrightable. For example, the Third Circuit rejected a defendant's argument that operating system programs are "per se" uncopyrightable because an operating system is a "method of operation" for a computer. Apple Computer, Inc. v. Franklin Computer Corp., 714 F.2d 1240, 1250–52 (3d Cir.1983). The court distinguished between the "method which instructs the computer to perform its operating functions" and "the instructions themselves," and found that the instructions were copyrightable. Id. at 1250–51. In its analysis, the court noted: "[t]hat the words of a program are used ultimately in the implementation of a process should in no way affect their copyrightability." Id. at 1252 (quoting CONTU Report at 21). The court focused "on whether the idea is capable of various modes of expression" and indicated that, "[i]f other programs can be written or created which perform the same function as [i]n Apple's operating system program, then that program is an expression of the idea and hence copyrightable." Id. at 1253. Notably, no other circuit has adopted the First Circuit's "method of operation" analysis.

...

Here, the district court recognized that the SSO "resembles a taxonomy," but found that "it is nevertheless a command structure, a system or method of operation-a long hierarchy of over six thousand commands to carry out pre-assigned functions." Copyrightability Decision, 872 F.Supp.2d at 999–1000. In other words, the court concluded that, although the SSO is expressive, it is not copyrightable because it is also functional. The problem with the district court's approach is that computer programs are by definition functional—they are all designed to accomplish some task. Indeed, the statutory definition of "computer program" acknowledges that they function "to bring about a certain result." See 17 U.S.C. § 101 (defining a "computer program" as "a set of statements or instructions to be used directly or indirectly in a computer in order to bring about a certain result"). If we were to accept the district court's suggestion that a computer program is uncopyrightable simply because it "carr[ies] out pre-assigned functions," no computer program is protectable. That result contradicts Congress's express intent to provide copyright protection to computer programs, as well as binding Ninth Circuit once law finding computer programs copyrightable, despite their utilitarian or functional purpose. Though the trial court did add the caveat that it "does not hold that the structure, sequence and organization of all computer programs may be stolen," Copyrightability Decision, 872 F.Supp.2d at 1002, it is hard to see how its method of operation analysis could lead to any other conclusion.

While it does not appear that the Ninth Circuit has addressed the precise issue, we conclude that a set of commands to instruct a computer to carry out desired operations may contain expression that is eligible for copyright protection. See Mitel, 124 F.3d at 1372. We agree with Oracle that, under Ninth Circuit law, an original work—even one that serves a function—is entitled to copyright protection as long as the author had multiple ways to express the underlying idea. ...

As the district court acknowledged, Google could have structured Android differently and could have chosen different ways to express and implement the functionality that it copied. Specifically, the court found that "the very same functionality could have been offered in Android without duplicating the exact command structure used in Java." Copyrightability Decision, 872 F.Supp.2d at 976. The court further explained that Google could have offered the same functions in Android by "rearranging the various methods under different groupings among the various classes and packages." Id. The evidence showed, moreover, that Google designed many of its own API packages from scratch, and, thus, could have designed its own corresponding 37 API packages if it wanted to do so.

Given the court's findings that the SSO is original and creative, and that the declaring code could have been written and organized in any number of ways and still have achieved the same functions, we conclude that Section 102(b) does not bar the packages from copyright protection just because they also perform functions.

3. Google's Interoperability Arguments are Irrelevant to Copyrightability

Oracle also argues that the district court erred in invoking interoperability in its copyrightability analysis. Specifically, Oracle argues that Google's interoperability arguments are only relevant, if at all, to fair use—not to the question of whether the API packages are copyrightable. We agree.

In characterizing the SSO of the Java API packages as a "method of operation," the district court explained that "[d]uplication of the command structure is necessary for interoperability." Copyrightability Decision, 872 F.Supp.2d at 977. The court found that, "[i]n order for at least some of [the pre-Android Java] code to run on Android, Google was required to provide the same java . package. Class. method( ) command system using the same names with the same 'taxonomy' and with the same functional specifications." Id. at 1000 (emphasis omitted). And, the court concluded that "Google replicated what was necessary to achieve a degree of interoperability—but no more, taking care, as said before, to provide its own implementations." Id. In reaching this conclusion, the court relied primarily on two Ninth Circuit decisions: Sega Enterprises v. Accolade, Inc., 977 F.2d 1510 (9th Cir.1992), and Sony Computer Entertainment, Inc. v. Connectix, Corp., 203 F.3d 596 (9th Cir.2000).

Both Sega and Sony are fair use cases in which copyrightability was addressed only tangentially. In Sega, for example, Sega manufactured a video game console and game cartridges that contained hidden functional program elements necessary to achieve compatibility with the console. Defendant Accolade: (1) reverse-engineered Sega's video game programs to discover the requirements for compatibility; and (2) created its own games for the Sega console. Sega, 977 F.2d at 1514–15. As part of the reverse-engineering process, Accolade made intermediate copies of object code from Sega's console. Id. Although the court recognized that the intermediate copying of computer code may infringe Sega's copyright, it concluded that "disassembly of copyrighted object code is, as a matter of law, a fair use of the copyrighted work if such disassembly provides the only means of access to those elements of the code that are not protected by copyright and the copier has a legitimate reason for seeking such access." Id. at 1518. The court agreed with Accolade that its copying was necessary to examine the unprotected functional aspects of the program. Id. at 1520. And, because Accolade had a legitimate interest in making its cartridges compatible with Sega's console, the court found that Accolade's intermediate copying was fair use.

Likewise, in Sony, the Ninth Circuit found that the defendant's reverse engineering and intermediate copying of Sony's copyrighted software program "was a fair use for the purpose of gaining access to the unprotected elements of Sony's software." Sony, 203 F.3d at 602. The court explained that Sony's software program contained unprotected functional elements and that the defendant could only access those elements through reverse engineering. Id. at 603. The defendant used that information to create a software program that let consumers play games designed for Sony's PlayStation console on their computers. Notably, the defendant's software program did not contain any of Sony's copyrighted material. Id. at 598.

The district court characterized Sony and Sega as "close analogies" to this case. Copyrightability Decision, 872 F.Supp.2d at 1000. According to the court, both decisions "held that interface procedures that were necessary to duplicate in order to achieve interoperability were functional aspects not copyrightable under Section 102(b)." Id. The district court's reliance on Sega and Sony in the copyrightability context is misplaced, however.

As noted, both cases were focused on fair use, not copyrightability. In Sega, for example, the only question was whether Accolade's intermediate copying was fair use. The court never addressed the question of whether Sega's software code, which had functional elements, also contained separable creative expression entitled to protection. Likewise, although the court in Sony determined that Sony's computer program had functional elements, it never addressed whether it also had expressive elements. Sega and Sony are also factually distinguishable because the defendants in those cases made intermediate copies to understand the functional aspects of the copyrighted works and then created new products. See Sony, 203 F.3d at 606–07; Sega, 977 F.2d at 1522–23. This is not a case where Google reverse-engineered Oracle's Java packages to gain access to unprotected functional elements contained therein. As the former Register of Copyrights of the United States pointed out in his brief amicus curiae, "[h]ad Google reverse engineered the programming packages to figure out the ideas and functionality of the original, and then created its own structure and its own literal code, Oracle would have no remedy under copyright whatsoever." Br. for Amicus Curiae Ralph Oman 29. Instead, Google chose to copy both the declaring code and the overall SSO of the 37 Java API packages at issue.

We disagree with Google's suggestion that Sony and Sega created an "interoperability exception" to copyrightability. See Appellee Br. 39 (citing Sony and Sega for the proposition that "compatibility elements are not copyrightable under section 102(b)" (emphasis omitted)). ...

As previously discussed, a court must examine the software program to determine whether it contains creative expression that can be separated from the underlying function. See Sega, 977 F.2d at 1524–25. In doing so, the court filters out the elements of the program that are "ideas" as well as elements that are "dictated by considerations of efficiency, so as to be necessarily incidental to that idea; required by factors external to the program itself." Altai, 982 F.2d at 707.

To determine "whether certain aspects of an allegedly infringed software are not protected by copyright law, the focus is on external factors that influenced the choice of the creator of the infringed product." Dun & Bradstreet Software Servs.,

Inc. v. Grace Consulting, Inc., 307 F.3d 197, 215 (3d Cir.2002) (citing Altai, 982 F.2d at 714; Mitel, 124 F.3d at 1375). The Second Circuit, for example, has noted that programmers are often constrained in their design choices by "extrinsic considerations" including "the mechanical specifications of the computer on which a particular program is intended to run" and "compatibility requirements of other programs with which a program is designed to operate in conjunction." Altai, 982 F.2d at 709–10 (citing 3 Melville B. Nimmer & David Nimmer, Nimmer on Copyright § 13.01 at 13–66–71 (1991)). The Ninth Circuit has likewise recognized that: (1) computer programs "contain many logical, structural, and visual display elements that are dictated by . external factors such as compatibility requirements and industry demands"; and (2) "[i]n some circumstances, even the exact set of commands used by the programmer is deemed functional rather than creative for purposes of copyright." Sega, 977 F.2d at 1524 (internal citation omitted).

Because copyrightability is focused on the choices available to the plaintiff at the time the computer program was created, the relevant compatibility inquiry asks whether the plaintiff's choices were dictated by a need to ensure that its program worked with existing third-party programs. Dun & Bradstreet, 307 F.3d at 215; see also Atari, 975 F.2d at 840 ("External factors did not dictate the design of the 10NES program."). Whether a defendant later seeks to make its program interoperable with the plaintiff's program has no bearing on whether the software the plaintiff created had any design limitations dictated by external factors. See Dun & Bradstreet, 307 F.3d at 215 (finding an expert's testimony on interoperability "wholly misplaced" because he "looked at externalities from the eyes of the plagiarist, not the eyes of the program's creator"). Stated differently, the focus is on the compatibility needs and programming choices of the party claiming copyright protection—not the choices the defendant made to achieve compatibility with the plaintiff's program. Consistent with this approach, courts have recognized that, once the plaintiff creates a copyrightable work, a defendant's desire "to achieve total compatibility . is a commercial and competitive objective which does not enter into the . issue of whether particular ideas and expressions have merged." Apple Computer, 714 F.2d at 1253.

Given this precedent, we conclude that the district court erred in focusing its interoperability analysis on Google's desires for its Android software. See Copyrightability Decision, 872 F.Supp.2d at 1000 ("Google replicated what was necessary to achieve a degree of interoperability" with Java.). Whether Google's software is "interoperable" in some sense with any aspect of the Java platform (although as Google concedes, certainly not with the JVM) has no bearing on the threshold question of whether Oracle's software is copyrightable. It is the interoperability and other needs of Oracle—not those of Google—that apply in the copyrightability context, and there is no evidence that when Oracle created the Java API packages at issue it did so to meet compatibility requirements of other pre-existing programs.

...

III. Google's Policy–Based Arguments

Many of Google's arguments, and those of some amici, appear premised on the belief that copyright is not the correct legal ground upon which to protect intellectual property rights to software programs; they opine that patent protection for such programs, with its insistence on non-obviousness, and shorter terms of protection, might be more applicable, and sufficient. Indeed, the district court's method of operation analysis seemed to say as much. Copyrightability Decision, 872 F.Supp.2d at 984 (stating that this case raises the question of "whether the copyright holder is more appropriately asserting an exclusive right to a functional system, process, or method of operation that belongs in the realm of patents, not copyrights"). Google argues that "[a]fter Sega, developers could no longer hope to protect [software] interfaces by copyright . Sega signaled that the only reliable means for protecting the functional requirements for achieving interoperability was by patenting them." Appellee Br. 40 (quoting Pamela Samuelson, Are Patents on Interfaces Impeding Interoperability ? 93 Minn. L.Rev.1943, 1959 (2009)). And, Google relies heavily on articles written by Professor Pamela Samuelson, who has argued that "it would be best for a commission of computer program experts to draft a new form of intellectual property law for machine-readable programs." Pamela Samuelson, CONTU Revisited: The Case Against Copyright Protection for Computer Programs in Machine–Readable Form, 1984 Duke L.J. 663, 764 (1984). Professor Samuelson has more recently argued that "Altai and Sega contributed to the eventual shift away from claims of copyright in program interfaces and toward reliance on patent protection. Patent protection also became more plausible and attractive as the courts became more receptive to software patents." Samuelson, 93 Minn. L.Rev. at 1959.

Although Google, and the authority on which it relies, seem to suggest that software is or should be entitled to protection only under patent law-not copyright lawseveral commentators have recently argued the exact opposite. See Technology Quarterly, Stalking Trolls, Economist, Mar. 8, 2014, http:// www.economist. com/ne ws/technology-quarterly/21598 321–intellectual–property–after–being–blamed -stymying-innovationamerica-vague ("[M]any innovators have argued that the electronics and software industries would flourish if companies trying to bring new technology (software innovations included) to market did not have to worry about being sued for infringing thousands of absurd patents at every turn. A perfectly adequate means of protecting and rewarding software developers for their ingenuity has existed for over 300 years. It is called copyright."); Timothy B. Lee, Will the Supreme Court save us from software patents?, Wash. Post,, Feb. 26, 2014, 1:13 PM, http:// www.washingtonpost.com/blogs/the-switch/wp/ 2014/02/26/will-the-supreme-court-save-us-from-softwarepatents/ ("If you write a book or a song, you can get copyright protection for it. If you invent a new pill or a better mousetrap, you can get a patent on it. But for the last two decades, software has had the distinction of being potentially eligible for both copyright and patent protection. Critics say that's a mistake. They argue that the complex and expensive patent system is a terrible fit for the fast-moving software industry. And they argue that patent protection is unnecessary because software innovators already have copyright protection available.").

Importantly for our purposes, the Supreme Court has made clear that "[n]either the Copyright Statute nor any other says that because a thing is patentable it may not be copyrighted." Mazer v. Stein, 347 U.S. 201, 217 (1954). Indeed, the thrust of the CONTU Report is that copyright is "the most suitable mode of legal protection for computer software." Peter S. Menell, An Analysis of the Scope of Copyright Protection for Application Programs, 41 Stan. L.Rev. 1045, 1072 (1989); see also CONTU Report at 1 (recommending that copyright law be amended "to make it explicit that computer programs, to the extent that they embody an author's original creation, are proper subject matter of copyright"). Until either the Supreme Court or Congress tells us otherwise, we are bound to respect the Ninth Circuit's decision to afford software programs protection under the copyright laws. We thus decline any invitation to declare that protection of software programs should be the domain of patent law, and only patent law.

Conclusion

For the foregoing reasons, we conclude that the declaring code and the structure, sequence, and organization of the 37 Java API packages at issue are entitled to copyright protection. We therefore reverse the district court's copyrightability determination with instructions to reinstate the jury's infringement verdict. Because the jury hung on fair use, we remand Google's fair use defense for further proceedings consistent with this decision.

With respect to Google's cross-appeal, we affirm the district court's decisions: (1) granting Oracle's motion for JMOL as to the eight decompiled Java files that Google copied into Android; and (2) denying Google's motion for JMOL with respect to the rangeCheck function. Accordingly, we affirm-in-part, reverse-in-part, and remand for further proceedings.

AFFIRMED–IN–PART, REVERSED–IN–PART, AND REMANDED

Nos. 2017-1118 and 2017-1202 (Fed. Cir. March 27, 2018)

ORACLE v. GOOGLE (II)

United States Court of Appeals, Federal Circuit

O'MALLEY, Circuit Judge:

a. Commercial Use

Analysis of the first factor requires inquiry into the commercial nature of the use. Use of the copyrighted work that is commercial "tends to weigh against a finding of fair use." Harper & Row, 471 U.S. at 562. Courts have recognized, however, that, "[s]ince many, if not most, secondary users seek at least some measure of commercial gain from their use, unduly emphasizing the commercial motivation of a copier will lead to an overly restrictive view of fair use." Am. Geophysical Union v. Texaco, Inc., 60 F.3d 913, 921 (2d Cir. 1994); see also Infinity Broad. Corp. v.

Kirkwood, 150 F.3d 104, 109 (2d Cir. 1998) ("[N]otwithstanding its mention in the text of the statute, commerciality has only limited usefulness to a fair use inquiry; most secondary uses of copyrighted material, including nearly all of the uses listed in the statutory preamble, are commercial."). Accordingly, although the statute requires us to consider the "commercial nature" of the work, "the degree to which the new user exploits the copyright for commercial gain—as opposed to incidental use as part of a commercial enterprise—affects the weight we afford commercial nature as a factor." Elvis Presley Enters., Inc. v. Passport Video, 349 F.3d 622, 627 (9th Cir. 2003).

"[I]t is undisputed that Google's use of the declaring code and SSO from 37 Java API packages served commer- cial purposes." Order Denying JMOL, 2016 WL 3181206, at *7. Although the jury was instructed that commercial use weighed against fair use, the district court explained that the jury "could reasonably have found that Google's decision to make Android available open source and free for all to use had non-commercial purposes as well (such as the general interest in sharing software innovation)." Id.

On appeal, Oracle argues that Android is "hugely profitable" and that "Google reaps billions from exploiting Java in Android." Appellant Br. 29. As such, Oracle maintains that no reasonable jury could have found Android anything but "overwhelmingly commercial." Id.5

Google responds that: (1) because it gives Android away for free under an open source license the jury could have concluded that Android has non-commercial purpos- es; and (2) the jury could have reasonably found that Google's revenue flows from the advertisements on its search engine which preexisted Android. Neither argu- ment has merit.

First, the fact that Android is free of charge does not make Google's use of the Java API packages non- commercial. Giving customers "for free something they would ordinarily have to buy" can constitute commercial use. A&M Records, Inc. v. Napster, Inc., 239 F.3d 1004, 1015 (9th Cir. 2001) (finding that "repeated and exploita- tive copying of copyrighted works, even if the copies are not offered for sale, may constitute a commercial use"). That Google might also have non- commercial motives is

Oracle also argues that Google conceded that its use was "entirely commercial" during oral argument to this court in the first appeal. Order Denying JMOL, 2016 WL 3181206, at *7 ("Q: But for purpose and character, though, you don't dispute that it was entirely a commercial purpose. A: No."). The district court treated this colloquy as a judicial admission that Google's use was "commercial." Id. (noting that the word "entirely" was "part of the give and take" of oral argument). The court therefore instructed the jury that Google's use was commercial, but that it was up to the jury to determine the extent of the commerciality. Id. at *8. Oracle does not challenge the district court's jury instructions on appeal. In any event, as the district court noted, "even a wholly commercial use may still constitute fair use." Id. at *7 (citing Campbell, 510 U.S. at 585).

...As the Supreme Court made clear when The Nation magazine published excerpts from Harper & Row's book, partly for the purpose of providing the public newsworthy information, the question "is not whether the sole motive of the use is monetary gain but whether the user stands to profit from exploitation of the copyrighted material without paying the customary price." Harper & Row, 471 U.S. at 562. Second, although Google maintains that its revenue flows from advertisements, not from Android, commerciality does not depend on how Google earns its money. Indeed, "[d]irect economic benefit is not required to demonstrate a commercial use." A&M Records, 239 F.3d at 1015. We find, therefore, that, to the extent we must assume the jury found Google's use of the API packages to be anything other than overwhelmingly commercial, that conclusion finds no substantial evidentiary support in the record. Accordingly, Google's commercial use of the API packages weighs against a finding of fair use.

b. Transformative Use

Although the Copyright Act does not use the word "transformative," the Supreme Court has stated that the "central purpose" of the first fair use factor is to determine "whether and to what extent the new work is trans- formative." Campbell, 510 U.S. at 579. Transformative works "lie at the heart of the fair use doctrine's guarantee of breathing space within the confines of copyright, and the more transformative the new work, the less will be the significance of other factors, like commercialism, that may weigh against a finding of fair use." Id. (internal citation omitted).

A use is "transformative" if it "adds something new, with a further purpose or different character, altering the first with new expression, meaning or message." Id. The critical question is "whether the new work merely super- sede[s] the objects of the original creation . . . or instead adds something new." Id. (citations and internal quota- tion marks omitted). This inquiry "may be guided by the examples given in the preamble to §107, looking to whether the use is for criticism, or comment, or news reporting, and the like." Id. at 578-79. "The Supreme Court has recognized that parodic works, like other works that comment and criticize, are by their nature often sufficiently transformative to fit clearly under the fair use exception." Mattel Inc. v. Walking Mountain Prods., 353 F.3d 792, 800 (9th Cir. 2003) (citing Campbell, 510 U.S. at 579).

"Although transformation is a key factor in fair use, whether a work is transformative is a often highly contentious topic." Seltzer, 725 F.3d at 1176. Indeed, a "leading treatise on this topic has lamented the frequent misuse of the transformation test, complaining that it has become a conclusory label which is 'all things to all people.'" Id. (quoting Melville B. Nimmer & David Nimmer, 4 Nimmer on Copyright § 13.05[A][1][b], 13168-70 (2011)).

To be transformative, a secondary work must either alter the original with new expression, meaning, or message or serve a new purpose distinct from that of the original work. Campbell, 510 U.S. at 579; Elvis Presley Enters., 349 F.3d at 629. Where the use "is for the same intrinsic purpose as [the copyright holder's] . . . such use seriously weakens a claimed fair use." Worldwide Church of God v. Phila.

Church of God, Inc., 227 F.3d 1110, 1117 (9th Cir. 2000) (quoting Weissmann v. Freeman, 868 F.2d 1313, 1324 (2d Cir. 1989)).

Although "transformative use is not absolutely necessary for a finding of fair use, the goal of copyright, to promote science and the arts, is generally furthered by the creation of transformative works." Campbell, 510 U.S. at 579 (citation and footnote omitted). As such, "the more transformative the new work, the less will be the significance of other factors, like commercialism, that may weigh against a finding of fair use." Id. Importantly, in the Ninth Circuit, whether a work is transformative is a question of law. See Mattel, 353 F.3d at 801 (explaining that parody—a well-established species of transformative use—"is a question of law, not a matter of public majority opinion"); see also Fox News Network, LLC v. TVEyes, Inc., No. 15-3885, 2018 WL 1057178, at *3-4 (2d Cir. Feb. 27, 2018) (reassessing whether the use in question was transformative and deciding it was as a matter of law).

In denying JMOL, the district court explained that "of course, the copied declarations serve the same function in both works, for by definition, declaring code in the Java programming language serves the [same] specific definitional purposes." Order Denying JMOL, 2016 WL 3181206, at *8.6 The court concluded, however, that the jury could reasonably have found that Google's selection of some, but not all, of the Java API packages—"with new

According to the district court, if this fact were sufficient to defeat fair use, "it would be impossible ever to duplicate declaring code as fair use and presumably the Federal Circuit would have disallowed this factor on the first appeal rather than remanding for a jury trial." Id. But in our prior decision, we remanded in part because Google represented to this court that there were disputes of fact regarding how Android was used and whether the APIs Google copied served the same function in Android and Java. Oracle, 750 F.3d at 1376. Without the benefit of briefs exploring the record on these issues, and Google's later agreement with respect to these facts, we concluded that we could not say that there were no material facts in dispute. Id. As explained previously, however, those facts are no longer in dispute. The only question that remains regarding transformative use is whether, on the now undisputed facts, Google's use of the APIs was, in fact, transformative.

...

On appeal, Oracle argues that Google's use was not transformative because it did not alter the APIs with "new expression, meaning, or message." Appellant Br. 29 (quoting Campbell, 510 U.S. at 579). Because Google concedes that it uses the API packages for the same purpose, Oracle maintains that it was unreasonable for either the jury or the court to find that Google sufficiently transformed the APIs to overcome its highly commercial use.

Google responds that a reasonable jury could have concluded that Google used a small portion of the Java API packages to create a new work in a new context— "Android, a platform for smartphones, not desktops and servers." Cross-Appellant Br. 37. Google argues that, although the declarations and SSO may perform the same functions in Android and Java, the jury could reasonably find that they have different purposes because the "point of Android was to create a groundbreaking platform for smartphones." Id. at 39.

Google's arguments are without merit. As explained below, Google's use of the API packages is not transform- ative as a matter of law because: (1) it does not fit within the uses listed in the preamble to § 107; (2) the purpose of the API packages in Android is the same as the purpose of the packages in the Java platform; (3) Google made no alteration to the expressive content or message of the copyrighted material; and (4) smartphones were not a new context.

...

That Google wrote its own implementing code is irrelevant to the question of whether use of the APIs was transformative. As we noted in the prior appeal, "no plagiarist can excuse the wrong by showing how much of his work he did not pirate." Oracle, 750 F.3d at 1375 (quoting Harper & Row, 471 U.S. at 565). The relevant question is whether Google altered "the expressive content or message of the original work" that it copied—not whether it rewrote the portions it did not copy. See Seltzer, 725 F.3d at 1177 (explaining that a work is not trans- formative where the user "makes no alteration to the expressive content or message of the original work"). That said, even where the allegedly infringing work "makes few physical changes to the original or fails to comment on the original," it will "typically [be] viewed as transformative as long as new expressive content or message is appar- ent." Id. Here, however, there is no suggestion that the new implementing code somehow changed the expression or message of the declaring code. While Google's use could have been transformative if it had copied the APIs for some other purpose—such as teaching how to design an API—merely copying the material and moving it from one platform to another without alteration is not trans- formative.

Google's primary argument on appeal is that Android is transformative because Google incorporated the declarations and SSO of the 37 API packages into a new context—smartphones. But the record showed that Java SE APIs were in smartphones before Android entered the market. Specifically, Oracle presented evidence that Java SE was in SavaJe mobile phones and that Oracle licensed Java SE to other smartphone manufacturers, including Danger and Nokia. Because the Java SE was already being used in smartphones, Google did not "transform" the copyrighted material into a new context and no reasonable jury could conclude otherwise.7

In any event, moving material to a new context is not transformative in and of itself—even if it is a "sharply different context." TCA Television Corp. v. McCollum, 839 F.3d 168, 181-83 (2d Cir. 2016) (finding that use "at some length, almost verbatim," of the copyrighted comedy routine "Who's on First?" in a dramatic play was not transformative where the play neither "imbued the Routine with any new expression, meaning, or message," nor added "any new dramatic purpose"). As previously explained, a use becomes transformative only if it serves a different purpose or alters the "expression, meaning, or message" of the original work. Kelly, 336 F.3d at 818. As such, "[c]ourts have been reluctant to find fair use when an original work is merely retransmitted in a different medium." A&M Records, 239

F.3d at 1015. Accordingly, although a change of format may be "useful," it "is not technically a transformation." Infinity Broad., 150 F.3d at 108 n.2 (finding that retransmitting copyrighted radio transmissions over telephone lines was not transformative because there was no new expression, meaning, or message).

...

To some extent, any use of copyrighted work takes place in a slightly different context than the original. And of course, there is no bright line identifying when a use becomes transformative. But where, as here, the copying is verbatim, for an identical function and purpose, and there are no changes to the expressive content or message, a mere change in format (e.g., from desktop and laptop computers to smartphones and tablets) is insufficient as a matter of law to qualify as a transformative use.

c. Bad faith

In evaluating the "purpose and character" factor, the Ninth Circuit applies "the general rule that a party claiming fair use must act in a manner generally compatible with principles of good faith and fair dealing." Perfect 10, 508 F.3d at 1164 n.8 (citing Harper & Row, 471 U.S. at 562-63). In part, this is based on the fact that, in Harper & Row, the Supreme Court expressly stated that "[f]air use presupposes 'good faith' and 'fair dealing.'" 471 U.S. at 562 (citation omitted). It is also in part true because, as the Ninth Circuit has said, one who acts in bad faith should be barred from invoking the equitable defense of fair use. Fisher, 794 F.2d at 436 (calling the principle of considering the alleged infringer's "bad conduct" as a "bar [to] his use of the equitable defense of fair use" a sound one)

...

Consistent with this authority, and at Oracle's request, the district court instructed the jury that it could consider whether Google acted in bad faith (or not) as part of its assessment of the first fair use factor. Order Deny- ing JMOL, 2016 WL 3181206, at *6. And, because Oracle was permitted to introduce evidence that Google acted in bad faith, the court permitted Google to try to prove its good faith. Id.

At trial, Oracle introduced evidence suggesting that "Google felt it needed to copy the Java API as an accelerant to bring Android to the market quicker" and knew that it needed a license to use Java. Id. For its part, Google presented evidence that it believed that the declar- ing code and SSO were "free to use and re-implement, both as a matter of developer practice and because the availability of independent implementations of the Java API enhanced the popularity of the Java programming language, which Sun promoted as free for all to use." Id. at *7.

...

On appeal, Oracle argues that there was ample evidence that Google intentionally copied Oracle's copyrighted work and knew that it needed a license to use Java. Google responds that the jury heard sufficient evidence of Google's good faith based on industry custom and was entitled to credit that evidence.

But, while bad faith may weigh against fair use, a copyist's good faith cannot weigh in favor of fair use. Indeed, the Ninth Circuit has expressly recognized that "the innocent intent of the defendant constitutes no defense to liability." Monge, 688 F.3d at 1170 (quoting 4 Melville B. Nimmer & David Nimmer, Nimmer on Copyright § 13.08[B][1] (Matthew Bender rev. ed. 2011)). If it were clear, accordingly, that the jury found fair use solely or even largely because it approved of Google's motives even if they were in bad faith, we would find such a conclusion improper. Because evidence of Google's good faith was relevant to rebut evidence of its bad faith, however, and there is no objection to the instructions to the jury on this or any other point, we must assume that the jury simply did not find the evidence of Google's bad faith persuasive.

The jury was instructed that, "[i]n evaluating the extent to which Google acted in good faith or not, you may take into account, together with all other circumstances, the extent to which Google relied upon or contravened any recognized practices in the industry concerning re- implementation of API libraries." Order Denying JMOL, denied permission to use a work does not weigh against a finding of fair use." Campbell, 510 U.S. at 585 n.18 ("If the use is otherwise fair, then no permission need be sought or granted.").

Ultimately, we find that, even assuming the jury was unpersuaded that Google acted in bad faith, the highly commercial and non-transformative nature of the use strongly support the conclusion that the first factor weighs against a finding of fair use.

Factor 2: Nature of the Copyrighted Work

The second factor—the nature of the copyrighted work—"calls for recognition that some works are closer to the core of intended copyright protection than others, with the consequence that fair use is more difficult to establish when the former works are copied." Campbell, 510 U.S. at 586. This factor "turns on whether the work is informational or creative." Worldwide Church of God, 227 F.3d at 1118; see also Harper & Row, 471 U.S. at 563 ("The law generally recognizes a greater need to disseminate factual works than works of fiction or fantasy."). Creative expression "falls within the core of the copy- right's protective purposes." Campbell, 510 U.S. at 586. Although "software products are not purely creative works," it is well established that copyright law protects computer software. Wall Data, 447 F.3d at 780 (citing Sega Enters. Ltd. v. Accolade, Inc., 977 F.2d 1510, 1519 (9th Cir. 1992) ("[T]he 1980 amendments to the Copyright Act unambiguously extended copyright protection to computer programs.")).

Here, the district court found that the jury could have concluded that the process of designing APIs was "highly creative" and "thus at the core of copyright's protection" or it could "reasonably have gone the other way and concluded that the declaring code was not highly creative." Order Denying JMOL, 2016 WL 3181206, at *10. While the jury heard testimony from Google's own expert that API design is "an art, not a science," other witnesses emphasized the functional role of the declaring code and the SSO and minimized the creative aspects. Id. Accordingly, the district court concluded that the "jury could reasonably have found that, while the declaring code and SSO were creative enough to qualify for copyright protection, functional considerations predominated in their design." Id.

On appeal, Oracle emphasizes that designing the APIs was a highly creative process and that the organization of the packages was not mandated by function. Indeed, this court has already held that the declaring code and the SSO of the 37 API packages at issue were sufficiently creative and original to qualify for copyright protection. Oracle, 750 F.3d at 1356. According to Oracle, the district court erred in assuming that, because the APIs have a "functional role," they cannot be creative.

As Google points out, however, all we found in the first appeal was that the declarations and SSO were sufficiently creative to provide the "minimal degree of creativity," Feist Publ'ns, Inc. v. Rural Tel. Serv. Co., 499 U.S. 340, 345 (1991), that is required for copyrightability. We also recognized that a reasonable jury could find that "the functional aspects of the packages" are "relevant to Google's fair use defense." Oracle, 750 F.3d at 1369, 1376- 77. On remand, Oracle stipulated that some of the declarations were necessary to use the Java language and presented no evidence explaining how the jury could distinguish the functionality and creativity of those declarations from the others. Google maintains that it presented evidence that the declarations and SSO were functional and the jury was entitled to credit that evidence.

Although it is clear that the 37 API packages at issue involved some level of creativity—and no reasonable juror could disagree with that conclusion—reasonable jurors could have concluded that functional considerations were both substantial and important. Based on that assumed factual finding, we conclude that factor two favors a finding of fair use.

The Ninth Circuit has recognized, however, that this second factor "typically has not been terribly significant in the overall fair use balancing." Dr. Seuss Enters., L.P. v. Penguin Books USA, Inc., 109 F.3d 1394, 1402 (9th Cir. 1997) (finding that the "creativity, imagination and originality embodied in The Cat in the Hat and its central character tilts the scale against fair use"); Mattel, 353 F.3d at 803 (similar). Other circuits agree. Fox News Network, 2018 WL 1057178, at *5 ("This factor 'has rarely played a significant role in the determination of a fair use dispute,' and it plays no significant role here." (quoting Authors Guild v. Google, Inc., 804 F.3d 202, 220 (2d Cir. 2015))). We note, moreover, that allowing this one factor to dictate a conclusion of fair use in all cases involving copying of software could effectively negate Congress's express declaration—continuing unchanged for some forty years—that software is copyrightable. Accordingly, though the jury's assumed view of the nature of the copyrighted work weighs in favor of finding fair use, it has less significance to the overall analysis.

Factor 3: Amount and Substantiality of the Portion Used

The third factor focuses on the "amount and substantiality of the portion used in . . . the context of the copy- righted work, not the infringing work." Oracle, 750 F.3d at 1375. Indeed, the statutory language makes clear that "a taking may not be excused merely because it is insubstantial with respect to the infringing work."

Harper & Row, 471 U.S. at 565. "[T]he fact that a substantial portion of the infringing work was copied verbatim [from the original work] is evidence of the qualitative value of the copied material, both to the originator and to the plagiarist who seeks to profit from marketing someone else's copyrighted expression." Id. Thus, while "whole- sale copying does not preclude fair use per se, copying an entire work militates against a finding of fair use." Worldwide Church of God, 227 F.3d at 1118 (citation and quotation marks omitted). But, there is no relevance to the opposite—i.e., adding substantial content to the copyrighted work is not evidence that what was copied was insubstantial or unimportant.

The inquiry under this third factor "is a flexible one, rather than a simple determination of the percentage of the copyrighted work used." Monge, 688 F.3d at 1179. The Ninth Circuit has explained that this third factor looks to the quantitative amount and qualitative value of the original work used in relation to the justification for its use. Seltzer, 725 F.3d at 1178. The percentage of work copied is not dispositive where the portion copied was qualitatively significant. Harper & Row, 471 U.S. at 566 ("In view of the expressive value of the excerpts and their key role in the infringing work, we cannot agree with the Second Circuit that the 'magazine took a meager, indeed an infinitesimal amount of Ford's original language.'" (citation omitted)). Google is correct that the Ninth Circuit has said that, "this factor will not weigh against an alleged infringer, even when he copies the whole work, if he takes no more than is necessary for his intended use." Id. (citing Kelly v. Arriba Soft Corp., 336 F.3d 811, 820-21 (9th Cir. 2003)). But the Ninth Circuit has only said that is true where the intended use was a transformative one, because the "extent of permissible copying varies with the purpose and character of the use." Id. (quoting Campbell, 510 U.S. at 586-87). Here, we have found that Google's use was not transformative and Google has conceded both that it could have written its own APIs and that the purpose of its copying was to make Android attractive to programmers. "Necessary" in the context of the cases upon which Google relies does not simply mean easier.

In assessing factor three, the district court explained that the "jury could reasonably have found that Google duplicated the bare minimum of the 37 API packages, just enough to preserve inter-system consistency in usage, namely the declarations and their SSO only, and did not copy any of the implementing code," such that Google "copied only so much as was reasonably necessary." Order Denying JMOL, 2016 WL 3181206, at *10. In reaching this conclusion, the court noted that the jury could have found that the number of lines of code Google duplicated was a "tiny fraction of one percent of the copyrighted works (and even less of Android, for that matter)." Id. We disagree that such a conclusion would have been reasonable or sufficient on this record.

On remand, the parties stipulated that only 170 lines of code were necessary to write in the Java language. It is undisputed, however, that Google copied 11,500 lines of code—11,330 more lines than necessary to write in Java. That Google copied more than necessary weighs against fair use. See Monge, 688 F.3d at 1179 (finding that, where the copyist "used far more than was necessary" of the original work, "this factor weighs against fair use"). And, although Google emphasizes that it used a small percentage of Java (11,500 lines of declarations out of roughly 2.86

million lines of code in the Java SE librar- ies), it copied the SSO for the 37 API packages in its entirety.

The district court emphasized Google's desire to "preserve inter-system consistency" to "avoid confusion among Java programmers as between the Java system and the Android system." Order Denying JMOL, 2016 WL 3181206, at *10-11. As we noted in the prior appeal, however, Google did not seek to foster any "inter-system consistency" between its platform and Oracle's Java platform. Oracle, 750 F.3d at 1371. And Google does not rely on any interoperability arguments in this appeal.11 Google sought "to capitalize on the fact that software developers were already trained and experienced in using the Java API packages at issue." Id. But there is no inherent right to copy in order to capitalize on the popu- larity of the copyrighted work or to meet the expectations of intended customers. Taking those aspects of the copy- righted material that were familiar to software developers to create a similar work designed to be popular with those same developers is not fair use. See Dr. Seuss Enters., 109 F.3d at 1401 (copying the most famous and well recognized aspects of a work "to get attention" or "to avoid the drudgery in working up something fresh" is not a fair use (quoting Campbell, 510 U.S. at 580)).

Even assuming the jury accepted Google's argument that it copied only a small portion of Java, no reasonable jury could conclude that what was copied was qualitatively insignificant, particularly when the material copied was important to the creation of the Android platform. Google conceded as much when it explained to the jury the importance of the APIs to the developers it wished to attract. See Tr. of Proceedings held on 5/16/16 at 106:8-

In the prior appeal, we noted that "Google's competitive desire to achieve commercial 'interoperability' . . . may be relevant to a fair use analysis." Oracle, 750 F.3d at 1376-77. But, although several amici in this appeal discuss interoperability concerns, Google has abandoned the arguments it once made about interoperability. This change in course is not surprising given the unrebutted evidence that Google specifically designed Android to be incompatible with the Java platform and not allow for interoperability with Java programs. Id. at 1371.

...

Factor 4: Effect Upon the Potential Market

The fourth and final factor focuses on "the effect of the use upon the potential market for or value of the copy- righted work." 17 U.S.C. § 107(4). This factor reflects the idea that fair use "is limited to copying by others which does not materially impair the marketability of the work which is copied." Harper & Row, 471 U.S. at 566-67. It requires that courts "consider not only the extent of market harm caused by the particular actions of the alleged infringer, but also whether unrestricted and widespread conduct of the sort engaged in by the defend- ant . . . would result in a substantially adverse impact on the potential market for the original." Campbell, 510 U.S. at 590 (citation and quotation marks omitted).

The Supreme Court once said that factor four is "un- doubtedly the single most important element of fair use." Harper & Row, 471 U.S. at 566. In its subsequent opinion in Campbell, however, the Court emphasized that none of the four factors can be viewed in isolation and that "[a]ll are to be explored, and the results weighed together, in light of the purposes of copyright." 510 U.S. at 578; see also Infinity Broad., 150 F.3d at 110 ("Historically, the fourth factor has been seen as central to fair use analysis, although the Supreme Court appears to have backed away from this position." (internal citation omitted)). The Court has also explained that "[m]arket harm is a matter of degree, and the importance of this factor will vary, not only with the amount of harm, but also with the relative strength of the showing on the other factors." Campbell, 510 U.S. at 590 n.21.

The Ninth Circuit recently indicated that likely mar- ket harm can be presumed where a use is "commercial and not transformative." Disney Enters., Inc. v. VidAngel, Inc., 869 F.3d 848, 861 (9th Cir. 2017) (citing Leadsinger, 512 F.3d at 531, for the proposition that, where a use "was commercial and not transformative, it was not error to presume likely market harm"). That presumption allegedly traces back to Sony Corp. of America v. Univer- sity City Studios, Inc., 464 U.S. 417, 451 (1984), where the Supreme Court stated that, "[i]f the intended use is for commercial gain, that likelihood [of future harm] may be presumed. But if it is for a noncommercial purpose, the likelihood must be demonstrated." The Supreme Court has since clarified that market impact, "no less than the other three [factors], may be addressed only through a 'sensitive balancing of interests'" and that earlier inter- pretations of Sony to the contrary were incorrect. Camp- bell, 510 U.S. at 590 n.21 (quoting Sony, 464 U.S. at 455 n.40);12 see also Monge, 688 F.3d at 1181 (cautioning against overemphasis on a presumption of market harm after Campbell). On this point, we must apply clear Supreme Court precedent rather than the more recent Ninth Circuit's statements to the contrary.

The Court noted, however, that "what Sony said simply makes common sense: when a commercial use amounts to mere duplication of the entirety of an original, it clearly 'supersede[s] the objects,' of the original and serves as a market replacement for it, making it likely that cognizable market harm to the original will occur." Id. at 591.

In evaluating the fourth factor, courts consider not only harm to the actual or potential market for the copyrighted work, but also harm to the "market for potential derivative uses," including "those that creators of original works would in general develop or license others to devel- op." Campbell, 510 U.S. at 592; see also A&M Records, 239 F.3d at 1017 ("[L]ack of harm to an established mar- ket cannot deprive the copyright holder of the right to develop alternative markets for the works."). A court can therefore consider the challenged use's "impact on poten- tial licensing revenues for traditional, reasonable, or likely to be developed markets." Swatch Grp. Mgmt. Servs. Ltd. v. Bloomberg L.P., 756 F.3d 73, 91 (2d Cir. 2014) (citation omitted); see also Seltzer, 725 F.3d at 1179 ("This factor also considers any impact on 'traditional, reasonable, or likely to be developed markets.'" (citation omitted)).

Also relevant to the inquiry is the fact that a copyright holder has the exclusive right to determine "when, 'whether and in what form to release'" the copyrighted work into new markets, whether on its own or via a licensing agreement. Monge,

688 F.3d at 1182 (quoting Harper & Row, 471 U.S. at 553). Indeed, the Ninth Circuit has recognized that "[e]ven an author who had disavowed any intention to publish his work during his lifetime" was entitled to copyright protection because: (1) "the relevant consideration was the 'potential market'" and (2) "he has the right to change his mind." Worldwide Church, 227 F.3d at 1119 (citing Salinger v. Random House, Inc., 811 F.2d 90, 99 (2d Cir. 1987)); see also Micro Star v. Formgen Inc., 154 F.3d 1107, 1113 (9th Cir. 1998) (noting that only the copyright holder "has the right to enter that market; whether it chooses to do so is entirely its business").

Here, the district court concluded that the jury "could reasonably have found that use of the declaring lines of code (including their SSO) in Android caused no harm to the market for the copyrighted works, which were for desktop and laptop computers." Order Denying JMOL, 2016 WL 3181206, at *10. In reaching this conclusion, the district court noted that, before Android was released, Sun made all of the Java API packages available for free and open source under the name OpenJDK, subject only to the terms of a general public license. Id. According to the district court, the jury could have concluded that "Android's impact on the market for the copyrighted works paralleled what Sun already expected via its Open- JDK." Id.

On appeal, Oracle argues that the evidence of actual and potential harm stemming from Google's copying was "overwhelming," and that the district court erred as a matter of law in concluding otherwise. Appellant Br. 52. We agree.

First, with respect to actual market harm, the evidence showed that Java SE had been used for years in mobile devices, including early smartphones, prior to Android's release. Specifically, the jury heard testimony that Java SE was already in smartphones, including Blackberry, SavaJe, Danger, and Nokia. That Android competed directly with Java SE in the market for mobile devices is sufficient to undercut Google's market harm arguments. With respect to tablets, the evidence showed that Oracle licensed Java SE for the Amazon Kindle. After Android's release, however, Amazon was faced with two competing options—Java SE and Android—and selected Android. ...

Google submits that the jury could have discounted this evidence because the Java SE APIs were available for free through OpenJDK. But Amazon moved from Java to Android—not to OpenJDK. And the evidence of record makes clear that device manufacturers did not view Amazon later used the fact that Android was free to negotiate a steep discount to use Java SE in its newer e- reader. In other words, the record contained substantial evidence that Android was used as a substitute for Java SE and had a direct market impact. Given this evidence of actual market harm, no reasonable jury could have concluded that there was no market harm to Oracle from Google's copying.

Even if there were a dispute about whether Oracle was licensing Java SE in smartphones at the time An- droid launched, moreover, "fair use focuses on potential, not just actual, market harm." Monge, 688 F.3d at 1181. Accordingly, although the district court focused exclusively on the market it found that Oracle had already en- tered—desktops and laptops—it should have considered how

Google's copying affected potential markets Oracle might enter or derivative works it might create or license others to create. ...

Of course, the fact that those negotiations were not successful does not factor into the analysis. Campbell, 510 U.S. at 585 n.18 ("If the use is otherwise fair, then no permission need be sought or granted. Thus, being denied permission to use a work does not weigh against a finding of fair use."). Such evidence was only relevant to show Oracle's interest in the potential market for smartphones. ..

Google argues that a reasonable jury could have concluded that Java SE and Android did not compete in the same market because Oracle: (1) was not a device maker; and (2) had not yet built its own smartphone platform. Neither argument has merit. That Oracle never built a smartphone device is irrelevant because potential markets include licensing others to develop derivative works. See Campbell, 510 U.S. at 592. The fact that Oracle had not yet developed a smartphone platform is likewise irrelevant as a matter of law because, as Oracle submits, a market is a potential market even where the copyright owner has no immediate plans to enter it or is unsuccessful in doing so. See Worldwide Church, 227 F.3d at 1119; Micro Star, 154 F.3d at 1113. Even assuming a reasonable jury could have found no current market harm, the undisputed evidence showed, at a minimum, that Oracle intended to license Java SE in smartphones; there was no evidence in the record to support any contrary conclusion. Because the law recognizes and protects a copyright owner's right to enter a "potential market," this fact alone is sufficient to establish market impact.

Given the record evidence of actual and potential harm, we conclude that "unrestricted and widespread conduct of the sort engaged in by" Google would result in "a substantially adverse impact on the potential market for the original" and its derivatives. See Campbell, 510 U.S. at 590 (citation and quotation marks omitted). Accordingly, the fourth factor weighs heavily in favor of Oracle.

Balancing the Four Factors

Having undertaken a case-specific analysis of all four factors, we must weigh the factors together "in light of the purposes of copyright." Campbell, 510 U.S. at 578. We conclude that allowing Google to commercially exploit Oracle's work will not advance the purposes of copyright in this case. Although Google could have furthered copyright's goals of promoting creative expression and innova- tion by developing its own APIs, or by licensing Oracle's APIs for use in developing a new platform, it chose to copy Oracle's creative efforts instead. There is nothing fair about taking a copyrighted work verbatim and using it for the same purpose and function as the original in a com- peting platform.

Even if we ignore the record evidence and assume that Oracle was not already licensing Java SE in the smartphone context, smartphones were undoubtedly a potential market. Android's release effectively replaced Java SE as the supplier of Oracle's copyrighted works and prevented Oracle from participating in developing mar- kets. This superseding use is inherently unfair.

On this record, factors one and four weigh heavily against a finding of fair use, while factor two weighs in favor of such a finding and factor three is, at best, neutral. Weighing these factors together, we conclude that Google's use of the declaring code and SSO of the 37 API packages was not fair as a matter of law.

We do not conclude that a fair use defense could never be sustained in an action involving the copying of computer code. Indeed, the Ninth Circuit has made it clear that some such uses can be fair. See Sony, 203 F.3d at 608; Sega, 977 F.2d at 1527-28. We hold that, given the facts relating to the copying at issue here—which differ materially from those at issue in Sony and Sega—Google's copying and use of this particular code was not fair as a matter of law. ...

13. Copyright on Databases

937 F.2d 700 (1991)

KREGOS v. The ASSOCIATED PRESS

United States Court of Appeals, Second Circuit

JON O. NEWMAN, Circuit Judge:

The primary issue on this appeal is whether the creator of a baseball pitching form is entitled to a copyright. The appeal requires us to consider the extent to which the copyright law protects a compiler of information. George L. Kregos appeals from the April 30, 1990, judgment of the District Court for the Southern District of New York (Gerard L. Goettel, Judge) dismissing on motion for summary judgment his copyright and trademark claims against the Associated Press ("AP") and Sports Features Syndicate, Inc. ("Sports Features"). We affirm dismissal of the trademark [702] claims, but conclude that Kregos is entitled to a trial on his copyright claim, though the available relief may be extremely limited.

Facts

The facts are fully set forth in Judge Goettel's thorough opinion, 731 F.Supp. 113 (S.D.N.Y.1990). The reader's attention is particularly called to the appendices to that opinion, which set forth Kregos' pitching form and the allegedly infringing forms. Id. at 122-24 (Appx. 1-4). Kregos distributes to newspapers a pitching form, discussed in detail below, that displays information concerning the past performances of the opposing pitchers scheduled to start each day's baseball games. The form at issue in this case, first distributed in 1983, is a redesign of an earlier form developed by Kregos in the 1970's. Kregos registered his form with the Copyright Office and obtained a copyright. Though the form, as distributed to subscribing newspapers, includes statistics, the controversy in this case concerns only Kregos' rights to the form without each day's data, in other words, his rights to the particular selection of categories of statistics appearing on his form.

In 1984, AP began publishing a pitching form provided by Sports Features. The AP's 1984 form was virtually identical to Kregos' 1983 form. AP and Sports Features changed their form in 1986 in certain respects, which are discussed in part I(d) below.

Kregos' 1983 form lists four items of information about each day's games — the teams, the starting pitchers, the game time, and the betting odds, and then lists nine items of information about each pitcher's past performance, grouped into three categories. Since there can be no claim of a protectable interest in the categories of information concerning each day's game, we confine our attention to the categories of information concerning the pitchers' past performances. For convenience, we will identify each performance item by a number from 1 to 9 and use that number whenever referring to the same item in someone else's form.

The first category in Kregos' 1983 form, performance during the entire season, comprises two items — won/lost record (1) and earned run average (2). The second category, performance during the entire season against the opposing team at the site of the game, comprises three items — won/lost record (3), innings pitched (4), and earned run average (5). The third category, performance in the last three starts, comprises four items — won/lost record (6), innings pitched (7), earned run average (8), and men on base average (9). This last item is the average total of hits and walks given up by a pitcher per nine innings of pitching.

It is undisputed that prior to Kregos' 1983 form, no form had listed the same nine items collected in his form. It is also undisputed that some but not all of the nine items of information had previously appeared in other forms. In the earlier forms, however, the few items common to Kregos' form were grouped with items different from those in Kregos' form. Siegel's 1978 form contained won/lost record (1) and earned run average for the season [703] (2), but contained no "at site" information (3, 4, 5) and no information for recent starts (6, 7, 8, 9). It contained only two of Kregos' nine items (1, 2). Fratas' 1980 form contained "at site" information for the previous season (differing from Kregos' "at site" information for the current season (3, 4, 5)) and contained no information for recent starts (6, 7, 8, 9). It contained only two of Kregos' nine items (1, 2). Eckstein's 1981 form, the only prior form to contain information for recent starts (using two of the four items in Kregos' form (6, 7)) lacked the third and fourth "recent starts" items (earned run average and men on base average (8, 9)), contained "at site" information only for won/lost record and did not report that data for the current season against the opposing team, and lacked earned run average for the season (2). It contained only three of Kregos' nine items (1, 6, 7).

Kregos' item (9), men on base average in recent starts, had not previously appeared anywhere. However, a supplier for the Associated Press Syndicate, Inc. had distributed on a weekly basis the men on base average for every pitcher for the entire season, rather than for the most recent three starts, as in Kregos' form.

District Court decision. The District Court granted summary judgment for the defendants on both Kregos' copyright and trademark claims. On the copyright side of the case, the Court ruled that Kregos lacked a copyrightable interest in his pitching form on three grounds. First, the Court concluded that Kregos' pitching form was insufficiently original in its selection of statistics to warrant a copyright as a compilation. Second, the Court concluded that, in view of the limited space available for displaying pitching forms in newspapers, the possible variations in selections of pitching statistics were so limited that the idea of a pitching form had merged into its expression. Third, the Court ruled that Kregos' pitching form was not entitled to a copyright because of the so-called "blank form" doctrine. On the trademark side of the case, the Court granted summary judgment for the defendants on the ground that Kregos' trademark claims encountered, as a matter of law, a functionality defense.

Discussion

I. Copyright Claim

A. Copyright for a Compilation of Facts.

The basic principles concerning copyright protection for compilations of facts are clear and have recently been authoritatively restated in the Supreme Court's decision rejecting copyright protection for telephone book white pages. Feist Publications, Inc. v. Rural Telephone Service Co., Inc., ____ U.S. ___, 111 S.Ct. 1282, 113 L.Ed.2d 358 (1991) ("Feist"). "A factual compilation is eligible for copyright if it features an original selection or arrangement of facts, but the copyright is limited to the particular selection or arrangement. In no event may copyright extend to the facts themselves." Id. at ____, 111 S.Ct. at 1290. "Original, as the term is used in copyright, means only that the work was independently created by the author (as opposed to copied from other works), and that it possesses at least some minimal degree of creativity." Id. at ____, 111 S.Ct. at 1287 (citation omitted).

In principle, this "independent creation" sense of the word "original" applies to the originality required to entitle a selection of factual information to a copyright. "A compiler may settle upon a selection or arrangement that others have used; novelty is not required. Originality requires only that the author make the selection or arrangement independently (i.e., without copying that selection or arrangement from another work)...." Id. at ____, 111 S.Ct. at 1294. In practice, however, as the Court in Feist made clear, application of the "originality" standard to compilations of facts is narrowed somewhat by the requirement of "some minimal level of creativity." Id. In Feist, for example, it would have [704] availed the compiler nothing to have persuaded a fact-finder that it came upon the idea of "selecting" all the telephone subscribers in town and "arranging" their names in alphabetical order without copying these features from any preexisting work. The widespread prior existence of white page lists of all telephone subscribers in a community, arranged alphabetically, precluded, as a matter of law, a finding of the requisite creativity. The white pages were deemed "entirely typical" and "garden-variety." Id. at ____, 111 S.Ct. at 1296. The selection of listings "could not be more obvious." Id. And "there is nothing remotely creative about arranging names alphabetically in a white pages directory.... It is not only unoriginal, it is practically inevitable." Id.

Thus, as to compilations of facts, independent creation as to selection and arrangement will not assure copyright protection; the requirement of minimal creativity becomes an important ingredient of the test for copyright entitlement. "[T]he selection and arrangement of facts cannot be so mechanical or routine as to require no creativity whatsoever." Id.

Prior to Feist, we had applied these principles to require some minimal level of creativity in two fairly recent cases that illustrate compilations of facts one of which is and one of which is not entitled to a copyright, Eckes v. Card Prices Update, 736 F.2d 859 (2d Cir.1984), and Financial Information, Inc. v. Moody's Investors Service, 808 F.2d 204 (2d Cir.1986) ("FII"), cert. denied, 484 U.S. 820, 108 S.Ct. 79, 98 L.Ed.2d 42 (1987). In Eckes we upheld a District Court's finding, made after trial, that a selection of 5,000 out of 18,000 baseball cards to be considered "premium" was entitled to a copyright. Eckes, 736 F.2d at 863. In FII we upheld a District Court's finding, also made after trial, that the listing of five items of information concerning municipal bond calls lacked sufficient selection to warrant a copyright; in almost all instances, the five items for the various bond issues had all appeared in "tombstone" ads, and only "minor additional research" was needed to complete the listings. FFI, 808 F.2d at 208.

Kregos' pitching form presents a compilation of facts that falls between the extremes illustrated by Eckes and FFI. Kregos has selected nine items of information concerning a pitcher's performance. The universe of known facts available only from inspection of box scores of prior games is considerably greater than nine, though perhaps not as great as the quantity of 18,000 cards in Eckes. For example, Kregos could have selected past performances from any number of recent starts, instead of using the three most recent starts. And he could have chosen to include strikeouts, walks, balks, or hit batters. By consulting play-by-play accounts of games, instead of box scores, he could have counted various items such as the number of innings in which the side was retired in order, or in which no runner advanced as far as second base. Or he could have focused on performance under pressure by computing the percentage of innings in which a runner scored out of total innings in which a runner reached second base, and he could have chosen to calculate this statistic for any number of recent starts. In short, there are at least scores of available statistics about pitching performance available to be calculated from the underlying data and therefore thousands of combinations of data that a selector can choose to include in a pitching form.[4]

It cannot be said as a matter of law that in selecting the nine items for his pitching form out of the universe of available data, Kregos has failed to display enough selectivity to satisfy the requirement of originality. Whether in selecting his combination of nine items he has displayed the requisite degree of creativity is a somewhat closer question. Plainly he has done better than the compiler in FFI who "selected" only the five facts about bond calls already grouped together in nearly all tombstone ads. Judge Goettel [705] was persuaded to rule against Kregos, at least in part, because "most of the statistics ... had been established in previously existing forms." 731 F.Supp. at 118. But that observation is largely irrelevant to the issue of whether Kregos' selection of statistics displays sufficient creativity to warrant a copyright. Nearly all copyrighted compilations of facts convey facts that have been published elsewhere. Each of the cards selected for the "premium" category in Eckes had previously been published. To hold a valid copyright, a compiler of facts need not be a discoverer of facts. Indeed, any discovered fact, or, in Kregos' case, any newly devised statistic, would not, in and of itself, be eligible for copyright protection.

The prior publication of some of the statistics on Kregos' form might indicate, however, that his selection is not sufficiently different from those grouped in earlier publications to satisfy minimal creativity. That conclusion cannot rest on just the prior appearance of the statistics Kregos chose to use, but might rest on the prior appearance of a selection of those statistics that either is identical to Kregos' selection or varies from his only to a trivial degree. In that event, the first issue would be whether Kregos could demonstrate originality, i.e., persuade the trier that he had not copied from the similar selection. Even if Kregos could satisfy that burden, the issue would then arise as to whether the previously published selections of statistics had reached the point where it could be said that Kregos' selection was insufficiently creative, or in the words of Feist, "entirely typical," "garden-variety," or "obvious." In view of the variety of pitching forms disclosed in the record, it is unlikely that such a conclusion could be reached and certainly could not be reached as a matter of law.

But these issues are not even likely to arise because the record discloses no prior pitching form with more than three of the pitching performance statistics that are included in Kregos' selection of nine statistics. There is no prior form that is identical to his nor one from which his varies in only a trivial degree. The validity of his copyright in a compilation of facts cannot be rejected as a matter of law for lack of the requisite originality and creativity.

B. Idea/Expression Merger.

The fundamental copyright principle that only the expression of an idea and not the idea itself is protectable, see Mazer v. Stein, 347 U.S. 201, 217, 74 S.Ct. 460, 470, 98 L.Ed. 630 (1954), has produced a corollary maxim that even expression is not protected in those instances where there is only one or so few ways of expressing an idea that protection of the expression would effectively accord protection to the idea itself. See Educational Testing Services v. Katzman, 793 F.2d 533, 539 (3d Cir.1986); Toro Co. v. R & R Products Co., 787 F.2d 1208, 1212 (8th Cir.1986). Our Circuit has considered this so-called "merger" doctrine in determining whether actionable infringement has occurred, rather than whether a copyright is valid, see Durham Industries, Inc. v. Tomy Corp., 630 F.2d 905, 916 (2d Cir.1980), an approach the Nimmer treatise regards as the "better view." See 3 Nimmer on Copyright § 13.03[B][3] at 13-58 (1990). Assessing merger in the context of alleged infringement will normally provide a more detailed and realistic basis for evaluating the claim that protection of expression would inevitably accord protection to an idea.

Determining when the idea and its expression have merged is a task requiring considerable care: if the merger doctrine is applied too readily, arguably available alternative forms of expression will be precluded; if applied too sparingly, protection will be accorded to ideas. Recognizing this tension, courts have been cautious in applying the merger doctrine to selections of factual information, see Educational Testing Services, 793 F.2d at 540 (doctrine inapplicable to selection of test questions); Toro Co., 787 F.2d at 1212 (doctrine inapplicable to selection of data for numbering parts), though the doctrine has been applied on occasion to selections of categories of data, see, e.g., Matthew Bender & Co. v. Kluwer Law Book Publishers, Inc., 672 F.Supp. 107, 110 (S.D.N.Y.1987) (categories of data concerning personal injury awards).

In one sense, every compilation of facts can be considered to represent a merger of an idea with its expression. Every compiler of facts has the idea that his particular selection of facts is useful. If the compiler's idea is identified at that low level of abstraction, then the idea would always merge into the compiler's expression of it. Under that approach, there could never be a copyrightable compilation of facts. However, if the idea is formulated at a level of abstraction above the particular selection of facts the compiler has made, then merger of idea and expression is not automatic. Even with an idea formulated at a somewhat high level of abstraction, circumstances might occur where the realistic availability of differing expressions is so drastically limited that the idea can be said to have merged in its expression.

In this case, Judge Goettel understood Kregos' idea to be "to publish an outcome predictive pitching form." 731 F.Supp. at 119. In dissent, Judge Sweet contends that Kregos' idea is that the nine statistics he has selected are the most significant ones to consider when attempting to predict the outcome of a baseball game. Unquestionably, if that is the idea for purposes of merger analysis, then merger of that idea and its expression has occurred — by definition.

Though there is room for fair debate as to the identification of the pertinent idea whenever merger analysis is applied to a compilation of facts, we think the "idea" in this case is the one as formulated by Judge Goettel. Kregos has not devised a system that he seeks to withdraw from the public domain by virtue of copyright. He does not present his selection of nine statistics as a method of predicting the outcome of baseball games. His idea is that of "an outcome predictive pitching form" in the general sense that it selects the facts that he thinks newspaper readers should consider in making their own predictions of outcomes. He does not purport to weight the nine statistics, much less provide a method for comparing the aggregate value of one pitcher's statistics against that of the opposing pitcher in order to predict an outcome or even its probability of occurring. He has not devised a system, as had the deviser of a bookkeeping system in Baker v. Selden, 101 U.S. (11 Otto) 99, 25 L.Ed. 841 (1879). He has compiled facts, or at least categories of facts.

Though formulating the idea as "an outcome predictive pitching form," Judge Goettel applied the merger doctrine, concluding that the idea of selecting outcome predictive statistics to rate pitching performance was capable of expression in only a very limited number of ways. He thought the case more attracted by Matthew Bender, involving categories of data for personal injury awards, than by the cases involving categories of statistics for performances of race horses, see Wabash Publishing Co. v. Flanagan, No. 89-C-1923 (N.D.Ill. Apr. 3, 1989) (1989 WL 32939); Triangle Publications, Inc. v. New England Newspaper Publishing Co., 46

F.Supp. 198, 201-02 (D.Mass.1942); see also Triangle Publications, Inc. v. Sports Eye, Inc., 415 F.Supp. 682, 684 (E.D.Pa.1976). In Matthew Bender, Judge Conner concluded that the categories in the plaintiff's chart (amount, case, plaintiff, event, injury, and relevant data) were "the only sensible ones which could have been used to compile the data." 672 F.Supp. at 112. That observation may well have been so as to categories of data for personal injury awards, but we think the same cannot be said of categories of pitching statistics.

As the various pitching forms in the record indicate, the past performances of baseball pitchers can be measured by a variety of statistics, as can the past performances of race horses. Kregos' selection of categories includes three statistics for the pitcher's current season performance against the day's opponent at the site of the day's game; other charts select "at site" performance against the opponent during the prior season, and some select performance against the opponent over the pitcher's career, both home and away. Some charts include average men on base per nine innings; others do not. The data for most recent starts could include whatever number of games the compiler [707] thought pertinent. These variations alone (and there are others) abundantly indicate that there are a sufficient number of ways of expressing the idea of rating pitchers' performances to preclude a ruling that the idea has merged into its expression.

In reaching this conclusion, we confess to some unease because of the risk that protection of selections of data, or, as in this case, categories of data, have the potential for according protection to ideas. Our concern may be illustrated by an example of a doctor who publishes a list of symptoms that he believes provides a helpful diagnosis of a disease. There might be many combinations of symptoms that others could select for the same purpose, but a substantial question would nonetheless arise as to whether that doctor could obtain a copyright in his list, based on the originality of his selection. If the idea that the doctor is deemed to be expressing is the general idea that the disease in question can be identified by observable symptoms, then the idea might not merge into the doctor's particular expression of that idea by his selection of symptoms. That general idea might remain capable of many other expressions. But it is arguable that the doctor has conceived a more precise idea — namely, the idea that his selection of symptoms is a useful identifier of the disease. That more limited idea can be expressed only by his selection of symptoms, and therefore might be said to have merged into his expression. Thus, as with the idea/expression dichotomy itself, see Nichols v. Universal Pictures Corp., 45 F.2d 119, 121 (2d Cir.1930) (Judge Learned Hand's formulation of the "abstractions test"), cert. denied, 282 U.S. 902, 51 S.Ct. 216, 75 L.Ed. 795 (1931), application of the doctrine of an idea merging with its expression depends on the level of abstraction at which the idea is formulated.

As long as selections of facts involve matters of taste and personal opinion, there is no serious risk that withholding the merger doctrine will extend protection to an idea. That was surely the case with the selection of premium baseball cards in Eckes. It is also true of a selection of prominent families for inclusion in a social directory. See Social Register Ass'n v. Murphy, 128 F. 116 (C.C.D.R.I.1904); see also New York Times Co. v. Roxbury Data Interface, Inc., 434 F.Supp. 217, 222 n. 2 (D.N.J.1977). However, where a selection of data is the first step in an analysis that yields a precise result or even a better-than-average probability of some result, protecting the "expression" of the selection would clearly risk protecting the idea of the analysis.

Kregos' pitching form is part way along the continuum spanning matters of pure taste to matters of predictive analysis. He is doing more than simply saying that he holds the opinion that his nine performance characteristics are the most pertinent. He implies that his selections have some utility in predicting outcomes. On the other hand, he has not gone so far as to provide a system for weighing the combined value of the nine characteristics for each of two opposing pitchers and determining a probability as to which is more likely to win. Like the compilers of horse racing statistics, Kregos has been content to select categories of data that he obviously believes have some predictive power, but has left it to all sports page readers to make their own judgments as to the likely outcomes from the sets of data he has selected. His "idea," for purposes of the merger doctrine, remains the general idea that statistics can be used to assess pitching performance rather than the precise idea that his selection yields a determinable probability of outcome. Since there are various ways of expressing that general idea, the merger doctrine need not be applied to assure that the idea will remain in the public domain.

C. "Blank Form" Doctrine.

The District Court also ruled that Kregos could not obtain a valid copyright in his pitching form because of the so-called "blank form" doctrine. The doctrine derives from the Supreme Court's decision in Baker v. Selden, supra. The Court there denied copyright protection to blank forms contained in a book explaining a system of double-entry bookkeeping. The forms displayed an arrangement of columns and headings that permitted entries for a day, a week, or a month to be recorded on one page or two facing pages. The Court made clear that the author could not obtain copyright protection for an "art" that "might or might not have been patented" and reasoned that since the "art" was available to the public, "the ruled lines and headings of accounts must necessarily be used as incident to it." Id. at 104. Then, in a concluding statement that is susceptible to overreading, the Court said that "blank account-books are not the subject of copyright." Id. at 107.

Though there are some statements suggesting broadly that no blank forms are copyrightable, see Bibbero Systems, Inc. v. Colwell Systems, Inc., 893 F.2d 1104, 1106-07 (9th Cir.1990), amended, reh'g denied, 1990 WL 1285, 1990 U.S.App.LEXIS 2562; M.M. Business Forms Corp. v. UARCO, Inc., 472 F.2d 1137, 1139 (6th Cir.1973), many courts have recognized that there can be protectable elements of forms that include considerable blank space. See, e.g., Harcourt, Brace & World, Inc. v. Graphic Controls Corp., 329 F.Supp. 517, 524 (S.D.N.Y.1971) (answer sheets); Norton Printing Co. v. Augustana Hospital, 155 U.S.P.Q. 133 (N.D.Ill.1967) (laboratory test forms). See generally Whelan Associates, Inc. v. Jaslow Dental Laboratory, Inc., 797 F.2d 1222, 1242-43 (3d Cir.1986), cert. denied, 479 U.S. 1031, 107 S.Ct. 877, 93 L.Ed.2d 831 (1987).

The regulations of the Copyright Office are careful to preclude copyright registration to:

Blank forms, such as ... account books, diaries, bank checks, scorecards, address books, report forms, order forms and the like, which are designed for recording information and do not in themselves convey information; 37 C.F.R. § 202.1(c) (1990) (emphasis added).

Of course, a form that conveys no information and serves only to provide blank space for recording information contains no expression or selection of information that could possibly warrant copyright protection. See, e.g., John H. Harland Co. v. Clarke Checks, Inc., 711 F.2d 966, 971-72 (11th Cir.1983) (check stubs). At the same time, it should be equally obvious that a writing that does contain a selection of categories of information worth recording, sufficiently original and creative to deserve a copyright as a compilation of facts, cannot lose that protection simply because the work also contains blank space for recording the information. When the Copyright Office denies a copyright to scorecards or diaries that "do not in themselves convey information," it must be contemplating works with headings so obvious that their selection cannot be said to satisfy even minimal creativity (a baseball scorecard with columns headed "innings" and lines headed "players"; a travel diary with headings for "cities" "hotels," and "restaurants"). Such a work conveys no information, not just because it contains blanks, but because its selection of headings is totally uninformative. On the other hand, if a scorecard or diary contained a group of headings whose selection (or possibly arrangement) displayed cognizable creativity, the author's choice of those headings would convey to users the information that this group of categories was something out of [709] the ordinary. See 1 Nimmer on Copyright § 2.18[C][1] at 2-201 (1990) ("Thus books intended to record the events of baby's first year, or a record of a European trip, or any one of a number of other subjects, may evince considerable originality in suggestions of specific items of information which are to be recorded, and in the arrangement of such items.") (emphasis added; footnote omitted).

The Ninth Circuit has rejected this approach, believing that the rule of cases like Norton Printing "is potentially limitless." Bibbero Systems, 893 F.2d at 1107. In the Ninth Circuit's view, "[a]ll forms seek only certain information, and, by their selection, convey that the information sought is important." Id. With deference, we suggest that this critique of Norton Printing and other cases recognizing a copyright in the selection of categories of information for forms is not well taken. All forms may convey that the information called for is important (or at least worth recording), but the form-maker does not necessarily display even minimal creativity by selecting categories of "important" information. The principle of cases like Norton Printing is not limitless because courts are obliged to determine as to forms, as with all compilations of information, whether the author's selection of categories of data to be recorded displays at least minimal creativity. The check stub in Clarke Checks was plainly deficient in this regard. Whether the forms in Bibbero Systems and Norton Printing displayed the requisite creativity are matters of fair dispute. But all forms need not be denied protection simply because many of them fail to display sufficient creativity.

In the pending case, once it is determined that Kregos' selection of categories of statistics displays sufficient creativity to preclude a ruling as a matter of law that it is not a copyrightable compilation of information, that same conclusion precludes rejecting his copyright as a "blank form."

D. Extent of Protection.

Our ruling that Kregos' copyright claim survives defendants' motion for summary judgment does not, of course, mean that he will necessarily obtain much of a victory. "Even if a work qualifies as a copyrightable compilation, it receives only limited protection.... [C]opyright protects only the elements that owe their origin to the compiler — the selection, coordination, and arrangement of facts." Feist, ____ U.S. at ____, 111 S.Ct. at 1294. If Kregos prevails at trial on the factual issues of originality and creativity, he will be entitled to protection only against infringement of the protectable features of his form. Only the selection of statistics might be entitled to protection. We agree entirely with Judge Goettel that nothing in Kregos' arrangement of the selected statistics displays the requisite creativity. As to the arrangement, Kregos' form is surely a "garden-variety" pitching form. The statistics are organized into the "obvious" arrangement of columns, and the form follows the pattern of most other forms: the statistics are organized into three groups, first the statistics about each pitcher's performance for the season, then the statistics about the pitcher's performance against the day's opponent, and finally the statistics concerning the pitcher's recent starts.

Even as to the selection of statistics, if Kregos establishes entitlement to protection, he will prevail only against other forms that can be said to copy his selection. That would appear to be true of the AP's 1984 form, which, as Judge Goettel noted, is "identical in virtually every sense to plaintiff's form." 731 F.Supp. at 115. Whether it is also true of the AP's current form, revised in 1986, is far less certain. That form contains six of Kregos' nine items (1, 2, 6, 7, 8, 9). It also includes four items that Kregos does not have. Three of these items concern performance against the day's opposing team — won-lost record, innings pitched, and earned run average; though these three statistics appear on Kregos' form, the AP's 1986 form shows data for the current season both home and away, whereas Kregos' form shows data [710] for the pitcher's current season at the site of that day's game. The fourth item on the AP's 1986 form and not on Kregos' form shows the team's record in games started by that day's pitcher during the season.

The reason for doubting that the AP's 1986 form infringes Kregos' form arises from the same consideration that supports Kregos' claim to a copyright. Kregos can obtain a copyright by displaying the requisite creativity in his selection of statistics. But if someone else displays the requisite creativity by making a selection that differs in more than a trivial degree, Kregos cannot complain. Kregos contends that the AP's 1986 form makes insignificant changes from its 1984 form. But Kregos cannot have it both ways. If his decision to select, in the category of performance against the opposing team, statistics for the pitcher's current season at the site of today's game displays, in combination with his other selections, enough creativity to merit copyright protection, then a competitor's decision to select in that same category performance statistics for the pitcher's season performance both home and away may well insulate the competitor from a claim of infringement. Thus, though issues remain to be explored before any determination can be made, it may well be that Kregos will have a valid claim only as to the AP's 1984 form.

...

Conclusion

The judgment of the District Court is reversed and remanded with respect to the copyright claim, and affirmed with respect to the trademark claims.

SWEET, District Judge, concurring in part and dissenting in part:

While I concur in the majority's conclusion that Kregos has displayed sufficient creativity to satisfy the Feist Publications standard for copyrightability, I would affirm the district court's grant of summary judgment because I conclude that Kregos' idea here has merged into his expression.

1. Kregos' Idea

I agree with the majority that Kregos displayed at least some creativity in selecting his nine statistics for his pitching form, and thereby satisfied the creativity standards of Feist Publications. However, I believe that this selection was not simply an expression of the idea that this information might be of interest to sports fans, but instead represented his very specific idea that these nine statistics were the most significant ones to consider when attempting to predict the outcome of a baseball game. I respectfully disagree with the majority's statement that Kregos' idea was the abstract "general idea that statistics can be used to assess pitching performance," because while I agree that the application of the merger doctrine will always depend on the level at which the idea is formulated, I do not believe that the majority has set forth convincing grounds for its determination as to the idea at issue here.

If few people had previously considered using pitching statistics to handicap baseball games, I would agree that Kregos' particular selection of statistics might indeed be entitled to protection as a detailed expression of his idea. Here, however, the format and the arrangement of data existed prior to his choice of particular items to report, and thus his "creation" was nothing more than that choice, which as an expression seems to me inseparable from its idea.

I have difficulty distinguishing between Kregos' work and the example of a doctor's identification of the symptoms to use in diagnosing a disease, which the majority suggests would be unprotectible because of merger. In making this suggestion, the majority eschews the notion that the doctor's idea is the "general idea that the disease in question can be identified by observable symptoms" in favor of the more precise formulation that the idea is that "his selection of symptoms is a useful identifier of the disease." Majority Opinion at 707. This reasoning would appear to apply equally well to Kregos' case. In both cases, the creators have conceived very precise "ideas" concerning the significant data which ought to be considered in predicting a given result, and those ideas can be expressed only by identifying the relevant data. Of course, there is the obvious distinction that a system for making medical diagnoses is more socially beneficial than system for estimating sports odds, but such a distinction does not offer a basis for denying copyright protection to one while granting it to the other.

...

I find this situation closer to that in Matthew Bender & Co. v. Kluwer Law Book Publishers, Inc., 672 F.Supp. 107 (S.D.N.Y.1987), in which the plaintiff sought protection only for its method of arranging information concerning personal injury awards. There, as here, there was no allegation that the defendant had copied the plaintiff's data, but merely that it had arranged its own data in a format which was similar to that used by the plaintiff. In denying relief to the plaintiff, Judge Conner held that the idea of the plaintiff's work was to provide useful information in a functional format, and that the copyright could not be used to preclude others from adopting that format. 672 F.Supp. at 110.

...

While I agree with the majority's statement that "[e]very compiler of facts has the idea that his particular selection of facts is useful," I believe that there is a difference between the idea that a selection is useful and the more precise idea that it is the most useful selection possible.

The less precise idea is found in cases of compilations which are based on aesthetic choices, such as a list of socially-prominent families, or those in which the value of the compilation is due more to the fact of compilation than to the intrinsic value of the data being compiled: this would include the parts numbering list at issue in Toro Co. v. R & R Products, where the numbers were not significant prior to being associated with the parts, the test questions in Educational Testing Services, where the questions were valuable to the defendants precisely because they had been used by the plaintiff, and, to the extent the selection was in fact subjective, the premium card list in Card Prices, where the defendants had no independent knowledge of which cards it would be profitable to update.

The more precise idea is found where the compiler's main purpose is to compile data which will allow a reader of the compilation to reach a clearly-defined goal, such as the case reports in Matthew Bender, where the goal was to estimate the possible settlement value of a case, or a doctor's diagnostic form, where the goal would be to diagnose the given disease, or Kregos' pitching form, where the goal is to predict the outcome of the game.

Finally, in light of the majority's agreement with the district court that Kregos' arrangement of the statistics was not itself creative or original, and therefore that his particular ordering is not protected, it is difficult to grasp exactly what "expression" the majority intends to protect, if not the fundamental expression that these nine items are valuable in predicting games. This difficulty becomes apparent as the majority speculates about the extent of protection to be given to Kregos' form.

...

44 F.3d 61 (2d Cir. 1994)

CCC V. MACLEAN

US Court of Appeals for the Second Circuit

LEVAL, Circuit Judge:

The appellant, publisher of a compendium of its projections of used car valuations, seeks to establish copyright infringement on the part of a competitor, which copied substantial portions of appellant's compendium into the computer data base of used car valuations it offers to its customers. Arising in the wake of the Supreme Court's decision in Feist Publications, Inc. v. Rural Telephone Serv. Co., 499 U.S. 340, 111 S. Ct. 1282, 113 L. Ed. 2d 358 (1991), this appeal raises the question of the scope of protection afforded by the copyright law to such compilations of informational matter. Finding no infringement, the district court granted summary judgment to the appellee. In our view, the copyright law offers more substantial protection to such compilations than envisioned in the district court's ruling. We therefore reverse.

Background

The Red Book. The appellant is Maclean Hunter Market Reports, Inc. ("Maclean"). Since 1911, Maclean, or its predecessors, have published the Automobile Red Book--Official Used Car Valuations (the "Red Book").1 The Red Book, which is published eight times a year, in different versions for each of three regions of the United States (as well as a version for the State of Wisconsin), sets forth the editors' projections of the values for the next six weeks of "average" versions of most of the used cars (up to seven years old) sold in that region. These predicted values are set forth separately for each automobile make, model number, body style, and engine type. Red Book also provides predicted value adjustments for various options and for mileage in 5,000 mile increments.

The valuation figures given in the Red Book are not historical market prices, quotations, or averages; nor are they derived by mathematical formulas from available statistics. They represent, rather, the Maclean editors' predictions, based on a wide variety of informational sources and their professional judgment, of expected values for "average" vehicles for the upcoming six weeks in a broad region. The introductory text asserts, "You, the subscriber, must be the final judge of the actual value of a particular vehicle. Any guide book is a supplement to and not a substitute for expertise in the complex field of used vehicle valuation."

CCC's computer services. Appellee CCC Information Services, Inc. ("CCC"), is also in the business of providing its customers with information as to the valuation of used vehicles. Rather than publishing a book, however, CCC provides information to its customers through a computer data base. Since at least 1988, CCC has itself been systematically loading major portions of the Red Book onto its computer network and republishing Red Book information in various forms to its customers.

CCC utilizes and resells the Red Book valuations in several different forms. CCC's "VINguard Valuation Service" ("VVS") provides subscribers with the average of a vehicle's Red Book valuation and its valuation in the NADA Official Used Car Guide (the "Bluebook"), the other leading valuation book, published by the National Automobile Dealers Association ("NADA"). The offer of this average of Red Book and Bluebook satisfies a market because the laws of certain states use that average figure as a minimum for insurance payments upon the "total loss" of a vehicle. CCC's "Computerized Valuation Service" ("CVS"), while it primarily provides its subscribers with CCC's independent valuation of used cars, also provides customers with the Red Book/Bluebook average and the Red Book values standing alone.

It is uncontested that CCC earns significant revenues through the sale of its services, in which it both directly and indirectly resells the figures it copies every few weeks from the Red Book. As the court found below, since 1988 numerous Red Book customers have canceled their subscriptions, opting instead to purchase CCC's services. Op. at 25 (JA 665).

Proceedings below. CCC brought this action in 1991, seeking, inter alia, a declaratory judgment that it incurred no liability to Maclean under the copyright laws by taking and republishing material from the Red Book. Maclean counterclaimed alleging infringement. CCC then pleaded various affirmative defenses, including that it used the Red Book for its intended purpose, fair use, and that the Red Book has come into the public domain as the result of its adoption in state statutes regulating the amount of insurance payments. CCC also made various contentions based on waiver, estoppel, consent, and untimeliness.

Both sides moved for summary judgment, and the motions were referred for report and recommendation to Magistrate Judge Arthur H. Latimer. Magistrate Judge Latimer recommended to the district court that CCC's motion for summary judgment be granted. Judge Latimer found (1) that the Red Book employed no originality or creativity in the selection, coordination or arrangement of data, and therefore did not constitute a protected "original work of authorship," 17 U.S.C.A. Sec. 101 (West 1977); (2) that the Red Book valuations were facts, or interpretations of facts, and were, therefore, not protected by copyright; (3) that, even if the entries were not facts, copyright protection was nonetheless precluded by the doctrine of "merger of idea and expression," because each entry in the Red Book is an idea--the idea of the value of the particular vehicle--and that idea is necessarily communicated by a dollar figure; and (4) that the Red Book had been placed in the public domain by being "incorporated into governmental regulations." District Judge Nevas then "approved, adopted and ratified" the Magistrate Judge's recommended ruling, and judgment was entered in CCC's favor. Endorsement at JA 671.

Discussion

1. Does the Red Book manifest originality so as to be protected by the copyright laws? The first significant question raised by this appeal is whether Maclean holds a protected copyright interest in the Red Book. CCC contends, and the district court held, that the Red Book is nothing more than a compilation of unprotected facts, selected and organized without originality or creativity, and therefore unprotected under the Supreme Court's teachings in Feist. We disagree.

...

The district court gave several reasons for its ruling that the Red Book failed the test for originality. First, the court stated, "Maclean Hunter has not persuasively demonstrated that the values published in the Red Book are anything more than interpretations or analyses of factual information.... While Maclean Hunter may have been the first to discover and report this material, the material does not 'owe its origin' to Maclean Hunter." (Citing Feist, 499 U.S. at 361, 111 S. Ct. at 1296; Op. at 16-17 (JA 656-57).)

The district court was simply mistaken in its conclusion that the Red Book valuations were, like the telephone numbers in Feist, pre-existing facts that had merely been discovered by the Red Book editors. To the contrary, Maclean's evidence demonstrated without rebuttal that its valuations were neither reports of historical prices nor mechanical derivations of historical prices or other data. Rather, they represented predictions by the Red Book editors of future prices estimated to cover specified geographic regions. According to Maclean's evidence, these predictions were based not only on a multitude of data sources, but also on professional judgment and expertise. The testimony of one of Maclean's deposition witnesses indicated that fifteen considerations are weighed; among the considerations, for example, is a prediction as to how traditional competitor vehicles, as defined by Maclean, will fare against one another in the marketplace in the coming period. (JA 209-12.) The valuations themselves are original creations of Maclean.

Recognizing that " [o]riginality may also be found in the selection and ordering of particular facts or elements," the district court concluded that none had been shown. Op. at 17 (JA 657). This was because the Red Book's selection and arrangement of data represents "a logical response to the needs of the vehicle valuation market." Id. at 18 (JA 658). In reaching this conclusion, the district court applied the wrong standard. The fact that an arrangement of data responds logically to the needs of the market for which the compilation was prepared does not negate originality. To the contrary, the use of logic to solve the problems of how best to present the information being compiled is independent creation. See Feist, 499 U.S. at 359, 111 S. Ct. at 1295 (originality is to be found unless the creative spark is so utterly lacking as to be "virtually nonexistent").

We find that the selection and arrangement of data in the Red Book displayed amply sufficient originality to pass the low threshold requirement to earn copyright protection. This originality was expressed, for example, in Maclean's division of the national used car market into several regions, with independent predicted valuations for each region depending on conditions there found. A car model does not command the same value throughout a large geographic sector of the United States; used car values are responsive to local conditions and vary from place to place. A 1989 Dodge Caravan will not command the same price in San Diego as in Seattle. In furnishing a single number to cover vast regions that undoubtedly contain innumerable variations, the Red Book expresses a loose judgment that values are likely to group together with greater consistency within a defined region than without. The number produced is necessarily both approximate and original. Several other aspects of the Red Book listings also embody sufficient originality to pass Feist's low threshold. These include: (1) the selection and manner of presentation of optional features for inclusion;7 (2) the adjustment for mileage by 5,000 mile increments (as opposed to using some other breakpoint and interval); (3) the use of the abstract concept of the "average" vehicle in each category as the subject of the valuation; and (4) the selection of the number of years' models to be included in the compilation.

We conclude for these reasons that the district court erred in ruling that the Red Book commands no copyright protection by reason of lack of originality.

2. The idea-expression dichotomy and the merger of necessary expression with the ideas expressed. CCC's strongest argument is that it took nothing more than ideas, for which the copyright law affords no protection to the author. According to this argument, (1) each entry in the Red Book expresses the authors' idea of the value of a particular vehicle; (2) to the extent that "expression" is to be found in the Red Book's valuations, such expression is indispensable to the statement of the idea and therefore merges with the idea, so that the expression is also not protectible, and; (3) because each of Red Book's valuations could freely be taken without infringement, all of them may be taken without infringement. This was one of the alternate bases of the district court's ruling in CCC's favor.

The argument is not easily rebutted, for it does build on classically accepted copyright doctrine. It has been long accepted that copyright protection does not extend to ideas; it protects only the means of expression employed by the author. As the Supreme Court stated in Mazer v. Stein, 347 U.S. 201, 74 S. Ct. 460, 98 L. Ed. 630 (1954),

Unlike a patent, a copyright gives no exclusive right to the art disclosed; protection is given only to the expression of the idea--not the idea itself. Thus, in Baker v. Selden, 101 U.S. 99 [25 L. Ed. 841] [(1879)], the Court held that a copyrighted book on a peculiar system of bookkeeping was not infringed by a similar book using a similar plan which achieved similar results where the alleged infringer made a different arrangement of the columns and used different headings. Id. at 217, 74 S. Ct. at 470 (footnote omitted).

It is also well established that, in order to protect the immunity of ideas from private ownership, when the expression is essential to the statement of the idea, the expression also will be unprotected, so as to insure free public access to the discussion of the idea. See Kregos, 937 F.2d at 705; Herbert Rosenthal Jewelry Corp. v. Kalpakian, 446 F.2d 738, 742 (9th Cir. 1971) ("When the 'idea' and its 'expression' are ... inseparable, copying the 'expression' will not be barred, since protecting the 'expression' in such circumstances would confer a monopoly of the 'idea' upon the copyright owner free of the conditions and limitations imposed by the patent law.").

We nonetheless believe the district court erred in granting judgment to CCC. We reach this conclusion based on the need to balance the conflicts and contradictions that pervade the law of copyright, and the need, where elements of the copyright law conflict, to determine, as a policy judgment, which of its commands prevails over the other.

... Among them is the issue raised by this appeal of the protection, if any, to be accorded to compilations. For if CCC's argument prevails, for reasons explained below, virtually nothing will remain of the protection accorded by the statute to compilations, notwithstanding the express command of the copyright statute.

Given the nature of compilations, it is almost inevitable that the original contributions of the compilers will consist of ideas. Originality in selection, for example, will involve the compiler's idea of the utility to the consumer of a limited selection from the particular universe of available data. One compiler might select out of a universe of all businesses those that he believes will be of interest to the Chinese-American community, see Key Publications, 945 F.2d at 514, another will select those statistics as to racehorses or pitchers that are believed to be practical to the consumer in helping to pick winners, see Kregos, 937 F.2d at 706-07; Wabash Publishing Co. v. Flanagan, No. 89 Civ. 1923, 1989 WL 32939, 1989 U.S.Dist. LEXIS 3546 (N.D. Ill. Mar. 31, 1989) (particular selection and arrangement of information relevant to horse races found copyrightable); Triangle Publications, Inc. v. New England Newspaper Publication Co., 46 F. Supp. 198, 201-02 (D. Mass. 1942) (same); another will offer a list of restaurants he suggests are the best, the most elegant, or offer the best value within a price range. Each of these exercises in selection represents an idea.

In other compilations, the original contribution of the compiler will relate to ideas for the coordination, or arrangement of the data. Such ideas for arrangement are generally designed to serve the consumers' needs, making the data more useful by increasing the ease of access to those data that answer the needs of the targeted customers, or dividing the data in ways that will efficiently serve the needs of more diverse groups of customers. For example, a listing of New York restaurants might be broken down by geographic areas of the city, specialty or type (e.g., seafood, steaks and chops, vegetarian, kosher, Chinese, Indian); price range; handicapped accessibility, etc.

It is apparent that virtually any independent creation of the compiler as to selection, coordination, or arrangement will be designed to add to the usefulness or desirability of his compendium for targeted groups of potential customers, and will represent an idea. In the case of a compilation, furthermore, such structural ideas are likely to be expressed in the most simple, unadorned, and direct fashion. If, as CCC argues, the doctrine of merger permits the wholesale copier of a compilation to take the individual expression of such ideas, so as to avoid the risk that an idea will improperly achieve protection, then the protection explicitly conferred on compilations by Section 103 of the U.S. Copyright Act will be illusory.

We addressed precisely this problem in Kregos, 937 F.2d 700. The plaintiff Kregos had created a form to be used to help predict the outcome of a baseball game by filling in nine statistics of the competing pitchers. The defendant contended, in terms similar to CCC's argument, that the copyright owner's idea was the utility of the nine selected statistics in helping a fan predict the outcome, and that the idea was merged in the expression of it--in the copyrighted form that listed those nine statistics. Judge Newman wrote:

In one sense, every compilation of facts can be considered to represent a merger of an idea with its expression. Every compiler of facts has the idea that his particular selection of facts is useful. If the compiler's idea is identified at that low level of abstraction, then the idea would always merge into the compiler's expression of it. Under that approach, there could never be a copyrightable compilation of facts. Kregos, 937 F.2d at 706.

Recognizing that the purpose of the doctrine of merger of expression with idea is to insure that protection not extend to ideas, the Kregos opinion went on to describe different categories of ideas. It distinguished between, on the one hand, those ideas that undertake to advance the understanding of phenomena or the solution of problems, such as the identification of the symptoms that are the most useful in identifying the presence of a particular disease; and those, like the pitching form there at issue, that do not undertake to explain phenomena or furnish solutions, but are infused with the author's taste or opinion. Kregos postulated that the importance of keeping ideas free from private ownership is far greater for ideas of the first category, directed to the understanding of phenomena or the solving of problems, than for those that merely represent the author's taste or opinion and therefore do not materially assist the understanding of future thinkers. As to the latter category, the opinion asserted that, so long as the selections reflected in the compilation "involve matters of taste and personal opinion, there is no serious risk that withholding the merger doctrine," 937 F.2d at 707 (emphasis added), would inflict serious injury on the policy underlying the rule that forbids granting protection to an idea. This was in contrast to analyses belonging to the first category--building blocks of understanding--as to which "protecting the [necessary] 'expression' of the selection would clearly risk protecting the idea of the analysis." Id at 707. Because Kregos's idea was of the soft type infused with taste or opinion, the court withheld application of the merger doctrine, permitting Kregos to exercise ownership. It accomplished this by assigning to the idea a different level of abstraction from the expression of it, so that the merger doctrine would not apply and the copyright owner would not lose protection. ("His 'idea,' for purposes of the merger doctrine, remains the general idea that statistics can be used to assess pitching performance rather than the precise idea that his selection yields a determinable probability of outcome." 937 F.2d at 707.)

Kregos, thus, makes a policy judgment as between two evils. Unbridled application of the merger doctrine would undo the protection the copyright law intends to accord to compilations. Complete failure to apply it, however, would result in granting protection to useful ideas. Kregos adopts a middle ground. In cases of wholesale takings of compilations, a selective application of the merger doctrine, withholding its application as to soft ideas infused with taste and opinion, will carry out the statutory policy to protect innovative compilations without impairing the policy that requires public access to ideas of a more important and useful kind.

Application of the Kregos approach to our facts leads us to the conclusion that the district court should, as in Kregos, have "withheld " the merger doctrine. As a matter of copyright policy, this was not an appropriate instance to apply the merger doctrine so as to deprive Red Book of copyright protection. The consequences of giving CCC the benefit of the merger doctrine are too destructive of the protection the Act intends to confer on compilations, without sufficient benefit to the policy of copyright that seeks to preserve public access to ideas.

In the first place, the takings by CCC from the Red Book are of virtually the entire compendium. This is not an instance of copying of a few entries from a compilation. This copying is so extensive that CCC effectively offers to sell its customers Maclean's Red Book through CCC's data base. CCC's invocation of the merger doctrine to justify its contention that it has taken no protectible matter would effectively destroy all protection for Maclean's compilation.

Secondly, the valuations copied by CCC from the Red Book are not ideas of the first, building-block, category described in Kregos, but are rather in the category of approximative statements of opinion by the Red Book editors. To the extent that protection of the Red Book would impair free circulation of any ideas, these are ideas of the weaker category, infused with opinion; the valuations explain nothing, and describe no method, process or procedure. Maclean Hunter makes no attempt, for example, to monopolize the basis of its economic forecasting or the factors that it weighs; the Red Book's entries are no more than the predictions of Red Book editors of used car values for six weeks on a rough regional basis. As noted above, Red Book specifies in its introduction that " [y]ou, the subscriber, must be the final judge of the actual value of a particular vehicle. Any guide book is a supplement to and not a substitute for expertise in the complex field of used vehicle valuation." This language is remarkably similar to our observation in Kregos, that the author "has been content to select categories of data that he obviously believes have some predictive power, but has left it to all sports page readers to make their own judgments as to the likely outcomes from the sets of data he has selected." 937 F.2d at 707.

The balancing of interests suggested by Kregos leads to the conclusion that we should reject CCC's argument seeking the benefit of the merger doctrine. Because the ideas contained in the Red Book are of the weaker, suggestion-opinion category, a withholding of the merger doctrine would not seriously impair the policy of the copyright law that seeks to preserve free public access to ideas. If the public's access to Red Book's valuations is slightly limited by enforcement of its copyright against CCC's wholesale copying, this will not inflict injury on the opportunity for public debate, nor restrict access to the kind of idea that illuminates our understanding of the phenomena that surround us or of useful processes to solve our problems. In contrast, if the merger doctrine were applied so as to bar Maclean's enforcement of its copyright against CCC's wholesale takings, this would seriously undermine the protections guaranteed by Sec. 103 of the Copyright Act to compilations that employ original creation in their selection, coordination, or arrangement. It would also largely vitiate the inducements offered by the copyright law to the makers of original useful compilations.

3. Public domain. We disagree also with the district court's ruling sustaining CCC's affirmative defense that the Red Book has fallen into the public domain. The district court reasoned that, because the insurance statutes or regulations of several states establish Red Book values as an alternative standard, i.e., by requiring that insurance payments for total losses be at least equal either to Red Book value or to an average of Red Book and Bluebook values (unless another approved valuation method is employed), the Red Book has passed into the public domain. The argument is that the public must have free access to the content of the laws that govern it; if a copyrighted work is incorporated into the laws, the public need for access to the content of the laws requires the elimination of the copyright protection.

No authority cited by CCC directly supports the district court's view. It relied on Building Officials & Code Adm. v. Code Tech. Inc., 628 F.2d 730 (1st Cir. 1980) ("BOCA"), which the Magistrate Judge found "virtually indistinguishable" from our case. Although the First Circuit Court of Appeals, in BOCA, indeed expressed sympathy with the arguments here advanced by CCC, its ruling is not a holding to that effect. The Court of Appeals merely vacated a preliminary injunction, expressing doubts as to the plaintiff copyright holder's likelihood of success, and remanding for a full hearing on whether the plaintiff had lost its copyright protection by reason of the adoption of its previously protected work (a construction code) as part of the laws of Massachusetts.

We are not prepared to hold that a state's reference to a copyrighted work as a legal standard for valuation results in loss of the copyright. While there are indeed policy considerations that support CCC's argument, they are opposed by countervailing considerations. For example, a rule that the adoption of such a reference by a state legislature or administrative body deprived the copyright owner of its property would raise very substantial problems under the Takings Clause of the Constitution. We note also that for generations, state education systems have assigned books under copyright to comply with a mandatory school curriculum. It scarcely extends CCC's argument to require that all such assigned books lose their copyright--as one cannot comply with the legal requirements without using the copyrighted works. Yet we think it unlikely courts would reach this conclusion. Although there is scant authority on CCC's argument, Nimmer's treatise opposes such a suggestion as antithetical to the interests sought to be advanced by the Copyright Act. See Nimmer Sec. 5.06 [C] at 5-60.

Conclusion

Because Maclean has demonstrated a valid copyright, and an infringement thereof, we direct the entry of judgment in Maclean's favor. We remand to the district court for further proceedings.

14. Moral Rights in Copyright Law

538 F.2d 14 (1976)

GILLIAM v. AMERICAN BROADCASTING COMPANIES

United States Court of Appeals, Second Circuit

LUMBARD, Circuit Judge:

Plaintiffs, a group of British writers and performers known as "Monty Python," appeal from a denial by Judge Lasker in the Southern District of a preliminary injunction to restrain the American Broadcasting Company (ABC) from broadcasting edited versions of three separate programs originally written and performed by Monty Python for broadcast by the British Broadcasting Corporation (BBC). We agree with Judge Lasker that the appellants have demonstrated that the excising done for ABC impairs the integrity of the original work. We further find that the countervailing injuries that Judge Lasker found might have accrued to ABC as a result of an injunction at a prior date no longer exist. We therefore direct the issuance of a preliminary injunction by the district court.

Since its formation in 1969, the Monty Python group has gained popularity primarily through its thirty-minute television programs created for BBC as part of a comedy series entitled "Monty Python's Flying Circus." In accordance with an agreement between Monty Python and BBC, the group writes and delivers to BBC scripts for use in the television series. This scriptwriters' agreement recites in great detail the procedure to be followed when any alterations are to be made in the script prior to recording of the program. The essence of this section of the agreement is that, while BBC retains final authority to make changes, appellants or their representatives exercise optimum control over the scripts consistent with BBC's authority and only minor changes may be made without prior consultation with the writers. Nothing in the scriptwriters' agreement entitles BBC to alter a program once it has been recorded. The agreement further provides that, subject to the terms therein, the group retains all rights in the script.

Under the agreement, BBC may license the transmission of recordings of the television programs in any overseas territory. The series has been broadcast in this country primarily on non-commercial public broadcasting television stations, although several of the programs have been broadcast on commercial stations in Texas and Nevada. In each instance, the thirty-minute programs have been broadcast as originally recorded and broadcast in England in their entirety and without commercial interruption.

In October 1973, Time-Life Films acquired the right to distribute in the United States certain BBC television programs, including the Monty Python series. Time-Life was permitted to edit the programs only "for insertion of commercials, applicable censorship or governmental . . . rules and regulations, and National Association of Broadcasters and time segment requirements." No similar clause

533

was included in the scriptwriters' agreement between appellants and BBC. Prior to this time, ABC had sought to acquire the right to broadcast excerpts from various Monty Python programs in the spring of 1975, but the group rejected the proposal for such a disjoined format. Thereafter, in July 1975, ABC agreed with Time-Life to broadcast two ninety- minute specials each comprising three thirty-minute Monty Python programs that had not previously been shown in this country.

Correspondence between representatives of BBC and Monty Python reveals that these parties assumed that ABC would broadcast each of the Monty Python programs "in its entirety." On September 5, 1975, however, the group's British representative inquired of BBC how ABC planned to show the programs in their entirety if approximately 24 minutes of each 90 minute program were to be devoted to commercials. BBC replied on September 12, "we can only reassure you that ABC have decided to run the programmes 'back to back,' and that there is a firm undertaking not to segment them." ABC broadcast the first of the specials on October 3, 1975. Appellants did not see a tape of the program until late November and were allegedly "appalled" at the discontinuity and "mutilation" that had resulted from the editing done by Time-Life for ABC. Twenty-four minutes of the original 90 minutes of recording had been omitted. Some of the editing had been done in order to make time for commercials; other material had been edited, according to ABC, because the original programs contained offensive or obscene matter.

In early December, Monty Python learned that ABC planned to broadcast the second special on December 26, 1975. The parties began negotiations concerning editing of that program and a delay of the broadcast until Monty Python could view it. These negotiations were futile, however, and on December 15 the group filed this action to enjoin the broadcast and for damages. Following an evidentiary hearing, Judge Lasker found that "the plaintiffs have established an impairment of the integrity of their work" which "caused the film or program . . . to lose its iconoclastic verve." According to Judge Lasker, "the damage that has been caused to the plaintiffs is irreparable by its nature." Nevertheless, the judge denied the motion for the preliminary injunction on the grounds that it was unclear who owned the copyright in the programs produced by BBC from the scripts written by Monty Python; that there was a question of whether Time-Life and BBC were indispensable parties to the litigation; that ABC would suffer significant financial loss if it were enjoined a week before the scheduled broadcast; and that Monty Python had displayed a "somewhat disturbing casualness" in their pursuance of the matter.

Judge Lasker granted Monty Python's request for more limited relief by requiring ABC to broadcast a disclaimer during the December 26 special to the effect that the group dissociated itself from the program because of the editing. A panel of this court, however, granted a stay of that order until this appeal could be heard and permitted ABC to broadcast, at the beginning of the special, only the legend that the program had been edited by ABC. We heard argument on April 13 and, at that time, enjoined ABC from any further broadcast of edited Monty Python programs pending the decision of the court.

In determining the availability of injunctive relief at this early stage of the proceedings, Judge Lasker properly considered the harm that would inure to the plaintiffs if the injunction were denied, the harm that defendant would suffer if the injunction were granted, and the likelihood that plaintiffs would ultimately succeed on the merits. See Hamilton Watch Co. v. Benrus Watch Co., 206 F.2d 738 (2d Cir. 1953). We direct the issuance of a preliminary injunction because we find that all these factors weigh in favor of appellants.

There is nothing clearly erroneous in Judge Lasker's conclusion that any injury suffered by appellants as a result of the broadcast of edited versions of their programs was irreparable by its nature. ABC presented the appellants with their first opportunity for broadcast to a nationwide network audience in this country. If ABC adversely misrepresented the quality of Monty Python's work, it is likely that many members of the audience, many of whom, by defendant's admission, were previously unfamiliar with appellants, would not become loyal followers of Monty Python productions. The subsequent injury to appellants' theatrical reputation would imperil their ability to attract the large audience necessary to the success of their venture. Such an injury to professional reputation cannot be measured in monetary terms or recompensed by other relief. See Coca-Cola Co. v. Gemini Rising, Inc., 346 F.Supp. 1183, 1189 (E.D.N.Y.1972); Estee Lauder, Inc. v. Watsky, 323 F.Supp. 1064, 1067 (S.D.N.Y.1970).

In contrast to the harm that Monty Python would suffer by a denial of the preliminary injunction, Judge Lasker found that ABC's relationship with its affiliates would be impaired by a grant of an injunction within a week of the scheduled December 26 broadcast. The court also found that ABC and its affiliates had advertised the program and had included it in listings of forthcoming television programs that were distributed to the public. Thus a last minute cancellation of the December 26 program, Judge Lasker concluded, would injure defendant financially and in its reputation with the public and its advertisers.

However valid these considerations may have been when the issue before the court was whether a preliminary injunction should immediately precede the broadcast, any injury to ABC is presently more speculative. No rebroadcast of the edited specials has been scheduled and no advertising costs have been incurred for the immediate future. Thus there is no danger that defendant's relations with affiliates or the public will suffer irreparably if subsequent broadcasts of the programs are enjoined pending a disposition of the issues.

We then reach the question whether there is a likelihood that appellants will succeed on the merits. In concluding that there is a likelihood of infringement here, we rely especially on the fact that the editing was substantial, i. e., approximately 27 per cent of the original program was omitted, and the editing contravened contractual provisions that limited the right to edit Monty Python material. It should be emphasized that our discussion of these matters refers only to such facts as have been developed upon the hearing for a preliminary injunction. Modified or contrary findings may become appropriate after a plenary trial.

Judge Lasker denied the preliminary injunction in part because he was unsure of the ownership of the copyright in the recorded program. Appellants first contend that the question of ownership is irrelevant because the recorded program was merely a derivative work taken from the script in which they hold the uncontested copyright. Thus, even if BBC owned the copyright in the recorded program, its use of that work would be limited by the license granted to BBC by Monty Python for use of the underlying script. We agree.

Section 7 of the Copyright Law, 17 U.S.C. s 7, provides in part that "adaptations, arrangements, dramatizations . . . or other versions of . . . copyrighted works when produced with the consent of the proprietor of the copyright in such works . . . shall be regarded as new works subject to copyright . . . ." Manifestly, the recorded program falls into this category as a dramatization of the script, and thus the program was itself entitled to copyright protection. However, section 7 limits the copyright protection of the derivative work, as works adapted from previously existing scripts have become known, to the novel additions made to the underlying work, Reyher v. Children's Television Workshop, 533 F.2d 87 (2d Cir. 1976), and the derivative work does not affect the "force or validity" of the copyright in the matter from which it is derived. See Grove Press, Inc. v. Greenleaf Publishing Co., 247 F.Supp. 518 (S.D.N.Y.1965). Thus, any ownership by BBC of the copyright in the recorded program would not affect the scope or ownership of the copyright in the underlying script.

Since the copyright in the underlying script survives intact despite the incorporation of that work into a derivative work, one who uses the script, even with the permission of the proprietor of the derivative work, may infringe the underlying copyright. See Davis v. E. I. DuPont deNemours & Co., 240 F.Supp. 612 (S.D.N.Y.1965) (defendants held to have infringed when they obtained permission to use a screenplay in preparing a television script but did not obtain permission of the author of the play upon which the screenplay was based).

If the proprietor of the derivative work is licensed by the proprietor of the copyright in the underlying work to vend or distribute the derivative work to third parties, those parties will, of course, suffer no liability for their use of the underlying work consistent with the license to the proprietor of the derivative work. Obviously, it was just this type of arrangement that was contemplated in this instance. The scriptwriters' agreement between Monty Python and BBC specifically permitted the latter to license the transmission of the recordings made by BBC to distributors such as Time-Life for broadcast in overseas territories.

One who obtains permission to use a copyrighted script in the production of a derivative work, however, may not exceed the specific purpose for which permission was granted. Most of the decisions that have reached this conclusion have dealt with the improper extension of the underlying work into media or time, i. e., duration of the license, not covered by the grant of permission to the derivative work proprietor. See Bartsch v. Metro- Goldwyn-Mayer, Inc., 391 F.2d 150 (2d Cir.), cert. denied, 393 U.S. 826, 89 S.Ct. 86, 21 L.Ed.2d 96 (1968); G. Ricordi & Co. v. Paramount Pictures Inc., 189 F.2d 469 (2d Cir.), cert. denied, 342 U.S. 849, 72 S.Ct. 77, 96 L.Ed. 641 (1951). Cf. Rice v. American Program Bureau, 446 F.2d

685 (2d Cir. 1971). Appellants herein do not claim that the broadcast by ABC violated media or time restrictions contained in the license of the script to BBC. Rather, they claim that revisions in the script, and ultimately in the program, could be made only after consultation with Monty Python, and that ABC's broadcast of a program edited after recording and without consultation with Monty Python exceeded the scope of any license that BBC was entitled to grant.

The rationale for finding infringement when a licensee exceeds time or media restrictions on his license the need to allow the proprietor of the underlying copyright to control the method in which his work is presented to the public applies equally to the situation in which a licensee makes an unauthorized use of the underlying work by publishing it in a truncated version. Whether intended to allow greater economic exploitation of the work, as in the media and time cases, or to ensure that the copyright proprietor retains a veto power over revisions desired for the derivative work, the ability of the copyright holder to control his work remains paramount in our copyright law. We find, therefore, that unauthorized editing of the underlying work, if proven, would constitute an infringement of the copyright in that work similar to any other use of a work that exceeded the license granted by the proprietor of the copyright.

If the broadcast of an edited version of the Monty Python program infringed the group's copyright in the script, ABC may obtain no solace from the fact that editing was permitted in the agreements between BBC and Time-Life or Time-Life and ABC. BBC was not entitled to make unilateral changes in the script and was not specifically empowered to alter the recordings once made; Monty Python, moreover, had reserved to itself any rights not granted to BBC. Since a grantor may not convey greater rights than it owns, BBC's permission to allow Time-Life, and hence ABC, to edit appears to have been a nullity. See Hampton v. Paramount Pictures Corp., 279 F.2d 100 (9th Cir.), cert. denied, 364 U.S. 882, 81 S.Ct. 170, 5 L.Ed.2d 103 (1970); Ilyin v. Avon Publications, 144 F.Supp. 368, 372 (S.D.N.Y.1956).

ABC answers appellants' infringement argument with a series of contentions, none of which seems meritorious at this stage of the litigation. The network asserts that Monty Python's British representative, Jill Foster, knew that ABC planned to exclude much of the original BBC program in the October 3 broadcast. ABC thus contends that by not previously objecting to this procedure, Monty Python ratified BBC's authority to license others to edit the underlying script.

Although the case of Ilyin v. Avon Publications, Inc., 144 F.Supp. 368, 373 (S.D.N.Y.1956), may be broadly read for the proposition that a holder of a derivative copyright may obtain rights in the underlying work through ratification, the conduct necessary to that conclusion has yet to be demonstrated in this case. It is undisputed that appellants did not have actual notice of the cuts in the October 3 broadcast until late November. Even if they are chargeable with the knowledge of their British representative, it is not clear that she had prior notice of the cuts or ratified the omissions, nor did Judge Lasker make any finding on the question. While Foster, on September 5, did question how ABC was to broadcast the entire program if it was going to interpose 24 minutes of commercials, she received

Argument 1: ratification

assurances from BBC that the programs would not be "segmented." The fact that she knew precisely the length of material that would have to be omitted to allow for commercials does not prove that she ratified the deletions. This is especially true in light of previous assurances that the program would contain the original shows in their entirety. On the present record, it cannot be said that there was any ratification of BBC's grant of editing rights. ABC, of course, is entitled to attempt to prove otherwise during the trial on the merits. *Argument 2: joint work*

ABC next argues that under the "joint work" theory adopted in Shapiro, Bernstein & Co. v. Jerry Vogel Music, Inc., 221 F.2d 569 (2d Cir. 1955), the script produced by Monty Python and the program recorded by BBC are symbiotic elements of a single production. Therefore, according to ABC, each contributor possesses an undivided ownership of all copyrightable elements in the final work and BBC could thus have licensed use of the script, including editing, written by appellants.

The joint work theory as extended in Shapiro has been criticized as inequitable unless "at the time of creation by the first author, the second author's contribution (is envisaged) as an integrated part of a single work," and the first author intends that the final product be a joint work. See 1 M. Nimmer, Copyright ss 67-73. Furthermore, this court appears to have receded from a broad application of the joint work doctrine where the contract which leads to collaboration between authors indicates that one will retain a superior interest. See Szekely v. Eagle Lion Films, Inc., 242 F.2d 266 (2d Cir.), cert. denied, 354 U.S. 922, 77 S.Ct. 1382, 1 L.Ed.2d 1437 (1957). In the present case, the screenwriters' agreement between Monty Python and BBC provides that the group is to retain all rights in the script not granted in the agreement and that at some future point the group may license the scripts for use on television to parties other than BBC. These provisions suggest that the parties did not consider themselves joint authors of a single work. This matter is subject to further exploration at the trial, but in the present state of the record, it presents no bar to issuance of a preliminary injunction.

Argument 3: Contract

Aside from the question of who owns the relevant copyrights, ABC asserts that the contracts between appellants and BBC permit editing of the programs for commercial television in the United States. ABC argues that the scriptwriters' agreement allows appellants the right to participate in revisions of the script only prior to the recording of the programs, and thus infers that BBC had unrestricted authority to revise after that point. This argument, however, proves too much. A reading of the contract seems to indicate that Monty Python obtained control over editing the script only to ensure control over the program recorded from that script. Since the scriptwriters' agreement explicitly retains for the group all rights not granted by the contract, omission of any terms concerning alterations in the program after recording must be read as reserving to appellants exclusive authority for such revisions.

Finally, ABC contends that appellants must have expected that deletions would be made in the recordings to conform them for use on commercial television in the United States. ABC argues that licensing in the United States implicitly grants a license to insert commercials in a program and to remove offensive or obscene material prior to broadcast. According to the network, appellants should have

Argument 4: standard practice in US

anticipated that most of the excised material contained scatological references inappropriate for American television and that these scenes would be replaced with commercials, which presumably are more palatable to the American public.

The proof adduced up to this point, however, provides no basis for finding any implied consent to edit. Prior to the ABC broadcasts, Monty Python programs had been broadcast on a regular basis by both commercial and public television stations in this country without interruption or deletion. Indeed, there is no evidence of any prior broadcast of edited Monty Python material in the United States. These facts, combined with the persistent requests for assurances by the group and its representatives that the programs would be shown intact belie the argument that the group knew or should have known that deletions and commercial interruptions were inevitable. Several of the deletions made for ABC, such as elimination of the words "hell" and "damn," seem inexplicable given today's standard television fare.[FN8] If, however, ABC honestly determined that the programs were obscene in substantial part, it could have decided not to broadcast the specials at all, or it could have attempted to reconcile its differences with appellants. The network could not, however, free from a claim of infringement, broadcast in a substantially altered form a program incorporating the script over which the group had retained control.

Our resolution of these technical arguments serves to reinforce our initial inclination that the copyright law should be used to recognize the important role of the artist in our society and the need to encourage production and dissemination of artistic works by providing adequate legal protection for one who submits his work to the public. See Mazer v. Stein, 347 U.S. 201, 74 S.Ct. 460, 98 L.Ed. 630 (1954). We therefore conclude that there is a substantial likelihood that, after a full trial, appellants will succeed in proving infringement of their copyright by ABC's broadcast of edited versions of Monty Python programs. In reaching this conclusion, however, we need not accept appellants' assertion that any editing whatsoever would constitute infringement. Courts have recognized that licensees are entitled to some small degree of latitude in arranging the licensed work for presentation to the public in a manner consistent with the licensee's style or standards. See Stratchborneo v. Arc. Music Corp., 357 F.Supp. 1393, 1405 (S.D.N.Y.1973); Preminger v. Columbia Pictures Corp., 49 Misc.2d 363, 267 N.Y.S.2d 594 (Sup.Ct.), aff'd 25 App.Div.2d 830, 269 N.Y.S.2d 913 (1st Dept.), aff'd 18 N.Y.2d 659, 273 N.Y.S.2d 80, 219 N.E.2d 431 (1966). That privilege, however, does not extend to the degree of editing that occurred here especially in light of contractual provisions that limited the right to edit Monty Python material.

II

It also seems likely that appellants will succeed on the theory that, regardless of the right ABC had to broadcast an edited program, the cuts made constituted an actionable mutilation of Monty Python's work. This cause of action, which seeks redress for deformation of an artist's work, finds its roots in the continental concept of droit moral, or moral right, which may generally be summarized as including the right of the artist to have his work attributed to him in the form in which he created it. See 1 M. Nimmer, supra, at s 110.1.

American copyright law, as presently written, does not recognize moral rights or provide a cause of action for their violation, since the law seeks to vindicate the economic, rather than the personal, rights of authors. Nevertheless, the economic incentive for artistic and intellectual creation that serves as the foundation for American copyright law, Goldstein v. California, 412 U.S. 546, 93 S.Ct. 2303, 37 L.Ed.2d 163 (1973); Mazer v. Stein, 347 U.S. 201, 74 S.Ct. 460, 98 L.Ed. 630 (1954), cannot be reconciled with the inability of artists to obtain relief for mutilation or misrepresentation of their work to the public on which the artists are financially dependent. Thus courts have long granted relief for misrepresentation of an artist's work by relying on theories outside the statutory law of copyright, such as contract law, Granz v. Harris, 198 F.2d 585 (2d Cir. 1952) (substantial cutting of original work constitutes misrepresentation), or the tort of unfair competition, Prouty v. National Broadcasting Co., 26 F.Supp. 265 (D.Mass.1939). See Strauss, The Moral Right of the Author 128-138, in Studies on Copyright (1963). Although such decisions are clothed in terms of proprietary right in one's creation, they also properly vindicate the author's personal right to prevent the presentation of his work to the public in a distorted form. See Gardella v. Log Cabin Products Co., 89 F.2d 891, 895-96 (2d Cir. 1937); Roeder, The Doctrine of Moral Right, 53 Harv.L.Rev. 554, 568 (1940). Lanham Act:

Here, the appellants claim that the editing done for ABC mutilated the original work and that consequently the broadcast of those programs as the creation of Monty Python violated the Lanham Act s 43(a), 15 U.S.C. s 1125(a). This statute, the federal counterpart to state unfair competition laws, has been invoked to prevent misrepresentations that may injure plaintiff's business or personal reputation, even where no registered trademark is concerned. See Mortellito v. Nina of California, 335 F.Supp. 1288, 1294 (S.D.N.Y.1972). It is sufficient to violate the Act that a representation of a product, although technically true, creates a false impression of the product's origin. See Rich v. RCA Corp., 390 F.Supp. 530 (S.D.N.Y.1975) (recent picture of plaintiff on cover of album containing songs recorded in distant past held to be a false representation that the songs were new); Geisel v. Poynter Products, Inc., 283 F.Supp. 261, 267 (S.D.N.Y.1968).

These cases cannot be distinguished from the situation in which a television network broadcasts a program properly designated as having been written and performed by a group, but which has been edited, without the writer's consent, into a form that departs substantially from the original work. "To deform his work is to present him to the public as the creator of a work not his own, and thus makes him subject to criticism for work he has not done." Roeder, supra, at 569. In such a case, it is the writer or performer, rather than the network, who suffers the consequences of the mutilation, for the public will have only the final product by which to evaluate the work. Thus, an allegation that a defendant has presented to the public a " garbled," Granz v. Harris, supra (Frank, J., concurring), distorted version of plaintiff's work seeks to redress the very rights sought to be protected by the Lanham Act, 15 U.S.C. s 1125(a), and should be recognized as stating a cause of action under that statute. See Autry v. Republic Productions, Inc., 213 F.2d 667 (9th Cir. 1954); Jaeger v. American Intn'l Pictures, Inc., 330 F.Supp. 274

(S.D.N.Y.1971), which suggest the violation of such a right if mutilation could be proven.

During the hearing on the preliminary injunction, Judge Lasker viewed the edited version of the Monty Python program broadcast on December 26 and the original, unedited version. After hearing argument of this appeal, this panel also viewed and compared the two versions. We find that the truncated version at times omitted the climax of the skits to which appellants' rare brand of humor was leading and at other times deleted essential elements in the schematic development of a story line. We therefore agree with Judge Lasker's conclusion that the edited version broadcast by ABC impaired the integrity of appellants' work and represented to the public as the product of appellants what was actually a mere caricature of their talents. We believe that a valid cause of action for such distortion exists and that therefore a preliminary injunction may issue to prevent repetition of the broadcast prior to final determination of the issues.

III

We do not share Judge Lasker's concern about the procedures by which the appellants have pursued this action. The district court indicated agreement with ABC that appellants were guilty of laches in not requesting a preliminary injunction until 11 days prior to the broadcast. Our discussion above, however, suggests that the group did not know and had no reason to believe until late November that editing would take place. Several letters between BBC and Monty Python's representative indicate that appellants believed that the programs would be shown in their entirety. Furthermore, the group did act to prevent offensive editing of the second program immediately after viewing the tape of the first edited program. Thus we find no undue delay in the group's failure to institute this action until they were sufficiently advised regarding the facts necessary to support the action. In any event, ABC has not demonstrated how it was prejudiced by any delay. See Emle Industries, Inc. v. Patentex, Inc., 478 F.2d 562, 574 (2d Cir. 1973).

Finally, Judge Lasker denied a preliminary injunction because Monty Python had failed to join BBC and Time-Life as indispensable parties. We do not believe that either is an indispensable party. ABC argues that joinder of both was required because it acted in good faith pursuant to its contractual rights with Time-Life in broadcasting edited versions of the programs, and Time-Life, in turn, relied upon its contract with BBC. Furthermore, ABC argues, BBC must be joined since it owns the copyright in the recorded programs.

Even if BBC owns a copyright relevant to determination of the issues in this case, the formalistic rule that once required all owners of a copyright to be parties to an action for its infringement has given way to equitable considerations. See Jaeger v. American International Pictures, supra, 330 F.Supp. at 279; 7 C. Wright & A. Miller, Federal Practice and Procedure, s 1614. In this case, the equities to be considered under Fed.R.Civ.P. 19(a) strongly favor appellants. Monty Python is relying solely on its copyright in the script and on its rights as an author. No claim is being made that Monty Python has rights derived from the copyright held by another. Compare First Financial Marketing Services Group, Inc. v. Field

Promotions, Inc., 286 F.Supp. 295 (S.D.N.Y.1968). One of the parties is an English corporation, and any action that appellants, a group of English writers and performers, might have against that potential defendant would be better considered under English law in an English court. Complete relief for the alleged infringement and mutilation complained of may be accorded between Monty Python and ABC, which alone broadcast the programs in dispute. If ABC is ultimately found liable to appellants, a permanent injunction against future broadcasts and a damage award would satisfy all of appellants' claims. ABC's assertion that failure to join BBC and Time-Life may leave it subject to inconsistent verdicts in a later action against its licensors may be resolved through the process of impleader, which ABC has thus far avoided despite a suggestion from the district court to use that procedure. Finally, neither of the parties considered by ABC to be indispensable has claimed any interest in the subject matter of this litigation. See Fed.R.Civ.P. 19(a)(2).

For these reasons we direct that the district court issue the preliminary injunction sought by the appellants.

...

988 F.Supp.2d 212 (2013)

COHEN v. G & M REALTY

United States District Court, E.D. New York.

BLOCK, Senior District Judge.

On November 12, 2013, the Court issued an order denying plaintiffs' application for a preliminary injunction and stated that a written opinion would soon follow.1 This is that opinion.

By issuing its order, the Court decided that the plaintiffs were not entitled to a preliminary injunction under the Visual Artists Rights Act of 1990 ("VARA"), 17 U.S.C. § 106A, to prevent the destruction of their paintings that adorned the exterior of the buildings owned by the defendants, which are scheduled for demolition. The case has received wide media coverage because the buildings, located in Long Island City, had become the repository of the largest collection of exterior aerosol art (often also referred to as "graffiti art") in the United States, and had consequently become a significant tourist attraction—commonly known as 5 Pointz.

This marks the first occasion that a court has had to determine whether the work of an exterior aerosol artist—given its general ephemeral nature—is worthy of any protection under the law.

Plaintiffs invoke that part of VARA which gives the "author of a work of visual art" the right to sue to prevent the destruction of his or her work if it is one of "recognized stature." VARA recognizes that a work of visual art "may be incorporated in or made part of a building," and includes within its protective reach any such work that was created after its enactment on June 1, 1991, unless a written waiver was obtained from the artist. See 17 U.S.C. § 113(d)(1).

Whether a protected work is of "recognized stature," is "best viewed as a gate-keeping mechanism." Carter v. Helmsley–Spear, Inc., 861 F.Supp. 303, 315 (S.D.N.Y.1994), rev'd and vacated in part and aff'd in part, by 71 F.3d 77 (2d Cir.1995). Accordingly, since plaintiffs' works post-dated VARA and no written waivers were obtained, the Court held a preliminary injunction hearing on November 6–8, and ordered the parties "to be prepared to address, inter alia, whether each plaintiff's work was of "recognized stature."

At the hearing, the Court heard testimony from three of the 17 plaintiffs, the defendant Gerald Wolkoff, who is the principal owner of the defendants' real estate development companies, and purported expert witnesses from each side. The Court also received as evidence a number of exhibits, including 24 photographs of the plaintiffs' paintings—which until two days ago were on the walls of 5Pointz—that they claim were works of "recognized stature." Several of the 24 works are reproduced in an appendix to this opinion. Before exploring the evidence in order to make the requisite relevant findings of fact under FED. R. CIV. P. 65, it would be useful to first examine the principal aspects of VARA for an understanding of its purpose and reach in its grand design to protect the work of the visual artist.

I

The Second Circuit's decision in Carter is the appropriate starting point. In sum, the court explained that VARA amended existing copyright law to add protections for two "moral rights" of artists; the rights of attribution and integrity. Moral rights are distinct from general copyrights, and they rest upon the "belief that an artist in the process of creation injects his spirit into the work and that the artist's personality, as well as the integrity of the work, should therefore be protected and preserved." Carter, 71 F.3d at 81. As noted by the circuit court in Carter, the right of attribution:

generally consists of the right of an artist to be recognized by name as the author of his work or to publish anonymously or pseudonymously, the right to prevent the author's work from being attributed to someone else, and to prevent the use of the author's name on works created by others, including distorted editions of the author's original work.

Id. The right of integrity "allows the author to prevent any deforming or mutilating changes to his work, even after title in the work has been transferred." Id. And "[i]n some [international] jurisdictions the integrity right also protects artwork from destruction." Id. By enacting VARA, Congress made the latter a federal right. Thus, whether viewed as a subset of the right of integrity, see 17 U.S.C. § 106A(a)(3), or, as conceptualized by the circuit court in Carter, as a separate right, VARA protects against the destruction of works of visual art, but only if they are works of "recognized stature." 71 F.3d at 83 ("With numerous exceptions, VARA grants three rights: the right of attribution, the right of integrity and, in the case of works of visual art of 'recognized stature' the right to prevent destruction.").

The Second Circuit in Carter noted that VARA carved out a number of exceptions. For example, it observed that a "work of visual art" is defined by the Act "in terms both positive (what it is) and negative (what it is not)." Id. at 83–84. Thus, the definition includes " 'a painting, drawing, print, or sculpture, existing in a single copy' or in a limited edition of 200 copies or fewer,' " but excludes " 'any poster, map, globe, chart, technical drawing, diagram, model, applied art, motion picture or other audio-visual work.' " Id. at 84 (quoting 17 U.S.C. § 101). Therefore, as explained in Carter, "Congress meant to distinguish works of visual art from other media, such as audio-visual works and motion pictures, due to the different circumstances surrounding how works of each genre are created and disseminated." Id. Although "this concern led to a narrow definition of works of visual art," id., the Second Circuit adopted the language of the House Report that:

[t]he courts should use common sense and generally accepted standards of the artistic community in determining whether a particular work falls within the scope of the definition. Artists may work in a variety of media, and use any number of materials in creating their work. Therefore, whether a particular work falls within the definition should not depend on the medium or materials used. Id. (quoting H.R.REP. NO. 514, at 11).

The circuit court also noted that for all covered works "the rights provided for endure for the life of the author or, in the case of a joint work, the life of the last surviving author," and, while they cannot be transferred, they "may be waived by a writing signed by the author." Id. at 83. Moreover, copyright registration is not required to bring a VARA infringement action, "or to secure statutory damages and attorney's fees." Id. In that regard, "[a]ll remedies available under copyright law, other than criminal remedies, are available." Id.

What the Second Circuit did not do in Carter was to address what constitutes a work of "recognized stature," since, unlike the district court, it found that the particular work—a very large "walk-through sculpture," installed in the lobby of a commercial building—was "a work made for hire," meaning "a work prepared by an employee within the scope of his or her employment." Id. at 85. As such, it was one of the proscribed exceptions to VARA, requiring reversal for that particular reason. The circuit court had no occasion, therefore, to determine whether the sculpture was of "recognized stature." By contrast, after having held that the work was not covered by the "work made for hire" exception, the district court did indeed conclude that the work was of "recognized stature." Its decision, therefore, marked the first time subsequent to the enactment of VARA that a court attempted to give some content and meaning to the phrase—which is not defined in the statute.

The lower court in Carter perceived "recognized stature" to implicitly require the plaintiff to make a two-tiered showing: "(1) that the visual art in question has 'stature,' i.e. is viewed as meritorious, and (2) that this stature is 'recognized' by art experts, other members of the artistic community, or by some cross-section of society." 861 F.Supp. at 325. In this latter regard, the court noted that an earlier version of VARA provided that a "court or other trier of facts may take into account the opinion of artists, art dealers, collectors of fine art, and other persons involved with the creation, appreciation, history, or marketing of works of recognized sources." Id. at 325 n. 10 (citations omitted). Although it believed that this provision was eliminated from VARA prior to enactment to provide courts "greater discretion with regard to what sources may be considered in determining whether a given work of visual art is a work of recognized stature," it nonetheless thought that a court "can, and should, consider these sources." Id.

The district court concluded that the plaintiffs' experts had established that the sculpture in the lobby was a work of "recognized stature" principally because (1) one of the experts, an art critic and professor of art history, testified that "this was [a] coherent ongoing program," he wanted "everyone to go and see it," the sculpture was "a work of art like almost nothing I've ever seen before," and that it "is an incredible phenomenon and I want to see it again and learn more about it;" (2) another expert, the president of the Municipal Art Society of New York, testified that the Society had organized a tour of the work and was anxious to make the work a permanent part of its tour schedule; (3) a third witness, a professor who taught two- and three-dimensional design, testified that he was "very exhilarated" by the work, "[t]he imagination of the work is tremendous," and it is "overall a very exciting piece." Id. at 325–26. He enumerated the standards, which unfortunately are not identified in the court's decision, that he used to judge whether a given work is a work of recognized stature.

Although the two-tier Carter test has been referenced in a handful of subsequent cases, the Court's research has located only one circuit court and two other district courts that have substantively evaluated whether a visual art work was one of "recognized stature." In Martin v. City of Indianapolis, 192 F.3d 608 (7th Cir.1999), the Seventh Circuit affirmed the district court's grant of summary judgment and its award of damages for a sculpture that had been destroyed. It noted, however, that as plaintiff contended, "the Carter v Helmsley–Spear test may be more rigorous than Congress intended." Id. at 612. But the court did not have to address the issue since it accepted as probative evidence of "stature," under the more vigorous Carter test utilized by the district court—in the face of defendant's hearsay objections—"certain newspaper and magazine articles, including a letter from an art gallery director and a letter to the editor of The Indianapolis News, all in support of the sculpture." Id. The circuit court also referenced a letter from the Director of Indiana University's Herron School of Art, who opined that the sculpture was "an interesting and aesthetic stimulating configuration of forms and structures," and an article by the visual arts editor of the The Indianapolis News describing the sculpture as "[g]leaming, clean and abstract, yet domestic in scale and reference," which "unites the area, providing a nexus, a marker, a designation, an identity and, presumably, a point of pride." Id. at 613.

In Pollara v. Seymour, 206 F.Supp.2d 333 (N.D.N.Y.2002), Judge Hurd held, as a matter of law, after a bench trial, that even under the Carter formulation, the particular mural in that case was not of recognized stature because "while plaintiff's work was unquestionably meritorious," it was "intended solely as a display piece for a one-time event." Id. at 336. The court reasoned, therefore, that "[i]t defies the underlying purpose of VARA to assume that the statute was intended to protect works of artistic merit without regard to whether such works were ever intended as 'art' or whether they were intended to be displayed as art or were otherwise intended to be preserved for posterity as works of artistic merit." Id. And in Scott v. Dixon, 309 F.Supp.2d 395 (E.D.N.Y.2004), the court dismissed plaintiff's VARA suit on the merits after a bench trial because the artist's sculpture had been commissioned for placement in the defendants' private backyard, which was obscured by hedges from public view. The court reasoned, therefore, that under VARA "it is not enough that works of art authored by the plaintiff, other than the work sought to be protected, have achieved [recognized] stature. Instead, it is the artwork that is the subject of the litigation that must have acquired this stature." Id. at 406. Thus, "while the Sculpture may have had artistic merit, it was not a work of recognized stature within the meaning of VARA" since it had never been exposed to the public. Id.

I

The evidence adduced at the preliminary injunction hearing in the present case reflects the following:

A. The Advent of 5Pointz

There is little disagreement about the origins of the aerosol art that adorned the defendants' buildings. Plaintiff Cohen and defendant Wolkoff—the effective owner of the several buildings comprising 5Pointz—collectively explained that the buildings—one of which is five stories high-had for many years housed various commercial businesses. Starting in the early or mid–1990s, the exterior walls had become a place for distasteful graffiti by many self-proclaimed aerosol artists; it was then known as the Phun Phactory. To control this festering problem, Cohen approached Wolkoff in 2002 to become the curator of the works that would be permitted to be painted on the walls. Wolkoff agreed; Cohen, known in the art world as "Meres One," was one of the principal contributors to the aerosol wall paintings and Wolkoff liked his work. Wolkoff "was supportive of creative efforts but wanted somebody responsible to manage it." Tr. at 21, Nov. 6, Cohen. But nothing was put in writing; it was just the "general understanding that [Cohen] would be allowed to select who would be permitted to paint on the walls." Id. at 22. Wolkoff, therefore, gave his oral blessings to permit qualified aerosol artists, under Cohen's control, to display their works on his buildings.

Soon the quality of the aerosol art vastly improved. The site became known as 5Pointz and evolved into a mecca for high-end works by internationally recognized aerosol artists. As Cohen described it:

In the time that I've been there, I've seen 5 to 10 artists on a very good day, until now up to 40 artists on a good day, and on our most craft [sic] day, a hundred ten artists painting. We have now 6 to 10 tour buses that come a day. There [are] foot tours, bike tours. Everyone wants to come and shoot a video there, and people come take engagement, wedding photos there. It's become a major attraction. Id. at 27.

Cohen personally conducted hundreds of school tours a year, which sold out months in advance, for students from as far as Canada. As he testified, there were also corporate and VIP tours; moreover, 5Pointz is listed in Time Out New York "as a New York must-see," and is in 150 tour guide books.

Marie Flageul, a professional event planner, lent further credence to the fact that 5Pointz had become a special public attraction. For example, she put together a number of events there, including a performance by the famous DJ "Kool Herc" which attracted 4,000 people, and "a good amount of fashion, editorial photo shoots, happen at 5Pointz;" moreover, the last 12 minutes of a movie, "Now You See Me," featuring the stars Morgan Freeman, Jessie Eisenberg, Woody Harrelson, and Michael Caine, were shot at 5Pointz "because of the artwork." Id. at 139, 146.

Cohen best summed up 5Pointz in a magazine interview he gave in 2010:

The 5 Pointz is a 200,000 square foot warehouse in Queens, New York, basically an entire city block. It was originally set up in 1993 as the Phun Phactory as a legit space for the tourists to come and drop pieces, but when it closed and fell in disrepair, I negotiated with the landlord to take the place over and reopened it as an outdoor exhibit space called the 5 Pointz—The Institute of Higher Burnin. 5 Pointz represents the coming together of the 5 New York boroughs and until a few months ago, we had about 90 resident artists who rented studio space in the building7 and we used the outside as a controlled canvas for local and international artists to come, drop pieces and contribute to the overall story. The building is 5 industrial stories high, and as you can see, we pretty much managed to cover the whole exterior in aerosol.

Pls.' Compl. Ex. A, Interview, London Street–Art Design Magazine (Feb. 16, 2010). There is little question, therefore, that 5Pointz had become a recognized tourist attraction, and the defendants do not contend otherwise.

To his credit, Wolkoff acknowledged his appreciation of the works of art at *220 5Pointz—describing them as "beautiful." Tr. at 146, Nov. 7, 2013. Nonetheless, the time had come to knock down the buildings to make room for two apartment complexes that are expected to provide approximately 1,000 residences. In response to community pressure, the City Planning Commission required, as a condition for the issuance of its building permit, that defendants include 75 affordable housing units and install 3,300 square feet of exterior art panels "to be used to maintain artist street wall art in the area." Wolkoff Aff. Ex. H. Final building permit approval was issued on August 21, 2013. Id.

When questioned by the court, Wolkoff testified that there was no feasible engineering way he could preserve the existing buildings, with their "beautiful" art work, and incorporate them into the new ones.

B. "Recognized Stature"

When it came to whether any of the 24 works were of "recognized stature," much of the testimony did not differentiate between these discrete words, and by and large assumed that if the work had artistic merit it was ipso facto of recognized stature. Thus, one of the plaintiffs, Danielle Mastrion, whose portrait of "Kool Herc" is among the 24, considered all of them to be of recognized stature because they satisfied factors such as "technical ability, composition, color, line work, detail and also the artist's credentials," Tr. at 20, Nov. 7, 2013; see the "Kool Herc" portrait at App. Ex. C. And Joe Conzo, Jr., a documentary photographer, who described himself as one of the "forefathers" of the hiphop culture reflected in the works at 5Pointz, essentially agreed, describing the works in general as "innovative" and "colorful," and in some cases, "pioneering." Tr. at 117, 119, 120, Nov. 6, 2013. He believed that each of the 24 paintings was deserving of VARA protection because of the common elements of their "details" and "hard work." Id. at 123.

Mastrion best expressed the notion that the artistic quality of the works alone qualified them as works of recognized stature in the following colloquy with the court:

THE COURT: So just intrinsic quality of the work, even if it's not exposed to the public, would still qualify, in your opinion, as something that should satisfy the statutory standard of the status, so to speak?

MASTRION: A beautiful piece of work, is a beautiful piece of work.

THE COURT: So the fact that it's been exposed to the public, you don't think it necessarily is a factor or a consideration?

MASTRION: I think it is. I think it elevates it even more.

THE COURT: Even without that, it would still qualify?

MASTRION: Yes.

Tr. at 60, Nov. 7, 2013.

This notion of the intrinsic quality of the work being the sine qua non for VARA protection was reinforced by Mastrion's testimony regarding the work of the artist Bernard Aptekar, currently gracing the courthouse's public gallery. Asked to opine on it, Mastrion believed that, although she did not know the artist, his works were certainly of recognized stature because she was "very blown away" by "the color work, the detail, the intricacies of them." Id. at 57. Regardless of whether the work had achieved any other recognition, Mastrion believed that "[i]t would be a tragedy to see any of that work destroyed" because "[i]t's beautiful work down there." Id. at 58.

The focus of whether any of plaintiffs' 24 paintings were not only works of stature, but had also achieved the requisite recognition to bring them within the embrace of VARA, centered on the testimony of each party's proffered art expert. The defendants' expert, Erin Thompson, an art history professor of impeccable academic credentials, took a restrictive view of both the concept of "stature" and "recognition." In her opinion, while "quality is certainly one of the factors in the stature" of a work of art, "stature is recognizing not particular qualities of objects, but the way these qualities are valued by the public." Id. at 100. And while she recognized that being "innovative" and possessing "uniqueness" are additional factors bearing upon a work's stature, ultimately to qualify as such a work, it should be at a level where scholars agree that it is "changing the history of art." Id. at 104.

As for the concept of "recognition," Professor Thompson' s inquiry focused on ascertaining whether any of 24 works had been mentioned in academic publications or on the Internet. She found that for 19 of the 24, "there were no dissertations, no journal articles, no other scholarly mentions of the work," and there were no Google results for either the name of the work or the artist: "no one at all had seen fit to put on the Internet the name of that work." Id. at 97. Of the other five, three were mentioned "by the artists themselves or on the 5Pointz web site," and "two of the remaining works each have one mention a piece on a street art web site, on a blog, or an artist's blog." Id. at 99. Although, in Thompson's opinion, none of the 24 works was of recognized stature, she believed that Lady Pink's work, "Green Mother Earth," came the closest because of all the artists, Lady Pink was the only one who "had been mentioned in a dissertation, or a scholarly book or a journal article." Id. at 98. See App. Ex. A.

Although acknowledging that the art at 5Pointz had indeed achieved widespread recognition as a tourist attraction, Professor Thompson believed that this would not satisfy VARA recognition unless the visitors came "to see a particular work of art." Id. at 100. If so, this would qualify as the requisite statutory recognition even in the absence of any academic recognition. As she acknowledged in response to the court's questioning:

THE COURT: So am I correct in understanding that recognition ... is somewhat an expansive concept? You can have academic recognition. You can have practical recognition by people flocking to see something. Even if it's not in any book, it would all be under the umbrella of this concept of recognition, right?

THOMPSON: Correct.

Thompson acknowledged that an aerosol artist's work, although a "subculture" of the art world, could be of recognized stature if there were a "consensus of the scholarly community and the art community," even if painted on the exterior of a building. Id. at 102. She gave as an example the work of the internationally recognized aerosol artist Banksy, who had been mentioned "in something like a hundred and thirty dissertations and more than 1500 scholarly articles," and whose recent work, completed on October 31, 2013, generated more than 400,000 Google results after only two weeks. Id. And she also acknowledged, when asked by defendants' counsel if the fact that works at 5Pointz have been painted over would "affect your opinion whether the works [presently on the walls] have achieved recognized stature," that "[s]omething can be ephemeral and achieve recognized stature." Id. at 107.

Plaintiffs' expert, Daniel Simmons, Jr., the head of the Rush Philanthropic Arts Foundation and the owner of two well-known New York City art galleries, agreed with Thompson that aerosol art can achieve recognized stature and gave credible testimony as to both stature and recognition. Simmons, a visual artist in his own right, has received many awards for his life-long commitment to art education. He has also amassed a personal collection of mostly contemporary art which he valued at $5 million; it includes a number of Meres One's works.

As for stature, Simmons' focus was, not surprisingly, also on the work's quality, such as "design, color, shape, form" and characteristics of "symmetry" and "innovation." Tr. at 18, 25, Nov. 8, 2013. He believed that all 24 works qualified as "real artworks." Id. at 15. Simmons heaped particular praise on Mastrion's portrait of "Kool Herc" as "absolutely fantastic" and instantly recognized "as a great piece of artwork," id. at 29, 33, as well as Meres One's works, and Lady Pink's "Green Mother Earth" mural. See App. Ex. A, B, and C for each of these works.

As for recognition, Simmons opined that it means "there's enough people that know what [the work] looks like, and feels like and what it's trying to impart; that it would be, to me, if it was missing from the canon of art history, that it would be a loss." Id. at 16. He testified that if a work of art "was exhibited in galleries, and museums, and in places where large number of people could see it, that would be recognized stature;" thus, "it would have to be significant public exposure." Id. at 16–17. When pressed by the Court to elaborate on the concept of public exposure, Simmons invoked the works of all the artists at 5Pointz:

"Well, recently, a few years ago the Brooklyn Museum had a big show on graffiti and acquired a lot of graffiti work into their collection, and a number of these artists that are on 5Pointz were in this exhibition in Brooklyn Museum. I think that the number of people around the world that come to the location where this—what I've been calling way before this the '5Pointz Museum of Street Art'—makes any work that's up on that building [of] recognizable stature." Id. at 17.

As for Lady Pink's "Green Mother Earth," Simmons classified it as "a great example of her work"; moreover, one of her works was part of the show at the Brooklyn Museum exhibit of great graffiti artists. Id. at 24. He described the painting as "a great example and a comparable example of the work that's been done since the '70s." Id. In particular, he thought its exposure at 5Pointz gave it great public recognition because "[i]t's probably one of the pieces that people come to see because she is so recognized." Id. at 25.

Plaintiffs' counsel then focused Simmons' attention on a number of other works included in the Appendix. He opined that Meres One's "Drunken Bulbs" was of recognized stature because the deployment of "these light bulbs are iconic and seen and known all over the world," and that "[a]ny time you see this piece of work or this icon ... you know it's Meres One." Id. at 26; see App. Ex. B. He testified that people came to see this work at 5Pointz "and anything that this artist does, because he is recognized. So whatever works that he has on that building, he would be a draw to come to that building along with Lady Pink." Id. at 27. Simmons heaped high praise on Meres One and Lady Pink by likening their works to a Picasso that was just "brought up from the basement," making their work "instantly famous because of the stature of the artist." Id. at 40.

As a specific example of Meres One's reputation, Simmons spoke about a documentary he made, The Collage of Imagination, in which he featured 5Pointz because it was "part of a movement." Id. at 28. The film, which included an interview with Meres One, was televised nationally and also got 20,000 hits on YouTube.

Simmons had no knowledge of whether the 5Pointz artists or their works were the subject of any academic works, but he believed that "everything is in flux from the old ways of doing things, and the way things are publicized and the way the media looks at things." Id. at 30. The thrust of his testimony regarding recognition for the

5Pointz artwork of Meres One, Lady Pink, and the other celebrated 5Pointz aerosol artists was that people are drawn to see their works because of the artists' reputations and the uniqueness of 5Pointz as an internationally recognized place to view the works at one location.

Simmons also praised "Manga Koi," a work by plaintiff Akiko Miyakami, also known as Shiro, which contains—like Meres One's light bulbs—an iconic figure "that's been seen all over the world." Id. at 34. As he explained: "This artist is a world-renowned artist, and this figure has itself, not this particular painting, but this figure, which is incorporated in this painting, has been seen by hundreds of thousands of people around the world." Id. And another work, "Dream of Oil" by Francisco Fernandez, was "probably seen more than any other piece" because of its size and location on top of one of the 5Pointz buildings where it had to be viewed every day by people riding the 7 train, making its visibility "tremendous." Id. at 37. See App. Ex. D and E for "Manga Koi" and "Dream of Oil."

At the end of his testimony, when asked by plaintiffs' counsel "what impact would the loss of the works of visual [art] have on the art world and Hip Hop community," Simmons responded: "I think New York City as a whole would be diminished. It's a major tourist attraction for Long Island City. Its part of the development of Long Island City. Just like, pretty much ... MoMa being there, it's a drawing point for artists and art lovers to come from all over the world to see." Id. at 46.

In Simmons' opinion, 5Pointz and its extraordinary aerosol art had become "[p]art of the urban landscape," and "should be preserved, if possible." Id.

...

III

The Court could not have issued a preliminary injunction unless the plaintiffs demonstrated "either (a) likelihood of success on the merits or (b) sufficiently serious questions going to the merits to make them a fair ground for litigation and a balance of hardships tipping decidedly in the [p]laintiff's favor." Salinger v. Colting, 607 F.3d 68, 79 (2d Cir.2010) (internal citation omitted). If so, "the court may issue the injunction only if the plaintiff has demonstrated that he is likely to suffer irreparable harm in the absence of the injunction." Id. at 80 (internal citation omitted). In that regard, the Court "must actually consider the injury the plaintiff will suffer if he or she loses in the preliminary injunction but ultimately prevails on the merits, paying particular attention to whether the remedies available at law, such as monetary damages, are inadequate to compensate for that injury." Id. (internal citation omitted). Next, a Court "must consider the balance of hardships between the plaintiff and defendant and issue the injunction only if the balance of hardships tips in the plaintiff's favor."8 Id. Finally, the Court "must ensure that the public interest would not be disserved." Id.

Picasso believed that "[t]he purpose of art is washing the dust of daily life off our souls." He surely would have supported applying VARA to protect the works of the modern aerosol artist. As Congress recognized, whether a particular work falls within the definition of visual art, "should not depend on the medium or materials used," since "[a]rtists may work in a variety of media, and use any number of materials in creating their work." See H.R. REP. NO. 514 at 11 (quoted in Carter, 71 F.3d at 84). This fits the aerosol artist to a "T," and our souls owe a debt of gratitude to the plaintiffs for having brought the dusty walls of defendants' buildings to life.

But VARA only protects a work of visual art. 17 U.S.C. § 106A; see also 17 U.S.C. § 202 ("ownership of a copyright, or any of the exclusive rights under a copyright, is distinct from ownership of any material object in which the work is embodied."). The Court regrettably had no authority under VARA to preserve 5Pointz as a tourist site. That authority is vested in state or local authorities, and since 5Pointz had become such a scenic attraction, the City probably could have exercised its power of eminent domain to acquire the site outright. It chose not to. Cf. Bunyan v. Commissioners of Palisades Interstate Park, 167 A.D. 457, 153 N.Y.S. 622, 628 (3d Dep't 1915) (affirming the purchase of a quarry for the purpose of preserving the "scenic beauty" of the Hudson River Palisades as a taking for "public use").9 Although the Court was taken by the breadth and visual impact of 5Pointz, its authority under VARA is consequently limited to determining whether a particular work of visual art that was destroyed was one of "recognized stature," and if so, what monetary damages the creator of each work is entitled to.

The evidence adduced at the preliminary injunction hearing leads the Court to conclude that at least some of the 24 works, which plaintiffs contend were of recognized stature, such as Lady Pink's "Green Mother Earth," present "sufficiently serious questions going to the merits to make them a fair ground for litigation." Salinger, 607 F.3d at 79. The final resolution of whether any do indeed qualify as such works of art is best left for a fuller exploration of the merits after the case has been properly prepared for trial, rather than at the preliminary injunction stage. Since VARA does not define "recognized stature," the court ultimately will have to decide whether to embrace the strictures of the academic views espoused by the defendants or the more expansive ones suggested by the plaintiffs. More testimony than that presented by the parties under the time constraints of the preliminary injunction hearing—where the pressures upon the parties and the Court circumscribed a full presentation and deliberation of this gate-keeping issue—will undoubtedly aid the Court in making its final decision.

The Court had to determine, therefore, whether the plaintiffs demonstrated that they were likely to suffer irreparable harm. Once again, as the circuit court in Salinger explained, this required the district court to consider "the injury the plaintiff will suffer if he or she loses on the preliminary injunction but ultimately prevails on the merits, paying particular attention to whether the remedies available at law, such as monetary damages, are inadequate to compensate for that injury." 607 F.3d at 80 (internal citation omitted).

Although the works have now been destroyed—and the Court wished it had the power to preserve them—plaintiffs would be hard-pressed to contend that no amount of money would compensate them for their paintings; and VARA—which makes no distinction between temporary and permanent works of visual art— provides that significant monetary damages may be awarded for their wrongful destruction. See 17 U.S.C. §§ 501–505 (providing remedies for VARA violations). In any event, paintings generally are meant to be sold. Their value is invariably reflected in the money they command in the marketplace. Here, the works were painted for free, but surely the plaintiffs would gladly have accepted money from the defendants to acquire their works, albeit on a wall rather than on a canvas.

Moreover, plaintiffs' works can live on in other media. The 24 works have been photographed, and the court, during the hearing, exhorted the plaintiffs to photograph all those which they might wish to preserve. All would be protected under traditional copyright law, see 17 U.S.C. § 106 (giving, inter alia, copyright owners of visual works of art the exclusive rights to reproduce their works, to prepare derivative works, and to sell and publicly display the works), and could be marketed to the general public—even to those who had never been to 5Pointz.

Finally, whether viewed as bearing upon the issue of irreparable harm or the balancing of the hardships, the ineluctable factor which precludes either preliminary or permanent injunctive relief was the transient nature of the plaintiffs' works. Regardless of Cohen's belief that the 24 works were to be permanently displayed on the buildings, he always knew that the buildings were coming down—and that his paintings, as well as the others which he allowed to be placed on the walls, would be destroyed. Particularly disturbing is that many of the paintings were created as recently as this past September, just weeks after the City Planning Commission gave final approval to the defendants' building plans. In a very real sense, plaintiffs' have created their own hardships.

But this does not mean that defendants do not share some responsibility. After all, Wolkoff gave his blessings to Cohen and the aerosol artists to decorate the buildings, and he did not choose to protect himself from liability by requiring VARA waivers. Moreover, while he was supportive of the artists and appreciated their work, he also stood to benefit economically from all the attention that had been drawn to the site as he planned to market the new buildings' residences. Since, as defendants' expert correctly acknowledged, VARA protects even temporary works from destruction, defendants are exposed to potentially significant monetary damages if it is ultimately determined after trial that the plaintiffs' works were of "recognized stature."

As for the public, its general interests will be served by the new apartments, including the 75 affordable housing units, and while the present walls will no longer exist, the public's aesthetic interests were addressed by the City Planning Commission by requiring 3,300 square feet of the exterior of the new buildings to be made available for art. Defendants can do even more. They can make much more space available, and give written permission to Cohen to continue to be the curator so that he may establish a large, permanent home for quality work by him and his acclaimed aerosol artists. For sure, the Court would look kindly on such largesse when it might be required to consider the issue of monetary damages; and 5Pointz, as reincarnated, would live.

APPENDIX

Exhibit A

"Green Mother Earth" by Sandra Fabara ("Lady Pink")

Exhibit B

"Drunken Bulbs" by Jonathan Cohen ("Meres One")

"7–Angle Time Lapse" by Jonathan Cohen

Exhibit C

"Kool Herc" by Danielle Mastrion

Exhibit D

"Manga Koi"

by Akiko Miyakami ("Shiro")

Exhibit E

"Dream of Oil"by Francisco Fernandez

15. Copyright Secondary Liability

76 F.3d 259 (1996)
FONOVISA v. CHERRY AUCTION
US Court of Appeals of the Ninth Circuit

SCHROEDER, Circuit Judge:

[1] This is a copyright and trademark enforcement action against the operators of a swap meet, sometimes called a flea market, where third-party vendors routinely sell counterfeit recordings that infringe on the plaintiff's copyrights and trademarks. The district court dismissed on the pleadings, holding that the plaintiffs, as a matter of law, could not maintain any cause of action against the swap meet for sales by vendors who leased its premises. The district court's decision is published. Fonovisa Inc. v. Cherry Auction, Inc., 847 F. Supp. 1492 (E.D. Cal. 1994). We reverse.

[2] Background

[3] The plaintiff and appellant is Fonovisa, Inc., a California corporation that owns copyrights and trademarks to Latin/Hispanic music recordings. Fonovisa filed this action in district court against defendant-appellee, Cherry Auction, Inc., and its individual operators (collectively "Cherry Auction"). For purposes of this appeal, it is undisputed that Cherry Auction operates a swap meet in Fresno, California, similar to many other swap meets in this country where customers come to purchase various merchandise from individual vendors. See generally, Flea Market Owner Sued for Trademark Infringement, 4 No. 3 J. Proprietary Rts. 22 (1992). The vendors pay a daily rental fee to the swap meet operators in exchange for booth space. Cherry Auction supplies parking, conducts advertising and retains the right to exclude any vendor for any reason, at any time, and thus can exclude vendors for patent and trademark infringement. In addition, Cherry Auction receives an entrance fee from each customer who attends the swap meet.

[4] There is also no dispute for purposes of this appeal that Cherry Auction and its operators were aware that vendors in their swap meet were selling counterfeit recordings in violation of Fonovisa's trademarks and copyrights. Indeed, it is alleged that in 1991, the Fresno County Sheriff's Department raided the Cherry Auction swap meet and seized more than 38,000 counterfeit recordings. The following year, after finding that vendors at the Cherry Auction swap meet were still selling counterfeit recordings, the Sheriff sent a letter notifying Cherry Auction of the on-going sales of infringing materials, and reminding Cherry Auction that they had agreed to provide the Sheriff with identifying information from each vendor. In addition, in 1993, Fonovisa itself sent an investigator to the Cherry Auction site and observed sales of counterfeit recordings.

[5] Fonovisa filed its original complaint in the district court on February 25, 1993, and on March 22, 1994, the district court granted defendants' motion to dismiss pursuant to Federal Rule of Civil Procedure 12(b)(6). In this appeal, Fonovisa does not challenge the district court's dismissal of its claim for direct copyright infringement, but does appeal the dismissal of its claims for contributory copyright infringement, vicarious copyright infringement and contributory trademark infringement.

[6] The copyright claims are brought pursuant to 17 U.S.C. § 101 et seq. Although the Copyright Act does not expressly impose liability on anyone other than direct infringers, courts have long recognized that in certain circumstances, vicarious or contributory liability will be imposed. See Sony Corp. of America v. Universal City Studios, Inc., 464 U.S. 417, 435 (1984) (explaining that "vicarious liability is imposed in virtually all areas of the law, and the concept of contributory infringement is merely a species of the broader problem of identifying circumstances in which it is just to hold one individually accountable for the actions of another").

...

[8] We analyze each of the plaintiff's claims in turn.

Vicarious Copyright Infringement

[10] The concept of vicarious copyright liability was developed in the Second Circuit as an outgrowth of the agency principles of respondeat superior. The landmark case on vicarious liability for sales of counterfeit recordings is Shapiro, Bernstein and Co. v. H. L. Green Co., 316 F.2d 304 (2d Cir. 1963). In Shapiro, the court was faced with a copyright infringement suit against the owner of a chain of department stores where a concessionaire was selling counterfeit recordings. Noting that the normal agency rule of respondeat superior imposes liability on an employer for copyright infringements by an employee, the court endeavored to fashion a principle for enforcing copyrights against a defendant whose economic interests were intertwined with the direct infringer's, but who did not actually employ the direct infringer.

[11] The Shapiro court looked at the two lines of cases it perceived as most clearly relevant. In one line of cases, the landlord-tenant cases, the courts had held that a landlord who lacked knowledge of the infringing acts of its tenant and who exercised no control over the leased premises was not liable for infringing sales by its tenant. See e.g. Deutsch v. Arnold, 98 F.2d 686 (2d Cir. 1938); c.f. Fromott v. Aeolina Co., 254 F.2d 592 (S.D.N.Y. 1918). In the other line of cases, the so-called "dance hall cases," the operator of an entertainment venue was held liable for infringing performances when the operator (1) could control the premises and (2) obtained a direct financial benefit from the audience, who paid to enjoy the infringing performance. See e.g. Buck v. Jewell-LaSalle Realty Co., 238 U.S. 191, 198-199 (1931); Dreamland Ballroom, Inc. v. Shapiro, Bernstein & Co., 36 F.2d 354 (7th Cir. 1929).

[12] From those two lines of cases, the Shapiro court determined that the relationship between the store owner and the concessionaire in the case before it

was closer to the dance-hall model than to the landlord-tenant model. It imposed liability even though the defendant was unaware of the infringement. Shapiro deemed the imposition of vicarious liability neither unduly harsh nor unfair because the store proprietor had the power to cease the conduct of the concessionaire, and because the proprietor derived an obvious and direct financial benefit from the infringement. 316 F.2d at 307. The test was more clearly articulated in a later Second Circuit case as follows: "even in the absence of an employer-employee relationship one may be vicariously liable if he has the right and ability to supervise the infringing activity and also has a direct financial interest in such activities." Gershwin Publishing Corp. v. Columbia Artists Management, Inc., 443 F.2d 1159, 1162 (2d Cir. 1971). See also 3 Melville Nimmer & David Nimmer, Nimmer on Copyright 1204(A)[1], at 1270-72 (1995). The most recent and comprehensive discussion of the evolution of the doctrine of vicarious liability for copyright infringement is contained in Judge Keeton's opinion in Polygram Intern. Pub., Inc. v. Nevada/TIG, Inc., 855 F. Supp. 1314 (D. Mass. 1984).

[13] The district court in this case agreed with defendant Cherry Auction that Fonovisa did not, as a matter of law, meet either the control or the financial benefit prong of the vicarious copyright infringement test articulated in Gershwin, supra. Rather, the district court concluded that based on the pleadings, "Cherry Auction neither supervised nor profited from the vendors' sales." 847 F. Supp. at 1496. In the district court's view, with respect to both control and financial benefit, Cherry Auction was in the same position as an absentee landlord who has surrendered its exclusive right of occupancy in its leased property to its tenants.

[14] This analogy to absentee landlord is not in accord with the facts as alleged in the district court and which we, for purposes of appeal, must accept. The allegations below were that vendors occupied small booths within premises that Cherry Auction controlled and patrolled. According to the complaint, Cherry Auction had the right to terminate vendors for any reason whatsoever and through that right had the ability to control the activities of vendors on the premises. In addition, Cherry Auction promoted the swap meet and controlled the access of customers to the swap meet area. In terms of control, the allegations before us are strikingly similar to those in Shapiro and Gershwin.

[15] In Shapiro, for example, the court focused on the formal licensing agreement between defendant department store and the direct infringer-concessionaire. There, the concessionaire selling the bootleg recordings had a licensing agreement with the department store (H. L. Green Company) that required the concessionaire and its employees to "abide by, observe and obey all regulations promulgated from time to time by the H. L. Green Company," and H. L. Green Company had the "unreviewable discretion" to discharge the concessionaires' employees. 316 F.2d at 306. In practice, H. L. Green Company was not actively involved in the sale of records and the concessionaire controlled and supervised the individual employees. Id. Nevertheless, H. L. Green's ability to police its concessionaire - which parallels Cherry Auction's ability to police its vendors under Cherry Auction's similarly broad contract with its vendors - was sufficient to satisfy the control requirement. Id. at 308.

[16] In Gershwin, the defendant lacked the formal, contractual ability to control the direct infringer. Nevertheless, because of defendant's "pervasive participation in the formation and direction" of the direct infringers, including promoting them (i.e. creating an audience for them), the court found that defendants were in a position to police the direct infringers and held that the control element was satisfied. 443 F.2d at 1163. As the promoter and organizer of the swap meet, Cherry Auction wields the same level of control over the direct infringers as did the Gershwin defendant. See also Polygram, 855 F. Supp. at 1329 (finding that the control requirement was satisfied because the defendant (1) could control the direct infringers through its rules and regulations; (2) policed its booths to make sure the regulations were followed; and (3) promoted the show in which direct infringers participated).

[17] The district court's dismissal of the vicarious liability claim in this case was therefore not justified on the ground that the complaint failed to allege sufficient control.

[18] We next consider the issue of financial benefit. The plaintiff's allegations encompass many substantive benefits to Cherry Auction from the infringing sales. These include the payment of a daily rental fee by each of the infringing vendors; a direct payment to Cherry Auction by each customer in the form of an admission fee, and incidental payments for parking, food and other services by customers seeking to purchase infringing recordings.

[19] Cherry Auction nevertheless contends that these benefits cannot satisfy the financial benefit prong of vicarious liability because a commission, directly tied to the sale of particular infringing items, is required. They ask that we restrict the financial benefit prong to the precise facts presented in Shapiro, where defendant H. L. Green Company received a 10 or 12 per cent commission from the direct infringers' gross receipts. Cherry Auction points to the low daily rental fee paid by each vendor, discounting all other financial benefits flowing to the swap meet, and asks that we hold that the swap meet is materially similar to a mere landlord. The facts alleged by Fonovisa, however, reflect that the defendants reap substantial financial benefits from admission fees, concession stand sales and parking fees, all of which flow directly from customers who want to buy the counterfeit recordings at bargain basement prices. The plaintiff has sufficiently alleged direct financial benefit.

[20] Our conclusion is fortified by the continuing line of cases, starting with the dance hall cases, imposing vicarious liability on the operator of a business where infringing performances enhance the attractiveness of the venue to potential customers. In Poloygram, for example, direct infringers were participants in a trade show who used infringing music to communicate with attendees and to cultivate interest in their wares. 855 F. Supp. at 1332. The court held that the trade show participants "derived a significant financial benefit from the attention" that attendees paid to the infringing music. Id.; See also Famous Music Corp. v. Bay State Harness Horse Racing and Breeding Ass'n, 554 F.2d 1213, 1214 (1st Cir. 1977) (race track owner vicariously liable for band that entertained patrons who were not "absorbed in watching the races"); Shapiro, 316 F.2d at 307 (dance hall cases hold

proprietor liable where infringing "activities provide the proprietor with a source of customers and enhanced income"). In this case, the sale of pirated recordings at the Cherry Auction swap meet is a "draw" for customers, as was the performance of pirated music in the dance hall cases and their progeny.

[21] Plaintiffs have stated a claim for vicarious copyright infringement.

[22] Contributory Copyright Infringement

[23] Contributory infringement originates in tort law and stems from the notion that one who directly contributes to another's infringement should be held accountable. See Sony v. Universal City, 464 U.S. at 417; 1 Niel Boorstyn, Boorstyn On Copyright 10.06[2], at 10-21 (1994) ("In other words, the common law doctrine that one who knowingly participates in or furthers a tortious act is jointly and severally liable with the prime tortfeasor, is applicable under copyright law"). Contributory infringement has been described as an outgrowth of enterprise liability, see 3 Nimmer 1204[a][2], at 1275; Demetrigdes v. Kaufmann, 690 F. Supp. 289, 292 (S.D.N.Y. 1988), and imposes liability where one person knowingly contributes to the infringing conduct of another. The classic statement of the doctrine is in Gershwin, 443 F.2d 1159, 1162: "[O]ne who, with knowledge of the infringing activity, induces, causes or materially contributes to the infringing conduct of another, may be held liable as a `contributory' infringer." See also Universal City Studios v. Sony Corp. of America, 659 F.2d 963, 975 (9th Cir. 1981), rev'd on other grounds, 464 U.S. 417 (1984) (adopting Gershwin in this circuit).

[24] There is no question that plaintiff adequately alleged the element of knowledge in this case. The disputed issue is whether plaintiff adequately alleged that Cherry Auction materially contributed to the infringing activity. We have little difficulty in holding that the allegations in this case are sufficient to show material contribution to the infringing activity. Indeed, it would be difficult for the infringing activity to take place in the massive quantities alleged without the support services provided by the swap meet. These services include, inter alia, the provision of space, utilities, parking, advertising, plumbing, and customers.

[25] Here again Cherry Auction asks us to ignore all aspects of the enterprise described by the plaintiffs, to concentrate solely on the rental of space, and to hold that the swap meet provides nothing more. Yet Cherry Auction actively strives to provide the environment and the market for counterfeit recording sales to thrive. Its participation in the sales cannot be termed "passive," as Cherry Auction would prefer.

[26] The district court apparently took the view that contribution to infringement should be limited to circumstances in which the defendant "expressly promoted or encouraged the sale of counterfeit products, or in some manner protected the identity of the infringers." 847 F. Supp. 1492, 1496. Given the allegations that the local sheriff lawfully requested that Cherry Auction gather and share basic, identifying information about its vendors, and that Cherry Auction failed to comply, the defendant appears to qualify within the last portion of the district court's own standard that posits liability for protecting infringers' identities. Moreover, we agree with the Third Circuit's analysis in Columbia Pictures

Industries, Inc. v. Aveco, Inc., 800 F.2d 59 (3rd Cir. 1986) that providing the site and facilities for known infringing activity is sufficient to establish contributory liability. See 2 William F. Patry, Copyright Law & Practice 1147 ("Merely providing the means for infringement may be sufficient" to incur contributory copyright liability).

...

464 U.S. 417 (1984)

SONY CORP. OF AMERICA V. UNIVERSAL CITY STUDIOS, INC.

United States Supreme Court

If vicarious liability is to be imposed on Sony in this case, it must rest on the fact that it has sold equipment with constructive knowledge of the fact that its customers may use that equipment to make unauthorized copies of copyrighted material. There is no precedent in the law of copyright for the imposition of vicarious liability on such a theory. The closest analogy is provided by the patent law cases to which it is appropriate to refer because of the historic kinship between patent law and copyright law.

In the Patent Act, both the concept of infringement and the concept of contributory infringement are expressly defined by statute. [Footnote 20] The prohibition against contributory infringement is confined to the knowing sale of a component especially made for use in connection with a particular patent. There is no suggestion in the statute that one patentee may object to the sale of a product that might be used in connection with other patents. Moreover, the Act expressly provides that the sale of a "staple article or commodity of commerce suitable for substantial noninfringing use" is not contributory infringement. 35 U.S.C. § 271(c).

When a charge of contributory infringement is predicated entirely on the sale of an article of commerce that is used by the purchaser to infringe a patent, the public interest in access to that article of commerce is necessarily implicated. A finding of contributory infringement does not, of course, remove the article from the market altogether; it does, however, give the patentee effective control over the sale of that item. Indeed, a finding of contributory infringement is normally the functional equivalent of holding that the disputed article is within the monopoly granted to the patentee.

For that reason, in contributory infringement cases arising under the patent laws, the Court has always recognized the critical importance of not allowing the patentee to extend his monopoly beyond the limits of his specific grant. These cases deny the patentee any right to control the distribution of unpatented articles unless they are "unsuited for any commercial noninfringing use." Dawson Chemical Co. v. Rohm & Hass Co., 448 U. S. 176, 448 U. S. 198 (1980). Unless a commodity "has no use except through practice of the patented method," id. at 448 U. S. 199, the patentee has no right to claim that its distribution constitutes contributory infringement. "To form the basis for contributory infringement, the item must almost be uniquely suited as a component of the patented invention." P. Rosenberg, Patent Law Fundamentals § 17.02[2] (2d ed.1982).

"[A] sale of an article which though adapted to an infringing use is also adapted to other and lawful uses, is not enough to make the seller a contributory infringer. Such a rule would block the wheels of commerce." Henry v. A. B. Dick Co., 224 U. S. 1, 224 U. S. 48 (1912), overruled on other grounds, Motion Picture Patents Co. v. Universal Film Mfg. Co., 243 U. S. 502, 243 U. S. 517 (1917).

We recognize there are substantial differences between the patent and copyright laws. But in both areas, the contributory infringement doctrine is grounded on the recognition that adequate protection of a monopoly may require the courts to look beyond actual duplication of a device or publication to the products or activities that make such duplication possible. The staple article of commerce doctrine must strike a balance between a copyright holder's legitimate demand for effective -- not merely symbolic -- protection of the statutory monopoly, and the rights of others freely to engage in substantially unrelated areas of commerce. Accordingly, the sale of copying equipment, like the sale of other articles of commerce, does not constitute contributory infringement if the product is widely used for legitimate, unobjectionable purposes. Indeed, it need merely be capable of substantial noninfringing uses.

IV

The question is thus whether the Betamax is capable of commercially significant noninfringing uses. In order to resolve that question, we need not explore all the different potential uses of the machine and determine whether or not they would constitute infringement. Rather, we need only consider whether, on the basis of the facts as found by the District Court, a significant number of them would be noninfringing. Moreover, in order to resolve this case, we need not give precise content to the question of how much use is commercially significant. For one potential use of the Betamax plainly satisfies this standard, however it is understood: private, noncommercial time-shifting in the home. It does so both (A) because respondents have no right to prevent other copyright holders from authorizing it for their programs, and (B) because the District Court's factual findings reveal that even the unauthorized home time-shifting of respondents' programs is legitimate fair use.

...

545 U.S. 913 (2005)

METRO-GOLDWYN-MAYER STUDIOS v. GROKSTER

United States Supreme Court

Justice Souter: Legal Q'·

The question is under what circumstances the distributor of a product capable of both lawful and unlawful use is liable for acts of copyright infringement by third parties using the product. We hold that one who distributes a device with the object of promoting its use to infringe copyright, as shown by clear expression or other affirmative steps taken to foster infringement, is liable for the resulting acts of infringement by third parties. Holding

I

A

Respondents, Grokster, Ltd., and StreamCast Networks, Inc., defendants in the trial court, distribute free software products that allow computer users to share electronic files through peer-to-peer networks, so called because users' computers communicate directly with each other, not through central servers. The advantage of peer-to-peer networks over information networks of other types shows up in their substantial and growing popularity. Because they need no central computer server to mediate the exchange of information or files among users, the high-bandwidth communications capacity for a server may be dispensed with, and the need for costly server storage space is eliminated. Since copies of a file (particularly a popular one) are available on many users' computers, file requests and retrievals may be faster than on other types of networks, and since file exchanges do not travel through a server, communications can take place between any computers that remain connected to the network without risk that a glitch in the server will disable the network in its entirety. Given these benefits in security, cost, and efficiency, peer-to-peer networks are employed to store and distribute electronic files by universities, government agencies, corporations, and libraries, among others.

Other users of peer-to-peer networks include individual recipients of Grokster's and StreamCast's software, and although the networks that they enjoy through using the software can be used to share any type of digital file, they have prominently employed those networks in sharing copyrighted music and video files without authorization. A group of copyright holders (MGM for short, but including motion picture studios, recording companies, songwriters, and music publishers) sued Grokster and StreamCast for their users' copyright infringements, alleging that they knowingly and intentionally distributed their software to enable users to reproduce and distribute the copyrighted works in violation of the Copyright Act, 17 U.S.C. § 101 et seq. (2000 ed. and Supp. II).2 MGM sought damages and an injunction.

Discovery during the litigation revealed the way the software worked, the business aims of each defendant company, and the predilections of the users. Grokster's eponymous software employs what is known as FastTrack technology, a protocol developed by others and licensed to Grokster. StreamCast distributes a very similar product except that its software, called Morpheus, relies on what is known as Gnutella technology. A user who downloads and installs either software possesses the protocol to send requests for files directly to the computers of others using software compatible with FastTrack or Gnutella. On the FastTrack network opened by the Grokster software, the user's request goes to a computer given an indexing capacity by the software and designated a supernode, or to some other computer with comparable power and capacity to collect temporary indexes of the files available on the computers of users connected to it. The supernode (or indexing computer) searches its own index and may communicate the search request to other supernodes. If the file is found, the supernode discloses its location to the computer requesting it, and the requesting user can download the file directly from the computer located. The copied file is placed in a designated sharing folder on the requesting user's computer, where it is available for other users to download in turn, along with any other file in that folder.

In the Gnutella network made available by Morpheus, the process is mostly the same, except that in some versions of the Gnutella protocol there are no supernodes. In these versions, peer computers using the protocol communicate directly with each other. When a user enters a search request into the Morpheus software, it sends the request to computers connected with it, which in turn pass the request along to other connected peers. The search results are communicated to the requesting computer, and the user can download desired files directly from peers' computers. As this description indicates, Grokster and StreamCast use no servers to intercept the content of the search requests or to mediate the file transfers conducted by users of the software, there being no central point through which the substance of the communications passes in either direction.

Although Grokster and StreamCast do not therefore know when particular files are copied, a few searches using their software would show what is available on the networks the software reaches. MGM commissioned a statistician to conduct a systematic search, and his study showed that nearly 90% of the files available for download on the FastTrack system were copyrighted works. Grokster and StreamCast dispute this figure, raising methodological problems and arguing that free copying even of copyrighted works may be authorized by the rightholders. They also argue that potential noninfringing uses of their software are significant in kind, even if infrequent in practice. Some musical performers, for example, have gained new audiences by distributing their copyrighted works for free across peer-to-peer networks, and some distributors of unprotected content have used peer-to-peer networks to disseminate files, Shakespeare being an example. Indeed, StreamCast has given Morpheus users the opportunity to download the briefs in this very case, though their popularity has not been quantified.

As for quantification, the parties' anecdotal and statistical evidence entered thus far to show the content available on the FastTrack and Gnutella networks does not say much about which files are actually downloaded by users, and no one can say how often the software is used to obtain copies of unprotected material. But MGM's evidence gives reason to think that the vast majority of users' downloads are acts of infringement, and because well over 100 million copies of the software in question are known to have been downloaded, and billions of files are shared across the FastTrack and Gnutella networks each month, the probable scope of copyright infringement is staggering.

Grokster and StreamCast concede the infringement in most downloads, Brief for Respondents 10, n. 6, and it is uncontested that they are aware that users employ their software primarily to download copyrighted files, even if the decentralized FastTrack and Gnutella networks fail to reveal which files are being copied, and when. From time to time, moreover, the companies have learned about their users' infringement directly, as from users who have sent e-mail to each company with questions about playing copyrighted movies they had downloaded, to whom the companies have responded with guidance.6 App. 559—563, 808—816, 939—954. And MGM notified the companies of 8 million copyrighted files that could be obtained using their software.

Grokster and StreamCast are not, however, merely passive recipients of information about infringing use. The record is replete with evidence that from the moment Grokster and StreamCast began to distribute their free software, each one clearly voiced the objective that recipients use it to download copyrighted works, and each took active steps to encourage infringement.

After the notorious file-sharing service, Napster, was sued by copyright holders for facilitation of copyright infringement, A & M Records, Inc. v. Napster, Inc., 114 F. Supp. 2d 896 (ND Cal. 2000), aff'd in part, rev'd in part, 239 F.3d 1004 (CA9 2001), StreamCast gave away a software program of a kind known as OpenNap, designed as compatible with the Napster program and open to Napster users for downloading files from other Napster and OpenNap users' computers. Evidence indicates that "[i]t was always [StreamCast's] intent to use [its OpenNap network] to be able to capture email addresses of [its] initial target market so that [it] could promote [its] StreamCast Morpheus interface to them," App. 861; indeed, the OpenNap program was engineered " 'to leverage Napster's 50 million user base,' " id., at 746.

StreamCast monitored both the number of users downloading its OpenNap program and the number of music files they downloaded. Id., at 859, 863, 866. It also used the resulting OpenNap network to distribute copies of the Morpheus software and to encourage users to adopt it. Id., at 861, 867, 1039. Internal company documents indicate that StreamCast hoped to attract large numbers of former Napster users if that company was shut down by court order or otherwise, and that StreamCast planned to be the next Napster. Id., at 861. A kit developed by StreamCast to be delivered to advertisers, for example, contained press articles about StreamCast's potential to capture former Napster users, id., at 568—572, and it introduced itself to some potential advertisers as a company "which is similar to what Napster was," id., at 884. It broadcast banner advertisements to users of other Napster-compatible software, urging them to adopt its OpenNap. Id., at 586. An internal e-mail from a company executive stated: " 'We have put this network in place so that when Napster pulls the plug on their free service ... or if the Court orders them shut down prior to that ... we will be positioned to capture the flood of their 32 million users that will be actively looking for an alternative.' " Id., at 588—589, 861.

Thus, StreamCast developed promotional materials to market its service as the best Napster alternative. One proposed advertisement read: "Napster Inc. has announced that it will soon begin charging you a fee. That's if the courts don't order it shut down first. What will you do to get around it?" Id., at 897. Another proposed ad touted StreamCast's software as the "#1 alternative to Napster" and asked "[w]hen the lights went off at Napster ... where did the users go?" Id., at 836 (ellipsis in original). StreamCast even planned to flaunt the illegal uses of its software; when it launched the OpenNap network, the chief technology officer of the company averred that "[t]he goal is to get in trouble with the law and get sued. It's the best way to get in the new[s]." Id., at 916.

The evidence that Grokster sought to capture the market of former Napster users is sparser but revealing, for Grokster launched its own OpenNap system called Swaptor and inserted digital codes into its Web site so that computer users using Web search engines to look for "Napster" or "[f]ree filesharing" would be directed to the Grokster Web site, where they could download the Grokster software. Id., at 992—993. And Grokster's name is an apparent derivative of Napster.

StreamCast's executives monitored the number of songs by certain commercial artists available on their networks, and an internal communication indicates they aimed to have a larger number of copyrighted songs available on their networks than other file-sharing networks. Id., at 868. The point, of course, would be to attract users of a mind to infringe, just as it would be with their promotional materials developed showing copyrighted songs as examples of the kinds of files available through Morpheus. Id., at 848. Morpheus in fact allowed users to search specifically for "Top 40" songs, id., at 735, which were inevitably copyrighted. Similarly, Grokster sent users a newsletter promoting its ability to provide particular, popular copyrighted materials. Brief for Motion Picture Studio and Recording Company Petitioners 7—8.

In addition to this evidence of express promotion, marketing, and intent to promote further, the business models employed by Grokster and StreamCast confirm that their principal object was use of their software to download copyrighted works. Grokster and StreamCast receive no revenue from users, who obtain the software itself for nothing. Instead, both companies generate income by selling advertising space, and they stream the advertising to Grokster and Morpheus users while they are employing the programs. As the number of users of each program increases, advertising opportunities become worth more. Cf. App. 539, 804. While there is doubtless some demand for free Shakespeare, the evidence shows that substantive volume is a function of free access to copyrighted work. Users seeking Top 40 songs, for example, or the latest release by Modest Mouse, are certain to be far more numerous than those seeking a free Decameron, and Grokster and StreamCast translated that demand into dollars.

Finally, there is no evidence that either company made an effort to filter copyrighted material from users' downloads or otherwise impede the sharing of copyrighted files. Although Grokster appears to have sent e-mails warning users about infringing content when it received threatening notice from the copyright holders, it never blocked anyone from continuing to use its software to share copyrighted files. Id., at 75—76. StreamCast not only rejected another company's offer of help to monitor infringement, id., at 928—929, but blocked the Internet Protocol addresses of entities it believed were trying to engage in such monitoring on its networks, id., at 917—922.

B

After discovery, the parties on each side of the case cross-moved for summary judgment. The District Court limited its consideration to the asserted liability of Grokster and StreamCast for distributing the current versions of their software, leaving aside whether either was liable "for damages arising from past versions of their software, or from other past activities." 259 F. Supp. 2d 1029, 1033 (CD Cal. 2003). The District Court held that those who used the Grokster and Morpheus software to download copyrighted media files directly infringed MGM's copyrights, a conclusion not contested on appeal, but the court nonetheless granted summary judgment in favor of Grokster and StreamCast as to any liability arising from distribution of the then current versions of their software. Distributing that software gave rise to no liability in the court's view, because its use did not provide the distributors with actual knowledge of specific acts of infringement. Case No. CV 01 08541 SVW (PJWx) (CD Cal., June 18, 2003), App. 1213.

The Court of Appeals affirmed. 380 F.3d 1154 (CA9 2004). In the court's analysis, a defendant was liable as a contributory infringer when it had knowledge of direct infringement and materially contributed to the infringement. But the court read Sony Corp. of America v. Universal City Studios, Inc., 464 U.S. 417 (1984), as holding that distribution of a commercial product capable of substantial noninfringing uses could not give rise to contributory liability for infringement unless the distributor had actual knowledge of specific instances of infringement and failed to act on that knowledge. The fact that the software was capable of substantial noninfringing uses in the Ninth Circuit's view meant that Grokster and StreamCast were not liable, because they had no such actual knowledge, owing to the decentralized architecture of their software. The court also held that Grokster and StreamCast did not materially contribute to their users' infringement because it was the users themselves who searched for, retrieved, and stored the infringing files, with no involvement by the defendants beyond providing the software in the first place.

The Ninth Circuit also considered whether Grokster and StreamCast could be liable under a theory of vicarious infringement. The court held against liability because the defendants did not monitor or control the use of the software, had no agreed-upon right or current ability to supervise its use, and had no independent duty to police infringement. We granted certiorari. 543 U.S. ___ (2004).

II

A

MGM and many of the amici fault the Court of Appeals's holding for upsetting a sound balance between the respective values of supporting creative pursuits through copyright protection and promoting innovation in new communication technologies by limiting the incidence of liability for copyright infringement. The more artistic protection is favored, the more technological innovation may be discouraged; the administration of copyright law is an exercise in managing the trade-off. See Sony Corp. v. Universal City Studios, supra, at 442; see generally Ginsburg, Copyright and Control Over New Technologies of Dissemination, 101

Colum. L. Rev. 1613 (2001); Lichtman & Landes, Indirect Liability for Copyright Infringement: An Economic Perspective, 16 Harv. J. L. & Tech. 395 (2003).

The tension between the two values is the subject of this case, with its claim that digital distribution of copyrighted material threatens copyright holders as never before, because every copy is identical to the original, copying is easy, and many people (especially the young) use file-sharing software to download copyrighted works. This very breadth of the software's use may well draw the public directly into the debate over copyright policy, Peters, Brace Memorial Lecture: Copyright Enters the Public Domain, 51 J. Copyright Soc. 701, 705–717 (2004) (address by Register of Copyrights), and the indications are that the ease of copying songs or movies using software like Grokster's and Napster's is fostering disdain for copyright protection, Wu, When Code Isn't Law, 89 Va. L. Rev. 679, 724–726 (2003). As the case has been presented to us, these fears are said to be offset by the different concern that imposing liability, not only on infringers but on distributors of software based on its potential for unlawful use, could limit further development of beneficial technologies. See, e.g., Lemley & Reese, Reducing Digital Copyright Infringement Without Restricting Innovation, 56 Stan. L. Rev. 1345, 1386–1390 (2004); Brief for Innovation Scholars and Economists as Amici Curiae 15–20; Brief for Emerging Technology Companies as Amici Curiae 19–25; Brief for Intel Corporation as Amicus Curiae 20–22.

The argument for imposing indirect liability in this case is, however, a powerful one, given the number of infringing downloads that occur every day using StreamCast's and Grokster's software. When a widely shared service or product is used to commit infringement, it may be impossible to enforce rights in the protected work effectively against all direct infringers, the only practical alternative being to go against the distributor of the copying device for secondary liability on a theory of contributory or vicarious infringement. See In re Aimster Copyright Litigation, 334 F.3d 643, 645–646 (CA7 2003).

One infringes contributorily by intentionally inducing or encouraging direct infringement, see Gershwin Pub. Corp. v. Columbia Artists Management, Inc., 443 F.2d 1159, 1162 (CA2 1971), and infringes vicariously by profiting from direct infringement while declining to exercise a right to stop or limit it, Shapiro, Bernstein & Co. v. H. L. Green Co., 316 F.2d 304, 307 (CA2 1963). Although "[t]he Copyright Act does not expressly render anyone liable for infringement committed by another," Sony Corp. v. Universal City Studios, 464 U.S., at 434, these doctrines of secondary liability emerged from common law principles and are well established in the law, id., at 486 (Blackmun, J., dissenting); Kalem Co. v. Harper Brothers, 222 U.S. 55, 62–63 (1911); Gershwin Pub. Corp. v. Columbia Artists Management, supra, at 1162; 3 M. Nimmer & D. Nimmer, Copyright, §12.04[A] (2005).

B

Despite the currency of these principles of secondary liability, this Court has dealt with secondary copyright infringement in only one recent case, and because MGM has tailored its principal claim to our opinion there, a look at our earlier holding is in order. In Sony Corp. v. Universal City Studios, supra, this Court addressed a claim that secondary liability for infringement can arise from the very distribution of a commercial product. There, the product, novel at the time, was what we know today as the videocassette recorder or VCR. Copyright holders sued Sony as the manufacturer, claiming it was contributorily liable for infringement that occurred when VCR owners taped copyrighted programs because it supplied the means used to infringe, and it had constructive knowledge that infringement would occur. At the trial on the merits, the evidence showed that the principal use of the VCR was for " 'time-shifting,' " or taping a program for later viewing at a more convenient time, which the Court found to be a fair, not an infringing, use. Id., at 423—424. There was no evidence that Sony had expressed an object of bringing about taping in violation of copyright or had taken active steps to increase its profits from unlawful taping. Id., at 438. Although Sony's advertisements urged consumers to buy the VCR to " 'record favorite shows' " or " 'build a library' " of recorded programs, id., at 459 (Blackmun, J., dissenting), neither of these uses was necessarily infringing, id., at 424, 454—455.

On those facts, with no evidence of stated or indicated intent to promote infringing uses, the only conceivable basis for imposing liability was on a theory of contributory infringement arising from its sale of VCRs to consumers with knowledge that some would use them to infringe. Id., at 439. But because the VCR was "capable of commercially significant noninfringing uses," we held the manufacturer could not be faulted solely on the basis of its distribution. Id., at 442.

This analysis reflected patent law's traditional staple article of commerce doctrine, now codified, that distribution of a component of a patented device will not violate the patent if it is suitable for use in other ways. 35 U.S.C. § 271(c); Aro Mfg. Co. v. Convertible Top Replacement Co., 377 U.S. 476, 485 (1964) (noting codification of cases); id., at 486, n. 6 (same). The doctrine was devised to identify instances in which it may be presumed from distribution of an article in commerce that the distributor intended the article to be used to infringe another's patent, and so may justly be held liable for that infringement. "One who makes and sells articles which are only adapted to be used in a patented combination will be presumed to intend the natural consequences of his acts; he will be presumed to intend that they shall be used in the combination of the patent." New York Scaffolding Co. v. Whitney, 224 F. 452, 459 (CA8 1915); see also James Heekin Co. v. Baker, 138 F. 63, 66 (CA8 1905); Canda v. Michigan Malleable Iron Co., 124 F. 486, 489 (CA6 1903); Thomson-Houston Electric Co. v. Ohio Brass Co., 80 F. 712, 720—721 (CA6 1897); Red Jacket Mfg. Co. v. Davis, 82 F. 432, 439 (CA7 1897); Holly v. Vergennes Machine Co., 4 F. 74, 82 (CC Vt. 1880); Renwick v. Pond, 20 F. Cas. 536, 541 (No. 11,702) (CC SDNY 1872).

In sum, where an article is "good for nothing else" but infringement, Canda v. Michigan Malleable Iron Co., supra, at 489, there is no legitimate public interest in its unlicensed availability, and there is no injustice in presuming or imputing an intent to infringe, see Henry v. A. B. Dick Co., 224 U.S. 1, 48 (1912), overruled on other grounds, Motion Picture Patents Co. v. Universal Film Mfg. Co., 243 U.S. 502 (1917). Conversely, the doctrine absolves the equivocal conduct of selling an item with substantial lawful as well as unlawful uses, and limits liability to instances of more acute fault than the mere understanding that some of one's products will be misused. It leaves breathing room for innovation and a vigorous commerce. See Sony Corp. v. Universal City Studios, supra, at 442; Dawson Chemical Co. v. Rohm & Haas Co., 448 U.S. 176, 221 (1980); Henry v. A. B. Dick Co., supra, at 48.

The parties and many of the amici in this case think the key to resolving it is the Sony rule and, in particular, what it means for a product to be "capable of commercially significant noninfringing uses." Sony Corp. v. Universal City Studios, supra, at 442. MGM advances the argument that granting summary judgment to Grokster and StreamCast as to their current activities gave too much weight to the value of innovative technology, and too little to the copyrights infringed by users of their software, given that 90% of works available on one of the networks was shown to be copyrighted. Assuming the remaining 10% to be its noninfringing use, MGM says this should not qualify as "substantial," and the Court should quantify Sony to the extent of holding that a product used "principally" for infringement does not qualify. See Brief for Motion Picture Studio and Recording Company Petitioners 31. As mentioned before, Grokster and StreamCast reply by citing evidence that their software can be used to reproduce public domain works, and they point to copyright holders who actually encourage copying. Even if infringement is the principal practice with their software today, they argue, the noninfringing uses are significant and will grow.

We agree with MGM that the Court of Appeals misapplied Sony, which it read as limiting secondary liability quite beyond the circumstances to which the case applied. Sony barred secondary liability based on presuming or imputing intent to cause infringement solely from the design or distribution of a product capable of substantial lawful use, which the distributor knows is in fact used for infringement. The Ninth Circuit has read Sony's limitation to mean that whenever a product is capable of substantial lawful use, the producer can never be held contributorily liable for third parties' infringing use of it; it read the rule as being this broad, even when an actual purpose to cause infringing use is shown by evidence independent of design and distribution of the product, unless the distributors had "specific knowledge of infringement at a time at which they contributed to the infringement, and failed to act upon that information." 380 F.3d, at 1162 (internal quotation marks and alterations omitted). Because the Circuit found the StreamCast and Grokster software capable of substantial lawful use, it concluded on the basis of its reading of Sony that neither company could be held liable, since there was no showing that their software, being without any central server, afforded them knowledge of specific unlawful uses.

This view of Sony, however, was error, converting the case from one about liability resting on imputed intent to one about liability on any theory. Because Sony did not displace other theories of secondary liability, and because we find below that it was error to grant summary judgment to the companies on MGM's inducement claim, we do not revisit Sony further, as MGM requests, to add a more quantified description of the point of balance between protection and commerce when liability rests solely on distribution with knowledge that unlawful use will occur. It is enough to note that the Ninth Circuit's judgment rested on an erroneous understanding of Sony and to leave further consideration of the Sony rule for a day when that may be required.

C

Sony's rule limits imputing culpable intent as a matter of law from the characteristics or uses of a distributed product. But nothing in Sony requires courts to ignore evidence of intent if there is such evidence, and the case was never meant to foreclose rules of fault-based liability derived from the common law. Sony Corp. v. Universal City Studios, 464 U.S., at 439 ("If vicarious liability is to be imposed on Sony in this case, it must rest on the fact that it has sold equipment with constructive knowledge" of the potential for infringement). Thus, where evidence goes beyond a product's characteristics or the knowledge that it may be put to infringing uses, and shows statements or actions directed to promoting infringement, Sony's staple-article rule will not preclude liability.

The classic case of direct evidence of unlawful purpose occurs when one induces commission of infringement by another, or "entic[es] or persuad[es] another" to infringe, Black's Law Dictionary 790 (8th ed. 2004), as by advertising. Thus at common law a copyright or patent defendant who "not only expected but invoked [infringing use] by advertisement" was liable for infringement "on principles recognized in every part of the law." Kalem Co. v. Harper Brothers, 222 U.S., at 62—63 (copyright infringement). See also Henry v. A. B. Dick Co., 224 U.S., at 48—49 (contributory liability for patent infringement may be found where a good's "most conspicuous use is one which will coöperate in an infringement when sale to such user is invoked by advertisement" of the infringing use); Thomson-Houston Electric Co. v. Kelsey Electric R. Specialty Co., 75 F. 1005, 1007—1008 (CA2 1896) (relying on advertisements and displays to find defendant's "willingness ... to aid other persons in any attempts which they may be disposed to make towards [patent] infringement"); Rumford Chemical Works v. Hecker, 20 F. Cas. 1342, 1346 (No. 12,133) (CC N. J. 1876) (demonstrations of infringing activity along with "avowals of the [infringing] purpose and use for which it was made" supported liability for patent infringement).

The rule on inducement of infringement as developed in the early cases is no different today. Evidence of "active steps ... taken to encourage direct infringement," Oak Industries, Inc. v. Zenith Electronics Corp., 697 F. Supp. 988, 992 (ND Ill. 1988), such as advertising an infringing use or instructing how to engage in an infringing use, show an affirmative intent that the product be used to infringe, and a showing that infringement was encouraged overcomes the law's reluctance to find liability when a defendant merely sells a commercial product suitable for some lawful use, see, e.g., Water Technologies Corp. v. Calco, Ltd., 850 F.2d 660, 668 (CA Fed. 1988) (liability for inducement where one "actively and knowingly aid[s] and abet[s] another's direct infringement" (emphasis omitted)); Fromberg, Inc. v. Thornhill, 315 F.2d 407, 412—413 (CA5 1963) (demonstrations by sales staff of infringing uses supported liability for inducement); Haworth Inc. v. Herman Miller Inc., 37 USPQ 2d 1080, 1090 (WD Mich. 1994) (evidence that defendant "demonstrate[d] and recommend[ed] infringing configurations" of its product could support inducement liability); Sims v. Mack Trucks, Inc., 459 F. Supp. 1198, 1215 (ED Pa. 1978) (finding inducement where the use "depicted by the defendant in its promotional film and brochures infringes the ... patent"), overruled on other grounds, 608 F.2d 87 (CA3 1979). Cf. W. Keeton, D. Dobbs, R.

Keeton, & D. Owen, Prosser and Keeton on Law of Torts 37 (5th ed. 1984) ("There is a definite tendency to impose greater responsibility upon a defendant whose conduct was intended to do harm, or was morally wrong").

For the same reasons that Sony took the staple-article doctrine of patent law as a model for its copyright safe-harbor rule, the inducement rule, too, is a sensible one for copyright. We adopt it here, holding that one who distributes a device with the object of promoting its use to infringe copyright, as shown by clear expression or other affirmative steps taken to foster infringement, is liable for the resulting acts of infringement by third parties. We are, of course, mindful of the need to keep from trenching on regular commerce or discouraging the development of technologies with lawful and unlawful potential. Accordingly, just as Sony did not find intentional inducement despite the knowledge of the VCR manufacturer that its device could be used to infringe, 464 U.S., at 439, n. 19, mere knowledge of infringing potential or of actual infringing uses would not be enough here to subject a distributor to liability. Nor would ordinary acts incident to product distribution, such as offering customers technical support or product updates, support liability in themselves. The inducement rule, instead, premises liability on purposeful, culpable expression and conduct, and thus does nothing to compromise legitimate commerce or discourage innovation having a lawful promise.

III

A

The only apparent question about treating MGM's evidence as sufficient to withstand summary judgment under the theory of inducement goes to the need on MGM's part to adduce evidence that StreamCast and Grokster communicated an inducing message to their software users. The classic instance of inducement is by advertisement or solicitation that broadcasts a message designed to stimulate others to commit violations. MGM claims that such a message is shown here. It is undisputed that StreamCast beamed onto the computer screens of users of Napster-compatible programs ads urging the adoption of its OpenNap program, which was designed, as its name implied, to invite the custom of patrons of Napster, then under attack in the courts for facilitating massive infringement. Those who accepted StreamCast's OpenNap program were offered software to perform the same services, which a factfinder could conclude would readily have been understood in the Napster market as the ability to download copyrighted music files. Grokster distributed an electronic newsletter containing links to articles promoting its software's ability to access popular copyrighted music. And anyone whose Napster or free file-sharing searches turned up a link to Grokster would have understood Grokster to be offering the same file-sharing ability as Napster, and to the same people who probably used Napster for infringing downloads; that would also have been the understanding of anyone offered Grokster's suggestively named Swaptor software, its version of OpenNap. And both companies communicated a clear message by responding affirmatively to requests for help in locating and playing copyrighted materials.

In StreamCast's case, of course, the evidence just described was supplemented by other unequivocal indications of unlawful purpose in the internal communications and advertising designs aimed at Napster users ("When the lights went off at Napster ... where did the users go?" App. 836 (ellipsis in original)). Whether the messages were communicated is not to the point on this record. The function of the message in the theory of inducement is to prove by a defendant's own statements that his unlawful purpose disqualifies him from claiming protection (and incidentally to point to actual violators likely to be found among those who hear or read the message). See supra, at 17—19. Proving that a message was sent out, then, is the preeminent but not exclusive way of showing that active steps were taken with the purpose of bringing about infringing acts, and of showing that infringing acts took place by using the device distributed. Here, the summary judgment record is replete with other evidence that Grokster and StreamCast, unlike the manufacturer and distributor in Sony, acted with a purpose to cause copyright violations by use of software suitable for illegal use. See supra, at 6—9.

Three features of this evidence of intent are particularly notable. First, each company showed itself to be aiming to satisfy a known source of demand for copyright infringement, the market comprising former Napster users. StreamCast's internal documents made constant reference to Napster, it initially distributed its Morpheus software through an OpenNap program compatible with Napster, it advertised its OpenNap program to Napster users, and its Morpheus software functions as Napster did except that it could be used to distribute more kinds of files, including copyrighted movies and software programs. Grokster's name is apparently derived from Napster, it too initially offered an OpenNap program, its software's function is likewise comparable to Napster's, and it attempted to divert queries for Napster onto its own Web site. Grokster and StreamCast's efforts to supply services to former Napster users, deprived of a mechanism to copy and distribute what were overwhelmingly infringing files, indicate a principal, if not exclusive, intent on the part of each to bring about infringement.

Second, this evidence of unlawful objective is given added significance by MGM's showing that neither company attempted to develop filtering tools or other mechanisms to diminish the infringing activity using their software. While the Ninth Circuit treated the defendants' failure to develop such tools as irrelevant because they lacked an independent duty to monitor their users' activity, we think this evidence underscores Grokster's and StreamCast's intentional facilitation of their users' infringement.12

Third, there is a further complement to the direct evidence of unlawful objective. It is useful to recall that StreamCast and Grokster make money by selling advertising space, by directing ads to the screens of computers employing their software. As the record shows, the more the software is used, the more ads are sent out and the greater the advertising revenue becomes. Since the extent of the software's use determines the gain to the distributors, the commercial sense of their enterprise turns on high-volume use, which the record shows is infringing.13 This evidence alone would not justify an inference of unlawful intent, but viewed in the context of the entire record its import is clear.

The unlawful objective is unmistakable.

B

In addition to intent to bring about infringement and distribution of a device suitable for infringing use, the inducement theory of course requires evidence of actual infringement by recipients of the device, the software in this case. As the account of the facts indicates, there is evidence of infringement on a gigantic scale, and there is no serious issue of the adequacy of MGM's showing on this point in order to survive the companies' summary judgment requests. Although an exact calculation of infringing use, as a basis for a claim of damages, is subject to dispute, there is no question that the summary judgment evidence is at least adequate to entitle MGM to go forward with claims for damages and equitable relief.

***

In sum, this case is significantly different from Sony and reliance on that case to rule in favor of StreamCast and Grokster was error. Sony dealt with a claim of liability based solely on distributing a product with alternative lawful and unlawful uses, with knowledge that some users would follow the unlawful course. The case struck a balance between the interests of protection and innovation by holding that the product's capability of substantial lawful employment should bar the imputation of fault and consequent secondary liability for the unlawful acts of others.

MGM's evidence in this case most obviously addresses a different basis of liability for distributing a product open to alternative uses. Here, evidence of the distributors' words and deeds going beyond distribution as such shows a purpose to cause and profit from third-party acts of copyright infringement. If liability for inducing infringement is ultimately found, it will not be on the basis of presuming or imputing fault, but from inferring a patently illegal objective from statements and actions showing what that objective was.

There is substantial evidence in MGM's favor on all elements of inducement, and summary judgment in favor of Grokster and StreamCast was error. On remand, reconsideration of MGM's motion for summary judgment will be in order.

The judgment of the Court of Appeals is vacated, and the case is remanded for further proceedings consistent with this opinion.

It is so ordered.

676 F.3d 19 (2012)

VIACOM v. YOUTUBE

United States Court of Appeals, Second Circuit

JOSÉ A. CABRANES, Circuit Judge:

This appeal requires us to clarify the contours of the "safe harbor" provision of the Digital Millennium Copyright Act (DMCA) that limits the liability of online service providers for copyright infringement that occurs "by reason of the storage at the direction of a user of material that resides on a system or network controlled or operated by or for the service provider." 17 U.S.C. § 512(c).

The plaintiffs-appellants in these related actions—Viacom International, Inc. ("Viacom"), The Football Association Premier League Ltd. ("Premier League"), and various film studios, television networks, music publishers, and sports leagues (jointly, [676 F.3d 26] the "plaintiffs") —appeal from an August 10, 2010 judgment of the United States District Court for the Southern District of New York (Louis L. Stanton, Judge), which granted summary judgment to defendants-appellees YouTube, Inc., YouTube, LLC, and Google Inc. (jointly, "YouTube" or the "defendants"). The plaintiffs alleged direct and secondary copyright infringement based on the public performance, display, and reproduction of approximately 79,000 audiovisual "clips" that appeared on the YouTube website between 2005 and 2008. They demanded, inter alia, statutory damages pursuant to 17 U.S.C. § 504(c) or, in the alternative, actual damages from the alleged infringement, as well as declaratory and injunctive relief.

In a June 23, 2010 Opinion and Order (the "June 23 Opinion"), the District Court held that the defendants were entitled to DMCA safe harbor protection primarily because they had insufficient notice of the particular infringements in suit. Viacom Int'l, Inc. v. YouTube, Inc., 718 F.Supp.2d 514, 529 (S.D.N.Y.2010). In construing the statutory safe harbor, the District Court concluded that the "actual knowledge" or "aware[ness] of facts or circumstances" that would disqualify an online service provider from safe harbor protection under § 512(c)(1)(A) refer to "knowledge of specific and identifiable infringements." Id. at 523. The District Court further held that item-specific knowledge of infringing activity is required for a service provider to have the "right and ability to control" infringing activity under § 512(c)(1)(B). Id. at 527. Finally, the District Court held that the replication, transmittal, and display of videos on YouTube constituted activity "by reason of the storage at the direction of a user" within the meaning of § 512(c)(1). Id. at 526–27.

These related cases present a series of significant questions of statutory construction. We conclude that the District Court correctly held that the § 512(c) safe harbor requires knowledge or awareness of specific infringing activity, but we vacate the order granting summary judgment because a reasonable jury could find that YouTube had actual knowledge or awareness of specific infringing activity on its website. We further hold that the District Court erred by interpreting the "right and ability to control" provision to require "item-specific" knowledge. Finally, we affirm the District Court's holding that three of the challenged YouTube software functions fall within the safe harbor for infringement that occurs "by reason of" user storage; we remand for further fact-finding with respect to a fourth software function.

BACKGROUND

A. The DMCA Safe Harbors

"The DMCA was enacted in 1998 to implement the World Intellectual Property Organization Copyright Treaty," Universal City Studios, Inc. v. Corley, 273 F.3d 429, 440 (2d Cir.2001), and to update domestic copyright law for the digital age, [676 F.3d 27] see Ellison v. Robertson, 357 F.3d 1072, 1076 (9th Cir.2004). Title II of the DMCA, separately titled the "Online Copyright Infringement Liability Limitation Act" (OCILLA), was designed to "clarif[y] the liability faced by service providers who transmit potentially infringing material over their networks." S.Rep. No. 105–190 at 2 (1998). But "[r]ather than embarking upon a wholesale clarification" of various copyright doctrines, Congress elected "to leave current law in its evolving state and, instead, to create a series of 'safe harbors[ ]' for certain common activities of service providers." Id. at 19. To that end, OCILLA established a series of four "safe harbors" that allow qualifying service providers to limit their liability for claims of copyright infringement based on (a) "transitory digital network communications," (b) "system caching," (c) "information residing on systems or networks at [the] direction of users," and (d) "information location tools." 17 U.S.C. § 512(a)-(d).

To qualify for protection under any of the safe harbors, a party must meet a set of threshold criteria. First, the party must in fact be a "service provider," defined, in pertinent part, as "a provider of online services or network access, or the operator of facilities therefor." 17 U.S.C. § 512(k)(1)(B). A party that qualifies as a service provider must also satisfy certain "conditions of eligibility," including the adoption and reasonable implementation of a "repeat infringer" policy that "provides for the termination in appropriate circumstances of subscribers and account holders of the service provider's system or network." Id. § 512(i)(1)(A). In addition, a qualifying service provider must accommodate "standard technical measures" that are "used by copyright owners to identify or protect copyrighted works." Id. § 512(i)(1)(B), (i)(2).

Beyond the threshold criteria, a service provider must satisfy the requirements of a particular safe harbor. In this case, the safe harbor at issue is § 512(c), which covers infringement claims that arise "by reason of the storage at the direction of a user of material that resides on a system or network controlled or operated by or for the service provider." Id. § 512(c)(1). The § 512(c) safe harbor will apply only if the service provider:

(A) (i) does not have actual knowledge that the material or an activity using the material on the system or network is infringing;

(ii) in the absence of such actual knowledge, is not aware of facts or circumstances from which infringing activity is apparent; or

(iii) upon obtaining such knowledge or awareness, acts expeditiously to remove, or disable access to, the material;

(B) does not receive a financial benefit directly attributable to the infringing activity, in a case in which the service provider has the right and ability to control such activity; and

(C) upon notification of claimed infringement as described in paragraph (3), responds expeditiously to remove, or disable access to, the material that is claimed to be infringing or to be the subject of infringing activity.

Id. § 512(c)(1)(A)-(C). Section 512(c) also sets forth a detailed notification scheme that requires service providers to "designate[ ] an agent to receive notifications of claimed infringement," id. § 512(c)(2), and specifies the components of a proper notification, commonly known as a "takedown notice," to that agent, see id. § 512(c)(3). Thus, actual knowledge of infringing material, awareness of facts or circumstances that make infringing activity apparent, or [676 F.3d 28] receipt of a takedown notice will each trigger an obligation to expeditiously remove the infringing material.

With the statutory context in mind, we now turn to the facts of this case.

B. Factual Background

YouTube was founded in February 2005 by Chad Hurley ("Hurley"), Steve Chen ("Chen"), and Jawed Karim ("Karim"), three former employees of the internet company Paypal. When YouTube announced the "official launch" of the website in December 2005, a press release described YouTube as a "consumer media company" that "allows people to watch, upload, and share personal video clips at www. You Tube. com." Under the slogan "Broadcast yourself," YouTube achieved rapid prominence and profitability, eclipsing competitors such as Google Video and Yahoo Video by wide margins. In November 2006, Google acquired YouTube in a stock-for-stock transaction valued at $1.65 billion. By March 2010, at the time of summary judgment briefing in this litigation, site traffic on YouTube had soared to more than 1 billion daily video views, with more than 24 hours of new video uploaded to the site every minute.

The basic function of the YouTube website permits users to "upload" and view video clips free of charge. Before uploading a video to YouTube, a user must register and create an account with the website. The registration process requires the user to accept YouTube's Terms of Use agreement, which provides, inter alia, that the user "will not submit material that is copyrighted ... unless [he is] the owner of such rights or ha[s] permission from their rightful owner to post the material and to grant YouTube all of the license rights granted herein." When the registration process is complete, the user can sign in to his account, select a video to upload from the user's personal computer, mobile phone, or other device, and instruct the YouTube system to upload the video by clicking on a virtual upload "button."

Uploading a video to the YouTube website triggers a series of automated software functions. During the upload process, YouTube makes one or more exact copies of the video in its original file format. YouTube also makes one or more additional copies of the video in "Flash" format, a process known as "transcoding." The transcoding process ensures that YouTube videos are available for viewing by most users at their request. The YouTube system allows users to gain access to video content by "streaming" the video to the user's computer in response to a playback request. YouTube uses a computer algorithm to identify clips that are "related" to a video the user watches and display links to the "related" clips.

...

DISCUSSION

We review an order granting summary judgment de novo, drawing all factual inferences in favor of the non-moving party. See, e.g., Paneccasio v. Unisource Worldwide, Inc., 532 F.3d 101, 107 (2d Cir.2008). "Summary judgment is proper only when, construing the evidence in the light most favorable to the non-movant, 'there is no genuine dispute as to any material fact and the movant is entitled to judgment as a matter of law.' " Doninger v. Niehoff, 642 F.3d 334, 344 (2d Cir.2011) (quoting Fed.R.Civ.P. 56(a)).

A. Actual and "Red Flag" Knowledge: § 512(c)(1)(A)

The first and most important question on appeal is whether the DMCA safe harbor at issue requires "actual knowledge" or "aware[ness]" of facts or circumstances indicating "specific and identifiable infringements," Viacom, 718 F.Supp.2d at 523. We consider first the scope of the statutory provision and then its application to the record in this case.

1. The Specificity Requirement

"As in all statutory construction cases, we begin with the language of the statute," Barnhart v. Sigmon Coal Co., 534 U.S. 438, 450, 122 S.Ct. 941, 151 L.Ed.2d 908 (2002). Under § 512(c)(1)(A), safe harbor protection is available only if the service provider:

(i) does not have actual knowledge that the material or an activity using the material on the system or network is infringing;

(ii) in the absence of such actual knowledge, is not aware of facts or circumstances from which infringing activity is apparent; or

(iii) upon obtaining such knowledge or awareness, acts expeditiously to remove, or disable access to, the material....

17 U.S.C. § 512(c)(1)(A). As previously noted, the District Court held that the statutory phrases "actual knowledge that the material ... is infringing" and "facts or circumstances from which infringing activity is apparent" refer to "knowledge of specific and identifiable infringements." Viacom, 718 F.Supp.2d at 523. For the reasons that follow, we substantially affirm that holding.

Although the parties marshal a battery of other arguments on appeal, it is the text of the statute that compels our conclusion. In particular, we are persuaded that the basic operation of § 512(c) requires knowledge or awareness of specific infringing activity. Under § 512(c)(1)(A), knowledge or awareness alone does not disqualify the service provider; rather, the provider that gains knowledge or awareness of infringing activity retains safe-harbor protection if it "acts expeditiously to remove, or disable access to, the material." 17 U.S.C. § 512(c)(1)(A)(iii). Thus, the nature of the removal obligation itself contemplates knowledge or awareness of specific infringing material, because expeditious removal is possible only if the service provider knows with particularity which items to remove. Indeed, to require expeditious removal in the absence of specific knowledge [676 F.3d 31] or awareness would be to mandate an amorphous obligation to "take commercially reasonable steps" in response to a generalized awareness of infringement. Viacom Br. 33. Such a view cannot be reconciled with the language of the statute, which requires "expeditious[ ]" action to remove or disable " the material " at issue. 17 U.S.C. § 512(c)(1)(A)(iii) (emphasis added).

On appeal, the plaintiffs dispute this conclusion by drawing our attention to § 512(c)(1)(A)(ii), the so-called "red flag" knowledge provision. See id. § 512(c)(1)(A)(ii) (limiting liability where, "in the absence of such actual knowledge, [the service provider] is not aware of facts or circumstances from which infringing activity is apparent"). In their view, the use of the phrase "facts or circumstances" demonstrates that Congress did not intend to limit the red flag provision to a particular type of knowledge. The plaintiffs contend that requiring awareness of specific infringements in order to establish "aware[ness] of facts or circumstances from which infringing activity is apparent," 17 U.S.C. § 512(c)(1)(A)(ii), renders the red flag provision superfluous, because that provision would be satisfied only when the "actual knowledge" provision is also satisfied. For that reason, the plaintiffs urge the Court to hold that the red flag provision "requires less specificity" than the actual knowledge provision. Pls.' Supp. Br. 1.

This argument misconstrues the relationship between "actual" knowledge and "red flag" knowledge. It is true that "we are required to 'disfavor interpretations of statutes that render language superfluous.' " Conn. ex rel. Blumenthal v. U.S. Dep't of the Interior, 228 F.3d 82, 88 (2d Cir.2000) (quoting Conn. Nat'l Bank v. Germain, 503 U.S. 249, 253, 112 S.Ct. 1146, 117 L.Ed.2d 391 (1992)). But contrary to the plaintiffs' assertions, construing § 512(c)(1)(A) to require actual knowledge or awareness of specific instances of infringement does not render the red flag provision superfluous. The phrase "actual knowledge," which appears in § 512(c)(1)(A)(i), is frequently used to denote subjective belief. See, e.g., United States v. Quinones, 635 F.3d 590, 602 (2d Cir.2011) ("[T]he belief held by the defendant need not be reasonable in order for it to defeat ... actual knowledge."). By contrast, courts often invoke the language of "facts or circumstances," which appears in § 512(c)(1)(A)(ii), in discussing an objective reasonableness standard. See, e.g., Maxwell v. City of New York, 380 F.3d 106, 108 (2d Cir.2004) ("Police officers' application of force is excessive ... if it is objectively unreasonable in light of the facts and circumstances confronting them, without regard to their underlying intent or motivation." (internal quotation marks omitted)).

The difference between actual and red flag knowledge is thus not between specific and generalized knowledge, but instead between a subjective and an objective standard. In other words, the actual knowledge provision turns on whether the provider actually or "subjectively" knew of specific infringement, while the red flag provision turns on whether the provider was subjectively aware of facts that would have made the specific infringement "objectively" obvious to a reasonable person. The red flag provision, because it incorporates an objective standard, is not swallowed up by the actual knowledge provision under our construction of the § 512(c) safe harbor. Both provisions do independent work, and both apply only to specific instances of infringement.

The limited body of case law interpreting the knowledge provisions of the § 512(c) safe harbor comports with our view of the specificity requirement. Most [676 F.3d 32] recently, a panel of the Ninth Circuit addressed the scope of § 512(c) in UMG Recordings, Inc. v. Shelter Capital Partners LLC, 667 F.3d 1022 (9th Cir.2011), a copyright infringement case against Veoh Networks, a video-hosting service similar to YouTube. As in this case, various music publishers brought suit against the service provider, claiming direct and secondary copyright infringement based on the presence of unauthorized content on the website, and the website operator sought refuge in the § 512(c) safe harbor. The Court of Appeals affirmed the district court's determination on summary judgment that the website operator was entitled to safe harbor protection. With respect to the actual knowledge provision, the panel declined to "adopt[ ] a broad conception of the knowledge requirement," id. at 1038, holding instead that the safe harbor "[r]equir [es] specific knowledge of particular infringing activity," id. at 1037. The Court of Appeals "reach[ed] the same conclusion" with respect to the red flag provision, noting that "[w]e do not place the burden of determining whether [materials] are actually illegal on a service provider." Id. at 1038 (alterations in original) (quoting Perfect 10, Inc. v. CCBill LLC, 488 F.3d 1102, 1114 (9th Cir.2007)).

Although Shelter Capital contains the most explicit discussion of the § 512(c) knowledge provisions, other cases are generally in accord. See, e.g., Capitol Records, Inc. v. MP3tunes, LLC, 821 F.Supp.2d 627, 635, 2011 WL 5104616, at *14 (S.D.N.Y. Oct. 25, 2011) ("Undoubtedly, MP3tunes is aware that some level of infringement occurs. But, there is no genuine dispute that MP3tunes did not have specific 'red flag' knowledge with respect to any particular link...."); UMG Recordings, Inc. v. Veoh Networks, Inc., 665 F.Supp.2d 1099, 1108 (C.D.Cal.2009) (" UMG II ") ("[I]f investigation of 'facts and circumstances' is required to identify material as infringing, then those facts and circumstances are not 'red flags.' "). While we decline to adopt the reasoning of those decisions in toto, we note that no court has embraced the contrary proposition—urged by the plaintiffs—that the red flag provision "requires less specificity" than the actual knowledge provision.

Based on the text of § 512(c)(1)(A), as well as the limited case law on point, we affirm the District Court's holding that actual knowledge or awareness of facts or circumstances that indicate specific and identifiable instances of infringement will disqualify a service provider from the safe harbor.

2. The Grant of Summary Judgment

The corollary question on appeal is whether, under the foregoing construction of § 512(c)(1)(A), the District Court erred in granting summary judgment to YouTube on the record presented. For the reasons that follow, we hold that although the District Court correctly interpreted § 512(c)(1)(A), summary judgment for the defendants was premature.

i. Specific Knowledge or Awareness

The plaintiffs argue that, even under the District Court's construction of the safe harbor, the record raises material issues of fact regarding YouTube's actual knowledge or "red flag" awareness of specific instances of infringement. To that end, the plaintiffs draw our attention to various estimates regarding the percentage of infringing content on the YouTube website. For example, Viacom cites evidence [676 F.3d 33] that YouTube employees conducted website surveys and estimated that 75–80% of all YouTube streams contained copyrighted material. The class plaintiffs similarly claim that Credit Suisse, acting as financial advisor to Google, estimated that more than 60% of YouTube's content was "premium" copyrighted content—and that only 10% of the premium content was authorized. These approximations suggest that the defendants were conscious that significant quantities of material on the YouTube website were infringing. See Viacom Int'l, 718 F.Supp.2d at 518 ("[A] jury could find that the defendants not only were generally aware of, but welcomed, copyright-infringing material being placed on their website."). But such estimates are insufficient, standing alone, to create a triable issue of fact as to whether YouTube actually knew, or was aware of facts or circumstances that would indicate, the existence of particular instances of infringement.

Beyond the survey results, the plaintiffs rely upon internal YouTube communications that do refer to particular clips or groups of clips. The class plaintiffs argue that YouTube was aware of specific infringing material because, inter alia, YouTube attempted to search for specific Premier League videos on the site in order to gauge their "value based on video usage." In particular, the class plaintiffs cite a February 7, 2007 e-mail from Patrick Walker, director of video partnerships for Google and YouTube, requesting that his colleagues calculate the number of daily searches for the terms "soccer," "football," and "Premier League" in preparation for a bid on the global rights to Premier League content. On another occasion, Walker requested that any "clearly infringing, official broadcast footage" from a list of top Premier League clubs—including Liverpool Football Club, Chelsea Football Club, Manchester United Football Club, and Arsenal Football Club—be taken down in advance of a meeting with the heads of "several major sports teams and leagues." YouTube ultimately decided not to make a bid for the Premier League rights—but the infringing content allegedly remained on the website.

The record in the Viacom action includes additional examples. For instance, YouTube founder Jawed Karim prepared a report in March 2006 which stated that, "[a]s of today[,] episodes and clips of the following well-known shows can still be found [on YouTube]: Family Guy, South Park, MTV Cribs, Daily Show, Reno 911, [and] Dave Chapelle [sic]." Karim further opined that, "although YouTube is not legally required to monitor content ... and complies with DMCA takedown requests, we would benefit from preemptively removing content that is blatantly illegal and likely to attract criticism." He also noted that "a more thorough analysis" of the issue would be required. At least some of the TV shows to which Karim referred are owned by Viacom. A reasonable juror could conclude from the March 2006 report that Karim knew of the presence of Viacom-owned material on

YouTube, since he presumably located specific clips of the shows in question before he could announce that YouTube hosted the content "[a]s of today." A reasonable juror could also conclude that Karim believed the clips he located to be infringing (since he refers to them as "blatantly illegal"), and that YouTube did not remove the content from the website until conducting "a more thorough analysis," thus exposing the company to liability in the interim.

Furthermore, in a July 4, 2005 e-mail exchange, YouTube founder Chad Hurley sent an e-mail to his co-founders with the subject line "budlight commercials," and stated, "we need to reject these too." Steve Chen responded, "can we please [676 F.3d 34] leave these in a bit longer? another week or two can't hurt." Karim also replied, indicating that he "added back in all 28 bud videos." Similarly, in an August 9, 2005 e-mail exchange, Hurley urged his colleagues "to start being diligent about rejecting copyrighted / inappropriate content," noting that "there is a cnn clip of the shuttle clip on the site today, if the boys from Turner would come to the site, they might be pissed?" Again, Chen resisted:

but we should just keep that stuff on the site. i really don't see what will happen. what? someone from cnn sees it? he happens to be someone with power? he happens to want to take it down right away. he gets in touch with cnn legal. 2 weeks later, we get a cease & desist letter. we take the video down.

And again, Karim agreed, indicating that "the CNN space shuttle clip, I like. we can remove it once we're bigger and better known, but for now that clip is fine."

Upon a review of the record, we are persuaded that the plaintiffs may have raised a material issue of fact regarding YouTube's knowledge or awareness of specific instances of infringement. The foregoing Premier League e-mails request the identification and removal of "clearly infringing, official broadcast footage." The March 2006 report indicates Karim's awareness of specific clips that he perceived to be "blatantly illegal." Similarly, the Bud Light and space shuttle e-mails refer to particular clips in the context of correspondence about whether to remove infringing material from the website. On these facts, a reasonable juror could conclude that YouTube had actual knowledge of specific infringing activity, or was at least aware of facts or circumstances from which specific infringing activity was apparent. See § 512(c)(1)(A)(i)-(ii). Accordingly, we hold that summary judgment to YouTube on all clips-in-suit, especially in the absence of any detailed examination of the extensive record on summary judgment, was premature.

We hasten to note, however, that although the foregoing e-mails were annexed as exhibits to the summary judgment papers, it is unclear whether the clips referenced therein are among the current clips-in-suit. By definition, only the current clips-in-suit are at issue in this litigation. Accordingly, we vacate the order granting summary judgment and instruct the District Court to determine on remand whether any specific infringements of which YouTube had knowledge or awareness correspond to the clips-in-suit in these actions.

ii. "Willful Blindness"

The plaintiffs further argue that the District Court erred in granting summary judgment to the defendants despite evidence that YouTube was "willfully blind" to specific infringing activity. On this issue of first impression, we consider the application of the common law willful blindness doctrine in the DMCA context.

"The principle that willful blindness is tantamount to knowledge is hardly novel." Tiffany (NJ) Inc. v. eBay, Inc., 600 F.3d 93, 110 n. 16 (2d Cir.2010) (collecting [676 F.3d 35] cases); see In re Aimster Copyright Litig., 33,4 F.3d 643 (7th Cir.2003) ("Willful blindness is knowledge, in copyright law ... as it is in the law generally."). A person is "willfully blind" or engages in "conscious avoidance" amounting to knowledge where the person " 'was aware of a high probability of the fact in dispute and consciously avoided confirming that fact.' " United States v. Aina-Marshall, 336 F.3d 167, 170 (2d Cir.2003) (quoting United States v. Rodriguez, 983 F.2d 455, 458 (2d Cir.1993)); cf. Global–Tech Appliances, Inc. v. SEB S.A., ––– U.S. ––––, 131 S.Ct. 2060, 2070–71, 179 L.Ed.2d 1167 (2011) (applying the willful blindness doctrine in a patent infringement case). Writing in the trademark infringement context, we have held that "[a] service provider is not ... permitted willful blindness. When it has reason to suspect that users of its service are infringing a protected mark, it may not shield itself from learning of the particular infringing transactions by looking the other way." Tiffany, 600 F.3d at 109.

The DMCA does not mention willful blindness. As a general matter, we interpret a statute to abrogate a common law principle only if the statute "speak[s] directly to the question addressed by the common law." Matar v. Dichter, 563 F.3d 9, 14 (2d Cir.2009) (internal quotation marks omitted). The relevant question, therefore, is whether the DMCA "speak[s] directly" to the principle of willful blindness. Id. (internal quotation marks omitted). The DMCA provision most relevant to the abrogation inquiry is § 512(m), which provides that safe harbor protection shall not be conditioned on "a service provider monitoring its service or affirmatively seeking facts indicating infringing activity, except to the extent consistent with a standard technical measure complying with the provisions of subsection (i)." 17 U.S.C. § 512(m)(1). Section 512(m) is explicit: DMCA safe harbor protection cannot be conditioned on affirmative monitoring by a service provider. For that reason, § 512(m) is incompatible with a broad common law duty to monitor or otherwise seek out infringing activity based on general awareness that infringement may be occurring. That fact does not, however, dispose of the abrogation inquiry; as previously noted, willful blindness cannot be defined as an affirmative duty to monitor. See Aina–Marshall, 336 F.3d at 170 (holding that a person is "willfully blind" where he "was aware of a high probability of the fact in dispute and consciously avoided confirming that fact"). Because the statute does not "speak[ ] directly" to the willful blindness doctrine, § 512(m) limits—but does not abrogate— the doctrine. Accordingly, we hold that the willful blindness doctrine may be applied, in appropriate circumstances, to demonstrate knowledge or awareness of specific instances of infringement under the DMCA.

The District Court cited § 512(m) for the proposition that safe harbor protection does not require affirmative monitoring, Viacom, 718 F.Supp.2d at 524, but did not expressly address the principle of willful blindness or its relationship to the DMCA safe harbors. As a result, whether the defendants made a "deliberate effort to avoid guilty knowledge," In re Aimster, 33,4 F.3d at 650, remains a fact question for the District Court to consider in the first instance on remand.

B. Control and Benefit: § 512(c)(1)(B)

Apart from the foregoing knowledge provisions, the § 512(c) safe harbor provides that an eligible service provider must "not receive a financial benefit directly attributable to the infringing activity, in a case in which the service provider has the right and ability to control such activity." 17 U.S.C. § 512(c)(1)(B). The District Court addressed this issue in a single paragraph, quoting from § 512(c)(1)(B), the so-called "control and benefit" provision, and concluding that "[t]he 'right and ability to control' the activity requires knowledge of it, which must be item-specific." Viacom, 718 F.Supp.2d at 527. For the reasons that follow, we hold that the District Court erred by importing a specific knowledge requirement into the control and benefit provision, and we therefore remand for further fact-finding on the issue of control.

1. "Right and Ability to Control" Infringing Activity

On appeal, the parties advocate two competing constructions of the "right and ability to control" infringing activity. 17 U.S.C. § 512(c)(1)(B). Because each is fatally flawed, we reject both proposed constructions in favor of a fact-based inquiry to be conducted in the first instance by the District Court.

The first construction, pressed by the defendants, is the one adopted by the District Court, which held that "the provider must know of the particular case before he can control it." Viacom, 718 F.Supp.2d at 527. The Ninth Circuit recently agreed, holding that "until [the service provider] becomes aware of specific unauthorized material, it cannot exercise its 'power or authority' over the specific infringing item. In practical terms, it does not have the kind of ability to control infringing activity the statute contemplates." UMG Recordings, Inc. v. Shelter Capital Partners LLC, 667 F.3d 1022, 1041 (9th Cir.2011). The trouble with this construction is that importing a specific knowledge requirement into § 512(c)(1)(B) renders the control provision duplicative of § 512(c)(1)(A). Any service provider that has item-specific knowledge of infringing activity and thereby obtains financial benefit would already be excluded from the safe harbor under § 512(c)(1)(A) for having specific knowledge of infringing material and failing to effect expeditious removal. No additional service provider would be excluded by § 512(c)(1)(B) that was not already excluded by § 512(c)(1)(A). Because statutory interpretations that render language superfluous are disfavored, Conn. ex rel. Blumenthal, 228 F.3d at 88, we reject the District Court's interpretation of the control provision.

The second construction, urged by the plaintiffs, is that the control provision codifies the common law doctrine of vicarious copyright liability. The common law imposes liability for vicarious copyright infringement "[w]hen the right and ability to supervise coalesce with an obvious and direct financial interest in the exploitation of copyrighted materials—even in the absence of actual knowledge that the copyright mono [poly] is being impaired." Shapiro, Bernstein & Co. v. H.L. Green Co., 316 F.2d 304, 307 (2d Cir.1963); cf. Metro–Goldwyn–Mayer Studios Inc. v. Grokster, Ltd., 545 U.S. 913, 930 n. 9, 125 S.Ct. 2764, 162 L.Ed.2d 781 (2005). To support their codification argument, the plaintiffs rely [676 F.3d 37] on a House Report relating to a preliminary version of the DMCA: "The 'right and ability to control' language ... codifies the second element of vicarious liability....

Subparagraph (B) is intended to preserve existing case law that examines all relevant aspects of the relationship between the primary and secondary infringer." H.R.Rep. No. 105–551(I), at 26 (1998). In response, YouTube notes that the codification reference was omitted from the committee reports describing the final legislation, and that Congress ultimately abandoned any attempt to "embark[ ] upon a wholesale clarification" of vicarious liability, electing instead "to create a series of 'safe harbors' for certain common activities of service providers." S.Rep. No. 105–190, at 19.

Happily, the future of digital copyright law does not turn on the confused legislative history of the control provision. The general rule with respect to common law codification is that when "Congress uses terms that have accumulated settled meaning under the common law, a court must infer, unless the statute otherwise dictates, that Congress means to incorporate the established meaning of those terms." Neder v. United States, 527 U.S. 1, 21, 119 S.Ct. 1827, 144 L.Ed.2d 35 (1999) (ellipsis and internal quotation marks omitted). Under the common law vicarious liability standard, " '[t]he ability to block infringers' access to a particular environment for any reason whatsoever is evidence of the right and ability to supervise.' " Arista Records LLC v. Usenet.com, Inc., 633 F.Supp.2d 124, 157 (S.D.N.Y.2009) (alteration in original) (quoting A & M Records, Inc. v. Napster, Inc., 239 F.3d 1004, 1023 (9th Cir.2001)). To adopt that principle in the DMCA context, however, would render the statute internally inconsistent. Section 512(c) actually presumes that service providers have the ability to "block ... access" to infringing material. Id. at 157; see Shelter Capital, 667 F.3d at 1042–43. Indeed, a service provider who has knowledge or awareness of infringing material or who receives a takedown notice from a copyright holder is required to "remove, or disable access to, the material" in order to claim the benefit of the safe harbor. 17 U.S.C. § 512(c)(1)(A)(iii) & (C). But in taking such action, the service provider would—in the plaintiffs' analysis—be admitting the "right and ability to control" the infringing material. Thus, the prerequisite to safe harbor protection under § 512(c)(1)(A)(iii) & (C) would at the same time be a disqualifier under § 512(c)(1)(B).

Moreover, if Congress had intended § 512(c)(1)(B) to be coextensive with vicarious liability, "the statute could have accomplished that result in a more direct manner." Shelter Capital, 667 F.3d at 1045.

It is conceivable that Congress ... intended that [service providers] which receive a financial benefit directly attributable to the infringing activity would not, under any circumstances, be able to qualify for the subsection (c) safe harbor. But if that was indeed their intention, it would have been far simpler and much more straightforward to simply say as much. Id. (alteration in original) (quoting Ellison v. Robertson, 189 F.Supp.2d 1051, 1061 (C.D.Cal.2002), aff'd in part and rev'd in part on different grounds, 357 F.3d 1072 (9th Cir.2004)).

In any event, the foregoing tension—elsewhere described as a "predicament" and a "catch22"—is sufficient to establish that the control provision "dictates" [676 F.3d 38] a departure from the common law vicarious liability standard, Neder, 527 U.S. at 21, 119 S.Ct. 1827. Accordingly, we conclude that the "right and ability to control" infringing activity under § 512(c)(1)(B) "requires something more than the ability to remove or block access to materials posted on a service provider's website." MP3tunes, LLC, 821 F.Supp.2d at 645, 2011 WL 5104616, at *14; accord Wolk v. Kodak Imaging Network, Inc., ––– F.Supp.2d ––––, ––––, 2012 WL 11270, at *21 (S.D.N.Y. Jan. 3, 2012); UMG II, 665 F.Supp.2d at 1114–15; Io Grp., Inc. v. Veoh Networks, Inc., 586 F.Supp.2d 1132, 1151 (N.D.Cal.2008); Corbis Corp. v. Amazon.com, Inc., 351 F.Supp.2d 1090, 1110 (W.D.Wash.2004), overruled on other grounds by Cosmetic Ideas, Inc. v. IAC/Interactivecorp., 606 F.3d 612 (9th Cir.2010). The remaining—and more difficult—question is how to define the "something more" that is required.

To date, only one court has found that a service provider had the right and ability to control infringing activity under § 512(c)(1)(B). In Perfect 10, Inc. v. Cybernet Ventures, Inc., 213 F.Supp.2d 1146 (C.D.Cal.2002), the court found control where the service provider instituted a monitoring program by which user websites received "detailed instructions regard[ing] issues of layout, appearance, and content." Id. at 1173. The service provider also forbade certain types of content and refused access to users who failed to comply with its instructions. Id. Similarly, inducement of copyright infringement under Metro–Goldwyn–Mayer Studios Inc. v. Grokster, Ltd., 545 U.S. 913, 125 S.Ct. 2764, 162 L.Ed.2d 781 (2005), which "premises liability on purposeful, culpable expression and conduct," id. at 937, 125 S.Ct. 2764, might also rise to the level of control under § 512(c)(1)(B). Both of these examples involve a service provider exerting substantial influence on the activities of users, without necessarily—or even frequently—acquiring knowledge of specific infringing activity.

In light of our holding that § 512(c)(1)(B) does not include a specific knowledge requirement, we think it prudent to remand to the District Court to consider in the first instance whether the plaintiffs have adduced sufficient evidence to allow a reasonable jury to conclude that YouTube had the right and ability to control the infringing activity and received a financial benefit directly attributable to that activity.

C. "By Reason of" Storage: § 512(c)(1)

The § 512(c) safe harbor is only available when the infringement occurs "by reason of the storage at the direction of a user of material that resides on a system or network controlled or operated by or for the service provider." 17 U.S.C. § 512(c)(1). In this case, the District Court held that YouTube's software functions fell within the safe harbor for infringements that occur "by reason of" user storage. Viacom, 718 F.Supp.2d at 526 (noting that a contrary holding would "confine[ ] the word 'storage' too narrowly to meet the statute's purpose"). For the reasons that follow, we affirm that holding [676 F.3d 39] with respect to three of the challenged software functions—the conversion (or "transcoding") of videos into a standard display format, the playback of videos on "watch" pages, and the "related videos" function. We remand for further fact-finding with respect to a fourth software function, involving the third-party syndication of videos uploaded to YouTube.

As a preliminary matter, we note that "the structure and language of OCILLA indicate that service providers seeking safe harbor under [§] 512(c) are not limited to merely storing material." Io Grp., 586 F.Supp.2d at 1147. The structure of the statute distinguishes between so-called "conduit only" functions under § 512(a) and the functions addressed by § 512(c) and the other subsections. See 17 U.S.C. § 512(n) ("Subsections (a), (b), (c), and (d) describe separate and distinct functions for purposes of applying this section."). Most notably, OCILLA contains two definitions of "service provider." 17 U.S.C. § 512(k)(1)(A)-(B). The narrower definition, which applies only to service providers falling under § 512(a), is limited to entities that "offer[ ] the transmission, routing or providing of connections for digital online communications, between or among points specified by a user, of material of the user's choosing, without modification to the content of the material as sent or received." Id. § 512(k)(1)(A) (emphasis added). No such limitation appears in the broader definition, which applies to service providers—including YouTube—falling under § 512(c). Under the broader definition, "the term 'service provider' means a provider of online services or network access, or the operator of facilities therefor, and includes an entity described in subparagraph (A)." Id. § 512(k)(1)(B). In the absence of a parallel limitation on the ability of a service provider to modify user-submitted material, we conclude that § 512(c) "is clearly meant to cover more than mere electronic storage lockers." UMG Recordings, Inc. v. Veoh Networks, Inc., 620 F.Supp.2d 1081, 1088 (C.D.Cal.2008) ("UMG I").

The relevant case law makes clear that the § 512(c) safe harbor extends to software functions performed "for the purpose of facilitating access to user-stored material." Id.; see Shelter Capital, 667 F.3d at 1031–35. Two of the software functions challenged here—transcoding and playback—were expressly considered by our sister Circuit in Shelter Capital, which held that liability arising from these functions occurred "by reason of the storage at the direction of a user." 17 U.S.C. § 512(c); see Shelter Capital, 667 F.3d at 1027–28, 1031; see also UMG I, 620 F.Supp.2d at 1089–91; Io Group, 586 F.Supp.2d at 1146–48. Transcoding involves "[m]aking copies of a video in a different encoding scheme" in order to render the video "viewable over the Internet to most users." Supp. Joint App'x I:236. The playback process involves "deliver[ing] copies of YouTube videos to a user's browser cache" in response to a user request. Id. at 239. The District Court correctly found that to exclude these automated functions from the safe harbor would eviscerate the protection afforded to service providers by § 512(c). Viacom, 718 F.Supp.2d at 526–27.

A similar analysis applies to the "related videos" function, by which a YouTube computer algorithm identifies and displays "thumbnails" of clips that are "related" to the video selected by the user. The plaintiffs claim that this practice constitutes content promotion, not "access" to stored content, and therefore falls beyond the scope of the safe harbor. Citing similar language in the Racketeer Influenced and Corrupt Organizations Act ("RICO"), 18 U.S.C. §§ 1961–68, and the Clayton [676 F.3d 40] Act, 15 U.S.C. §§ 12 et seq., the plaintiffs argue that the statutory phrase "by reason of" requires a finding of proximate causation between the act of storage and the infringing activity. See, e.g., Holmes v. Sec. Investor Prot. Corp., 503 U.S. 258, 267–68, 112 S.Ct. 1311, 117 L.Ed.2d 532 (1992) (holding that the "by reason of" language in the RICO statute requires proximate causation). But even if the plaintiffs are correct that § 512(c) incorporates a principle of proximate causation—a question we need not resolve here—the indexing and display of related videos retain a sufficient causal link to the prior storage of those videos. The record makes clear that the related videos algorithm "is fully automated and operates solely in response to user input without the active involvement of YouTube employees." Supp. Joint App'x I:237. Furthermore, the related videos function serves to help YouTube users locate and gain access to material stored at the direction of other users. Because the algorithm "is closely related to, and follows from, the storage itself," and is "narrowly directed toward providing access to material stored at the direction of users," UMG I, 620 F.Supp.2d at 1092, we conclude that the related videos function is also protected by the § 512(c) safe harbor.

The final software function at issue here—third-party syndication—is the closest case. In or around March 2007, YouTube transcoded a select number of videos into a format compatible with mobile devices and "syndicated" or licensed the videos to Verizon Wireless and other companies. The plaintiffs argue—with some force— that business transactions do not occur at the "direction of a user" within the meaning of § 512(c)(1) when they involve the manual selection of copyrighted material for licensing to a third party. The parties do not dispute, however, that none of the clips-in-suit were among the approximately 2,000 videos provided to Verizon Wireless. In order to avoid rendering an advisory opinion on the outer boundaries of the storage provision, we remand for fact-finding on the question of whether any of the clips-in-suit were in fact syndicated to any other third party.

D. Other Arguments

1. Repeat Infringer Policy

The class plaintiffs briefly argue that YouTube failed to comply with the requirements of § 512(i), which conditions safe harbor eligibility on the service provider having "adopted and reasonably implemented ... a policy that provides for the termination in appropriate circumstances of subscribers and account holders of the service provider's system or network who are repeat infringers." 17 U.S.C. § 512(i)(1)(A). Specifically, the class plaintiffs allege that YouTube "deliberately set up its identification tools to try to avoid identifying infringements of class plaintiffs' works." This allegation rests primarily on the assertion that YouTube permitted only designated "partners" to gain access to content identification tools by which YouTube would conduct network searches and identify infringing material.[14]

Because the class plaintiffs challenge YouTube's deployment of search technology, [676 F.3d 41] we must consider their § 512(i) argument in conjunction with § 512(m). As previously noted, § 512(m) provides that safe harbor protection cannot be conditioned on "a service provider monitoring its service or affirmatively seeking facts indicating infringing activity, except to the extent consistent with a standard technical measure complying with the provisions of subsection (i)." 17 U.S.C. § 512(m)(1) (emphasis added). In other words, the safe harbor expressly disclaims any affirmative monitoring requirement—except to the extent that such monitoring comprises a "standard technical measure" within the meaning of § 512(i). Refusing to accommodate or implement a "standard technical measure" exposes a service provider to liability; refusing to provide access to mechanisms by which a service provider affirmatively monitors its own network has no such result.

In this case, the class plaintiffs make no argument that the content identification tools implemented by YouTube constitute "standard technical measures," such that YouTube would be exposed to liability under § 512(i). For that reason, YouTube cannot be excluded from the safe harbor by dint of a decision to restrict access to its proprietary search mechanisms.

2. Affirmative Claims

Finally, the plaintiffs argue that the District Court erred in denying summary judgment to the plaintiffs on their claims of direct infringement, vicarious liability, and contributory liability under Metro–Goldwyn–Mayer Studios Inc. v. Grokster, Ltd., 545 U.S. 913, 125 S.Ct. 2764, 162 L.Ed.2d 781 (2005). In granting summary judgment to the defendants, the District Court held that YouTube "qualif[ied] for the protection of ... § 512(c)," and therefore denied the plaintiffs' cross-motion for summary judgment without comment. Viacom, 718 F.Supp.2d at 529.

The District Court correctly determined that a finding of safe harbor application necessarily protects a defendant from all affirmative claims for monetary relief. 17 U.S.C. § 512(c)(1); see H.R.Rep. No. 105–551(II), at 50; S.Rep. No. 105–190, at 20; cf. 17 U.S.C. § 512(j) (setting forth the scope of injunctive relief available under § 512). For the reasons previously stated, further fact-finding is required to determine whether YouTube is ultimately entitled to safe harbor protection in this case. Accordingly, we vacate the order denying summary judgment to the plaintiffs and remand the cause without expressing a view on the merits of the plaintiffs' affirmative claims.

CONCLUSION

To summarize, we hold that:

(1) The District Court correctly held that 17 U.S.C. § 512(c)(1)(A) requires knowledge or awareness of facts or circumstances that indicate specific and identifiable instances of infringement;

(2) However, the June 23, 2010 order granting summary judgment to YouTube is VACATED because a reasonable jury could conclude that YouTube had knowledge or awareness under § 512(c)(1)(A) at least with respect to a handful of specific clips; the cause is REMANDED for the District Court to determine whether YouTube had knowledge or awareness of any specific instances of infringement corresponding to the clips-in-suit;

(3) The willful blindness doctrine may be applied, in appropriate circumstances, to demonstrate knowledge or awareness of specific instances of infringement under § 512(c)(1)(A); the cause is REMANDED for the [676 F.3d 42] District Court to consider the application of the willful blindness doctrine in the first instance;

(4) The District Court erred by requiring "item-specific" knowledge of infringement in its interpretation of the "right and ability to control" infringing activity under 17 U.S.C. § 512(c)(1)(B), and the judgment is REVERSED insofar as it rests on that erroneous construction of the statute; the cause is REMANDED for further fact-finding by the District Court on the issues of control and financial benefit;

(5) The District Court correctly held that three of the challenged YouTube software functions—replication, playback, and the related videos feature—occur "by reason of the storage at the direction of a user" within the meaning of 17 U.S.C. § 512(c)(1), and the judgment is AFFIRMED insofar as it so held; the cause is REMANDED for further fact-finding regarding a fourth software function, involving the syndication of YouTube videos to third parties.

On remand, the District Court shall allow the parties to brief the following issues, with a view to permitting renewed motions for summary judgment as soon as practicable:

(A) Whether, on the current record, YouTube had knowledge or awareness of any specific infringements (including any clips-in-suit not expressly noted in this opinion);

(B) Whether, on the current record, YouTube willfully blinded itself to specific infringements;

(C) Whether YouTube had the "right and ability to control" infringing activity within the meaning of § 512(c)(1)(B); and

(D) Whether any clips-in-suit were syndicated to a third party and, if so, whether such syndication occurred "by reason of the storage at the direction of the user" within the meaning of § 512(c)(1), so that YouTube may claim the protection of the § 512(c) safe harbor.

We leave to the sound discretion of the District Court the question of whether some additional, guided discovery is appropriate in order to resolve "(C)" ("[w]hether YouTube had 'the right and ability to control' infringing activity"), and "(D)" ("[w]hether any clips-in-suit were syndicated to a third party"). As noted above, for purposes of this case, the record with respect to "(A)" ("[w]hether ... YouTube had knowledge or awareness of any specific infringements") and "(B)" ("[w]hether. YouTube willfully blinded itself to specific infringements") is now complete.

Each party shall bear its own costs.

APPENDIX ARELEVANT PROVISIONS OF THE DIGITAL MILLENNIUM COPYRIGHT ACT 17 U.S.C. § 512

(c) Information residing on systems or networks at direction of users.—

(1) In general.—A service provider shall not be liable for monetary relief, or, except as provided in subsection (j), for injunctive or other equitable relief, for infringement of copyright by reason of the storage at the direction of a user of material that resides on a system or network controlled or operated by or for the service provider, if the service provider—

(A) (i) does not have actual knowledge that the material or an activity using the material on the system or network is infringing;

[676 F.3d 43] (ii) in the absence of such actual knowledge, is not aware of facts or circumstances from which infringing activity is apparent; or

(iii) upon obtaining such knowledge or awareness, acts expeditiously to remove, or disable access to, the material;

(B) does not receive a financial benefit directly attributable to the infringing activity, in a case in which the service provider has the right and ability to control such activity; and

(C) upon notification of claimed infringement as described in paragraph (3), responds expeditiously to remove, or disable access to, the material that is claimed to be infringing or to be the subject of infringing activity.

(2) Designated agent.—The limitations on liability established in this subsection apply to a service provider only if the service provider has designated an agent to receive notifications of claimed infringement described in paragraph (3), by making available through its service, including on its website in a location accessible to the public, and by providing to the Copyright Office, substantially the following information:

(A) the name, address, phone number, and electronic mail address of the agent.

(B) other contact information which the Register of Copyrights may deem appropriate.

The Register of Copyrights shall maintain a current directory of agents available to the public for inspection, including through the Internet, and may require payment of a fee by service providers to cover the costs of maintaining the directory.

(3) Elements of notification.—

(A) To be effective under this subsection, a notification of claimed infringement must be a written communication provided to the designated agent of a service provider that includes substantially the following:

(i) A physical or electronic signature of a person authorized to act on behalf of the owner of an exclusive right that is allegedly infringed.

(ii) Identification of the copyrighted work claimed to have been infringed, or, if multiple copyrighted works at a single online site are covered by a single notification, a representative list of such works at that site.

(iii) Identification of the material that is claimed to be infringing or to be the subject of infringing activity and that is to be removed or access to which is to be disabled, and information reasonably sufficient to permit the service provider to locate the material.

(vi) Information reasonably sufficient to permit the service provider to contact the complaining party, such as an address, telephone number, and, if available, an electronic mail address at which the complaining party may be contacted.

(iv) A statement that the complaining party has a good faith belief that use of the material in the manner complained of is not authorized by the copyright owner, its agent, or the law.

(v) A statement that the information in the notification is accurate, and under penalty of perjury, that the complaining party is authorized to act on behalf of the owner of an exclusive right that is allegedly infringed.

(B)(i) Subject to clause (ii), a notification from a copyright owner or from a person authorized to act on behalf of the copyright owner that fails to comply substantially with the provisions of subparagraph

[676 F.3d 44] (A) shall not be considered under paragraph (1)(A) in determining whether a service provider has actual knowledge or is aware of facts or circumstances from which infringing activity is apparent.

(ii) In a case in which the notification that is provided to the service provider's designated agent fails to comply substantially with all the provisions of subparagraph (A) but substantially complies with clauses (ii), (iii), and (iv) of subparagraph (A), clause (i) of this subparagraph applies only if the service provider promptly attempts to contact the person making the notification or takes other reasonable steps to assist in the receipt of notification that substantially complies with all the provisions of subparagraph (A).

(i) Conditions for Eligibility.—

(1) Accommodation of technology.—The limitations on liability established by this section shall apply to a service provider only if the service provider—

(A) has adopted and reasonably implemented, and informs subscribers and account holders of the service provider's system or network of, a policy that provides for the termination in appropriate circumstances of subscribers and account holders of the service provider's system or network who are repeat infringers; and

(B) accommodates and does not interfere with standard technical measures.

(2) Definition.—As used in this subsection, the term "standard technical measures" means technical measures that are used by copyright owners to identify or protect copyrighted works and—

(A) have been developed pursuant to a broad consensus of copyright owners and service providers in an open, fair, voluntary, multi-industry standards process;

(B) are available to any person on reasonable and nondiscriminatory terms; and

(C) do not impose substantial costs on service providers or substantial burdens on their systems or networks.

(k) Definitions.—

(1) Service provider.—

(A) As used in subsection (a), the term "service provider" means an entity offering the transmission, routing, or providing of connections for digital online communications, between or among points specified by a user, of material of the user's choosing, without modification to the content of the material as sent or received.

(B) As used in this section, other than subsection (a), the term "service provider" means a provider of online services or network access, or the operator of facilities therefor, and includes an entity described in subparagraph (A).

(2) Monetary relief.—As used in this section, the term "monetary relief" means damages, costs, attorneys' fees, and any other form of monetary payment.

(m) Protection of privacy.—Nothing in this section shall be construed to condition the applicability of subsections (a) through (d) on—

(1) a service provider monitoring its service or affirmatively seeking facts indicating infringing activity, except to the extent consistent with a standard technical measure complying with the provisions of subsection (i); or

(2) a service provider gaining access to, removing, or disabling access to material [676 F.3d 45] in cases in which such conduct is prohibited by law.

(n) Construction.—

Subsections (a), (b), (c), and (d) describe separate and distinct functions for purposes of applying this section. Whether a service provider qualifies for the limitation on liability in any one of those subsections shall be based solely on the criteria in that subsection, and shall not affect a determination of whether that service provider qualifies for the limitations on liability under any other such subsection.

508 F.3d 1146 (2007)

PERFECT 10, INC. v. GOOGLE INC

US Court of Appeals of the Ninth Circuit

IKUTA, Circuit Judge:

In this appeal, we consider a copyright owner's efforts to stop an Internet search engine from facilitating access to infringing images. Perfect 10, Inc. sued Google Inc., for infringing Perfect 10's copyrighted photographs of nude models, among other claims... The district court preliminarily enjoined Google from creating and publicly displaying thumbnail versions of Perfect 10's images, but did not enjoin Google from linking to third-party websites that display infringing full-size versions of Perfect 10's images. ... Perfect 10 and Google both appeal the district court's order. We have jurisdiction pursuant to 28 U.S.C. § 1292(a)(1).

The district court handled this complex case in a particularly thoughtful and skillful manner. Nonetheless, the district court erred on certain issues, as we will further explain below. We affirm in part, reverse in part, and remand.

I

Background

Google's computers, along with millions of others, are connected to networks known collec- tively as the "Internet." "The Internet is a world-wide network of

593

networks . . . all sharing a common communications technology." Computer owners can provide information stored on their computers to other users connected to the Internet through a medium called a webpage. A webpage consists of text interspersed with instructions written in Hypertext Markup Language ("HTML") that is stored in a computer. No images are stored on a webpage; rather, the HTML instructions on the webpage provide an address for where the images are stored, whether in the webpage publisher's computer or some other computer. In general, webpages are publicly available and can be accessed by computers connected to the Internet through the use of a web browser.

Google operates a search engine, a software program that automatically accesses thousands of websites (collections of webpages) and indexes them within a database stored on Google's computers. When a Google user accesses the Google website and types in a search query, Google's soft- ware searches its database for websites responsive to that search query. Google then sends relevant information from its index of websites to the user's computer. Google's search engines can provide results in the form of text, images, or videos.

The Google search engine that provides responses in the form of images is called "Google Image Search." In response to a search query, Google Image Search identifies text in its database re- sponsive to the query and then communicates to users the images associated with the relevant text. Google's software cannot recognize and index the images themselves. Google Image Search provides search results as a webpage of small images called "thumbnails," which are stored in Google's servers. The thumbnail images are reduced, lower-resolution versions of full-sized images stored on third-party computers.

When a user clicks on a thumbnail image, the user's browser program interprets HTML instruc- tions on Google's webpage. These HTML instructions direct the user's browser to cause a rectangular area (a "window") to appear on the user's computer screen. The window has two separate areas of information. The browser fills the top section of the screen with information from the Google webpage, including the thumbnail image and text. The HTML instructions also give the user's browser the address of the website publisher's computer that stores the full-size version of the thumbnail. By following the HTML instructions to access the third-party webpage, the user's browser connects to the website publisher's computer, downloads the full-size image, and makes the image appear at the bottom of the window on the user's screen. Google does not store the images that fill this lower part of the window and does not communicate the images to the user; Google simply provides HTML instructions directing a user's browser to access a third-party web- site. However, the top part of the window (containing the information from the Google webpage) appears to frame and comment on the bottom part of the window. Thus, the user's window appears to be filled with a single integrated presentation of the full-size image, but it is actually an image from a third-party website framed by information from Google's website. The process by which the webpage directs a user's browser to incorporate content from different computers into a single win- dow is referred to as "in-line linking." Kelly v. Arriba Soft Corp., 336 F.3d 811, 816 (9th Cir. 2003). The term "framing" refers to the process by which information from one computer appears to frame and annotate the in-line linked content from another computer.

Google also stores webpage content in its cache. For each cached webpage, Google's cache contains the text of the webpage as it appeared at the time Google indexed the page, but does not store images from the webpage. Google may provide a link to a cached webpage in response to a user's search query. However, Google's cache version of the webpage is not automatically updated when the webpage is revised by its owner. So if the webpage owner updates its webpage to remove the HTML instructions for finding an infringing image, a browser communicating directly with the webpage would not be able to access that image. However, Google's cache copy of the webpage would still have the old HTML instructions for the infringing image. Unless the owner of the com- puter changed the HTML address of the infringing image, or otherwise rendered the image unavail- able, a browser accessing Google's cache copy of the website could still access the image where it is stored on the website publisher's computer. In other words, Google's cache copy could provide a user's browser with valid directions to an infringing image even though the updated webpage no longer includes that infringing image.

In addition to its search engine operations, Google generates revenue through a business pro- gram called "AdSense." Under this program, the owner of a website can register with Google to become an AdSense "partner." The website owner then places HTML instructions on its webpages that signal Google's server to place advertising on the webpages that is relevant to the webpages' content. Google's computer program selects the advertising automatically by means of an algorithm. AdSense participants agree to share the revenues that flow from such advertising with Google.

...

Perfect 10 markets and sells copyrighted images of nude models. Among other enterprises, it operates a subscription website on the Internet. Subscribers pay a monthly fee to view Perfect 10 images in a "members'" area of the site. Subscribers must use a password to log into the members' area. Google does not include these password-protected images from the members' area in Google's index or database. Perfect 10 has also licensed Fonestarz Media Limited to sell and distribute Per-fect 10's reduced-size copyrighted images for download and use on cell phones.

Some website publishers republish Perfect 10's images on the Internet without authorization. Once this occurs, Google's search engine may automatically index the webpages containing these images and provide thumbnail versions of images in response to user inquiries. When a user clicks on the thumbnail image returned by Google's search engine, the user's browser accesses the third- party webpage and in-line links to the full-sized infringing image stored on the website publisher's computer. This image appears, in its original context, on the lower portion of the window on the user's computer screen framed by information from Google's webpage.

Procedural History. In May 2001, Perfect 10 began notifying Google that its thumbnail images and in-line linking to the full-size images infringed Perfect 10's copyright. Perfect 10 continued to send these notices through 2005.

On November 19, 2004, Perfect 10 filed an action against Google that included copyright infringement claims. This was followed by a similar action against Amazon.com on June 29, 2005. On July 1, 2005 and August 24, 2005, Perfect 10 sought a preliminary injunction to prevent Amazon.com and Google, respectively, from "copying, reproducing, distributing, publicly displaying, adapting or otherwise infringing, or contributing to the infringement" of Perfect 10's photographs; linking to websites that provide full-size infringing versions of Perfect 10's photographs; and infringing Perfect 10's username/password combinations.

The district court consolidated the two actions and heard both preliminary injunction motions on November 7, 2005. The district court issued orders granting in part and denying in part the preliminary injunction against Google and denying the preliminary injunction against Amazon.com. Perfect 10 and Google cross-appealed the partial grant and partial denial of the preliminary injunction motion, and Perfect 10 appealed the denial of the preliminary injunction against Amazon.com. On June 15, 2006, the district court temporarily stayed the preliminary injunction.

...

III

Direct Infringement

Perfect 10 claims that Google's search engine program directly infringes two exclusive rights granted to copyright holders: its display rights and its distribution rights. "Plaintiffs must satisfy two requirements to present a prima facie case of direct infringement: (1) they must show ownership of the allegedly infringed material and (2) they must demonstrate that the alleged infringers violate at least one exclusive right granted to copyright holders under 17 U.S.C. § 106." Even if a plaintiff satisfies these two requirements and makes a prima facie case of direct infringement, the defendant may avoid liability if it can establish that its use of the images is a "fair use" as set forth in 17 U.S.C. § 107.

Perfect 10's ownership of at least some of the images at issue is not disputed.

The district court held that Perfect 10 was likely to prevail in its claim that Google violated Perfect 10's display right with respect to the infringing thumbnails. However, the district court con- cluded that Perfect 10 was not likely to prevail on its claim that Google violated either Perfect 10's display or distribution right with respect to its full-size infringing images. We review these rulings for an abuse of discretion.

A. Display Right

In considering whether Perfect 10 made a prima facie case of violation of its display right, the district court reasoned that a computer owner that stores an image as electronic information and serves that electronic information directly to the user ("i.e., physically sending ones and zeroes over the [I]nternet to the user's browser," is displaying the electronic information in violation of a copyright holder's exclusive display right. Conversely, the owner of a computer that does not store and serve the electronic information to a user is not displaying that information, even if such owner in- line links to or frames the electronic information. The district court referred to this test as the "server test."

Applying the server test, the district court concluded that Perfect 10 was likely to succeed in its claim that Google's thumbnails constituted direct infringement but was unlikely to succeed in its claim that Google's in-line linking to full-size infringing images constituted a direct infringement. As explained below, because this analysis comports with the language of the Copyright Act, we agree with the district court's resolution of both these issues.

We have not previously addressed the question when a computer displays a copyrighted work for purposes of section 106(5). Section 106(5) states that a copyright owner has the exclusive right "to display the copyrighted work publicly." The Copyright Act explains that "display" means "to show a copy of it, either directly or by means of a film, slide, television image, or any other device or process . . . ." 17 U.S.C. § 101. Section 101 defines "copies" as "material objects, other than phonorecords, in which a work is fixed by any method now known or later developed, and from which the work can be perceived, reproduced, or otherwise communicated, either directly or with the aid of a machine or device." Finally, the Copyright Act provides that "[a] work is 'fixed' in a tangible medium of expression when its embodiment in a copy or phonorecord, by or under the authority of the author, is sufficiently permanent or stable to permit it to be perceived, reproduced, or otherwise communicated for a period of more than transitory duration."

We must now apply these definitions to the facts of this case. A photographic image is a work that is "'fixed' in a tangible medium of expression," for purposes of the Copyright Act, when embodied (i.e., stored) in a computer's server (or hard disk, or other storage device). The image stored in the computer is the "copy" of the work for purposes of copyright law. See MAI Sys. Corp. v. Peak Computer, Inc., 991 F.2d 511, 517-18 (9th Cir. 1993) (a computer makes a "copy" of a software program when it transfers the program from a third party's computer (or other storage device) into its own memory, because the copy of the program recorded in the computer is "fixed" in a manner that is "sufficiently permanent or stable to permit it to be perceived, reproduced, or otherwise com- municated for a period of more than transitory duration" (quoting 17 U.S.C. § 101)). The computer owner shows a copy "by means of a . . . device or process" when the owner uses the computer to fill the computer screen with the photographic image stored on that computer, or by communicating the stored image electronically to another person's computer. 17 U.S.C. § 101. In sum, based on the plain language of the statute, a person displays a photographic image by using a computer to fill a computer screen with a copy of the photographic image fixed in the computer's memory. There is no dispute that Google's computers store thumbnail versions of Perfect 10's copyrighted images and communicate copies of those thumbnails to Google's users. Therefore, Perfect 10 has made a prima facie case that Google's communication of its stored thumbnail images directly infringes Perfect 10's display right.

Google does not, however, display a copy of full-size infringing photographic images for purposes of the Copyright Act when Google frames in-line linked images that appear on a user's computer screen. Because Google's computers do not store the photographic images, Google does not have a copy of the images for purposes of the Copyright Act. In other words, Google does not have any "material objects . . . in which a work is fixed . . . and from which the work can be perceived, reproduced, or otherwise communicated" and thus cannot communicate a copy. 17 U.S.C. § 101.

Instead of communicating a copy of the image, Google provides HTML instructions that direct a user's browser to a website publisher's computer that stores the full-size photographic image. Pro- viding these HTML instructions is not equivalent to showing a copy. First, the HTML instructions are lines of text, not a photographic image. Second, HTML instructions do not themselves cause infringing images to appear on the user's computer screen. The HTML merely gives the address of the image to the user's browser. The browser then interacts with the computer that stores the infringing image. It is this interaction that causes an infringing image to appear on the user's computer screen. Google may facilitate the user's access to infringing images. However, such assistance raises only contributory liability issues, and does not constitute direct infringement of the copyright owner's display rights.

Perfect 10 argues that Google displays a copy of the full-size images by framing the full-size images, which gives the impression that Google is showing the image within a single Google webpage. While in-line linking and framing may cause some computer users to believe they are viewing a single Google webpage, the Copyright Act, unlike the Trademark Act, does not protect a copy- right holder against acts that cause consumer confusion. Cf. 15 U.S.C. § 1114(1) (providing that a person who uses a trademark in a manner likely to cause confusion shall be liable in a civil action to the trademark registrant).

Nor does our ruling that a computer owner does not display a copy of an image when it commu- nicates only the HTML address of the copy erroneously collapse the display right in section 106(5) into the reproduction right set forth in section 106(1). Nothing in the Copyright Act prevents the various rights protected in section 106 from overlapping. Indeed, under some circumstances, more than one right must be infringed in order for an infringement claim to arise. For example, a "Game Genie" device that allowed a player to alter features of a Nintendo computer game did not infringe Nintendo's right to prepare derivative works because the Game Genie did not incorporate any portion of the game itself. See Lewis Galoob Toys, Inc. v. Nintendo of Am., Inc., 964 F.2d 965, 967 (9th Cir. 1992). We held that a copyright holder's right to create derivative works is not infringed unless the alleged derivative work "incorporate[s] a protected work in some concrete or permanent 'form.'" In other words, in some contexts, the claimant must be able to claim infringement of its reproduc- tion right in order to claim infringement of its right to prepare derivative works.

Because Google's cache merely stores the text of webpages, our analysis of whether Google's search engine program potentially infringes Perfect 10's display and distribution rights is equally applicable to Google's cache. Perfect 10 is not likely to succeed in showing that a cached webpage that in-line links to full-size infringing images violates such rights. For purposes of this analysis, it is irrelevant whether cache copies direct a user's browser to third-party images that are no longer available on the third party's website, because it is the website publisher's computer, rather than Google's computer, that stores and displays the infringing image.

B. Distribution Right

The district court also concluded that Perfect 10 would not likely prevail on its claim that Google directly infringed Perfect 10's right to distribute its full-size images. The district court reasoned that distribution requires an "actual dissemination" of a copy. Because Google did not communicate the full-size images to the user's computer, Google did not distribute these images.

Again, the district court's conclusion on this point is consistent with the language of the Copyright Act. Section 106(3) provides that the copyright owner has the exclusive right "to distribute copies or phonorecords of the copyrighted work to the public by sale or other transfer of ownership, or by rental, lease, or lending." 17 U.S.C. § 106(3). As noted, "copies" means "material objects . . . in which a work is fixed." 17 U.S.C. § 101. The Supreme Court has indicated that in the electronic context, copies may be distributed electronically. See N.Y. Times Co. v. Tasini, 533 U.S. 483, 498, (2001) (a computer database program distributed copies of newspaper articles stored in its computerized database by selling copies of those articles through its database service). Google's search engine communicates HTML instructions that tell a user's browser where to find full-size images on a website publisher's computer, but Google does not itself distribute copies of the infringing photographs. It is the website publisher's computer that distributes copies of the images by transmitting the photographic image electronically to the user's computer. As in Tasini, the user can then obtain copies by downloading the photo or printing it.

Perfect 10 incorrectly relies on Hotaling v. Church of Jesus Christ of Latter-Day Saints and Napster for the proposition that merely making images "available" violates the copyright owner's distribution right. Hotaling v. Church of Jesus Christ of Latter-Day Saints, 118 F.3d 199 (4th Cir. 1997); Napster, 239 F.3d 1004. Hotaling held that the owner of a collection of works who makes them available to the public may be deemed to have distributed copies of the works. Similarly, the distribution rights of the plaintiff copyright owners were infringed by Napster users (private indi-viduals with collections of music files stored on their home computers) when they used the Napster software to make their collections available to all other Napster users.

This "deemed distribution" rule does not apply to Google. Unlike the participants in the Napster system or the library in Hotaling, Google does not own a collection of Perfect 10's full-size images and does not communicate these images to the computers of people using Google's search engine. Though Google indexes these images, it does not have a collection of stored full-size images it makes available to the public. Google therefore cannot be deemed to distribute copies of these images under the reasoning of Napster or Hotaling. Accordingly, the district court correctly concluded that Perfect 10 does not have a likelihood of success in proving that Google violates Per- fect 10's distribution rights with respect to full-size images.

C. Fair Use Defense

Because Perfect 10 has succeeded in showing it would prevail in its prima facie case that Google's thumbnail images infringe Perfect 10's display rights, the burden shifts to Google to show that it will likely succeed in establishing an affirmative defense. Google contends that its use of thumb- nails is a fair use of the images and therefore does not constitute an infringement of Perfect 10's copyright. See 17 U.S.C. § 107.

...

In applying the fair use analysis in this case, we are guided by Kelly v. Arriba Soft Corp., which considered substantially the same use of copyrighted photographic images as is at issue here. In Kelly, a photographer brought a direct infringement claim against Arriba, the operator of an Internet search engine. The search engine provided thumbnail versions of the photographer's images in response to search queries. We held that Arriba's use of thumbnail images was a fair use primarily based on the transformative nature of a search engine and its benefit to the public. We also concluded that Arriba's use of the thumbnail images did not harm the photographer's market for his image.

In this case, the district court determined that Google's use of thumbnails was not a fair use and distinguished Kelly. We consider these distinctions in the context of the four-factor fair use analysis.

Purpose and character of the use. The first factor, 17 U.S.C. § 107(1), requires a court to con- sider "the purpose and character of the use, including whether such use is of a commercial nature or is for nonprofit educational purposes." The central purpose of this inquiry is to determine whether and to what extent the new work is "transformative." A work is "transformative" when the new work does not "merely supersede the objects of the original creation" but rather "adds something new, with a further purpose or different character, altering the first with new expression, meaning, or message." Conversely, if the new work "supersede[s] the use of the original," the use is likely not a fair use. Harper & Row Publishers, Inc. v. Nation Enters., 471 U.S. 539, 550-51, 105 S. Ct. 2218, 85 L. Ed. 2d 588 (1985) (internal quotation omitted) (publishing the "heart" of an unpublished work and thus supplanting the copyright holder's first publication right was not a fair use); see also Wall Data Inc. v. L.A. County Sheriff's Dep't, 447 F.3d 769, 778-82 (9th

Cir. 2006) (using a copy to save the cost of buying additional copies of a computer program was not a fair use).

As noted in Campbell, a "transformative work" is one that alters the original work "with new expression, meaning, or message." "A use is considered transformative only where a de- fendant changes a plaintiff's copyrighted work or uses the plaintiff's copyrighted work in a different context such that the plaintiff's work is transformed into a new creation."

Google's use of thumbnails is highly transformative. In Kelly, we concluded that Arriba's use of thumbnails was transformative because "Arriba's use of the images serve[d] a different function than Kelly's use--improving access to information on the [I]nternet versus artistic expression." Although an image may have been created originally to serve an entertainment, aesthetic, or informative function, a search engine transforms the image into a pointer directing a user to a source of information. Just as a "parody has an obvious claim to transformative value" because "it can provide social benefit, by shedding light on an earlier work, and, in the process, creating a new one," Campbell, 510 U.S. at 579, a search engine provides social benefit by incorporating an original work into a new work, namely, an electronic reference tool. Indeed, a search engine may be more transforma- tive than a parody because a search engine provides an entirely new use for the original work, while a parody typically has the same entertainment purpose as the original work. See, e.g., id. at 594-96 (holding that 2 Live Crew's parody of "Oh, Pretty Woman" using the words "hairy woman" or "bald headed woman" was a transformative work, and thus constituted a fair use); Mattel, Inc. v. Walking Mountain Prods., 353 F.3d 792, 796-98, 800-06 (9th Cir 2003) (concluding that photos parodying Barbie by depicting "nude Barbie dolls juxtaposed with vintage kitchen appliances" was a fair use). In other words, a search engine puts images "in a different context" so that they are "transformed into a new creation." Wall Data, 447 F.3d at 778.

The fact that Google incorporates the entire Perfect 10 image into the search engine results does not diminish the transformative nature of Google's use. As the district court correctly noted, we determined in Kelly that even making an exact copy of a work may be transformative so long as the copy serves a different function than the original work. For example, the First Circuit has held that the republication of photos taken for a modeling portfolio in a newspaper was transformative be- cause the photos served to inform, as well as entertain. See Nez v. Caribbean Int'l News Corp., 235 F.3d 18, 22-23 (1st Cir. 2000). In contrast, duplicating a church's religious book for use by a differ- ent church was not transformative. See Worldwide Church of God v. Phila. Church of God, Inc., 227 F.3d 1110, 1117 (9th Cir. 2000). Nor was a broadcaster's simple retransmission of a radio broadcast over telephone lines transformative, where the original radio shows were given no "new expression, meaning, or message." Infinity Broad. Corp. v. Kirkwood, 150 F.3d 104, 108 (2d Cir. 1998). Here, Google uses Perfect 10's images in a new context to serve a different purpose.

The district court nevertheless determined that Google's use of thumbnail images was less trans- formative than Arriba's use of thumbnails in Kelly because Google's use of thumbnails superseded Perfect 10's right to sell its reduced-size images for use on cell phones. The district court stated that "mobile users can download and save the thumbnails displayed by Google Image Search onto their phones," and concluded "to the extent that users may choose to download free images to their phone rather than purchase [Perfect 10's] reduced-size images, Google's use supersedes [Perfect 10's]."

Additionally, the district court determined that the commercial nature of Google's use weighed against its transformative nature. Although Kelly held that the commercial use of the photographer's images by Arriba's search engine was less exploitative than typical commercial use, and thus weighed only slightly against a finding of fair use, the district court here distinguished Kelly on the ground that some website owners in the AdSense program had infringing Perfect 10 images on their websites. The district court held that because Google's thumbnails "lead users to sites that directly benefit Google's bottom line," the AdSense program increased the commercial nature of Google's use of Perfect 10's images.

In conducting our case-specific analysis of fair use in light of the purposes of copyright, we must weigh Google's superseding and commercial uses of thumbnail images against Google's significant transformative use, as well as the extent to which Google's search engine promotes the purposes of copyright and serves the interests of the public. Although the district court acknowledged the "truism that search engines such as Google Image Search provide great value to the public," the district court did not expressly consider whether this value outweighed the significance of Google's superseding use or the commercial nature of Google's use. The Supreme Court, however, has directed us to be mindful of the extent to which a use promotes the purposes of copyright and serves the interests of the public.

We note that the superseding use in this case is not significant at present: the district court did not find that any downloads for mobile phone use had taken place. Moreover, while Google's use of thumbnails to direct users to AdSense partners containing infringing content adds a commercial dimension that did not exist in Kelly, the district court did not determine that this commercial element was significant. The district court stated that Google's AdSense programs as a whole contributed "$ 630 million, or 46% of total revenues" to Google's bottom line, but noted that this figure did not "break down the much smaller amount attributable to websites that contain infringing content."

We conclude that the significantly transformative nature of Google's search engine, particularly in light of its public benefit, outweighs Google's superseding and commercial uses of the thumbnails in this case. In reaching this conclusion, we note the importance of analyzing fair use flexibly in light of new circumstances. Sony, 464 U.S. at 431-32; id. at 448 n.31 ("'[Section 107] endorses the purpose and general scope of the judicial doctrine of fair use, but there is no disposition to freeze the doctrine in the statute, especially during a period of rapid technological change.'" (quoting H.R. Rep. No. 94-1476, p. 65-66 (1976), U.S. Code Cong. & Admin. News 1976, p. 5680)). We are also mindful of the Supreme Court's direction that "the more transformative the new work, the less will be the significance of other factors, like commercialism, that may weigh against a finding of fair use." Campbell, 510 U.S. at 579.

Accordingly, we disagree with the district court's conclusion that because Google's use of the thumbnails could supersede Perfect 10's cell phone download use and because the use was more commercial than Arriba's, this fair use factor weighed "slightly" in favor of Perfect 10. Instead, we conclude that the transformative nature of Google's use is more significant than any incidental superseding use or the minor commercial aspects of Google's search engine and website. Therefore, this factor weighs heavily in favor of Google.

...

The amount and substantiality of the portion used. "The third factor asks whether the amount and substantiality of the portion used in relation to the copyrighted work as a whole . . . are reasonable in relation to the purpose of the copying." In Kelly, we held Arriba's use of the entire photo- graphic image was reasonable in light of the purpose of a search engine. Specifically, we noted, "[i]t was necessary for Arriba to copy the entire image to allow users to recognize the image and decide whether to pursue more information about the image or the originating [website]. If Arriba only copied part of the image, it would be more difficult to identify it, thereby reducing the usefulness of the visual search engine." Accordingly, we concluded that this factor did not weigh in favor of either party. Because the same analysis applies to Google's use of Perfect 10's image, the district court did not err in finding that this factor favored neither party.

Effect of use on the market. The fourth factor is "the effect of the use upon the potential market for or value of the copyrighted work." 17 U.S.C. § 107(4). In Kelly, we concluded that Arriba's use of the thumbnail images did not harm the market for the photographer's full-size images. We reasoned that because thumbnails were not a substitute for the full-sized images, they did not harm the photographer's ability to sell or license his full-sized images. Id. The district court here followed Kelly's reasoning, holding that Google's use of thumbnails did not hurt Perfect 10's market for full- size images. We agree.

Perfect 10 argues that the district court erred because the likelihood of market harm may be presumed if the intended use of an image is for commercial gain. However, this presumption does not arise when a work is transformative because "market substitution is at least less certain, and market harm may not be so readily inferred." As previously discussed, Google's use of thumbnails for search engine purposes is highly transformative, and so market harm cannot be presumed.

Perfect 10 also has a market for reduced-size images, an issue not considered in Kelly. The district court held that "Google's use of thumbnails likely does harm the potential market for the down- loading of [Perfect 10's] reduced-size images onto cell phones." The district court reasoned that persons who can obtain Perfect 10 images free of charge from Google are less likely to pay for a down- load, and the availability of Google's thumbnail images would harm Perfect 10's market for cell phone downloads. As we discussed above, the district court did not make a finding that Google users have downloaded thumbnail images for cell phone use. This potential harm to Perfect 10's mar-ket remains hypothetical. We conclude that this factor favors neither party.

Having undertaken a case-specific analysis of all four factors, we now weigh these factors together "in light of the purposes of copyright." In this case, Google has put Perfect 10's thumbnail images (along with millions of other thumbnail images) to a use fundamentally different than the use intended by Perfect 10. In doing so, Google has provided a significant benefit to the public. Weighing this significant transformative use against the unproven use of Google's thumbnails for cell phone downloads, and considering the other fair use factors, all in light of the purpose of copy-right, we conclude that Google's use of Perfect 10's thumbnails is a fair use. Because the district court here "found facts sufficient to evaluate each of the statutory factors . . . [we] need not remand for further factfinding." We conclude that Google is likely to succeed in proving its fair use defense and, accordingly, we vacate the preliminary injunction regarding Google's use of thumbnail images.

IV

Secondary Liability for Copyright Infringement

We now turn to the district court's ruling that Google is unlikely to be secondarily liable for its in-line linking to infringing full-size images under the doctrines of contributory and vicarious infringement. The district court ruled that Perfect 10 did not have a likelihood of proving success on the merits of either its contributory infringement or vicarious infringement claims with respect to the full-size images. In reviewing the district court's conclusions, we are guided by the Supreme Court's recent interpretation of secondary liability, namely: "[o]ne infringes contributorily by inten-tionally inducing or encouraging direct infringement, and infringes vicariously by profiting from direct infringement while declining to exercise a right to stop or limit it." Grokster, 545 U.S. at 930 (internal citations omitted).

Direct Infringement by Third Parties. As a threshold matter, before we examine Perfect 10's claims that Google is secondarily liable, Perfect 10 must establish that there has been direct infringement by third parties. See Napster, 239 F.3d at 1013 n.2 ("Secondary liability for copyright infringement does not exist in the absence of direct infringement by a third party.").

Perfect 10 alleges that third parties directly infringed its images in three ways. First, Perfect 10 claims that third-party websites directly infringed its copyright by reproducing, displaying, and distributing unauthorized copies of Perfect 10's images. Google does not dispute this claim on appeal.

Second, Perfect 10 claims that individual users of Google's search engine directly infringed Perfect 10's copyrights by storing full-size infringing images on their computers. We agree with the district court's conclusion that Perfect 10 failed to provide sufficient evidence to support this claim. There is no evidence in the record directly establishing that users of Google's search engine have stored infringing images on their computers, and the district court did not err in declining to infer the existence of such evidence.

Finally, Perfect 10 contends that users who link to infringing websites automatically make "cache" copies of full-size images and thereby directly infringe Perfect 10's reproduction right. The district court rejected this argument, holding that any such reproduction was likely a "fair use." The district court reasoned that "[l]ocal caching by the browsers of individual users is noncommercial, transformative, and no more than necessary to achieve the objectives of decreasing network latency and minimizing unnecessary bandwidth usage (essential to the [I]nternet). It has a minimal impact on the potential market for the original work ...." We agree; even assuming such automatic copy- ing could constitute direct infringement, it is a fair use in this context. The copying function per- formed automatically by a user's computer to assist in accessing the Internet is a transformative use. Moreover, as noted by the district court, a cache copies no more than is necessary to assist the user in Internet use. It is designed to enhance an individual's computer use, not to supersede the copy- right holders' exploitation of their works. Such automatic background copying has no more than a minimal effect on Perfect 10's rights, but a considerable public benefit. Because the four fair use factors weigh in favor of concluding that cache copying constitutes a fair use, Google has established a likelihood of success on this issue. Accordingly, Perfect 10 has not carried its burden of showing that users' cache copies of Perfect 10's full-size images constitute direct infringement.

Therefore, we must assess Perfect 10's arguments that Google is secondarily liable in light of the direct infringement that is undisputed by the parties: third-party websites' reproducing, displaying, and distributing unauthorized copies of Perfect 10's images on the Internet.

A. Contributory Infringement

In order for Perfect 10 to show it will likely succeed in its contributory liability claim against Google, it must establish that Google's activities meet the definition of contributory liability recently enunciated in Grokster. Within the general rule that "[o]ne infringes contributorily by intentionally inducing or encouraging direct infringement," Grokster, 545 U.S. at 930, the Court has defined two categories of contributory liability: "Liability under our jurisprudence may be predicated on actively encouraging (or inducing) infringement through specific acts (as the Court's opinion de-velops) or on distributing a product distributees use to infringe copyrights, if the product is not capable of 'substantial' or 'commercially significant' noninfringing uses." Id. at 942 (Ginsburg, J., con- curring).

Looking at the second category of liability identified by the Supreme Court (distributing products), Google relies on Sony, 464 U.S. at 442, to argue that it cannot be held liable for contributory infringement because liability does not arise from the mere sale of a product (even with knowledge that consumers would use the product to infringe) if the product is capable of substantial non- infringing use. Google argues that its search engine service is such a product. Assuming the princi- ple enunciated in Sony is applicable to the operation of Google's search engine, then Google cannot be held liable for contributory infringement solely because the design of its search engine facilitates such infringement. Grokster, 545 U.S. at 931-

32 (discussing Sony, 464 U.S. 417. Nor can Google be held liable solely because it did not develop technology that would enable its search engine to automatically avoid infringing images. However, Perfect 10 has not based its claim of infringement on the design of Google's search engine and the Sony rule does not immunize Google from other sources of contributory liability.

We must next consider whether Google could be held liable under the first category of contributory liability identified by the Supreme Court, that is, the liability that may be imposed for inten- tionally encouraging infringement through specific acts. Grokster tells us that contribution to infringement must be intentional for liability to arise. Grokster, 545 U.S. at 930. However, Grokster also directs us to analyze contributory liability in light of "rules of fault-based liability derived from the common law,"id. at 934-35, and common law principles establish that intent may be imputed. "Tort law ordinarily imputes to an actor the intention to cause the natural and probable consequences of his conduct."DeVoto v. Pac. Fid. Life Ins. Co., 618 F.2d 1340, 1347 (9th Cir. 1980); RESTATEMENT (SECOND) OF TORTS § 8A cmt. b (1965) ("If the actor knows that the conse- quences are certain, or substantially certain, to result from his act, and still goes ahead, he is treated by the law as if he had in fact desired to produce the result."). When the Supreme Court imported patent law's "staple article of commerce doctrine" into the copyright context, it also adopted these principles of imputed intent. Grokster, 545 U.S. at 932 ("The [staple article of commerce] doctrine was devised to identify instances in which it may be presumed from distribution of an article in commerce that the distributor intended the article to be used to infringe another's patent, and so may justly be held liable for that infringement."). Therefore, under Grokster, an actor may be contributorily liable for intentionally encouraging direct infringement if the actor knowingly takes steps that are substantially certain to result in such direct infringement.

Our tests for contributory liability are consistent with the rule set forth in Grokster. We have adopted the general rule set forth in Gershwin Publishing Corp. v. Columbia Artists Management, Inc., namely: "one who, with knowledge of the infringing activity, induces, causes or materially contributes to the infringing conduct of another, may be held liable as a 'contributory' infringer," 443 F.2d 1159, 1162 (2d Cir. 1971). See Ellison, 357 F.3d at 1076; Napster, 239 F.3d at 1019; Fonovisa, Inc. v. Cherry Auction, Inc., 76 F.3d 259, 264 (9th Cir. 1996).

We have further refined this test in the context of cyberspace to determine when contributory liability can be imposed on a provider of Internet access or services. See Napster, 239 F.3d at 1019- 20. In Napster, we considered claims that the operator of an electronic file sharing system was contributorily liable for assisting individual users to swap copyrighted music files stored on their home computers with other users of the system. We stated that "if a computer system operator learns of specific infringing material available on his system and fails to purge such material from the system, the operator knows of and contributes to direct infringement." Because Napster knew of the availability of infringing music files, assisted users in accessing such files, and failed to block access to such files, we concluded that Napster materially contributed to infringement.

The Napster test for contributory liability was modeled on the influential district court decision in Religious Technology Center v. Netcom On-Line Communication Services, Inc. (Netcom), 907 F. Supp. 1361, 1365-66 (N.D. Cal. 1995). In Netcom, a disgruntled former Scientology minister posted allegedly infringing copies of Scientological works on an electronic bulletin board service. The messages were stored on the bulletin board operator's computer, then automatically copied onto Netcom's computer, and from there copied onto other computers comprising "a worldwide community" of electronic bulletin board systems. Netcom held that if plaintiffs could prove that Netcom knew or should have known that the minister infringed plaintiffs' copyrights, "Netcom [would] be liable for contributory infringement since its failure to simply cancel [the former minis- ter's] infringing message and thereby stop an infringing copy from being distributed worldwide constitute[d] substantial participation in [the former minister's] public distribution of the message."

Although neither Napster nor Netcom expressly required a finding of intent, those cases are consistent with Grokster because both decisions ruled that a service provider's knowing failure to prevent infringing actions could be the basis for imposing contributory liability. Under such circumstances, intent may be imputed. In addition, Napster and Netcom are consistent with the longstand- ing requirement that an actor's contribution to infringement must be material to warrant the imposition of contributory liability. Both Napster and Netcom acknowledge that services or products that facilitate access to websites throughout the world can significantly magnify the effects of otherwise immaterial infringing activities. The Supreme Court has acknowledged that "[t]he argument for im- posing indirect liability" is particularly "powerful" when individuals using the defendant's software could make a huge number of infringing downloads every day. Grokster, 545 U.S. at 929. Moreo- ver, copyright holders cannot protect their rights in a meaningful way unless they can hold providers of such services or products accountable for their actions pursuant to a test such as that enunci- ated in Napster. See id. at 929-30 ("When a widely shared service or product is used to commit in- fringement, it may be impossible to enforce rights in the protected work effectively against all direct infringers, the only practical alternative being to go against the distributor of the copying device for secondary liability on a theory of contributory or vicarious infringement."). Accordingly, we hold that a computer system operator can be held contributorily liable if it "has actual knowledge that specific infringing material is available using its system," Napster, 239 F.3d at 1022, and can "take simple measures to prevent further damage" to copyrighted works, Netcom, 907 F. Supp. at 1375, yet continues to provide access to infringing works.

Here, the district court held that even assuming Google had actual knowledge of infringing material available on its system, Google did not materially contribute to infringing conduct because it did not undertake any substantial promotional or advertising efforts to encourage visits to infringing websites, nor provide a significant revenue stream to the infringing websites. This analysis is erroneous. There is no dispute that Google substantially assists websites to distribute their infringing copies to a worldwide market and assists a worldwide audience of users to access infringing materials. We cannot discount the effect of such a service on copyright owners, even though Google's assistance is available to all websites, not just infringing ones. Applying our test, Google could be held contributorily liable if it had knowledge that infringing Perfect 10 images were available using its search engine, could take simple measures to prevent further damage to Perfect 10's copyrighted works, and failed to take such steps.

The district court did not resolve the factual disputes over the adequacy of Perfect 10's notices to Google and Google's responses to these notices. Moreover, there are factual disputes over whether there are reasonable and feasible means for Google to refrain from providing access to infringing images. Therefore, we must remand this claim to the district court for further consideration whether Perfect 10 would likely succeed in establishing that Google was contributorily liable for in-line linking to full-size infringing images under the test enunciated today.

B. Vicarious Infringement

Perfect 10 also challenges the district court's conclusion that it is not likely to prevail on a theory of vicarious liability against Google. Grokster states that one "infringes vicariously by profiting from direct infringement while declining to exercise a right to stop or limit it." As this formulation indicates, to succeed in imposing vicarious liability, a plaintiff must establish that the defendant ex- ercises the requisite control over the direct infringer and that the defendant derives a direct financial benefit from the direct infringement. See id. Grokster further explains the "control" element of the vicarious liability test as the defendant's "right and ability to supervise the direct infringer." Thus, under Grokster, a defendant exercises control over a direct infringer when he has both a legal right to stop or limit the directly infringing conduct, as well as the practical ability to do so.

We evaluate Perfect 10's arguments that Google is vicariously liable in light of the direct infringement that is undisputed by the parties, namely, the third-party websites' reproduction, display, and distribution of unauthorized copies of Perfect 10's images on the Internet. See supra Section IV.A. In order to prevail at this preliminary injunction stage, Perfect 10 must demonstrate a likeli- hood of success in establishing that Google has the right and ability to stop or limit the infringing activities of third party websites. In addition, Perfect 10 must establish a likelihood of proving that Google derives a direct financial benefit from such activities. Perfect 10 has not met this burden.

With respect to the "control" element set forth in Grokster, Perfect 10 has not demonstrated a likelihood of showing that Google has the legal right to stop or limit the direct infringement of third-party websites. Unlike Fonovisa, where by virtue of a "broad contract" with its vendors the defendant swap meet operators had the right to stop the vendors from selling counterfeit recordings on its premises, Perfect 10 has not shown that Google has contracts with third-party websites that empower Google to stop or limit them from reproducing, displaying, and distributing infringing copies of Perfect 10's images on the Internet. Perfect 10 does point to Google's AdSense agreement, which states that Google reserves "the right to monitor and terminate partnerships with entities that violate others' copyright[s]." However, Google's right to terminate an AdSense partnership does not give Google the right to stop direct infringement by third-party websites. An infringing third-party website can continue to reproduce, display, and distribute its infringing copies of Perfect 10 images after its participation in the AdSense program has ended.

Nor is Google similarly situated to Napster. Napster users infringed the plaintiffs' reproduction and distribution rights through their use of Napster's proprietary music-file sharing system. There, the infringing conduct was the use of Napster's "service to download and upload copyrighted music." Because Napster had a closed system requiring user registration, and could terminate its users' accounts and block their access to the Napster system, Napster had the right and ability to prevent its users from engaging in the infringing activity of uploading file names and downloading Napster users' music files through the Napster system. By contrast, Google cannot stop any of the third- party websites from reproducing, displaying, and distributing unauthorized copies of Perfect 10's images because that infringing conduct takes place on the third-party websites. Google cannot terminate those third-party websites or block their ability to "host and serve infringing full-size images" on the Internet.

Moreover, the district court found that Google lacks the practical ability to police the third-party websites' infringing conduct. Specifically, the court found that Google's supervisory power is limited because "Google's software lacks the ability to analyze every image on the [I]nternet, compare each image to all the other copyrighted images that exist in the world . . . and determine whether a certain image on the web infringes someone's copyright." The district court also concluded that Perfect 10's suggestions regarding measures Google could implement to prevent its web crawler from indexing infringing websites and to block access to infringing images were not workable. Rather, the suggestions suffered from both "imprecision and overbreadth." We hold that these findings are not clearly erroneous. Without image-recognition technology, Google lacks the practical ability to police the infringing activities of third-party websites. This distinguishes Google from the defendants held liable in Napster and Fonovisa. See Napster, 239 F.3d at 1023-24 (Napster had the ability to identify and police infringing conduct by searching its index for song titles); Fonovisa, 76 F.3d at 262 (swap meet operator had the ability to identify and police infringing activity by patrolling its premises).

Perfect 10 argues that Google could manage its own operations to avoid indexing websites with infringing content and linking to third-party infringing sites. This is a claim of contributory liability, not vicarious liability. Although "the lines between direct infringement, contributory infringement, and vicarious liability are not clearly drawn," in general, contributory liability is based on the defendant's failure to stop its own actions which facilitate third-party infringement, while vicarious liability is based on the defendant's failure to cause a third party to stop its directly infringing activities. Google's failure to change its operations to avoid assisting websites to distribute their infringing content may constitute contributory liability, see supra Section IV. A. However, this failure is not the same as declining to exercise a right and ability to make third-party websites stop their direct infringement. We reject Perfect 10's efforts to blur this distinction.

Because we conclude that Perfect 10 has not shown a likelihood of establishing Google's right and ability to stop or limit the directly infringing conduct of third-party websites, we agree with the district court's conclusion that Perfect 10 "has not established a likelihood of proving the [control] prong necessary for vicarious liability."

C. Digital Millennium Copyright Act

Google claims that it qualifies for the limitations on liability set forth in title II of the DMCA, 17 U.S.C. § 512. In particular, section 512(d) limits the liability of a service provider "for infringement of copyright by reason of the provider referring or linking users to an online location containing in- fringing material or infringing activity, by using information location tools, including a directory, index, reference, pointer, or hypertext link" if the service provider meets certain criteria. We have held that the limitations on liability contained in 17 U.S.C. § 512 protect secondary infringers as well as direct infringers.

The parties dispute whether Google meets the specified criteria. Perfect 10 claims that it sent qualifying notices to Google and Google did not act expeditiously to remove the infringing material. Google claims that Perfect 10's notices did not comply with the notice provisions of section 512 and were not adequate to inform Google of the location of the infringing images on the Internet or iden- tify the underlying copyrighted work. Google also claims that it responded to all notices it received by investigating the webpages identified by Perfect 10 and suppressing links to any webpages that Google confirmed were infringing.

Because the district court determined that Perfect 10 was unlikely to succeed on its contributory and vicarious liability claims, it did not reach Google's arguments under section 512. In revisiting the question of Perfect 10's likelihood of success on its contributory infringement claims, the district court should also consider whether Google would likely succeed in showing that it was entitled to the limitations on injunctive relief provided by title II of the DMCA.

...

VI

We conclude that Google's fair use defense is likely to succeed at trial, and therefore we reverse the district court's determination that Google's thumbnail versions of Perfect 10's images likely con- stituted a direct infringement. The district court also erred in its secondary liability analysis because it failed to consider whether Google and Amazon.com knew of infringing activities yet failed to take reasonable and feasible steps to refrain from providing access to infringing images. Therefore we must also reverse the district court's holding that Perfect 10 was unlikely to succeed on the merits of its secondary liability claims. Due to this error, the district court did not consider whether Google and Amazon.com are entitled to the limitations on liability set forth in title II of the DMCA. The question whether Google and Amazon.com are secondarily liable, and whether they can limit that liability pursuant to title II of the DMCA, raise fact-intensive inquiries, potentially requiring further fact finding, and thus can best be resolved by the district court on remand. We therefore remand this matter to the district court for further proceedings consistent with this decision.

Because the district court will need to reconsider the appropriate scope of injunctive relief after addressing these secondary liability issues, we do not address the parties' arguments regarding the scope of the injunction issued by the district court. For the same reason, we do not address the parties' dispute over whether the district court abused its discretion in determining that Perfect 10 satis- fied the irreparable harm element of a preliminary injunction.

Therefore, we reverse the district court's ruling and vacate the preliminary injunction regarding Google's use of thumbnail versions of Perfect 10's images. We reverse the district court's rejection of the claims that Google and Amazon.com are secondarily liable for infringement of Perfect 10's full-size images. We otherwise affirm the rulings of the district court. We remand this matter for further proceedings consistent with this opinion. Each party shall bear its own costs on appeal.

AFFIRMED IN PART; REVERSED IN PART; REMANDED.

572 F.Supp.2d 1150

LENZ v. UNIVERSAL

United States District Court, N.D. California, San Jose Division

JEREMY FOGEL, District Judge.

I. BACKGROUND

On February 7, 2007, Plaintiff Stephanie Lenz ("Lenz") videotaped her young children [1152] dancing in her family's kitchen. The song "Let's Go Crazy" by the artist professionally known as Prince ("Prince") played in the background. The video is twentynine seconds in length, and "Let's Go Crazy" can be heard for approximately twenty seconds, albeit with difficulty given the poor sound quality of the video. The audible portion of the song includes the lyrics, "C'mon baby let's get nuts" and the song's distinctive guitar solo. Lenz is heard asking her son, "what do you think of the music?" On February 8, 2007, Lenz titled the video "Let's Go Crazy # 1" and uploaded it to YouTube.com ("YouTube"), a popular Internet video hosting site, for the alleged purpose of sharing her son's dancing with friends and family. YouTube provides "video sharing" or "user generated content." The video was available to the public at http://www.youtube.com/watch?v=N1KfJHFW1hQ.

Universal owns the copyright to "Let's Go Crazy." On June 4, 2007, Universal sent YouTube a takedown notice pursuant to Title II of the Digital Millennium Copyright Act ("DMCA"), 17 U.S.C. § 512 (2000). The notice was sent to YouTube's designated address for receiving DMCA notices, "copyright@youtube.com," and demanded that YouTube remove Lenz's video from the site because of a copyright violation. YouTube removed the video the following day and sent Lenz an email notifying her that it had done so in response to Universal's accusation of copyright infringement. YouTube's email also advised Lenz of the DMCA's counter-notification procedures and warned her that any repeated incidents of copyright infringement could lead to the deletion of her account and all of her videos. After conducting research and consulting counsel, Lenz sent YouTube a DMCA counter-notification pursuant to 17 U.S.C. § 512(g) on June 27, 2007. Lenz asserted that her video constituted fair use of "Let's Go Crazy" and thus did not infringe Universal's copyrights. Lenz demanded that the video be re-posted. YouTube re-posted the video on its website about six weeks later. As of the date of this order, the "Let's Go Crazy # 1" video has been viewed on YouTube more than 593,000 times.

In September 2007, Prince spoke publicly about his efforts "to reclaim his art on the internet" and threatened to sue several internet service providers for alleged infringement of his music copyrights. Lenz alleges that Universal issued the removal notice only to appease Prince because Prince "is notorious for his efforts to control all uses of his material on and off the Internet." Lenz's Opposition Brief at 3. In an October 2007 statement to ABC News, Universal made the following comment:

Prince believes it is wrong for YouTube, or any other user-generated site, to appropriate his music without his consent. That position has nothing to do with any particular video that uses his songs. It's simply a matter of principle. And legally, he has the right to have his music removed. We support him and this important principle. That's why, over the last few months, we have asked You-Tube to remove thousands of different videos that use Prince music without his permission. Second Amended Complaint ("SAC"), ¶ 30; see also J. Aliva et al., The Home Video Prince Doesn't Want You to See, ABC NEWS, Oct. 26, 2007...Lenz asserts in her complaint that "Prince himself demanded that Universal seek the removal of the ["Let's Go Crazy # 1"] video ... [and that] Universal sent the DMCA notice at Prince's behest, based not on the particular characteristics of [the video] or any good-faith belief that it actually infringed a copyright but on its belief that, as `a matter of principle' Prince `has the right to have his music removed.'" SAC ¶ 31.

On July 24, 2007, Lenz filed suit against Universal alleging misrepresentation pursuant to 17 U.S.C. § 512(f) and tortious interference with her contract with You-Tube. She also sought a declaratory judgment of non-infringement. Universal filed a motion to dismiss, which the Court granted on April 8, 2008, 2008 WL 962102. Lenz was given leave to amend her complaint to replead her first and second claims for relief. On April 18, 2008, Lenz filed the operative SAC, alleging only a claim for misrepresentation pursuant to 17 U.S.C. § 512(f). On May 23, 2008, Universal filed the instant motion.

II. LEGAL STANDARD

"Dismissal under Rule 12(b)(6) is appropriate only where the complaint lacks a cognizable legal theory or sufficient facts to support a cognizable legal theory." Mendiondo v. Centinela Hosp. Medical Center, 521 F.3d 1097, 1104 (9th Cir.2008). "While a complaint attacked by a Rule 12(b)(6) motion to dismiss does not need detailed factual allegations, a plaintiffs obligation to provide the `grounds' of his `entitle[ment] to relief requires more than labels and conclusions, and a formulaic recitation of the elements of a cause of action will not do." Bell Atlantic Corp. v. Twombly, ___ U.S. ___, 127 S.Ct. 1955, 1964-65, 167 L.Ed.2d 929 (2007) (internal citations omitted).

III. DISCUSSION

The DMCA requires that copyright owners provide the following information in a takedown notice:

(i) A physical or electronic signature of a person authorized to act on behalf of the owner of an exclusive right that is allegedly infringed.

(ii) Identification of the copyrighted work claimed to have been infringed, or, if multiple copyrighted works at a single online site are covered by a single notification, a representative list of such works at that site.

(iii) Identification of the material that is claimed to be infringing or to be the subject of infringing activity and that is to be removed or access to which is to be disabled, and information reasonably sufficient to permit the service provider to locate the material.

(iv) Information reasonably sufficient to permit the service provider to contact the complaining party, such as an address, telephone number, and, if available, an electronic mail address at which the complaining party may be contacted.

(v) A statement that the complaining party has a good faith belief that use of the material in the manner complained of is not authorized by the copyright owner, its agent, or the law.

(vi) A statement that the information in the notification is accurate, and under penalty of perjury, that the complaining party is authorized to act on behalf of the owner of an exclusive right that is allegedly infringed. 17 U.S.C. § 512(c)(3)(A) (emphasis added).

Here, the parties do not dispute that Lenz used copyrighted material in her video or that Universal is the true owner of Prince's copyrighted music. Thus the question in this case is whether 17 U.S.C. § 512(c)(3)(A)(v) requires a copyright owner to consider the fair use doctrine in formulating a good faith belief that "use of the material in the manner complained of is not authorized by the copyright owner, its agent, or the law."

Universal contends that copyright owners cannot be required to evaluate the question of fair use prior to sending a takedown notice because fair use is merely an excused infringement of a copyright rather than a use authorized by the copyright owner or by law. Universal emphasizes that Section 512(c)(3)(A) does not even mention fair use, let alone require a good faith belief that a given use of copyrighted material is not fair use. Universal also contends that even if a copyright owner were required by the DMCA to evaluate fair use with respect to allegedly infringing material, any such duty would arise only after a copyright owner receives a counternotice and considers filing suit. See 17 U.S.C. § 512(g)(2)(C).

Lenz argues that fair use is an authorized use of copyrighted material, noting that the fair use doctrine itself is an express component of copyright law. Indeed, Section 107 of the Copyright Act of 1976 provides that "[n]otwithstanding the provisions of sections 106 and 106A, the fair use of a copyrighted work ... is not an infringement of copyright." 17 U.S.C. § 107. Lenz asserts in essence that copyright owners cannot represent in good faith that material infringes a copyright without considering all authorized uses of the material, including fair use.

Whether fair use qualifies as a use "authorized by law" in connection with a takedown notice pursuant to the DMCA appears to be an issue of first impression. Though it has been discussed in several other actions, no published case actually has adjudicated the merits of the issue. See, e.g., Doe v. Geller, 533 F.Supp.2d 996, 1001 (N.D.Cal.2008) (granting motion to dismiss for lack of personal jurisdiction).

A. Fair Use and 17 U.S.C. § 512(c)(3)(A)(v).

When interpreting a statute, a court must begin "with the language of the statute and ask whether Congress has spoken on the subject before [it]." Norfolk and Western Ry. Co. v. American Train Dispatchers Ass'n, 499 U.S. 117, 128, 111 S.Ct. 1156, 113 L.Ed.2d 95 (1991). If "Congress has made its intent clear, [the court] must give effect to that intent." Miller v. French, 530 U.S. 327, 336, 120 S.Ct. 2246, 147 L.Ed.2d 326 (2000) (internal quotation marks and citation omitted). Here, the Court concludes that the plain meaning of "authorized by law" is unambiguous. An activity or behavior "authorized by law" is one permitted by law or not contrary to law. Though Congress did not expressly mention the fair use doctrine in the DMCA, the Copyright Act provides explicitly that "the fair use of a copyrighted work ... is not an infringement of copyright." 17 U.S.C. § 107. Even if Universal is correct that fair use only excuses infringement, the fact remains that fair use is a lawful use of a copyright. Accordingly, in order for a copyright owner to proceed under the DMCA with "a good faith belief that use of the material in the manner complained of is not authorized by the copyright owner, its agent, or the law," the owner must evaluate whether the material makes fair use of the copyright. 17 U.S.C. § 512(c)(3)(A)(v). An allegation [1155] that a copyright owner acted in bad faith by issuing a takedown notice without proper consideration of the fair use doctrine thus is sufficient to state a misrepresentation claim pursuant to Section 512(f) of the DMCA. Such an interpretation of the DMCA furthers both the purposes of the DMCA itself and copyright law in general. In enacting the DMCA, Congress noted that the "provisions in the bill balance the need for rapid response to potential infringement with the end-users [sic] legitimate interests in not having material removed without recourse." Sen. Rep. No. 105-190 at 21 (1998).

Universal suggests that copyright owners may lose the ability to respond rapidly to potential infringements if they are required to evaluate fair use prior to issuing takedown notices. Universal also points out that the question of whether a particular use of copyrighted material constitutes fair use is a fact-intensive inquiry, and that it is difficult for copyright owners to predict whether a court eventually may rule in their favor. However, while these concerns are understandable, their actual impact likely is overstated. Although there may be cases in which such considerations will arise, there are likely to be few in which a copyright owner's determination that a particular use is not fair use will meet the requisite standard of subjective bad faith required to prevail in an action for misrepresentation under 17 U.S.C. § 512(f). See Rossi v. Motion Picture Ass'n of America, Inc., 391 F.3d 1000, 1004 (9th Cir.2004) (holding that "the `good faith belief requirement in § 512(c)(3)(A)(v) encompasses a subjective, rather than objective, standard").

... Undoubtedly, some evaluations of fair use will be more complicated than others. But in the majority of cases, a consideration of fair use prior to issuing a takedown notice will not be so complicated as to jeopardize a copyright owner's ability to respond rapidly to potential infringements. The DMCA already requires copyright owners to make an initial review of the potentially infringing material prior to sending a takedown notice; indeed, it would be impossible to meet any of the requirements of Section 512(c) without doing so. A consideration of the applicability of the fair use doctrine simply is part of that initial review. As the Ninth [1156] Circuit observed in Rossi, a full investigation to verify the accuracy of a claim of infringement is not required. Rossi, 391 F.3d at 1003-04.

The purpose of Section 512(f) is to prevent the abuse of takedown notices. If copyright owners are immune from liability by virtue of ownership alone, then to a large extent Section 512(f) is superfluous. As Lenz points out, the unnecessary removal of non-infringing material causes significant injury to the public where timesensitive or controversial subjects are involved and the counter-notification remedy does not sufficiently address these harms. A good faith consideration of whether a particular use is fair use is consistent with the purpose of the statute. Requiring owners to consider fair use will help "ensure[] that the efficiency of the Internet will continue to improve and that the variety and quality of services on the Internet will expand" without compromising "the movies, music, software and literary works that are the fruit of American creative genius." Sen. Rep. No. 105-190 at 2 (1998).

...

IV. ORDER

Good cause therefor appearing, IT IS HEREBY ORDERED that the motion to dismiss is DENIED.

Made in the USA
Coppell, TX
20 August 2020

34063106R00337